HOSPITAL MERGERS
in the Making

health
administration
press

HOSPITAL MERGERS
in the Making

David B. Starkweather

Health Administration Press
Ann Arbor, Michigan
1981

Library of Congress Cataloging in Publication Data

Starkweather, David B.
    Hospital mergers in the making.

    Bibliography: p.
    Includes index.
    1. Hospital mergers. 2. Hospital mergers—United
States. I. Title. [DNLM: 1. Health facilities—Organization and
administration—United States. 2. Hospital administration—United
States. WX 150 S795h]
RA971.S73   338.8'36136211'0973   81-4245
ISBN 0-914904-54-X   AACR2

Health Administration Press
The School of Public Health
The University of Michigan
Ann Arbor, Michigan 48109
(313) 764-1380

To some of my respected colleagues who understand merger: Dwight Barnett (deceased), a person brave enough to take on a merger that most said was impossible; Glenn Mitchell, a manager whose professionalism is exceeded only by his humanity; List Witherill, a public servant of the first order; Joe Hafey, a planner who understands health organizations; Wanda Jones, a consultant who calls things as she sees them.

To Faye, with whom I have been happily merged since 1960.

Contents

PART III. THE RAMIFICATIONS

List of Figures

Preface

This book is my attempt to blend the worlds of theory and practice. There is a rough symmetry between this effort and my own career pathway. My twenty years of engagement with health administration have been split almost equally between the administration of a large medical center, comprised of two merged hospitals, and full-time teaching and research. For most of this time my professional hobby has been mergers, approached first as an administrator and second as an academic.

As Paul White aptly put it, "The grafting of theory on practice—or vice versa—is a very loose affair." While granting the difficulties of achieving such a graft, it is the goal for this book. My approach takes three forms.

Part I consists of three chapters of concepts. In the first, I put mergers in the context of current realities and future trends in health care organization. This is followed by two chapters in which I state my theoretical bases for speculation and then present numerous hypotheses about hospital mergers. These propositions are derived both from pure theories and my personal "impure" experience. Reliance on personal observation will inevitably get me in trouble with some theorists, who will charge that it is idiosyncratic. Reliance on theory invites the practitioner's charge that it is irrelevant. I willingly run the gauntlet between these, since I have little regard for the hair splitters of the social sciences who end up talking only to each other, and I get frustrated with the anecdotalists of the practicing world who never quite get to generalizing from their "unique" experiences.

The second part of the book, chapters 4 through 9, consists of six case studies, each reflecting a different view of the merging phenomenon as well as the variety of settings in which hospital mergers transpire and the different pathways they take. I make no pretense of statistical representation in this selection, having abandoned that when I chose the research method of case study rather than large-sample survey. Nonetheless, I believe the cases present a reasonable spread of circumstances, and I submit that a trade off of case study depth for survey research breadth is appropriate to this early stage of elucidation.

In the third part of the book, chapters 10 through 13, I compare and contrast the six cases, using as a baseline the propositions presented in chapter 3. I am up to two things here: testing the fit of my propositions to the reality of the cases, and discussing the implications of the fit to each case. The discussion is aimed at four groups of people: those concerned with the development of policies about the role of mergers in health care reorganization, those involved in planning specific hospital integrations, those concerned with the management of merged hospitals, and those social scientists, primarily sociologists of the interorganizational stripe, who might be interested.

Behavioral scientists' concern with interorganization is very new, representing part of the shift to an open-systems view. Theories about mergers have been developed mostly by economists and thus are primarily relevant to business enterprises. The literature on hospital mergers is authored mainly by persons involved in their creation or operation. The resulting gap has been well summarized by White:

> Immersed as many of the authors are in specific local problems and their solutions, much of the writing on inter-organizational behavior in health is exhortive, consisting of reports on "how we did it" without sufficient explanation of the factors which produce or facilitate the success. In general, the results . . . contribute more to our understanding of necessary cause than to that of sufficient cause. . . . We can now spell out many of the conditions that will impede interaction among health organizations. Specifying the sufficient causes of organizational interaction is a more difficult task. ["Critique of Conceptual Frameworks and Empirical Studies Relevant to Interorganizational Relationships in Health." In *A Critical Evaluation of Research On the Interrelationships Among Health Care Institutions*. Baltimore: Johns Hopkins University School of Hygiene and Public Health, 1971.]

Specifying these sufficient causes is the goal of this book. My effort falls short of White's specification of rational and systematic development of useful theory, but it is a beginning. My approach is purposely middle range, and I hope it responds to the growing call from social scientists and practitioners for such approaches.

There is a selectivity in this book that I should make clear from the start. Many types of integrations occur in the health field; I offer a typology in chapter 1. This book is about the most extreme type—complete merger—not the most frequent form, but the most revealing. Dynamics will be obvious in the complete merger situation that are not so apparent in looser forms of integration, though they are there. I believe the differences between these forms are those of degree, not kind.

The research leading up to this book has been of the vest-pocket type. I have enjoyed—or been saddled by—virtually no grant funds with which to assemble a research staff and conduct a large-scale undertaking. Although this was not my original intent, this approach has proven to have considerable benefits. Because I have had to be selective in both my theoretic pursuits and my real world observations—the former tied closely to teaching the application of organization theory, and the latter tied closely to problem solving as an administrator and a consultant—I have been forced to think as perceptively as possible about what is going on.

Since I have depended upon my own resources, I cannot explain away the limitations of this book to circumstances, including those imposed by funding. While I have been on my own financially, many persons have been most helpful in other ways. Larry Prybil helped make possible a sabbatical at the Medical College of Virginia which yielded access to one of my case study mergers and time in which to think and write. Others have willingly opened up their organizations to my scrutiny or that of my colleagues, providing ample doses of time, searching old files, lining up key persons, and assuming the risk that comes with allowing organizational snoops into their corporate closets. I thank Glenn Mitchell, List Witherill, Jane Robertson, and Bob DuPar. There is a final group of people whose contributions have been more precious than money: my student and faculty colleagues who have studied and written about mergers and whose results are published herein: Joe Coyne, Len Dougherty, Joe Hafey, JoAnn Johnson, Mark Secord, and Jennie Stone. Their sense of inquiry has provided me with stimulation and renewal.

DAVID B. STARKWEATHER
Berkeley, 1981

PART I.

Concepts

1.

Hospital Mergers and
Health Care Organization

In the field of health care . . . the last quarter of the
century will be the era of the merger. Virtually every
health institution will be involved in one or more mergers.

Sieverts and Sigmond (1970)

A. CONSOLIDATION AND PUBLIC POLICY

Integration among providers of health care is now national policy. This became so with enactment of Public Law 93–641; the National Health Planning
and Resources Development Act, passed by Congress in late December of
1974 and signed into law by President Ford on 4 January 1975. Within eighteen months of this latter date the Secretary of Health, Education and Welfare
issued guidelines based on ten national health priorities contained in the
legislation, one of which is "the development of multi-institutional systems
for coordinating or consolidating institutional health services."

Why is it now a public policy to consolidate institutional providers? For
some time the nation has had too many small hospitals, each with limitations
in its ability to serve and many below the size necessary for efficient operations. Yet, comprehensive health care can only be delivered by either large
single institutions or well-coordinated networks of providers. To some, the
accomplishment of this reorganization is a necessary prelude to a national
health insurance for the U.S.; hence its inclusion in a legislation generally
designed to anticipate such a program.

Put in terms of political economics, there is the dilemma of choosing
between goals of efficiency and goals of effectiveness. Concerning efficiency,
we know that our nation spends more of its national resources on health care
than almost any nation in the world, and we regularly ask whether its citizens
are getting their money's worth. This concern is behind a wide variety of
regulations aimed at containing costs. One way to increase efficiency is for
health care providers, primarily hospitals, either to share in the development
and operation of expensive services, or to consolidate.

Concerns for effectiveness focus more on the distribution of decent medical care. Proponents of this line conclude that the U.S. can afford and should provide some minimal standard of health care uniformly to all of its citizens, even if spending levels go still higher. But no more money would be needed, say these advocates, if providers were to emphasize primary and ambulatory care rather than the secondary and tertiary services found in hospitals, and if they would emphasize preventive as well as diagnostic and curative services.

Thus, the proponents of effectiveness measures stress decentralization of health services, while those concerned with efficiency emphasize their concentration. But this distinction is deceptive. Consolidations among hospitals potentially can respond to both of these goals because such integrations lead to an essential critical mass—a necessary foundation for the outreach programs envisioned by those devoted to comprehensive, uniformly available care.[1]

This situation is summarized in figure 1. 1. The vertical axis represents the goal of effectiveness, emphasizing access and comprehensiveness. The horizontal axis represents the goal of efficiency, emphasizing the institutional costs of producing medical care, with particular reference to relations among hospitals. The figure highlights the relationship of output, i.e., the scope of services available, to input, i.e., the organization of production.

FIGURE 1.1   Future Patterns of Health Care Organization

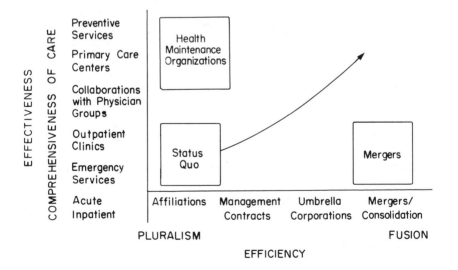

The figure suggests that combinations among health service organizations of the several types listed on the horizontal axis are important to the dual objectives of medical care cost containment and the extension of services to those without reasonable access. This thinking is based on the assumptions that (1) important gains in efficiency and quality can be achieved by combining certain health services; (2) in order to achieve these gains, new, formal mechanisms are necessary to bind together traditionally autonomous organizations; and (3) these new combinations will not only constitute efficient concentration of certain health care resources but also lead to effective decentralization and extension of services through properly linked outreach operations.

We will examine each of these assumptions in subsequent portions of this book.

B.   THE MERGING PHENOMENON

Information gathered in a special survey of all U.S. hospitals (American Hospital Association, 1974) shows a definite trend in corporate consolidations among hospitals during the period 1960 to 1973 and indicates that the trend since 1973 has accelerated. Hospitals counted in the survey as having entered a multihospital system had done one or more of the following: 1) previously separate hospitals incorporated into one new organization with a common board; 2) previously separate hospitals became part of a chain with a board of directors which determines policy and provides centralized administration; or 3) previously separate hospitals entered a major affiliation agreement or management contract with an organization that assumes a major policy role.

By these criteria, the number of hospitals entering a consolidation in 1961 was 5 and the number per year rose steadily through 1972 when it was approximately 50: an average rate of increase of 10 percent per year. In 1973 the number dropped dramatically to 20, probably due to that year's economic stabilization program which led to a cautionary stand among many hospitals. This lull in the merger pace was temporary, however. The harsh economic realities which the stabilization program brought to the attention of many hospitals led subsequently to an increase in various forms of consolidation. In 1976 Money et al. stated that "the total number of hospitals involved in or considering some form of cooperative management . . . approaches 2,500" (p. 30). In 1977 the American Hospital Association confirmed this dramatic resurgence (Portney, 1977).

In 1979, the American Hospital Association conducted another survey (Brown et al., 1980). Unlike previous surveys, this one excluded all federal and state government facilities as well as psychiatric and long term care institutions. It concentrated instead on community hospitals of different types: investor-owned, Catholic, other religious, voluntary, university, and local government. This survey yielded 1,505 hospitals that were in multi-institution systems, as defined above. There were 245 systems that accounted for 26 percent of all community hospitals and 31 percent of all community hospital beds. Of these, 50 percent were under Catholic ownership, 12 percent under the auspices of other religious groups, and 11 percent investor-owned. The average number of hospitals in investor-owned systems was 17.7, with an average size of 133 beds. When the investor-owned group was excluded, the average number of hospitals per system was 4.5. Almost half of the systems have more than 900 beds, while 15 percent, primarily Catholic and investor-owned, have more than 2,000 beds per system.

The AHA survey distinguished between two main types of managements: those managed centrally, where the corporate office appoints or approves the individual hospital managers, and those organized along affiliation lines where the hospital operates and is managed independently of the corporation. The systems that are managed centrally are substantially larger, while the systems that operate on an affiliated basis have larger individual hospitals within them. Over half of all these 245 systems surveyed were managed centrally. These grew to a much larger extent between 1975 and 1979, both in number of beds and number of hospitals per system, than did the affiliated systems. As for geographic distribution, in New England only 10 percent of all community hospitals were in systems, while in the mountain and Pacific states the comparable figures were 41 percent and 40 percent, respectively. Other regions were within this range.

The history of consolidations among for-profit hospitals is dramatic, revealing a special dynamic of a subindustry as well as a reflection of the larger trend. As late as the mid-1960s virtually all of the nation's proprietary hospitals were owned singly by individuals or small, privately held partnerships or corporations. Most owners were physicians. In the late 1960s, the great majority of these privately held hospitals were sold to larger stock corporations. These can be considered public corporations in that their financial issues were traded on the New York and other stock exchanges. This industry restructuring provided advantages for both sellers and purchasers. For sellers, it not only eliminated the burden of management, which had become more complex than practicing physician-owners wanted to undertake, but also provided a new source of much needed fixed and working capital for their typically small, obsolete hospitals. For corporate buyers, the hospital industry suddenly appeared as a growth industry with great financial potential. Medicaid and Medicare laws had provided a reimbursement for the hospital market which reduced much of the risk for investors in the form of a baseline, guaranteed operating income to hospitals which assured return on investors' dollars. In addition, the general economy was humming at this time, and investors were looking for new investment opportunities. With the economic downturn of the early 1970s, another phase of selling and buying occurred: many of the 25 to 30 stock corporations which had been formed in the 1960s to purchase and run hospitals were sold to a smaller number of the largest hospital corporations, notably Hospital Corporation of America, American Medicorp, Hospital Affiliates, Humana, and American Medical International. This concentration avoided bankruptcy for some, and for others it recognized the realities of ownership in a market in which gain would now have to come from operating performance rather than stockmarket glamor. As of 1976, this consolidation had reached the point that the five corporations named above had acquired ownership of 60 percent of all investor-owned hospital beds. In 1978, the degree of concentration moved higher with the merger of two of these five corporations, American Medicorp and Humana. Then, in 1981, the two largest of these, Hospital Corporation of America and Hospital Affiliates, merged. Now, this one corporation owns approximately one-third of all investor-owned hospital beds, and two others own another one-third. Further, the largest corporation almost doubles its control of hospital beds through contracts to manage hospitals owned by others.

Williams's (1976) study of hospital closures and mergers in New York City between 1960 and 1975 is the most detailed. Forty-six institutions satisfied his merger definition: 1) two or more hospitals combined to form a new corporate entity with a consolidation of governance; or 2) a stronger hospital acquired the assets and beds of a weaker hospital. Williams found that

> in 1960 there were 143 general care hospitals in the city. By 1975 there were 111, a net reduction of 32 general care hospitals, or a decrease of 22 percent.
>
> The net decrease takes into account 11 new hospitals which opened during this period and the redesignation of selected chronic care hospitals as acute care institutions.
>
> Closures outnumbered mergers, 34 to 12.
>
> Of the 46 closed or merged hospitals, 24 were under voluntary auspices, 19 were proprietary, and 3 were under local government control.
>
> The number of general care beds in the system remained about the same over the decade and a half. In other words, beds lost through closures in this period were more than offset by beds gained in new hospitals and in existing hospitals.
>
> Nine of the closed or merged hospitals were specialty institutions—three for ophthalmology, two for the exclusive treatment of women, two for the treatment of cancer, one for children's orthopedic problems, and one for the treatment of the ear. This is a continuation of the long trend towards the disappearance of isolated specialty hospitals.
>
> Closed and merged hospitals tended to be small: 13 hospitals—about 40 percent—had 50 beds or less; 23 hospitals—about 80 percent—had 100 beds or less. [p. 2]

Several findings of the American Hospital Association and Williams surveys are similar. One, that relatively small hospitals are typically involved, supports the economic explanation that hospitals seek through integration the advantages of scale not otherwise available. Another is the relatively large proportion of religious hospitals that are in multi-unit systems, suggesting that since many of these systems have been in existence for decades the trend is not as dramatic as the statistics suggest. Another finding is the wide variation in the trend by regions of the country. Finally, concerning the development of critical masses many of the respondents to the American Hospital Association survey indicated that they undertook consolidation in part to develop the capacity to provide progressive patient care, such as outpatient services, health maintenance and health education programs, extended care and rehabilitation facilities.

C. UNDERLYING REASONS

A trend as fundamental as this—leading eventually to a substantial restructuring of one of the nation's largest industries—has its genesis in three basic forces: economic, technological, and demographic.

Few dispute the inefficiency of the present hospital industry structure: the average sized hospital of 166^3 beds is approximately half the size regarded as necessary for optimum efficiency. Although it is not economical for one small hospital to spend huge sums of capital and operating money for specialized facilities and services already acquired by another nearby hospital, this is commonplace. Eventually, this inefficiency will challenge the small hospital's very survival: it must either grow from within or combine with another institution in order to capture economies of scale.

Health planning and regulatory agencies are increasingly challenging internal growth. If most small hospitals were to take this pathway to survival, another flaw in the nation's health systems would be exacerbated: an excess of beds in most communities. Consolidation, then, emerges as a salvation formula for competing hospitals in hundreds of American communities.

Changes in the source and nature of operating income compound the economic problems of survival for a free-standing small hospital. Starting in the mid-1960s, the proportion of governmental health care expenditures grew, increasing the flow of funds for the purchase of hospital services. This stimulated some sponsors, notably for-profit corporations, to enter the market, typically with small and sometimes unnecessary facilities. There then followed pressures to achieve rationalization and cost containment through various regulatory devices. What seemed in the late 1960s to be a benign market had become harsh by the mid-1970s.

Even if small hospitals survive in the short run, they face a long-term threat when obsolete facilities or equipment require new capital investments. Increasingly, private donors, commercial lenders, and planning agencies question whether several independent hospitals in a community should undertake major replacements or expansion that could lead to or perpetuate overcapacity. Lenders prefer larger-volume operations where there is higher likelihood that full utilization will generate sufficient cash flow to insure pay back. When the market for hospital capital monies is tight, money flows first or only to lower-risk projects represented by new consolidations.

As for technology, the acute care hospital is the house of wonders where advances in applied science have found perhaps their greatest application: innovations in medical technology continue at a rate which exceeds that of most other fields of endeavor, and investments in this technology are increasingly expensive. It requires increasingly larger hospital operations to make these investments economically feasible. Consolidation is one way of obtaining this scale. Further, the larger institutions which have these technologies need a referral system of patients to assure the continued volumes necessary to support their investments. Corporate integration is one way to obtain these referrals.

The recent demography of many urban populations has rendered the prior pattern of autonomous institutions unstable. The flight of wealthy and middle class people to suburbs has left the core cities of most metropolitan areas inhabited by poor people who have greater relative need for care but lesser ability to pay for services and to contribute to hospital upkeep and development. Physicians too have joined the exodus. Suburban hospitals have welcomed them and gradually developed the specialized services which previously attracted patients to inner-city hospitals. Now, however, with pressures against this continued development by suburban hospitals, their affiliation with large, inner-city tertiary hospitals offers increasing mutual benefits.

These underlying forces—economic, technological, and demographic— create a turbulent environment for hospitals, and where there is turbulence there is likely to be change.[4] Since this turbulence affects different hospitals in different ways, their responses will vary. A stimulus to larger urban hospitals will likely be population shifts, while the impetus to change for smaller rural institutions may be the imperatives of technology or the economics of capital markets (Shortell, 1977; Wegmiller, 1978). Brown (1976) has teased out of these forces a profile of institutions most likely to consolidate.

> Under this new strategy, vigorous, existing hospitals will probably expand their sphere of influence by bringing into their system (or creating new systems) those hospitals that fit some combination of 1) chronic low occupancy, 2) deficit operations, 3) rural or inner-city location, 4) changing patient clientele with increasing medical needs but a reduced ability to pay for services, 5) geographical area having trouble attracting skilled and trained administrators and

physicians, 6) new suburbs and new towns without a well-developed community group to pursue health care needs aggressively and furnish the start-up capital, 7) hospitals of small bed size and 8) hospitals with older, deteriorating physical plants. [pp. 52–53]

Clearly, as predicated by the underlying forces and evidenced by the numerous examples, there is a strong trend toward integration.[5]

D. THE FUTURE

Numerous experts in health care organization have agreed that, at least for the next ten years, the trend towards integration will not only remain prominent but accelerate. In early 1975, 20 experts on U.S. health care organization, organized into a Delphi forecasting panel, made the following predictions (Starkweather et al., 1975):

> Seventy-five percent of the panel gave a 90% likelihood to the occurrence within the next 10 years of more specific organizational ties between medical groups, hospitals, ambulatory care, and specialized facilities as a result of hospital consolidations."

> Sixty-five percent of the panel gave a 90% likelihood, and another 30% gave a 50% likelihood, to the occurrence, again within 10 years, of "greater voluntary coordination, cooperation and functional specialization among hospitals regarding all services, research, and education."

> Fifty-five percent of the panel gave a 90% likelihood, and another 35% a 50% likelihood, to the 10-year occurrence of "stronger management alliances."

> Thirty-five percent gave a 90% likelihood, and another 40% a 50% likelihood, to the 10-year occurrence of "formal consortia of hospitals which will jointly assume financial risk."

> Fifteen percent gave a 90% likelihood, and another 40% gave a 50% likelihood, to the 10-year occurrence of "physical consolidations and complete organizational merger" as a pattern of development. [p. 41]

The pattern of development for the 1980s appears to be one in which hospitals will seek the advantages of consolidation without the complete surrender of institutional autonomy. Shortell's (1977) thoughtful analysis and predictions include the following:

> During the period 1961 through 1974 there has been a net decrease of 25 percent in not-for-profit short term general hospitals with fewer than 100 beds, and a 41 percent decrease in the number of investor-owned hospitals with fewer than 200 beds. This trend is likely to be sustained in the future, with controls on operating and capital funds provided by new planning legislation and proposed national health insurance legislation. In brief, there will be fewer hospitals in the 1980's, but those that do exist will be larger. . . . These large hospitals will tend to be part of multiunit systems. The idea that "small is beautiful" will be replaced by "less is best."

Already, approximately 1900 hospitals belong to one of approximately 371 multiunit systems. Investor-owned hospitals will increasingly be organized as part of investor-owned chains, and management contracts will continue to grow. . . . Other systems will be organized around religious ties, urban-rural linkages, and teaching hospital-primary care linkages. Some hospitals will simultaneously belong to two systems. For example, a hospital may be a part of a religious-owned system but at the same time be participating as a primary care hospital for a locally based hospital network. [pp. 43–44]

For the time beyond the 1980s there are several possible patterns. Speculation and opinion vary as to the likelihood and worth of each. One view holds that the trend of the 1970s and 1980s will continue, both in number of institutions involved and in the degree of integration. This is the view of Seiverts and Sigmond (1970), as quoted in the epigraph of this chapter. This view assumes that the mixed strategy of hospitals of the 1980s, i.e., multiunit systems that obtain some advantages of scale while preserving some institutional authority, will lead naturally to more complete forms of consolidation. DeVries (1978) believes in a developmental continuum: "Chances are greater that hospitals that are interested in the benefits of consortia or system will begin at one of the simpler, less committed levels . . . and over time and with experience move to the right (i.e., to tighter forms) of the continuum . . ." (p. 84). Brown (1976) makes the same forecast:

Single-community hospitals and those with small branches will increasingly make alliances with neighboring hospitals for shared services, and as these less formal arrangements increase trust and interaction, more will consider contract management which will lead to more eventual mergers. As management becomes a more centralized organization, trustees' and medical staff's fears will be lessened, thus overcoming a major hurdle in the move to further system integration. Just as merger and common ownership can lead to centralized direction and control, common management should lead to common ownership. [p. 49]

Connors (1978) sees a similar future.

We are at the beginning of a long term trend toward multi-hospital arrangements. Multi-hospital systems have in the past and will, to a greater degree in the future, out-perform the single free standing organization. In the longer term, consortia, loose sharing arrangements, and mergers without teeth will give way to organizations with ownership obligations or tighter management arrangements capable of committing an entire system to a course of action and direction of change. Competition will develop among and between systems, while at the same time there will be significant cooperation and joint effort. [p. 4]

A quite different view holds that the consolidation momentum could in the future reach the limits of its own usefulness. Just as growth and size have been virtues in the American culture of the past, so can future peoples come to feel that small is beautiful (Schumacher, 1973). Hospitals must be particularly sensitive to this, since they are at once large "health factories" and also places where the most intimate of services are rendered in highly individualized encounters (Freidson, 1967). Aside from inflexibility in patient care which is the inevitable consequence of bigness, the corporate power of large merged health enterprises may come eventually to be questioned (Starkweather et al., 1979). In the language of antitrust, present day integrations among hospitals yield savings in social resources and other public benefits which offset what might otherwise be regarded as unlawful restraint of trade. Yet "such claims are properly viewed with skepticism, for there has never been an antitrust sinner who did not claim that he was serving the public good" (Areeda, 1972, p. 42). Shortell (1977) believes that although multiunit hospital systems will grow, in part as a response to increased regulation and external forces, "their very presence may well lead to further regulation by means of antitrust legislation. The possibility of such perversities . . . should not be ignored" (pp. 45–46).

Another view stresses the development of community-based comprehensive health care systems, with multiunit hospital arrangements as the developmental base. This is the notion of critical mass and vertical integration presented earlier in this chapter. Stull (1977) states that "existing multihospital systems appear to be strategies for coping with managerial deficiencies and financial imperatives rather than strategies for developing comprehensive health care systems" (p. 43). Shortell (1977) predicts that, by the mid-1980s when health maintenance organization experience is acquired, horizontally-integrated hospital systems will begin to regionalize and to develop vertical health care delivery systems. (See I. Definitions later in this chapter.)

All of this means that there is a basic trend toward integration that will continue into the future. It also means that the trend will be represented by great variety in corporate forms. What is more important, the evolution is multistaged, with considerable doubt as to what in the long run can and should be made to follow from the short run trend of the 1980s.

E.   Advantages of Merger

We can classify the claimed advantages of hospital consolidation according to the goals of efficiency and effectiveness: those reasons relating to use of resources and those relating to outputs of hospital and medical activity. The first set is economic, the second service-related. We can also identify those gains that result from the process of merging regardless of efficiency or effectiveness.

THE ADVANTAGES OF EFFICIENCY

May (1970) neatly categorized the efficiency reasons for consolidation by placing them in the context of economic theory.[6] The categories are: 1) economies of scale, 2) market share, and 3) substitutability or complementarity among items in a hospital's service lines.

Much has been written concerning economies of scale. Some practicing administrators believe that a hospital with 400–600 beds is more efficient than either smaller or larger hospitals. Numerous health economists have studied the behavior of hospital costs per unit of output over different sizes and have failed to come to specific agreement. However, it has been demonstrated that average costs generally decrease as hospital size increases from very small to somewhat greater than 300 beds, indicating the existence of economies of scale in hospital operation, primarily among smaller hospitals and most dramatically in those under the U.S. average size of 166 beds. Unit costs begin to increase again at the size of 600 to 700 beds, indicating diseconomies of scale. Health economists have not explored this latter phenomenon thoroughly as these larger facilities pose greater problems of controlling for quality, i.e., scope of services. Diseconomies of size are generally attributed to higher costs of coordination, communication, and organizational control.

Factors leading to economies of scale or, as they are sometimes called, increasing returns to scale, are five in number. First, there may be some unavoidable excess capacity in a hospital, such as a renal dialysis unit or an open-heart surgery suite. Equipment and personnel must be on hand when needed, but efficient operation requires a much higher utilization rate than that of the present scale of operation. If two hospitals merge, each contributing expensive, complementary, but seldom-used equipment, economies of scale may follow. Second, many items of equipment and supply become cheaper when purchased on a larger scale. Third, more specialized processes, whether performed by people or machines, become possible as the scale of operation increases. For example, two small hospital laboratories each employing three technologists doing a variety of different kinds of tests can, after combining, assign each of the six technologists to a specialized task. This should result in higher quality of test results and in lower cost per test since, as the skill level with respect to the specialized process increases, tests take less time to perform and are completed with fewer spoiled results. Fourth, the cost of capital to a merged organization would probably be lower than it would be to either of the smaller organizations which existed prior to the merger. The larger, presumably more stable, organization presents a better risk to lenders, or often can present itself as more deserving to receive gifts or grants because of its activities. Finally, the statistical law of large numbers gives rise to certain economies of scale. Occupancy levels in large hospitals are generally higher than those in small hospitals. Furthermore, occupancy rates of specialized units and of the hospital as a whole vary less in large hospitals than in small ones. This can be demonstrated statistically as well as empirically: if one observes a large sample from a given distribution, variance is smaller relative to the mean than it is for a small sample.

The second efficiency factor concerns changes or modifications of market share. Among manufacturing corporations, mergers frequently occur when one firm has outlets or a distribution system which another firm wishes to tap. In the hospital industry, an institution in a core city area may have historically served a clientele of middle and upper class persons. If it now faces a situation in which its own geographical area requires a new form of delivery and new emphasis in the type of care delivered, it may choose to change its program and adapt itself to the new needs. On the other hand, it may be unable or unwilling to adapt and, instead, look for new markets for its services. One way to obtain those is to merge with an existing organization already operating in such markets.

The final economic factor has to do with substitutability or complementarity of services. If two services are substitutes, then as more of one is used, less of the other will be used. If the relationship between the two is complementary, an increase in the use of one causes an increase in the use of the other. Suppose that services of a surgical suite and those of a surgeon are complementary in the sense just described. Then, if one party to a proposed merger has surgeons who want to operate but who cannot get adequate time in the schedule, and the other party has low usage of its surgical facilities, the economic viability of the proposed merger increases as a result. On the other hand, suppose that internists are good substitutes for family practitioners and that one of the hospitals has many of the former on its staff and the other has a large number of the latter. In this case, the merger is likely to be impeded by whichever group of physicians is threatened by the increased possibilities of substitution.

Any consideration of these three economic factors must be made in the context of the economic interests of the groups concurrently involved in either encouraging or thwarting merger attempts. We can categorize these interested parties into: 1) external groups such as planning or regulatory agencies which purport to represent society at large; 2) organizational groups such as boards, administrators, and sometimes medical staffs which are primarily concerned with the welfare of the hospital qua hospital; and 3) personal groups such as employees and physicians whose special economic interests are affected by a merger.

These various groups react in different ways to merger plans—occasionally even diametrically opposing each other. For instance, the first advantage of merger, the achievement of efficiency through economies of scale, should be viewed positively by all concerned—except, perhaps, by employee groups who might lose jobs or seniority, or by physicians who might find fewer beds available for their patients as a result of the proposed merger.

Similarly, from the points of view of society and the organization, elimination of excess capacity should have positive implications. But will this also be the case for the gynecologist who will no longer have access to the previously unoccupied maternity beds, or to patients and visitors who must now travel farther to the new, merged hospital?

Integrations among hospitals can deal advantageously with duplication of facilities and services which regulatory bodies often view as unnecessary. Redundant equipment in many cases was not installed casually. To produce the necessary quantity and quality of x-ray diagnostic procedures, a hospital may have had to buy x-ray therapy equipment in order to attract or hold radiologists. In this case, the diagnostic and therapeutic procedures are complements in production. In eliminating unnecessary duplication of therapy machines, the merging process may inadvertently reduce the complementary diagnostic services as well.

Elimination of personnel shortages may help the hospital but reduce the rate of increase in wages and thus be opposed by employee groups. Improvement in quality and quantity of hospital care rendered may benefit the individual receiving the care but raise costs to society or restrict the scope of practice for some physicians.

Many more examples could be cited. The point is not that consolidation fails to bring real economic advantages to hospitals, but that the net gain combines many pluses and minuses, each calculated differently by the numerous parties which have something at stake.

Roos (1975) puts it well, in commenting on Reid's (1968) study of business mergers:

> Reid's work suggests that hospital mergers could also be analyzed from the perspective of which member of the coalition's—hospital administrators, medical schools, physicians, the patient, and the public—interests are most served. For example, do mergers help hospital administrators win higher salaries, more prestige, and more control, as do their counterparts in private business? Do physicians win higher fees, access to costlier equipment, and the possibility for increased specialization? Does the patient win higher quality treatment? Does the public win lower or contained costs as well as better access to medical facilities? These questions are far from academic and suggest a framework within which hospital mergers should be evaluated. It seems clear now that the public's representative, the national government, is pushing mergers in the hope of advancing the public's interest in cost containment. Using Reid as a guide, it will be important to monitor the mergers to discover what the actual outcomes are. [pp. 20–21]

THE ADVANTAGES OF SERVICE AND QUALITY

Keairens and Murphy (1970) and Acton (1967) have summarized the possible clinical, patient, and community-oriented advantages of merger[7] as follows:

1) Centralization makes it possible to increase depth and expand scope of services, leading to improvements in quality. For example, the addition of microchemistries to support pediatrics adds depth, and and the addition of a home care or extended care program adds scope.

2) Conversely, a poor-quality duplicate service is likely to be eliminated. Indeed, merger may be the only way to dispatch it.

3) Formal training programs are likely to be encouraged; they generally upgrade all physicians' medical knowledge. Education programs directly improve quality of care. And, indirectly, training programs require organization, faculty, and facilities which in turn improve quality.

4) Though centralization can reduce geographic access to some services, it can also improve access by providing services not previously available, such as the development of special programs in community medicine and organized primary care.

5) A major medical center can overcome problems associated with the care of indigent and other high-risk populations by mobilizing programs and services and more effectively dealing with financial and bureaucratic constraints.

6) Coordinated control over a larger bed capacity and bed utilization can lead to decreased waiting lists and increased flexibility in use of specialized beds, benefiting patient care as well as reducing costs.

7) Physicians reduce lost time as they devote time and energies to one rather than two or three medical staffs. This leaves more time for direct patient management.

Of these seven service-oriented advantages, only the second, the opportunity to dispatch a poor quality activity, is clearly related to merger and not to increased size.

Westerman (1978) believes that quality improvements will be the second generation concern of multihospital systems, once efficiency-related gains of the first generation are achieved. He narrates the following plausible scenario.

> The hospital industry seems to be moving from 7,000 individual units to a network of far fewer systems. As systems develop, they will need to attract free-standing units. Early system development tended to pull together natural groupings based on ownership, geography, beliefs and economic incentives. As the second phase of groupings take place the larger systems will offer a more attractive package to relatively well-off free-standing units. This more attractive package will address difficult operating problems of the free-standing unit. Rating high among difficult areas is the issue of quality assurance. Small institutions with limited numbers of medical staff can only do a finite number of audits, even at the rate of only four a year. Multi-unit systems have

the capacity to fulfill conventional wisdom in quality assurance and develop innovative measures utilizing peer review among a larger number of physicians. PSROs will have a far easier time working with individual hospitals in larger systems. Larger systems will have the data base and technology to be compared one with another. New system methodologies should emerge to elevate the effectiveness of quality systems. As the improved data emerge, government policy makers will be in a better position to explore various policy alternatives. [p. 11]

THE ADVANTAGES OF PROCESS

Aside from efficiency or effectiveness gains, a merger may yield what Sieverts and Sigmond (1970) call institutional renewal. They point out not only that many health organizations are governed and run through structures that are obsolete to current functions and community demands, but also that people in leadership positions can become out-of-date, resistant to change, or tired.

> What do you do about obsolete organizational patterns or exhausted leadership? Frequently an organization can generate new leadership or unilaterally (often with expensive outside help) redesign its own organizational structures. The process of corporate merger, however, with its necessary negotiations of competing interests, involves new looks at purposes, programs, and partnerships—and can be a deliberate device to elevate a new leadership group into authority, thereby creating an institution with the vigor of newness coupled with solidity of experience. [p. 262]

F.   SOME DISADVANTAGES OF MERGER

As with the advantages outlined above, we need to distinguish between size-related disadvantages and those deriving from merger per se.

Concerning the former, we have already mentioned the diseconomies of largeness. Unit costs of operations go up for hospitals of 600 or 700 beds and more, due to the increased problems of coordination, communication, and control in an organization now so big that the left hand doesn't know what the right is doing.

More pervasive and serious are the nonaccounted costs of human indifference and impersonality that can creep into an organization so large that few people comprehend the whole, much less feel a sense of responsibility for or loyalty to it—a most serious matter in the intensely human factory called a hospital.[8] "The larger the system the more danger a patient can get lost in it. Consolidations may keep patients from getting care through layers of bureaucracy" (Schweiker, 1978).

Patient access to care may also be adversely affected by some forms of consolidation. Results of a National Opinion Research survey reflect public alarm over removing immediate access to services such as emergency rooms and cardiac units (Schweiker, 1978).

Again, while some sort of integration among hospitals may have produced these several size-related effects, the disadvantages are not those of the integration itself. Most of the drawbacks of mergers per se run to the process of integration. Further, most are in that elusive realm of institutional identity, culture, and personality—not to be diminished in their importance by their resistance to measurement.

The process of growth by merger causes losses that do not occur when comparable size is achieved by internal expansion of one of the parties. Consolidations cause severe rifts. People loyal to and familiar with an organization are more likely to be set aside, or put in a new environment where they may not perform as well. Mergers can more readily produce people over or underqualified for jobs than can comparable change made more deliberately and predictably by organizational growth from within (Grube, 1971). This has its effect on hospital performance.

Further, inefficiency may result from the new organization's loss of group work experience and knowledge of informal employee interaction necessary for developing an efficient working relationship (Packer, 1964). Money et al. (1976) concluded from their study of hospital mergers that the organizational processes that evolve after merger satisfy the conditions of alienation, i.e., powerlessness, meaninglessness, normlessness, isolation from satisfying social relations, and self-estrangement (p. 58).

Then there are the organizational consequences of identity and reputation losses among parties to merger—losses which would not take place were hospital restructuring done by means other than consolidation of existing entities. Potential donors who feel loyal to prior institutions are indifferent to the new. In addition connections—important political relationships—may be severed for the old entities and difficult to replace by the newly formed and novel entity. Franklin (1971), describing the changing political inputs to a hospital during the formation of a multihospital system, states that public support of a unique institution will initially drop as its identity is submerged into a larger organization and as its perceived relevance to the community's goals drops.

Beyond immediate institutional results, cultural effects influence the merging entities more broadly and more subtly. Most U.S. communities reflect national values of pluralism and choice. A merger may destroy the hospital as a community's symbol of shared effort, pride, and ownership (Stone, 1978). A merger can lead to alienation by removing an institution important to the structure of a community and replacing it with an unknown. Further, we must ask, with Schweiker (1978), "Will the differing needs of individual communities be overshadowed by the broader demands of larger systems?" (p. 8)

Most of the disadvantages or barriers to merger are behavioral. Since they appear to be controlling factors in most situations, much of the remainder of this book is about them.

G.   THE MARKETPLACE EFFECT OF MERGERS

Economists use the phrase market structure to denote the distribution and marketplace effect of economic power among firms in an industry. Hospitals seldom compete directly for patients, although they usually do so indirectly through medical staff appointments and efforts to attract new or young physicians with growing practices. But they do compete with one another for other resources, notably specialized personnel. One effect of a merger of two hospitals is to increase, however infinitesimally, the monopsonistic power of the combination with respect to the purchase of specialized labor and other resources. This goes beyond the ability of a large buyer to purchase a needed resource at a lower price than a small buyer; additionally, the sheer bargaining or market power of the new and larger organization vis-à-vis that of the sellers of services will increase. For example, two nonmerged hospitals may compete for the services of registered nurses by offering higher salaries or better working hours. After the two have merged, the situation is as if they had previously colluded with respect to salaries: the price is not likely to rise as rapidly as it would have otherwise.

Hospital market structure effect can be explained by the example of a community with four institutions: Hospital A with 50 beds, B with 150, C with 150, and D with 325. Applying the list of advantages presented above, A's future is gloomy indeed without merger or growth; however, if it merged with B or C the new combine would likely survive and possibly prosper, leaving the nonmerged 150-bedder to fare a precarious future. If B and C combined, they would effectively challenge D's dominant position, which D might hedge by picking up A. If either B or C merged with D, both A and the remaining nonmerged 150-bedder are put into something of a dependency state.

In addition to these market structure effects for individual hospitals, there is also the community-wide effect. The least significant merger—numerically speaking, A plus D—would increase D's size by over 15 percent without increasing the community's bed capacity. In the most significant merger, B plus C, either hospital would grow by 100 percent with the same nil effect on community growth. If, in the least significant example, D were to add 50 beds instead of merging with A, the community growth would be in the order of 7 percent; in the most significant the community effect would be 22 percent. A number of merged institutions reported to Brown and Lewis (1976) that the total number of beds in the new organization was significantly less than they would have needed had they not merged.

Thus, the effects of institutional growth by merger and institutional growth from within are quite different, leading to varying states of relative efficiency, capacity for future performance, and relative disperson or concentration of power.

There is disagreement over whether market dominance is good or bad. In classical economics, merger is a strategy to reduce competition, reduce output, reduce costs, and raise prices (Stigler, 1950). Yet some (Cooney and Alexander, 1975) argue that since in the not-for-profit hospital industry major portions of production can be considered a public service, domination by merger turns into an advantage not only for the merged institutions but for the community at large.

> The advantage rests in the fact that this domination, if it is realized, can provide the resources and power base for the system to play the role of a planning authority. . . . It can design the scope, quantity, quality, and distribution of services it provides in such a fashion as to serve the community it dominates and avoid duplication of facilities and services by better utilizing hospital services. [Part 1, p. 3]

Here we have a real debate. There seems little doubt that merged hospitals acquire greater control over their market environments than nonmerged hospitals in comparable circumstances. But there is no guarantee that the kinds of public benefits outlined by Cooney and Alexander will follow. We will further discuss the relative benefits of private and public regulation of hospital markets in chapter 10.

H.   THE EVALUATION OF MERGER RESULTS

We simply do not know the real benefits of merger because we lack solid evaluation. Only three studies in the literature draw conclusions from objective and comparative data. Numerous others simply report the answers to questions asked of administrators or other merger officials about what they think the results of merger to have been. We will first present results of three studies in the second category, despite their strong respondent bias; we will follow these by the three studies in the first category.

THREE SURVEY STUDIES

Harris's (1970) study is worthwhile because it compares merger administrator's opinions of results with the apparent motives for merging. Harris's respondents were 79 administrators of what he calculated to be the universe of 93 mergers that had transpired in the foregoing five years. The administrators' reasons for integration fell into six areas: financial, managerial, manpower, education and research, service, and external. Respondents indicated whether a reason was "highly sigificant," "significant," or "insignificant." Another part of the survey asked for the effect of merger, using the same categories but with a "yes"/"no" response. Some of the results are shown in table 1.1.[9]

TABLE 1.1.   Reasons and Results of Hospital Mergers

Category of Reason Reason Result	Percentage Indicating Reason "Highly Significant" or "Significant"	Percentage Indicating "Yes" as Result
Financial		
Save institution in financial trouble.	47	
Was one or more saved from disaster?		41
Is the merger on a sound financial basis?		98
Pool beds for greater efficiency.	74	
Did pooling result in economy?		78
Eliminate duplication of services.	68	
Has duplication been avoided?		86
Increase borrowing power.	12	
Has borrowing power been increased?		61
Enhance fund raising power.	36	
Were fund raising drives successful?		35
Enhance opportunities to receive government grants.	42	
Have qualified for government grants?		49
Achieve economies through standardization.	66	
Has standardization resulted in savings?		65
Economize by consolidations of money, manpower, etc.	57	
Have savings been realized?		69
Managerial		
Broaden governing board representation.	18	
Has broadening been achieved?		39
Utilize sophisticated management techniques.	24	
Able to attract highly qualified managers?		84
Able to use modern management techniques?		63
Refine facility and program planning.	32	
Has more coordinated planning resulted?		88

Continued

TABLE 1.1.   Continued

Category of Reason Reason Result	Percentage Indicating Reason "Highly Significant" or "Significant"	Percentage Indicating "Yes" as Result
Manpower		
Conserve time and energy of physicians.	56	
Has such been saved?		73
Improve personnel selection opportunities.	53	
Have opportunities been improved?		71
Combat personnel shortages.	43	
Has merger helped overcome shortages?		49
Lower high staffing costs.	63	
Have staffing costs been lowered?		43
Service		
Develop better services through resource pooling.	75	
Are more comprehensive services now offered?		75
Develop clinical programs and facilities.	65	
Has development occurred?		63
Coordinate services.	76	
Has coordination been achieved?		75
Education and research		
To elevate educational standards.	45	
Have such been raised?		41
To broaden educational programs.	44	
Has paramedical education been improved?		57
To develop clinical research programs.	30	
Have research efforts more fully developed?		33
External		
To meet demands of outside agencies.	45	
Does the merger meet outside demands?		33

Source: Harris, 1970.

In general, service-oriented reasons (service, education, and research) were listed more frequently as "highly significant" or "significant," as compared to efficiency-oriented categories (financial, managerial, manpower). Even so, almost half of the mergers were undertaken to save at least one of the hospitals from financial disaster. In general, results were as originally desired, although the high success rates reported on features reflecting managerial performance support our suspicion of nonvalidity. Outcomes that differed markedly from original expectations had to do with increased borrowing power, where merger results were much higher than original expectations, and the lowering of staffing costs, where original expectations were higher than results.

Harris's results were approximately the same as those of a study conducted by Dagnone (1967) of 40 multiple unit hospital systems, 24 of which were mergers. Seventy-nine percent of these institutions had reorganized primarily for what we have called service-oriented reasons, with efficiency-oriented reasons again secondary. Contrary to Harris' results, 63 percent of Dagnone's respondents reported problems with absentee administration, intra-unit competition, and friction between line and staff.

> Even if management has developed a sound plan of allocation of powers, devised the most logical organizational arrangements, skillfully adopted these to fit available personnel, and although the entire hospital system is capably directed by the chief executive officer, human problems will prevail . . . it is inevitable that friction, disagreement, some positioning for power and detectable resistance to change (will occur) on the part of those who see it (merger) as a threat to their status. Problems such as these exist in all hospital organizations but they are accentuated by occurring more frequently and taking on special forms. [pp. 62–63]

A before-after study of a single widely publicized merger of three hospitals in Wilmington, Delaware also reported mixed results (McGrath et al., 1970). In a survey conducted three years after merger there was wide disagreement as to whether consolidation had achieved improved quality of care, availability of specialized equipment, etc. Most of the survey's respondents were physicians who had originally voted for or against the merger (66 percent for, 34 percent against) and then participated in a medical staff merging in which three separate staffs were unified into a single new one. Physicians holding staff appointments in any of the three hospitals were granted similar status in the new medical center, which carried access to all hospitals in the merger.

Three years after merger there was still strong resistance. Of the 76 doctors who originally opposed merger, 82 percent were still opposed. Of the 130 who originally supported merger, 35 percent had come to oppose it. Thus, three years after merger, only a minority—48 percent of respondents—favored the three-hospital combination. Respondents were asked whether merger had caused improvement, decline, or did not affect selected aspects of health care and professional considerations. The proportion perceiving a decline is shown in table 1.2.

TABLE 1.2.   Wilmington Medical Center: Physician Respondents Perceiving Decline in Health System After Merger, by Position on Merger

| | Position on Merger Before and After | | | |
Aspect of Health System	Stable Opposition (%)	Opposition to Support (%)	Stable Support (%)	Support to Opposition (%)
Quality of patient care	61	36	12	53
Control of outpatient care	36	21	8	22
Administration of individual facilities	56	14	14	56
Utilization of all health personnel	37	14	11	38
Ability to operate as autonomous professionals	50	29	11	47
Individual status in medical community	43	0	4	33

Source: McGrath et al. (1971).

The data suggest that premerger patterns of opposition or support had a strong influence on postmerger appraisals. Notably, the 62 doctors who were stable in their opposition were consistently more likely to see negative consequences than the 85 who were stable in their support. Quite possibly this bias was strong enough to block successful accommodation to change. McGrath and colleagues concluded:

> However, the fact that fairly substantial numbers of respondents, regardless of their initial position, perceived a decline suggests that the merger had not yet measured up to pre-merger expectations. One possible interpretation is that during pre-merger discussions backers, confronted with a generally skeptical and conservative audience, over-emphasized the potential advantages and underplayed the disadvantages in an attempt to win support of the physicians. This could have generated unrealistic expectations. . . . Combining this problem with transition problems such as scheduling and bed allocation set the stage for frustration and disenchantment. [pp. 53, 54]

Perhaps all we can conclude from these three studies is that obtaining valid appraisal of merger benefits by survey is difficult indeed, given the complexity of the situations, the lapsed times incurred, the shortage of good outcome measures, and the professional and managerial identities involved. Yet, these survey results suggest that the array of important merger benefits is heavily laced with shortcomings, and that the mix of each depends strongly on who is doing the evaluating.

THREE COMPARATIVE STUDIES

Neumann (1974) reported on a financial study of the eight merged hospitals of the Samaritan Health Service, Arizona, conducted by a team of researchers drawn from Northwestern University and the American Hospital Association. An abstract of Neumann's findings follows:

> Four hospitals, located in or near Phoenix, were merged into Samaritan Health Service, a nonprofit corporation. Four other hospitals with less than 35 beds each, located in remote rural areas of Arizona, are leased by Samaritan Health Service. The research involved 1) an evaluation of the financial history of the individual Samaritan hospitals and 2) a comparison of the merged Samaritan system with a control group of unmerged hospitals.

> Audited financial statements and other Samaritan operating reports were used as data inputs for the evaluation of the financial position of each Samaritan hospital during the entire period (1967–1971). The second part of the financial analysis was based on a comparative evaluation of average costs of Samaritan Health Service when compared to the average costs of other unmerged hospitals. The merged Samaritan hospitals were compared with similar (control) hospitals that were not merged. A variety of qualitative attributes such as bed-size categories, accreditation status, and program approvals were used to select sets of unmerged (control) hospitals that were similar to each respective Samaritan hospital. By matching hospitals on this basis the control groups included hospitals that provided services similar to those provided by each of the merged Samaritan hospitals.

> The financial evaluation of each of the Samaritan hospitals prior to merger (1968) indicated that only Good Samaritan Hospital was in sound financial condition; the other seven smaller hospitals all had varying degrees of financial weakness. . . . The formation of Samaritan Health Service can, therefore, be characterized as the merger of a large, financially strong hospital with smaller hospitals that were, for the most part, experiencing severe crises. Each of the smaller Samaritan hospitals required some form of capital input in order to survive. The required capital financing put an immediate strain on Samaritan Health Service.

> The synergistic effect of the merger has had three results: 1) spreading the risk of financial bankruptcy over a larger asset base, 2) stabilizing the flow of funds from operations for the entire Samaritan system, and 3) providing additional external sources of capital funds to individual Samaritan hospitals. External capital funds were provided by institutional investors who had not previously loaned funds to individual unmerged Samaritan hospitals.

> The second aspect of this research was to determine the impact of the merger on operating costs. That is, did average costs increase as a result of the merger? The question that is relevant is whether average costs increased or decreased after the merger as compared to similar unmerged hospitals. The

rate of increase in average cost per stay for Samaritan Health Service both before and after the merger was not significantly different from the rate of increase in average cost per stay for the control hospitals for the same periods.

This conclusion is not consistent with the theories of traditional economics; hospital mergers would be expected to yield economies of scale that would moderate any increases in average costs. In Neumann's view, this curious phenomenon can be attributed largely to the observation that, since the merger, Samaritan Health Service provided substantially more services than it did before the merger: the growth in services provided by Samaritan Health Service was 21.6 percent (1968–1970) as compared to 10.8 percent for the control hospitals. Further, although providing no data in support, Neumann concluded that the additional costs of increased services at Samaritan Health Service appear to have been offset by documented cost savings in the areas of purchasing and materials management, personnel administration, and food services that were a direct result of the merger. Neumann concluded:

> The results of this study can be generalized to other hospitals that may contemplate mergers. It should be noted, however, that cost savings may not manifest themselves in the form of lower average operating costs where these two conditions exist: 1) the merged hospitals include small hospitals that could not previously afford to provide accredited health care, and 2) the scope and/ or quality of service at these small hospitals is upgraded as a result of the merger. These two conditions militate against a reduction in average costs when available resources are used to finance changes in health services capabilities. However, the impact of the merger can be judged financially beneficial, as mergers may permit increments to service that individual hospitals could not afford prior to merger. [p. 987]

Neumann's study reveals both the methodologic difficulties of such analyses and the qualifications that must be attached to the conclusions. The Northwestern-American Hospital Association researchers had difficulty controlling for quality and scope of service changes which were covarying with the merger. Further, their conclusion that the merger provided financial survival for otherwise precarious hospitals begs the question whether such hospitals should in fact have continued—a determination that presumably would involve many noneconomic factors.

Treat's (1976) study is similar to Neumann's, except that his sample size was larger and he concentrated more on effectiveness questions, i.e., capability to deliver care,[10] a weakness in Neumann's study. Treat also examined merger effects over a longer period of time for each institution studied. He applied 14 criteria to 32 pairs of merged and unmerged hospitals, drawn from the list developed by Harris (1970) and others, for the period 1956 to 1970. Data were collected on each merger for the year before merger, and for three, five, and seven years afterward.

Treat tested the null hypothesis that no significant difference exists in efficiency and effectiveness between hospitals that merge and those which remain independent. Fifteen pairings of merged and nonmerged hospitals yielded significant differences at the 1 percent level, 53 pairings were statistically different at the 5 percent level, 36 instances allowed for rejection of the null hypothesis at the 10 percent level, and 68 instances allowed for rejection at the 20 percent level.

The findings concerning average cost per case strongly suggested that merged hospitals experienced greater increases in costs than their paired independent counterparts. The findings held for the overall comparison by time frame and for all of the separate comparisons except the one involving non-SMSA (Standard Metropolitan Statistical Area) hospitals. These same findings held with regard to the average cost per day and total expense indicators.

These findings do not support the assertion that mergers improve hospital efficiency, except for those hospitals located in non-SMSA areas. Treat felt that one plausible explanation has to do with the idea of prospective costs, a factor identified in studies of mergers among banks. Such costs include

> the salary cost of a suitable replacement for top management, the cost of fringe benefits that have never actually been provided for the employees, the cost of meeting the competition . . . , the costs of mechanization and modernization which have never been undertaken. These are costs which a successful (institution) must pay in a competitive situation if it is to provide the services offered by other (institutions), but they are costs which dismay the . . . directors of many small institutions who have not faced up to obsolescence of their management practices and their physical plant. [Smith 1971, p. 108]

Another explanation offered by Treat is that rather than trying to reduce anything, merged hospitals may be intent on enlarging and expanding their capacities. Therefore, total expenses would be expected to rise more in study hospitals than in control hospitals, to support their larger organizations. Curiously, while total expense had been increasing, output had in many cases been declining. This inverse relationship between patient days and total expense calls into question the wisdom of hospital merger on grounds of improved efficiency, or at least lends credence to the factors of coordination costs and diseconomies of scale mentioned in the literature.

Whereas most of the performance associated with Treat's efficiency indicators was less than promising, the reverse was generally true with regard to his effectiveness indicators. Both services and approvals[11] increased significantly over all time frames and in most categories. With the exception of the larger hospitals, which supposedly already had many of the approvals, merged hospitals consistently gained more approvals than their paired independent counterparts. In the case of non-SMSA and small hospitals, the labor intensity indicator increased significantly during the time frames studied, suggesting a useful result for these hospitals which often are unable to attract and hold even minimal numbers of qualified personnel to staff their facilities.

On balance, Treat's findings indicated that merger tends to reduce efficiency while enhancing effectiveness. Small, rural hospitals fared better on his effectiveness indicators, suggesting that merger is a useful strategy for such facilities. However, we must recognize a shortcoming of Treat's model: his effectiveness measures did not include prospective and time/travel costs. Increased travel and communication problems are often cited as two of the most vexing problems in mergers. Treat concluded:

> The findings of this study suggest that many of the alleged benefits of mergers, especially in the area of cost savings, while playing a major part in merger deliberations and expectations, do not materialize after merger. . . . The concept appears more encouraging for non-SMSA (rural) hospitals, especially in view of the evidence suggesting that the benefits seem to extend over the long run. . . . Many desirable benefits involving improved hospital efficiency and effectiveness will accrue to such institutions. Mergers of large, short-term, urban hospitals, on the other hand, should be viewed with caution. Although such mergers succeed in increasing the service capability of the hospitals involved, the evidence overwhelmingly suggest that such service improvements are gained only with a concomitant increase in costs and expenses. Merger does not appear a promising answer to the financial problems of urban hospitals. [p. 208]

Treat's conclusions are sobering. His summary conclusion about urban hospitals may be premature; the benefits of mergers involving large, complex, urban hospitals may take more time to shake out than those of their smaller, rural counterparts—even longer than the substantial time frames provided by Treat's analysis.

The third comparative study—actually two related substudies—focused on the amount of time it takes for a merger to realize its advantages. The studies were part of a larger examination of multi-hospital systems conducted by researchers of the Health Services Research Center, sponsored by the American Hospital Association's Research and Education Trust and Northwestern University (Cooney and Alexander, 1975).

The AHA-Northwestern group examined Neumann's study described above and were perplexed by the findings, notably that 1) average cost increases after merger were greater than those before, and 2) there were no discernable differences between the rates of cost increase at Samaritan Health Service as compared with the set of unmerged hospitals. Further, their own gross cost comparison of the Samaritan Health Service with various groupings of U.S. hospitals (nationwide, Arizona, and Phoenix area) showed that the nation's community hospitals, in aggregate, experienced a faster rate of cost increase during Samaritan's premerger years than during the period after 1969, while the Samaritan system experienced the opposite pattern: it had the lowest relative case cost growth rates during the premerger period of 1967 to 1969 and the highest growth rates during the postmerger years of 1970 to 1972. Finally, the Chicago researchers noted that in Neumann's study less than two full years had passed since the merger under study had taken place.

The researchers designed an extension and expansion of Neumann's methodology aimed at analyzing the cost patterns of more mature mergers. One examination focused on the same study site but extended the study period by one and one-half years. The other study examined seven other multihospital systems scattered throughout the U.S. The first study analyzed the differences between the economic performance of the Samaritan system and those of a corresponding group of analogous but nonmerged hospitals over the period January 1967 through June 1973. Two different techniques were used to calculate the levels and growth rates of the total expense per adjusted admission. The first was a simplified ratio analysis of the system's economic experience to that of its control set in two points in time: 1) the first six months of both premerger and postmerger periods, and 2) the last six months of both periods. The second technique was a linear regression analysis which determined the absolute level (constant) and growth rate (trend) of the total expense per adjusted admission over the two periods (premerger and postmerger) for both the Samaritan system and its control set.[12]

It was hypothesized that the cost patterns of the two sets of hospitals should resemble those shown in figure 1.2.

This model shows that three distinct time periods must be considered when the effects of merger on hospital costs are considered: (a) the premerger period, (b) the adjustment period, and (c) the postadjustment or new equilibrium period. The theoretical experiences of the two sets of equivalent hospitals are identical in the first period. During the second period the two sets start from the same point but follow different paths, depending on local circumstances. Some systems might experience little resistance and low setup costs after merger and begin immediately to realize economies of scale, reduction of facility and service duplication, increased operational flexibility, etc. Other systems, however, might have to spend significant amounts of money intially to set up corporate offices, upgrade and expand their hospitals' services to corporate standards, establish standardized procedures, and overcome internal and external opposition to merger. The hump shown in the average cost of System A during its adjustment period in figure 1.2 represents the possible setup and initial upgrading costs of a newly formed merger. Finally, in the third period the two sets of hospitals (system A and set B) follow the same path, but the merged system, A, starts at a lower level than set B.

FIGURE 1.2   Theoretical Cost Patterns of Merged and
Non-Merged Hospitals, Over Time

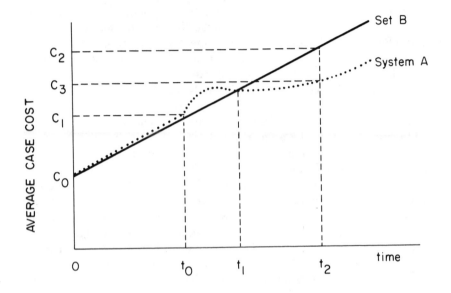

The study revealed that after the merger the Samaritan system experienced a higher actual level and growth rate in average case cost than its control set. The differences were statistically significant for the entire post-merger period of 33 months. Adding 18 months to the Neumann study produced no real change in the findings.[13]

An analysis of the behavior of the two components of the average case cost ratio revealed that, although total expenses for the system experienced a relative increase, there was a relative decrease in admissions (adjusted) during the postmerger period. This was probably the result of initial internal and external opposition to the system. When the effects of a declining number of admissions were taken into consideration, analysis of postmerger expense patterns experienced by the various functional areas within the hospitals produced a clearer picture of where the major cost increases occurred.

The functional areas considered in this analysis were patient-related services, hotel services, and administrative services. The Samaritan system paid more for its patient-related and administrative services and less for its hotel-type services than its control set, over the period of time studied. The fastest relative growth was in the patient-related services area.

When the total expense per admission variable for each functional category was broken down into its two primary components, salary and other direct expense, it was found that the bulk of the postmerger cost differences between Samaritan and its control group were in the latter category: supplies, small equipment, and professional services for the financially weaker hospitals. The relative decrease in salary experienced by the System stemmed from a relative decrease in the wage rates paid rather than from a relative decrease in man-hours worked. In fact, the relative increase in man-hours per adjusted admission experienced by the System provided indirect evidence that the Samaritan hospitals offered higher quality services during the postmerger period relative to their control hospitals.

The data show the economic consequences experienced by Samaritan during its initial formative stage, a subsequent period of organizational trauma and adverse external reaction, and its attempts to upgrade some of its weaker hospitals. The AHA-Northwestern researchers concluded that "the adjustment period for this system might be lengthened slightly because of the more altruistic motives of the System, and the amount of economies of scale realized might be less than those attained by a more economically oriented System. Nevertheless, the System has the potential for receiving many of the economic benefits that multihospital systems, in general, theoretically acquire in the long run" (p. 36).

The Chicago group's second substudy was of seven multihospital systems, derived primarily from mergers, located in different regions of the country. The data sources and general methodology used in these comparative case studies were identical to those utilized in the economic analysis of the Samaritan Health Service, except that the analysis used data for postmerger periods only. The systems selected for case study varied in age so that the actual economic patterns experienced at different points of development could be evaluated in order to draw inferences about the length of the postmerger adjustment period. Economic patterns for the years 1967 through 1972 were studied.

Findings from this study came closer to fitting the performance of merged hospitals hypothesized in figure 1.2. The seven systems also exhibited some common economic characteristics and behaviors. Specifically:

1) The levels of average case cost for the older systems were relatively lower than the levels of their control sets, while two younger systems experienced relatively higher levels of average cost over the study period.

2) The growth rates of average case cost experienced by the multihospital systems declined in relation to the rates of their control sets except in situations where the model predicted higher or equal relative rates of growth. Two younger systems experienced higher relative rates of cost growth owing in part to a dominance of initial

setup costs, while the oldest system experienced an equal relative cost growth rate owing to its having reached the postmerger state of economic equilibrium before the beginning of the study period.

3) The levels of average gross patient-generated revenue per adjusted admission (price) received by the multihospital systems were lower than those received by their control sets at the end of the study period in all but the three youngest systems.

4) The growth rates of prices charged by the systems for various hospital services declined relative to their control sets in all cases.

5) The amounts of output (measured by admissions adjusted for ambulatory services) of all systems, except one, were relatively higher over the study period than those experienced by their control sets.

6) The average lengths of stay experienced by the multihospital systems were generally lower than those of their control sets over the study period. This finding implies a more intensive rate of utilization of system hospital facilities as well as a generally lower occupancy rate. Brown (1978) believes this also suggests tighter controls of medical practice patterns resulting from strong management.

7) Economies of scale were realized most consistently by the multihospital systems in the functional area of hotel type services. There were some economies of scale realized by the systems in their patient-related and administrative areas, but these were generally less significant and less consistent. The multihospital systems usually showed a relatively lower growth rate in the number of total man-hours per case.

8) The length of the immediate postmerger adjustment period seemed to vary considerably from system to system.

The findings of this study are more supportive of merger benefits than any of the others. The overall conclusion is that there are economic benefits to mergers, but that they take a long time to be realized.[14] The AHA-Northwestern and Treat findings are consistent in suggesting that organizational complexity is a strong variable. Treat's rural, less complex hospitals apparently realized merger benefits earlier. His time frame, extended as it was (seven years postmerger), did not allow for a final verdict on the more complex urban hospitals. The study of more mature systems by the AHA-Northwestern researchers indicates that certain benefits are eventually realized (Trustee, 1976).

The two studies of the Samaritan Health Service were, in retrospect, ill-advised. As a sample of one, the System was an unfortunate choice for concentrated research. The number of hospitals merged almost simultaneously was extraordinary. Whatever the reasons were for this, they certainly could have been expected to accentuate initial merger traumas. In addition, the System became the target of inordinate external criticisms and pressures which diverted its managers' attentions from improving the merger as an operating entity. Even so, the two research reports and the considerable descriptive literature on Samaritan Health Services (Astolfi and Edwards, 1973) indicate that service and quality-oriented gains were obtained, primarily at the smaller rural hospitals in the System; efficiency-oriented gains were nebulous at best and clearly not those that had originally been heralded.

Indeed, all hospital merger studies are vague on whether the increases in service capacity that typically come with integration are gained with concomitant, less-than-concomitant, or more-than-concomitant increases in costs—crucial questions, most difficult to determine.[15] In the seven-system study conducted by the AHA-Northwestern group there were "no apparent differences noted in the composition of services between the systems and the corresponding control sets except . . . [one system] seems to have produced a less comprehensive composition of services at a very low cost and price, and . . . [another system] appears to have offered a very comprehensive composition of services at very high cost and price" (Cooney and Alexander, 1975, part 1, p. 48). Neumann (1974) believes that "the additional costs of increased services at Samaritan Health Services appear to have been offset by documented cost savings" (p. 997) in the efficiency realms—not a bad deal, if true. His study was of an eight-hospital merger balanced roughly equally between larger urban and smaller rural institutions. Treating these two types of hospitals separately, Treat (1976) concluded that rural hospital mergers provide gains in both efficiency and effectiveness realms, and only in respect to large urban hospitals did "the evidence overwhelmingly suggest that such service improvements were gained only with concomitant increase in costs and expenses" (p. 208). This is still not a bad deal (although undoubtedly not the deal that originally was sold) if the additional services were needed and could have been provided in no other way.

These two important "ifs" bring us back to the market structure and timing aspects of merger—those features which, unlike size and complexity, can fairly be attributed to merger as a process. If the additional services were needed, could they have been provided within the same time frame and with the same costs without merger? And, if the answer is yes, would the resulting structure of each community's hospital industry be more or less *pro bono publico*? What would the differences be in excess capacities, relative dispersal vs. concentration of health care, and long-run capacity of all institutions for effective performance?

These are knotty questions indeed, but ones that relate hospital mergers per se to the larger context of health care organization. It will be a long time before we know the answers. Meanwhile, we can make some inferences from the studies performed to date.

Considerable debate surrounds what actually happens following a merger. Many persons who have gone through mergers are convinced that their resulting benefits outweigh the costs. However, the actual benefits and costs of multihospital integrations appear to be quite different from those expected (Roos, 1975), including the likelihood that a newly formed merger will experience a period immediately after its creation during which its expenses increase because of system setup costs and organizational trauma associated with change. Because of this, it is tempting to conclude, as do most social scientists (Guetzkow, 1966), that mergers should proceed only with deliberate gradualism—to do otherwise would simply wastes money. Yet it may be politically essential to proceed with haste—to do otherwise would simply be to forego a merger and thus its eventual potential gains. However, in no case should the formation of a merger provide the excuse to purchase unneeded equipment, build or maintain unneeded facilities, or establish an unnecessarily expensive structure of decision making and control.

The area of hotel services seems to yield economies of scale most easily. This is a fertile cost-saving realm because of labor-saving technology, use of volume purchasing, and the lower levels of opposition to change. Yet, this conclusion is drawn from studies of multihospital mergers involving corporate integration but not complete physical integration. Without denying the benefits of multiple-hospital facilities under single management, these looser forms of integration cannot obtain the more significant benefits that come with integration of professional and patient care activities under one roof (or connected roofs). The real gains can be made only in these realms (Terrenzio, 1973).

Finally, there is the important question of who is the primary beneficiary of merged operations—the institutions and parties associated with them, patients, or the community at large. Brown (1976) believes that benefits from scale accrue to profit and nonprofit systems alike. "The benefits from superior performance seem likely to go to the owners—community or investors" (p. 94). The AHA-Northwestern researchers feel that "multihospital systems do not appear to act as monopolists. The savings realized through their relatively larger operational bases are, in general, passed on to the people they serve" (Cooney and Alexander, 1975, part 1, p. 32). By their own admission, the evidence for this conclusion is scanty. The opposite possibility, dominance for its own sake, has already been briefly discussed and will be discussed further in chapter 10.

The overall conclusion of the Chicago researchers is a reasonable one:

> Indeed, the multi-hospital system approach is not the answer to all the economic woes of the health care field. It does appear, however, to be a promising

alternative which begins to attack some of the problems that have long plagued the delivery of health services in this country. [p. 49]

I. Definitions

Mergers have been termed "centralizations of hospital management and operations" (Berman, 1971); "a situation where assets and liabilities are legally consolidated or where the combination, by purchase, lease, or other means, of two or more organizations results in the transfer of managerial prerogatives to a single governing board" (Shirley, 1973); "the formation of multihospital units under the same management—whether the units are located in the same city, different cities, or even in different states" (Crosby, 1967); and "any of various methods of combining two or more . . . hospitals wherein an acquired hospital either dissolves into merger with a surviving hospital or the old hospitals dissolve after consolidation into a new hospital" (Treat, 1976).[16] There are other descriptions, but these show the imprecision that abounds in most of them.

Another set of definitions, drawn from business rather than from the health field, places all integrations into three broad patterns: vertical, horizontal, and conglomerate. Vertical integration refers to the linking of enterprises at immediately related stages of production. Thus, a firm may merge with or acquire a company on which it either relies for supplies or to which it sells much of its output. Horizontal integration refers to the linking of firms at the same stage in the productive process in the same industry. Conglomerate merger refers to firms acquiring or merging with firms in unrelated product lines or industries.

The unique features of the health field may obscure the direct parallels among health service organizations of all three types (Schultz and Johnson, 1976). Examples of vertical integration in the health field include the purchase of a laboratory or a pharmacy by a hospital, or integration of a hospital and a group practice of physicians. Mergers of hospitals and extended care facilities (ECFs) also fall into this category. The second type, horizontal integration, is very common. Hospital-to-hospital mergers and ECF-to-ECF combinations are included in this category, as well as many for-profit chain corporations. Examples of the third type include the ownership of drug companies by large chemical corporations, and the integration of medicine and insurance in some prepayment corporations. The ownership of Catholic hospitals by religious communities could be considered a combination of eleemosynary units from medicine and religion.

Another approach to definition is to view each of several types of combination as falling on a spectrum, as shown at the bottom of figure 1.3. The left extreme of this spectrum represents pluralism, involving no formal relationships whatsoever between two or more hospitals. The right extreme denotes complete fusion. Distinctive points can be identified on this spectrum that represent formal combinations between U.S. health institutions, as shown by the middle horizontal line of figure 1.3. Of no less importance are the great variety of informal arrangements which either enhance or mitigate the establishment of formal relationships. For instance, the situation where physicians of a community hold multiple medical staff appointments at several hospitals, rather than single appointments at one, represents an informal interlocking between the hospitals that probably enhances formal relationships the institutions might undertake.

FIGURE 1.3   Informal and Formal Linkages between Hospitals

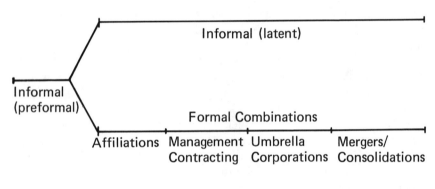

These natural linkages are of two types. One type is preformal—the relationships exist prior to and constitute a supportive or hostile environment for initial formal association. Another type is latent—it is not limited to the readiness stage of formal relations but is a concomitant of all stages and types of organizational combinations. This type of informality is created by formalization, rather than existing prior to it and, again, may be functional or dysfunctional. As shown in figure 1.3, the relationship between formal and informal linkages is represented by a single horizontal line at the left of the scale (preformal), dividing into parallel lines at the point of formalization (latent informal relations, and formal combinations).

A hospital combination, a generic term, represents any point on our spectrum to the right of preformal; an affiliation falls toward the left-middle, management contracting at the middle, an umbrella corporation toward the right middle, and a merger/consolidation at the right end of the spectrum.[17]

Affiliations are combinations among institutions designed for specific and limited joint undertakings. The agreements, entered voluntarily, are formal, but contain easily executed escape clauses for each party. The services shared are commonly supportive or logistic in nature, and require minimal investments of corporate assets. They may represent voluntary subscriptions to peripheral services offered by trade and professional associations (i.e., group insurance, uniform accounting systems), joint development by two or more hospitals of shared services with the objective of efficiency (e.g., shared services of radiologists, common laundries), or joint development of new services on the part of a small number of institutions and requiring some initial input of capital. These can also be proposed or executed by an agency which is distinct from the health facilities involved (e.g., centralized data processing, visiting nurse or home care services, affiliations for medical or paramedical teaching). Another type of affiliation fulfills the purpose of agreeing to certain trade-offs in services to be developed and offered. Hospitals that affiliate for purposes of shared services often span distinct jurisdictions or separate communities, while those developed for the purpose of allocating or shifting specialized clinical services usually have common or overlapping patient service areas. Affiliations are organizational not physical combinations. The organizational impact on the participating entities is minimal; only a few individuals' tasks, job methods, or work rules are changed.

A second type of combination is management contracting. Hospitals share administrations in this arrangement (Brown, 1976). The contract typically runs for several years, although it contains a short-term cancellation clause. The arrangement retains the cooperating members not only as distinct legal entities but also as operational bodies. The prior ownership of the participating hospitals remains intact. Unified management exists to serve these distinct governing bodies and the policies and goals they determine. The combined services are primarily administrative, although management is broadly defined and not limited to business services. The contracting institutions are typically drawn from separate communities, although they are often within the same general region. The organizational impact on participants goes beyond task revisions; there is also reorganization of departments and often the introduction of new hospitalwide procedures that promote management and operating efficiencies.

Our third type of combination is an umbrella corporation. In this arrangement a newly formed corporation spans but does not replace prior entities. The integration is considered permanent although the separate hospitals retain enough identity to split if the combination appears unworkable. There are two important subtypes of the umbrella corporation. One grants only limited authorities to the new corporation, but in these realms the umbrella corporation's decisions are final. These arrangements often deal with planning or allocation of services among otherwise distinct hospitals. There is usually no central management or central fiscal control. The other subtype grants the umbrella corporation more general and complete authority, usually exercised through unified management, policy, and fiscal control. This type is akin to the parent-subsidiary form found commonly in the business world. This arrangement requires the participating hospitals to turn over all assets to the new corporation which in turn assumes their liabilities. Newly developed assets are typically owned by the umbrella corporation. Services combined in this arrangement include hospital support and administrative activities as well as professional services. In addition to these aspects of horizontal integration, the new corporation may engage in vertical integration by developing or acquiring diagnostic clinics, group practices, home health services, extended care facilities, etc. Hospitals entering umbrella corporations sometimes serve the same population with different types of care, e.g., general care, tertiary care, or care dispersed among regional hospitals. The organizational impact on the participating institutions involves systemswide changes, introduced by planned intervention and changes in structure, activities, and perhaps goals.

A merger or consolidation is a combination of previously separate entities in which at least one organization is dissolved and absorbed by another or by a new corporation. The prerogatives of the successor organization are enumerated in formal agreements which assume permanence and which prohibit the autonomous activity of existing units. In consolidations, a new corporation completely replaces the prior corporate entities, while in merger the surviving corporation is one of the existing entities. Such an arrangement encompasses all hospital services including those previously mentioned as well as direct patient care operations. If the institutions involved serve the same community, as is typical, the facilities often end up being physically integrated into one replacement institution. The organizational impact is systemwide, involving new structures, unpredictable consequences, and simultaneous rather than sequential change. A summary of the characteristics of the four types of combinations is shown in figure 1.4 and table 1.3.[18]

J.   Discussion

In 1969 an official of the American Hospital Association said, "It is not unreasonable for hospitals to expect a savings of about ten percent in their operating cost through merger." This official saw the "beginning of a trend" as "the powers in communities around the country begin to realize the money to be saved through application of the same management principles as are applied in industry" (*Wall Street Journal*, Jan. 2, 1969, p. 12).

FIGURE 1.4 Corporate Relationships: Different Types
of Hospital Combinations

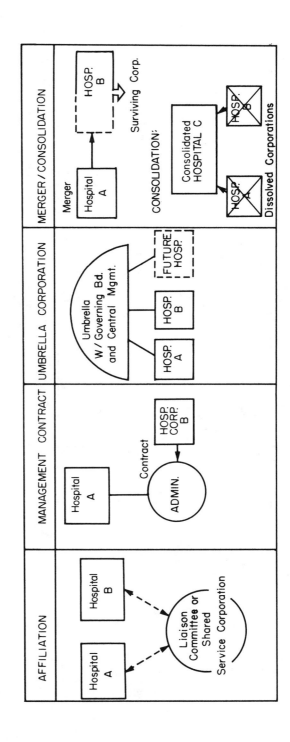

TABLE 1.3.   Characteristics of Different Hospital Combinations

	Pluralism			Fusion
	Affiliations	Management contracts	Umbrella corporations	Mergers / consolidations
Organizational pattern	Voluntary subscription or joint development, usually involving a third party; trade-off agreements	Preserve prior ownerships; new management	Delegation of policy making to new agency; new ownership and financial development	Absorption of one or more prior entities; loss of prior identities and functions
Legal bonds	Implied agreements, contracts, and formal agreements with escape clauses	Contract, typically for several years	Transferred assets; prior corporate entities continue	Replacement agreements; prior entities abolished
Services combined	Support, logistic	Administrative, broadly defined	Administrative, professional services	Administrative, professional, direct patient care operations
Geography	Dispersed or local	Separate communities; often same region	Sometimes serve same population; often regionally organized	Often a common geographic population; physical integration often intended
Organizational impact	Minimal changes of tasks, jobs, rules	Reorganization of departments; new efficiency procedures	Substantial change—new functions, accomplished by planned intervention	Evolutionary, systemwide; involving new structures; change may be spontaneous, involving unpredictable consequences

Implying that hospital enterprises are sufficiently like their business counterparts to be amenable to the same good results, this statement overlooked at least four important differences which impact heavily on the process of corporate restructuring. The quasi-independence of the medical staff of a typical hospital is unknown in the business world. A hospital is entirely dependent upon this group—its members control the business the hospital receives and indirectly control much of its operating costs. Further, the medical staff represents an intricate power system which is brought to bear on every merger. All mergers dislocate medical practices in some way; understandably, physicians respond according to the interest they have invested in their practices. Yet, beyond this obvious effect, physicians also have a pervasive influence on hospital affairs based on considerations of professional status and power (Rothman et al., 1971); widespread opposition is likely to develop which can threaten the very viability of a hospital integration. Obviously, the structure and process of consolidation must bow to this circumstance.

Second, the dominant type of hospital corporation is nonprofit, which begs the question of what is the substitute for the profit motivation said to be at the root of business enterprise behavior. Health economists disagree as to what are the true motives of hospitals (which debate we will review in chapter 2). Despite these differences, they all give prominence to the factors of prestige, community identity, and social and personnel satisfaction of trustees, administrators and physicians. For those who control hospitals, advancement of these goals partially substitutes for the dollar gains pursued by their business counterparts.

A third major difference lies in the environment of regulations in which hospitals operate. Questions as to whether hospitals survive, grow, or merge are very much clothed with the public interest. Their operations are increasingly supervised and their reimbursements controlled to the point that they operate less in the free market place of the typical business firm and more in the regulated environment of a public utility. Even entry to the hospital market is now controlled by franchising procedures which substitute the slow and cumbersome process of public decision-making for the business realities of prices, profits, and supply vs. demand.

Finally, in the business community there are many balance sheet mergers in which the important factors are ownership and control of equity. Also, there are numerous product mergers, evidenced most dramatically by the conglomerate phenomenon of the late 1960s in which the prime interest was in markets and sales penetration rather than in the nature of the merged organizations. The contrary holds true in the health field where corporate integration combines essentially a large variety of professional skills. Value is placed neither on equity nor on manufactured goods, but rather on a set of human beings who deliver highly personalized services. The crucial forces, therefore, are more likely to be rooted in the psychologies and sociologies of people than in control of material things.

Reflecting on the distinction between business and health field mergers, an experienced administrator of several hospital mergers states (Rosenberger, circa 1970):

> In much of the discussion of our present health care system, there is an implicit assumption that it could be made more efficient if only it were managed in the same way large corporations are managed. People are not aware of the fact that many of our largest corporations are just beginning to face the kind of problems that have confronted us in the health field for many decades, and are responding to these problems by behaving less like monolithic power systems and more like complex cooperative systems. We do not yet understand that . . . our hospitals have traveled further than anyone else along the road that leads to the kind of post-industrial professional service society that is gradually evolving. [p. 5]

The integrations we have classified and described in this chapter constitute a mere present-day snapshot of a long-run trend. We do not know where this trend will end, nor do we know all the permutations that will evolve along the way. We do not know its final significance. It is possible that corporate restructuring in the health field will be the means by which the nation finally achieves that illusive but important end so long sought: regionalized health care delivery. If this is to be so, then two broad aspects of development will have to be advanced simultaneously: 1) the legal and financial aspects of corporate formation, succession, and dissolution, and 2) the political and behavioral aspects of power, control, exchange, and the mediation of organizational conflict. Corporate planning—planning about corporations rather than the traditional planning by corporations—is emerging as a major strategy of health care reform.

NOTES

1. Some strongly disagree. Granting that organized primary care is a weak element in the U. S. health care system, in the late 1960s and early 1970s the federal government funded numerous health centers unrelated to the medical and hospital establishments of the communities in which they were located. This was by design, to avoid being contaminated by the establishment's orientation to a hospital-based and specialty-based health care system. Consumer control of these primary care centers contrasted with provider domination of hospitals. Many of these experiments flopped. When federal monies were withdrawn, they had no alternate basis of support; they were not linked to the rest of the system and could not function well without its various supports—professional, administrative, financial, and political. From this natural experiment many students of U. S. health care organization concluded that the full spectrum of services embraced by the phrase "comprehensive health care," in particular primary medical care, can be achieved only with the developmental strengths residing in the nation's hospitals.

2. On this distinction, Williams observed, "Although ordinarily a hospital merger might be expected to be a different kind of event from a hospital closing, in some cases the outcome was the same. The merged hospital simply closed its doors, having donated to another stronger institution its useable assets and perhaps also the right to incorporate its bed capacity into proposed new construction. The survival sought by the hospital seeking merger often turned out to be no more than a plaque on the wall of the stronger institution" (pp. 4–5).

3. In 1979, the average size of all nonfederal short-term general and special hospitals was 166 beds. In 1964 the average size for the same group was 126.

4. The New York City situation summarized by Williams (1976) illustrates this: "A reading of the records shows that the frequent catalyst leading to closure or merger was apt to be bankruptcy or the threat of bankruptcy. . . ."

    "A few of the hospitals which closed or merged were not-for-profit community hospitals with long histories of service to their neighborhoods. The record shows that these hospitals were at least partially the victims of the unprecedented demographic shift that occurred in New York City during the 1960's—the in-migration of two million Blacks and Puerto Ricans, and the equally momentous out-migration of a predominantly white middle-class population to the suburbs. Many hospitals found themselves in changed neighborhoods, separated from their former constituencies, often abandoned by their medical staff, and unable to raise philanthropic funds. . . . The infusion of federal money . . . undoubtedly helped some major voluntary hospitals to adapt successfully to changing neighborhoods, making it possible for them to finance broad community out-patient programs. On the other hand, the record shows that Medicaid reimbursement became the main financial underpinning for the continued existence of inadequate and redundant institutions which offered the most limited kind of inpatient services. In many cases this financial support only postponed a hospital's closing" (pp. 5–6).

5. How long this trend has been in place, statistically, is impossible to determine. But the causes seem to have varied over time (Brown, 1968; White and Vlasak, 1970). During the interwar decades, 1920–1940, a great number of specialty hospitals merged into general hospitals as hospital leaders recognized that their institutions required complex equipment as a result of changing technology in medical care, and as many wanted the prestige of large and more complete facilities. Then, in the post-World War II period from the late 1940s and through the 1950s and in some areas in the early 1960s, the prevailing motivation was the hope of capturing manpower. Typically, the combination would be a merger or affiliation with a teaching base in order to get house staff. Now, in most instances from the early or mid-1960s on, this trend seems to be diminishing and mergers are motivated primarily by the twin pressures of economics and technology, with small hospitals increasingly unable to survive the crunch between the two.

6. With May's permission, the several paragraphs which follow are an abstract of his formulation.

7. Keairens and Murphy offer numerous matrices suggesting the benefits, disbenefits, and ramifications of each of the seven items which follow.

8. For evidence of the disfunctions of larger hospitals using measures of patient care service rather than accounting costs, see Starkweather (1973).

9. The responses of "highly signfiicant" and "significant" have been combined. In general, the percentages for each were about equal: i.e., a response of 50 percent

in table 1.1 is made up of 25 percent "highly significant" and 25 percent "significant" responses.

10. Treat's measures of efficiency were: 1) lower average costs per case; 2) lower average costs per day; 3) shorter patient lengths of stay; 4) fewer employees needed to care for each patient; 5) lower total expenses; 6) higher occupancy rates; 7) lower bed turnover intervals; 8) higher labor productivity; 9) fewer beds; 10) higher bed turnover rates. Treat's measures of effectiveness were: 1) higher indices of services; 2) higher number of approvals; 3) higher labor intensity; 4) higher total units of output in terms of patient days.

11. "Approvals" refers primarily to educational programs in medicine, nursing, etc., certified by various national professional associations.

12. Because matching efforts showed that no two hospitals are identical, statistical matchings were obtained by the selection of groups of hospitals that were similar to a corresponding Samaritan system hospital. Selection was based on the matching of hospital experience on a number of cost-related variables shown by the hospitals in 1969, the year of the merger.

   The major design limitation involved use of retrospective data and the resulting problems surrounding the control group matching process. The variable-by-variable matching could take place at only one point in the study period, and some crucial variables could not be matched at all because of an insufficient number of observations. The study did examine several matched characteristics considered to be most influential to a hospital's cost experience: geographic location, changes in average length of stay, changes in occupancy rate, and increase in bed size. Differences in these characteristics found between the Samaritan system and its control set were handled subjectively when the findings and conclusions were interpreted.

   Another point of matching that some scientists believe is important but that was not included in these analyses is case complexity, or case mix. The assumption was made by the researchers that the hospitals' case mixes did not change significantly over the study period.

   The primary environmental problem imposed on the study was the Economic Stabilization Program established by the federal government in 1971. In theory, the changes in the average hospital's cost pattern brought about by the ESP should have been reflected equally in both the study hospitals and the control hospitals. It was impossible, however, to determine the real impact of ESP on the hospitals included in this study.

13. A study by Whittaker (1974) revealed the same approximate results, i.e., post-merger increase in costs and services.

14. Just how long has always been vague. Matti (1976), a participant in the AHA-Northwestern research, estimates seven years.

15. Another portion of the AHA-Northwestern studies deals extensively with questions of comprehensiveness, availability, and quality of care in multihospital systems, focusing again primarily on the Samaritan Health Services. Aside from serious questions of methodology in these studies, they do not relate the service and quality-oriented benefits to costs.

16. On the subtleties of words, Mace and Montgomery (1962) note that "when management representatives of an acquiring company, A, talk with executives of a potential acquisition, B, the conversation is always in terms of merger, although it is implicit and apparent that company A proposes to take over company B" (p. 4).

17. I am indebted to Ross Stromberg, Esq., for collaboration in developing this typology and the material which follows to the end of the section. Our classification is not the same as several others that have been offered, although there are commonalities. Cook (1975) classifies all hospital combinations as associations, voluntary memberships formed to deal with specific and limited activities; consortia, groups of institutions brought together for a specific purpose; federations, several institutions joined together having autonomy over local affairs but giving up the role of developing separate major plans or policies; and mergers, two or more institutions joined as a single entity. Clark (1971) deals more with function than corporate structure. His spectrum includes replication, each institution produces services on its own; assignment, one hospital provides services to another; pooling, hospitals share joint management of services through a new and separate corporation; and purchasing, services obtained from an outside source which is formed by the collaborating hospitals. Brown and Lewis (1976) offer a five-way classification of shared services, contract service, contract management, merger, and multiple-hospital systems. Showing their preference for the fifth, Brown and Lewis state that the first four represent system trends: "Not all of these trends lead to the development of hospital systems, but they represent steps in that direction" (p. 25). DeVries (1978) offers a seven way classification, distinguished from the one used herein by 1) adding a category called formal affiliation to cover activites such as patient transfer agreements and house officer affiliations; 2) splitting management contracts into two categories in order to distinguish contract management from leasing; and 3) adding a category called consortia for planning or education. Finally, Reynolds and Stunden (1978) provide four types: consortium, similar to Cook's and DeVries' forms of the same name; overlapping board membership, where one chief executive reports to two or more distinct boards that meet together and conduct business sequentially; holding company, the same as described in the text as umbrella corporation; and corporate model, the same as described in the text as merger/consolidation.

18. This schema also accommodates several popular types of aggregations not represented by the cases selected for this book but well described in the literature. For discussion of groupings of Catholic hospitals, see Brown (1975). For discussion of contract management by for-profit corporations, see Downey (1974) and Federation (1976*b*). For brief descriptions of 27 different arrangements including five public hospital systems, two for-profit corporations, and twenty not-for-profit combinations (both religious and nondenominational), see Brown and Lewis (1976).

As with most typologies, there are some unusual integrations that do not appear to fit in any one class, or are a combination of types. One is a condominium arrangement where separate hospital corporations occupy the same physical structure(s) that they jointly own (Brown and Gelinas, 1978). This is partly the case with the Palo Alto-Stanford Hospital integration described in chapter 4. A closely related situation occurs when one hospital owns the physical assets and operates a hospital within, but also leases a portion of the building(s) to another licensed hospital corporation. Such is the case with the Kaiser Medical Plan and several non-Kaiser hospitals. Another unusual integration reported in 1977 was between a Catholic hospital and a municipal hospital, with a for-profit hospital corporation operating the merged facility on a management contract (*Modern Healthcare*, 1977).

REFERENCES

Acton, Harvey. "The Multiple-Unit in Theory and Practice." Master's thesis, Graduate Program in Hospital and Health Administration, University of Iowa, 1967.
American Hospital Association. "Status of Multi-Hospital Systems." *Hospitals*, June 1, 1974.
Areeda, Philip E. "Anti-Trust Laws and Public Utility Regulation." *The Bell Journal of Economics*, Spring 1972.
Astolfi, Adrienne A., and Edwards, Sam A. "Study Analyzes Effects of Merger." *Hospitals*, February 16, 1973.
Bastnagel, G., et al. "Hospitals Consolidate Medical Services." *Hospitals*, July 1, 1973.
Berman, Howard. "Mergers and Consolidations: A Solution?" *Hospital Administration*, Winter 1971.
Boston, J.R., and Edwards, S.A. "Hospital Mergers: A Model for Third Party Funding." *Hospital Administration*, Summer 1974.
Brown, M. "Contract Management: Latest Development in the Trend Toward Regionalization of Hospital and Health Services." *Hospital and Health Services Administration*, Winter 1976.
————. "Multi-Hospital Systems and Shared Services: Some Questions and Issues." Paper presented at Invitational Conference on Multi-Hospital Systems, Washington, D.C., June 15–16, 1978.
————. "Multi-Unit Systems Under Single Management." *Hospital and Health Services Administration*, Spring 1976.
————, et. al. "Trends in Multi-Hospital Systems: A Multi-Year Comparison." *Health Care Management Review*, Fall, 1980.
————, and Gelinas, M. "The Condominium: Time for Applications to Hospitals and Other Health Care Organizations." *Health Care Management Review*, Summer 1978.
————, and Lewis, H.L. *Hospital Management Systems*. Germantown, Maryland: Aspen, 1976.
————, and Money, W.H. "The Promise of Multi-Hospital Management." *Hospital Progress*, August 1975.
Brown, Ray E. "Realigning the Hospital System: Emerging Forces and Evolving Patterns." Speech given at the 79th Annual Meeting of the Association of American Medical Colleges, Houston, Texas, November 2, 1968.
Clark, John R. "A Coordinated System for Institutionally Based Health Care Services." Hospital Education and Research Foundation of Pennsylvania, 1974.
Clark, W. "The Semantics of Multi-Hospital Aggregations." *Hospitals*, July 1, 1971.
Connors, Edward J. "Generic Problems in the Development and Operation of Multi-Hospital Systems." Presented at Sixth Annual Invitational Conference on Multi-Hospital Systems, San Francisco, June 17–19, 1978.
Cook, H.F. "Shared Services—Complex but Rewarding." *Hospitals*, February 1, 1975.
Cooney, J.P., and Alexander, T.L. "Multihospital Systems: An Evaluation." Health Services Research Center of the Hospital Research and Educational Trust and Northwestern University, (in four parts), 1975.
Crosby, Edwin L. "Improving the Delivery of Health Care Services." *Hospitals*, September 1, 1967.
Dagnone, Antonio. "A Study of Multiple Unit Hospital Systems." Unpublished thesis, Program in Hospital Administration, University of Toronto, 1967.

DeVries, R.A. "Strength in Numbers." *Hospitals*, March 16, 1978.

Doody, M.F. "Guidelines for Implementing Cooperative Programs." *Hospitals*, June 1, 1974.

Downey, G.W. "For Sale: Hospital Management." *Modern Healthcare*, June 1975.

Federation of American Hospitals. *Annual Report*. Washington, D.C., 1976a.

Federation of American Hospitals Review. "National Medical Enterprises, Inc., Aids Tax-Supported Facilities with Problems." June 1976b.

Franklin, C.L. "The Urban Multi-Hospital System: Necessary Conditions." *Hospital Administration*, Winter 1971.

Friedson, E. "Health Factories: A Review Essay." *Social Problems*, Spring 1967, pp. 493–500.

Grube, Edward F. "Hospital Mergers." *Hospitals*, May 1, 1971.

Guetzkow, Harold. "Relations Among Organizations." In *Studies on Behavior in Organizations*, ed. by Bowers, A. Athens: University of Georgia Press, 1966.

Harris, Allyn R. "Mergers Are Made to Add Service and Save Money—And They Do." *Modern Hospital*, May 1970, pp. 92–96.

Health Services Research Center. *Demonstration and Evaluation of Integrated Health Care Facilities, Samaritan Health Service, Phoenix, Arizona*. Chicago: The Center, 1972.

Hospitals, August 16, 1976 (Part II), *American Hospital Association Guide to the Health Care Field*, 1980 Edition. The Association, Chicago.

Hospital Topics, August 1973.

Keairens, Harold, and Murphy, R. "Clinical Aspects of Mergers." In *Conference on Analysis of Hospital Mergers: Transcript of Proceedings*, ed. by D.B. Starkweather and D.C. Walden. Rockville, Md.: National Center for Health Services Research and Development, 1970.

Littauer, David. "Case Report of A Hospital Merger." In *Trends in Hospital Mergers*. Dayton, Ohio: Proceedings of Annual Scientific Session, American Association of Hospital Consultants, 1967.

Mace, Myles L., and Montgomery, George G. *Management Problems of Corporate Acquisitions*. Boston: Harvard University Press, 1962.

Matti, L.B. "Multihospital Arrangements: Planning for a New Way of Life." *Hospitals*, June 16, 1976.

May, Joel J. "Economic Variables in Hospital Mergers." In *Conference on Analysis of Hospital Mergers: Transcript of Proceedings*, ed. by D.B. Starkweather and D.C. Walden. Rockville, Md.: National Center for Health Services Research and Development, 1970.

McGrath, J.H.; Rothman, R.A.; and Schwartzbaum, A.M. "Factors Associated With Physicians' Vote on the Wilmington Hospital Merger." *Delaware Medical Journal*, February 1970.

Modern Healthcare, March 1970.

Modern Hospital. "The Multiple Hospital is the Only Way to Go." November 1973.

Money, William H., et al. "A Comparative Study of Multi-Unit Health Care Organizations." In *Organization Research in Hospitals*. Chicago: Chicago Blue Cross Association, 1976.

Neumann, Bruce. "A Financial Analysis of a Hospital Merger: Samaritan Health Service." *Medical Care*, December 1974.

Packer, D.W. *Resource Acquisition in Corporate Growth*. Cambridge: M.I.T. Press, 1964.

Platou, C.N., and Rice, J.A. "Multi-Hospital Holding Companies." *Harvard Business Review*, May-June 1972; Platou, et al. "Consecutor Theory of Hospital Development: An Examination of the Multi-Unit System of the Fairview Hospitals." *Hospital Administration*, Spring 1972.

Portney, Steven. "The Swelling Tide: Services and Management in Systems." *Hospitals*, May 16, 1977.

Reid, Samuel R. *Mergers, Managers, and the Economy*. New York: McGraw-Hill, 1968.

Reynolds, James, and Stunden, Ann. "The Organization of Not-For-Profit Hospital Systems." *Health Care Management Review*, Fall 1978.

Roos, Noralou P. "Two Models for Understanding the Hospital." Working Paper No. 75–71. Chicago: Northwestern University Graduate School of Management, 1975.

Rosenberger, D.M. "A New Look at Hospital Mergers in Relation to the Evolution of Our Health Care System." New England Hospital Assembly, 1970.

Rothman, R.A., et al. "Physicians and a Hospital Merger: Patterns of Resistance to Organizational Change." *Journal of Health and Social Behavior*, March 1971.

Schweiker, R.S. Washington, D.C.: Conference on Multi-Hospital Systems and Shared Service Organizations, June 16, 1978.

Schultz, R., and Johnson, A. *Management of Hospitals*. New York: McGraw-Hill, 1976.

Schumaker, E.F. *Small is Beautiful: Economics as if People Mattered*. New York: Harper and Row, 1973.

Seiverts, S., and Sigmond, R. "On the Question of Mergers." (Editorial), *Medical Care*, July-August 1970.

Shirley, Robert. "Analysis of Employee and Physician Attitude Toward Hospital Merger." *Academy of Management Journal*, September 1973.

Shortell, Stephen. "The Researcher's View." In *Hospitals in the 1980s: Nine Views*. Chicago: American Hospital Association, 1977.

Smith, David L. "The Performance of Merging Banks." *Journal of Business*, February 1971.

Starkweather, D.B. "Beyond the Semantics of Multi-Hospital Aggregations." *Health Services Research*, Spring 1972.

————. "Health Facility Mergers: Some Conceptualizations." *Medical Care*, November-December 1971.

————. "Hospital Organization Performance and Size." *Inquiry*, September 1973.

————, Gelwicks, L., and Newcomb, R. "Delphi Forecasting of Health Care Organization." *Inquiry*, March 1975.

————, Greenawalt, L., and Mehringer, A. "Mergers and Anti-Trust Laws in the Health Industry: A Review and Discussion." Chicago: Blue Cross Association, 1979.

Stigler, G.J. "Monopoly and Oligopoly by Merger." *American Economic Review*, May 1950.

Stone, A.J. "Why Hospitals Don't Merge." Occasional Paper, Division of Administrative Health Sciences, School of Public Health, University of California, Berkeley, 1978.

Stull, Richard. "Many Concepts Mold Multi-Institutional Systems." *Hospitals*, April 1, 1977.

Terrenzio, J.V. "Sharing Professional Services." *Hospital Forum*, March 1973.

Tibbetts, Pamela. Administrative Director, Health Management Cooperative of California. Personal correspondence, August 18, 1978.

Treat, Thomas F. "The Performance of Merging Hospitals." *Medical Care*, March 1976.

Trustee. "Multi-Hospital Systems: The Older They Get, The Better They Run." December 1976.

Wall Street Journal. "Caring Together: Many Hospitals Merge in Midst of Spiraling Health Care Costs." January 2, 1969.

Wegmiller, Donald C. "Multi-Institutional Packs Offer Rural Hospitals Do-Or-Die Options." *Hospitals*, January 16, 1978.

Westerman, John H. "Quality of Care." In *Summary Proceedings, Washington Invitational Conference on Multihospital Systems and Shared Services Organizations, Washington, D.C., June 17–18, 1978*, Center for Multihospital Systems and Shared Services Organizations, American Hospital Association, September 1978.

White, Paul E., and Vlasak, George J. "Interorganizational Research in Health: Conference Proceedings." National Center for Health Science Research and Development and the Department of Behavioral Sciences. Baltimore: Johns Hopkins University School of Hygiene and Public Health, 1970.

Whittaker, G.F. "An Economic and Statistical Evaluation of the Performance of Hospitals in a Merged System: An Application of a Quasi-Experimental Design." Ph.D. Dissertation, Northwestern University, 1974.

Williams, Herbert. "Hospital Closures and Mergers, New York City, 1960–1975." New York: Health and Hospital Planning Council of Southern New York, Inc., 1976.

2.

Some Theoretic Assumptions

No matter what you have to do with an organization—
whether you are going to study it, work in it, consult for
it, subvert it, or use it in the interest of another organization—you must have some view of the nature of the
beast with which you are dealing. This constitutes a
perspective on organizations.

Charles Perrow (1970)

This book has a conceptual base of two parts. Several general assumptions
are presented in this chapter; they form the basis for numerous specific
propositions about hospital mergers advanced in chapter 3. Neither chapter
is complete without the other.

A. THE ASSUMPTION OF BEHAVIORISM:
    MERGERS ARE A POLITICAL PHENOMENON

This assertion contrasts with the view that mergers result from rational analysis and conclusion, based generally on economic theories of optimality and
management science techniques of decision making.

As we have seen in chapter 1, there is little evidence that hospital
mergers achieve all that is acclaimed for them in benefits and costs. This is
not to deny that benefits exist, but to argue that mergers proceed on the basis
of motivations quite different from those explained by the theories of rational
decision making. These motivations are sociological, psychological, and cultural in nature, and are logical only with respect to behavioral rationality.

Central to this distinction is the difference between institutional "motivating" goals and social "legitimating" goals (Miller, 1968). The descriptive
literature on mergers stresses the dominance of motivating goals of survival,
the upgrading or downgrading of status and power, and the bartering of institutional identities. This is summarized by Franklin (1971):

> In the past, hospitals have evolved so as to maintain the capacity of responding
> to virtually any demand placed upon them. This condition, while not objec-
> tively desirable, musters the support of some groups within the hospital as a

necessary and desirable state. If the benefits of the (larger) system are to be realized the hospital must abandon this objective. The problem . . . is the hospital's loss of identity as a legal entity and as regards its stature and function in a community . . . the pertinent question concerns defining the point at which the hospital legally and practically loses its identity. [pp. 28–29]

If consolidations among hospitals defy empirical explanation, how then are we to know their ultimate benefit? This question is serious, since such integrations are now a matter of national public policy, are being actively and seriously pursued by competent professionals, and have become a part of the established rhetoric of those who deal with health care reorganization.

The answer: mergers are good if they survive.

Clearly, there are health institutions that survive at least for a while despite their lack of enduring social benefit. Yet, a link between organizational survival and economic rationality can be established. In economic theory those enterprises sized near the optimal point on a long-run average cost curve for their market will and should prevail; these firms are of greater benefit because they operate at peak efficiency for whatever level of quality and scope of service is specified.[1] Economic theory goes on to say that rational decision making within the firm advances this social optimality, through shorter run actions taken in the context of the longer run.

Our argument is that these short run and enterprise-based decisions are essentially based in behavior rather than management science, because of both the special turbulence of the hospital's environment and its decision-making structure. The end result is roughly the same—very roughly the same—and amounts to what economists call industry restructuring. There is a long-run trend in the health industry toward rationalization. To the extent that the merging phenomenon permits institutions to respond to these forces and in some way survive,[2] then the process is rational.

At the individual enterprise level, these differing theories about organizational reality may be compared in three realms: goal orientation, use of information, and decision making. We will first state what the rational model has to say about each of these features and then argue that the character of hospitals makes the behavioral model a better fit, at least in the instance of mergers.

GOAL ORIENTATION

The rational model assumes that organizational goals are clear, relatively uncomplicated, and that inconsistencies have been resolved. Further, goals are decomposable: they can be broken down into subgoals to ensure that advancing subgoals simultaneously enhances general goals.

But the typical hospital does not possess a clear or unified goal structure.

This can be demonstrated on both theoretical and empirical grounds. Despite a good deal of analysis, conducted primarily by economists, there remains widespread disagreement as to the real motivations of hospitals (Jacobs, 1974). One ascribed goal is that of growth—long-run increase in output. A closely related theory holds the same for hospitals but within specified cost restraints. Other theorists identify two goals of quantity and quality, subject to budget constraints. They grant that these goals conflict, but say little about how conflicts are resolved beyond the sweeping assumption that some final resolution is obtained (Newhouse, 1970). Another approach does not even attribute to the hospital its own distinct goals, but instead sees the hospital as the agent of another entity—a cooperative of physicians called the medical staff (Pauley and Redisch, 1973). The goals of this physician group are dominant, and they are to increase personal profits. In this model the hospital is seen as a nonprofit subcontractor, performing on terms specified by the general contractor, the profit-seeking physicians.[3]

In short, there is no theoretical agreement that the hospital has a goal structure sufficiently unified to produce the objective functions needed for rational decision making.

If the hospital's unifying goal structure is deficient or weak, then the institution can best be viewed in terms of a survival model of organizational behavior rather than a goal-seeking model (Etzioni, 1960). This theory views the hospital as a composite of different and semiautonomous groups engaged in constant exchange. These groups are in both perpetual conflict and coalition, with the degree of each varying substantially over time and across institutions. Much of the decision making that goes on is undertaken separately by the several parties to this hospital coalition—governing boards, administration, physicians—pursuing different ends but pursuing them simultaneously. The important dimensions of this game are the differential uses of power and influence rather than the different means of obtaining common goals (Pfeffer and Salanck, 1974). This makes the process of decision making one of politics rather than enterprise rationality.

With respect to merging, this means that no single posture can be attributed to each hospital involved. Indeed, the ultimate motivating goal in organizations—survival—is not an institutionwide one, but one shared by several distinct components. These components may survive separately or in combination, depending upon the coalitions which form for mutual benefit, but the sum of these will not necessarily equal organizationwide survival. This explains why hospitals will willingly pursue their own demise under certain circumstances—a most unusual organizational phenomenon.

In another respect the hospital is a special case of weak goal formation. The relationship between organizational and individual goals has been well considered (Barnard, 1938). Granting that individual motivations differ, participants in an organization are induced to conform to organizational goals and discipline by payments, most commonly money, which are then used to pursue individual interests. An organizational reward structure is thus carefully designed to overcome problems associated with diverse individual and subgroup goals, and effectiveness in this depends generally on how much the organization can pay. Conflict can be stimulated by a reward system that places individual members or subgroups in competition for scarce resources. On the other hand, unlimited resources tend to decrease the need for joint action, be it through conflict resolution or cooperation, and increase differentiation (March and Simon, 1958). Organizations functioning in a benign or supportive environment can satisfy their enterprise objectives with less than a complete expenditure of organizational energy, with reserves left over to satisfy relatively distinct and varying individual or subgroup goals. Organizational slack permits this, since, when resources are relatively unlimited, enterprises need not resolve the merits of subgroup claims: substantially different goals can be sustained. Conversely, when resources are restricted organizational slack is taken up, and the relationship between subgroups within an enterprise becomes more competitive. It follows that when mergers are the result of economic hardship, the behavioral assumptions of conflicting and unresolved goals become more germane.

USE OF INFORMATION

The rational model assumes that complete information is available and that an organization can process data so that it can know the consequences of each of its proposed courses of action, i.e., that cause and effect are predictable. This assumption is held not only for internal organizational process, converting inputs to outputs, but also to feedback from the environment sufficient to know the effect of outputs. The behavioral model challenges the rational model's assumption 1) that information is widely available and 2) that such information will be processed objectively.

We have already characterized the general uncertainty of the health field, which can be attributed not to a shortage of raw data made available to hospitals, but to confusion about what to do with these data. Given their lack of clear goals, how can they know what data to use in pursuit of optimizing results? As stated, knowledge is missing on the full costs and benefits of hospital mergers. Further, instead of unbiased information handling, hospitals, filter data that are heavily conditioned by the coalition of subgroups which constitute hospital power. Thus, intelligence gathering about reality is done not for the organization as a whole but for those elements represented most strongly in the coalition. Organizational evaluation of what has been done in the past and what can be done in the future depends very much on who is doing the evaluating.

PROBLEM SOLVING AND DECISION MAKING

The rational model assumes that an organization both desires and can achieve optimizing of its goals, can call forth a problem-solving and decision-making process in which a set of consequences is attached to each of many alternatives, can compare simultaneously the consequences of each alternative, and has the criteria for selecting the most preferred course of action.

The behaviorists base their challenge to this on the premise that organizational decision making derives from the individual human problem-solving process. Central to this premise is the concept of bounded rationality (March and Simon, 1958), the notion that the human mind, incapable of knowing or dealing with all information and all possibilities, instead bases cognition on limited data and a repertory of responses based on experience. Since not all information is available or can be processed, and since human cognition will likely introduce biases which correlate imperfectly with objective reality, the resulting decision will generally be satisfactory but not optimal. Attributing this same cognition process to organizations, it follows that there are bounds to organizational reality; that since not all factors can be considered in making decisions, some are taken to be strategic and others thereby reduced in importance or eliminated; that this selection is dictated by organizational processes built up over time; and that the results are "satisficing" rather than "optimizing."

In this adaptive system of decision making 1) an organization develops repertories of action which dictate the choices to be examined, 2) each problem-solving effort addresses a restricted range of circumstances and consequences, 3) alternative courses of action and their consequences are pursued sequentially rather than simultaneously, and 4) each approach is executed in semi-independence of the others, with the first minimally satisfactory alternative likely to be accepted. As summarized by Lindbloom (1959), "decision making is based on successive limited comparisons which largely substitute experience for theory in predicting the consequences of making small changes for the very near future." [p. 258]

Further, this whole process is generally characterized by a problem-avoidance rather than problem-solving posture, which leads to incomplete resolution of conflict, to narrowly rather than widely shared responses to problems, to slow rather than rapid organizational learning, and to uncertain decision making (Cyert and March, 1965).

In summary, the three organizational features of goal structure, processing of data, and decision making all strongly influence the way an enterprise goes about adapting to a changing environment. The rational model assumes that an organization both wants to and can define reality, knows where it wants to go based on that definition, has information not only readily available but amenable to calculations such that consequences of all proposed actions can be predicted, has an internal discipline sufficient to move all its parts in the same direction, and is capable of redesigning the enterprise to take advantage of its assessment of its environment. Behavioral theory argues that institutions are severely constrained in this process by the uncertainty of their environments, their need to maintain a viable internal coalition in order to avoid instability, and their limitations as assemblers, storers, and utilizers of information.

Each theoretical approach—rational and behavioral—leads to some organizational truths, but neither alone affords an adequate understanding. Without denying the substantial abilities of some organizations as problem-solving and decision-making institutions, we argue that the behavioral model is particularly adaptable to hospital mergers since each party to a potential merger knows little of its full consequences, the information they gather and use is strongly biased, and the decision-making coalitions using these data are themselves unstable.

B.   THE ASSUMPTION OF SOCIOLOGY: MERGERS ARE AN ORGANIZATIONAL TRANSACTION

This book focuses on behavior of the organization, using as its unit of analysis the enterprise or its major parts, instead of on organizational behavior, which focuses on individuals' behavior in an organized context. Behavioral scientists dispute over whether an organization should be viewed as anything more than the sum of its individual interactions. The resulting confusion stems in part from the proclivity of industrial psychologists to extend to the organizational and even interorganizational level concepts and findings derived from interpersonal and small group behavior. While some of these concepts are relevant, others have been stretched too far (Perrow, 1970).

For some, this application renders organization theory irrelevant; those interested in the applications of such theories are usually themselves individuals in organizations. Yet, the reverse is true: individuals are more likely to obtain whatever ends they seek through organized endeavor if they understand the larger dynamics of such entities.

This assumption will lead us to exclude certain perspectives on mergers. Much of microeconomic theory, while relating to the organization of production, is not concerned with organizations *per se*. For example, it is sufficient in the micro-economic view to consider the firm an undifferentiated unit— certainly a limiting assumption in hospitals contemplating merger. In another realm, much of the psychological and social psychological theory placed under the organizational rubric merely uses that rubric to study human behavior. Notions about small group dynamics exemplify this tendency. We will deal only tangentially with these theories and findings because our unit of analysis is the whole enterprise or some large subsystem thereof. We will be interested in individual and group psychology, but only as these help predict organizational behavior rather than explain human behavior.

C. THE ASSUMPTION OF CONDUCT:
MERGERS CAN BEST BE VIEWED AS A PROCESS

A process view differs from one that emphasizes form, common in the sociology of formal organizations, or outcome, common in microeconomics. This view emphasizes organizational adaptation: efforts made by an enterprise threatened by a changing environment[4] to obtain a new stability involving new relationships (Terryberry, 1968). That organizations change by seeking a new status quo is an ironic yet continuous occurrence. "Processes involved in organizing must continually be reaccomplished. Organizations continue to exist only to the degree that they are able to maintain a balance between flexibility and stability" (Weick, 1974, p. 36). "Central to the natural-system approach is the concept of homeostasis, or self-stabilization, which spontaneously, or naturally, governs the necessary relationships among parts and activities and thereby keeps the system viable in the face of disturbances stemming from the environment" (Thompson, 1967, p. 7).

This concept is explored by Hage (1974) in a book about organizational communication and control in hospitals. Hage observed changes in how a hospital under his study conducted its affairs during a time in which it was in transition from a mechanical steady state to an organic steady state. The first condition refers to an organization with relatively few occupations and a simple division of labor; it is thus easy to program the enterprise's operations with a small elite that makes decisions and gets things done based on a distribution of rewards and punishments. There is a clear hierarchy of authority, with feedback relating primarily to questions of production. Hage saw his study hospital moving away from this condition to one described by a progressively more rapid rate of change and a more complex division of labor, leading to a lag in the adjustment of mechanical state coordination and control systems to the point of organizational breakdown over a series of conflicts. In Hage's hospital this movement was stimulated by the introduction of a teaching program, with associated new relationships relative to a medical school faculty, and the consequent introduction of new centers of influence.

Hage believed this anomic state of instability to be part of the transition process to an organic state characterized by still further specialization, more rapid change, and larger proportions of professional rather than production activities. Importantly, coordination and control in this second type of enterprise occurs via a large number of committees rather than by a hierarchy, with emphasis placed on continuous learning and socialization rather than the distribution of sanctions.[5] "The study allows us to tell the story about organization and evolution, or what systems theorists would label the problem of the moving equilibrium between one steady state and another." (p. 73)

The merger phenomenon seems to invoke even more dramatic adjustments in this process of adaptation. The kind of conflict-ridden anomic instability described by Hage is pervasive in mergers; indeed, there is an acceleration of this normal transition to the point that change is often abortive rather than evolutionary.[6]

Viewing the combining of institutions as a process rather than as a pattern of static relationships allows expression of the important dimension of time. Merging may be seen as a sequence that runs from time of anonymity, when each health facility is unaware of the other as a potential party to combination, to a time of outcome, when complete integration has occurred. Many institutions initiate the merging process but few carry it through to total fusion. Examination of the several junctures along the time-path can reveal the critical decisions that have been made for or against more complete integration. Why do certain health facilities follow one pathway as compared to another? What organizational computations are made? What interhospital dynamics transpire? By backward induction the pathway which led them to whatever end they reached can be examined, along with the changes in organizational characteristics which took place in the process, i.e., attrition of key members, roles of different influentials, changes in structure, etc. A case study approach reveals much of this.

A process model also reveals the importance of different decisions at different times. For instance, the middle-range types of formal combinations (management contracts, umbrella corporations) discussed in chapter 1 can be viewed as transitional steps between strictly limited and more complete forms. Such a view implies a multistage strategy in which middle-range relationships are taken as means to more distant ends. Many observers of interorganizational relations in the health field predict this pattern. A quite different view holds middle-range combinations to be alternatives to complete merger, i.e., not transitional means to other ends but ends in themselves. Such a model suggests that at least some hospitals can proceed from relative autonomy to complete fusion without transitional processes. The research has not been conducted which would indicate whether middle-range forms of organization are necessary or merely contributing conditions to more complete forms. Yet, the practical implications of the two patterns are important: they involve quite different lengths of time, require national health leaders to promulgate different policies, and call for different incentive and penalty designs to be drawn up by local planning and regulatory agencies.

D. The Assumption of Discord: Mergers Precipitate Severe and Inordinate Conflict

Conflict is ubiquitous in organizations and endemic to hospitals. It is said to be both good and bad. The question is whether large amounts of it at certain points can render an organization functionless. By social conflict we mean disagreement of various types, from simple arguments that are eventually resolved, to more advanced levels of continuous antagonism, to extreme stages of strike, sabotage, or even physical combat. Social conflict can be distinguished from interpersonal antagonism. When groups conflict, the reasons usually lie less frequently in personality differences than in structural features: organizational power, control of information, etc. Conflict is the struggle to alter their distribution, usually expressed as antagonism over policies and procedures that evolve from their exercise.

While an unusual amount of conflict can be tolerated for a short time without organizational change, a combination of intensity and duration leads to discontinuity: control breaks down and a new stability gradually reemerges as effort is consciously directed toward resolution.[7]

March and Simon (1964) identify four ways in which an organization reacts to conflict. Problem solving assumes that objectives are shared and that the task is to identify a solution that satisfies the shared criteria. Persuasion assumes that objectives may differ but need not be taken as fixed— that at some level objectives are shared and that a disagreement over subgoals can be mediated. Where bargaining is used, disagreement over goals is taken as fixed, and agreement without persuasion is sought through the parlaying of strength, bluffing, and other processes that acknowledge conflict of interest, threats, falsifications of position, and gamesmanship. In the fourth type, politics, the participants perceive the arena of bargaining to be flexible: the strategy of lesser powers is to expand the arena of conflict to include potential allies.

The first two of these, problem solving and persuasion, are analytic processes. The latter two, bargaining and politics, can be called bartering. The more organizational conflict represents individual rather than intergroup conflict, the greater will be the use of analytic procedures. Conversely, the more conflict represents intergroup differences, the greater will be the use of bartering. Bartering necessarily strains an enterprise's status and power systems. It also acknowledges a heterogeneity of goals, thus reducing a possible means of control or stabilization. Because of these consequences, March and Simon predict that an organizational hierarchy will perceive or react to all conflict as though it were individual rather than intergroup, and that disputes will be defined whenever possible as problems of analysis instead of bartering (explaining, perhaps, why consultants are so frequently used in potential mergers), and that such reactions will persist even when they appear to be inappropriate. Further, there will be a greater explicit emphasis on common goals where they do not exist than where they do. Bartering, when it occurs, will frequently be concealed within an analytic framework.

In a similar but more operational vein, Thompson (1967) discusses the strategies decision makers will likely adapt under varying circumstances. Where there is certainty about which causes lead to which effects and organizational agreement on outcomes, a computational strategy will be adapted. Where outcome preferences are clear but cause/effect relationships are uncertain, a judgmental strategy will be used as the basis of decision making. In the reverse situation, where cause/effect is certain but desired results not agreed upon, organizational problems call for a compromise strategy. Finally, when there is uncertainty on both dimensions, Thompson speaks of an inspirational strategy for decision making, if any decisions are to be made.

Hospital mergers, or possible mergers, could be classified on these two dimensions of relative cause/effect certainty and relative agreement on outcomes, and the strategies of key decision makers could be predicted accordingly. Indeed, chapter 3 contains specific propositions about this, and the case study in chapter 6 is a test of these notions.

E.   THE ASSUMPTION OF EXCHANGE:
MERGERS ARE THE OUTCOME OF BARGAINING

THE THEORY OF EXCHANGE

As stated by Homans (1950), an early conceptualizer of exchange theory, "of all our many social approaches to behavior, the one that sees it as an economy is the most neglected, and yet it is the one we use every moment of our lives . . ." (p. 606). The central thesis of exchange theory is that an individual is motivated to interact with another if he expects that the association will result in a positive outcome. The more mutually rewarding and less costly the behavior of the two individuals, the more desirable the outcome will appear to be. If the calculated outcome exceeds the individuals' relevant comparison levels, the participants will highly value the relationship and will seek similar exchange behavior in the future. Rewards are defined as gratification of a person's needs, intrinsic or extrinsic. Costs are defined as any negative reinforcement, including unfulfilled expectations, fatigue, or anxiety, that derive from exchanging; they also include the value of rewards foregone by engaging in such activity—opportunity cost. Comparison level refers to the degree to which the outcome of a particular interaction satisfies the individual in relation to his expectations, the outcomes received by others similar to him, and the alternative choices available.

THEORIES OF DOMAINS

Exchange theory is made more specific to interorganizational relationships, as compared to interpersonal, by the theories of domain and domain consensus. Organizational domains are defined areas within which exchange transpires. They represent the stakes each organization claims for present and future activity. Domain consensus between two or more enterprises is the degree to which they accept each others' claims. The bargaining which leads to domain consensus results in a contract, usually unwritten, which specifies the parties' expected future behavior and performance. Organizations seek domain consensus because the resulting contracts reduce uncertainty and thus obtain for organizations greater control over their environment. Yet, in this process organizations acquire new dependencies: the price for reduced uncertainty is a commitment to specified future behavior.

As an elementary example, consider the physician's affiliation with a hospital. It reduces uncertainty for both: it increases the practitioner's assurance that his patients will have a bed and related services when needed, and it increases the hospital's assurance that its facilities will be used. In the process, each is dependent on the other, and both commit themselves to future behaviors, primarily through medical staff activity. Sometimes this mutuality becomes imbalanced. In mergers this imbalance is virtually guaranteed.[8]

There have been several applications of exchange and domain theories to the health field, including the works of Elling (1963, 1972) on the nature of community support for hospitals, of Levine and White (1961) on interorganizational relationships among health agencies, and of Shortell (1974) on physician referral patterns.

TYPES OF INTERDEPENDENCIES

The links that organizations develop to manage and monitor their interdependencies constitute varying types of cooperation, classified by Thompson (1967) as contracting, co-opting, and coalescing. Contracts are negotiated agreements for the exchange of future performances. These agreements rest either on faith and belief that each party will perform in order to maintain its reputation or prestige, or on specific documents which third parties can evaluate and assess penalties for failure, as in a binding legal contract. In co-opting, one organization absorbs new elements into its leadership from another to avoid threats to its stability or existence and to increase the certainty of support by the co-opted organization. This act is more constraining than contracting inasmuch as it places an element previously in the organization's environment in a position to exert internal influence. Coalescing is a combination or a joint venture between two or more organizations wherein they act as one with respect to certain goals. This not only provides the bases for exchange but requires commitment to future joint decision making; thus, it is even more constraining than the other two forms.[9]

These three general types of cooperation conform roughly to three of the four types of hospital combinations presented in chapter 1: affiliations are examples of contracting, management contracts are examples of co-opting, and umbrella corporations are examples of coalescing.[10] The fourth type of hospital combination, merger or consolidation, goes beyond Thompson's three forms. In this arrangement the price paid for reduction of uncertainty is surrender of decision-making autonomy; the organization actually loses its independent identity. Thompson might have called this consumption of one enterprise by another.

The importance to organizations of striking the appropriate form of co-operation, or of cooperating at all, is underscored by Thompson (1964):

> The organization that adopts a strategy of competition where cooperation is called for may lose all opportunity to realize its goals, or may finally turn to cooperation or coalition at a higher cost than would have been necessary originally. On the other hand, an organization may lose part of its integrity and therefore some of its potentiality if it unnecessarily shares power in exchange for support. Hence, the establishment of the appropriate form of interaction with its environment can be a major organizational consideration in a complex society. [p. 187][11]

Thompson believes that an organization's attainment of viable domain is essentially a political problem. The compromises and maneuverings that are necessary to obtain and defend domains are disruptive and costly, and therefore organizations seek to minimize their necessity. Unless driven by circumstances, they will instead attempt to maintain their status quo.

If we are to see all of this in Homans' terms, as an economy, then the media of exchange become important. To Homans these were nonmaterial as well as material, and generally rooted in the complex psychology of personal gratification. In the interorganizational realm, specifically in the health field, media of exchange have been classified by Levine and White (1961) as 1) problems or diseases covered, 2) populations served, and 3) services rendered. Elling and Halebsky (1961) specify funds, patients, and community partici-pation as the media, the last emphasizing the role which sponsorship and ownership serve in differentiating community organizations and linking them to segments of their environment which offer varying amounts and types of support.

RESOURCES VS. GOALS

Etzioni's (1960) summary classification of theories about organizations distin-guishes between effectiveness models that emphasize goal pursuit and survival models that emphasize the enterprises' capacity to obtain resources. In his latter category bargaining position is important: a good bargaining position enhances an organization's ability to attain its own and its members' personal goals. The highest kind of organizational effectiveness is reached when an organization maximizes its bargaining position and optimizes its resource procurement (Yuchtman and Seashore, 1967). The optimum point is the one beyond which the organization endangers itself by depleting its resource producing environment or by stimulating countervailing forces within the environment. Thus, institutional goals are seen not as criteria of effectiveness but as strategies adopted by members and groups for enhancing their organization's bargaining position. Those persons who are significant to this process are in the dominant coalition, and organizational goals can be seen as the future domains intended by this coalition (Thompson, 1967). "This view gives us a way of explaining the often noted tendency of organizations to seek survival and growth. So long as the organization presents favorable spheres of action to individuals in highly discretionary jobs, we have a strong motivation for them to avoid decisions which would end those spheres of action" (p. 128).

In short, goals are seen as means to ends rather than ends in themselves. Goal consensus is not a precondition of an organization's activity. Parties deal with goals only to the extent that goals represent projections of activities in which they are already engaged and would like to continue. These activities become strong or weak chips to be played in the game of conflict bargaining.

Long (1958) explores this idea even further in an intriguing proposition that stresses the game-playing behavior of man.[12] Long recognized different types of exchange—economic, political, etc.—but placed the social game in a class by itself.

> The local community can be usefully conceptualized in an ecology of games. In the territorial system a variety of games goes on: banking, newspaper publishing, contracting, manufacturing, etc. The games give structure, goals, roles, strategies, tactics, and publics to the players. Players in each game make use of players in the others for their particular purposes. . . . The interaction of the games produces unintended but systematically functional results for the ecology. . . . The organizations of society produce satisfactions with both their products and their processes. The two are not unrelated, but, while the production of the product may in the larger sense enable players and onlookers to keep score, the satisfaction in the process is the satisfaction of playing the game and the sense in which any activity can be grasped as a game.

> Far from regarding games as trivial, the writer's position would be that man is both a game-playing and game-creating animal, that his capacity to create and play games and take them deadly seriously is of the essence, and that it is through games or activities analogous to game-playing that he achieves a

satisfactory sense of significance and a meaningful role. [p. 261]

We will not enter here the theoretical debate engaged elsewhere as to whether these survival models constitute views of organizations that are essentially goalless (Georgiou, 1973), or whether their missing purpose is simply a lack of clear definition of aims which nonetheless exist in obscurity (Biddle, 1964). "It is tempting to assume, as many theorists have, that purposes are always present to justify the organization. It would follow from such an assumption that the purpose precedes the organization in time, and that any organization which loses its purpose will soon dissolve. Yet organizations exist—and prosper—with no clearly defined purpose" (p. 164).

A decent theoretical middle ground is that taken by White and Vlasak (1970): "Whereas goals once seemed a determinant of organizational behavior, they are increasingly (in open system approaches) being regarded as only one consequence among many of outside factors affecting the organization." If one views goals on a spectrum with social or legitimating purposes at one end and institutional or motivating ones at the other (Miller, 1968) the descriptive literature on hospital mergers (Starkweather and Taylor, 1970) makes it clear that motivating goals of survival and preservation of identity figure prominently in the dynamics (Gottshall, 1966).[13] Exchange theory and bargaining theory de-emphasize goal congruence as an important factor in organizational relations.

It follows that the parties to exchange will have different relative strengths. A dominant position by one institution may result either from an aggressive or competitive posture by that enterprise or from some form of consensus on the part of other organizations in its environment to support it. This support may come in the form of encouragement to expand its function, inducement to include new populations, or the offer of resources (Levine, 1965). The relationships of hospitals to health systems agencies make these concepts entirely relevant.

And, as has been noted, various parts of each enterprise can be differentiated by their relative dependence on the organization as a whole (Gouldner, 1959), and thus their strength. Certain parts are relatively dependent, not having direct access to elements outside the enterprise with which to exchange, whereas others possess higher degrees of independence because they do have such access. For hospitals comtemplating mergers this means that bargaining strength in exchange will be different for various subpowers, i.e., medical staff departments, employee groups, etc., when dealing with their counterpart units in other hospitals.[14] Thus, intraorganizational stress is heightened by interorganizational transactions, to the point that sometimes the two realms, inter and intra, cannot be distinguished.

A key feature in this process is the various players' perceptions of their relative strength or weakness. If parties see themselves as weak they will generally adopt the survival-of-the-parts approach; if strong, they will attempt to preserve the entirety.[15] So, the process is based on a constantly rolling and generally crude (because imperfectly informed) assessment of perseverance into the future. In this bargaining process the more powerful enterprises can better predict their own future life space, while the converse is true for the weaker parties; they thus behave differently in the merger process. The activities and goals of the more powerful subunits will persevere and their subpowers will remain more stable or, if change occurs, it will be by choice rather than by external intervention. For this reason Roos (1975) suggests that the conduct of more powerful parties will more closely fit the rational model of organization decision making, and that of the less powerful parties more closely the behavioral model.[16]

EXCHANGE AS A BASIS FOR ANALYSIS

Finally, an exchange/bargaining approach to mergers can take several analytic pathways that reveal true organizational dynamics.[17] One approach is to concentrate on the specific resources being exchanged: information, funds, influence, futures, etc.[18] Another, already stressed in the Assumption of Conduct, is to focus on process rather than intent: the modes of transaction. Another is to identify the time periods for which agreements are binding, as an indication of their importance. Another is to examine the persons involved: their agendas, their personal qualities of commitment and ego structure, their rewards and stimulations, and their impact on the organizations. Another focus can be on the issues over which there is conflict: the ebb and flow in intensity of certain issues, and the real meaning of various *causes célèbres*. Another focus can be on the norms and values lying within institutions that come to the fore—indeed, are tested—by the bargaining and exchange process.[19] Yet another focus could be on boundary definitions and redefinitions, seen best through the behavior of boundary personnel (Evans, 1972). Finally, we could focus on the posturing of exchange: are the organizations negotiating as sovereign entities, or is one or more subordinate to some other formal or informal hierarchy?[20]

These different analytic pathways are related; insights gained by one will lend clarity to another. Each is explored in various segments of this book, and chapter 3 presents a number of propositions relating to each.

F. THE ASSUMPTION OF POWER: MERGERS REQUIRE THE ATTENTION OF A COMMUNITY'S NETWORK OF ELITES

There is little doubt that communities have power networks, although there is widespread debate over their nature. The study of community power has developed along two apparently distinct lines, generally referred to as elitist and pluralist theories. The elitist tradition maintains that community life is dominated by a relatively small group of persons with economic and political power. Members of this group initiate, direct, and resolve all key issues. Citizen participation is relatively insignificant, exercised through powerless voluntary associations which serve as vehicles for legitimizing the actions taken by elites. Hunter's (1953) study of health planning in a small eastern city is strongly in this tradition. The pluralist view sees power distributed among several community groups with dominance shifting according to issues rather than residing with a single stable network (Dahl, 1961; Polsby, 1963).

Undoubtedly these distinctions are overdrawn; community power networks with different characteristics can be placed on a spectrum ranging from diffusion to concentration.[21] Further, as Perrucci and Pilisuk (1970) have pointed out, there is a certain reductive absurdity to this distinction. Proponents of the elitist theory assume that once persons are identified with a reputation for power, it automatically follows that they are dealing with the most salient community issues. Pluralists accept this view, for it becomes their justification for seeking out the most controversial community issues. Thus, elitists look for individuals most identified with important values of a community—those persons who hold prestige, wealth, position, etc.—and pluralists look for issues that will smoke out those who seek to influence the distribution of these values.

Both assumptions miss an essential point: that community power resides in a network of individuals who represent institutional influence (Turk, 1970). Since community power deals with situations affecting large and heterogeneous segments of a community, it follows that no one person through his personal qualities or the resources of his own position can be sufficiently instrumental: he or she does not command the resources sufficient for influencing others. Persons who influence decision making, whether in one issue or across many, must therefore draw upon others' resources as well as their own, in order to exercise power. Control is vested in the relationships, not the individuals (Weick, 1974). We can say, then, that the resources relevant to the existence and exercise of power are dispersed and reside in interorganizational connections that may be mobilized in situations involving important community values.[22] Hospitals are value-laden institutions, and a hospital merger typically involves a genuine conflict over major community values; thus, a community's power structure(s) must become involved. The question of whether there is one tightly knit elite structure or several different and loosely coordinated networks is not as important as the basic fact that most communities have a system or systems of enduring power and that the power of influentials residing in these networks either to make policy or block new directions in policy taken up by others is not to be minimized.

If a community has a generic power structure, it can generally be distinguished from a para-elite medical power network which regularly operates in health affairs to influence major institutional activities (Freeborn and Darsky, 1974). Yet, when merger is contemplated a new pattern of communication must be established between these distinct but usually overlapping systems, which substantially complicate the merging phenomenon.

G.   THE ASSUMPTION OF ORGANIZATIONAL EFFECT:
      MERGERS CAUSE PERVASIVE DEFICITS IN
      COMMUNICATION AND COORDINATION

Communication and coordination are two edges of the same management sword. The problems they present are central to organizational adaptation, in this instance, running more to internal integration than external affairs. Theorists of a variety of persuasions have approached the matter, but their different languages have obscured their considerable insights. We will endeavor here to synthesize them through their application to mergers.

Mergers increase both the complexity and the load of communication. The merged organization has new tasks to perform and there is a new combination of multiple power centers, creating a strong need for centralized and well-functioning coordination and control. But there are also critical problems to be solved—difficulties not before encountered that seem best addressed by those closest to the problems. Improved problem solving calls for dispersed decision making.

The problem is that improvements in one of these needs are made at the expense of the other, and the job of balancing these dual organizational requirements demands great management skill. The free flow of communication improves problem solving but impedes coordination. Unrestricted communication creates a battleground of ideas; the battle helps to identify alternatives, but it impedes agreement. Coordination requires eventual agreement on one plan, even though different plans might do equally well. Relatively unrestricted communication makes the performance of groups superior to that of individuals when the task is finding the best solution to a problem, but inferior when the task is one of coordinating action. As put by Blau and Scott (1962): "These conclusions point to a fundamental dilemma in formal organizations. Organizations require, of course, both effective coordination and effective problem-solving to discharge their functions. But the very mechanism through which hierarchical differentiation improves coordination—restricting and directing the flow of communications—is what impedes problem-solving. This dilemma posed by the need for unrestricted and for restricted communication cannot be resolved—it must be endured" (p. 196).

When faced with a rapid growth of communication problems, management usually responds by breaking an organization into more or less self-contained pieces. If these are relatively more self-contained, creating a federated-type of reorganization, problem solving is maximized at the expense of overall coordination and control. If the pieces are established along lines of function or specialization, often called a composite-type of reorganization, they contribute more to overall organizational control, but are less capable of local problem solving since each specialized unit is more dependent on other units for a full repertoire of responses. To March and Simon (1964) the crucial difference between the two is the level of integration, which is lower in a federated-type reorganization and higher in a composite-type. These two management structures have been applied to hospitals of different size, with remarkably different results in organizational performance (Starkweather, 1970, 1973).

These views stressing management structure are derived in part from classical management theory and in part from newer theories that view organizations as information processing entities. A pair of open system theorists have turned much of their attention to the same problem, stated as the dilemma of differentiation vs. integration. Briefly, Lawrence and Lorsch (1967) studied six plastics firms with a rapidly changing market and technology. They found quite different time conceptions and goal orientations among the production, marketing, and research divisions of these firms. These differences inhibited coordination and cooperation between the units. Significantly, the most successful of the six firms were those in which the three functions were most distinctive as well as the most integrated. To Lawrence and Lorsch, integration did not mean a fusing together of the various units, thus producing a common outlook, even though such a result would appear to be the common sense solution. Rather, their view of integration was to allow each division to be as different in its outlook and structure as its environment and task demanded, and to use various mediating devices that stood midway between the outlook of any two departments. The successful firms in their study used many such devices—committees, ad hoc groups, and assigned integrators—who were not dominated by the perspective of any single group.

Accepting this degree of differentiation within an organization seems to be a problem for many top executives, who often believe that coordination would be easier if all units were structured alike and were viewed as having the same goals. Lawrence and Lorsch's contingency model, where structures depend upon the nature of the tasks to be done, challenges this approach. Most analyses of this sort have limited application to the hospital situation, although one application by Baldwin (1972) to a group of Florida hospitals yielded the same findings as to organizational effectiveness as those of Lawrence and Lorsch. And Hage's study, discussed previously, is strongly suggestive. Beyond these, most analysts do not adequately account for the differences in professional vs. institutional control mechanisms embodied in hospital medical staff and administrative structures. The distinctiveness yet the mutuality of these control systems most properly characterizes the hospital (Starkweather, 1970).[23] Even without the medical staff complication, production functions in hospitals clearly vary as much or more than in business enterprises; different parts of different hospitals face quite as varying uncertainties as do their counterparts in plastics companies.[24] "The problem remains, however, that some operations have little variety yet quite a bit of uncertainty, while others have little uncertainty but a great deal of variety. These two types are neither highly routine nor highly non-routine; they are in the middle, somehow, but they are not in the same middle for they differ substantially from each other" (Perrow, 1970, p. 75). This will often be the case in hospital mergers, since they involve integrating institutions of quite different size, mix of patients, general complexity, and environmental dependency.

The final realm of communication and coordination crucial to the merging phenomenon is the impact of communication on individuals' attitude, morale, and performance. We will skip over a great bulk of theory on this subject, much of it derived from the study of informal organization,[25] and deal only with individuals' responses insofar as they affect mergers as organizational events.

The response of lower level members to organizational change is conditioned by two factors: the nature of communication channels and the information transmitted therein. Together, they represent an intelligence system. At a critical stage in the merger process—the time surrounding implementation—the intelligence system for most participants is deficient. This is so for a variety of reasons. New power centers and new power relationships have yet to be resolved. A new organizational structure, along which lines most official communication is channeled, has yet to be settled. In short, there is organizational lag.

Under such circumstances, official expectations of conduct are not properly or sufficiently disseminated or acknowledged, resulting in confusion and conflict based on differential perceptions of what is wanted.[26] In the extreme, these will constitute a state of pluralistic ignorance: a wholly mistaken view of organizational expectations that is widely shared. Schanck (1952) observed that for pluralistic ignorance to occur, either communication or behavioral observation must be restricted. Hospitals in merger are likely to have both, the first for the reasons cited above and the second because of the extreme functional compartmentalization that characterizes hospitals even when merger is not at hand.

Money et al. (1976) have reported on employees' responses in several mergers:

It is apparent that creation of a larger organization through merger, and the formalization and proceduralization that accompany such a merger can lead to both an increase in a feeling of powerlessness and an increase in fragmentation to the task, and the disconnection of the task from larger organizational as well as personal goals. Thus, a mild form of alienation may result.

Alienation is not irrelevant to efficiency. The more quickly alienation situations are discovered and eliminated within a merged organization, the sooner the organization can develop into an equilibrium condition and enjoy the benefits of merger. [p. 58]

Thus, at some point in the merger proceeding, false impressions must be adjusted to reality. Since misunderstanding is widespread, and in some instances purposely generated, this readjustment time in mergers is one of low morale and performance for those persons whose perceptions were at greatest odds. It is also a time of heightened organizational tension, conflict, and instability. At its worst, the entire undertaking is at jeopardy; at its best a new period of testing and restabilization is ushered in.

H.   SUMMARY

We have pictured the hospital merging phenomenon as a means by which organizations adapt to changing environments. This adaptation is usually dramatic, often involving complete and simultaneous adjustment of all organizational parts, instead of partial and sequential adjustment of some parts. We have argued that while this adaptation is rational in the long run, i.e., it represents essential hospital industry restructuring, in the short run it can be seen as a behavioral phenomenon. This view contrasts with many prevailing concepts of how organizations do or should take actions based on rational decision making.

Mergers can best be seen through the lens of a moving rather than a still camera—as a process rather than a static state. The process features exchange, conflict, and bargaining. The media of exchange are both material and nonmaterial, with questions of social prestige and organizational identity figuring prominently.

In open systems theories of organizations, environment affects both structure and process, which in turn result in some sort of outcome. The aspect of this sequence which seems most important to hospital mergers is that of interorganizational exchange: that which is most directly affected by environmental factors and which dictates new structures and processes. The structures in turn develop first as "trial balances" between subpowers to a new coalition; the trial balances usually contain imperfections that are revealed in a follow-on phase of intraorganizational dynamics in which problems of communication, coordination and problem solving are severe, all exacerbated by misinformation and false perceptions. In all of this—from early inter-organization relations to an outcome—actions are based less on goal performance than on organizational maintenance.

The array of theories discussed in this chapter is by no means inclusive; rather it is intentionally selective of those concepts which have particular bearing on mergers in the health field. The theories selected constitute a set of assumptions which have been explicitly stated so that our basis for proceeding is made as clear as possible.

We have, then, the beginnings of a flight map. We have charted the general terrain and have even established a direction of journey. It remains to establish an exact route.[27] In chapter 3 we will design and file such a plan, and in subsequent chapters we will take several case study journeys, some of which can be predicted to proceed more or less according to theoretical flight plan, and others which will not. In the final section of the book we will focus on the deviations and will contemplate, in retrospect, whether what happened was due to the navigational tools used, the flight plan, unexpected weather, or simply judgments of the flight crew.

NOTES

1. This refers to the survivor technique of economics, advanced by Stigler (1958), Saving (1961), and Weiss (1964). Stigler argued that if a particular size class of firm increased in relative importance over time, it had advantages of scale over smaller or larger firms whose size classes declined in relative importance. Saving used the same method to estimate plant scales. In both cases, optimal meant competitively most effective, i.e., an efficiently sized firm is one that meets any and all problems an entrepreneur actually faces: strained labor relations, rapid innovation, government regulation, etc. Of course, social efficiency may be a different thing: the most efficient firm entrepreneurially may arise from possession of monopoly power, undesirable labor practices, discriminatory legislation, etc. Large firms may survive and grow by means of predatory or restrictive policies or because of their ability to exploit suppliers. Or, they may decline because their market position forces them to hold an umbrella over the firms on the fringe of the industry or because they are threatened by antitrust authorities. Small firms may survive and grow because of their ability to exploit local labor markets or to circumvent the law. The survival technique makes no distinction between social optimality and entrepreneurial optimality, but it does serve as one basis for evaluating the general efficiency of an industry in terms of resource use.
2. The phrase "in some way" is crucial, since many consolidations foreclose on previously autonomous organizations. The difference between survival of the organization in total and survival of one or more of its parts is discussed later.
3. This economic theory parallels medical sociology's view of hospitals as the physicians' workshop, restated sarcastically by some as the "doctors' playpen."
4. At a minimum, the environment is comprised of suppliers, competitors, clients, potential or actual unions, government regulatory agencies on a local or national basis, new technologies, and the complex social and political milieu of the community in which an organization exists (Perrow, 1970, p. 54).

5. Dichotomizing organizations into these two states has been popular in the literature. The distinction has been overdrawn, perhaps to enhance the preference of many social scientists, notably those of the human relations school, for organic approaches. An excellent review and discussion of the several views of bureaucracy, structure, and technology is provided by Perrow (1970), who writes, "But the main point . . . is not whether there are three or four or more types of firms, . . . but that firms differ according to the kind of work they do and thus differ in their structure. Once this is realized, it becomes possible to selectively utilize the many techniques offered for solving organizational problems" (p. 91).

6. Rather than "running the film at a faster speed," to use Hage's analogy (p. 60), the imagery is of "running the film fast, but it unexpectedly breaks, showing blank on a screen that must be filled in immediately." Another of Hage's analogies visualizes an organization's structure as a mobile with various parts, one for each major power group. The absorption of one new part introduces only minor adjustment, but the addition of several more parts at the same time clearly upsets the balance of the entire structure. Extending Hage's analogy to what we mean by abortive change, a merger can be visualized as two or more previously free-hanging mobiles that are either gradually or suddenly relocated to the same pendant. Some parts clash directly and immediately and others are affected indirectly, but the total effect is to cause the new integrated mobile to collapse in a tangle of parts, none performing properly, until the structure is rebuilt and rebalanced to accommodate the new parts.

7. "Here everything is laid bare as we observe conflicts as a process over time. Conflicts make the basis upon which social structures are built crystal clear. This is the great advantage of studying organizations during periods of instability" (Hage, 1974, p. 98).

8. The manner in which this imbalance evolves, and the many ramifications thereof, is illustrated in a case study of a merger of two hospitals in Philadelphia (Goodwin, 1972), showing the dependency of one hospital on a certain big-admitter doctor and the dilemma posed by the question of his quality of medical practice.

9. Of course coalescing may be solely for obtaining resources, without any real integration. Dunaye (1970) describes health organizations that agree to rules of future decision making for dividing federal funds provided for cooperative endeavors, but do not agree to rules affecting integration of resources. See also White's (1970) comments on Turk's (1962, 1970) studies of community integration, which suggest a refinement of Thompson's typology. Adrian and Press (1968) distinguish between the admission of an individual into the decision making circle of an organization, cooptation, and joint decision making by representatives of organizations, coalition. In the latter, the relationship derives solely from separate collective decisions made by each of the two or more organizations, with individuals participating as representatives under specific constraints imposed by their organizations. Thus, Thompson's use of the term coalescing in conjunction with coalition may be confusing, for the reason that coalescing implies more permanent and complete arrangements than coalition, which Thompson defines as limited (White, 1970).

10. White (1970) states: "The relationship of cooptation and coalition with respect to affecting vertical and horizontal relationships appears to be uninvestigated. One might hypothesize that cooptation, almost by definition, occurs in potential vertical relationships and coalition in potential horizontal ones" (p. 31).

11. An example of Thompson's point is provided by Money et al. (1976). In a merger of numerous hospitals in Arizona, they found the perception of uncertainty re-

duced at the smaller, rural hospitals, and increased at the larger, urban (Phoenix) hospitals.

12. Note also the title of Elling's (1963) case study: "The Hospital Support Game in Urban City."

13. As one consultant put it: "Whatever the reasons are for starting mergers, the reason for stopping them is always identity."

14. In game theory models drawn from the management sciences, note the difference between two-person interactions and n-person interactions with coalitions. (See Coyne and Starkweather, 1978.)

15. One observer likened this to sailors on a ship in danger: first, all hands work to save the ship; then all hands turn to saving themselves by taking to life boats. By then rescue boats may be at hand.

16. She also asserts that the rational model may be more helpful in dealing with uncertainty than with conditions of unresolved goals.

17. Several of the pathways which follow were suggested by discussants at a conference on interorganizational research in health (White and Vlasak, 1970) attended by the author.

18. Alberts and Segall (1966) offer a classification of these for business mergers: 1) forecast bargains, meaning the stream of dividends the different parties expect to materialize; 2) cost of capital bargains, i.e., capitalization rates; 3) tax bargains, meaning how the merger is arranged to minimize future tax burdens; 4) mismanagement bargains, i.e., which management will control and which can be expected to lead the merger to its best performance; and 5) negotiation bargains, i.e., a merger price that must be struck when there is no active market price for shares of the companies upon which to base an exchange.

19. In this connection, White and Vlasak (1970) caution that "health organizations often do not know what scores are important to the other organizations with which they would interact, for the latter's criteria may be masked" (p. 53).

20. As is often the case in mergers involving religious hospitals.

21. Walton (1966) has offered a typology which is more discreet than the pluralist/elitist dichotomy. He classified the findings of 33 studies of community power structure according to their pyramidal, fractional, coalitional, and amorphous features.

22. For community welfare institutions, the degree of connectedness between organizations is different, though obviously related, to the amount of overlapping from memberships on boards. After reviewing the several studies on this latter topic, White (1970) concluded that "the question of the effects of overlapping memberships remains unanswered" (p. 22).

23. In this regard, note Scott's (1965) distinction between heteronomous and autonomous professional organizations.

24. In hospitals, for example, obstetrics is a relatively routine department which even has something like an assembly line where mothers move from room to room and nurse to nurse during the course of their labor, delivery, and postpartum. The other extreme is exotic surgery, such as organ transplantation. Here, there is little to be considered routine by either staff or patient. Yet, in many hospitals, the basic organization and rules are much the same. Coser's (1958) insightful comparison of a hospital's medical and surgical wards shows the variations which do informally take place despite similar organizational structures; indeed, her study invites the question of whether performance would not substantially increase if structures were altered in the manner outlined by Lawrence and Lorsch (1967).

25. Not to diminish its importance. Indeed, informal organization is a spontaneous and functional development, absolutely necessary in complex organizations for survival and adaptation.
26. March and Simon (1958) assert that three variables create the conditions necessary for intergroup conflict in an organization: 1) the existence of positive felt need for joint decision making, 2) a difference in goals, and 3) a difference in perceptions of reality.
27. White and Vlasak (1970) itemize the difficulties of using such a map for successful flight. In a critique of the general literature on interorganizational relations in health, they muse: "When, after surveying much of the literature in the given area, one looks back in search of some simple graphic image to sum up the overall impression, the one that (seems most) . . . fitting is that of a large relief map, or rather a potential map. Most of it, by far, is still blank, of course, but more significantly, those small sections of roads and paths that have been entered in the map have the following properties: they are marked with different and disparate color codes and other symbols; they are drawn to widely differing scales; they are positioned at different vertical levels; and they only very rarely yield to the observer's attempts to extrapolate, at least faintly, some possible connections from one section to another." [Part 1, p. 7]

REFERENCES

Adrian, Charles, and Press, Charles. "Decision Costs in Coalition Formation." *American Political Science Review*, October 1972.
Alberts, William W., and Segall, Joel E. *The Corporate Merger*. Chicago: University of Chicago Press, 1966.
Baldwin, L.E. "An Empirical Study: The Effect of Organizational Differentiation and Integration on Hospital Performance." *Hospital Administration*, Fall 1972.
Barnard, Charles I. *Functions of the Executive*. Cambridge: Harvard University Press, 1938.
Belknap, Ivan, and Steinle, John G. *The Community and Its Hospitals*. Syracuse, New York: Syracuse University Press, 1963.
Biddle, Bruce. "Roles, Goals, and Value Structures in Organizations." In *New Perspectives in Organization Research*, ed. by Cooper, et al. New York: Wiley, 1964.
Blau, Peter M., and Scott, Richard W. *Formal Organizations*. San Francisco: Chandler, 1962.
Burns, T., and Stalker, G.M. *The Management of Innovation*. London: Tavistuck, 1961.
Coser, R.L. "Authority and Decision Making in a Hospital: A Comparative Analysis." In *Comparative Studies in Administration*, ed. by Thompson, J.D. Pittsburgh: University of Pittsburgh Press, 1958.
Coyne, Joseph, and Starkweather, D.B. "A Game Theoretic Analysis of Hospital Mergers." Occasional Paper No. 9, Hospital and Health Services Administration, School of Public Health. Berkeley: University of California, November 1978.
Cyert, Richard M., and March, James G. *A Behavioral Theory of the Firm*. Englewood Cliffs, New Jersey: Prentice-Hall, 1965.
Dahl, Robert. *Who Governs?* New Haven: Yale University Press, 1961.
Dunaye, Thomas. *Community Planning Impact on Areawide Systems of Health Facilities and Services*. Ph.D. Dissertation, School of Public Health, University of California, Los Angeles, 1970.

Elling, Ray H. "The Hospital Support Game in Urban Center." In *The Hospital in Modern Society*, ed. by E. Freidson. Glencoe: The Free Press, 1963.
————, and Halebsky, Sandor. "Organizational Differentiation and Support: A Conceptual Framework." *Administrative Science Quarterly*, Fall, 1961.
————, and Lee, Ollie J. "Formal Connections of Community Leadership to the Health System." In *Patients, Physicians, and Illness*, 2nd. ed., ed. by Jack E. Gartly. New York: The Free Press, 1972.
Etzioni, Amatai. "Two Approaches to Organizational Analysis: A Critique and Suggestion." *Administrative Science Quarterly*, September 1960.
Evans, William M. "An Organization-Set Model of Interorganizational Relations." In *Interorganizational Decision-Making*, ed. by Matthew Tuite et al. Chicago: Aldine, 1972.
Feldstein, Paul J. "An Analysis of Reimbursement Plans." *Reimbursement Incentives for Hospital and Medical Care: Objectives and Alternatives*, U.S. Department of Health, Education, and Welfare, Social Security Administration, Office of Research and Statistics, Research Report #26, Washington, D.C., 1968.
Franklin, Carter L. "The Urban Multi-Hospital System: Necessary Conditions." *Hospital Administration*, Winter 1971.
Freeborn, D.K., and Darsky, Ben J. "A Study of the Power Structure of the Medical Community." *Medical Care*, January 1974.
Georgiou, Petro. "The Goal Paradigm and Notes Towards a Counter Paradigm." *Administrative Science Quarterly*, September 1973.
Goodwin, J. *Doctor Amos and Western Hospital*. Case #9–374–753, Harvard Intercollegiate Case Clearing House, Boston, Massachusetts, 1972.
Gottshall, Ralph K. "Merger Benefits Outnumber the Problems." *Hospitals*, February 16, 1966.
Gouldner, Alvin. "Reciprocity and Autonomy in Functional Theory." In *Symposium on Sociological Theory*, ed. by Llewellyn Gross. Evanston, Illinois: 1959.
Hage, Jerald. *Communication and Organizational Control: Cybernetics in Health and Welfare Settings*. New York: Wiley and Sons, 1974.
Homans, George C. "Social Behavior as Exchange." *American Journal of Sociology*, September 1958.
Hunter, Floyd. *Community Power Structure*. Chapel Hill: University of North Carolina Press, 1953.
Jacobs, Philip. "A Survey of Economic Models of Hospitals." *Inquiry*, June 1974.
Lawrence, Paul, and Lorsch, Jay. *Organization and Environment: Managing Differentiation and Integration*. Boston, Harvard University, 1967.
Levine, Sol, and White, Paul E. "Exchange as a Conceptual Framework for the Study of Inter-Organizational Relationships." *Administrative Science Quarterly*, March 1961.
Lindbloom, Charles E. "The Science of Muddling Through." *Public Administrative Review*, Spring 1959.
Long, Norton. "The Local Community as an Ecology of Games." *American Journal of Sociology*, November 1958.
March, James G., and Simon, H.A. *Organizations*. New York: Wiley, 1950.
Miller, Walter B. "Inter-Institutional Conflict as a Major Impediment to Delinquency Prevention." *Human Organization*, Fall 1968.
Money, William H., et al. "A Comparative Study of Multi-Unit Health Care Organizations." In *Organization Research in Hospitals*. Chicago: Blue Cross Association, 1976.
Newhouse, J.P. "Toward a Theory of Non-Profit Institutions: An Economic Model of a Hospital." *American Economic Review*, March 1970.

Pauley, M.V., and Redisch, M. "The Not-For-Profit Hospital as the Physician's Cooperative." *American Economic Review*, March 1973.

Perrow, C. *Organizational Analysis: A Sociological View*. Belmont, California: Wadsworth, 1970.

Perrucci, Robert, and Pilisuk, Marc. "Leaders and Ruling Elites: The Interorganizational Basis of Community Power." *American Sociological Review*, December 1970.

Pfeffer, Jeffrey. "Merger as a Response to Organizational Interdependence." Faculty Working Paper, College of Commerce and Business Administration, University of Illionis at Urbana-Champaign, April 1972.

Pfeffer, J., and Salanck, G. "Organizational Decision Making as a Political Process: The Case of a University Budget." *Administrative Science Quarterly*, June 1974.

Polsby, Nelson. *Community Power and Political Theory*. New Haven: Yale University Press, 1963.

Roos, N.P. "Two Models for Understanding the Hospital Merger." Working Paper No. 75–71, Northwestern University Graduate School of Management, Chicago, 1975.

Saving, T.R. "Estimation of Optimal Size of Plant by the Survivor Technique." *Quarterly Journal of Economics*, November 1961.

Schanck, R.L. "A Study of a Community and Its Groups and Institutions Conceived of as Behaviors of Individuals." *Psychological Monographs*, February 1932.

Scott, W.R. "Reactions to Supervision in a Heteronomous Professional Organization." *Administrative Science Quarterly*, June 1965.

Shortell, Stephen. "Determinants of Physician Referral Rates: An Exchange Theory Approach." *Medical Care*, January 1974.

Starkweather, D.B. "Hospital Size, Complexity, and Formalization." *Health Services Research*, Winter 1970.

————, and Taylor, Shirley J. *Health Facility Mergers and Combinations: An Annotated Bibliography*. Chicago: American College of Hospital Administrators, 1970.

Stigler, George J. "The Economies of Scale." *Journal of Law and Economics*, October 1958.

Terryberry, Shirley. "The Evolution of Organizational Environments." *Administrative Science Quarterly*, March 1968.

Thompson, James D. "Decision-Making, The Firm, and The Market." In *New Perspectives on Organizational Research*, ed. by W.W. Cooper et al. New York: Wiley, 1964.

————. *Organizations in Action*. New York: McGraw-Hill, 1967.

Turk, Herman. "Interorganizational Networks in Urban Society: Initial Perspectives and Comparative Research." *American Sociological Review*, February 1970.

————. "Social Cohesion Through Variant Values: Evidence from Medical Role Relations." *American Sociological Review*, February 1962.

Walton, John. "Substance and Artifact: The Current Status of Research on Community Power Structure." *American Journal of Sociology*, January 1966.

Weick, Karl E. *The Social Psychology of Organizing*. Redding, Massachusetts: Addison-Wessley, 1974.

Weiss, Leonard W. "The Survival Technique and the Extent of Suboptimal Capacity." *Journal of Political Economy*, June 1964.

Whisler, Thomas L. "Organizational Aspects of Corporate Growth." In *The Corporate Merger*, ed. by W.W. Alberts and J.E. Segalls. Chicago: University of Chicago Press, 1966.

White, Paul. "Critique of Conceptual Frameworks and Empirical Studies Relevant to Interorganizational Relationships in Health." In *A Critical Evaluation on the Interrelationships Among Health Care Institutions*, Paul White, Principal Investigator, Johns Hopkins University, School of Public Health, Baltimore, Maryland, 1960.

————, and Vlasak, George J., eds. *Interorganizational Research in Health.* Conference Proceedings, Johns Hopkins University National Center for Health Services Research and Development, U.S. Department of Health, Education and Welfare, 1970.

Yuchtman, Ephram, and Seashore, Stanley. "A Systems Resource Approach to Organizational Effectiveness." *American Sociological Review*, April 1967.

3.
The Merging Process: Some Propositions

A. A MODEL OF THE PROCESS

There is no such thing as a typical merger. Yet, the conditions which set the stage, the sequence of events which lead up to, and the actions which flow from merger can be placed in an overall scheme.

The merging process can be viewed as consisting of four stages, each of which encompasses several factors. These have a sequential relationship to each other, as is seen in table 3.1.

TABLE 3.1.   Four Stages of the Merging Process

Stage	Beginning event	Factors	Ending event
Pre-existing condition	Anonymity	Environmental, community, economic	Initial contact
Enabling forces	Initial formal contact	Sociological: interorganizational, intraorganizational, bargaining	Initial integration of resources
Dynamics of implementation	Initial integration of resources	Managerial, psychological, individual	Full integration of resources
Stabilization	Full integration of resources	Institutional, evaluative	Revised and accepted organization

The full evolution of these stages is a long-run process, taking ten to twenty years in most instances. The first stage, Preexisting Conditions, runs from the time of anonymity, when two or more hospitals are unaware of each other as potential merger partners, to initial formal contact. Factors pertinent in this stage relate to the broad environment of health care organization as well as to the community in which the merger transpires: the network of formal and informal power centers, and community decision-making processes. Economic variables are also important at this stage: the relative obsolescence of hospital plants, financial viability of entities involved, perceived economies of scale, and opportunities to establish broader financial bases for new activities.

The second stage, Enabling Forces, spans the time from initial formal contact to initial integration of resources. A significant event that occurs sometime within this period is the decision whether or not to merge. Factors prominent in this stage are sociological: status and power of groups such as hospital boards, medical staffs, and administrations. The interaction of these as groups is important: bargaining and exchange both between and within organizations contemplating merger. Conflict and accommodation are significant processes, played out on the organizational battleground of identity vs. integration. Economic factors continue to be considered at this stage, particularly the impact of special studies of economies of scale, synergistic effects, and availability of monies.

The span encompassed by the third stage, Dynamics of Execution, starts with the time of initial integration of resources and runs to the time of full integration of resources. Factors prominent in this stage are psychological: the responses of individuals in the merged enterprise, intraorganizational strain, and individual-organization relations. For instance, actions typically taken to protect individuals and subgroups as they enter a merged operation are antithetical to actions subsequently necessary to secure the merger.

The final stage, Stabilization, spans the period of time from full integration of resources to outcome. During this stage there is a period of reappraisal, of varying length, when the several parties to the merger—still identifiable as separate groups—have second thoughts about the worth of the new venture. During this period a wait-and-see attitude is taken on the part of some, and intense jockeying for position occurs. Power relationships are tested, revised, and reestablished. Also, during this stage, the merger parties roughly assess performance based on comparison of results to date with original expectations. This assessment contributes to the determination of whether the merger survives in its existing form. The stage ends when all significant power and identity of one or more of the organizational contestants are submerged and a permanent order is established and commonly recognized.

This model assumes the most complete form of integration defined in chapter 1: merger or consolidation.[1] This type of combination has characteristics not entirely present in other forms. We concentrate on it in this book because of the dramatic changes it imposes on the organizations involved; analysis under these conditions of intensity reveals factors which are not as apparent in the less complete forms of integration, but do nonetheless exist.

Another way of conceptualizing the merging process is to view it by organizational level. The first stage focuses primarily on environmental and community characteristics and the second spans inter and intraorganizational levels. The third deals with intraorganizational issues and individuals' behavioral response. The fourth stage focuses on outcomes, primarily at the organizational level. There is a cause-effect relationship between the factors of each stage, as shown in figure 3.1.

FIGURE 3.1   Organizational Levels of the Merging Process

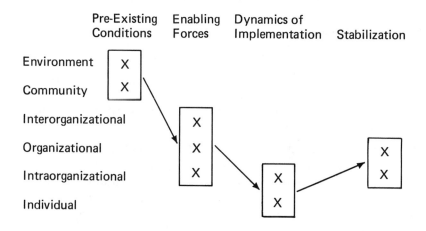

B.   SOME PROPOSITIONS ABOUT HOSPITAL MERGERS

Table 3.1 and figure 3.1 provide the format of this chapter. Each of four sections will be devoted to a stage of the merging process. A series of middle-range propositions will be presented which are based on the theoretical assumptions stated in chapter 2 as well as the descriptive literature on mergers in the health field.[2] The propositions which emerge from this melding of theory and practice will then be applied to the cases presented in chapters 4 through 9. The testing of these for goodness of fit will then be presented in chapters 10 through 13, through cross-case analysis, discussion, and conclusions. As discussed in the Preface, the desired result is a contribution to 1) policy developments concerning the rationalization of health delivery systems, 2) effective management of the merging process and of merged institutions, and 3) new knowledge about interorganizational relations.[3]

STAGE I: PRE-EXISTING CONDITIONS

Rate of Merger Activity
The economic, technical, and demographic causes of merger have been pre-

sented in chapter 1. These spring from the general conditions of the larger environment, but their impact on health institutions is specific.

Economics. It is alternately held that the health service industry is capital-shy or capital-excessive. During several periods in recent decades the nation's hospital plant has been either insufficient, obsolete, or both. It was this condition at the end of World War II that stimulated the Hill-Burton Act, the first major federal funding program for the health field. During other periods there have been spurts of new construction, expansion, or modernization, leading to pressures for control over capital allocations based on assumptions that excess supply creates unnecessary demand (Galbraith, 1967). These spurts appear to be related to times of heightened business activity and expansion of the general economy. The construction of many suburban hospitals in the late 1950s, the replacement and modernization of urban hospitals in the 1960s, and the construction of new proprietary hospitals in the early 1970s are all examples of this phenomenon.

The relationship of these conditions to merger activity can be expressed as follows:

Proposition 1a.   Merger activity among nonprofit health enterprises is greater during periods of reduced economic activity.
An inactive economy results in minimal flows of capital to the health field, making it more difficult for marginal institutions to continue themselves as free-standing entities; instead, they seek merger as a means of obtaining funds to perpetuate at least certain parts of the enterprise (Berman, 1971). Conversely, an expanding economy results in increased flows from both public and private sources, enabling the upgrading and expansion of institutions as separate units. There is a lag in both effects. Decision making in the health field is usually slow on such matters, and it can easily take five years after the decisions have been made to implement any plan involving physical facilities.

The proposition specifies nonprofit firms, suggesting a different cause-effect relationship for proprietary hospitals. Integrations that have taken place among these firms are seldom community based; instead they are among institutions dispersed broadly throughout a region or the nation. For this reason few of these combinations are full mergers involving physical integration. Further, the owners' motivation is self gain, which is specifically prohibited in nonprofit corporations and public agencies. For these reasons, many of the variables relating to community dynamics discussed in chapter 2, notably the Assumption of Behaviorism (A.) and the Assumption of Exchange (E.), do not dominate.

However, the economic variables do hold, resulting in the more typical business effect of heightened economic activity resulting in increased mergers activity[4]—the reverse of that stated in Proposition 1a.[5] This is witnessed by the active consolidation movement of the late 1960s which saw most individual or partnership-held proprietary hospitals sold to large national corporations. This form of integration paralleled the conglomerate movement in the business community of the same period of time, which in turn followed immediately on economic good times.[6]

The impact of this free market effect will be less in the future than it has been in the past, both for profit and nonprofit hospitals, due to increased control of capital developments through regulation. At least for the near future, the effect of this regulation will be a movement toward merger. Following national policy, available capital funds will be channeled towards institutions in some way integrated with others, leaving those not so linked at greater risk of obtaining the funds necessary for self-perpetuation. Therefore:

Proposition 1b. The economic impact on hospital merger activity is reflected in two conditions: availability of capital monies and manner of distribution. The first is a necessary but insufficient condition; the second is a reflection of public policy rather than market enterprise.

Technology.   A visible technological gap between what is known to be feasible and what actually exists will induce health organizations, particularly those active in the development of new medical science, to strive to close the gap. The most feasible ways to do this may be through merger, since larger size increases a health enterprise's financial capacity to establish and support new technology and merger can make available needed specialized human resources.

In the health field, institutional pressures to close the technology gap are entwined with physicians' organized interest to improve quality. This interest is served both by new technology and by educational programs involving full-time clinical personnel—both residents in training and technology-linked superspecialists.

Lewis (White and Vlasak, 1970) points out that the interest of doctors in quality of care is in part real and in part an effort to obtain production assistance. He sees combinations deriving from interests in advancing medical quality as vertical mergers in medical practice to obtain a factor of production—medical manpower—often in short supply to private practicing physicians in community hospitals.

These are the forces behind mergers involving medical schools: previously separate hospitals obtain access to new technologies, physical and human, possessed by universities, and in the process risk the price of university dominance. The medical schools, in turn, obtain access to more patients for their faculty and students through the use of beds and clinics financed and constructed by others, but risk having to share control over patient care operations and, perhaps, teaching. This is a straightforward illustration of the new dependencies which result from revised domain consensus, as discussed in chapter 2 under the title Assumption of Exchange.

While medical institutions depend on technology, and merger rate is influenced by its change, the influence is economic; it is economic conditions which permit or block health enterprises from investing in and maintaining high technology. The medical school situation is again illustrative. When federal funding for medical education facilities became available in the early 1960s, there was a spurt of development from the previous plateau of approximately 80 university medical centers to a new level of over 100; and many existing medical schools expanded their output. During this period of heightened activity university-owned teaching hospitals were generally expanded and most new schools constructed teaching hospitals. However, with the general economic decline of the early 1970s there was a diminished flow of federal funds for these purposes. Also, state legislatures began to question the maintenance of complete university-owned teaching hospitals in the face of community hospitals with excess capacity. So, a combination of circumstances rooted in economics—declining prospects for medical schools wishing to maintain separately controlled hospitals, increased need for teaching patients, and escalating costs for community hospitals of keeping up with technology—all produced a new phase of town-gown integrations.

The malpractice crisis is another example of the relation of technology to economics, and both to the practice of medicine. The costs of malpractice insurance and the wish to avoid malpractice exposure puts greater pressure on hospitals from physicians to obtain those technologies which, when used, will either reduce the risk of malpractice or show evidence of prudent professional conduct. Thus, to the extent that the malpractice issue contributes to the pressure already applied to hospitals to close the technological gap, and to the extent that merger is the most plausible means of so doing, the interests of physicians in quality—whether for positive professional reasons or defensive economic ones—are supportive.

The trickling of new technology into any field is an obscure process; useful generalizations about it are hard to come by. At least we can say that its impact is both direct and indirect, and multistaged. Investments necessary for new direct technology impinge most heavily on large urban tertiary hospitals, often operating in a university environment. A second effect might be called referred technology which impacts medium-sized urban and suburban hospitals where the environment of dependency and support is the local community rather than a university. Yet, typically these hospitals have informal links to tertiary facilities for the diagnosis and treatment of complicated cases.[7] A third effect, reflex technology, impinges on smaller and rural institutions where the problem of making sufficient capital investment in technology is accentuated by shortages of specialized manpower. These institutions make little effort to capture direct technologies, but rather invest to avoid the organizational demise which comes with total technological obsolescence. White and Vlasak (1970) comment on the plight of these third-level institutions, often built with federal Hill-Burton funds after World War II.

> These smaller and medium-sized institutions originally built as medical "manpower traps" . . . have lost their attractiveness for the new type of physician who, while perhaps equally individualistic and free-enterprising, is, technologically, no longer a generalist doing everything for everybody but rather a determined specialist who must be properly backed up by other specialists and a lot of equipment if he is to "do his own thing" in a competitive manner. [Part III, p. 12]

The general effect of technology on hospital mergers will be even greater in the future than it has been in the past, since there will be "more rigorous evaluation of new medical technologies and less dispersion of new technology" (Shortell, 1977).

To summarize:

Proposition 2a.   Mergers will occur when and where the technological gap between hospitals is wide.

Proposition 2b.   The impact of technological differences between potential merger parties is modulated by economic conditions and by characteristics of medical practice. The current direction of both of these variables is towards closing technological differences among hospitals.

Proposition 2c.   Since the diffusion of technology is from tertiary to general to primary care institution, the effect on merger dynamics is that of an asset held by a higher level hospital which is preferred by a lower level institution.

Demographics.   While the economic and technological derivations of merger are broadly environmental in origin, mergers caused by demographic changes stem more directly from local conditions.

Proposition 3.   Rapid change in the demographic composition of a community stimulates merger activity.

Changes in a community population's composition alter the community's needs for health services. Adjustment of the mix of services to match changing population requirements introduces the possibility of trade-offs between facilities, which in turn might lead to combination. An example is the shifting among hospitals of responsibility for obstetrics services, due both to geographic shifts of child-bearing women, as in the flight to the suburbs, and changes in attitudes about child bearing. Another example is that of urban neighborhoods that previously housed middle- and upper-class residents but have changed to industrial or commercial activity. These neighborhoods become unable to support private hospitals; the hospitals search for either alternate locations or new sources of patients, and may merge with other hospitals as a result.

In the past, rapid population expansion has been inversely related to merger activity, i.e., positively related to hospital proliferation. This is because in rapidly growing communities there is demand for more services, often met by new firms entering the market. In the future, increasingly, certificate of need legislation or other regulations will operate to insist that such demands be met with satellites or relocations of existing hospitals.

The Nature of Competition and the Size of Hospitals
An extension of the theory of domains discussed in the Assumption of Exchange (chap. 2, sec. E) relates to the degree of competition/dominance existing in the hospital industry. In cities with numerous hospitals there are forces that lead both to open competition among many facilities and to dominance by a few, i.e., oligopoly. It is possible that hospitals conform to a theory of exchange and competition enunciated by Galbraith (1962) and Blau and Scott (1962). As summarized by the latter:

> Looking at these processes of development from another perspective, one can see that the outcome of competition at one stage changes the object of the competition at the next. In the earlier stages, all units compete against all others. Differential success in this competition for relative standing has the result that the least successful are no longer able to compete with the most successful, and this change leads to the establishment of symbiotic relations that aid both parties in their continued competition. But now the two groups have different objects in their competition: the more successful units compete with one another for dominance, while the less successful units compete for survival. . . . Relations between units have also changed, since some former competitors have now become partners in exchange. Differential success in further competitive processes enables a few large organizations to dominate a given market. At this advanced stage when dominance has been achieved, a new object of competition emerges, namely, the ability to exercise controlling power in exchange relations. [p. 22]

Does this model fit the long-run hospital ecology of urban areas? And, if so, what is the value and nature of the symbiotic relationship between the parties? The evidence is suggestive only, based on the very few longtitudinal studies of hospital industry evolution.[8] The theory is more persuasive then the evidence.

Merger is of course only one way by which this dominance/competition circumstance may evolve—the other being growth from within enterprises.[9] Given an opportunity, a firm will instinctively move towards a larger and more dominant position. Size brings stability, removing some of the risks which small enterprises must undertake. Competition is reduced as an organization grows (Caplow, 1957). Large organizations are more widely dispersed or engage in more activities, leaving them less at the mercy of destructive forces working on one localized segment. Status is associated with bigness and is thus enhanced by growth. Finally, most communities cannot tolerate the collapse of very large institutions and will extend forms of support that would not be forthcoming to smaller firms.

Pfeffer (1972) summarizes the relationship of merger to these factors as follows:

> We have, then, three distinct issues. First, there are the propositions in the literature that organizations take actions to control or manage their environments, or at least their dependency on the environment. Secondly, there appears . . . the pervasive theme of the objective of growth. Finally, there is the issue of how to grow . . . internally, or through merger, and also the simultaneous question of which areas in the environment to expand into. . . . [pp. 1–2] Merger, then, is just one possible strategy for managing the organization's dependence with the environment. Merger may be pursued for objectives of growth, of course, and growth *per se* may be part of a strategy of dealing with the environment. The intertwining of these makes conclusive resolution impossible. [p. 6]

Precisely how dominance is achieved by some is only dimly perceived. Lee (1971), one of several economists who have contemplated hospitals' economic motivations (Jacobs, 1974) focuses on relative prestige as the driving force.

The ability to capture resources, i.e., money and medical specialists, and the ability to control resources that have been captured are two obvious mechanisms. Price (1968), in an analysis of several studies dealing with organizational environment relationships, offers a number of relevant propositions: organizations which have an ideology are more likely to have a high degree of effectiveness than organizations which do not. Those which have major elite co-optation are more likely to be effective.[10] Organizations which have a high degree of representation are more likely to be effective than those which have a low degree.[11] And, organizations which have a major elite constituency are more likely to be effective than organizations which do not.

Evan (1972) believes that it is "essential to descend to a lower level of aggregation of social structure and examine the system linkages . . . of boundary personnel": executives, lawyers, purchasing agents, marketing specialists, personnel officers, etc. It is here that various environmental interactions are mediated.

> If the boundary personnel of the focal organization are not commensurate in number, quality of education or expertise, position in the organization hierarchy, and . . . reference group orientation with the boundary personnel of organizations comprising the input and output organization-set, the effectiveness of the focal organization will be impaired. [p. 190]

A proposition advanced by Lefton and Rosengren (1966) is that service organizations with broad and lateral interests in clients are more likely to extend their interests by expanding their domains than by increasing inter-agency relations.

Further, as discussed in the Assumption of Exchange (chap. 2, sec. E), a more dominant position of one organization relative to others may result either from aggressive or competitive behavior by that organization or from some form of consensus on the part of others about it. Levine (1965) states:

> If the goals of a specific agency are accepted by other agencies of the health and welfare system, they may encourage the organization in question to expand its functions or include new population groups, and offer it appropriate elements to perform these functions. Eventually, however, should an agency not respond to this encouragement, it may be forced to forfeit its claim to a particular part of its domain. [pp. 65–66]

Whether dominance results from aggressive behavior of an organization in the face of opposition from others or from acceptance of an expanded role thrust upon it by others is an important matter in the case of hospital mergers, given the important role of health planning and regulatory bodies.

White (1970) places the physician at the center of interorganizational dynamics.

> Characteristically, the physician who insists on having his alternative work-shops retained unmerged, also tends to insist that the hospital be "alternative" or secondary only in terms of his own personal decision, certainly not in terms of the hardware and service complement he would have at his disposal, and significantly, not in terms of dependence on another institution, particularly not on the institution from which he is, in the given instance, temporarily "shut off," for whatever reason, or on one in which he has no significant influence. . . . Yet, the same physician's desire, or need, for a full complement of equipment and staff . . . will under certain conditions, operate as a force working . . . toward greater integration of hospitals or even toward merger. What are these conditions? Crudely put, . . . the integration-fostering conditions arise at the point, and only at the point, at which the more primary, more "natural" forces of differentiation, institutional individuation, or feudal-ism according to some, begin to bring greatly diminishing returns. That is, when the physician's (and the sponsoring group's) *first* preference—the alter-native workshop that is "as good as . . ." or that, at least, has a "90% com-pleteness of services"—has been rendered unattainable by the superior controlling forces of the environment; the social ecology of the institution has changed beyond salvage and all the traditional sources of financial nourish-ment have withered away. The consequences set in motion a vicious circle of decline in service, equipment and prestige, leading to inability to develop new sources of nourishment capable of restoring the institution to competitive health. [pp. 50–51]

Pfeffer and Leblebici (1973) believe that actions taken by enterprises to reduce competitive behavior are most likely when industrial concentration, i.e., the number of firms, is at an intermediate range. At very low levels of concentration, when there are many firms in a market, interorganizational linkages through joint ventures and other devices will accomplish little because there are so many organizations that must be linked. On the other hand, with only a few firms, merger or other formal linkages are not necessary; in these highly concentrated markets tacit interfirm coordination is sufficient as only a few other firms must be monitored. From this Pfeffer and Leblebici conclude that the proportion of joint venture activity "will be negatively related to the difference in industry concentration from a median value" (p. 406).

Extending these several views to hospitals, we can assert:

Proposition 4a. *Mergers will take place in communities where there are sufficient hospitals to permit dominance by a few without eliminating competition.*

Proposition 4b. *Merger activity is more likely in large cities and metropolitan areas than in small cities and rural areas.*

As documented in chapter 1, section B, most mergers of recent times have involved small or medium-sized hospitals. This fact, in combination with Propositions 4a and 4b, indicates that merger activity is conditioned by both community size and hospital size. The two are related. Rural communities frequently have only one small hospital. In small cities and suburban areas there are usually several small or medium-sized hospitals. In large cities and metropolitan areas there is usually a mix of small, medium, and large hospitals, with dispersion among neighborhoods and differentiation among facilities as to type of patients served and services rendered.

In rural areas there are insufficient hospital candidates for merger. Other types of integration are likely, particularly during harsh economic times, but these will be with urban institutions or will be looser forms of affiliation such as federations, management contracts, or umbrella corporation arrangements. This is because of the need for geographic dispersion of such facilities; complete physical integration would reduce geographic access.

In small cities the merger of hospitals will often eliminate competition.[12] In large cities within metropolitan areas there are sufficient candidates for merger without destroying competition. In new metropolitan suburbs, many hospitals have experienced rapid growth. For these, there is a point beyond which independent growth becomes difficult. As the hospital grows, it successfully adds services (in business terms, it expands its product line). However, it reaches a point where only complicated and expensive services are left to be added, ones which are difficult to support without a larger base of operations and ones which do not need to be offered in each of several hospitals.[13] At this point, integration of some sort is seen as a possible solution to both concerns—continued expansion of services and rationalization of services—as well as a method of achieving a new degree of market domination. This may be matched by the emerging of organized interest in quality on the part of medical staffs, for the reasons discussed previously, coupled perhaps with the availability of downtown hospitals with teaching programs involving full-time clinical personnel. Add to this the introduction of professional management, usually present in medium- and large-sized hospitals but not in small facilities,[14] and the constellation of forces will sometimes lead to merger.[15] This leaves the question of why small hospitals located in large cities and metropolitan areas do not merge more frequently, and why large hospitals in the same areas are not involved more frequently.

Reasons concerning large hospitals are obvious. They have already captured scale economies and achieved a degree of market dominance. Further, others resist consolidation among large hospitals assuming that competition would be reduced or eliminated—usually voiced as a fear of bigness—and that geographic dispersion of hospitals among populations would be reduced.

The reasons why small hospitals in densely populated areas do not merge more frequently are more obscure. Some of these hospitals are specialty hospitals able to survive on the basis of symbiotic exchange with larger hospitals. Others are protected from merger by special interests: physicians, often generalists, who feel they would be swallowed up by merger (see Proposition 15b), or sponsors who are not concerned about economic self-sufficiency.[16] These two reasons apply particularly to small hospitals which intend to remain small over time. Their strategy is merely to survive.

Summary
The forces that effect interorganizational hospital dynamics are rooted in economics, technology, and demographics. These are forcing new dependencies among hospitals; each must consider the exchange of independence for new resources and the reduction of future risk, most of which is analyzed in the context of strong motives of institutional survival. Which of these considerations end up in merger is indeed a complex matter, determined in part by enlightened self-interest among institutions in private exchange, and in part through regulation by public bodies. The long-run trend appears to be increased concentration, perhaps settling at a level of balance of dominance by relatively few, leaving room for standard competition among others. This condition applies only to urban areas, and merger is only one way in which it is achieved.

A factor which serves to enhance this trend is what might be called the coincidence of crises. Given the variables and the relationships discussed above, significant interorganizational change will more likely occur if crises in each of the potential merger parties occur roughly simultaneously. It is unlikely that the same crises will occur within two or more organizations, but crises of different types will happen at the same time. Obviously, if both or several parties are in need of change, merger is more likely to result. The situation is well stated by Morris (1963):

> Planning is facilitated if action is initiated when each of the involved agencies is undergoing a major internal change or crisis in its operations. This may be due to changes in financial support, personnel, leadership, technology, demands for service, or other events which are not subject to internal control. [p. 471, II]

Dagone's (1967) study of the motives for merger among 24 multiple hospital combinations documents this. The catalyst in 85 percent of the institutions proved to be change in its various disguises:

> A matter of necessity was the common theme . . . All of these hospitals were experiencing a financial plight due to either a high operating cost index, low occupancy, inability to attract medical staff, or the need for retaining accreditation status. One administrator summed up the situation which faced his hospital as "merge or disband." [p. 24]

Proposition 5. Merger will more likely occur when all potential merger parties face crises in their respective organizations.

STAGE II: ENABLING FORCES

To restate, this second stage of the merging process spans the time from initial formal contact to initial integration of resources. A significant event that occurs sometime within this period is the decision whether or not to merge. Prominent factors in this stage are sociological: status and relative power of groups such as hospital boards, medical staffs, and administrations. The interaction of these parties as groups is important: bargaining and exchange both between and within organizations contemplating merger. Conflict and accommodation are significant processes. Economic factors continue to be considered at this stage, particularly the impact of special studies that are usually commissioned.

Merger Motives
We have dwelled thus far on the causes of consolidations in the health field, viewed ecologically. We discuss here the motives which guided the actions of influentials and decision makers in institutions contemplating merger.

The history of business consolidations offers various possible motives for merger (Young, 1963; Gort, 1969). Contrary to what might be expected, these do not focus exclusively on economic factors. May (1970) reports that in the combination movement around the turn of the century, and again in the 1920s, two factors were influential, though neither was typically admitted publicly: (1) to restrict competition and (2) to make profit for the promoters, who hoped to get a generous fee for combining companies. The two reasons were related because some of the promoters' profits were what the buyers of the stock would pay to receive the additional long-run earnings expected from the reduction of competition.

There is some question as to whether these combinations of economic enterprises were also designed to bring about greater operating efficiency. Consolidations among railroads were often designed, at least in part, to improve operations. But another factor played a very important part: the desire of leaders to build industrial empires and to gain power and prestige by controlling larger organizations.

The numerous and widespread business mergers of recent years—many of local and regional scope only—spring from more complex factors, including the desire to 1) diversify product lines; 2) get a foothold in an industry with a high growth potential; 3) expand geographical markets; 4) acquire management, physical facilities, or research capacity; 5) assure sources of supplies or marketing organization and obtain the synergistic effects thereof; 6) utilize retained profits in business from improved growth possibilities; 7) meet a variety of tax problems; 8) obtain company assets below their true value; 9) access otherwise unavailable financing; and 10) avoid bankruptcy (May, 1970; Treat, 1973).

The theory of synergism (Alberts, 1966) says that individual enterprises do not separately have as much value as they do when put into particular combinations. Entrepreneurs see these opportunities and combine elements in new and different ways.

The bargaining theory (Ansoff and Weston, 1962) denies the ability to make such accurate valuations, stating instead that different judgments can be made about the future, that some people are right and some wrong, and that the people who are right can profit from the errors of others. The theory assumes that there are wide variations in the valuation of assets and that the purchase price of firms to be acquired in mergers result more from negotiations between the parties than from objective valuations of worth. This theory better explains the large number of mergers that seem to be based on manipulation of stocks rather than on the intrinsic economics of the combination.[17]

In something of the same vein, Reid (1968) holds that classic synergy benefits are either nonexistent or serendipitous: "Since mergers (in the business world) do not, in fact, occur with greatest frequency during business contractions when the pressure for more efficient operations is greatest, the hypothesis that the achievement of economies is a strong motive for merger remains unsupported" (p. 143).

Reid suggests that managers, stockholders, and the public have different and, in fact, conflicting interests in a business merger. Managers seek affluence, prestige, community and social recognition, and continuity of their established positions of power and control; they are more likely to obtain these by maximizing the size of their firm than by maximizing its profitability—which is the primary goal of stockholders.[18] He makes the same case for mergers promoting management's interests at the expense of the public's interests.

Reid's ideas suggest that hospital mergers could also be analyzed from the perspective of which members of dominant coalitions—administrators, trustees, physicians, medical school officials, patients, the general public—are being served by merger, and how. "Do mergers help hospital administrators gain higher incomes, more prestige, or more control? Do physicians obtain higher fees, access to costlier equipment, and the possibility of increased specialization? Do patients gain higher quality treatment? Does the public win lower costs as well as better access to medical care? These questions are far from academic and suggest a framework within which hospital mergers should be evaluated" (Roos, 1975, p. 21).

The discussion in support of the Assumption of Behaviorism (chap. 2, A.) suggests that motives for merger among hospitals will be multiple and definitely will include those stressed by Reid. Even health economists, who would be expected to stress the synergistic or bargaining theories, grant the prominent place of sociological and psychological factors in the motivations of hospitals as enterprises.

Indeed, this suggests that the pursuit of social status may be an end in itself, with community welfare a secondary and perhaps unintended result. It is even possible, by the Assumption of Exchange and the Assumption of Power (chap. 2, E., F.), that the play of the interorganizational game provides sufficient satisfactions for community influentials to initiate or sustain merger activity when no other purposes seem compelling or even apparent.

An example from the Boston culture of elites is provided by Wittrup (*Health Care Management Review*, 1976):

> I work on the assumption that they're volunteers, so they aren't in it for money, but it's a position of community leadership and what they aspire to, in effect, is the respect of their "community." Our term for it down here is "conversations at lunch on State Street." State Street is sort of a symbol of the Boston downtown, a high powered community, and those guys down there have lunch, and that's a little minipublic. . . . Now, during the last several years the general social environment has been conducive to mergers. In other words merger is, generally speaking, a good word. It sounds like you're . . . attending to public interest, recognizing the evil of duplication of services and the proliferation of facilities. . . . And so board members don't want to be cast in the image of being parochial and out of the main stream. . . . Now, you have to remember that everyone of those people has a duty to look after his own thing. . . . You learn when you pick up the telephone and try to manipulate other people, other people are trying like hell to manipulate you and that makes life fun, so long as it's open and fair and in the interests of a worthy purpose. [pp. 92–93]

These conclusions are verified by several empiric studies of interhospital relations (Harris, 1969, 1970; Dagnone, 1967; Weil, 1969). A study by Morris (1963) of interorganizational dynamics among six health institutions revealed the full spectrum of possible institutional motivations. Morris concluded that successful combinations always first involve financial incentives; yet he was careful not to place economic factors as controlling. Cooperation can be furthered by financial inducements only if a general meeting of minds has been achieved. Financial incentives alone cannot bring about coordination.

Concerning social prestige, Morris found that although most institutions seek to broaden the base of their support by bringing representation from many groups into board membership, in fact the control of most remains in the hands of an originating subgroup or its derivatives. Such subgroups, in turn, are "motivated by social and cultural influences to which organizational rationality may be subverted" (p. 252).

In summary, the motives for merger among hospitals can be placed in three broad categories:

1) Economic efficiency—enhanced ability to acquire capital, opportunities for operating efficiencies, ability to attract needed manpower resources, etc.

2) Community effectiveness—provisions of greater scope and quality medical services, contribution to the training of health personnel, etc.

3) Behavioral gain—heightened social status and visibility of influentials, including civic leaders, physicians, management, etc.

These several motivations have varying impacts, depending upon the stage of the merger process.

Proposition 6a.   Economic factors control the initial stages of merger consideration, and the perception of economic advantage is necessary though not sufficient for merger to transpire.

Proposition 6b.   Prestige factors control transitional stages of the merger process, and the perception of improved or at least equivalent status for participating community and organizational influentials is necessary for merger to proceed.

Proposition 6c.   During all stages of the merger process, community betterment is a contingent condition legitimating the process. Only during the last stages does it, in some cases, become a controlling factor.

Organizational Identity

Proposition 6b highlights the opportunities presented by merger for the maintenance or acquisition of personal social prestige. A related matter is that of organizational identity.

In the marketplace of goods, identity tends to be linked to a product. However, in service industries the product is not well identified: output is often vague, and the consumer is ignorant of precisely what has been rendered in his/her behalf. Identity, thus, becomes a function of the organization.

Identity is a particularly strong force in hospitals. Boards are composed of volunteers whose efforts evoke feelings of strong allegiance, based partly on the natural defense of any cause to which time and energy have been donated, and partly on the link between hospital image and personal status and community standing. Strong identity results from physician attitudes, since hospital facilities are critical to their practices. Employees often count hospital traditions of altruism and relief of human suffering as an important concomitant of employment. Volunteer groups glorify a variety of peripheral activities which gradually assume importance. And, beyond specific subgroups, a general gestalt develops and persists.[19] "Hospitals, like people, take on a character and a personality. Once it (the community) forms an impression of the character of the hospital, that interpretation clings and is very hard to change" (Burling et al., 1956, p. 15).

Proposition 7.   The probability of merger is enhanced if the identity of prior institutions is initially preserved.

This preservation can take a number of forms: retention of prior institutional names, appointment of persons to the new organization strongly identified with prior organizations, recognition of some physical area or structure, or preservation of parts of prior organizations such as boards of directors, medical staffs, or volunteer groups.

Some subgroups possess identity strength which must be honored during organizational transition. Georgopoulos and Matejko (1967) have observed:

> It is significant that in the hospitals studied, the higher the position of a group in the internal power structure, the stronger its tendency to assume that the hospital has an excellent reputation in the community, or that it is an excellent or very good place in which to work. Those who, because of their organizational role, are more concerned with the performance of professional obligations than with the hospital's public image are also more critical of the hospital's standing on both counts. [p. 82]

Proposition 7 deals only with initial preservation of identity of prior institutions. Initial efforts to accommodate prior identities in order to accomplish merger will likely lead to subsequent organizational stress, since it simply defers the necessary process of destroying prior identities.

What Happens to Goals in the Merging Process?
Probably no subject is as extensively developed in the sociology of formal
organizations as that of goals; yet there is practically no treatment of the
subject regarding the disposition of former goals and the formation of new
ones in combined organizations.

In most instances hospitals' charitable goals are relatively unassailable,
but the merger process directly challenges and examines institutional purposes and functions. Further, the peculiar diffuse authority system of most
health institutions makes institutional conflicts over purpose both inevitable
and intense in the merger situation—to the point that, as concluded by Morris
and Binstock (1966), "attention to factions and their interests is more likely
to provide an understanding . . . than an analysis that is built upon identification of an organization's responsibilities in the community" (p. 112).[20]

This suggests two dimensions of goal analysis pertinent to the merging
process. One, discussed in connection with the Assumption of Behaviorism
(chap. 2, sec. A), views goals on a spectrum with social or legitimate purposes
at one end and institutional or motivating ones at the other. We have argued
in a number of ways that the motivating goals of institutional survival and
preservation of identity figure prominently in the dynamics of merger. To put
it succinctly:

*Proposition 8.   Even though community-oriented goals are offered in
order to legitimize mergers, institutional goals dominate their formation.*

The other dimension of goal analysis specifies their relative intangibility
or specificity. This feature is related to the distinction between social and
institutional purposes made in Proposition 8. Legitimating purposes are usually expressed in intangible terms—"expressions of intended states of affairs
that do not adequately describe the desired states or activities that would
constitute their achievement" (Warner and Havens, 1968). While we are
tempted to say that goals should always be stated with clarity and precision,
there are definite advantages to their intangibility, particularly in the early
phases of merger. Intangible goals are often stated in idealized terms, which
inspire people to action. Diverse and even inconsistent subgoals can temporarily be accommodated through flexibility and adaptation. Superiors can exert greater discretionary control over subordinates. Intangible goals allow
people to assume that their organization is effective, since evidence which
would support or deny the assumption often cannot be obtained.

There are drawbacks, however. As the new organization progresses,
the need for more functional statements of goals emerges. Original lofty expectations remain unfulfilled, leading to disillusionment. Intangible goals are
eroded by neglect and an inability to realize them. Since their effectiveness
cannot be tested, their lack of evaluation may ultimately deny the organization

important guides to required changes (Sills, 1957).

A phenomenon associated with intangibility is goal displacement, wherein the major claimed goals are neglected in favor of peripheral goals associated with maintaining the organization. This displacement occurs because of an emerging need for goals which are more easily comprehended, more tangible, and more easily computed. The Assumption of Exchange (chap. 2, sec. E) suggests that pure goals are displaced by some combination of an extension of prior and current activities, combined with future domains intended by those in the dominant coalition. A classic example of this succession of goals is Sills' (1957) study of the National Foundation for Infantile Paralysis. After polio was eliminated, partly due to its efforts, the Foundation had to formulate new goals or dissolve. Sills documents how its motivating goal of organizational growth was maintained, as well as its organizational structure comprised of a highly centralized and powerful national office with decentralized local leadership and open membership. The new goals—research and treatment of childhood diseases—allowed the Foundation's top executives to preserve their positions of power and prestige in the national health field so they could shape the nature of the country's health activities; shifting from polio to other diseases was merely a means to this end, as was the decision to retain the same organizational structure.

Relative to others, health organizations' intangible goals survive as the presumed basis for activity for relatively longer periods of time. Several factors perpetuate these goals, such as the assumed social goodness of health organizations, as well as their complexity, wherein "the general goals specify an area of activity instead of a specific activity and therefore are subject to wide differences in interpretation" (Thompson and McEwen, 1958, pp. 29–30). A third factor involves the high proportion of professionals in hospitals. The motives and activities of these persons tend to supplant those of the organization: the public accepts their personal professional goals as those of the organization, which in turn reduces the hospital's need deliberately to examine and specify its own purposes. Also, the highly operational nature of hospitals—their routine dealings with life and death—demands a set of specific guidelines. General goals can persist while remaining ignored.[21]

Whether because original intangible goals are allowed to persist, or because operational characteristics detract from attention to goal formation, it appears that central, tangible goals are not well enunciated in hospitals. As a consequence, goals relating to systems maintenance must meet the organization's need for tangibility.

The pursuit of such goals, however, is not ultimately sufficient in the case of mergers, since they, by definition, challenge institutional survival. For a critical period of time in the merger process, two goal systems, each with its institutional function, clash. One system represents organizational transformation: new adaptation to a changing environment. The other represents organizational stability: survival in order to perpetuate community tradition, established networks of social power, etc. Neither system emerges as controlling without organizational stress.

To summarize thus far:

Proposition 9a.   Goals of proposed mergers will be deliberately intangible.

Proposition 9b.   After merger, originally stated intangible goals will not be translated into tangible goals and subgoals.

Proposition 9c.   In the absence of these there will be intraorganizational tension, due in part to carryover of existing organizations' goals.

Proposition 9d.   In the absence of tangible goals, evaluation activities will be minimal, original organizational expectations will remain unfulfilled with unanticipated consequences.

Goal pursuit in hospital mergers is complicated not only by the incongruencies that derive from new relations between organizations but also by those that stem from within each hospital. The several subpowers within a hospital are each pursuing, to some degree, different goals, and the organizationwide mix of these will produce a pattern of relative congruence or incongruence.

Proposition 10a.   Parties entering merger consideration with internal goal congruence will, relative to those entering with goal dissonance, enhance their bargaining position.

Proposition 10b.   Mergers entered by two parties with goal congruence are more likely to succeed than those in which goal dissonance is high.

The reason for this last proposition is that, during a crucial time in the exchange process between hospitals, the party or parties with irreconciled internal goals must turn away from external bargaining in order to deal with internal conflict generated in the process.[22]

Whether such conflicts are reconciled depends upon the orientation of the leaders of the several subpowers. By the Assumption of Exchange (chap. 2, sec. E), such leaders are part of a dominant coalition and are, in part, boundary personnel (Evan, 1972) in positions to obtain those crucial resources necessary for organizational continuance. Such boundary persons may orient themselves strongly to their own focal organization, in part because of their dependence on it, or to some other role-set organization, or to both. Evan's theory predicts that if there is goal similarity between the focal organization and members of its role set, they will compete rather than cooperate. However, with an overlap in membership, the reverse will take place, i.e., the combined effects of goal similarity and overlapping membership will lead to cooperation or collaboration (Evan, 1966). This local-cosmopolitan distinction in reference group orientation (Gouldner, 1957) will obviously vary among important hospital subgroups, but the distinctions will generally be heightened by the turbulence of merger considerations. In the extreme, this will lead to the predemise of a hospital contemplating merger, where local-oriented parties strongly motivated by institutional survival realize that the key cosmopolitan-oriented subgroups have abandoned the organization in favor of new coalitions. This, in turn, changes the dynamics of interorganizational bargaining and exchange, particularly as the other institution(s) realizes the situation.

Proposition 10c.   In mergers involving goal congruence in one party and dissonance in the other, bargaining proceeds on the assumption that one institution is dominant and the other submissive.

We will call this an incongruent merger: one party realizes that it does not hold its key organizational elements in sufficient control to maintain its essential core technology (Thompson, 1967) and survive as a whole.[23] In general, the difference between congruent and incongruent mergers is identical to the difference between merger and takeover.

Proposition 10d.   In the case of incongruent mergers, the negotiating strategy for the submissive institution is survival of parts, and the organizational dynamics involve the formation of new coalitions, both external and internal.

We can visualize the results of this as a hierarchy of survivorship. Organizational survival of the weaker party is impossible, but survival of one or several of the following subsets is possible: a constellation of subpowers; a single subpower; informal groups within formal subpowers; and/or individuals.

Proposition 10e.   In the case of congruent mergers, each organization remains intact during bargaining, with the negotiating activity centering on mutual cooptation and the bargaining issues centering on the hospitals' redundant elements.

Figure 3.2 summarizes the relationships described by Propositions 10a through 10e. Because of the screen of vague and intangible goals (and despite their prominence in the language of merger talks), direct examination of institutional statements will reveal few of the above actions and reactions. Such can be determined only by observing 1) the parties active in exchange; 2) who they bargain with, both within and between organizations; 3) the information sought and obtained; 4) the issues at stake; and 5) who allocates resources where.[24] We should get a strong sense of these from the case studies in chapters 4 through 9.

Figure 3.2   A Coalition View of Hospital Mergers

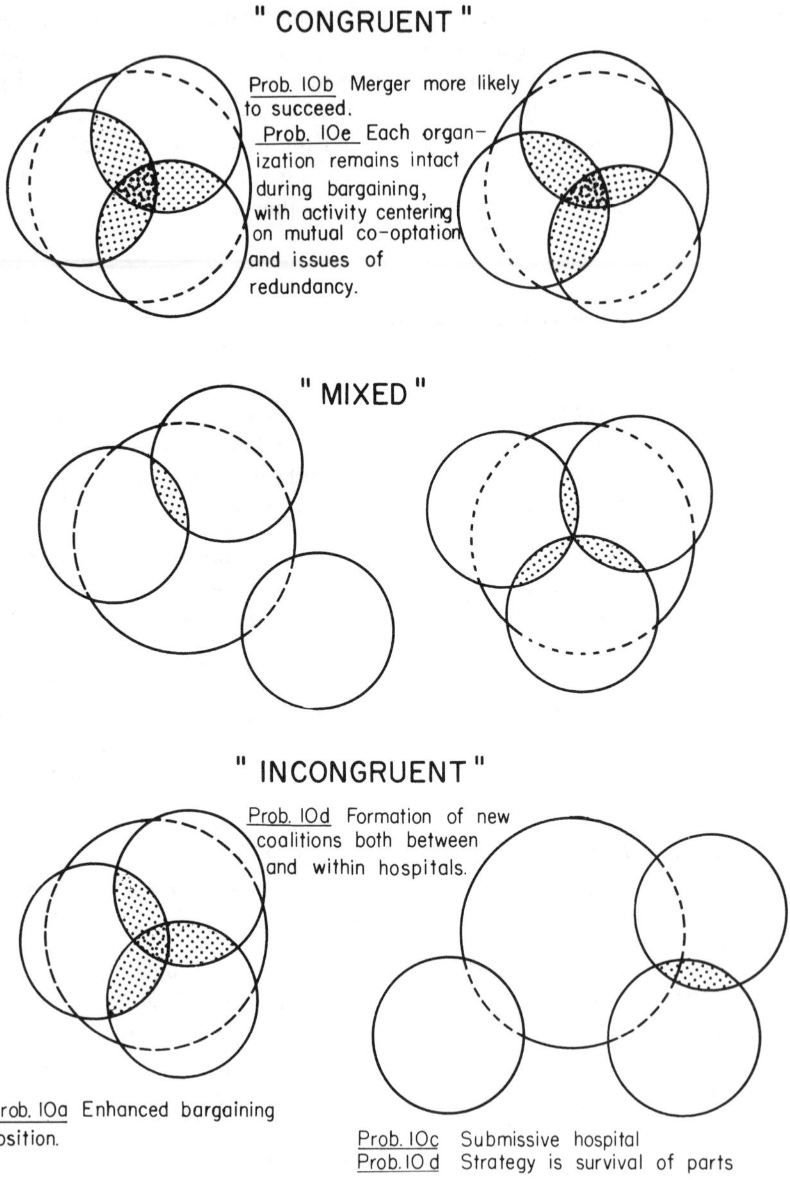

" CONGRUENT "

Prob. 10b Merger more likely
to succeed.
 Prob. 10e Each organ-
ization remains intact
during bargaining,
with activity centering
on mutual co-optation
and issues of
redundancy.

" MIXED "

" INCONGRUENT "

Prob. 10d Formation of new
coalitions both between
and within hospitals.

Prob. 10a Enhanced bargaining
position.

Prob. 10c Submissive hospital
Prob.10 d Strategy is survival of parts

Power and its Correlates

The preceding discussion of congruent and incongruent mergers was presented in the context of organizational goals. Yet, goals in themselves appear to be a weak guidance system for organizational behavior; they explain little in the absence of an understanding of power. Weber defined power as one party's ability to realize its will against opposition (Gerth and Mills, 1946). Parties to a merger can be of relatively balanced or imbalanced power.

Further, as we have noted in connection with Propositions 10b and 10c, parties to a potential merger might survive as wholes or only as parts. We will call this relative continuance: the capacity of a potential merger party to persevere as a whole without merger. This capacity can be measured roughly by a scale that runs from irredeemable—merger is essential to continued survival of parts—to autonomous—survival of the whole is assured with or without merger.[25] Autonomy allows an organization to pursue its activities with a high degree of adaptability, resulting in a greater likelihood of sustained effectiveness on its own terms (Price, 1968).

Third, the negotiating process and the results of merger are influenced by the relative complementarity of the parties. Complementarity among merger parties refers to their mutual filling of each other's needs. Several features among merger candidates could be either complementary or redundant: financial well-being, fund-raising ability, age of plant, scope of services, quality of management, amount and type of teaching, geographic location, ability to attract patients, prestige, etc.[26] A scale which measures this feature would run from complete redundancy to complete complementarity.[27]

These three variables—power, continuance, and complementarity—strongly influence whether initial merger contacts and exchange will proceed to reorganization. The relationship between successful merger, power, complementarity, and continuance is as follows:

$$\text{Merger} = f \left[\frac{\text{power balance} \times \text{complementarity}}{\text{continuance}} \right].$$

From this a number of propositions can be advanced:

Proposition 11a.   Between units of balanced power, merger is a function of complementarity, given that all parties are interested in continuance.[28]

Proposition 11b.   Where units are of balanced power and low complementarity, i.e., redundant, few mergers will transpire unless continuance of one or more units is threatened.

Proposition 11c.   If continuance of one or more parties is seriously threatened, merger will likely result even though complementarity is low and power is imbalanced.

These hypotheses underscore organizations' strong will to survive: if survival is threatened, merger will tend to be undertaken even though no power leverage is available nor synergistic combination of functions will result. This phenomenon, however, is likely only if the threat to survival is conclusive.

Proposition 11d. Hospitals with low continuance will first vigorously pursue support as autonomous institutions and not until this possibility has been exhausted will they enter merger.

Who Makes the Merger Decisions, and How?

Community Influentials.   From the discussion surrounding the Assumptions of Power (chap. 2, sec. F), we know that many communities have a network of elites who strongly influence important community restructuring, who number relatively few persons, and who can bring institutional as well as individual resources to bear.

Research is inconclusive as to what specific types of institutional power are linked into community networks, although the two categories of business and political organizations are usually included, as is communications, i.e., owners of newspapers (Hunter, 1953; Altshuler, 1969).

The relative visibility of such elites is an important question in the study of hospital mergers. Studies show that this visibility, i.e., agreement as to which influentials constitute the network, varies among communities.[29] Widespread consensus as to which persons are leaders improves community decision-making processes: the time necessary to achieve a new set of relationships among hospitals might be shortened, since decisive actions about merger are usually not taken until an established community power network is tapped and members of that network are granted, or acquire, influence in the situation (Elling and Halebsky, 1961).

For most communities, one can visualize a paraelite network of medical influentials making the regular decisions of health organizations. Such networks are sufficient for most decision making, but when merger is contemplated, the organizational issues break out and intrude upon the general community power reserves. There are often a number of false starts in this process before the appropriate community influentials become identified and involved. Indeed, the discovery and functioning of this larger power structure is often in itself a major organizational learning task for hospitals involved in merger activity, and the escalation from the more issue-oriented to the more general system adds new complications and dimensions to the merger phenomenon. This explains, in part, the long period of time which most hospital mergers take—often 10 to 20 years.

To summarize:

Proposition 12a. Involvement of a community's general elite is necessary to successful merger.

Proposition 12b. During the initial stages of merger consideration there is low consensus among merger parties as to which community influentials must be involved in decision making.

Proposition 12c. Merger parties initially tend to confine communication and bargaining to a subnetwork of influentials which operates primarily in medical affairs.

Proposition 12d. Because of these two phenomena (low consensus, restriction of decision making) the merger process is protracted and typically involves one or more inconclusive attempts to arrive at a definitive course of action.

Proposition 12e. These attempts often involve 1) consultant's studies, followed by 2) initial bargaining between the parties to merger, followed by 3) escalation to the larger network of community influentials.

This sequence fits the theory of organization reaction to intergroup conflict discussed in the Assumption of Discord (chap. 2, sec. D). Disputes will first be defined as problems in analysis and the initial reactions to them will be problem solving and persuasion. Such reactions will persist even when they appear to be inappropriate. The explicit emphasis placed on common goals will be greater where they do not exist than where they do. And bargaining, when it occurs, will be concealed within an analytic framework. All of this is caused by the strain which bargaining and conflict impose on an organization's power system and the inherent avoidance mechanisms that exist to disguise the problem.

The Influence of Third Parties.   Propositions 12a through 12e suggest that a well-established network of influentials within a community is needed to decide a hospital merger. Can the same be accomplished by outside parties, or can they serve as brokers or mediators?

Mergers in the business world occur largely as a result of private and usually secret negotiations. By contrast, mergers among health facilities are often initiated and even transacted by third parties. Consulting firms recommend such actions. Religious bodies act as brokers. Philanthropic bodies encourage merger on the grounds that better use of donated monies will result (Littauer, 1967). Medical schools play a prominent role, using education as a common denominator among institutions (Sheldon, 1974). Prominant industrialists act as initiators (Elling, 1963), and planning and regulatory bodies play prominent roles in the merger process.

For mergers occurring in the decade of the 1970s, Starkweather and

Taylor found 12 instances where consolidations had been internally generated, and 19 where merger had been recommended and urged by external groups. Most of the external stimuli came from community or areawide planning groups without statutory power, or from religious sources (i.e., Catholic diocese or religious federations).[30]

Undoubtedly, these statistics will be altered for the 1980s and the future, due to the changes in statutory powers of planning and regulatory agencies. In general the role of third parties can be expected to increase, although such might be hard to determine: mergers apparently arranged by internal parties could in fact be stimulated by the likelihood of external sanctions of one form or another.

Either way, the involvement of third parties complicates the process. According to White (1970): "The relationship of A to B depends on their knowledge, singly and mutually, of who controls the resources, their respective constraints in obtaining them, and consequently the alternative decisions open to each of them at a given time. Their relationships are complicated by the decisions of other actors who may perceive A and B as ideally related in another manner" (p. 15). Whether a complication or not, the intervention of third parties is often crucial.

Proposition 13a.   Merger activity is greater in communities where private or statutory planning bodies are strong.

What it takes to make a planning body strong is another large subject. Suffice it to say that it may be inherently strong, or it may appear to be strong because it reflects power located elsewhere. In Hunter's (1953) early study of health planning he found a voluntary health planning agency acting as a front organization, serving merely to legitimate the actions of more powerful but less visible forces.

Proposition 13b.   In communities where potential merger parties have relatively balanced power, a third party must intervene to achieve merger.

This proposition appears to be refuted by Morris (1963), who indicates that the prime function of planning councils is to "reassure weaker organizations about their relative positions vis-a-vis more powerful ones. . . . This function is especially important in the health field when it touches upon nonhospital organizations (i.e., proposed vertical integrations). Hospitals are usually so powerful that related organizations become fearful of that power and resist with special vigor all efforts at coordination" (pp. 462–63).

We can agree that third party agencies of various types may contribute to the merger of unequal parties.[31] Proposition 13b states that their intervention is essential when the partners have balanced power.

Institutional Influentials.   Influentials residing within organizations contemplating merger can usually be distinguished from those of the larger community environment. While the discussion that follows distinguishes between these two groups, we must recognize that essential links between them exist to some degree in every organization. Pfeffer's (1972) study of hospital boards emphasizes the linking role of trustees and documents the relationship of well-linked boards to organizational performance. Propositions 12a through 12e indicate that such linking will smooth the merger pathway.

Thompson's (1967) discussion of dominant coalitions pertains to internal power. Positions containing discretion over structure, resource allocation, domain commitment, etc., may be termed highly discretionary. Incumbents of these positions seek to maintain power equal to or greater than their dependence on others in the organization. When the individual's power in a highly discretionary job is less than this dependence, he/she will seek a coalition. Such coalitions are formed under conditions of conflict and high aspirations. Thus, dominant coalitions are linkages of two or more individuals, or sets of individuals, in highly discretionary positions who believe that their abilities to satisfy organizational dependencies are greater in combination than alone, and where the results of increased power can be shared.[32]

Hospital mergers can be seen both as a consequence of changes in interorganizational dependencies and as a cause of changes in intraorganizational dependencies because such coalitions are viable only at an organization's vulnerable points—where it has important dependencies—and merger is associated with organizational vulnerability.

Proposition 14a. Merger forces new conflict, new distribution of power, and new interdependencies upon the dominant coalitions of the hospitals involved.

Since the formation of coalitions is based on the wish of individuals and groups to increase power, the more numerous the sources of uncertainty and contingency, the more numerous the bases for power and the political positions. The converse is also true. Thus, merger both results from and causes different concentrations of power.

Further, when inputs necessary for organizational survival and growth are widely available in the environment, those responsible for obtaining them will have little basis for organizational power; conversely, the scarcity of those same inputs will endow such individuals with greater power. Such inputs may be patient referrals, technologies, or something as vague as legitimacy (Selznick, 1949). Given the desire of individuals and groups to enhance power, under extremes of scarcity those in high discretion positions may form new coalitions with essential elements of the environment. These coalitions will obtain power to the extent that the needed inputs are hard to get.

Typically, mergers are associated with these extremes of scarcity whose impact on the differential power of influentials can be predicted.

Proposition 14b.   At the early stages of potential mergers, those who initiate new relations between hospitals are those who seek increased power within their dominant coalition.

Proposition 14c.   In the early stages of merger, the high uncertainty caused by conditions that suggest merger lead to a diffusion of power bases, increasing the number of potential influentials and causing merger dynamics to focus on those parties who are politically necessary to the proceedings.

Proposition 14d.   As merger negotiations proceed, those who control the scarcest elements necessary for survival or growth obtain greatest influence. These persons hold veto over the proceedings and become the target of cooptation efforts.

When power is widely distributed a large and diverse dominant coalition usually exists from which an inner circle (Thompson, 1967) emerges to conduct coalition business. This may be a formal or informal group, but in either case the composition reflects the power distribution of the larger body. An organization with a dispersed base of power can be immobilized unless the inner circle is effective. The subtle processes of negotiation and compromise cannot work when they include large numbers. Such issues can be ratified but not decided by the larger group.

This is precisely the case in the typical hospital, where power must be concentrated. The internal organization of the typical hospital is run by a junta of three relatively well-balanced power centers representing the authorities of knowledge (medical staff), office (administration), and ownership (board). In order for the hospital to run at all, given its complexity and this pattern of shared authority, power has to be rather closely held by a few members of each of the three groups; otherwise, few decisions will be made and little will be accomplished.[33] Yet, this concentration does not go as far as it does in the typical business corporation, where it concentrates at the top of a pyramidal management structure.

It follows that the organizational change necessitated by merger is made more difficult by the need to satisfy several dominant interests. According to Morris and Binstock (1966), "It is difficult for coalition-dominated organizations to make change at all; it is far easier to overcome the resistance of an organization that is dominated by a single faction" (p. 110).

Proposition 14e.   In the latter stages of the merging process, uncertainty has been reduced and predictability increased, leading to a reduction in the bases of power (a concentration of power), reducing the number of influentials, and causing merger dynamics to focus on the resolution of conflicts and issues.

Finally, there is the matter of the leadership of the dominant coalition. Does our conceptualization of the merging hospital as a complex organization mean that it inevitably lacks a central power symbol—a recognized leader?

Clearly, unilateral power cannot fall to one person in such an organization; yet, we know that an individual can cast a long shadow: he/she can symbolize the power of the organization and can exercise significant leadership. If such a central power figure exists, she/he will manage the dominant coalition. But that person can do so only with the consent and approval of the coalition. "The highly complex organization is not the place for the dictator or the commander to emerge. . . . Neither the central power figure nor the inner circle can reverse the direction of organizational movement at will" (Thompson, 1967, pp. 142–43). Instead, the circumstances call for the kind of leader which Thompson calls the superb politician—a term he uses in its most positive sense.

The situation is well described by Wittrup (*Health Care Management Review*, 1976):

> The common rule is that the main negotiators in the merger have got to be a small group of trustees who are prepared to see it happen. . . . In merger negotiations . . . there needs to be a figure who has enormous credibility. By credibility I simply mean that people tend to believe that if he's for it, it must be good and that he's not out to feather his own nest. The paid people always have an axe to grind and even if they succeed in rising above that, nobody will believe them. . . . Sometimes it will be the elected chairman of the board, sometimes it will be a grand old man, somebody let's say who is 68 years old, who maybe would announce in advance that he or she will not take a seat on the new board, and who thereby establishes enough credibility in the situation to be able to deal with everybody. [p. 91]

Influentials' Personalities. Organizational characteristics have been the subject of discussion thus far. Here we focus on the personal attributes of participants in the merger process. Earlier we stated that, at the organizational level, complementarity contributes to merger success. In respect to personal characteristics, however, the opposite is true:

Proposition 15a. Homogeneity in influentials' personal characteristics contributes to successful merger.

This applies to the qualities of two particular subgroups: to the social, economic, and cultural background of boards of directors; and to physicians.

Homogeneity eases communication between groups by providing common grounds for mutual understanding. In particular, it removes an element of threat to one or more parties which would otherwise prevail. If personal characteristics of subgroups were vastly different, one party would perceive a possible diminution of status if merged with the other—a condition which would cause it to resist merger. If, on the other hand, each party perceived opportunities for maintaining existing status, or enhancing status, merger will be viewed more favorably (Einstein, 1964).

Proposition 15b. Resistance to merger will come from parties of lower socioeconomic or professional status.

All of this underscores again the power of identity as a motivator in merger dynamics, as discussed in the Assumption of Sociology (chap. 2, B.) and in Proposition 7.

Patterns of Exchange
Initial Contact and Follow Through.   Horizontal interorganizational contact is made at the earliest stage of the merger process, usually between like subpowers of each organization and often between key board members (Weil, 1969).[34]

Proposition 14b states that those who initiate new relations between hospitals are seeking increased power within their own enterprises. The observation that board members, presumably the occupants of the power positions, often initiate contact, appears to contradict the proposition that power seekers do the initiating. There is probably a difference between simple initial contact, often ascribed to trustees, and pursuit of the more serious type of relationship suggested by Proposition 14b—the difference between a casual contact and a tactical initiative. At any rate, the parties making first contact are not necessarily the most influential within their respective hospitals.

More important, the notion that there is a most powerful party is inconsistent with the dominant coalition form of hospital leadership. As we have noted, even the coalition manager can declare little without others' consent. Further, the influence of various subpowers comes to bear at different times and in different ways: the power of a de facto veto can be as strong at one time as the power of initiative at another.

It remains true, however, that:

Proposition 16a.   The members of each institution's power center who maintain contact between organizations contemplating merger will retain an important influence on subsequent proceedings that take place within their organizations.

Proposition 16b.   By virtue of their control over information flow, such persons increase their standing in the dominant coalitions of their hospitals.

Once initial communication between organizations is established and initial postures taken, there follows a period of intense intraorganizational realignment, channeled along vertical lines within each hospital, e.g., between medical staff and board. In this debate, each power center attempts to secure the strongest position for itself, based on its perception of what its ultimate domain is likely to be if the merger transpires.[35] Since the issues at hand are extra- rather than intraorganizational, the postures and strategies of each subpower may be quite different than they normally would be. For instance, the medical staff of Hospital A may ordinarily dispute with the board or administration over operating matters, but when faced with the possibility of reorganization involving Hospital B's medical staff, its posture relative to A's board and A's administration may change.

Further, the less secure parties tend to communicate lesser amounts and/or less realistic information. Thus, greater inner group conflict and greater differential internal conflict develops between two or more merger parties, with the consequences outlined in Propositions 10a through 10e.[36]

Theoretically, in mergers among highly congruent enterprises, intraorganizational solidarity is greater when faced with pending interorganizational dealings than would otherwise by the case. Further, efforts are made to establish advance commitment on key issues known to be surfacing, particularly in realms where interdependencies are essential. These commitments bind the power centers together for purposes of strength in external negotiations. The subject and nature of these commitments reveal much about the relative influence of the several power centers and provide clues to the topics of subsequent, postmerger organizational tension. Even the pathways of communication and the type of bargaining used are revealing.

The weaker powers tend to cling more strongly and for longer duration to the established intraorganizational (vertical) linkages, while the stronger parties move to interorganizational (horizontal) relations with their counterpart members and subgroups.[37] This recoalescing is dictated by the perceived relative dependencies and relative cosmopolitan/local orientation of the several power centers within each organization. If this settles out in such a way that no revised coalition can be assembled whose members represent essential core technologies, then predemise of the existing organization(s) will have taken place.

The next phase emphasizes the bonds which must be forged between organizations; its topic is the new organization rather than the existing ones. The commitments made construct the merged unit and destroy the old. These relationships tend to conflict with those established in prior stages. Again, the issues proclaimed by the parties which cling to their "vertical" relationships will reveal future organizational tensions.

Taylor (1978) has cast this process differently by extending to hospital mergers some of the concepts of adaption to innovation (Rogers and Shoemaker, 1971). The parties to a potential innovation like merger can be classified as 1) innovators with a venturesome and external hospital orientation; 2) early adapters who are highly respected opinion leaders; 3) early majority persons who are very deliberate in their decision-making; 4) late majority persons who tend to be skeptical and need peer pressure in order to adapt a new approach; and 5) laggards who are tradition-bound and not easily convinced by either sound argument or peer pressure.

When the merger idea is introduced to the decision making group the opinion leaders will have to adapt and endorse the concept—if the climate is right.

While opinion leaders tend to have greater exposure to external communications than their followers, greater social accessibility, higher status, and are more innovative, at the same time they tend to represent the group's norms. They can lose their following if they go too far beyond the group or become identified with forces outside the group. Opinion leaders seem to have a sense of when the merger idea will have an accepting audience. . . . If the climate is not right, the merger idea will not be picked up. . . .

Close analysis of the diffusion process reveals that in order for a system to decide on an issue as a whole, a decision must first be made by individuals, one at a time, each person reaching his or her own conclusion to accept or reject the idea. At its core, understanding the process of (organizational) change requires an understanding of how people change. An extensive organizational change such as merger may overload individuals beyond their capacity to accommodate, . . . or may represent the extreme of their adaptive efforts. [Taylor, 1978, pp. 28–29]

Proposition 16c.   One of the several power centers of each hospital will appropriate the formal interorganizational relationships concerning merger. This power center will, on the one hand, be a party to intraorganizational debate which has as its purpose the preservation of prior hospital identity and domain, and on the other hand to interorganizational debate, which has as its purpose the development of the newly merged organization.

Proposition 16d.   Conflict between these two sets of relationships will develop, revealing both the issues of and parties to future organizational tension.

Proposition 16e.   The issues will become topics of negotiation between the merger parties, and the parties will become the target of 1) cooptation, in the instance of power-balanced mergers, and 2) absorption, in the instance of imbalanced mergers.

Proposition 16f.   A new dominant coalition and new inner circle will emerge out of this dynamic which reflects a new domain consensus and new interdependencies.

The emergence of these new groups signals the basic decision made by influentials to proceed with merger. These groups will commit future control over resources as a solution to present-day exigencies.

Proposition 16g.   A central figure will emerge to manage the coalition. If several people are candidates for this leadership, it will devolve to the person with superior political skills.

Means of Influence.   What mechanisms do influentials use to deal with merger? The Assumption of Discord (chap. 2, D) stressed the pervasiveness of conflict in interhospital transactions. Different response patterns were identified, including one that distinguished between problem solving, persuasion, bargaining, and politics, and a parallel one that distinguished between computational strategy, judgmental strategy, compromise strategy, and inspirational strategy. Levine and White (1961) suggest a similar typology for the health field. When the functions of the interacting organizations are diffuse, achieving consensus requires constant readjustment and compromise—negotiation. For more specific activities, attainment comes from exchange of information about procedures—mutual orientation. A less frequent and more formal process is the empowering or licensing of one organization by another, such as by a certificate of need process—legitimation.

Integrating and extending these several typologies to hospital mergers, we can classify the means of influence available to parties on a spectrum ranging from those involving closed, private channels to those involving open, visible mechanisms:

1. Use of personal relationships
   a. Friendship: the wish of one party to gratify the other
   b. Collusion

2. Use of bargaining
   a. Rational argument and persuasion
      Directly between parties
      Under sponsorship of third party
   b. Selling or inducement[38]
      Positive
      Negative

3. Use of force of public opinion
   a. Appeal to sense of obligation to community betterment
   b. Focus on public demand for change

These are not mutually exclusive categories. Reference to public demand could enter into rational-type bargaining, or various forms of inducement might be involved in private discussions resulting from collusion.[39]

Further, circumstances dictate heavily the pathways selected. There appear to be typical patterns of means used at different stages of the merging process.

Proposition 17a.   As the merging process unfolds, forms of influence necessary to bring about change will vary.

Proposition 17b.   In earlier stages, merger parties use influence based on personal and private relationships. In subsequent stages, they use bargaining. In the final stages, they may invoke forms of public persuasion.

Proposition 17c.   At whatever stage of merger development, parties who see themselves as weaker will more readily escalate the means of dealing with conflict to more open, visible, and public mechanisms.

This last hypothesis is based on observations by social scientists of organizational conflict during the heightened period of community advocacy of the late 1960s (Fainstein and Fainstein, 1972; Lipsky, 1968). What distinguished these conflicts from the more traditional sorts was that control of change was not securely in the hands of established organization leaders and that the response to conflict—indeed, the generation of it—was quite different in establishment institutions than in the new advocacy organizations. From this we can impute certain behaviors to the weaker parties of a merger, or those that perceive themselves as such, particularly the tendency to escalate both issues and means of dealing with them to wider publics with the hopes of attracting increased attention to their cause, obtaining more resources, and attracting new constituents—all strategies designed to obtain greater negotiating power.

The different conflict resolution pathways can themselves become the object of negotiation, being matters of great sensitivity to the parties involved, since both have strongly held notions of what represents fair play. If one party switches tactics on the other, particularly without warning, the result will be a high order of transactional noise which delays the proceedings and can itself become a major item of contention.

This is not uncommon: during periods of heightened conflict, there is often a switching in agenda topics between substantive and due-process issues. This acts as a cooling mechanism during times of hottest contention; yet, it can also jeopardize the proceedings by giving the parties reason to question each other's good faith and motives, interfering with their ability to bargain over objective issues.[40] There are numerous examples of this in the cases reported in chapters 5 and 6.

Proposition 17d. In incongruent and/or imbalanced merger proceedings, switches in method of influence will take place which are not communicated.

Proposition 17e. This will divert the attention of parties from substantive issues to questions of process, both delaying the proceedings and increasing the conflict.

Proposition 17f. This conflict will involve questions of mutual trust and confidence which will erode merger proceedings unless a third party mediates the conflict.

The parties to conflict will on such matters share their feelings with third parties rather than directly confronting each other, making the role of a third party crucial to returning negotiations to substantive issues.

STAGE III: DYNAMICS OF IMPLEMENTATION

This stage will focus on individuals' behavioral responses in the merged organization, specifically on the intense intraorganizational strain and conflict between the individual and the organization. This occurs because prior policies and actions taken to protect individuals and subgroups entering merger are antithetical to those necessary to establish stability in the new organization.

Managing the Merger

Proposition 18a. During developmental stages of merger, control resides outside of the top administration, but passes to it once the merged organization commences operation.

Every organization can be conceived as having three distinct levels of responsibility and control: technical, managerial, and institutional (Parsons, 1960). The managerial level services the technical suborganization by mediating between the technical producers and those who use their products, and by obtaining resources necessary for the technical function. The managerial level controls the technical suborganization by deciding scale of operations, employment policies, and the broad tasks to be performed. The institutional level provides meaning, legitimization, higher level support, and rights. This level relates the organization to agencies of the community.

Yet, the institutional level provides little formal or operational control, the feature which is crucial at the implementation of merger. So, essential control transfers from the institutional level to the managerial level. As put by Thompson (1964), "I hope I have presented a case for the hot-potato aspect of uncertainty absorption, i.e., which parts of the organization are to absorb the uncertainties stemming from the environment" (p. 348).[41]

The enterprises involved in this venture have just gone through a period of extreme instability, and there is a pervasive organizational will to restabilize (Hage, 1974). It is the job of new leadership to establish this stability, and in so doing, it must deal with three major problems: 1) change too rapid for the complexity of the situation; 2) organizational restructuring, the introduction of a new distribution of power which existing parties resist; and 3) insufficient communication and coordination.

Coping with these problems devolves to the top administration.

Proposition 18b. The successful implementation of hospital mergers depends on top management.

This is for a number of reasons. First, those in control of and responsible for management—boards—do not clearly perceive the new goals that the merged organization has acquired and underestimate the administrative task of developing the skills necessary to work out chains of means and ends between avowed goals and the activities necessary to achieve them.[42] The new board is likely to be drawn from prior policy setting bodies whose members in turn have been familiar with organizational problems of smaller scale and lower complexity. Also, board members are part-time volunteers with limited exposure to the merged organization, as reported by Reynolds and Stunden (1978).

Second, as suggested previously, there remain in the merged organization a variety of nonoperating problems which demand management attention. These fall into two categories: intraorganizational problems stemming from the merger of previous groups, and new issues relating to the ecology of the merged organization, such as the establishment of boundaries, obtaining public support, providing information about the new venture, and justifying its existence and programs.

Third, there is a heavy requirement for dealing with difficult day-to-day management problems brought on by an organization with built-in intraorganizational strain and by pressures for greater efficiencies and the provision of new services. These also demand imaginative attention.

Finally, there is a particular requirement at the early stage of a new organization's development for personal and positive leadership: "The task of central management is no longer one of running the entire organization, but of intervening in a few crucial areas, and of setting the tone of the organization" (Penrose, 1959). Yet, this form of charisma may not be available to a hospital merger. It may have existed during the premanagement phase in the person of a community leader, then disappeared in the transition to the operational phase where personal leadership must be integrated with executive-based institutional power. Further, the shared power context within which leadership must be developed complicates a hospital merger.

This latter point suggests that some form of multiple leadership is most suitable. This has been best stated by Perrow (1963), in his perceptive case study of an urban hospital.

> While social scientists have been reluctant to consider the possibility of an organization without some *de facto* single source of power, it is possible for two or more groups to share power and leadership, to divide up the organization into segments where each has control. . . . It is different from fractionated power where several groups have small amounts of power in an unstable and temporary situation. With multiple leadership there are a small number—perhaps two or three—of recognized centers of power. It is different from a contest of power, for the groups do not seek—at least over the short run—to vanquish each other, but recognize each other's sphere of interests. . . . In multiple leadership there is no single ultimate authority in fact, even though there is in the official constitution.
>
> Multiple leadership, as a stable system of goal determination and policy setting, is most likely to be found in organizations where there are multiple goals and where these goals lack precise criteria of achievement and allow considerable tolerances with regard to achievement. . . .
>
> These considerations have two consequences: the accommodation of group interests in such a situation can easily lead to organizational drift, ambiguity of purpose, and opportunism. Furthermore, the important lubricant of such

a system is some kind of facilitating leadership, someone who keeps explosive issues from erupting too often and maintains easy, comfortable relations among the groups. For the threat to multiple leadership is open confrontation of competing interests that could lead to a debilitating power struggle and vanquishment of one or more groups. [pp. 132–133]

A review of the literature on hospital mergers reveals no general pattern of leadership. The only clear tendency is most merger parties' failure to recognize or concern themselves with particular leadership traits or requirements.[43]

Some of the management skills needed are obvious and straightforward: 1) problem solving—finding the best, quickest, and cheapest way of getting something done, or at least some satisfactory mix of these; 2) communication—either directly task-oriented or indirectly to do with staff morale and motivation; and 3) value setting—the attachment of values to necessary choices and the establishment of an organization's norms (Whisler, 1970). A fourth management activity is vital, but dimly understood: the formation of order out of chaos. This skill is closest to that of creativity. For managers it involves the discernment of hitherto unnoticed relationships or patterns in the complex environment of the organization, calculating their cause effect relationships, and translating them into appropriate programs of action. Discerning these relationships and fashioning the appropriate response is what Thompson (1967) judges to be the most crucial administrative function—coalignment. If it is crucial in complex organizations generally, it is doubly so in mergers, and we can surmise that those managers who possess this trait will more likely survive and perform effectively than those who do not.

The new merger's stability requires a new control mechanism with two essential features: 1) a pattern of authority and 2) the channeling of information. The first concentrates on structural features, dominated by questions of power and centralization/decentralization. The second relates more to communication, both organizational and interpersonal, dominated by questions of expression. The two are closely related: information flow is dictated by a communication network which, in turn, reflects the new distribution of power and authority. Conversely, decisions made by those in power are based on information provided, in the main, by persons in the rank and file who alter and bias its flow in light of their own perceptions and organizational needs (see chap. 2, secs. A and G). Both have differential impact on two realms of institutional dynamics: professional and bureaucratic. We will take them up separately.

Communication in a Professionalized Organization
Hage's (1974) study of cybernetics in professional organizations, using a hospital as case in point, is revealing. As presented in connection with the Assumption of Conduct (chap. 2, sec. C), his main theme is the wide divergence

between mechanical and organic communication and control, and the need in professionalized organizations for the communication network to be one of high socialization/feedback.

> In professional organizations, the prototype of an organic steady state, the professionals are coordinated via a large number of committees. Considerable emphasis is placed on continuous learning, and a variety of socialization procedures are established to keep the professional abreast of current technological developments. Usually, however, the professionals teach each other and thus are controlled even more than they would be by a system of sanctions. As long as they are given work autonomy, professionals accept socialization as desirable, and their behavior is in effect monitored and modified when found wanting. [p. 48]

Proposition 19a. As a merger evolves there will be instability and heightened conflict during a time of increased professionalization without corresponding decline in centralization.

Proposition 19b. Increased professionalization in mergers will increase the conflict between efficiency (administrative) goals and quality (professional) goals, and require new forms of organizational control.

Proposition 19c. Such control requires 1) less dependence on sanctions and more on socialization, and 2) less dependence on vertically structured pathways of communication and more on horizontal pathways which allow for feedback.

Proposition 19d. During this period of merger some professionals will leave; those remaining will vigorously attempt to establish a more stable state, which will be achieved when a new and more organic control and communication structure is established.

The Management Dilemma

For a merger, the problem with Hage's rather idealized concept is that as the merged organization becomes more complex and more differentiated it becomes increasingly difficult to develop agreement on direction and standards and procedures by which the behavior of all members can be regulated. The word members is in itself significant, as it properly characterizes the view physicians have of their place in the organization. In a merger the problems of institutional control of these members are immense, not only because of the normal conflicts of professional vs. bureaucratic authority but because of the likelihood that physicians have entered merger with widespread disagreement over both the desirability and expected results (McGrath et al., 1970). Further, as discussed in chapter 1, they have invested more than economic self-interest; professional status and influence are at stake.

As if this were not enough for the new leadership, the merged hospital is also a health factory (Friedson, 1967), with large numbers of employees (usually called, in the obsequious language of sociology, lower level participants) and operating processes which need more of a mechanical-type structure than is appropriate to the professional ranks.[44] Furthermore, the nature of a hospital, and in particular a merger of two or more, requires not only attention to the two different methods of institutional regulation—one for professional members and one for factory employees—but the artful joining of them for those many realms of hospital activity where both types of persons work in concert (Georgopoulos, 1972).

This calls for management skills of the highest order and places hospital mergers in a different, more demanding, and more challenging category than their counterparts in most other realms of enterprise.

The methods identified by management theorists for the administration of merged organizations are based on their varying assessments of the greatest organizational problems. Whisler (1966) identifies two sets of critical problems—those relating to communications and those relating to computation, i.e., problem solving (chap. 2, G.). Improvements in one are made at the expense of the other. Rapid growth of both types of problems leads management to break the organization into more self-contained units with the intent of reducing the communication load on top management. However, the increased computational capacity of dispersed units raises expenses by duplicating staffs. The typical reaction to this problem is to establish cheaper and perhaps more effective centralized corporate level staff departments. This, in turn, increases communications problems. Staff officials tend to assume gradually expanded authority. This tendency, coupled with communication difficulties, eventually leads back to recentralization of decision making.

Concerning business enterprises, Whisler found that when organizational growth by internal expansion reached the point where divisionalization appeared appropriate,[45] the problem becomes finding or developing executives capable of autonomous action. Conversely, growth by merger requires effort to make certain centralized staff services work effectively in the new organization where separate staff worked before—a quite different need in executive selection. The problem is difficult enough when the merger is between entities with a similar prior size and function providing compatible perspectives on this choice, but when size and function are dissimilar, the management selection problem is exacerbated.

Although centralized and dispersed functions can vary considerably, financial control is almost always centralized, including asset management, capital financing, budgeting, accounting, and data processing (Reynolds and Stunden, 1978). Operations management typically remains decentralized.

Merged hospitals appear to have an initial tendency toward centralization, placing an extremely heavy communications burden on top management.[46] The normal reaction would be to decentralize, as discussed above.

Yet, in most hospital mergers this is limited by the administration's uncertainty of authority. The relatively dispersed power coalitions, both those lingering from prior units and those of the new organization, pose greater limits on management discretion than those found in business mergers. Top management cannot delegate to subordinate levels powers which it does not itself possess, and it tends to hold tightly onto all available prerogatives in order to cope with situations which present a challenge to authority.

Coyne's (1978) comparative study of multiunit hospital systems yielded findings that generally support this view. The corporations in his study with highly centralized managements were less efficient than those with various forms of delegation; more autonomously structured corporations were more efficient.

Findings from a study of multihospital systems reported by Money et al. (1976) reveal similar effects. The older systems in their study were perceived to be less formalized and to have lower levels of hierarchy and authority than the newer systems. This may indicate that the newer systems were making misguided attempts to cope with uncertainty by becoming centralized and more rigid, while the older systems had shifted more responsibility for decision making to lower levels. The researchers also found strong differences in corporate staff executives' and line hospital managers' perceptions. The corporate staff persons felt that, relative to line managers, they had less than sufficient data available on which to base their decisions, there was more accurate communication up and down the hierarchy and more two-way communication, they had more influence on decisions, there was a higher level of role conflict, and there was a lower level of job satisfaction. This seemingly inconsistent set of perceptions bears witness to the difficulty with which merged hospital systems determine what can and should be dispersed and decentralized.

In summary, on the one hand, new mergers require strength of leadership, but on the other hand, they place constraints on the full development and exercise of management functions. This results in:

Proposition 20a. Control tends to remain centralized in top management of merged hospitals, despite operating circumstances calling for decentralization.

Proposition 20b. Management personnel of merged hospitals are often unable to meet the expectations placed on them.

Proposition 20c. A concomitant of hospital merger is management attrition, typically occurring after full integration of the combined organizations. [47]

Communication Within the Rank and File:
What's Going On?
Thus far, the discussion of individuals involved in mergers has been limited

to community influentials and top institutional policy makers. We focus here on the large and varied number of hospital paid employees.

Proposition 21a. Early in the merging process, persons in rank and file have little influence; only in the later stages (notably, stabilization stage) do their concerns attract priority attention, and only at these times do they obtain influence.

Of the several forms of influence that employees might have on organizations, Mechanic (1964) suggests that lower level participants influence primarily through powers of veto and punishment. He proposes that their influence is a function of 1) access to information, persons, and instrumentalities (i.e., nonhuman resources); and 2) the relative importance of these three to organizational performance. The rank and file can achieve power by obtaining, maintaining, and controlling access to these variables, thus making higher ranking participants dependent upon them.[48]

The complexity of hospital lines of authority often creates situations where lower level participants must, for the sake of continued functioning, grasp various forms of organizational influence. If such is the case with hospitals generally, it will be even more so in the merged hospital situation.

As noted in the Assumption of Effect (chap. 2, sec. G), the response of lower level participants to formal organizational change is conditioned by two broad factors: the nature of communication channels and the information transmitted therein. Together, they represent an intelligence system for the rank and file.

Research conducted by the AHA-Northwestern group (Money et al., 1976) shows that in merged hospitals, during the time immediately after merger, persons high in the hierarchy perceive that communication is generally accurate, accepted, and useful, while persons low in the hierarchy have a much more jaundiced view of the communication situation. Thus:

Proposition 21b. During merger implementation when resources are being integrated early in the stabilization stage, the intelligence system for the rank and file is underdeveloped.

This occurs for a variety of reasons (noted in chap. 2, sec. G), primarily that of organizational lag (Evan, 1966), which leads to confusion and conflict based on the differing expectations[49] or pluralistic ignorance.[50]

A prominent merger manager, Richard Witrup, reveals how this comes about (*Health Care Management Review*, 1976):

> But you should try desperately to avoid deciding questions like how exactly you're going to merge services or who is going to be director of what. You have the almost physical problem of getting them settled at the same time because you get one thing settled and by the time you've got another thing settled, the first one has come unglued. The other thing is, every one which is settled alienates somebody, so you have the problem of losing support everytime you

settle something. We call it the principle of the omnibus bill: you put forty issues in a piece of legislation and any one of them might pass, but the accumulated opposition to all forty of them is enough to kill the whole bill. [p. 96]

Based on whatever intelligence sources are used, each participant makes what Humpal (1968) calls a fate assessment of his/her future in the merger. The individual assesses two qualities of the merger critical to his or her response and to subsequent action.

1) Redundancy: the identity or comparability of resources. Total redundancy exists if all positions and functions are replicated in each organization that is party to merger. Redundancy means interchangeability of jobs, with commensurate threat to job holders.

2) Integration: the physical combination of elements from the two or more organizations to be merged, and the control over the resources represented by those elements. If, for instance, all persons in organization life space A are moved to organization B, and in so doing members of B obtain control over them, then complete integration will have taken place.

An employee's perception of integration and redundance will lead to an assessment of the persistence of both the subunit within which he or she works and the job, i.e., retained organizational identity. From this perception he or she determines the probable impact of the merger on personal organization life space.

Proposition 22a. *Hospital mergers involve high degrees of integration and redundancy, leading to disintegration of prior organizational subunits and changes in organizational life space.*

Proposition 22b. *In an effort to mitigate the impact of such change and reduce the dysfunctional consequences calculated to ensue, superiors manifest certain protections to key subgroups, suggesting that persistence of their prior organizational structure is possible, or even guaranteed, in the merger.*

This results in temporary reduction of organizational strain and tension which would otherwise jeopardize the merger, but also leads to incongruity between participants' perceptions of what is likely to take place and what in fact transpires.[51]

Proposition 22c. *Rank and file participants enter merger with inaccurate fate assessments followed by sudden reappraisal, which causes high personal and organizational stress and contributes to spontaneous change.*

Spontaneous change is one of serveral types. Micro change is minimal: alteration of individual duties, jobs, methods, work rules, etc. Function change focuses on organizational subunits rather than individual jobs: it deals with the reorganization of departments and modification of cross-departmental activities. Evolutionary change is systemwide concerning new organizational structures planned to take place sequentially and according to a predetermined schedule. Spontaneous change is systemwide, pervasive, sudden, and unpredictable: tasks, policies, work locales, informal work groups, and formal structures are upset, with change occurring simultaneously rather than sequentially. Anomie may prevail during this time—a social vacuum marked by the absence of norms or values (Durkheim, 1933).

What individuals in the rank and file do when faced with spontaneous change reflects their relative dependence on the merged organization, and this dependence varies by type of participant.

Proposition 22d. Participants with high dependence remain in the merged organization, but resist integration by striving to preserve, through formal or informal means, prior subgroup identity and organizational life space.

For physicians, there is typically high integration in respect to medical staff organization and low redundancy because private practices are based outside of the institution. Dependency is high because in most instances a hospital is an essential resource to modern medical practice; merger further increases this by reducing the number of alternate facilities. Because of this, and for the reasons discussed in chapter 1, we conclude:

Proposition 22e. Hospital mergers allow continuing separate identity of medical staffs.

Proposition 22f. Organizational attrition is both functional, eliminating individuals who might otherwise sabotage the organization, and dysfunctional, causing loss of important information and expertise.[52]

STAGE IV: STABILIZATION

The final stage of the merging process spans the period of time from full integration of resources to outcome.

Proposition 23a. The consequences of merger are other than anticipated, leading to postmerger reappraisal.

During this time the several parties to the new enterprise—still identifiable as prior subpowers—adopt a wait-and-see posture, reserve their full support, and reappraise the new venture's worth and their positions in it. There is a general jockeying for position. Also, there is rough assessment of organizational performance: a comparison of end results with original goals, both legitimating and motivating. This assessment determines whether the merger survives in its existing form. This period may be as short as several months, but more typically endures for several years.

Proposition 23b.   During this time all important relationships are tested; some are revised.

Many streams of organizational dynamics converge in this period as represented by several of the propositions previously advanced. They can be as basic as unanticipated changes in community demographics, economics, or technology, or as topical as the influence of one person. Some of the forces that can lead to reappraisal are 1) changes in the general economy or in the community, making more possible a postmerger split-off of some subgroup that is in schism (Propositions 2d, 3, 11d); 2) fear on the part of one merged party of dominance by another merged party, due possibly to inaccurate assessment of the merger, or possibly to an inappropriate organizational structure (Propositions 14d, 15b); 3) failure to achieve original goals of merger, either legitimating or motivating (Proposition 9d); 4) consequences of management and operating exigencies (Propositions 20c, 22b, 22c, 22d); and 5) medical staff dynamics (Propositions 19a, 22e).

In addition to these hypotheses about a period of postmerger inconclusiveness, there is also direct evidence from merger studies. First, we have the findings of economic studies (chap. 1, H) to the effect that results of merger are other than anticipated: claimed efficiencies are not realized. Second, we have the data on remarkably high rates of attrition among employees of both operating and managerial ranks, at levels which a priori mean unanticipated and pervasive consequences. Third, we have the before/after evidence from a study of a Wilmington, Delaware merger (chap. 1, sec. H),[53] admittedly a sample of one, but with corroborating evidence from many other mergers reported in the literature. This study found that physicians—those persons in a position to link the output of the merged hospitals to the clients they serve—found many things about the arrangement that were other than planned or expected. Three years after the merger, 62 of the 76 physicians who had earlier opposed the merger were still opposed, and 45 of the 130 doctors who originally supported the merger had come to oppose it. Fourth, there are a series of attitude studies which all point in the same direction; the evidence is spotty but strongly suggestive.

Costello et al. (1963) determined employee attitudes towards a pending merger of two large banks. Fifty-six percent of those surveyed had unfavorable attitudes toward the merger. More successful persons (as measured by pay and position) had more unfavorable attitudes, contradicting the expectation that the more successful would feel more assured about the change. The less successful apparently looked upon the merger as a second chance that aroused their long forgotten hopes for advancement and recognition. Older persons were more favorably inclined than younger—apparently they were more settled and secure, thus less adverse to risk. Also, there was some indication that older persons hoped for more favorable retirement benefits. In contrast, younger persons feared blocked promotions. The findings from a personality test were that both strongly independent and strongly dependent employees had less favorable attitudes toward merger, interpreted to mean that independent people were more confident of their ability to face change on their own and unhappy about the regimentation they forsaw in merger, while dependent personalities feared the upset of existing relationships. Costello and colleagues concluded:

> An interesting hypothesis for subsequent testing is suggested by our study: the more favorable the attitude toward a planned merger, the less satisfactory will be the subsequent adjustment to the actual merger. The characteristics . . . associated with favorable expectancies are those which . . . are likely to make later adjustment to a trying situation difficult—older age, a previous lack of success, and an authoritarian personality. In addition, as common sense has long dictated, highly favorable expectations about a stressful change can result in sharp disappointment and subsequent difficult adjustment. [p. 249]

Shirley's (1973) study of the series of mergers creating the Samaritan Health Services of Arizona is helpful both because it compares several of Costello's findings of before-merger attitudes with after-merger attitudes toward combination, and because it is a study of hospitals rather than of banks. The thrust of Shirley's study was to identify factors associated with initial acceptance or rejection of merger by employees and physicians. Two instruments were used: a questionnaire distributed to all management, supervisory, and operative employees affected by the merger, and a questionnaire distributed during structured interviews with 90 physicians selected by stratified random sample to represent all doctors.[54] Six hypotheses were tested, many of them drawn from Costello's research. On the strength of findings elsewhere that the degree of trust in management significantly affects initial reaction to plans for change, Shirley found that employees who saw top management as concerned for their interests showed a significantly greater tendency to support the merger decision. The importance of this for postmerger dynamics is that employees who did not trust management prior to merger could be expected to find fault with actions taken after integration.[55] For physicians, trust in management did not appear to be significant one way or the other, reflecting their relative independence from hospital administration as an employer and the irrelevance of job security for most doctors. Shirley's findings were the same as Costello's concerning premerger job satisfaction: those who were positive about the merger were those previously satisfied with their duties, pay, work conditions, chances for development, and supervision. This correlation of high morale with positive merger attitudes contradicts Sayle's (1962) reasoning that employees under stress will more likely welcome a change, and suggests that postmerger resistance will come from those who were previously unhappy.

Shirley found no correlation between promerger attitude on the part of employees and prior involvement in merger discussions and plans; however, the very large proportion of employees who had no opportunities for involvement (532 out of 568) makes this finding unreliable. For physicians, those who had involvement viewed merger more favorably. As for the anticipation of benefits, those that were optimistic about potential gains in pay, conditions of work, duties, and personal development were also strongly promerger in attitude. As for age of employees, the findings were roughly the same as Costello's: older employees agreed with the merger decision while younger did not. Shirley's findings suggested the same reasons for this as did Costello's. Data on this correlation among physicians were scant, but suggested that older physicians showed no greater tendency to have disagreed with the merger decision than younger—contradicting the conclusion reached by McGrath et al. (1970) that older doctors are less favorably inclined toward merger because they have vested interests in the maintenance of premerger arrangements.[56]

Finally, Shirley found that longer service employees did not resist merger more than shorter service workers; in fact, there was a slight tendency for them to be more supportive. The same was true for physicians.

A final bit of evidence comes from a two-stage study of the integration of a clinical pathology laboratory in connection with a 1972 merger of two large hospitals in Chicago. Wortman (1975) tested the hypothesis that the predicted strong negative perceptions immediately upon consolidation would diminish in the few months available for the investigation. Such was not the case; there was no reduction in level of dissatisfaction, as had been predicted. This held for both employees and physicians. The major problems that produced these attitudes were reported to be increased workload, lack of uniformity in test procedures, inadequate space, insufficient personnel to handle the new work, and poor communication.[57] Further, those relocated by the move had increased their negative perception of the merger. "Whether this represents some sort of boomerang effect caused by disappointment in the violation of prior expectations . . . is not clear" (p. 12).

To summarize, it seems clear that neither the beginning nor ending of the stabilization stage occurs at a single point in time,[58] but rather at several points in time for different elements of the merger. The initial integration of resources is likely to be at a different time for management than for any one of several operating departments, and these in turn will differ from the medical staff, etc. Similarly, outcome occurs at different time points.

Nonetheless, there is sufficient covariance to establish a predictable stage of continuing merger evolution—a moving equilibrium toward a more stable state—which ends only when all significant identity and influence of existing contestants are submerged and a revised order is not only established

but commonly recognized.
At this time and only at this time is the merging process complete.

NOTES

1. Taylor (1978) has elaborated on this four-stage approach in his excellent human dynamics model of the merger process. Phase I, "creating an environment," consists of four stages: environmental conditions, recognition of motivation, co-operative efforts, and conceptualization. Phase II, "deciding to merge," consists of three stages: merger decision, negotiations, and consummation. Phase III, "realization," consists of three stages: implementation, integration, and stabilization.

2. This literature is extensive, though largely descriptive and exhortative. An annotated bibliography is available of all material published between 1946 and 1969 (Starkweather and Taylor, 1969). Another annotated bibliography covers the ten years since 1969, approximately, to 1977 (services shared . . . , 1977). A list of 125 selected references, current to 1978, has been published by the American Hospital Association (1978).

3. These propositions seek to advance the theory of health services organization rather than to refine conceptualizations of sociology, economics, political science, psychology, etc. Notwithstanding, the study of mergers constitutes a fertile field for organizational analysis, with the potential for contributing new insights to these basic social sciences. For full analysis and comment on the history of interorganizational studies in the health field, see Berry (1970). He scores health field studies for their lack of theoretic base and criticizes interorganizational studies for their tendency to use personal experience rather than objective data collection. Berry concludes that emphasis should be placed on developing new theories of interorganizational behavior. The propositions developed in this chapter constitute such an effort.

4. Nelson (1959), in a study of the episodic nature of the occurrence of business mergers, concluded that mergers occur at times of favorable conditions in the capital markets: ". . . the rise of technological innovation, and the growth of interregional transportation were not important immediate factors in the merger waves. Peaks in the expansion of merger activity were found to be closest in timing to those in industrial stock prices, stock market trading, and new business incorporations" (pp. 6–7).

5. This contrast between for-profit and not-for-profit hospitals points to the difficulty of making generalizations about mergers in the health field: the theories of merger have been developed primarily by economists, which means that they are relevant to economic organizations. As observed by Pfeffer (1972): "This has led to only a relatively few focused questions being asked and to a neglect of the development of a theory of merger which is generalizable across types of organizations." White's review (c. 1972) of the sociology literature on interorganizational relations reveals the same problem, although his two schema are helpful.

6. The economic stimulation in the for-profit health industry was both the guaranteed reimbursement which came with passage in 1965 of Titles 18 and 19 of the Social Security Act, and the flow of investor capital derived from the sale of company shares through stock exchanges. This led in time to a dramatic

restructuring of the for-profit element of the hospital field, resulting in a high degree of concentration. This phenomenon started when the economy was flush and continued when it was in recession, revealing a typical pattern in business mergers (McCarthy, 1961). In boom years, acquiring companies usually make the first move in a proposed combination. In such a situation there is heavy bidding for attractive smaller companies and purchase prices are usually generous. During depression periods, or within depressed industries, the reverse is usually the situation: sellers take the initiative in order to survive bankruptcy, and prices paid are typically lower.

7. In the case of specialized hospitals, notably pediatric facilities, these links became formalized in a phase of mergers in the late 1940s and early 1950s (Blumberg, 1965).

8. One such study, reviewed in chapter 1, is of New York City hospitals. Of 143 hospitals in 1960, 46 had closed or merged by 1975. Most of these were small hospitals. The total bed complement of the city did not change during this time.

9. Evan (1972) hints that the pressures that emerge to transform the dominance-submission relationships into a bargaining relationship depend on the type of network already in place between organizations: dyad, wheel, all-channel, or chain. Thompson (1967) distinguishes between three kinds of technologies—long-linked, mediating, intensive—as to how domains are expanded.

10. For empirical evidence concerning hospitals, see Belnap and Steinle (1963) and Elling and Halebski (1961). Price also suggests that cooptation can be dysfunctional, since organizations which practice cooptation may have to adjust to the viewpoints of the parties coopted. "It is highly unlikely that the coopted members will be culturally similar to each other and/or to the remaining members of the organization" (p. 111).

11. Cooptation and representation are different mechanisms. In cooptation, individuals from the environment are brought into the organization. In the case of representation, individuals from the organization go into the environment and join organizations (Price, 1968).

12. For a lively account which illustrates the small-city situation see Elling (1963).

13. This line of reasoning is supported by the health economist, Berry (1967): ". . . hospitals should be considered as small or large not only in an absolute sense but also relative to the scope of services that they are producing. A 200-bed hospital may be the optimal size for producing a narrow range of services but an exceedingly inefficient size for producing a wide range of services" (pp. 129–30).

14. Neuhauser (1966) asserts that medium-sized hospitals are in a stage of administrative ascendancy, while large hospitals are in a stage of professional ascendancy.

15. Richard Wittrup, administrator of a three-hospital merger in Boston that took fifteen years to realize, has this to say about the constellation of forces (*Health Care Management Review*, 1976): "Viewing the dynamics of a merger as a set of social pressures you can guide is the most productive approach. If you're trying to quarterback this thing, the main thing to recognize is that the merger isn't happening because you willed it. The merger is happening because there are a lot of planets out there with the right alignment. If you stay out of their way and just nudge them, you get your results. If the planets are not in their right alignment, you might as well forget it—it's not going to happen, at least if they're so far out of alignment that even with a little nudge from you they won't get in" (p. 94).

16. The state of Nevada has 21 short-term general hospitals. Two are religious hospitals, one near Las Vegas and the other in Reno; four are federal government hospitals, one Air Force, one Veteran's Administration, two Indian Health Service; two are for-profit hospitals, both in Las Vegas; and one is a community sponsored hospital, a facility in Boulder City turned over by the federal government upon completion of construction of the Hoover Dam. The remaining 14 are county owned and operated, and, with the exception of two larger hospitals in Clark (Las Vegas) and Washoe (Reno) counties, are all under 75 beds. Most are much smaller. These 12 hospitals, 57 percent of the State's total, are generally regarded as the political fiefdoms of the several county boards of supervisors.

17. Such was the case in the numerous conglomerate mergers of the late 1960s and early 1970s which combined firms operating in totally different industries. By definition, these could not have been based on synergism in the production or distribution process.

18. This distinction between the motives of managers and stockholders in respect to mergers is a reflection of a similar one identified by a long list of commentators (Berle and Means, 1932; Gordon, 1961; Galbraith, 1967) in respect to enterprises generally: investor-controlled firms seek to maximize profits, whereas those dominated by managers seek to maximize growth and security.

19. We are speaking here of an organizational self, a concept that has not been well explored by sociologists. One worthwhile discussion, relevant to health organizations, is by Stanton (1970).

20. Elling (1963) concludes a case study of community hospital planning with the following statement: "Under the present rules of the hospital-support game, it is difficult to see how the much-trumpeted notion of the hospital as a community health center can be actualized. While an important part of the game's strategy is to announce that the hospital is serving 'the whole community', and while no doubt each hospital does do so to a considerable degree, an equally important part is to gain attachments to particular segments of the community and to compete with other teams in this respect" (pp. 107–8).

21. This is not surprising to Perrow (1961), who argues that an understanding of how goals actually influence activity can only be determined by examining "operative goals, those that are imbedded in the major operating policies and daily decisions of the personnel" (p. 855).

22. March and Simon (1958) specify three factors leading to internal conflict. The first, the experience of a positive felt need for joint decision making, is occasioned by the possibility of merger. The second, a difference in goals, derives from the junta aspect of hospitals discussed in the Assumption of Behaviorism (chap. 2, A.) and the Assumption of Discord (chap. 2, D.). The third is a difference in perceptions of reality. We will discuss this in detail subsequently; we have already noted it in the Assumption of Effect (chap. 2, G.).

23. We need to distinguish here between internal goal dissonance and multiple goals. There can be agreement to pursue several goals; indeed, this is the typical case. In the dissonant situation there is no agreement.

24. These five lend specificity to Hage's (1974) vague prescription to social scientists that determining what goals are being pursued by different power centers can be answered only by learning: 1) which priorities are paramount when goals are in conflict and 2) the basis of decision making regarding allocation of scarce resources.

25. Continuance is related to power, since powerful organizations can presumably acquire whatever is necessary to guarantee survival. However, per the discus-

sion leading to Propositions 4a and 4b, in some instances institutional power is used to grow and expand rather than merely to survive, while in others an organization is capable of survival only because of protective relationships established with others. There are small hospitals which are not powerful but which, for significant periods of time, seem to persevere. Thus, continuance is a factor to be distinguished from power. Continuance can also be distinguished from goal dissonance. As March and Simon (1958) point out, an organization can exist and persist with little need for joint decision making and with widespread disagreement among its participants.

26. For an analysis of relations between alcoholism agencies that was explained by the principle of complementarity see Klonglan et al. (1968).

27. In business, mergers without complementarity are said to be unlikely since the dominant party has little to gain—expansion by redundancy is not as attractive as expansion from within through new product lines. In the hospital industry this does not necessarily follow, because of market entry regulation. Under certificate of need regulations based on assumptions of excess bed supply, absorption of existing franchised beds is seen increasingly as the only way for larger hospitals to grow.

28. In this proposition the influence of relative power is related to initial merger activity, as compared to ultimate merger success. It is possible that a factor which initially enhances the likelihood of merger, balanced power, will subsequently complicate the merger process: the combined presence of equally strong and potentially viable subunits will lower the likelihood that tension will be resolved.

29. In a study of 67 cities, Crain et al. (1969), found some cities in which there was relatively little agreement. High-visibility cities tend to be concentrated in the Midwest, low-visibility cities on the West Coast. High status suburbs are too pluralistic to support single leadership groups.

30. This breakdown is provided by Treat (1973). He found that of the 12 internally generated mergers, four were by boards of directors, one by a medical staff, two by heterogeneous planning committees within one of the merged hospitals, and five by joint planning groups spanning two or more hospitals.

31. Also, the study upon which Morris drew this conclusion was limited to agencies which were all members of Jewish philanthropic federations. The same role for third party agencies may not apply when the focal organizations are of widely varying sponsorship. Not all planning agencies would support a weak organization in the same manner that a philanthropy would in the instance where the philanthropy had been instrumental in its establishment.

32. Hickson et al. (1960) classify the sources of intraorganizational power as 1) the ability to control uncertainties, 2) lack of substitutability, 3) centrality of position within an organization, and 4) pervasiveness of work product.

33. It is interesting that Weick (1969) believes that triads are the basic unit of analysis in organization theory. "The reason three is central is that it is the basic unit needed to demonstrate conditionality. . . . Organization is a mediated causal relationship between two items, in which the relationship . . . is influenced by the state of the third item" (p. 38).

34. For some reason hospital administrators, usually the respondents in studies like Weil's, like to ascribe the initiation of merger considerations to chance contact between old line trustees, but these have proven to be either false or unimportant. I have concluded that it is not very important which parties actually held the first conversation about a merger idea.

35. In this connection three perceptions are possible (March and Simon, 1958). In the case of unacceptability, the party knows at least the probability distribution of outcomes associated with different alternatives, in this case to merge or not, and may even be able to identify a preferred outcome, but the preferred outcome is not satisfactory. When the party knows the probability distribution of outcomes but cannot identify a preference, we have incomparability. In uncertainty the probability distributions cannot be known or estimated. In the merger situation, the kind of perception available to different subpowers will vary, in part for reasons of different access to information, leading to a mix of responses— which variety is only suggested by Miller's (1951) categories of approach-approach, approach-avoidance, and avoidance-avoidance tactics.

36. March and Simon stress the important role of information gathering units of an organization: "In an organization of any size at all, there will be different amounts and types of information at different points. This incomplete sharing of information leads to intra-organizational disagreement where there is pressure toward joint decision-making within the organization. . . . The greater the number of independent information sources, the greater the differentiation of perceptions within the organization. Thus, we would expect less perceptual conflict in an organization when one outside individual or group of individuals holds an acknowledged monopoly of relevant information than where there are a number of external sources" (pp. 127–28).

37. "Medical staff attitudes remind me of Columbus' sailors at the half-way point: some wanted to mutiny; the others wanted to turn back," said Shortcliffe (1967) of the four-hospital merger that created the Wilmington Medical Center.

38. For definition of terms, and distinction between selling and inducement, see Morris and Binstock (1966), p. 117.

39. Note, for instance, the different forms of influence used in three stages of community hospital development in urban city (Elling, 1963).

40. It is this aspect of interorganizational relationships which has closest analogue to the psychiatric theories of communication between individuals (Berne, 1972). Just as there is a limit to the application of the theories of interpersonal behavior to the inter-organizational realm, as discussed in the Assumption of Sociology (chap. 2, sec. B), so also is there a limit to the application of transactional analysis to enterprises—despite the founder's efforts (Berne, 1973). Organizations do not have the script formation imbedded at a very early age that transactional analysis theory holds people to have. Nor can organizations be classified with anywhere near the articulation that transactional analysis offers in its parent, adult, and child "states." Nonetheless, organizations do have identities which are derived from their particular sociologic origins. Our propositions about incongruent and imbalanced merger parties is suggestive of different dependency states between individuals. Our propositions about different pathways of influence and negotiation are similar to some games of transactional analysis. And the process of establishing new consensus on organizational domains has its parallels in re-scripting. Finally, there is Long's (1958) suggestive title, "The Local Community as an Ecology of Games." In short, though the roots of theoretic development are different and it cannot be said that one application is the logical extension of the other, the parallels are instructive.

41. March and Simon (1958) suggest that the absorption of uncertainty is frequently used, consciously or unconsciously, as a technique for acquiring and exercising power. "In a culture where direct contradiction of assertions of fact is not approved, an individual who is willing to make assertions, particularly about mat-

ters that do not contradict the direct perceptions of others, can frequently get these assertions accepted as premises of decisions" (p. 166). "The facts he communicates can be disbelieved but they can only rarely be checked. Hence, by the very nature and limits of the communication system, a great deal of discretion and influence is exercised by those persons who are in direct contact with some part of the "reality" that is of concern to the organization. Both the amount and the locus of uncertainty absorption affect the influence structure of the organization" (p. 165).

42. Penrose (1959, pp. 46–47) has discussed a similar limitation in business growth, either by internal or external expansion. For further support of this notion in terms of risk-aversion and reduction of likelihood of "response errors" on the part of managerial subordinates, see Knight (1946), p. 311.

43. For discussion of the matching of organizational requirements for leadership in health organizations with personal attributes of managers, both of which vary at different life cycle stages, see Starkweather and Kisch (1971).

44. In particular, the often discussed distinction between coordination by plan vs. coordination by feedback (March and Simon, 1958).

45. This is possibly the same point that Weston (1966) has identified for mergers: "There is an awkward age in the growth of a company that comes when it moves from a condition of essentially direct, informal, personal control to a condition of formal control. Let's say that it is in the $25 to $35 million sales range that you run into these diseconomies of trying to make the transition from a small company to a big company. However, once you get beyond this adolescent stage, I would argue that there are very substantial economies in size, from a management standpoint" (pp. 50–51).

46. For illustration, see Smith (1968).

47. Nor is this phenomenon limited to hospital mergers. See Karr (1969).

48. A number of characteristics possessed variably by different subgroups dictate their ability to manipulate this dependency. Mechanic offers six factors: "Expertise: Experts have tremendous potentials for power by withholding information, providing incorrect information, and so on, and to the extent that experts are dissatisfied the probability of organizational sabotage increases. . . . Effort and interest: Willingness to exert effort in areas where higher-ranking persons are reluctant to participate. . . . Attractiveness: Personality. . . . Location and Position: Propinquity to communications networks. . . . Coalitions: Informal arrangements between persons in various organizational sub-groups, which permit things to get done. . . . Rules: While rules are usually functional to organizational performance, they can often be used to support the contention by a lower level participant that he or she does not have to do what is asked, and they can be used as a rationalization for inaction" (p. 144).

49. March and Simon (1958) posit that "the greater the number of information sources the greater the differentiation of perceptions within the organization" (p. 127).

50. One form of pluralistic ignorance occurring in mergers is the development of opinions and facts on the part of employees which reflect community appraisal of the new venture (McQueen, 1967). These external signals are sought in the absence of sufficient communication or consistent information from internal sources. Since this community perception, particularly at the outset, is based on relative ignorance and, to some extent, on what persons want to know based on prior opinions about the mergers, the body of knowledge taken as true by participants can be at variance with organizational reality. Morale, devotion to

duty, etc, will vary according to this outside view of the hospital, despite actions taken within the institution. This difference between perception and reality can work to heighten or reduce the performance of members for the new organization. In the long run it is dysfunctional because it is nonvalid.

51. As described by Humpal (1968), this is incongruity between the individual's map and the organization's map. Humpal has developed some worthwhile submaps having to do with process, redundancy, expected behavior, and end state.

52. Attrition rates vary substantially across mergers. In general, there are differences between middle management and workers, and between acquired and parent enterprises. The rates often differ dramatically where this latter distinction is clear, with the rates for the acquired institution being three to five times the rates of the enterprise taking over. Further, attrition usually is higher than expected and does not have to do with failures to equalize and upgrade wages, fringe benefits, and personnel policies (Humpal, 1968).

53. The reader desiring more information on the setting of this study may review Cannon (1961, 1968), Shortcliff (1967), Gottshall (1967), and McKillop (1966).

54. For the employee questionnaire, 2050 surveys were distributed and 1971 returned (81.5 percent response). Of these, only 694 were from persons who had been employed prior to the merger. This reveals two important things. First, apparently the attrition rate was over 40 percent for the approximate two-year period from the time of merger to time of study. Second, this was not a two-stage study: the after-merger questionnaire asked respondents to indicate what their opinion of the merger had been some two years previous. This is a major weakness of the study, due to the limitations of retrospective responses.

55. On the matter of trust, theorists of organizational development focus on freeing up the communication process in organizations, based on the fact that uncertainty causes distrust among subunits. Since both are likely to be exacerbated by the merging process, the normal distrust in organizations is magnified (Roos, 1975). Organizational development practitioners strive to overcome this by explicit recognition and treatment of these problems in a group setting. Blumberg and Weiner (1971) took this approach to two geographically separate units of a national voluntary community organization that were about to be merged. Their approach was to engage the two groups in a three-dimensional confrontation exercise (Golembiewski and Blumberg, 1967). This allowed the consultants to identify organizational problems which would have to be dealt with if merger were to be effective. For example, one agency was more task oriented—concerned with getting the job done—than the other, which was much more concerned with interpersonal relations. These problems were treated in a way that opened up communication and reduced previous distrust. While there was only an informal follow-up on the postmerger results, Blumberg and Weiner found satisfaction among participants in what was done: "the participants felt that they are quite a bit ahead of the other organizational units that have merged through one process or another" (p. 100).

56. However, significant to Proposition 22e dealing with lag in medical staff integration is the fact that the Samaritan Health Service merger did not alter medical staff autonomy in the various hospitals, whereas the Wilmington Center merger examined by McGrath et al. mandated a single new medical staff to replace prior medical staffs.

57. Roos (1975) reviewed both the merged laboratory situation and Wortman's analysis of it. She commented as follows: "In any case, the distrust which is normally present in organizations is undoubtedly magnified when a hospital approaches

130   CONCEPTS

merger. In a laboratory merger, attending physicians worry that the pathologist may take advantage of their relative independence from the hospital and be less responsive to the physicians' complaints. However, this worry would probably be communicated as 'We don't want to lose the close professional rapport which now exists between physicians and pathologists.' Communication problems between two merging institutions will undoubtedly be greater yet. In a laboratory consolidation, the attempt to set up a uniform fee schedule raises immediate suspicion about interpreting each other's books. When two separate laboratories are to be merged into one unit, a very major question is 'Who gets the top position?' " (p. 17).

58. It has been pointed out that: "Some of the oldest, biggest, and most prestigious institutions in the country can be seen by an organizational historian as giant capstones superimposed upon a whole congeries of small hospitals which had been absorbed at some past period in history. In some cases, the seams of these mergers are still clearly visible, and occasionally they are, in fact, carefully preserved as cherished dividing lines of relative prestige, staff power, teaching fame, or financial contribution, whether through original endowment or through present-day ability to attract grants. Hence, can one perhaps see some of these cases as 'incomplete mergers?' They seem to offer illustrations of tenacity of some of the particularistic forces in the organizational world which, while too weak to prevent mergers at the critical time, manage to survive in vestigial forms through generations of boards, administrators, and staff" (White and Vlasak, 1970, pp. 50–51).

REFERENCES

Alberts, William W. "The Profitability of Growth by Merger." In *The Corporate Merger*, ed. by W. W. Alberts and J. E. Segall. Chicago: University of Chicago Press, 1966.

Altshuler, A. *The City Planning Process: A Political Analysis.* Cornell University Press, Ithica: Cowell Books, 1969.

Ansoff, H. Igor, and Weston, J. Fred. "Merger Objectives and Organization Structure." *Quarterly Review of Economics and Business*, Fall 1962.

Belknap, Ivan, and Steinle, John G. *The Community and Its Hospitals.* Syracuse, New York: Syracuse University Press, 1963.

Berle, A.A., and Means, G.C. *The Modern Corporation and Private Property.* New York: Macmillan, 1932.

Berman, Howard. "Mergers and Consolidation: A Solution?" *Hospital Administration*, Winter 1971.

Berne, Eric. *What Do You Say After You Say Hello?* New York: Grove Press, 1972.
————. *The Structure and Dynamics of Organizations and Groups.* New York: Ballantine, 1973.

Berry, Charles C. "Analysis of Citation Patterns in the Literature Associated with the Study of Interorganizational Relationships in the Health Field." In *Interorganizational Research in Health: Conference Proceedings*, ed. by P.E. White and G. Vlasak. Baltimore: Johns Hopkins School of Public Health, 1970.

Berry, Ralph E. "Returns to Scale in the Production of Hospital Services." *Health Services Research*, Summer 1967.

Biddle, Bruce. "Roles, Goals, and Value Structures in Organizations." In *New Perspectives in Organization Research*, ed. by R. Cooper et al. New York: Wiley 1964.

Blau, Peter M., and Scott, Richard W. *Formal Organizations.* New York, San Francisco: Chandler, 1962.
————, and Shoenherr, Richard. *The Structure of Organizations.* New York: Basic Books, 1971.
Blumberg, Arthur, and Wiener, William. "One from Two: Facilitating an Organizational Merger." *Journal of Applied Behavioral Science*, January-February 1971.
Blumberg, Mark S. "Changing Times Spur Hospital Mergers." *Modern Hospital*, July 1965.
Burling, Temple; Lentz, Edith; and Wilson, Robert. *The Give and Take in Hospitals.* New York: Putnam, 1956.
Cannon, Norman L. "The Case for Hospital Merger." *Delaware Medical Journal*, vol. 33, 1961.
————. "Three Years After Merger: An Appraisal and a Look Ahead." *Hospitals*, September 15, 1968.
Caplow, T. "Organization Size." *Administrative Science Quarterly*, Spring 1957.
Costello, Timothy W.; Kubis, Joseph F.; and Shaffer, Charles L. "An Analysis of Attitudes Toward a Planned Merger." *Administrative Science Quarterly*, September 1963.
Coyne, Joseph. *A Comparative Study of the Performance and Characteristics of Multi-hospital Systems.* Dr. Ph. dissertation, School of Public Health, University of California, Berkeley, 1978 (unpublished).
Crain, Robert; Morlock, Laura; and Vaneck, James J. "The Influence of Reputational, Positional, and Decisional Elites in Northern Cities." Paper delivered at 64th annual meeting, American Sociological Association, San Francisco, 1969.
Dagnone, Antonio. *A Study of Multiple Unit Hospital Systems.* Diploma Thesis, (unpublished), University of Toronto, 1967.
Durkheim, Emile. *The Division of Labor in Society.* Translated by George Simpson. Glencoe, Illinois: Free Press, 1933.
Einstein, M.B. *History of the Development of the Jewish Hospital of Saint Louis Medical Center.* Jewish Federation of Saint Louis, 1964.
Eisenstadt, S.N. "Bureaucracy and Bureaucratization, A Trend Report and Bibliography." *Current Sociology*, 7, no. 2 (1958), pp. 325-348.
Elling, Ray H. "The Hospital Support Game in Urban Center." In *The Hospital in Modern Society*, ed. by E. Friedson. Glencoe: The Free Press, 1963.
————, and Halebsky, Sandor. "Organizational Differentiation and Support: A Conceptual Framework." *Administrative Science Quarterly*, Fall, 1961.
Etzioni, Amatai. "Two Approaches to Organizational Analysis: A Critique and Suggestion." *Administrative Science Quarterly*, September 1960.
Evan, William. "Organizational Lag." *Human Organization*, Spring 1966.
————. "An Organization-Set Model of Inter-Organizational Relations." In Tuite, Matthew et al., *Inter-Organizational Decision Making.* Chicago: Aldine, 1972.
Fainstein, Norman I., and Fainstein, Sandra. "Innovation in Urban Bureaucracies." *American Behavioral Scientist*, March/April 1972.
Flanagan, John J. "Trends in Hospital Mergers." *Proceedings of the Annual Scientific Session*, American Association of Hospital Consultants, The Association, Chicago, 1967.
French, John R.P., and Raven, Bertram. "The Bases of Social Power." In *Group Dynamics, Research, and Theory*, 2nd. ed., ed. by D. Cartwright and A. Zander. Evanston, Illinois: Row, Peterson, 1960.
Friedson, E. "Health Factories: A Review Essay." *Social Problems*, Spring, 1967.
Galbraith, John K. *American Capitalism.* Cambridge: Houghton Mifflin, 1962.

_____. *The New Industrial State*. Boston: Houghton Mifflin, 1967.
Georgopoulos, Basil S. "The Hospital as an Organization and Problem Solving System." In *Organization Research on Health Institutions*, ed. by Basil S. Georgopoulos. Ann Arbor: Institute for Social Research, The University of Michigan, 1972.
_____, and Matejko, Aleksander. "The American General Hospital as a Complex Social System." *Health Services Research*, Spring 1967.
Gerth, Hans H., and Mills, C. Wright (tr. and eds.). *From Max Weber: Essays in Sociology*. New York: Oxford University Press, 1946.
Golembiewski, R., and Blumberg, A. "Confrontation as Training Design Complex Organizations: Attitudinal Changes in a Diversified Population of Managers." *Journal of Applied Behavioral Science*, October-November-December, 1967.
Gordon, R.A. *Business Leadership in the Large Corporation*. Berkeley: University of California Press, 1961.
Gort, Michael. "Diversification, Mergers, and Profits." In *The Corporate Merger*, ed. by W.W. Alberts and J.E. Segall. Chicago: University of Chicago Press, 1963.
_____. "An Economic Disturbance Theory of Mergers." *Quarterly Journal of Economics*, November 1969.
Gottshall, Ralph K. "Merger Benefits Outnumber the Problems." *Trustee*, November 1967.
Gouldner, A.W. "Cosmopolitans and Locals: Toward an Analysis of Latent Social Role." *Administrative Science Quarterly*, December (Part I) and March (Part II), 1957, 1958.
_____. "Reciprocity and Autonomy in Functional Theory." In *Symposium on Sociological Theory*, ed. by Llewellyn Gross. Evanston, Illinois: 1959.
Hage, Jerald. *Communication and Organization Control: Cybernetics in Health and Welfare Settings*. New York: Wiley, 1974.
Harris, Allyn R. "Causes and Effects of Hospital Mergers." Unpublished thesis, Trinity University, San Antonio, Texas, 1969.
_____. "Mergers are Made to Add Services and Save Money—And They Do." *Modern Hospital*, May 1970.
Health Care Management Review. "The Way Dick Wittrup Sees It." Winter, 1976.
Hickson, D.J., et al. "A Strategic Contingencies Theory of Intra-Organizational Power." *Administrative Science Quarterly*, April 1960.
Humpal, John J. "The Study of Mergers: Notes Toward A Theory and Conceptual Framework." Working Paper, University of Chicago, Behavioral Science Organizational Workshop, December 1968.
Hunter, Floyd. *Community Power Structure*. Chapel Hill: University of North Carolina Press, 1953.
Jacobs, Philip. "A Survey of Economic Models of Hospitals." *Inquiry*, June 1974.
Karr, Albert. "More Executives Get Caught in Job Shuffles as Merger Pace Climbs." *Wall Street Journal*, March 16, 1969.
Katz, Daniel, and Kahn, Robert L. *The Social Psychology of Organizations*. New York: Wiley, 1966.
Klonglan, Gerald E., et al. "Agency Interaction Patterns and Community Alcoholism Services." Sociology Report No. 73. Ames: Iowa State University, 1969.
Knight, F.H. *Risk, Uncertainty, and Profit*. Reprint no. 16. London: London School of Economics and Political Science.
Lee, Maw Lin, "A Conspicuous Production Theory of Hospital Behavior." *Southern Economic Journal*, July 1971. Health Information Foundation of the Graduate School of Business. Chicago: University of Chicago, 1971.

Lefton, Mark, and Rosegren, William R. "Organization and Clients: Lateral and Longitudinal Dimensions." *American Sociological Review*, December 1966.
Levine, Sol. "Organization Structure Related to Illness Behavior." In *Conference on Medical Sociology and Disease Control*, ed. by G. Gordon. Chicago: Health Information Foundation of the Graduate School of Business, University of Chicago, 1965.
_____, and White, Paul E. "Exchange As A Conceptual Framework for the Study of Inter-Organizational Relationships." *Administrative Science Quarterly*, March 1961.
Lipsky, M. "Protest as a Political Resource." *American Political Science*, December, 1968.
Littauer, David. "Case Report of a Hospital Merger." In *Trends in Hospital Mergers: Annual Scientific Session, American Association of Hospital Consultants*. Chicago: The Association, 1967.
Long, Norton E. "The Local Community as an Ecology of Games." *American Journal of Sociology*, November 1958.
March, James G., and Simon, H.A. *Organizations*. New York: Wiley, 1958.
May, Joel J. "Economic Variables in Hospital Mergers." In *Conference on Analysis of Hospital Mergers: Transcript of Proceedings*, ed. by D.B. Starkweather and D.C. Walden. Rockville, Maryland: National Center for Health Services Research and Development, 1970.
McCarthy, George D. "Premeditated Merger." *Harvard Business Review Merger and Acquisition Series*, Boston: Harvard University, 1961.
McGrath, John H.; Rothman, Robert A.; and Schwartzbaum, Allan A. "Factors Associated with Physicians' Vote on the Wilmington Hospital Merger." *Delaware Medical Journal*, February 1970.
McKillop, William. "Three Hospitals Merge to Create New Medical Center." *Hospitals*, February 16, 1966.
McQueen, R.J. "Trends in Hospital Mergers." *Hospital Administration in Canada*, December, 1967.
Mechanic, David. "Sources of Power of Lower Level Participants in Complex Organizations." In *New Perspectives on Organizational Research*, ed. by W.W. Cooper et al. New York: Wiley, 1964.
Michels, Robert. *Political Parties*. Glencoe: Free Press, 1949.
Miller, N.E. "Comments on Theoretical Models, Illustrated by the Development of Conflict Behavior." *Journal of Personality*, Winter 1951.
Money, W.H., et al. "A Comparative Study of Multi-Unit Health Care Organizations." In *Organization Research in Hospitals*. Chicago: Blue Cross Association, 1976.
Morrill, Richard L., and Erickson, Robert. "Variation in the Character and Use of Chicago Area Hospitals." Research Notes, *Health Services Research*, Fall 1968.
Morris, Robert. "Basic Factors in Planning for the Coordination of Health Services." *American Journal of Public Health*, February (Part I) and March (Part II), 1963.
_____, Binstock, Robert H. *Feasible Planning for Social Change*. New York: Columbia University Press, 1966.
Nelson, Ralph. *Merger Movements in American Industry: 1895–1956*. Princeton, New Jersey: Princeton University Press, 1959.
Neuhauser, Duncan. "Hospital Size and Structure." *Hospital Size and Efficiency*, Proceedings of Ninth Annual Symposium on Hospital Affairs, Center for Health Administration Studies, University of Chicago, 1966.

Parsons, Talcott. *Structure and Process in Modern Societies*. New York: The Free Press of Glencoe, 1960.

Penrose, Edith. *The Theory of the Growth of the Firm*. New York: Wiley, 1959.

Perrow, Charles. "Goals in Complex Organizations." *American Sociological Review*, November 1961.

————. "Goals and Power Structure: A Historical Case Study." In *The Hospital in Modern Society*, ed. by E. Friedson. Glencoe: Free Press, 1963.

————. *Organizational Analysis: A Sociological View*. Belmont, California: Wadsworth, 1970.

Perrucci, Robert, and Pilisuk, Marc. "Leaders and Ruling Elites: The Inter-Organizational Basis of Community Power." *American Sociological Review*, December 1970.

Pfeffer, Jeffrey. "Size, Composition, and Function of Hospital Boards of Directors: A Study of Organizational–Environmental Linkages." *Administrative Science Quarterly*, September 1972.

————, and Leblebici, Hujeyin. "Executive Recruitment and the Development of Interfirm Organizations." *Administrative Science Quarterly*, December 1973.

Price, James L. *Organizational Effectiveness: An Inventory of Propositions*. Homewood, Illinois: Irwin, 1968.

Reid, Samuel R. *Mergers, Managers, and the Economy*. New York: McGraw-Hill, 1968.

Reynolds, James, and Stunden, Ann. "The Organization of Not-For-Profit Hospital Systems." *Health Care Management Review*, Summer 1978.

Rogers, Everett M., and Shoemaker, Floyd F. *Communication of Innovation, A Cross-Cultural Approach*. 2d ed. New York: The Free Press, 1971.

Roos, Noralou. "Two Models for Understanding the Hospital Merger." Working Paper No. 75–71, Graduate School of Management, Northwestern University, Chicago, 1975.

Sayles, Leonard. "The Change Process in Organizations: An Applied Anthropology Approach." *Human Organization*, Summer 1962.

Schanck, R.L. "A Study of a Community and its Groups and Institutions, Conceived of as Behaviors of Individuals." *Psychologic Monographs*, 43, no. 2, 1932.

Scott, Richard W. "Some Implications of Organization Theory for Research on Health Services." *Milbank Memorial Fund Quarterly*, October 1966.

Selltiz, Claire, et al. *Research Methods in Social Relations*. New York: Holt, Rinehart, and Winston, 1965.

Selznik, Philip. *TVA and the Grass Roots*. Berkeley: University of California Press, 1949.

Services Shared by Health Care Organizations. Health Services Research Center of the Hospital Research and Education trust and Northwestern University, U.S. Department of Health, Education and Welfare, Publication # (HRA) 77–14552, 1977.

Sheldon, Alan. "Union Hospitals, Inc." Case #9–474–003, Harvard Business School, 1974.

Shirley, Robert C. "Analysis of Employee and Physician Attitudes Toward Hospital Merger." *Academy of Management Journal*, September 1973.

Shortcliffe, Ernest. "Hospital Merger—Some Personal Observations." In *Trends in Hospital Mergers*, Proceedings of the Annual Scientific Session, American Association of Hospital Consultants, The Association, Chicago, 1967.

Shortell, Stephen. "The Researcher's View." In *Hospitals in the 1980's: Nine Views*. Chicago: American Hospital Association, 1977.

Sills, David L. *The Volunteers: Means and Ends in a National Organization.* Glencoe: Free Press, 1957.
Smith, John A. *Hospital Mergers: Presbyterian—St. Luke's (Chicago).* Unpublished thesis, University of Chicago School of Business, 1968.
Smith, Randall, and Brooks, Dennis. *Mergers: Past and Present.* London: Acton Society Trust, 1963.
Stanton, Esther. *Clients Come Last.* Beverly Hills: Sage, 1970.
Starkweather, David, and Kisch, Arnold. "A Model of the Life Cycle Dynamics of Health Service Organizations." In *Administered Health Systems*, ed. by Arnold et al. New York: Atherton Press, 1971.
————, and Taylor, Shirley. *Health Facility Mergers and Consolidations: An Annotated Bibliography.* Chicago: American College of Hospital Administrators, 1970.
Taylor, Robert J. *Human Dynamics in Hospital Mergers.* Research Fellowship Paper, American College of Hospital Administrators, Chicago, 1978.
Thompson, James D. "Decision-Making, The Firm, and The Market." In *New Perspectives on Organizational Research*, ed. by W.W. Cooper. New York: Wiley, 1964.
————. *Organizations in Action.* New York: McGraw-Hill, 1967.
————, and McEwen, William J. "Organization Goals and Environment: Goal Setting As an Interaction Process." *American Sociological Review*, February 1958.
Treat, T. *A Study of the Characteristics and Performance of Merging Hospitals in the United States.* Ph.D. Dissertation, Texas A. and M. University, 1973.
Wallace, Forest D. "Principles of Acquisition." In *The Corporate Merger*, ed. by W.W. Alberts and J.E. Segall. Chicago: University of Chicago Press.
Warner, W. Keith, and Havens, A. Eugene. "Goal Displacement and the Intangibility of Organizational Goals." *Administrative Science Quarterly*, March 1968.
Weick, Karl E. *The Social Psychology of Organizing.* Redding, Massachusetts: Addison Wesley, 1969.
Weil, Peter A. *An Investigation of the Preconditions and Effects of Mergers Among Hospitals in the United States as Perceived by Hospital Administrations.* Master's thesis, University of Iowa, June 1969.
Weston, Fred. Discussant to Gort, Michael, "Diversification, Mergers, and Profits." In *The Corporate Merger*, ed. by W.W. Alberts and J.E. Segall. Chicago: University of Chicago Press, 1966.
Whisler, Thomas L. *Information Technology and Organizational Change.* Belmont, California: Wadsworth, 1970.
————. "Organizational Aspects of Corporate Growth." In *Corporate Growth*, ed. by W.W. Alberts and J.E. Segall. Chicago: University of Chicago Press, 1966.
White, Paul E. "Critique of Conceptual Frameworks and Empirical Studies Relevant to Organizational Relations in Health." In White, Paul E., "A Critical Evaluation of Research on the Interrelationships Among Health Care Organizations." Johns Hopkins University School of Public Health, c. 1972.
————, and Vlasak, George. *Interorganizational Research in Health: Conference Proceedings.* The Johns Hopkins School of Hygenic and Public Health and National Center for Health Services Research and Development, U.S. Department of Health, Education and Welfare, 1970.
Wortman, Paul M. *Merger Implementation: An Organizational Evaluation.* Unpublished manuscript, Department of Psychology, Northwestern University, Chicago, c. 1975.

Young, C. Richard, ed. *Mergers and Acquisitions: Planning and Action.* Study and report for Financial Executives Research Foundation, Arthur D. Little, Inc. New York: The Foundation, 1963.

Yuchtman, Ephram, and Seashore, Stanley. "A Systems Resource Approach to Organizational Effectiveness." *American Sociological Review*, April 1967.

PART II.

Six Cases

Introduction

A delightful thing for someone studying hospital mergers is that virtually everybody wants to be analyzed. Perhaps it is the nonproprietary aspect of most health institutions. There is also a laudable sense of self-scrutiny pervading much of the health administration community.

Though the main organizational doors of the sixteen enterprises involved in these six merger studies were readily and willingly opened, it did not follow that all the back hallways and closets could be easily entered. There were old tensions long since laid to rest that few wished to recall, wounded egos whose rewounding served no useful purpose, and private compromises that many felt should remain undisclosed.

Yet, probing all of these is essential to a full understanding of our six case studies. Dealing with these sensitivities is the challenge of the case method—and the fun. It requires the analyst to adhere to an ethic that is different and more demanding than that of the more typical survey research approach (Dalton, 1959). And even when taking the greatest of care, one can always misunderstand a case history. For this reason, one of our cases has been made anonymous; we believe the essence of the situation has been preserved while special sensitivities have been respected.

In no instance have we wished to slur anyone's character or motives. Nor have we meant to imply good or bad practice. Rather, to use the standard language of the Harvard Intercollegiate Cases, our examples are intended to serve as a basis for discussion rather than as illustrations of either effective or ineffective handling of a situation.

The case studies have multiple uses. One is to aid in university teaching. The cases are fairly long, incorporating numerous aspects of each situation; therefore, each has been divided into distinct subparts to enable the alternation of assigned case reading with classroom theory or seminar discussion. Each case has an introduction and one or more postlude commentaries which suggest lines of discussion. Each case has been classroom tested at least once for clarity.

Hospital decision makers, broadly defined to include managers, physicians, trustees, and regulators, can also use the cases. They contain a spread of issues, problems, approaches, and outcomes. The six case introductions should allow interested decision makers to select those most relevant to their circumstances.

The planner and policy maker in health care organization can also use the studies which, although they do not yield the broad sweep of aggregated data policy makers typically seek, demonstrate the real impact of policy on organizational behavior. The slip between policy and implementation is often great; policy makers can find some lessons, albeit painful ones, in these cases.

Finally, social scientists can view these cases through their various conceptual lenses. Chapters 2, 3, and 10 through 13 only begin to mine the theoretic proofs or disputes found in these descriptions. There is little here for economists, much for political scientists and sociologists, less for social psychologists, and more for anthropologists than seems obvious.

A brief comment on the pros and cons of case method analysis is in order (Penchansky, 1968). Case studies inevitably risk the perceptual bias of observations that support the analyst's preconceived notions, and the rejection of those that do not. Yet, as put by Hage (1974), "While the measures are not as exacting as in (large sample) comparative work, the time ordering of changes is very clear. Longitudinal study allows us to see the actual process of change in all its detail. . . . It is somewhat analogous to putting dye in the water and watching where the currents take it. The system reveals itself largely by these currents of change" (p. 61). We agree. These cases lead to no statistically significant conclusions, but they are revealing.

These cases can be classified in a number of ways. One is by the stages of merger evolution outlined at the beginning of chapter 3. Two cases run the full sequence of four stages, from preexisting conditions to stabilization: Palo Alto–Stanford and Los Angeles County. Another, Medical Center Hospitals of Norfolk, describes events through merger and several postmerger years, but not to a final settlement. In the remaining three we know only of the dynamics of formation but nothing of implementation. In the Seattle case, merger is certain, but the ink is hardly dry on the official papers. Westhaven-Riviera is a case study of nonmerger, as is the study of Davenport, Iowa; in each instance the outcome hangs in the balance until the end. In brief, three are accomplished mergers, one is in process, and two are accomplished nonmergers.

Another classification is by focus: what has the case author chosen to highlight, given the rich array of possibilities? The thread that runs through the Palo Alto-Stanford case is a set of issues common to many mergers involving medical schools. Palo Alto-Stanford is the most complex of all our situations. Indeed, a full grasp of the merger can only be approached after a study of three reports, one that concentrates on the hospital, an original contribution for this book, and two that center on the medical school, both reprints of articles published in *Science*. The Los Angeles County case illustrates an organizational dilemma that characterizes most mergers: centralization vs. decentralization. The public agency features of the situation are also notable. In Medical Center Hospital of Norfolk the concentration is on community power structure and the pervasive effect this has on all aspects of the merger. A second thread exists—the interplay of hospital merging with some unusual merging and demerging among groups of physicians. In the Seattle case, author Secord accentuates the role of a consultant. This case also reveals the whale-guppie syndrome of mergers involving hospitals of different sizes, as do the Los Angeles County and Medical Center Hospitals of Norfolk descriptions. These three cases involving institutions of different sizes contrast with the other three involving hospitals of similar size. So we have a good test of our propositions (chap. 3, 11a–d) about balance, complementarity, and perseverance. The Davenport, Iowa, case focuses on prominent issues, as does the Palo Alto-Stanford case; however, the issues in this instance are community based, whereas those of the Palo Alto-Stanford case run more to management and operations. Finally, the Westhaven-Riviera case exemplifies issues of negotiation, exchange, and bargaining. Here we come closest to examining the impact of individual personalities. In addition, this case examines the role of a planning agency and, again, that of a consultant.

Our third descriptive classification is by institution size and ownership. The immensity of the Los Angeles County merger is almost beyond imagining. Like the elephant of the jokes, we have grabbed it in only one place, and it sleeps wherever it wants. This merger combined four previously separate departments of one government. Here we are interested in whether the dynamics of a government reorganization are any different than those of the private sector, and whether they are any different from those involving previously autonomous entities. The Westhaven-Riviera case concerns two small hospitals, one public and one private, and therein lies much of the rub. The ownership at Palo Alto-Stanford is also mixed, being split between a city and a university. The merger survived these differences, but at very considerable cost in organizational strife. The eight institutions involved in the remaining three cases are all private, but hardly similar otherwise. The events in Davenport, Iowa hang considerably on the provincial house's influence on one of the hospitals, a Catholic institution. And another hospital in that case is owned by its doctors of osteopathy. In both the Norfolk and Seattle instances the general practice vs. specialist character of the hospitals is a stronger dynamic than the legalities of corporate form. So likewise is the influence of physician educators at Palo Alto-Stanford and Norfolk, but the medical schools in these latter two situations are markedly different.

One ownership type is missing: the for-profit hospital. We have excluded a case study of merger among proprietary hospitals because this type is much more like those of the business sector, about which there are numerous books and case studies. Chapter 1 outlines these essential differences, to which we held in the selection of cases for Part II.

There are sixteen different authors, coauthors, and commentators involved in the six case studies in Part II. While they have all generally adapted the format of reporting and analysis presented at the beginning of chapter 3—the merging process model—they also evidence a variety of backgrounds and outlooks.

John Walsh and Richard Knox reveal their skills as professional journalists in appendixes to the Palo Alto-Stanford case (chap. 4). Joe Hafey reveals the view of an experienced health care planner in his coauthorship of the Westhaven-Riviera case (chap. 5). Mark Secord shows his interest in the application of organization theory in his reporting of events in the merger of three hospitals in Seattle (chap. 6); and hospital consultant Wanda Jones, hospital trustee Robert Dupar, and hospital regulator Ludwig Lobe wind up the case with markedly different views of the same situation. The Davenport, Iowa, study (chap. 7) was written by Joe Coyne while he was a doctoral student at U.C. Berkeley; his writing illustrates his sensitivity to institutional sociology. Interestingly, Joe's case study was written almost entirely from newspaper reports. A commentator on this case, Anna Jane Stone, also looked on the situation while a student; her analysis evidences her educational background in cultural anthropology.

The author of the Los Angeles case study (chap. 8), is a member of the faculty of the Department of Nursing, California State University, Los Angeles. Jo Ann Johnson wrote her case study in partial fulfillment of the doctoral degree at the University of Southern California. This degree was in public administration—yet another view, and one entirely appropriate to a study of governmental reorganization. Her background in nursing also provided an operational reality to the case study that could easily have been lost in the reporting of such an immense undertaking. This case study is augmented by comments on the situation by two top administrators, Lister Witherill and Donald Avant, as well as by a firing-line manager within the agency, Leslie Smith. In the last of our case studies, a description of merger events in Norfolk, Virginia (chap. 9), chief executive Glenn Mitchell's views are not demarked by a separate postlude to the case, but instead are dispersed throughout the text.

Though this mix of case authors and commentators shows variety in viewpoints, the sixteen writers only begin to reveal the different interpretations that can be brought to bear. We leave this remaining opportunity to the reader.

REFERENCES

Dalton, Melvin. *Men Who Manage*. New York: John Wiley, 1959.
Hage, Jerald. *Communication and Organizational Control: Cybernetics in Health and Welfare Settings*. New York: Wiley and Sons, 1974.
Penchansky, Roy. *Health Services Administration: Policy Cases and the Case Method*. Cambridge: Harvard University Press, 1968.

4.

Hospital Merger and Medical Education:
The Palo Alto-Stanford Hospital

David B. Starkweather

Appendices by John Walsh and Richard A. Knox

A.   INTRODUCTION

The period of time covered by this case is 15 years, from 1953 to 1968. Though it is over a decade old it is not outdated; the issues remain current. The case focuses on a single merger, which included at least four subintegrations: 1) merger of two previously established hospitals; 2) merger of practicing and academic medicine, with practicing medicine further subdivided into solo practice and group practice; 3) commingling of two capital financing mechanisms, private financing through university philanthropy and public financing through bond issue; and 4) merger of two different forms of governance, publicly elected city councilmen and privately appointed university trustees. Viewed another way, this case involves one institution trying to serve two environments, a university and a community, with all relationships strained by the fact that there were no other teaching or community hospitals to which any of the participants could flee; there were no institutional escape valves.

    This case focuses primarily on the hospital portion of a univeristy-community medical center. There is another focus of equal interest and importance: the Stanford University School of Medicine. Fortunately, two excellent case studies have been made of this school, one written in 1971 and the other in 1979. The first is a three-part series that appeared in *Science*, describing the pattern and policies of medical school expansion since World War II and examining the effects of internal and external pressures for change. The 1979 study also appeared in *Science*[1]; both are included here, as appendices A and B.

    Taken together, the three case studies represent a varied and complete picture of almost three decades in the organizational life of a prominent medical center, highlighting major financial, educational, and social issues relating to medical schools, teaching hospitals, and university-community relations.

In order to reduce the complexity of the 15-year history of the Palo Alto-Stanford Hospital, six key issues have been chosen to reveal its underlying dynamics: 1) the manner in which institutional policies are set, i.e., the allocation of decision-making authority between hospital owners and directors; 2) medical staff organization, in particular, how chiefs of services should be selected when there are two semiautonomous medical staffs; 3) control of professional services in a hospital where goal conflict between patient care and teaching had been institutionalized; 4) the approach to clinical education by a medical school faculty oriented to teaching on indigent patients, but now faced with a hospital population of upper middle-class private patients; 5) financial policies in respect to both capital—whether hospital plant should be financed from private donations or from public bond issue—and operations—whether rates for a teaching hospital should be comparable with other community hospitals or whether they should be higher in recognition of costs of teaching and expanded scope of services; and 6) management unity, i.e., whether the hospital should be operated as one entity or as two.

These six issues will be traced through the fifteen-year time period, subdivided into the four stages of the merging process presented in chapter 3: prior conditions, enabling forces, dynamics of implementation, and stabilization.

PERSONS FIGURING PROMINENTLY IN THE CASE

Robert Alway, M.D., Dean, Stanford University School of Medicine, 1958–65

Dwight Barnett, M.D., Administrator, Palo Alto-Stanford Hospital, 1958–60

Leroy Bates, M.D., Director, Palo Alto-Stanford Hospital, 1964–68

Alvin Cox, M.D., Chairman, Department of Pathology, Stanford University School of Medicine, until 1965

Oliver Deehan, Administrator, Palo Alto-Stanford Hospital, 1960–63

Stanton Eversole, M.D., Surgical Pathologist, Palo Alto-Stanford Hospital, 1960–65

Robert Glaser, M.D., Dean, Stanford University School of Medicine, 1965–69

William Hewlett, Second president, Board of Directors, Palo Alto-Stanford Hospital; Vice-president, Hewlett-Packard Corporation

Andrew Hunt, M.D., Director, Stanford University Clinics, 1959–64

Henry Kaplan, M.D., Chairman, Department of Radiology, Stanford University School of Medicine

Russell Lee, M.D., Founder and president of Palo Alto Medical Clinic

David Packard, Trustee, Stanford University; President, Hewlett-Packard Corporation

Lowell Rantz, M.D., Associate Dean for Clinical Affairs, Stanford University School of Medicine; Chairman, Clinical Committee, Stanford University School of Medicine, until 1964

J. Wallace Sterling, Ph.D., President, Stanford University

Edward D. Stone, Architect of Stanford Medical Center

Richard Wilbur, M.D., Chief of Palo Alto Medical Staff, 1963–64

SEQUENCE OF IMPORTANT EVENTS

1955   Stanford University decides to move its medical school from San Francisco to the Palo Alto campus.

1956   City of Palo Alto and Stanford University decide to create the Palo Alto-Stanford Hospital Corporation and jointly construct a merged hospital.

1957   Packard Agreements established, resolving conflict over hospital-based specialty services.

1958   Dwight Barnett, M.D., appointed first hospital administrator.

1959   Pathologist Stanton Eversole, M.D., arrives.

Stanford Medical Center (including Palo Alto-Stanford Hospital) dedicated.

1960   Joint Professional-Administrative council formed.

Unified inpatient services established in surgery, pediatrics, and other specialties.

Hospital in debt one million dollars.

Dwight Barnett resigns; second hospital administrator, Oliver Deehan, appointed.

1962   Hospital Board meetings opened to public.

Plan for a unified medical staff proposed and defeated.

Hospital Medical Board formed.

Five Board principles proposed.

Administrator Deehan resigns, then returns.

1963 Joint committee of two owners appointed to consider proposal for hospital autonomy.

Citizens' Committee appointed by City of Palo Alto to consider proposal for hospital autonomy.

Stanford endorses proposals for hospital autonomy, stipulating a Hospital/Medical School affiliation agreement.

Administrator Deehan resigns permanently.

1964 Hospital submits annual budget for owners' approval without line-item details; budget is approved.

Medical School Dean Robert Alway resigns.

Roy Bates, M.D., appointed third hospital administrator.

1965 Affiliation agreement between Hospital and Medical School approved.

Owners approve grant of additional authorities to Hospital Board.

Robert Glaser, M.D., appointed Dean of Stanford Medical School and University Vice-president for Health Affairs.

1966 Dr. Eversole, hospital pathologist, resigns.

1967 City of Palo Alto agrees to Stanford's purchase of its five million dollar interest in the Hospital.

1968 Palo Alto-Stanford Hospital becomes Stanford University Hospital.

Roy Bates resigns as third hospital administrator and is replaced by a Stanford professor of psychiatry.

1969 Citizens of Palo Alto reject a zoning variance necessary to construct a new hospital to be owned by the Palo Alto Medical Clinic.

B.   PRIOR CONDITIONS

The time covered by this period runs from the early 1900s to the mid-1950s. It is characterized by a long history of informal relationships between town and gown in respect to medical affairs, coupled with several specific formal arrangements between the city of Palo Alto and Stanford University.

NFORMAL TIES

A phrase commonly heard in Palo Alto in the 1950s was that to know the relationship within and between three families was to understand most of the important influences on medical affairs in the midpeninsula. One family was the Lees, headed by Russell Lee, M.D., founder of the Palo Alto Medical Clinic, one of the largest fee-for-service group practices in the United States. Dr. Lee had four sons and one daughter, all phsyicians, two of whom figured prominently in this case. These two were Hewlett, a surgeon in the Palo Alto Medical Clinic, and Philip, who at the time of this case was an internist in the clinic but later became the Under Secretary of Health in HEW, and subsequently, the Chancellor of the University of California, San Francisco.

A second family was the Barnetts, starting with George Barnett, a popular and powerful member of the Stanford Medical School faculty during much of the early 1900s. His nephew, Charles, also became a member of Stanford's Medical School faculty; he was director of Stanford's outpatient clinics during the time immediately prior to this case. Dwight Barnett, another nephew, became the first administrator of the Palo Alto-Stanford Hospital. Anna Barnett, a niece, was a cardiologist with the Palo Alto Medical Clinic.

The third family was the Wilburs, starting with Ray Lyman Wilbur, Jr., who at various times had been president of the California Medical Association, Secretary of the Interior (during the Hoover administration), and chairman of the famous 1932 Committee on the Cost of Medical Care. Dr. Wilbur had also been Dean of Stanford Medical School and President of Stanford University. His son, Blake Wilbur, was the most prominent surgeon in Palo Alto, and a member of Dr. Lee's Palo Alto Medical Clinic. One of Blake's sons, Richard Wilbur, was an internist with the Palo Alto Clinic and active in medical society affairs. After this case he became a prominent member of the staff of the American Medical Association and was also for a time the Medical Director of the Department of Defense. During the time of this case, he was chief of one of the Hospital's two medical staffs, and President of California Blue Shield. Another of Blake Wilbur's sons, Ray Lyman Wilbur II, was an executive of the Hewlett-Packard Corporation, a large electronics firm whose principals, William Hewlett and David Packard, figure prominently in this case.

THE HISTORY OF STANFORD'S HOSPITALS

During this early period, Stanford University's teaching hospital was in San Francisco. It dated to the early part of the century when, in response to the Flexner Report, Stanford University took over the Cooper Medical College. Since this medical school and its hospital were 35 miles distant from the main campus in Palo Alto, a semiautonomous operation developed, including deep involvement with the private practicing medical community in San Francisco. The university's hospital consisted of two buildings, both built in the early part of the century. In 1954 one of these, the Lane Hospital, was condemned by the city of San Francisco as an earthquake hazard; all patients had to be immediately removed. This sudden reduction in the medical school's hospital capacity was one of the precipitating factors in the merger.

The Stanford Hospital in San Francisco cost the university approximately $500,000 per year in operating debt. Hospital policies were established by a Clinical Committee consisting of the heads of all clinical services of the Medical School—an unofficial board of directors for the hospital.

In 1955, Stanford University decided to move its medical school from San Francisco to Palo Alto. This was partly in response to the obsolete physical plant and annual operating debt, but primarily in response to the growing need for medical students to gain access to general campus courses and for faculty to join medical research with basic research being conducted on the main campus.[2]

THE HISTORY OF PALO ALTO'S HOSPITALS

In the late 1890s, Dr. William Snow, an instructor at Stanford University, conceived the idea of a student hospital guild. By assessing every undergraduate and faculty member a small sum each semester, Dr. Snow was able to furnish low-cost hospitalization in a renovated home near the center of Palo Alto.

The success of Dr. Snow's plan attracted the attention of the San Francisco medical profession. Several physicians saw definite investment possibilities in the establishment of a private hospital in Palo Alto which, in addition to serving the city of Palo Alto and Stanford University, would draw patients from other Peninsula cities and Santa Clara Valley ranch communities.

In 1908, the first full-fledged hospital was built by a group of local physicians. This 48-bed facility was called the Peninsula Hospital, and for some years it catered satisfactorily to Palo Alto's health needs. Although at no time was the Peninsula Hospital able to pay dividends to its shareholders, it met its operating costs each year until World War I, when occupancy suddenly dropped and the hospital began to lose money.

In 1921, the stockholders of the Peninsula Hospital approached the Palo Alto City Council with an offer to sell the institution. As the council was considering the offer, a plan for city-Stanford cooperation was presented. The plan, advanced by a San Francisco physician practicing at Stanford's hospital in San Francisco, called for Stanford to operate the institution while the city retained ownership. The plan was approved by the city council, and a $55,000 hospital bond issue was passed by the voters to buy the Peninsula Hospital.

During the 1920s, the Peninsula Hospital did well under city ownership and Stanford administration, but problems were beginning to appear: the old frame building was no longer adequate, and a new site was needed. A citizens' committee, headed by Dr. Russell Lee, urged the construction of a new hospital.

In 1928, Stanford offered a 10-acre portion of its 9,000 acre holdings for such a new hospital, to be constructed and owned by the city of Palo Alto, on a site immediately adjacent to the business district of Palo Alto but on the quiet acreage of the campus. A land lease was struck to cover a period of 99 years. Stanford was again to operate the new hospital under terms similar to those which had existed for the management of the Peninsula Hospital.

The plan was strongly endorsed by local doctors and, in 1929, a $250,000 bond issue was approved by Palo Alto's voters. The bonds covered only about half the cost of erecting the 100-bed structure; the remaining money came from donations.

The Palo Alto Hospital opened in 1931. Palo Alto continued to grow, and in 1937 a $175,000 bond issue was approved to finance an 80-bed addition. The four story wing was completed in 1942. By now the 200-bed Palo Alto Hospital was the largest on the Peninsula south of San Francisco. But again, it did not take long for the area's population to outgrow the hospital's capacity.

But inadequate size was not the only problem. Since 1929, the city had been financing its hospital constructions through bond issues that would be retired from operating revenues of the hospital. Because the city's assets were pledged to pay the investors if the hospital failed, it had a keen interest in the financial operations of the institution. The city council insisted on approving the annual budget for the hospital—both the operating budget and all capital items. In effect, the board of directors of the Palo Alto Hospital was the Palo Alto City Council. Yet the agreement between the city and the university called for Stanford to administer the hospital. Stanford's administration of the Palo Alto Hospital was an exercise in benign neglect. The university's interests in hospital matters were entirely in San Francisco. At no time during this contract did Stanford locate a medical, nursing, or any other teaching program in the hospital.

The Palo Alto Hospital was run by a Stanford-employed administrator whose prime orientation was to the city. For many years this person was an active, colorful Irishman, adept at the necessary political relationships but not professionally competent in management. A great deal of day-to-day hospital supervision evolved to the director of nurses. Over the 25-year period, from 1930 to 1955, the Palo Alto Hospital became seriously obsolete. The city authorized very few equipment purchases and the hospital was unable to generate reserves from its operation because all net income was immediately transferred to the city for repayment of construction bonds. By 1955, the Palo

Alto Hospital was in unsafe physical condition and seriously undersized: surgeries were performed in operating rooms without adequate air control and patients were bedded in halls.

In 1954, Palo Alto again decided to expand its hospital. At the same time Stanford University was considering the move of its medical school from San Francisco to the main campus.

A CONVERGENCE

Viewing the two hospital situations together, there was in the mid-1950s something of a simultaneous crisis: both Stanford and Palo Alto needed new hospitals, and both recognized in some vague way that they were approaching an era when hospitals should have substantially enlarged scopes of facilities and services, teaching programs, professional management, and a new approach to capital and operating finance. In addition, there was an available network of influential people which could be used as a conduit for discussions on how parties could solve their mutual problems.

C. ENABLING FORCES

This second stage covers the period of time from initial formal contact between the two parties to the initial integration of resources: 1954 to 1959.

THE IDEA

It is not clear where the idea of the Palo Alto-Stanford Hospital was born. Many feel it was initiated in private conversations between Dr. Russell Lee and J. Wallace Sterling, President of Stanford University. Lee was Sterling's personal physician, and the university contracted with the Palo Alto Medical Clinic for its student health service.

The idea had several dimensions. Stanford had a large campus, only a portion of which was used for academic functions. In recent years Stanford had expanded its practice of leasing portions of its land for nonuniversity or quasiuniversity purposes. One such lease was for the Stanford Industrial Park, a large acreage containing electronic and other industrial corporations. Scientists of many of these successful post-Sputnik companies were Stanford faculty members in physics and engineering. The Stanford Industrial Park was incorporated by the city of Palo Alto, even though the land belonged to the university. The city developed utilities for the area and the corporations paid taxes to the city. Stanford derived income from the leases, for general support of the university. One of the large industrial firms in the industrial park was the Hewlett-Packard Corporation, a very successful electronic firm started by two Stanford graduates, both of whom remained actively involved in Stanford affairs.

In short, the availability and deployment of Stanford's land, and the relationships with Palo Alto in connection therewith, offered a basis for further town-gown cooperation in the realms of medical education and community hospital services.

Another early idea was that a separate corporation should be formed to develop and run the proposed new hospital. This corporation would be non-profit and would be jointly owned by the city and the university. This would allow Stanford to "get out of the hospital business," which it desired to do because of its experience in San Francisco, by transferring direct responsibility for hospital affairs to a separate entity. A new corporation distinct from the university would also allow the city to continue its method of hospital capital financing, bonding, which would be impossible if hospital control remained with a private corporation over which the city had no ultimate influence.

Another early idea was that there should be two hospital medical staffs. There seemed to be no reason why medical school and community physicians could not remain in distinct groups, although it was unique. Each group insisted on controlling its own affairs, or at least not being controlled by the other group.

A final important early decision by the Stanford trustees related to finance: the university would no longer support the care of patients in its teaching hospital, as it had done in San Francisco. This meant that the new hospital and medical school would have to exist on revenues from private paying patients.

THE DECISION

These early and basic decisions were made by the university and not by the medical school faculty, most of whom were isolated in San Francisco during many of these discussions and remained largely ignorant of the discussions in Palo Alto. The hospital administration at Stanford's San Francisco hospitals was of a caretaker type and the Clinical Committee was primarily interested in teaching and professional affairs, not organizational, financial, or legal matters. As for the city, negotiations were conducted by a few members of the city council and the city manager. As in the case of Stanford, the hospital administrator of the Palo Alto Hospital was excluded from the discussions, partly because he was opposed to the idea. The practicing physicians in Palo Alto were not actively involved, aside from some members of Russell Lee's Palo Alto Medical Clinic; they were not well organized, and many opposed the idea.

With these key parties not involved in the discussions, how were basic decisions made so quickly? One explanation is the coincidence of personal relationships and influences, including several members of the three families described above. Other influential people were David Packard, President of Hewlett-Packard Corporation and a prominent trustee ȯf Stanford University; Noel Porter, an executive of Hewlett-Packard who was at the time mayor of the city of Palo Alto; and William Hewlett, Vice-President of the Hewlett-Packard Corporation, who was active in community affairs and had indicated his willingness to be on the board of directors of the new hospital.

There was also a clear logic to the merger: here was an opportunity for a dramatic synthesis of patient care, teaching and research—a three-legged stool that would not only synthesize these three activities in one center, but incorporate them in an organizational form such that no one element could obtain dominance over the other. These checks and balances included dual ownerships; two medical staffs with different orientations and responsibilities; shared policy making between the city council, hospital directors and university trustees; and shared management, both between the medical school dean and the hospital administrator and between those two parties and the city management and the university president's office.

It was, then, with a high sense of imagination, innovation, and importance that the many parties to the Palo Alto-Stanford Hospital idea decided in early 1956 to merge.

PLANS FOR THE MERGER—AND ROOTS OF PROBLEMS

The more specific plans which quickly evolved embodied adjustments and compromises among the many groups which vied for influence and position in the new hospital. The actions of these individuals and groups, in turn, reflected the university and community context of the merger. The result was a unique and highly complex town-gown hospital partnership. Those who knew of it—and it attracted great interest locally and nationally—marvelled at its organizational design and speculated on whether it would work.

The Physical Plan
The Stanford Medical Center, of which the Palo Alto-Stanford Hospital would be a part, was to consist of seven different buildings, each with a different function and several with different ownership. The entire plan was drawn up by the famous architect, Edward D. Stone, and was widely heralded as one of the most beautiful medical complexes ever designed.[3]

The Center is H shaped, with seven three-story buildings arranged as an integrated whole (see figure 4.1).

The purposes of the seven buildings were to be as follows:

1) The Hospital West Pavilion, or Palo Alto Pavilion was designed to house patients of the 500-physician Palo Alto Medical Staff. It con-

FIGURE 4.1   Physical Plan of Palo Alto-Stanford Medical Center

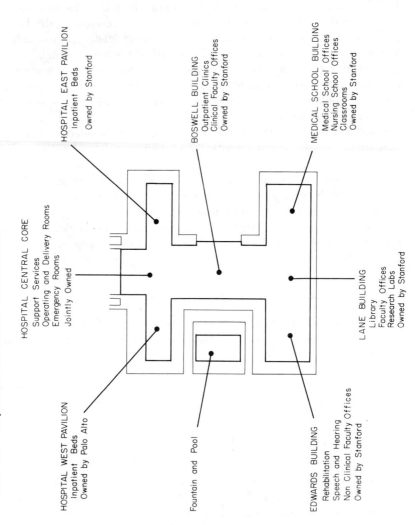

HOSPITAL EAST PAVILION
Inpatient Beds
Owned by Stanford

BOSWELL BUILDING
Outpatient Clinics
Clinical Faculty Offices
Owned by Stanford

MEDICAL SCHOOL BUILDING
Medical School Offices
Nursing School Offices
Classrooms
Owned by Stanford

HOSPITAL CENTRAL CORE
Support Services
Operating and Delivery Rooms
Emergency Rooms
Jointly Owned

HOSPITAL WEST PAVILION
Inpatient Beds
Owned by Palo Alto

Fountain and Pool

EDWARDS BUILDING
Rehabilitation
Speech and Hearing
Non Clinical Faculty Offices
Owned by Stanford

LANE BUILDING
Library
Faculty Offices
Research Labs
Owned by Stanford

tains 220 beds, was financed by the city of Palo Alto, and was built on part of an 18-acre patch of land leased to the city by Stanford University.

2) The Hospital East Pavilion, or Stanford Pavilion, was designed to house the teaching patients of the Stanford faculty. It was financed and owned outright by Stanford University and was built on Stanford land.

3) The Hospital Central Core Building was designed to contain the basic administrative and professional services necessary for patient care: laboratories, operating rooms, support services, dietary, business and administrative offices, etc. It was set up to be jointly owned by the city and the university as an indivisible asset: if the hospital corporation were ever dissolved this building could not be separated and allocated in parts to one or the other owner. It was built on Stanford land which was in part leased to the city and in part retained by the university. Each function in the Core building was calculated to represent a different percentage of investment by each owner. For instance, the operating rooms were invested in by Stanford in the proportion of 60 percent and by Palo Alto in the proportion of 40 percent.

4) The Boswell Building was planned to contain outpatient clinics and offices of clinical faculty members of the Medical School. It was owned completely by Stanford.

(These four buildings and the functions contained therein were to be under the control of the hospital board of directors because these buildings contained virtually all of the patient care activities of the medical center. The rest would be the responsibility of the medical school. However, allocation of authorities was more blurred and complex than this, confusing as it might already seem from an ownership and lease point of view. For instance, the Boswell Building contained nonpatient care as well as patient care activities. And, since it was agreed that the outpatient clinics would undoubtedly be run at a deficit for many years, the hospital's patient care authority in this building was closely supervised and occasionally superseded by the medical school which was picking up the deficit as a part of its university budget.)

5) The Edwards Building was owned by Stanford and constructed on Stanford land. It contained a rehabilitation center, speech and hearing activities, and numerous medical school nonclinical departments. The building was not under the jurisdiction of the hospital, though several of the functions contained therein were.

6) The Lane Building contained a large medical library, numerous faculty offices and research labs, and the pathology department, in-

cluding autopsy facilities. It was owned by Stanford, on university land, and operated by the medical school.

7) The Medical School Building was owned by Stanford and contained administrative offices and classrooms for the Schools of Nursing and Medicine.

The difficulties the two owners experienced in constructing the physical facilities were manifold. Two instances are illustrative. The original Edward D. Stone design was extravagant and exceeded the budget of both owners. As a result, the owners decided simply to reduce the module of design from fourteen to eleven feet, i.e., all spaces in the entire center that were originally planned as multiples of fourteen feet would now be multiples of eleven feet. This worked out fairly well except in patients' rooms, where it left doorways so narrow that neither beds nor wheelchairs could pass through them. Because of the confusion of planning in the context of dual ownership, this error was not discovered until late in construction, and it caused expensive remodeling.

A second example had to do with visual appearance. The entire outside of the medical center was to be covered with a Grecian design consisting of hundreds of six-foot squares, each fabricated offsite in concrete and subsequently attached with the help of cranes. Architect Stone specified small, anodized aluminum metal squares to be placed at the center of each of these large designs, the gold color of which would add a visual brilliance to the entire set of buildings. When the city councilmen of Palo Alto heard of this, they regarded it as an extravagance and prohibited any of the squares from being placed on the West Pavilion or the city's portion of the Central Core Building, even though the squares had been special ordered, paid for, and were available for installation. Stanford officials argued that it was a basic part of the architect's overall design and the squares should be installed throughout. After endless discussions and negotiations within the joint committee which was responsible for building the center, the city council finally relented.

The Organization Plan

The Palo Alto-Stanford Hospital, a nonprofit corporation, was established with an eight-member board of directors, four appointed by the city of Palo Alto and four by the trustees of Stanford University. While these eight directors held certain authorities, the hospital corporation was in turn jointly owned by the city and university. Several essentials of the hospital were determined separately by the two parties as partners. These matters were decided at annual and special meetings, at which the city's vote was cast by its mayor and the university's vote cast by its president. The eight directors, then, comprised a management board. The hospital held no assets unto itself: all land, buildings, equipment, and even supplies were held separately or jointly by the owners. Thus, in both asset control and legal authority there were limitations on the authority of the hospital directors.

Further details of the organizational plan are shown in figure 4.2.

This figure shows the montage of multiple relationships. Two medical staffs were independently responsible to the hospital center board. The hospital administration was formally responsible to the board, but in practice was also responsible to the city manager of Palo Alto and the university president. The board of directors had a dual responsibility to its two appointing authorities; and, in the case of the city, this responsibility was both direct to the city council and indirect through a subcommittee of the council established to deal with hospital affairs.

The Financial Plan

The city of Palo Alto financed its four million dollar investment in the medical center by a bond issue that was approved by its residents. Stanford's approximately twenty million dollar investment in both the hospital and other buildings of the medical center was obtained primarily from gifts and endowments.

How were these investments to be returned? The city had established a precedent with the 1930 Palo Alto Hospital of paying off such borrowed monies with hospital operating revenues, and it insisted on this method of bond retirement as a feature of the merged hospital's operation. Partly because the city had taken this position, Stanford decided that its investment in the hospital should be amortized and that it too would expect monies from the hospital operation.

The sum of these two obligations was approximately $500,000 per year, constituting a heavy debt burden on initial and subsequent financial operations. In addition, both owners agreed to require fund depreciation of physical plant and equipment. They did this in recollection of the obsolete state of their previous hospitals and the wish not to have the same circumstance repeat itself in a subsequent hospital generation. The Palo Alto-Stanford Hospital was thus burdened with a double capital finance requirement: one for repayment of monies for the existing plant and another for future replacements.

Administration

The merger obviously called for a skilled administrator with unusual background and qualifications. The hospital board specified that this person should be a physician with a record of effective administration. And the board hoped to find someone with knowledge of the personalities and forces involved in the development of the new venture. Through a nationwide search, one man emerged with qualifications perfectly tailored for the situation. He was Dwight

FIGURE 4.2   Organization Chart of Palo Alto-Stanford
Medical Center

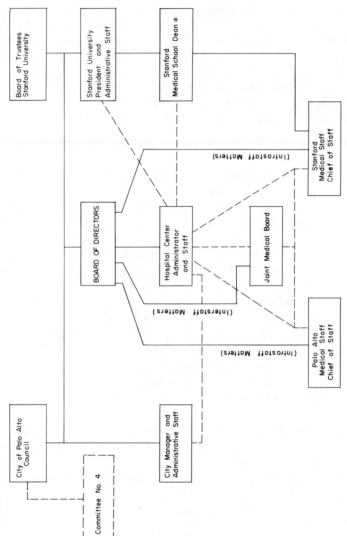

Board of Trustees
Stanford University

Stanford University
President and
Administrative Staff

Stanford
Medical School Dean *

Stanford
Medical Staff
Chief of Staff

(Intrastaff Matters)

BOARD OF DIRECTORS

Hospital Center
Administrator
and Staff

Joint Medical Board

(Interstaff Matters)

Palo Alto
Medical Staff
Chief of Staff

(Intrastaff Matters)

City of Palo Alto
Council

Committee No. 4

City Manager and
Administrative Staff

* Dean of Medical School also Chief of Staff of
Stanford Medical Staff.

Barnett, M.D., a man who had been administrator of an established teaching hospital in Detroit and professor of hospital administration at Columbia University. It was expected that his M.D. degree would assist him in his relations with physicians, and his professorship would place him in high regard in the academic community. In particular, however, he was a member of one of the three medical families. His uncle had been a prominent member of the medical school faculty and his brother was currently a faculty member. His cousin was a practitioner with the Palo Alto Clinic. Another relative was professor and head of the cardiology division of Stanford Medical School. In addition, a long time family friend, a leading plastic surgeon in the area, was Chief of the Palo Alto Medical Staff at the time of his appointment.

Dr. Barnett arrived in February 1958 to find: 1) the major dimensions of the medical center already cast, without any input from an administrative viewpoint; 2) an organization which provided little flexibility for hospital management; and 3) splits in authority at several levels. Dr. Barnett wondered whether the new hospital was organizationally viable, but waded in with enthusiasm and the head start of a strong set of informal relationships and professional credentials.

Hospital-Based Professional Services

Although the decision on physician organization had been to have separate but equal medical staffs for Palo Alto and Stanford doctors, there remained the matter of core hospital professional services to serve both groups: surgeries, delivery suite, radiology, pathology, etc. These became the subject of heated controversy early in the planning, particularly as regards radiology and pathology. Both staffs wanted to run these services. The strife reached the point where the entire merger was in jeopardy. The matter was referred to a special committee of both owners, of which David Packard became chairman. The Packard Agreements stipulated that all core services would be directed by the hospital board, but that the appointment of professionals to these services must be acceptable to the medical school in order to assure that these services be appropriate to Stanford's teaching and research programs.

Two unusual solutions then developed in radiology and pathology. In radiology there were two competent groups, one previously operating in the Palo Alto Hospital and the other, the Medical School Department of Radiology. This latter department was complete with diagnostic radiology and with sophisticated radiation therapy equipment invented by Dr. Henry Kaplan, world renowned cancer therapist and developer of clinical uses of the linear accelerator. The solution was that both radiology services would be continued: Dr. Kaplan indicated that he did not want the heavy work load which would be necessary if his department served all community patients, and the principals of the Palo Alto radiology group stipulated that they were not interested in radiation therapy and would limit their practice to diagnostics. The architect was then directed to design two diagnostic x-ray services and one radiation therapy facility with the two diagnostic facilities back-to-back. With only a thin wall between, the cost of changing the two diagnostic departments into one at some future time would not be great.

In pathology the situation was complicated in quite another way. Again, there were two sets of contenders. On the Palo Alto side, pathology services had been rendered for years by a partnership of two physicians which held a contract with the old Palo Alto Hospital. Unknown to the hospital, there was another agreement between the two pathologists that if their partnership ever dissolved, the junior partner would move his practice to no less than five miles' distance from the hospital. It was this junior partner who was the more professionally competent and aggressive and with whom the new hospital administration had entered discussions about revised contractual relationships. The senior partner became jealous and broke the partnership, which drove the junior partner out of the area. The hospital then broke off negotiations with the remaining partner on the grounds that a single person was incapable of providing the services needed by the new institution. Under the terms of the Packard Agreements this provided Stanford with the option of nominating a new chief pathologist, who had to be acceptable to the hospital. The job of identifying and nominating such a person fell to Professor Alvin Cox, chairman of the Medical School's Department of Pathology.

Thus, dissolution of the Palo Alto pathology partnership permitted the cooling of an issue that had become a cause célèbre to many, threatening the very continuance of the merger.

Teaching

It was clear that there would be a great deal of medical education in the new hospital; indeed, teaching was in many ways its reason for being. Since Palo Alto is an upper middle class community, there were virtually no indigent patients for Stanford to use for teaching in the traditional method of medical education, as there had been in San Francisco. The faculty would have to involve private patients extensively in its teaching activities. But this ran contrary to the interests of many private practitioners and intensified town-gown conflict.

Another aspect of teaching was the shift in medical school faculty from a relatively large proportion of part-time to full-time professors. This was both the practical result of the loss of many practice-oriented faculty who were unable or unwilling to move from San Francisco to Palo Alto, and a deliberate intent of the university to obtain new faculty of national reputations and research-oriented capacities.

This caused its own severe tension within the Medical School, whose new Dean in 1959—pediatrician Robert Alway—replaced three department chiefs, created a new Department of Genetics, and added eleven new full professors.

D.   DYNAMICS OF IMPLEMENTATION

The Stanford Medical Center, including the new hospital, was dedicated in September 1959. The ceremonies were the highlight of tours of the beautiful and impressive facilities and were keynoted by William McPeak, president of the Ford Foundation, who expressed his concern for the "wee small voice of the patient" amidst the complex and grandiose features of not only Palo Alto's and Stanford's facilities but those of most university teaching hospitals.[4]

This third stage of the case study covers the period of time from initial integration of resources to full integration: late 1959 to September 1960.

POLICY SETTING

The Palo Alto-Stanford Hospital board of directors became an active and effective group. Contrary to many predictions, there were no tie votes due to the equally numbered appointments by the city and the university; the concern on the part of the directors that this could happen seemed to stimulate efforts toward consensus. It was often difficult to determine who was appointed by which owner.

Another factor was the board's second president, William Hewlett. Hewlett's partner in business was David Packard, and Packard also was president of Stanford's Board of Trustees. Further, a top Hewlett-Packard Corporation executive, Noel Porter, was mayor of the city of Palo Alto.

Hospital board activities during this time related primarily to the city of Palo Alto, due to several city council members' suspicions that the hospital board was running things in favor of Stanford. Cost allocations between the two owners were established in great detail. All budgets and rates had to be submitted to and approved by the city. These were not simple matters, since the city operated on a cash flow accounting system and the university on an accrual system.

Another issue which the hospital board faced related to the press, and indirectly to the general community. The editor of the *Palo Alto Times*, the local, widely read newspaper, was hostile to the entire development. His hostility stemmed primarily from his connection that the Brown Act—a California law which requires that meetings of all public bodies be open to the public—applied to the hospital's board and committee meetings. The editor asserted this on the grounds that the board was directing a corporation which was created in part by a public body, the city of Palo Alto. It soon became obvious that the *Palo Alto Times* would report a negative view of all events concerning the hospital unless the matter of the application of the Brown Act was resolved in favor of public meetings.

MEDICAL STAFF ORGANIZATION

The Stanford faculty members arrived in Palo Alto from San Francisco suddenly to realize that they were responsible not only to the university, via their dean, but to a separate hospital corporation and board.[5] Although clinical department heads had previously been advised of this, and some were directly involved in the organizational decisions, this represented a new accountability for most faculty members. Their general opinion was that their own university had done them in. Led informally by the influential Henry Kaplan, chairman of the Medical School's Department of Radiology, the faculty became resistant virtually to all means of linking clinical faculty members to the hospital in the traditional manner of private teaching hospital medical staff organizations. With two distinct and semiautonomous medical groups, yet numerous hospital activities which had to be run as one, the hospital board and administration faced serious problems.

One example of this was staffing of the emergency room. The previous pattern for the Palo Alto Medical Staff had been the typical one for community hospitals: private physicians taking turns at being on call for emergencies. The practice for the Stanford Medical School was that of a teaching hospital: an emergency room staffed by interns and residents in surgery and other specialties. The Palo Alto Medical Staff did not wish to give up its pattern, partly because it threatened a source of revenue for young doctors starting practice in the community. Further, many Palo Alto physicians believed that Stanford's doctors were in some cases incompetent because the emergency room was often staffed by inexperienced interns. Stanford faculty members, in turn, were critical of private doctors for not being readily available when emergencies occurred. A complex arrangement was finally worked out in which responsibility for emergency room coverage alternated between private practicing and faculty physicians. Private physicians were required to be on the premises while on call, including bunking within the hospital at nights, and the faculty agreed to raise the level of competence of house officers assigned to the emergency room. Interns and residents could be used in the emergency room at all times, to be supervised on alternate days by private practicing physicians and faculty members.

This situation was typical of many throughout the hospital: scheduling operating rooms, anesthesia coverage for deliveries, and so on. They were all characterized by a high level of initial conflict followed by resolution in favor of improved patient care. The hospital's organizational check and balance seemed to be working: each medical group could and did call the other to task for some professional inadequacy, and the resolution was usually a significant improvement. However, such was obtained at the considerable expense of interpersonal and intergroup friction.

In order to deal with these issues, a new Joint Professional-Administrative Council was formed, composed of the officers of both medical staffs. It had numerous subcommittees to recommend policies for the operation of all activities which served both medical staffs. There were soon 26 of these groups. Since subcommittees had no authority unto themselves but merely represented the two separate staffs, virtually all issues were referred out of subcommittee to both the council and the two medical staffs. During any one month there could be up to 78 separate meetings, 26 for each of the areas covered by the Joint Professional-Administrative Council and twice that many for discussion of the same topics within the clinical departments of two medical staffs.

All of this evolved because neither medical staff would permit any supervision or control by the other medical staff. In the absence of any individual in each of the several clinical specialities with authority over such matters, elaborate coordination, negotiation and consensus taking devices were necessary.

CONTROL OF HOSPITAL-BASED PROFESSIONAL SERVICES

Following the break-up of the Palo Alto pathology partnership, Dr. Cox, chairman of Stanford's Department of Pathology, located an academic pathologist from Johns Hopkins University and brought him to Palo Alto for interviews with a number of key physicians of the Palo Alto and Stanford medical staffs. The candidate seemed acceptable, and Dr. Cox hired Dr. Stanton Eversole.

Partly because of the way in which he had been brought to Palo Alto and partly at his own preference, Dr. Eversole did not seek a specific and permanent contract with the hospital. Instead, his services were arranged under a temporary memorandum of agreement which called for paying him one-third of the surgical pathology revenue of the hospital, in the traditional manner of hospital-specialist contract relationships.

In short, the problem in pathology seemed to have been solved by a combination of informal good will and almost chance identification of a pathologist whose competence seemed obvious. Recourse to the formal and elaborate Packard Agreements seemed unnecessary.

TEACHING

The insufficiency of teaching material remained a problem for the medical school. The Stanford outpatient clinics were smaller than those in San Francisco. In order to avoid offending Palo Alto physcians, Stanford established a policy of accepting only those clinic patients who were referred by private practitioners. Further, there was an internal problem within the medical center relating to management of the clinics; was it the hospital's or the medical school's responsibility? After consultation with hospital officials, Dean Robert Alway appointed a medical director of the Stanford Clinics—a new position within the school which, though it challenged the authority of clinical department heads over their separate outpatient activities, held the potential for increasing the flow of patients to the clinics.

A series of town-gown meetings were scheduled, led jointly by Dr. Hunt, the new director of clinics, and Dr. Hewlett Lee, one of Dr. Russell Lee's sons. The appointment of Dr. Lee to this task was consistent with the active involvement of Palo Alto Clinic physicians as volunteer faculty members in Stanford's teaching programs. This committee finally concluded that, given the population growth of the Palo Alto area at the time, the medical school was no real threat to the private practice of medicine and that Stanford could proceed to expand its clinics without resistance from Palo Alto physicians.

But there remained an insufficiency of patients for inpatient teaching: during the first nine months of the hospital's operation, only 15 percent of the total patient complement was admitted by Stanford faculty members and house staff. One reason was the University's decision not to allocate any funds for the direct support of patient care; the faculty was forced to involve private patients in its teaching program. But this ran counter to a provision in the articles of incorporation of the hospital: no patient admitted by a member of the Palo Alto Medical Staff could be used for teaching purposes without his/her consent. This proviso was construed to mean that a private patient's physician could consent for the patient, rather than requiring the hospital to seek directly the patient's permission. Further, consent was implied by the act of admitting a patient to one of the several teaching services. A private physician could thus admit a patient to a teaching service or a private service, and this might be in either the Palo Alto (West) Pavilion or the Stanford (East) Pavilion. This option gave tremendous leverage to community physicians: private patients were needed by the medical school, but private doctors were under no obligation to give up control of their patients to the faculty's interns and residents. Yet, such was essential to the house officers' educational and professional development. This produced intense conflict between the two groups of physicians and resentment on the part of the medical school faculty.

Various arrangements were worked out in different clinical specialties. In medicine a small 27-bed teaching service was developed and run by the medical school. Private physicians could admit patients to this service if they wished, but if they did, they could only follow their patients; they retained no direct responsibility for patient management.

In surgery the resolution was easier, due perhaps to the fact that patients are fundamentally ignorant of what goes on in the operating room. Several teams of house officers were developed, some of which were assigned to faculty members and others to community practicing surgeons. In both cases, members of the house staff teams operated as assistant surgeons.

The most complete integration was developed in pediatrics: the Unified Pediatrics Service. In this arrangement the pediatric activities of both the private medical community and the faculty, as well as those of the nearby Stanford Children's Convalescent Hospital, were run as one operation headed by the chairman of Stanford's Department of Pediatrics. This chairman was in turn responsible to a board of the Unified Pediatric Service which included elected representatives of both faculty and community pediatricians. In the operation of the service there were no procedural differences in the handling of private and teaching cases: there was one acute inpatient pediatric unit of approximately 40 beds, one set of newborn nurseries, and one subacute unit. Distinctions within the service were by function rather than by category of admitting physician and patient. Private patients admitted to the hospital became the direct responsibility of the pediatric house staff, working under the close supervision of a full-time chief of inpatient services who was acceptable to both private and faculty pediatricians. Private pediatricians actively consulted with house staff members and the chief of service and usually obtained agreement on treatment regimes. While either professional group could initiate care in emergency situations without consultation, this was regarded as a breakdown in normal good practice and was seldom done. The accommodation in pediatrics was highly successful.

In these three clinical realms and others, town-gown accommodations were imaginative, varied, and hard-won. In the process the medical school faculty adjusted to university-based teaching with private patients, and private patients and physicians became knowledgeable and enthusiastic about a teaching hospital. By the end of the first full year of hospital operation, 45 percent of all patients were involved in teaching, although only 15 percent were admitted by Stanford faculty members and house staff. The proportion of privately admitted teaching patients was steadily increasing.

FINANCES

Prior to the opening of the hospital, the Palo Alto City Council had stipulated that patients of Palo Alto Medical Staff members who were not residents of Palo Alto—comprising two-thirds of all hospital admissions—should pay higher rates in order to match the taxes which residents of Palo Alto were paying for a portion of the large bond issue that had funded construction of the city's portions of the hospital. The council's stipulation required a second set of differential rates for patients admitted by Stanford faculty members, depending on whether such patients resided in Palo Alto. Hospital billing clerks could scarcely administer the rate schedules which were developed, much less explain them to confused patients.

All of this was an irritant. More crucial was the basic financial structure of the hospital. The university no longer subvened patient care, except in the clinics. Yet the faculty members continued their practice of treating patients for humane and teaching reasons without regard for ability to pay. High bad debts developed for Stanford patients. Further, the great variety of services offered, coupled with heavy intern and resident stipend costs, forced the hospital to charge rates that were higher than neighboring hospitals. Despite the medical center character of the hospital, it was still regarded by many as a community hospital. The rate differences were played up by the hostile *Palo Alto Times* and became a burning issue in the Palo Alto City Council. Many residents and their private physicians felt that care at the Palo Alto-Stanford Hospital was too expensive; the hospital began to lose patients. By the end of the first year of operations, the Hospital was one million dollars in debt.

OPERATIONAL UNITY

The central question which threaded through the professional, administrative and financial issues discussed above became whether the hospital could or should be operated as a single enterprise—ignoring the differences in ownership and land lease.

The question of a unified hospital operation centered on the authority and role of the Hospital Board of Directors. It was now clear that the mechanism of the Joint Professional-Administrative Council, effective as it had been for solving some initial problems, could not be counted on to resolve the basic differences in goals and authority which ran between the two medical staffs. In order to deal with these, it was necessary to invoke the ultimate authority of the hospital board. The problem was that the board's authority was not ultimate: it was responsible to two owners, and both medical staffs knew it. In particular, many members of the Stanford faculty had reservations: they would not accept the authority of the hospital board, even in patient care matters. They would translate matters of patient care into matters of teaching, and in respect to teaching the medical faculty could deal entirely with Dean Alway and the university, ignoring the hospital board and administration.

Even so, the formal authority system continued to infuriate Stanford faculty members, including Henry Kaplan, who had now concluded that they were not only working for a hospital over which they had no direct influence but that the hospital, in turn, was responsive to politicians, members of the

City Council of Palo Alto. This arrangement was untenable to Dr. Kaplan. He was a widely repsected physician, teacher, and researcher. And, it was speculated that he had the ear of Stanford University's president, J. Wallace Sterling.[6]

Through this entire period, one person on the Stanford medical faculty was inclined toward the hospital and worked tirelessly to bring his colleagues into it: Associate Dean Lowell Rantz. Dr. Rantz had come to this viewpoint because of his previous position in San Francisco as chairman of the Clinical Committee—the group which had acted as a board of directors for the Stanford Hospital. As a result of this background, he saw the problems of running the new institution and the importance of medical faculty participation.

In this matter of hospital authority, two features of Administrator Barnett's background and approach became crucial. In his previous hospital executiveship in Detroit, Dr. Barnett had become used to a strong hospital board which exercised its proper and full authority in medical staff affairs. His Detroit experience provided little guidance for this situation. Further, the Detroit hospital was a community nonprofit institution which, like many hospitals in the late 1930s and 40s, deliberately operated in the red in order to sustain the interest of wealthy donors. So, Dr. Barnett had not previously had to concern himself with sharp-pencil financial management.

What resulted in July of 1960 was a situation in which Dr. Barnett felt that the hospital board had failed to invoke the full authorities which it possessed, particularly over the medical staffs; hospital directors, on the other hand, felt that Dr. Barnett had not been handling properly the hospital's difficult financial plight. In a shirtsleeve session one hot summer afternoon, board president Hewlett expressed his exasperation with Dr. Barnett's financial management, and Dr. Barnett charged Hewlett and his colleagues with insufficient exercise of their corporate responsibility. The next day Dr. Barnett resigned.

To summarize, this crucial stage of merger implementation involved: 1) two owners dedicated to a new venture and willing to conduct a grand town-gown experiment; 2) a hospital board with deep concern for proper hospital policies and affairs, but with limited fundamental authority; 3) magnificent physical resources; 4) a new management charged with operating the venture without having participated in many of the key decisions leading to it; 5) one medical group—the Palo Alto Medical Staff—generally dedicated to the hospital, partly because it had no choice, and evidencing its interest through involvement of private patients in teaching; and 6) another medical group—the Stanford Medical School clinical faculty—that was initially ignorant of the relationships which had been struck by the university in its behalf and was subsequently distrustful of it.

E.   STABILIZATION

The final stage of this case, stabilization, runs from the time of complete integration of merged resources to a time called outcome: from late 1960 to 1968. The period can best be described in terms of a sequence of events relating to the six issues outlined in section A.

PUBLIC VS. PRIVATE POLICY SETTING

The *Palo Alto Times'* opposition to the hospital, based on its interest in having the Brown Act applied, was seriously affecting the hospital's public image at a time when financial exigencies called for a high level of physician and public support. After a great deal of debate, the board decided to open its meetings to public attendance, not in legal recognition of the Brown Act, but as a decision of a private organization. The effect was to drive the discussion of essential matters underground to a variety of committees and informal meetings. Real decisions were made at times and in locations other than official board meetings. This seemed to be an organizational necessity rather than an antipublic contrivance, due to the highly professional and personal nature of many items with which the board was dealing.

This had two effects. First, it accentuated to some Stanford Medical faculty members the error of their having been placed in this "political lash-up." Second, the official board meetings became something of a farce, with all the actors going through the proper motions of decisions made elsewhere, and dealing in trivia.

The *Palo Alto Times* editor soon argued that it was public debate of hospital issues which was called for, not public attendance at meetings; the hospital thus failed to obtain any real change for the better in the newspaper's influence on public opinion and support.

MEDICAL STAFF ORGANIZATION

The 27th Joint Professional Administrative Council subcommittee was a committee on committees, revealing the shortcomings of the council's organization and approach. Two basic problems remained: 1) neither medical staff was willing to let the other obtain any formal influence over it, and 2) the hospital needed an improved mechanism for obtaining professional input and decision making.

Two efforts to solve these problem were undertaken. One occurred in late 1962, consisting of private efforts by a group of responsible physicians of both medical groups. The effort was initiated by a member of the Palo Alto medical staff; Dr. Kaplan was active in the discussions. Results of these deliberations were published in a brief two-page memorandum, excerpted as follows:

After the fourth year of its existence, shortcomings of the Stanford Medical Center were brought into sharp focus by the increasing shortage of hospital beds, the resignation of its first administrator, and the fact that most of the original members of the Board of Directors of the Hospital have resigned. A member of the Palo Alto Medical Staff became very impressed with this sequence of events and thought that yet another approach to the dilemma might be tried.

Five meetings occurred between the dates of May 28 and November 4. . . . At each meeting we found that the medical staffs were related to nearly every question concerning the Medical Center. . . . We came to agreement that solution of the major present-day problems probably would not begin until the medical staffs improved their organization. . . . The next obvious step was to consider the possibility of uniting both staffs into a single medical staff.

The structure of the new medical staff would be similar to the usual medical staff structure: a chief of staff, a vice-chief of staff, secretary and treasurer, an executive committee, clinical divisions of the staff headed by their own chiefs. The chief of staff, vice-chief and secretary-treasurer would be elected from the staff. The chiefs of the clinical departments would be executives of the respective clinical departments of the Stanford Medical School. (It is to be noted that the executive of each Medical School department is appointed on a yearly basis by the Medical School and is not a permanent appointment.) Each chief would administer his own department with an executive committee, one half of whom he would appoint, and an equal number of whom would be elected by members of the respective department.

Appointment to the medical staff at the beginning would include all members of the present medical staffs. We foresaw no special problems for staff appointment of physicians new to the community.

There should be certain safeguards for the individual members of the staff. These safeguards appear also to be interchangeable as standards for the medical staff. 1) Equal opportunity for admitting patients. 2) Equal voice in staff organization structure agreed upon by the majority of a department or of the medical staff. 3) Provision of the most modern x-ray and laboratory facilities.[7]

It is not clear why the proposal failed. It was not well received by the Palo Alto Medical Staff because it had been developed in private, completely outside the medical staff structure. Further, it had been developed by a group of physicians who were active in teaching and supportive of Stanford's position in the hospital; thus, it was seen as lacking sufficient protection for private practitioners who were not involved in teaching.

The document was never endorsed by the Palo Alto Medical Staff; the unification proposal thus failed.

The second major effort was by the hospital administration, now in the hands of Oliver Deehan, a trained hospital administrator who had been a member of Dr. Barnett's administrative staff and who was skilled in management and financial affairs. Deehan attempted to move quickly toward a resolution of some of the organizational problems. He was broadly supported in these efforts by both the hospital board and the Palo Alto Medical Staff. He recognized that the Joint Professional-Administrative Council possessed too many committees and that, in the last analysis, each staff could appeal any decision to its owner. He believed there needed to be a new medical leadership empowered to deal with common operating problems facing both professional groups and those trying to run the institution.

A Medical Board was proposed, with a complete set of by-laws. Excerpts are as follows:

Purpose

The purpose of this organization shall be to formulate medical policy subject to the approval of the Board of Directors of the Palo Alto-Stanford Hospital.

Membership

The Dean or his delegate and three other members of the Clinical Committee of the Stanford Medical Staff, the three officers of the Palo Alto Medical Staff, the immediate past Chief of Staff of the Palo Alto Medical Staff and the Administrator of the Palo Alto-Stanford Hospital. The Administrator shall be an ex-officio member without a vote.

Officers

The Chairman of this organization shall be the Administrator of the Palo Alto-Stanford Hospital or his delegate. He shall have the responsibility for preparing the agenda of all meetings, including all items submitted by members at least one week in advance of the meeting at which time the item is to be discussed.

Committees

The nine designated standing committees of the Medical Board shall meet from time to time; shall recommend policy for their respective area to the Medical Board and shall not exercise executive authority except when specifically recommended by the Medical Board and approved by the Board of Directors. Members of each committee shall be appointed by the Dean as Chairman of the Clinical Committee of the Stanford Medical Staff and the Chief of the Palo Alto Medical Staff. The number of members of each committee shall be determined by the Medical Board but shall have equal representation from each Medical Staff.

The key feature of Deehan's plan was a simple one: in all areas of common professional concern the Medical Board would have professional authority which ran directly to the hospital board and nowhere else.

The plan obtained easy endorsement of the Palo Alto Medical Staff, partly because of the efforts of Richard Wilbur, M.D., a member of one of the three medical families, who was now chief of the Palo Alto Medical Staff. But the scheme encountered rough sledding in the medical school, particularly in the Clinical Committee—the same committee that had existed in San Francisco and now operated as the executive committee of the Stanford Medical Staff.

A tense Clinical Committee meeting was chaired by Dr. Rantz, who was pushing the plan. There was a direct confrontation between the president of the hospital board, William Hewlett, and Henry Kaplan, chairman of Stanford's Radiology Department. The key issue became whether all professional matters concerning patient care were under the jurisdiction of the Medical Board or whether they could be dealt with separately by the two medical staffs. After heated debate and a close showdown vote, the Medical Board plan was approved.

The Medical Board was quickly formed up and proceeded to reduce the proliferation of committees and directly resolve crucial issues. The Medical Board became an effective organizational unit in the evolution of the Palo Alto-Stanford Hospital toward a viable whole.

POLICY-MAKING AUTHORITY

By means of the Medical Board, the hospital could act decisively in professional matters. But in relation to its owners, the hospital board was still faced with harassment and challenge of its authority. The viability of the hospital as an effective organization was at stake.

Administrator Deehan's response was, again, to propose a document which, if accepted, would settle the matter in favor of the hospital. He advanced five Principles of the Board to be used as a policy guide for subsequent action by the many concerned parties. Excerpts of the Principles are as follows:

Patient Care
. . . The first and foremost function of the Hospital is to care for sick people. The Board has full responsibility for the scope and quality of such care. Its members naturally respond to this need because as laymen they identify themselves with patients or potential patients and tend to guide policies in the best interest of the patients. From this viewpoint, Board members can best balance and coordinate the efforts of the community and university physicians and hospital administration, to whom actual patient care activities are delegated. The Hospital's status as an institution dedicated to healing emanates from these three groups.

Education and Research
The quality of care ultimately depends upon the quality of the physicians associated with the Hospital. In turn, the quality of the physicians depends upon the ability of the institution to attract and train such doctors, both as interns and residents and as members of the medical staffs. The Hospital can only attract them by a continuing emphasis on the highest standards of patient care, associated teaching programs and opportunities for learning through research. . . .

Unity of Operation
The Board believes that the unified operation of the Hospital has proven successful during the past four years and will pursue it as a permanent policy. Although the owners originally felt the Center could encompass two hospitals, it has become apparent that such an operation would not be in the best in-

terests of the patients, their physicians, or the owners. Patient care would suffer from the confusion of double standards. Rates would probably be higher than at present. Cooperation between community and University medical staffs would be seriously hampered by the artificial barriers of a dual operation. The owners' fiscal positions would be damaged by less efficient use of beds and related facilities.

Authority

The Board of Directors reaffirms its intention of fully using its explicit legal authority (embodied in by-laws and operating agreements with the owners) and its implied authority (based on knowledge, competence and persuasive ability) to reach independent and final decisions on matters relating to operation and policy of the Hospital. . . .

Financing

The Board is determined to find and develop adequate sources of income for the Hospital. . . . At present, the Hospital generates enough income from patient care to cover traditional hospital expenditures, namely operating costs and essential equipment needs. This income is not sufficient to amortize original construction costs, provide funds for major new equipment, pay for future plant improvements and additions, and develop new programs.

Initial reaction to the Principles branded them glittering generalities unlikely to inspire substantial redirection or reorganization of the hospital. But as discussion of the document expanded, it became clear that different principles had been specifically aimed at different constituencies.

To the school of medicine the document stated that the faculty did not participate in the hospital purely as a research or teaching laboratory, able to ignore essential patient care responsibilities. To the private community it was saying the opposite: the hospital would move toward integration of educational programs in which virtually all physicians would be expected to participate. In respect to unity of operational authority, the implication for both owners was that the hospital needed to increase the scope of its authortiy and decision making, particularly in respect to financial operations. Deehan's proposal implied that the heavy debt burden imposed by the owners had to be lifted.

At a special hospital board meeting scheduled to discuss the principles, the general comment was favorable, but no action was taken. Deehan felt that there was no way in which the principles would be accepted by the two medical staffs and owners unless the board was prepared both strongly to support the ideas and force the issues. In a second special board meeting, Deehan resigned. After six weeks of intense discussion, the board decided to pursue the principles actively and to urge Deehan to return as administrator and lead them in this effort. He did so. The *Palo Alto Times* published the principles in a full page advertisement paid for personally by hospital board members. This precipitated wide debate in both the community and the university.

As far as the city of Palo Alto was concerned, a key feature was the assumption of financial responsibility for retirement of hospital construction bonds, using the city's tax revenue for full repayment rather than hospital operating revenues. Another item of debate was the hospital's insistence that differential rates be eliminated on grounds that it was impossible to administer them fairly.[8]

The board proposed a special meeting of the two owners and asked for the appointment of a joint committee to study the proposal for hospital autonomy. The city council appointed a citizens' advisory committee which concluded with a general endorsement of the hospital's proposals. The committee recommended to the city that it transfer the authorities requested by the board to the hospital and lift the debt burden. The city council took no action on its citizens' committee advisory report, awaiting action from the joint committee which had also been established.

On the Stanford side the issue was not so much finance but organizational control. Stanford endorsed the proposals on the condition that an affiliation agreement be developed between the hospital and the university. This agreement could be typical of many which existed between medical schools and private teaching hospitals. Again Oliver Deehan became frustrated at the slow pace of deliberation and resigned for a second and permanent time. David Starkweather, who had been in the hospital administration since its opening in 1959, was appointed acting administrator.

This put the burden of decision back with the Palo Alto City Council. More time passed and Starkweather too despaired of the inaction. His strategy was to submit a budget to both owners for the next fiscal year which contained no support for bond repayment from hospital operations and assumed all authorities which the hospital board had requested. He knew that by law the hospital budget had to be acted upon prior to the beginning of the fiscal year; thus, for better or worse, the key issues would have to be resolved. The budget for 1964–65, then, was an entirely different document than the owners' had become used to: no debt retirement, only a summary of expenses rather than line-item detail, allocation of capital equipment by the hospital board rather than by the owners, and revised cost accounting features. The budget was well received by the university, but not by the city council. After 23 different hearings and presentations in the spring of 1964, the city council finally approved the budget and, de facto, the Hospital's plan for increased authority.

At this point, with some assurance that hospital finances were improvable, the Hospital board turned its attention to relationships with the medical school: the affiliation agreement. The details of these negotiations had to be pursued by a new cast of personalities; virtually none of the officials who had originally been involved in the establishment of the Medical Center were now on the scene. Robert Alway, M.D., first dean of the Medical School, had resigned, although he remained in office while the university sought his replacement. Oliver Deehan, second administrator, had resigned, as had Andrew Hunt, M.D., director of Stanford's clinics, to become dean of Michigan State Univeristy Medical School. Another key associate dean of the medical school had resigned. In short, few persons who were familiar with Deehan's original proposal or the events of the recent past were available. There remained one key person who knew the issues and was actively dedicated to their resolution: Associate Dean Lowell Rantz. In late 1964, while at the rostrum of a professional meeting in the East, Dr. Rantz collapsed and died.

For the hospital board's part, it sought and appointed an experienced physician administrator, reasoning as it had six years previous that a person with such credentials would be able to deal effectively with professional relationships. Shortly after, Associate Administrator Starkweather resigned. It fell to the new director, Dr. Leroy Bates, to develop and propose the affiliation agreement necessary to obtain Stanford's final agreement. He found that the hospital wanted a loose agreement and the medical school wanted a tight one that would bind the hospital to support certain expenses of medical teaching and research.

Dr. Bates' proposal was conciliatory. It reviewed and underscored the goals shared by the medical school and hospital. It preserved the two medical staff organizations while at the same time making it clear that the Stanford faculty would be expected to participate in the hospital according to a complete set of medical staff by-laws. Bates' phraseology on this point was a clear attempt to smooth over prior differences. He distinguished between holding one appointment that involves serving two institutions with distinct missions and dual appoints simultaneously responsible to both institutions for the goals they share. Bates' draft agreement gave each staff separate access to the hospital board without excluding those activities which had previously been disputed and finally put under the jurisdiction of the medical board. The document provided some exceptions to the hospital board's authority for patient care. One was the Stanford Clinics, on grounds that the medical school was financing its deficits. Another was the Clinical Research Unit, a small hospital inpatient unit that was financed by federal funds and run by members of the faculty entirely for research purposes. A third was the rehabilitation service, on grounds that it was housed in the Edwards Building which was outside of the scope of the hospital's authority.

The section dealing with hospital professional service contracts was crucial to the issue of surgical pathology. Bates reinforced the Packard Agreements in respect to both hospital and medical school satisfaction with the services. But he proposed a modification in them to cover the case where the medical school might not be satisfied with the services of a person whom they had originally appointed—precisely the situation which had developed with Dr. Eversole. The proposed agreement called for three-way contracts between hospital, school, and the individuals involved: subtly different than Packard's two-way contract between the hospital and the physician which had to be satisfactory to the school.

As for finances, Bates proposed a rather clear shift in all identifiable educational expenses, from hospital to school. This was an effort to reduce some of the hospital's extraordinary expenses. With the shift, however, went some of the hospital's prior authority for approval and control of internship and residency programs.

Finally, Dr. Bates proposed a new small and powerful group that would resolve all important differences between the university and hospital in respect to finance:

> The financial shares of the respective institutions in the expenses, income, or capital financing of joint programs, facilities or equipment will be recommended by majority of those voting in a committee known as the Medical Planning and Development Committee, which will consist of the President of the University, the President of the Hospital Board, the Dean of the Medical School, the Hospital Director, the Chief of the Stanford University Medical Staff of the Hospital, and the Chief of the Palo Alto Staff of the Hospital, or their designated representatives. Any other matter may be placed on the agenda of the Committee by any member.

The full ramification of Bates' last sentence did not go unnoticed. In effect, the proposal would shift decision making away from what had become a very cumbersome bureaucratic process—one in which the hospital-university mechanisms had to parallel the hospital-city procedures—toward a small group which could be expected to resolve crucial differences and take definitive action. Given the faculty's extreme dissatisfaction with the prior organizational arrangements, this new form was well received.

Bates' draft was general to the point of vagueness on some points; the prevailing point of view saw value in not forcing every issue to sharp resolution.

Stanford's approval of the affiliation agreement cleared the last hurdle to joint-owner approval of the hospital board's proposals for increased authority and autonomy. The joint owners' committee that had been formed to study the matter so recommended, and the powers were granted. Ironically, so much time had elapsed, so many personalities had changed, and the issues had become so general, that the meaning of this action was obscure to many and the implications for its follow-through were unclear.

CONTROL OF PROFESSIONAL SERVICES: PATHOLOGY REVISITED

One person who had remained in administrative and professional limbo during this extended time was Dr. Eversole, the hospital pathologist. More than four years had now passed since his arrival. Features of the new hospital-school affiliation agreement, coupled with his now strained relationships with Alvin Cox, M.D., chairman of the School's Department of Pathology, made him uneasy.

Dr. Eversole announced that he now wanted a firm contract with the hospital, or he would quit. Dr. Cox had concluded that Eversole's appointment was unacceptable to the school; to Cox, Eversole had shown himself to be a poor teacher and had a truculent personality. Cox's stand was not endorsed by several key members of the Stanford Department of Surgery who worked closely with Eversole; they were not particularly concerned with whether Eversole was a good teacher but had developed high regard for him as a surgical tissue diagnostician. Partly because of this but primarily for unrelated reasons, Cox submitted his resignation as Pathology Department chairman. In accepting his resignation, Acting Dean Alway assumed direct involvement in the surgical pathology issue.

The matter was highly symbolic on both sides. The Palo Alto Medical Staff maintained that Eversole's continuance was essential to its support of the hospital. Palo Alto physicians viewed the "Eversole Affair" as a test of the hospital's newly established authority vis-a-vis the Medical School; they did not intend to become organizationally subservient to the faculty. Acting Dean Alway maintained that, by virtue of both the old "Packard Agreements" and the new affiliation agreement, the Hospital could not sign a contract with Eversole without School participation and approval.

When, after another year of negotiations, Dr. Eversole did in fact resign, many viewed his resignation as a victory for Stanford and a defeat for the Palo Alto Medical Staff. Such was not the medical school's view. Alway was now faced with the difficult obligation of providing pathology services for a busy hospital surgical schedule through a department that had no chief and was staffed with academics with little enthusiasm for the day-to-day routine of examining surgical tissues.

TEACHING

The issue in medical education now most closely related to hospital operations was control of beds. The hospital's occupancy problems had now been reversed; continuing population growth in the area and the medical center's growing reputation had lead to a serious insufficiency of beds. Tensions between community and university physicians over admitting privileges were reaching the breaking point. With newly established authority stemming from acceptance of the Five Principles, and a Medical Board in place with responsibility for such matters, hospital officials decided to allocate beds on the basis of patient care need. This meant that beds unused on one teaching service could be reallocated to clinical services of greater need. It also meant

that patients would be admitted to the hospital on the basis of their requirement for care rather than their teaching value, if the two were in conflict.
This policy was strongly resisted by medical school chiefs of clinical departments, who were in the habit of having their own clearly defined bed services.
Despite strong argument that good medical education required control of
teaching beds by educators, the hospital policy prevailed. This caused continuing tension between the two medical staffs, but under the circumstances
no other policy would have yielded less conflict. Both medical staffs called
for the construction of additional beds. Hospital officials agreed but were
powerless to take specific action because the two owners remained responsible for major facility changes.

A BASIC REAPPRAISAL

Approximately ten years after the Palo Alto-Stanford Hospital corporation
had been created, and six years after the two prior hospital operations had
been fully merged, both owners conducted basic reappraisals of their positions. These were not the result of formal decisions to do so, nor joint commitment to rational analysis, but rather the evolutionary result of the various
proposals and counterproposals, changes in key personalities, and both formal
and informal negotiations.

The first step in this process was taken by the university in early 1965
with the appointment of a new dean of the medical school, Robert Glaser,
M.D. Glaser was also appointed University Vice-president for Health Affairs.
This new authority altered the relationships between the hospital board and
university trustees and the university president's office. It meant that communication on all hospital matters would henceforth be channeled through
Vice-President Glaser. But the appointment had even more significance: it
appeared to close observers that Glaser had been charged by the university
with getting the medical school organizationally extricated from the Palo Alto-
Stanford Hospital, and with doing so in a way that left the university with a
teaching hospital.

Not long after his arrival Dr. Glaser suggested that the university purchase Palo Alto's share of the hospital. This idea was received with interest
by the Palo Alto city manager and council; the money obtained from the sale
could be used to repay hospital bonds, thus reducing the tax rate. At the
insistence of private physicians, a crucial issue within the city council became
whether, if Stanford obtained full control of the hospital, beds could be guaranteed for the patients of Palo Alto Medical Staff physicians. It became clear
that Palo Alto would not go for the purchase unless some guarantee was made
on this matter.

Another joint committee was appointed by the two owners, in this case
composed of administrative rather than professional persons. Two key indi-

viduals were Dean Glaser and City Manager George Morgan. Meetings were held without the participation of hospital board or administrative personnel. Quick agreement was reached on a recommendation: the university should purchase the city's hospital equity for five million dollars (the original four million in fixed assets plus one million in pipeline inventory and equipment purchased since opening). This was viewed by many as a good price for the city and therefore evidence of Stanford's strong desire to obtain a new hospital arrangement more supportive of its goals.

On the bed access question, two agreements were struck. One was that the medical school would agree to reserve sufficient beds for city of Palo Alto residents who were patients of Palo Alto Medical Staff physicians—the patient group for which the city council had chief concern. The second was an informal understanding: the city would not stand in the way of construction of a new hospital by Russell Lee's Palo Alto Medical Clinic.[9] This would expand the total number of beds available to the immediate and larger community and create something of a safety valve for private physicians should there be difficulties in practicing medicine in a hospital owned by the university.[10]

These understandings were accepted by the complaining Palo Alto physicians; all significant remaining opposition to the purchase disappeared. By the end of 1967 Stanford's purchase of the city's interests was made formal.

F. A NEW STABILITY

In approximately six years a situation characterized by an unusual commitment to shared university and community hospital objectives had changed to one of mutual suspicion followed by commitment to separation.

On July 1, 1968, the Palo Alto-Stanford Hospital became the Stanford University Hospital, a more typical university institution. Shortly after this, another change occurred in the hospital administration: Dr. Bates left and a Medical School Professor of psychiatry and former department head took over as hospital administrator. The Palo Alto Medical Staff continued as an organization but with severely reduced influence in clinical or hospital affairs. The hospital board also continued as an entity, but its name and functions were changed to advisory. The hospital's administrative departments—finance, personnel, etc.—started becoming those of Stanford University.

In short, the Hospital's organization and operation were greatly simplified but at the expense of the built-in checks and balances previously designed into the institution.

On the community side, a Palo Alto citizens' group strongly devoted to keeping the city residential in character, rather than industrial or commercial, took up active opposition to the Palo Alto Medical Clinic's hospital project. The group did not challenge the need for another hospital but was opposed to its location. The citizens' group argued that the Palo Alto Clinic hospital would increase traffic in their area and that the inevitable additional construction of hospital-related facilities would destroy the residential features of this portion of the city.[11]

The issue was widely debated, with the *Palo Alto Times* again playing a crucial role. In April 1969 the citizens of Palo Alto rejected the zoning change necessary for construction of a hospital by the Palo Alto Medical Clinic.

So, whatever the future held for clinical practice, teaching, and research, and whatever the ebb and flow of passions and loyalties, Palo Alto and Stanford doctors were destined to practice medicine under the same hospital roof for a continued and indefinite period of time. Fifteen years had seen great achievement, much conflict, and unprecedented change. It had taken so long, and there were so many details, many persons forgot that there had also been a remarkable merger.

NOTES

1. John Walsh, "Stanford School of Medicine 1): Problem over More than Money,"*Science*, Feb. 12, 1971; "Stanford School of Medicine 2): Clinicians Make an Issue," *Science*, Feb. 19, 1971; "Stanford School of Medicine 3): Varieties of Medical Experience," *Science*, Feb. 26, 1971. Richard A. Knox, "Stanford Medical School Suffers Fiscal Ideological Crises," *Science*, January 19, 1979.
2. There were two important sets of relationships that would be enhanced by the move: the proximity of clinical faculty members and their students located in San Franciso to general university campus resources, and the integration of San Francisco-based clinical teaching and research with medical school pre-clinical activities located on the main campus.
3. As described in *Time* March 31, 1958, which dubbed the Center "Medicine's Taj Mahal."
4. *Medical Care, the University, and Society*: Speeches delivered at the dedication of the Stanford Medical Center, September 17, 18, 1959, pp. 19–29.
5. Many members of the Palo Alto Medical Staff were also surprised by the arrangements. But they did not seem as concerned, rather expecting perhaps that consultation with several hundred practitioners in dispersed locations would have been difficult, and not as dependent on hospital arrangements for teaching and clinical research.
6. After reviewing a draft of this case study, Robert Alway offered the following recollection of the attitudes of Medical School faculty members and the influence of Henry Kaplan: "[In reading the case], although I get a bit of the flavor, I certainly do not get the impact of the markedly different interests and patterns of approach . . . in the different clinical departments. Although Henry Kaplan certainly was painfully consistent in his objections to many of the apparent intentions of hospital administration and the community practitioners, I do not feel at all, let alone the major, force of dissention should be read as though it was Henry's. The different personalities and wishes and approaches of the sev-

eral clinical department executives seemed to me to be at least as effective in maintaining our slow progress toward a smoothly functioning medical school with its essential clinical (hospital) activities" (personal correspondence, July 13, 1973).

7. Shidler, Frederic. Correspondence to Executive Committee, Palo Alto Hospital Medical Staff, Dec. 27, 1963.

8. By now insurance companies were ignoring the differentials. Stanford students were vocal in their complaints: some were admitted to teaching services and others to private services, with different charges.

9. Design and development funds had already been obtained for such a hospital, through a substantial research grant made to the Palo Alto Medical Research Foundation, a nonprofit spin-off of the Palo Alto Medical Clinic. This USPHS grant was obtained during the time when the senior Dr. Lee's son, Philip, was Undersecretary of Health in the Department of Health, Education, and Welfare.

10. In order for this "safety valve" to mean anything to many solo practitioners, a hospital constructed by the Palo Alto Medical Clinic would have to "open its doors" to non-Clinic practitioners. Dr. Lee so stated at a Palo Alto Medical Staff meeting at which the whole series of formal and informal negotiations were reviewed and discussed. Yet, this was a reversal of prior statements to the effect that in order for a group practice to operate optimally it must control hospital beds. Therefore, Dr. Lee's statement to the Palo Alto Medical Staff was suspect in several quarters.

11. Indeed, architectural plans for the hospital called for unusual "interstitial" spaces that increased the vertical rise of a ten-story hospital to the equivalent of almost twenty floors.

APPENDIX A: THREE ARTICLES ON THE STANFORD SCHOOL
OF MEDICINE

1. "PROBLEMS OVER MORE THAN MONEY"

In less than a decade Stanford University School of Medicine made a national reputation as a model of the research-oriented medical school. The names the public identify most readily with Stanford are those of cardiac surgeon Norman Shumway and of Nobel laureates Arthur Kornberg and Joshua Lederberg. But in its medical-school peer group Stanford has a broad-spectrum reputation for research and advanced techniques in other forms of surgery, radiology, psychiatry, and some types of medicine, and also for curriculum innovation. Stanford's dean during the 1960's, Robert S. Glaser, and some other members of the faculty belonged to that group of medical school representatives, foundation officers, and government officials who dominate the *haute politique* of academic medicine. And all in all, Stanford became one of the half-dozen schools generally regarded as setting the pace in American medical education.

These three articles are by John Walsh. Reprinted, with permission, from *Science*, February 12, 19, and 26, 1971.

Like other medical schools in the 1960's, Stanford depended heavily on federal funds to finance expansion. . . . Then in the later years of the decade, Stanford was hit by the squeeze on federal funds and by demands on the school to exercise a greater measure of social responsibility by providing new forms of training and community service. As a consequence Glaser, who resigned last year after 5 years as the university's chief administrator for health affairs, says that "Stanford has an acute form of the problems of American medical schools." And Lederberg, who has been deeply involved in policy issues in both the medical school and university in the last decade, observes that Stanford "has problems of identity and leadership which override the money problems."

Ironically, these problems of identity and leadership, of which Lederberg speaks, result in large part from the two decades of federal funding of research which created the modern medical school. And the frictions tend to be particularly severe at schools which by prevailing criteria are most successful, like Stanford.

If by self-diagnosis Stanford has big problems, they arise in part because the medical school has big personalities and big expectations. Through the 1960's, Stanford attracted faculty members whose talents and prestige enabled them to bring in funds which gave them and their colleagues a measure of independence. A "star system" emerged at Stanford which, to extend the metaphor, made the medical school organizationally more like a galaxy than a universe, which a medical school resembled under the old dean-centered system.

This did not happen accidentally. For Stanford the die was cast when the decision was made in the early 1950's to consolidate the medical school on the Stanford campus. The university in 1908 had taken over the 50-year-old Cooper Medical College in San Francisco and had continued the 2-year clinical phase of the M.D. training in the city. Preclinical courses were given on the campus. Wallace Sterling, who moved into the Stanford University presidency after World War II, was a key figure in carrying through the consolidation. Sterling recalls that a link with the campus science departments was recognized as necessary if medical education and service were to advance scientifically, but also some far-sighted advisers convinced him that "the day was going to come when social sciences, engineering, law, and business administration were going to be more important in medicine."

The medical school had developed a strong clinical tradition in San Francisco, and the debate over the move from the city split the faculty. When the move was made in 1959 many of the clinical partisans remained in the city, while faculty members committed to greater emphasis on research generally went south to Stanford.

New faculty members had to be recruited to fill the ranks, and not surprisingly these tended to be people who shared the vision of Stanford as a new avatar of scientific medicine. The arrival in 1959 of Lederberg and Kornberg, famous for their work in the then scientifically white-hot field of molecular biology, proved to have more than symbolic significance, since both men, in rather different ways, exercised a formative influence on the school. Kornberg was recruited with his whole microbiology group from Washington University in St. Louis, and the transplant of a big, productive biochemistry department into a medical school set a precedent for Stanford and other schools. Kornberg also was active in recruiting, especially in the early years, and is regarded by his colleagues as an insistent and effective spokesman for basic research. Lederberg, although he has been active outside Stanford as a commentator on scientific and political issues in addition to carrying on his own research and administrative work at the medical school, is also said to have been a knowledgeable and hardworking member of groups grappling with basic issues in both the medical school and the university.

That recruiting for the medical school should go successfully is hardly surprising since the recruiters represented a new and apparently amply-financed enterprise in very attractive physical and professional circumstances. In 1959 Stanford opened a medical center complex combining medical education, research, and hospital facilities. The medical center was designed by Edward Durrell Stone, then ascending the heights of his profession with his embassy and international exhibit architecture. The Stone style is evident in the center's columns and textured walls, but it is not mentioned on the architect's list of triumphs. The plan is essentially a grid of fairly narrow, interconnecting buildings. The center, considering its massive size, does not obtrude on the Stanford landscape, and there are pleasant, quiet courtyards and some bright, sunlit rooms. But there are complaints about endless corridors and a lack of usable space, and local opinion is summed up by a university administrator who says the medical center "aesthetically is fine, functionally. . . ."

But the design of the center perhaps had less profound effect than the cost of building and running it. Construction costs had been seriously underestimated by medical school planners. As a result there was not enough money to construct a clinical sciences research building in the first phase, which cost well over $20 million, and the clinical sciences research wing was not completed until 1966. The effect was to retard the buildup of faculty, and so, when federal funding tightened in the later 1960's, Stanford was left with some imbalances in its faculty.

Equally important was the university trustees' reaction to the unexpectedly high costs of the move to the campus. By the late 1950's, as one observer puts it, "the trustees felt they had a tiger by the tail." The cost of construction of the medical center was essentially covered by money raised from government and private sources, but the trustees saw the budgets of the medical school and the hospital as an open-ended demand. As a result, they put a ceiling on general university funds to be allocated to the medical school. This meant that the medical school was to be dependent primarily on the funds it generated itself, and this added even greater importance to the entrepreneurial drive of the faculty.

A further serious implication of the move from San Francisco was that the school cut ties not only with individuals but with institutions, primarily with the county hospital on which the school depended for "clinical material," the euphemism for the indigent patients who occupy the teaching beds in most medical schools.

In moving to Stanford, the medical school gambled on attracting enough fee-paying patients to provide clinical material and also to pay the costs of operating the university hospital, and part at least of the cost of intern and residency training programs. The center not only started out with zero patients but also faced the task of overcoming the suspicion, if not the hostility, of local physicians who alone could send referral patients whom any medical center needs for its training programs. The town-and-gown situation was particularly complicated since the peace treaty with the local community was based on an agreement to include a community hospital financed by Palo Alto in the new medical center complex.

The community hospital was merged with the university hospital in the late 1960's under an agreement that guarantees priority in a large block of beds to patients from the community and assures local physicians of staff rights. Criticism persists that the university hospital, with something over 500 beds, is too small by teaching hospital standards. One medical student said "there are more people in white coats than patients." Defenders of the system point out that Stanford also has arrangements with a nearby veterans hospital and a county hospital in San Jose which provide highly satisfactory training experience for students, interns, and residents. In addition there is a small, separate pavillion for chronically ill children on the campus, and the medical school provides some services for San Mateo County Hospital, although that relationship seems to be on the wane.

The trajectory of expansion at Stanford in the 1960's can be traced in the figures for budget and personnel. The budget rose from $5.7 million in 1959-60 to $25.5 million in 1969-70. Over the same period, income from federal grants rose from $2.3 million to $14 million, or from 41 percent of the total budget to 60 percent. The hospital budget increased at about the same rate as the medical school's, so that now the combined budget tops $50 million a year.

The reliance on federal funding has obviously influenced the shape of Stanford's educational program. The number of medical students increased only from 230 to 357 between 1959 and 1970. In the same years the interns and residents rose from 152 to 279—with the big increase affecting residents, who now number 240. The greatest percentage increase came in the number of postdoctoral fellows, which went up from 44 at the beginning of the decade to 218 in the current year. There were 35 Ph.D. candidates 10 years ago and there are 76 this year, but that number represents a sharp drop from 110 last year and reflects the cuts in federal support of research and training. Full-time faculty numbers 375 of whom 193 are tenured.

In all, the medical school has slightly over 1000 students in various categories. Only about a third are in the M.D. program. There is a small nursing school which has only about 62 students, down about a third from a decade ago, and a relatively small number of students are taking subprofessional training. Stanford, therefore, has an unusually large number of postgraduate students.

The mix was achieved deliberately and through the maximum use of federal and hospital service funds. As one financial official phrased it, "We couldn't afford a conservative financial program. We're living on soft money." Up to now the medical school has managed to avoid an operating deficit. Research just about paid for itself. But now expenses are increasing more rapidly and federal funding is not keeping up. And the administrator observes, "We're dug in for a sustaining operation. I don't think everybody realizes that."

Just as Stanford has depended on funds from federal research grants to underwrite graduate students and pay part of faculty salaries, it has had to follow an even older practice of "bootlegging" the costs of clinical training, including the salaries of interns and residents, from funds paid by patients for hospital service. This is standard practice among medical schools and the funds, in effect, are paid for services rendered, but now, because of inflation in medical costs including the salaries of house staff, the budget for clinical training is under very heavy pressure.

Things look particularly tight for Stanford in the immediate future. California Governor Ronald Reagan has ordered a sharp cut in funds for MediCal, the state's version of the federal Medicaid program for medical indigents. In addition there is a dispute over government billing requirements on surgical cases, which specify that the faculty member named as attending surgeon must himself perform the operation. Under the surgical-team system of teaching used at Stanford and elsewhere, a resident learns by wielding the scalpel under close supervision. Accounts receivable of some $1.5 million are tied up in the dispute.

Stanford, incidentally, cannot look to the state government for support, in the way that other private medical schools in several states have done, since the California constitution specifically prohibits such assistance.

At Stanford, however, almost everyone agrees that the problems run deeper than the threat of deficits. For example, departmental chairmanships in anatomy and physiology have remained unfilled for several years. In part this is because the cutback in federal funds has made it impossible to offer the inducements in space and staff positions that have been proffered to high-level recruits in earlier days. But there are also disagreements about what direction research and teaching in anatomy and physiology should take at Stanford, and the difficulty in settling issues such as these make some faculty feel that the medical school is suffering from a case of arrested development. And the feeling is sharpened by the fact that the search for a dean to replace Glaser has been on for almost a year.

The days when medical school policy was decided by the dean and a few influential-senior faculty are over. One effect of the flow of federal funds into the medical schools has been a redistribution of power. This has created pressures for major change in governance and even in the structure of the medical school which will be discussed in forthcoming articles.

2.   "CLINICIANS MAKE AN ISSUE"

Modern medical education was created when high-quality instruction and research in the biomedical sciences was united with clinical training, but, even at a research-oriented medical school like Stanford, the alliance remains an uneasy one. Some faculty members contend that the research ideal has triumphed at the expense of medical care. Professional pride and prejudice doubtless inspire part of it, but the criticism is potentially strong enough to change the structure of the medical school.

In oversimplified terms, the objections are that some clinical faculty are spending too much time on the wrong kind of research, with the result that they are not pulling their weight scientifically or financially. As inflation and the cutbacks in federal funding put heavy pressure on medical school budgets, this kind of dissatisfaction has mounted and some clinical departments, which have become power centers because of the income they generate from fees, are seeking greater control over their own finances and policy. This is a complex, multilevel argument, which is probably best approached by looking at the anatomy of the medical school.

Some friction persists because medical schools operate under their own double standard. Faculties are divided between Ph.D.'s and M.D.'s, concentrated in the basic sciences and clinical programs, respectively. Top administrative posts in academic medicine continue to go to physicians rather than Ph.D.'s, and in most schools substantial salary differentials favor the M.D.'s.

Since World War II, however, the second-class status of the basic sciences faculty has been considerably assuaged by large-scale funding of basic research by the federal government, principally through the National Institutes of Health (NIH) and also by such victories of research as polio vaccine and by the apparently boundless promise of such disciplines as molecular biology.

The availability of federal funding and prestige accruing from research has caused a blurring of the demarcation line between basic science and clinical programs. Clinicians found it possible to get their own research grants, and clinical departments tooled up programs of clinical research—efforts to apply the results of basic research and technology to medical care. Across the country, the trend has been particularly evident in departments of medicine. The number of subspecialties has multiplied, and developments in chemical therapy and instrumentation have opened new avenues for clinical research in almost all areas. To achieve interdisciplinary breadth, some clinical departments added Ph.D.'s to their rolls, on occasion outbidding basic sciences departments for their services. Many clinicians, of course, had been doing research, very good research, before NIH support became available. The famous report on medical schools by Abraham Flexner early in the century had urged on physician members of the medical school faculty the self-image of teacher-researcher-clinician. What had changed was that making at least a modest mark in research became obligatory for anyone hoping for tenure and advancement in academic medicine.

At Stanford, critics of clinical research do not fault the clinicians for doing research but for taking the basic sciences departments as their model and straining to make their work as "basic" as possible. The effort to emulate work done in labs headed by men such as Nobel laureates Arthur Kornberg and Joshua Lederberg is understandable, but the result, say the critics, is that many of the clinical researchers are neither very good researchers nor very good clinicians.

Clinical departments, of course, remain responsible for care of patients in medical center hospitals as well as for the training of medical students, interns, and residents—and, as research and training activities have increased, so, not surprisingly, has the size of clinical faculties.

This has inevitably affected the budget and a score of interviews at Stanford yielded the impression that the criticism of clinical research was directed not so much at its quality but at its cost in the context of medical school financing.

In the leading medical schools there has been a steady trend away from the old practice of basing clinical faculty members' salaries in part on fees they earn through providing medical service. The alternative is the so-called "full-full-time" system under which faculty members are paid set salaries while fees go into medical school coffers. The full-time system permits losses in some sectors to be counterbalanced by surpluses in others and, theoretically, at least, an equalization of quality in departments to be achieved throughout the school.

One of the constants of academic medicine is that some departments, notably surgery, radiology, and anesthesiology, make money on their services, while others, especially pediatrics, produce deficits. In private practice, surgeons, radiologists, and anesthesiologists are the most highly paid specialists. Stanford salaries for senior clinical faculty—in the $30,000 to $40,000 range— look more than adequate by university standards but amount to only about a half or a third of what their colleagues in the premium specialties earn in private practice. The main complaint in these clinical departments is not that they are underpaid, although they are not oblivious of that aspect, but that what they regard as a fair share of funds earned by their departments is not returned to finance research and needed expansion or renovations of facilities. And what they seem to find most galling is their belief that their colleagues in other departments are not putting sufficient time and effort into medical care to pay their department's way.

It is worth emphasizing that the animus is not directed toward researchers in the basic sciences departments. Those engaged in fundamental research at Stanford have not only imparted an aura of excellence but have been sufficiently successful in competing for available NIH funds to be still regarded as self-financing.

The strongest expression of resentment comes from the surgeons. Considering the surgeons' earning power and the proverbial "surgical personality," this should not be unexpected. Self-confidence and an extreme sense of the value of his work are, after all, basic qualifications for a surgeon; tempermentally, the surgeons are to medicine what fighter pilots are to air forces.

Roy B. Cohn, a distinguished renal surgeon whose tenure at Stanford predates the move from San Francisco and who plays the irascible elder statesman with zest, says, "The full-time system denigrates medical care. The exception is the surgeons. Surgeons would do [their work] for nothing. We work harder." Speaking of some of his colleagues in other departments, Cohn says, "Those fellows are very intellectual—once they establish a diagnosis, they lose interest."

Robert A Chase, chairman of the department of surgery, emphasizes the interdependence of departments in a good medical school by saying, for example, "The department of surgery can be no better than the weakest department in the school." But in discussing the issue there is no mistaking the firmness of his views. "Care of patients is a tough job. There should be appropriate recognition in the institution, and it is not always given. Surgery makes a greater effort than any department." And Chase footnotes a Rand study which, he says, found that Stanford per patient costs are high and that faculty in general don't spend a great deal of time in the clinics. "An economic incentive is not provided," says Chase, "in fact, the incentive is perverse." Chase goes on to insist that Stanford medical school cannot maintain its position if salaries are not competitive with peer medical schools across the country. Chase gave some examples of medical schools with higher salaries and noted, "The men in the department feel the full-time system is best so long as the constraints don't become terribly discouraging."

The critique of clinical research and the claim that the full-time system has an adverse effect on medical care must, of course, be examined for fairness.

Even the sharpest critics concede that clinical research is both necessary and difficult. No matter how intellectually challenging, basic research customarily uses such relatively amenable experimental objects as bacteria, viruses, or laboratory animals, whereas clinical researchers must ultimately work on human beings. The primary concern for the patient's well-being infinitely complicates the clinical researcher's task in designing and carrying out his work. And the critics tend to ignore the large amount of good clinical work being done. A few of the names that were frequently cited for high quality research in clinical departments at Stanford were Thomas C. Merigan for his work on interferon inducers, Rose O. Payne for advances in tissue typing for human organ transplants, and Judith G. Pool, an expert in the pathophysiology of blood typing, for developing a simplified method of preparing cryoprecipitated antihemophiliac globulin which makes surgery possible for hemophiliac patients. Work on immunology by department of medicine chairman Halsted R. Holman and his colleagues was often mentioned.

The charge that clinicians are not working hard enough to pay their own way apparently should be amended in many cases to a complaint that money due them is not collected. It is relatively easy to compute and bill charges for surgery or for radiological examination and treatment. The nature of treatment required by patients of the departments of pediatrics, psychiatry, and medicine often make it much harder. In the case of medical treatment, patients' insurance may provide for only marginal reimbursement. Physicians in these services may be faced with a large number of patients and may decide to see more patients and fill out fewer forms. Other dimensions of the issue are opened when the rewards of anesthesiologists or the total resources required for sophisticated surgery are questioned. But the point is not so much whether the critics are justified but that they feel intensely aggrieved and tend to be those who, because they are big earners for the school, exert real leverage.

Norman E. Shumway, head of the division of cardiovascular surgery and a pioneer in the heart transplant operation, is a strong proponent and participant of research in surgery. His view of how to organize it is a highly personal one. "I don't think you can do good research while carrying a heavy clinical schedule," says Shumway. "Research is a young man's game, and you find yourself providing a place for younger and brighter guys."

An ideal way to do this, Shumway thinks, would be to establish a cardiac center, "a miniature Manhattan project," which would combine preclinical teaching with research and care on "cross-departmental lines." Shumway says the center "would have more to do with cardiology than surgery. It can't be a specialty hospital—there's too much overlap in areas such as infectious diseases." Such a center he sees as necessarily a part of the university medical center.

Understating it somewhat, Shumway admits, "Some people won't like this, but suppose a whole school goes this way. It might be very attractive to federal agencies."

Rather similar views are held by Henry S. Kaplan, the astute and tough-minded chairman of the department of radiology. Kaplan was one of the engineers of the medical school's consolidation on the Stanford campus in 1959, and he has remained influential in the policy counsels of the medical school.

Kaplan, like Shumway, is attracted by the prospects of establishing a center or institute which would focus treatment and interdisciplinary research in a particular field. Kaplan envisions a cancer center and thinks that the push for a massive attack on cancer advocated in Congress and now proposed in the President's budget (*Science*, 12 February 1971) may provide the funds. The real question, says Kaplan, is "how to create an institute which is a fiscal and physical entity yet is still in the main stream of the educational process. I would not want to see a cancer center or cardiac center which is not part of the teaching process. We don't want watertight compartments."

Kaplan also bluntly concurs with the surgeons in saying, "A heavy degree of subsidization of those departments is going on needlessly. We wouldn't mind so long as people in those departments were working as hard as possible. It's time to blow the whistle," says Kaplan.

As critic, Kaplan's flanks are well covered. His department not only operates deeply in the black but has a strong reputation for clinical research. He himself is a successful researcher who pioneered development of the linear medical accelerator for radiation treatment of cancer and is, among other things, an authority on Hodgkin's disease and malignant lymphoma.

Kaplan's analysis of the ills of the medical schools is broader than a simple indictment of the handling of fees. In the period of rapid growth he feels that "too much reliance was placed on the federal government." A source of the trouble was the "extension into the NIH easy money era of the Flexner concept of the triple threat man" (teaching, research, patient care). In some departments the feeling that a man should be a great clinician fell into disuse. If you stay with the idea of the triple threat man, as patient load increases you must increase the staff. But where is the lab space and free time to work in the labs coming from?

"This is the problem of the medical schools. We must find a way to diversify the function of the faculty. One solution would be to create two kinds of faculty appointments. You might create a postgraduate medical school to exist side by side with the undergraduate medical school."

An immediate problem, as Kaplan sees it, is to create an incentive plan to provide Stanford with competitive salaries and funds for research.

The problem of incentives and the question of such new departures in organization as the creation of a cancer center or cardiac center are in abeyance while Stanford searches for a new dean to replace Robert S. Glaser, who resigned last spring to become a Commonwealth Fund executive.

The acting dean is John L. Wilson, who came to Stanford as an associate dean when Stanford took on administration of a regional medical program. Wilson is held in generally high regard by the faculty. In style he is anything but a confrontationist, but he is credited with taking relatively strong initiatives in the area of budget and day-to-day administration, considering his acting capacity. But the tougher policy problems have been tabled in the interim.

Internal pressures building at Stanford, such as those for creation of semiautonomous cancer and cardiac centers, some pessimists feel could dismember the medical school. Others, like geneticist Joshua Lederberg, think it may be possible to establish a new form of specialized treatment center connected to medical schools which would allow the schools to increase income without breaching the integrity of medical education.

Those familiar with the realpolitik of medical schools feel that something substantial must be done soon, since the resentments that produced the demand for an incentive plan and the center proposals are near the flash point in many schools. How Stanford deals with these problems or fails to deal with them will be important beyond Stanford, because, in making its reputation, Stanford inevitably made itself a model for other schools.

Stanford is being subjected to other strong centrifugal forces. Among the strongest is the demand from activists that the school commit itself more deeply to meeting the needs of the community. The implications for research and governance at Stanford of these demands will be the subject of a third article.

3.   "VARIETIES OF MEDICAL EXPERIENCE"

In the late 1950's Stanford medical school broke with convention by lengthening the regular 4-year course for the M.D. degree to 5 years. A decade later

Stanford switched to an elective system which offers the medical student an option of acquiring his M.D. in about 3 years.

This reversal was seen by many as representing a swing away from a research bias in the Stanford curriculum and toward a greater stress on clinical training and community service. The shift occurred during a period when social and political awareness was growing at Stanford and at other medical schools, but the causes of the shift were too complex to be attributed simply to a surge in medical populism.

Improved teaching in the sciences in high school and college produced a better prepared and more scientifically sophisticated incoming medical student. And the fact that almost all new M.D.'s go on to specialty training these days means that medical schools no longer need concentrate on producing physicians ready to enter practice after a year's internship.

Medical schools have also been faced with the task of preparing their graduates for a proliferating variety of careers in academic medicine, medical administration, and group and private practice. Stanford's 5-year plan, in fact, was devised in part to break the lockstep system of medical education and to allow a variety of study plans.

The key to flexibility under the 5-year program was to have been a block of open time in both the basic science and clinical training programs. The idea was that the student would spend about half the assigned time at any stage learning what the department or teaching group felt was important and the other half pursuing his special medical interests.

The Stanford plan developed an essential pattern of 3 years of basic sciences and 2 years of clinical training. Students complained that there was no early, meaningful exposure to patients, and there were a lot of wry, local jokes about Stanford offering the "DNA degree."

What was ambiguous from the start was whether open time was to be devoted to elective courses or was to be really free time. With Stanford's strength in basic research, there was a perhaps inevitable emphasis on research experience for the medical student. As one former medical school administrator put it, "The kids saw the free time as an opportunity to get out into the community; the faculty saw it as an opportunity to get the kids into the lab."

For all those reasons and because of the accelerating increase in medical knowledge, it was becoming more difficult for the faculty to agree on core material for the curriculum. Bernard W. Nelson, associate dean for student affairs, who watched the process from this special perspective, thinks the fact that the faculty could not agree on a body of knowledge essential to the training of a physician hastened an overhaul of curriculum. But the major factor in bringing about modification, he suggests, was the better preparation of students—with a resulting dissatisfaction with the heavy emphasis on basic sciences. The students who benefitted especially from the 5-year plan proved to be a relatively small, research-oriented group but by the mid-1960's student complaints were growing about the unevenness of teaching and the limitations of the free-time options.

Revision Necessary

By 1966 it became clear that a major effort at revision of the curriculum was necessary. The existing curriculum committee was disbanded and a new, blue-ribbon committee formed. Robert A. Chase, chairman of the department of surgery, who served on this new committee on medical education, recalls that at first the group made another attempt at developing the ideal core curriculum, but soon gave that up. A consensus developed in the committee that a totally elective system would provide the best chance of achieving the original aims of the Stanford plan. The major aims had been to make medical education more like graduate education by creating a preceptor-student relationship between the faculty member and medical student and to open alternative "pathways" through medical school to fit graduates for the differing roles played by physicians today.

To qualify for a degree under the elective system the student had to satisfy the requirements of 4000 hours of instruction laid down by California law, pass all the sections of the National Board examinations, and satisfy school requirements on competence. There was no legislation of which courses the student had to take, and a flexible pass-fail grading system was prescribed.

The changeover to the elective system was made in 1968 with less opposition than might have been anticipated. Some observers say that a general acceptance by faculty of the difficulty of establishing a viable core curriculum did much to move the faculty to acquiesce.

The flexibility provided by the 5-year plan is preserved under the elective system. Students may complete the M.D. course in about 3½ years, but they may also take 4, 5, or 6 years.

In the theoretical model of the new plan it was essential that faculty advisers maintain close contact with students, helping them to plan their studies with close references to the student's background and career goals. In practice, the advisory system appears not to have developed as planned, and many students, in fact, seem to obtain the advice they need from their peers.

The elective system has not, as a matter of fact, ushered in an era of wild improvisation in curriculum at Stanford. Anything but, it seems. Nelson and others observe that the students have proved quite conservative in curriculum matters. If anything, the trend is toward a heavier concentration on traditional medical school studies.

For the faculty, the elective system creates a new market situation and, because there are no captive audiences, a potential ego problem. The results seem to be mixed. On the one hand, faculty members are offering courses in what most interests them and what they feel is most important, and there is some indication that the quality of teaching has improved. On the other hand, as one faculty member said of his colleagues, "People are allowed to do what they damn well please without regard to what it does to total education." Some students complain that faculty members don't take the trouble to integrate material and give it continuity.

The elective system was adopted at a time when the demand for social relevance in medical education was growing. At a research-oriented medical school like Stanford the idea went somewhat against the grain, but during the later years of the decade a number of things were done to advance the claims of "social medicine." Probably the most significant event was the arrival in 1969 of Count Gibson who, while at Tufts, had been involved in setting up trailblazing community health centers in Boston and Mound Bayou, Mississippi. Gibson came to Stanford to establish a division of community medicine in the department of preventive medicine. Stanford soon had links with three Office of Economic Opportunity-sponsored health centers. These were in east Palo Alto, whose inhabitants are predominantly low income black people; in Alviso at the foot of San Francisco Bay, with a largely Mexican-American population; and in King City in a rural area.

Another "Outreach" Program
Another form of "outreach" program was established at Livingston, about a 2-hour drive from Stanford in agricultural Merced County. An unusual plan for a group practice based on a partnership between the medical school and people living in the area evolved when the town's only physician, an overworked Stanford alumnus, gave up his practice and turned over his office facilities to the medical school for use as a clinic. Livingston is not a poor community, and what has developed is a unique group practice staffed by medical school faculty members, residents, and medical students serving an economically heterogeneous population defined by high school district lines.

The community medicine program at Stanford is in its early stages and has not yet, for example, developed residencies, master's, or doctoral programs. The future of the program would seem to depend on how seriously the medical school pursues experimentation with new forms of delivery of medical care.

Participation in community health projects is, of course, not the only way in which students and faculty members have expressed the impulse toward greater political and social engagement. But until the Cambodia incursion last spring, few Stanford medical school students or faculty members had been actively involved in protest actions which had erupted on the Stanford campus fairly frequently. The events of last spring, however, led to the organization of a Stanford Medical Community for Peace involving students, faculty, and staff in a variety of nonviolent political activities, on and off campus, against the war.

Jeff Brown, president of the medical school student body at the time, observed that one effect of the Cambodia crisis was to raise in a nontheoretical way the "question of the responsibility of the medical student and physician to the profession and society." Many students and faculty members were willing to suspend professional training during the Cambodia reaction, but there was a free choice of whether to carry on with classes or to engage in political activity. Brown noted that there was some friction between groups. "Those who were heavily involved in political activity sacrificed education and resented those who did not." Brown says the experience forced consideration of the "fundamental question of the relation of medicine to the rest of society. Is it the responsibility of the physician to get involved in politics, education, mental health programs, social criticism?" After Cambodia the price of involvement was better understood, and some faculty members think the passion for activism was tempered.

This year's student body president, John Battista, says that organized political activity at the medical center has gone downhill since the peak period during Cambodia, but he feels that the upheaval of the spring did "teach the necessity for the medical school to have a superordinate goal."

The role of medical students in establishing goals and setting policy for the medical school has increased substantially in recent years. Students serve on many committees but complain that they still have relatively little impact on such basic issues as budget and admissions. The size of the entering class was increased about 65 to 75, and 10 places were allotted for admission of minority students on special terms. A separate admissions subcommittee was established to deal with these applicants, and a dispute has simmered over whether the special committee should have acceptance powers or should revert to an advisory capacity, as the faculty last year voted.

If the power of students, including graduate students, interns, and residents, is still limited, their influence is considerable. This influence is exercised less through the formal apparatus of student government than by the weight of their background, attitudes, and choices. The intellectual quality of Stanford applicants is very high—about 3000 applicants for 77 places in the entering medical school class last year. Medical students, graduate students, and interns and residents tend to come from the country's elite institutions where the index of social and political consciousness is highest, and Stanford, like other elite medical schools, tries to live up to its students' expectations.

It would be an error to regard Stanford medical students as a homogeneous lot. Battista, for example, thinks his classmates fall into three fairly distinct categories. First, there are the "competitive" types aiming at a rather standard medical school experience followed by the best possible specialty training and, probably, careers on rather traditional lines. Next are a smaller group, whom Battista calls "individualistic," who are attracted by Stanford's reputation in biomedical research and are headed for careers in research or, at any rate, in academic medicine. Finally, there is a new breed of medical student interested in community medicine and committed to entering practice as a member of group. It was characteristic of students of this persuasion that a number of them wanted to start a national campaign to refuse to serve in a fee-for-service system.

Interest in Social Issues

Stanford's 5-year plan, especially in the early 1960's, seems to have attracted a group of students who, typically, were very bright but lacked the conventional premedical training and medical student orientation. Many of them had particular interest in the social and behavioral sciences and social issues, and the longer training period made it possible for them to follow these interests while at the same time training as physicians.

The elective system seems to have had most effect on this group. One administrator observed, "We're getting fewer social relations types from Harvard and more scientifically oriented types." Administrators deny an assertion by some students that the admissions office is showing a new partiality to the conventionally prepared and motivated applicant. An increase in the numbers of applicants with backgrounds in the physical sciences and engineering, a fair number with Ph.D.'s, is noted, but the reasons for this have not been adequately analyzed.

In this area, as in others at Stanford, the trends are hardly clear. Stanford set out more than a decade ago with the primary objective of achieving excellence in training medical scientists and specialists. As preceding articles have suggested, the school's development has shown a decided unevenness, but by ordinary criteria, and particularly in postgraduate areas, its performance has been impressive. At the same time, Stanford's program for training M.D.'s has had shortcomings. The medical curriculum has been under almost constant revision, and David Korn, chairman of the pathology department, expresses a fairly general view when he says, "We're in an evolutionary phase. Maybe we overshot. I don't feel that we're necessarily on the optimal path in curriculum." The elective system, however, seems to be regarded by a majority as the best hope for maintaining genuine flexibility in the curriculum.

A matter of real concern at the moment at Stanford among many faculty members, especially basic science researchers like Arthur Kornberg, is that the demand for social relevance will cause a shift in resources and emphasis away from research.

Retrenchment in research funding has had an undeniable impact on Stanford, but there seems little danger of NIH's going out of business or of Stanford losing its competitive edge in garnering research grants.

The real problem at Stanford is not to avoid the extremes of becoming a research institute, on the one hand, or a staffing agency for storefront clinics, on the other. It is to find better ways to provide students with varieties of medical experiences, which will prepare them to meet the multiple responsibilities imposed on physicians today, and to enable them to improve the ailing American medical care system.

To do this at Stanford means altering the way decisions are made. The effect of federal support so far has been to create departmental fiefdoms, to relegate the dean to the role of mediator and power broker, and to put the premium and priority almost uncritically on growth.

What has happened at Stanford and at other medical schools is put in longer perspective by Joshua Lederberg, who thinks, "It is no longer possible to follow a policy of maximum growth." He traces a basic flaw in the relation between the federal government and the medical schools to the fact that "we never had a mandate to pursue a balanced program of medical training, research, and service." In the long run, only federal funds and a change in federal policy can foster such a balance.

APPENDIX B: STANFORD MEDICAL SCHOOL
               SUFFERS FISCAL IDEOLOGICAL CRISES

When General Eisenhower was president of Columbia University, the story is told, he once offered to swap jobs with President Harold Willis Dodds of Princeton. Dodds asked why. "Because you don't have a medical school," the general allegedly sighed.

President Richard W. Lyman of Stanford might be forgiven if he feels like Ike these days. Stanford's prestigious medical school and its 668-bed teaching hospital, which together account for 42 percent of the entire university's $380-million operating budget, are in the throes of a fiscal and administrative crisis that offers no ready or painless resolution and shows every prospect of worsening. Last month the situation moved Lyman to ask for the resignation of his dean and vice president for medical affairs, Clayton Rich, who has held the jobs since 1972.

Stanford's current problems are indeed extreme; nonetheless they are representative of issues that face major medical centers nationwide.

Appendix B is by Richard A. Knox. Reprinted, with permission from *Science*, Jan. 12, 1979.

Stanford's plight is not only financial; it is inevitably ideological as well, involving as it does who cuts and serves the pieces of a shrinking pie. It concerns the viability of a private institution with a frankly elitist vision of itself. As a recent Stanford manifesto proclaims, the school is devoted far more to biomedical reserach and the training of the next generations of medical "innovators and pioneers" than to turning out nonacademic physicians, caring for patients, or studying the role of medicine in society. One high-level Stanford administrator said in an interview with *Science*: "I think you would get an argument around here that doctors are even the principal product of Stanford Medical School."

The lines between those who consider general medical training paramount and those who think basic and clinical research of greatest importance at Stanford are drawn. As yet it is not clear what kind of accommodation can be reached. Kenneth Melmon, who was recently lured to Stanford from the University of California at San Francisco, is concerned about what he sees as diminishing public enthusiasm for basic research. He accepted the chairmanship of medicine at Stanford because of the school's reputed commitment to basic research as the underpinning of medical progress. "I really felt this was the place that would outlive the pressure to downplay research and do it royally," he told *Science*. "I still do, but I'm goddamned worried."

Nineteen seventy-eight has been a watershed year for Stanford University Medical Center, a time of gloomy portents from within and thunderbolts from without. "The fiscal problem was on the horizon last fall," said Deputy Dean Lawrence G. Crowley, who will become acting dean 1 January, "but the speed and magnitude of it took us by surprise." Last spring, medical center finance officers concluded that the medical school faced mounting deficits in the years ahead; unless drastic steps were taken, they said, the cumulative shortfall would reach more than $7 million by 1982 to 1983. A key reason lay in the amount of income generated by the school's clinical faculty— the ones who care for patients as opposed to those who only do basic research. In a memo dated 8 June, Dean Rich told the clinical chiefs that soaring expenses had far outstripped the hospital's net revenue, which rose only 2 percent over the previous year; outlays for the clinicians' salaries, for instance, jumped 23 percent this year.

"There has been a reduction in the number of patients seen this year and little price increase, but continued escalation of costs," the dean wrote. "There appears to have been a reduction nationally in the number of office visits and hospital admissions. Locally we see the effects of increasing competition from well-trained private practitioners, and may suffer from reduced referrals as HMO's [health maintenance organizations] are organized in this region, and because of increasingly tight price control and regulations."

Into this perilous situation charged two troublemakers with their view of reform. Eugene Dong, a renegade faculty heart surgeon, and Robert L.

Weinmann, an ultraconservative Stanford-trained community neurologist, have been attacking the very basis of Stanford's faculty billing system, a regime that Crowley, who's in charge of it, acknowledges is "a little bizarre." Like perhaps half of all U.S. medical schools, Stanford's full-time clinical faculty are on salary in a medical universe that operates according to the time-honored laws of fee-for-service. That is, Stanford clinicians turn over all their fees to the institution, which allocates salaries and applies the rest for activities such as unfunded research and teaching. Under this system, cross-subsidizations within the medical center have become so intricate over the past decade that it seems doubtful that even the administration fully understands who is being paid how much for doing precisely what.

Dong and Weinmann have persisted all year long in raising awkward public questions about the way Stanford bills Medicare and Medi-Cal for patient care: where the money goes, who controls it, how faculty members really spend their government-reimbursed time. Most crucially, they have dredged up the charge that makes all medical educators squirm: double-billing. The charge commonly arises out of the difficulty of sorting out which functions are supposed to be paid for through the professional fee, ostensibly tied to personal service rendered to the patient, and which through hospital cost-reimbursement funds, a category that wraps in such ineluctables as teaching and supervision of house staff and other personnel.

Dong, who is best known outside Stanford as coauthor of a recent science fiction thriller on artificial hearts, stopped doing heart surgery years ago because of "changing goals." He says he has a grand aim: "I want to reorganize the direction of this school. It's not going in the direction I've been raised to believe in—delivering first-quality individualistic medical care." He also has a grand ambition: to enter "state or national" politics. "There are well-meaning people in legislatures," he explained in an interview, "but they don't have the expertise to know when they're being conned by people with apparently altruistic motives." To further his new ambition, he is currently going to law school in his free time now that he no longer performs much surgery.

From yet another quarter Stanford suffered the most telling blow to date in early September. Federal Medicare officials announced they would not pay Stanford $2.4 million in anticipated reimbursement. The Medicare fees that Stanford faculty received for their professional services and turned over to the institution were now to be considered "restricted funds" and deducted from the hospital's Medicare cost-reimbursement. Stanford is appealing the action but the medical center's finance director told the faculty that "our chances of a successful appeal . . . are not great."

One immediate effect of the Medicare bombshell was to wipe out the clinical faculty's accustomed end-of-the-year bonuses, up to 40 percent of base salary for the highest-paid specialists. That was the beginning of the end for the dean. Many of the clinicians were incensed; and since they do not generally consider Clayton Rich their staunchest ally and defender—a former clinical chief calls him "the dean for biochemistry"—they naturally blamed him.

On 3 November, with his future uppermost in his mind, Rich had an especially unpleasant task. He appeared before 350 Stanford medical students to tell them that tuition would jump next year by 27 percent for entering students (from the current $5388 to $7373 for the academic year) and 15 percent for those currently enrolled (up to $6373); and also that it will take longer to win a Stanford M.D. (a minimum of 13 quarters, or just over 4 years). The average attendance now for students in Stanford's unique, all-elective program is 12.9 quarters, but there has been a growing tendency for students to leave after 3½ years to take clinical clerkships elsewhere. The net effect of the tuition changes, after adding 9 percent annual inflation to next year's "catch-up" increase, will be to add $6500 to the cost of a Stanford medical education. And Rich had to admit he didn't know where the school was going to get additional student aid funds.

Although the increase would not place Stanford ahead of what many private medical schools levy, the students' response was predictably angry. They assumed, in part correctly, that they were paying for the Medicare disallowance they had heard about.

By the time Rich appeared before the students, President Lyman had received emissaries from the medical faculty. Consulting key faculty on his own, Lyman discovered a quiet mutiny. One faculty member later said: "It's not the style here to have open discussions and votes of no-confidence." In individual conferences, some of the most influential clinical chairmen are said to have imparted the same message: "Things can't go on like this."

Lyman got the message. On 8 November he announced Rich's resignation.

"It was clear that there was going to be a confrontation within the school if I didn't resign and that I would need the substantial support of Lyman," Rich explained recently to *Science*. "Neither of us felt it would be the best course for the school at this point. . . . It's absolutely essential not to have the departments pulling in different directions and pointing the finger at each other."

Two days later the other shoe fell. The chief fraud and abuse official for Medi-Cal reportedly told Stanford officials in private the results of the double-billing investigation instigated by Dong and Weinmann. On the basis of a reveiw of "effort report" forms, which are supposed to reflect how much time a faculty member spends in "direct patient care" of the "hands-on" variety, California officials are said to have concluded that there was double-billing of Medi-Cal over a 3-year span. One Medi-Cal official told *Science* that Stanford has also been informed that the state may seek restitution for the double-billed amount, which could amount to several million dollars. Crowley, the deptuy dean, who was at the meeting, says he did not hear that message; but he and several other medical center officials acknowledge Stanford's vulnerability to the charge. "We may come to feel we used some funds we shouldn't have on the basis of those time reports," Rich said. A medical center lawyer added: "Our answer is that the [effort report] form wasn't very well designed."

As the dean hinted last spring, government reimbursement difficulties are not the only ones that bedevil Stanford these days, nor even the thorniest. A grocery list of others would include:

1) Declining demands for Stanford's services. Fewer patients are coming to Stanford's clinics and hospital. The hospital was budgeted for 188,000 patient-days last year but counted only 166,000. The trend is especially pronounced in the "community" beds of the hybrid teaching-community hospital, which account for about half the total. Last year the community beds were filled only somewhat more than 60 percent of the time. As Rich suggested, the growth of several fledgling prepaid health plans on the San Francisco Peninsula threatens to accelerate the exodus, since Stanford is too expensive a place for routine hospitalization under prepaid plans.

2) Wretched town-gown relations. Last summer, at the urging of clinical faculty members, Stanford Hospital directors voted to close off hospital privileges for certain services—radiology, anesthesiology, and labs such as neurology, nuclear medicine, and cardiac catheterization—to community doctors not already on the staff. Access to inpatient beds would remain open to qualified outside clinicians "for the foreseeable future"—a phrase that despite repeated disavowals sounded to community physicians "like a week from Thursday," as one Stanford official put it. The decision angered and alarmed area doctors, especially the 120-doctor Palo Alto Medical Clinic group which sends patients nowhere else but Stanford. Many of these community doctors are Stanford-trained; they view the recent action as an abrogation of the university's promises back in 1959, when the medical school moved here from San Francisco, and 1968, when the university bought out Palo Alto's interest in the community hospital component. President Lyman and other Stanford officials have denied bad faith but they are clearly worried about the threats from community doctors to take their patients down the road to some quite respectable nonteaching hospitals where the welcome is warmer.

3) Clinical facilities problems. According to James H. Stanford, the medical center's finance director, 20-year-old Stanford Hospital requires more than $12 million in renovations (after just losing millions on a new addition in cost overruns and delays) to meet accreditation and licensure standards. Yet the hospital has no separate endowment, he said, and the time is not propitious to be launching any community fund drives "given the current [town-gown] tensions." Moreover, Stanford is worried about the future of another vital resource, the county-owned Santa Clara Valley Medical Center. A quarter of Stanford's medical students and an equal proportion of its residents rotate through Valley Medical Center at any one time. But Proposition 13 has frozen salaries at the public hospital, causing an exodus of nurses and occasional shutdowns of intensive care units, and no one is sure how California governments are going to meet next year's Proposition-13 crunches. More ominously, the conservative fiscal mood impinges on the chances of an $84-million reconstruction program for the county institution, without which it cannot maintain accreditation and licensure.

Stanford University can't do much about the San Andreas Fault except to try to make its buildings "earthquake-proof." Likewise, Stanford University Medical Center cannot wish away inflation, competition, Proposition 13-ism, or lurking threats such as federal demands for more primary-care doctors or the Carter Administration's contemplated cutbacks in medical school capitation grants and research funds (see *New York Times*, Sunday, 3 December, p. 1). That means the school and hospital face some sort of fiscal earthquake-proofing; or as the exiting dean characterizes it, "significant reprogramming and rebudgeting."

As any initiate of faculty politics knows, those are fighting words. In terms of the medical school, the sibling rivalry is between those who see patients and those who do not—the clinicians and the researchers—and also between "have" departments, such as surgery and radiology, and "have-nots," such as pediatrics and many subspecialties.

The struggle has been a long time coming, arguably since 1959, when Stanford Medical School moved from San Francisco to Palo Alto and was reincarnated as the very model of a research-oriented medical school. For 10 years the decision paid off stunningly; by 1969 federal research funds supported 60 percent of the budget. But as everyone knows, or should have known, what goes up must come down. By 1974 research funds paid 41 percent of the faculty's salaries; since then the ratio of research-derived to clinically derived support has dwindled from 1.5 to parity.

For years Stanford weatherd the shift by virtue of its complex administrative structure, which allowed the dean to reallocate revenues according to his priorities. But such a structure is vulnerable at a time of across-the-board and increased fiscal accountability, a lesson that Stanford has seemed slow to learn.

Rich had hoped to meet the emergency without much structural reform. Lately he had been pushing for a plan to organize the clinical faculty into a large corporate group practice, apparently on the theory that government agencies and statutes, such as a California law against "the corporate practice of medicine" that Stanford is accused of violating, would thereby be satisfied. Under such a group practice, the faculty would technically no longer be "on salary" from the university, but the dean, as executive head of the corporation, might presumably maintain a good deal of redistributive discretion.

With Rich's departure that resolution of the problem may be down the drain too. The more powerful clinical chiefs, such as heart surgeon Norman Shumway, are said to be designing departmental group practices that would keep firm control of departmental revenues.

The implications of these plans are not lost upon basic researchers, who of course see no patients, nor upon have-not clinical departments that depend on cross-subsidization from their more prosperous brethren. "Basic research just can't survive if the dean loses his discretion to shift funds," argues one of the nonclinical department chiefs, Eric Shooter of neurobiology. "We aren't exactly the poor relations but we've got to have some subsidy. There has to be a transfer from the clinical side to the basic side." Resentful of the surgeons' boasts that they bring in the lion's share, and groping for solutions, Shooter even suggests plaintively that researchers "get some kind of incentives too, like some part of the indirect [research grant] costs coming back to the investigator as an incentive to write the next grant." It is an idea unlikely to excite the interest of the Department of Health, Education, and Welfare.

Creeping unease about a change in Stanford's mission—a natural and perhaps inevitable consequence of the funding and power shifts within the school—is emerging in other contexts these days. Last summer Nobel Laureate Arthur Kornberg, the faculty's most forceful exponent of the Stanford status quo, complained in the alumni magazine about the "erosion of our scientific enterprise" and the "inordinate control over school policy" exercised by clinicians just because they bring in "a major fraction of the school's budget."

"I am concerned," Kornberg wrote, "when there is a proliferation of teaching, clinical service or administrative activity far beyond what is appropriate for an institution with a major mission to create new knowledge."

And the ideological debate extends beyond fiscal power. Two years ago Kornberg and a number of like-minded faculty concluded that Stanford was admitting far too many students who were more interested in practicing medicine than in "creating new knowledge." As Shooter put it recently, echoing many others, "In the early seventies the admissions committee went overboard in the admission of students who knew from the day they came that they wanted to be general medical practitioners. Stanford is not the place to train that kind of individual."

Those who felt this way engineered a restructuring of the school's admissions procedure that many believe has corrected the trend, though one department chief recently lamented: "Lately I find students drifting toward the practice of medicine. I don't object to that," he added quickly, "but I thought originally that Stanford was more research-oriented."

There is some evidence, however, that sharply calls into question whether Stanford Medical School has ever turned out a preponderance of scientists and academicians, even in the biomedical boom days of the sixties. Lawrence Horowitz, a staffer for Senator Edward M. Kennedy's Senate Health Subcommittee, did a survey of Stanford alumni while he was a Robert Wood Johnson Clinical Scholar at Stanford from 1974 to 1977. Horowitz found that the "new," post-1959 Stanford Medical School did indeed graduate significantly more M.D.'s who ended up in medical research and teaching than the old San Francisco-based school had. Even so, he found, only one out of five Palo Alto-period alumni became full-time medical school faculty members. Moreover, a majority of those who graduated between 1960 and 1972 do no medical research, and a majority of those who do spend less than a quarter of their time at it.

"If it is clear that the majority of Stanford students do not want to become scientists or do research in a meaningful way," Horowitz asked in an article published last summer, "then does it not follow that Stanford's education is unbalanced because of a research and subspecialty bias?"

The "Horowitz Report" is not much talked about at Stanford Medical School; out of two dozen interviews with *Science* recently, no one brought it up spontaneously and most brushed it aside when it was mentioned. Last month, however, as if in rebuttal to Horowitz's question, a curriculum reform committee chaired by Robert A. Chase, a surgeon, said the school should take firm steps to ensure more research-oriented and scientifically competent graduates. Specifically, the committee frowned on the growing tendency of Stanford students to get through medical school as rapidly as possible and get on to clinical training; to reverse this state of affairs, it recommended that all students be required to write and defend a thesis, and to stay at least 13 quarters to do it.

The recommendation has not yet been acted upon by the school's faculty senate. So far its critics have been found mostly among the students, who question whether the thesis requirement will produce better doctors, diminish diversity among the student body or even, given its coercive aspect, lead to scientific competency and useful work. Proponents tend to take the attitude that it matters not one whit what the current students think: in the future, if the thesis requirement is adopted, Stanford will attract only those students who *want* to engage in "a scholarly investigative experience." The students' self-appointed ombudsman and faculty spokesman, William Creger, sees it a different way. Creger, who was dean of student affairs at the medical school until he had a falling out with Rich over admissions procedures and other matters 2 years ago, calls the proposed thesis requirement "more depressing than a required religion" and adds caustically: "I think we've got some scientists around here who feel threatened because students don't think they're the only gods any more."

Apart from the particulars of the "thesis" debate, however, the interesting thing about the Chase committee's report is the set of underlying "assumptions" which the authors took the trouble to lay out. Two of the 13 assumptions stand out:

1) "Stanford should specifically address the public's need for medical scientists"; and
2) "It should not be Stanford's function to meet specific societal needs through production of the number and proportion of various kinds of M.D.'s needed in today's maldistributed pool."

If this language sounds a tad defiant at a time when HEW Secretary Joseph A. Califano is telling the Association of American Medical Colleges to curb "the runaway growth of specialists and subspecialists," the implication is entirely deliberate. In discussions of the Chase committee's report among the faculty leaders recently, someone reportedly pointed out that the school should consider how such statements would read "on the front page of the *New York Times*." But after due consideration, the faculty decided to let it stand.

The document is merely symptomatic, in an unusually stark way, of the tensions within academic medicine in the late 1970's. Stanford traditionalists see their plight as tragic and their resistance as noble. But even one of Stanford's own, health economist Victor Fuchs, sees it in quite a different light. Speaking before the New Orleans convention of the Association of American Medical Colleges in late October, Fuchs said:

"Even a sympathetic, friendly observer can't help but get the impression that academic medicine's interest in health policy begins and ends with two commandments:

"First, 'give us money,'

"Second, 'leave us alone.' "

5.
Forced Merger Negotiations:
Westhaven and Riviera, California

David B. Starkweather and Joseph Hafey

A. INTRODUCTION

We have chosen this title for two reasons. First, the parties involved, two hospital boards, were unwilling to deal directly with each other, creating the need for a third party's intervention. This party provided a communication pathway where none existed, and in the process imposed its own set of outcome preferences. Second, the third party was in this instance a comprehensive health planning association, possessed of certain powers which it brought to bear that went well beyond the traditional forum role commonly attributed to such agencies.[1] The case, then, has particular relevance to health planning activists, given the increasing prominence of such agencies and the continuing debate over whether their role should be one of political involvement or detached planning.

The outcome of the merger negotiations described herein was not at all apparent until the very last: the intricate balance of forces for and against merger was about even. Because of this, we will concentrate on the details of negotiation between the two parties, since the outcome appeared to rest in these details.

Both of the authors were prominent actors in this situation—one as a consultant and the other as the executive of the comprehensive health planning agency. We were close enough to see and possibly understand what was going on, yet also close enough to imprint our biases on the events reported. The value of the first does not deny the possibility of the second; the conduct of any good case study rests on the horns of this dilemma.

The negotiations described in this case were intense and highly controversial. They were held in private and frequently involved personality clashes. For these reasons there is ample room for misunderstanding, selective viewing of what took place, and invalid assignment of motives. We have not intended any of these. To reduce the risk of having seemed to, we have rendered anonymous all persons and places in the case by providing fictitious names. This applies throughout except to our own names, which remain real.

PERSONS FIGURING PROMINENTLY IN THE CASE

Roland Becker, M.D., Director of Medical Services, Los Medanos County; member, board of directors, Comprehensive Health Planning Association

Ronald Coss, Vice-president of Gow Chemical, Riviera; president (sometime), board of trustees, Dana Memorial Hospital

Charles Eames, M.D., Chief of medical staff, Dana Memorial Hospital; member, Joint Negotiating Committee

Gregory Fall, Architect, Westhaven Community Hospital District

William Forrest, Businessman in Riviera and East County, president (sometime), Dana Memorial Hospital board of trustees

Joseph Hafey, Executive director, Comprehensive Health Planning Association of Los Medanos County

Melissa Honor, Member, board of directors, Westhaven Community Hospital District

Daniel Modrow, Member and president, board of directors, Westhaven Community Hospital District

David Starkweather, Consultant to Westhaven Community Hospital, Dana Memorial Hospital, and Comprehensive Health Planning Association

Zig Wagner, Secretary, Central Labor Council of Los Medanos County; member, board of directors of Comprehensive Health Planning Association; Comprehensive Health Planning Association appointee, Joint Negotiating Committee

SEQUENCE OF IMPORTANT EVENTS

1946   Westhaven Community Hospital opened in surplus Army barracks purchased from federal government.

1961   Annexation election held to expand Westhaven Hospital District; defeated.

1964   Bay Area Health Facility Planning Association approves construction of Dana Memorial Hospital.

1971   Westhaven Hospital District purchases nineteen acres of land from federal government, at former Camp Brendham.

1972   Physicians of East County urge a single hospital.

1973   Comprehensive Health Planning Association issues moratorium on hospital construction (February).

1974   CHPA Study Committee recommends single hospital be built at Brendham site and recommends new unified hospital corporation (March).

CHPA denies Westhaven application for certificate of need for new 78-bed hospital; Dana withdraws its proposal for certificate of need to expand to 109 beds (May).

CHPA sues State of California for having permitted Westhaven to proceed with hospital discussion (October).

1975   Merger negotiations committee established (March).

William Forrest elected president of Dana Memorial Hospital (June).

Daniel Modrow elected president of Westhaven Hospital District (July).

Joint Commission on Accreditation of Hospitals grants one-year accreditation to Westhaven Hospital (July).

Consultant Starkweather presents two-corporation unification plan: East Los Medanos Health Authority and Los Medanos Regional Hospital; negotiating committee decides to recommend plan to both hospital boards (August).

Dana Memorial Hospital approves unification plan (August).

Westhaven Hospital board defers decision on unification plan, pending board elections (September).

Westhaven Hospital District elections held: Daniel Modrow reelected and Melissa Honor elected (November).

1976   Negotiations resume (February).

Lawyers report to Negotiating Committee on legality of two-corporation plan (April).

Consultant Starkweather proposes revised unification plan: East Los Medanos Regional Hospital Consortium ("option #4") (May).

Negotiating Committee recommends plan to both hospital boards (May).

Westhaven counterproposes a plan: East Los Medanos Health Care Federation (June).

Final locked doors Negotiating Committee meeting; compromise unification plan evolved (July).

Dana Hospital board rejects compromise plan (August).

Westhaven Hospital reproposes its Federation plan, demanding a decision by Dana in one week (September).

Westhaven Hospital directors vote to proceed with new Westhaven Hospital (September).

CHPA-Westhaven lawsuit decided in favor of Westhaven (October).

CHPA board decides to abandon its prior policy on Westhaven Hospital construction (November).

1977   Los Medanos County Grand Jury decides not to investigate Westhaven Hospital District (January).

Citizens of Westhaven Hospital District vote for tax override to finance construction of new hospital (March).

1979   Westhaven Community Hospital is opened (July).

1980   Westhaven and Freemont Hospital Districts sign shared management agreement, and commit to a new joint powers authority and a new nonprofit corporation to administer the four-powers agreement.

B.   BACKGROUND: CIRCUMSTANCES AND EVENTS BEFORE 1970

THE TWO COMMUNITIES

Westhaven and Riviera are both small communities of about the same size, located five miles apart on the American River. The river's deep water channel makes it an important cargo route to several of California's inland cities, and the state's vast agricultural valley.

The two communities rest on the southern edge of a large agricultural region geographically subdivided, roughly, into a hilly western portion in which cattle grazing predominates, and a flat eastern portion, where vegetable and fruit production predominate. Over one-third of the population of this latter area is people with Spanish surnames, one-third of whom do not speak English.

There are thus three populations of equal size but unequal area—Westhaven, Riviera and the agricultural hills and flats. Together they form an informal jurisdiction known locally as East County. This area comprises a total of 84,000 people—small enough to ensure the constant interaction of industrial, residential and agricultural interests. Los Medanos is the name of the county in which this region is located. East County is dwarfed by this larger jurisdiction of 580,000 people, residing to the west in several suburban communities and industrial cities. The seat of county government is in Ignacio, a small industrial city ten miles distant from Westhaven and Riviera, with an economic history somewhat akin to Westhaven's. Figure 5.1 is a map of the area.

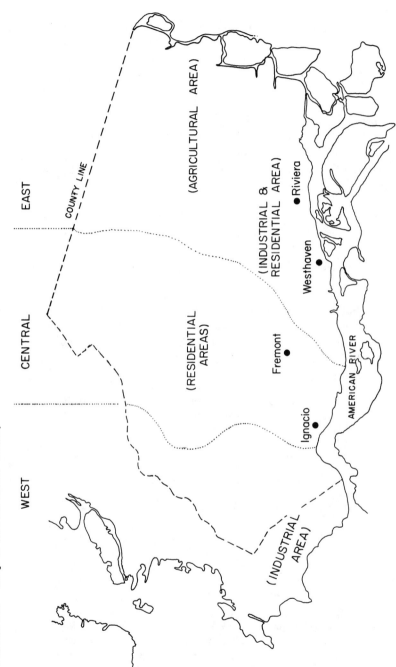

FIGURE 5.1   Map of Los Medanos County

East County is dominated by agriculture and small-business conservatism, coupled with disdain for the encroaching metropolitan development of the area immediately to the west. In this vein, the countywide comprehensive health planning agency is seen as an instrument of governmental and metropolitan intervention in the private life of East Los Medanos residents, yet is also regarded as one of those agencies with which East County individuals and institutions must relate in order to obtain the region's proper due.

The similarity between Westhaven and Riviera ends with their equal size and common maritime location. They are markedly different in racial composition and economic bases. These and other factors result in different forms of civic leadership.

Westhaven's 25,000 population is made of 48 percent whites and 52 percent nonwhite. Over 99 percent of East County's black persons live in Westhaven. These figures do not describe the significant population of Spanish surname persons. Nor do they reveal the prominent Italian population of Westhaven stemming from immigrations of the late 1800s and early 1900s relating to an active fishing industry. Westhaven's economic base is principally industrial—steel, chemicals, paper products, and glass.

Political and economic power in Westhaven is held tightly by a relatively small and long-established clique whose members operate sometimes in public office and other times by indirect influence. An experienced political observer of Westhaven described the situation as follows:

> In ethnic terms, there is an organized Chicano community which is constantly pressing the controlling interests for a piece of the action. The black community is not well organized and is under represented in most political realms, with the exception of the school board. The ruling majority is made up of Caucasians, who are primarily Italians. The Italian "sub–government" consists of a network of families which have both heavy financial ties, relating to land ownership, and strong blood ties. This describes a socio-economic spectrum which has a prominent wealthy establishment and a large poor population, with the middle class both proportionately smaller and much less represented in civic leadership than is the case in Riviera.

> The Italian "sub-government" is derived from the old "Westhaven Promotion League" headed by a coalition of these landed interests, including Bill Donnati, who is one of two attorneys in town "to see", a several-times member of the City Council and a prominent landowner. Another is Sal Buffi, a builder. A third is Bill Sora another old time landowner who is part-owner in Buffi's construction company. There are others.

> These people retain power because of 1) their willingness to spend money on elections, and 2) their pride in Westhaven. They believe Westhaven is a good place to live and feel that Italians who leave town, some of whom move to Riviera, are traitors. This group has heavy political muscle: several federal facilities located in Westhaven are outsized: the post office, a job training center, etc.

Riviera is a newer, more typically middle class small town—suburban, with an Anglo-Saxon, Protestant population of 33,000, composed of 98 percent Caucasian and 2 percent nonwhite. The 1970 census recorded 47 blacks residing in Riviera. Riviera's economic base is both industrial and residential.

The same political observer described Riviera's power structure as follows:

> It is not along ethnic lines at all. It is composed primarily of white corporation types who are constantly moving around the country as executives, engineers, etc. Many of these are Southerners, because they come from and are transferred between Gow Chemical's many plants in the South.

> There is not the permanent structure in Riviera that there is in Westhaven with its ruling families, nor are the vested interests so obvious. Riviera is led by middle class civic do-gooder and Chamber of Commerce types, with industry always there in the background.

In short, Riviera is not only markedly different from Westhaven, but in many ways developed as a reaction to the racial, economic, and residential features of Westhaven. Further, the third subpopulation of East Los Medanos, rural and isolated, contains many residents who are suspicious of both Westhaven's and Riviera's decision making, which disregards their agricultural neighbors.

MEDICAL CARE DELIVERY

East Los Medanos is served primarily by older general practice physicians. Of the 46 physicians practicing in the area, 54 percent are generalists and 46 percent specialists. Most have their offices in either Westhaven or Riviera. The two are relatively distinct medical communities: there are few patient referrals between the two groups, based partly on preference and partly on the absence of specialists. Even so, virtually all physicians enjoy medical staff privileges at the hospitals of both communities.

The Westhaven Community Hospital contains 78 beds, purchased in 1945 from the federal government which had built barracks-type facilities for the Army's nearby Camp Brendham. Since the facilities had been constructed prior to the creation of state licensing requirements, there were numerous hospital building code deficiencies; but the facility was still being operated under a variety of grandfather clauses and state approved exceptions. A major remodelling or new construction would trigger the stricter licensing requirements which had developed since 1945, making it impractical to include much of the present structure in any redevelopment plans. In 1975, the Joint Commission on Accreditation of Hospitals listed numerous serious deficiencies in the physical plant and granted only a one-year accreditation, pending their correction.

This hospital is owned and operated by a hospital district, an unusual form of governmental organization akin to a local school district, created by California state enabling legislation in 1948. Essential features of hospital districts are: 1) public election of five or more directors; 2) conduct of all business in public; 3) authority of the district directors to tax the residents of the district, without public vote, for the general planning and development of a hospital; and 4) authority to issue bonds to obtain funds for capital construction, upon approval by a majority vote of the districts' residents. Such hospital districts, common in California, are often called quasipublic hospitals because they have a publicly elected governance and accountability yet must operate financially as if they were private institutions. This arises from a stipulation in the state enabling law requiring that hospital revenues meet expenses and that bonds be paid off from hospital operations rather than from general tax levies.

In Riviera, as of the early 1960s, the community was served by a 26-bed nonprofit hospital located in an antiquated structure. This facility also failed to meet minimum state licensing standards, and was forced to remodel substantially or forfeit its license. For the prior ten years it had been run by a group of physicians who had rescued the hospital from bankruptcy proceedings. Efforts at building a new and more appropriate facility had been unsuccessful, and in late 1961 an election was held throughout all of East Los Medanos , including Riviera, to annex the area to the Westhaven Community Hospital District. This expansion of the tax district would have provided a sufficient financial base for construction of a single new hospital to serve the entire region. The measure passed by a simple majority in Westhaven but was defeated in all other communities by a lopsided 9–1 vote. Public information and concerted community action in favor of the proposal was not well organized, and subsequent to the election the belief became widespread that the lopsided defeat was due to a last minute campaign of a coalition of a few Riviera physicians, who did not want Westhaven's form of hospital governance imposed on their practice, and a few prominent Riviera industrialists, who saw that the district would increase their companies' taxes.

Following defeat of the measure, representatives of industry and the medical community in and around Riviera joined to form a nonprofit community hospital corporation which planned, financed, and constructed a 50-bed hospital on the outskirts of the city. It was named the Dana Memorial Hospital. By the time construction started, hospital trustees proudly announced that 40 percent of the needed dollars had been donated (the rest borrowed). The donated funds were received from the following sectors: residential—21 percent, commercial—11 percent, medical—26 percent, and industrial—42 percent.

This construction was approved in 1964 by the fledgling Bay Area Health Facility Planning Association, the predecessor organization to the Comprehensive Health Planning Association of Los Medanos County. During these deliberations, Dana officials expressed interest in seeing that a single hospital be formed in the near future to serve the entire area. The Association recommended that a Committee be established immediately, to be made up of representatives of Riviera's and Westhaven's hospitals, to work toward this end. This resulted a year later in a memorandum of understanding between the Association and Dana which urged that efforts be made to consolidate the interests of Riviera and Westhaven towards the eventual establishment of a single hospital to serve East Los Medanos, and that if this did not come about immediately it should eventually, even at the cost of discontinuing the Westhaven hospital. The memorandum added that in view of existing freeways and forecasted growth of population east of Riviera, the Dana Memorial site was ideally located for the establishment of such a hospital. In June of 1966 the Health Facilities Planning Association adopted an official position which enlarged even further on Dana's mantle: future developments in the region should be coordinated to ensure an orderly transition of responsibility from existing facilities to the board of Dana Memorial Hospital. In return for this designation, the Association stipulated that Dana's service area had to include all of East Los Medanos and that its governing board had to obtain adequate membership from each of the communities located in the expanded service area.

Four years passed.

In late 1970 a patient origin study was conducted by the Planning Association that showed that only 35 percent of all patients from Riviera admitted to any California hospital were cared for at Dana Memorial. The comparable figure for Westhaven was 37 percent. Apparently, many residents of East Los Medanos were willing to suffer the inconvenience of hospitalization in facilities considerably distant, revealing their lack of commitment to the local medical and hospital establishment. This situation bore most directly on the Westhaven Community Hospital which was now facing a declining occupancy. Its board members interpreted this to mean a drift of doctors and patients to Dana's new facility, as well as the continued flow of patients over the hill; the board members informally resolved to recapture the communities' just proportion of local hospital care.

This goal of Westhaven hospital was not supported by the Comprehensive Health Planning Association of Los Medanos County, which succeeded the Bay Area Health Facilities Planning Association in 1971. CHPA viewed East County as part of a larger medical care referral system in which the metropolitan hospitals of West County should continue to serve as important resources. It wanted to avoid replicating full hospital services in East County, especially duplicating expensive specialty developments in two suboptimally sized facilities.

In summary, Riviera and Westhaven are communities with known incompatibilities, based on different demographies, different economies, and different forms of civic leadership. Both have hospitals with different forms of supervision, one rooted in public government and the other in private civic volunteerism. A voluntary health planning agency had been active, but held insufficient power to obtain what it believed would be a rational medical care system for the area.

Despite these several circumstances which argued against hospital merger there were also several supporting it: 1) the obvious deficiencies in number and type of medical practitioners for the region; 2) a new planning agency with increased power and a new staff prepared to use its powers to the maximum; and 3) an emerging hospital economics that would make continuance of two inefficient small hospitals increasingly difficult.

C.   1971 TO 1975: THE CONVERGENCE OF FIVE EVENTS

The merging process during this period can be best described in a chronology of five important actions, all taking place among and between the two hospitals and CHPA.

WESTHAVEN REACTS

The directors of Westhaven Community Hospital did not acquiesce to the Bay Area Health Facilities Planning Association's designation of Dana as the growth hospital for the region. Starting in 1971, they began developing plans for replacing Westhaven's facility. The District purchased nineteen acres of land at Camp Brendham, a large World War II Army camp that had been declared surplus and was being parceled for sale to various civic and industrial buyers. Westhaven's plot was desirable in many respects: it was within the hospital district boundaries, although near its eastern edge; it was approximately midway between the cities of Westhaven and Riviera; an adjacent plot had been selected by a junior college district for construction of a new campus; and, the location was immediately next to the main east-west highway serving the region.

THE DOCTORS SPEAK OUT

With both hospitals apparently girding for separate futures, the medical community took action for the first time. A two-hospital joint medical staff liaison committee was formed, physicians were surveyed, and in December of 1972 a report was issued to both boards which included a petition signed by 95 percent of all East County practitioners. Basing their conclusion on the dual needs to improve medical services[2] and avoid duplication of facilities, the physicians underscored the need for a single facility to serve the entire area as the only feasible course of development.

CHPA ENTERS THE FRAY

Based partly on this evidence to support, and noting also the agreement in principle of both hospital boards to the single facility concept, the new Comprehensive Health Planning Agency of Los Medanos County officially declared a moratorium on all hospital construction in East County until a single application would reflect joint planning of both hospitals. This moratorium was adopted in February of 1973.

Yet, both hospitals continued to pursue their separate interests, and in October of the same year, CHPA received formal application from Westhaven for a certificate of need to construct a 109-bed facility on the Camp Brendham site. Knowing that this was coming, Joseph Hafey, CHPA executive, moved quickly to establish an Eastern Los Medanos County Study Committee, charged with the responsibility of resolving the dispute over the construction of a single facility. Membership on the 12-person committee was carefully'selected and included board members from each hospital and several physicians and hospital officials from outside the area to assure a broad regional viewpoint and to mitigate the continuing pressures from East County for a separate health services area. Both hospitals had reservations about the committee's composition, particularly Dana officials, who believed that the committee was stacked with Westhaven interests and was unnecessarily weighed by outside influences who would not respond appropriately to East County's special problems. Joseph Hafey's staffing of the committee was assisted by Melissa Honor, executive of Westhaven's Model Cities Health Policy Board.

THE STUDY COMMITTEE DELIBERATES

The study committee called for full presentation by each hospital of its plans for the future, including their individual approaches to unifying hospital services. Westhaven was first. Between October and December of 1973 it had scaled down its construction plans to a 78-bed hospital costing 6.3 million dollars to be financed by a bond issue retired out of patients' fees, which bonds would be offered by a new joint powers authority to be created by the hospital district and the County of Los Medanos.

Westhaven's presentation emphasized a single facility as the ultimate goal and stated its willingness and full capability to develop a health care system for the area, allowing that developments in this direction would be accelerated if the Study Committee endorsed the Brendham site. Hospital spokesmen stressed the benefits of cooperation with San Benito Junior College that were inherent in Westhaven's location: the college and hospital plots were contiguous. The hospital also outlined the advantages of a tax district and proposed that annexation of all East County to Westhaven's district again be submitted to a vote of the people.

Dana's presentation also underscored the desirability of a single larger hospital. Its plans called for expansion of its 53 beds to a 109-bed facility, at a cost of 2.5 million dollars, to be financed through a community fund drive and a commercial loan that would be retired from hospital operating revenues. The plans also included the development of satellite primary care centers designed to meet the needs of particular geographic and socioeconomic population groups. Significantly, Dana officials did not mention collaboration with Los Medanos County in the development of these services.

Dana officials stressed that their hospital was operating on a financially sound basis with a high occupancy of 95 percent in medical/surgical services. They went on to argue that, inasmuch as Dana Memorial was only five years old and was rendering care which was well regarded by patients and professionals, they "could not help but consider whether the single hospital concept could best be achieved by further development on the Antioch site." Dana trustees reported the results of studies conducted by two prominent consulting firms,[3] one of which justified this conclusion on grounds of population projections and demographic analysis showing the hospital's geographic suitability, the other of which documented the sufficient expansion capacity of Dana's building site.

The Study Committee now faced different arguments for site designation, each with merit. After two meetings of discussion and hot debate, it received a CHPA staff report outlining possible alternative uses for the Dana facility which included a family health center, an extended care facility or convalescent home, and several nonhealth related possibilities. The committee voted 7–4 to recommend that the major acute care facility for East County be located at the Camp Brendham site. Dana officials noted that all of the CHPA appointees to the committee voted for the Camp Brendham designation.

In reporting this action to the hospital boards and CHPA, the committee noted the advantages of access to the Brendham site, its location on the Riviera/Westhaven city boundary lines, and the proximity of San Benito Community College. The committee also concluded that the opportunities for architectural innovation made possible with a new facility at Westhaven's site compensated for its higher initial capital cost.

The committee also recommended that a new health care corporation be developed to plan and manage the entire health care system for East

County. This corporation should direct the consolidation of existing hospital services and supersede both existing boards. All future plans for hospital services should be developed by this new entity. The committee thus came down forcefully for a complete and immediate organizational integration but did not specify whether the corporation to accomplish this should be public or private.

The committee's report concluded with the recommendation that a joint planning group be formed to begin the transition to a new corporation, to be composed of three persons appointed by each hospital and four by CHPA, and that this interim body address itself immediately to the composition of the new corporation's board.

CHPA DECIDES

It was now March of 1974. Armed with the Study Committee's recommendations, the CHPA board put Westhaven's application on the agenda for its April meeting. The CHPA staff report was scathing. It noted that application of the Hill-Burton bed population formula to the local service area would result in 375 excess beds in 1979, if Westhaven's 78 beds were included. The report included five-year occupancy trends that showed a declining pattern for Westhaven's hospital. The staff went on to support the single facility concept by showing how one rather than two hospitals would reduce the total number of beds from 131 to 109, with commensurate savings in operating costs of at least 6.7 million dollars over a 40-year period.

In May of 1974, the CHPA board adapted its staff's recommendations and denied Westhaven's application. Five days after this decision, Dana officials advised CHPA that it was shelving its proposed application for expansion "in the hope that this action, coupled with the Westhaven application denial, would produce efforts toward the formation of a new corporation to establish and govern a single hospital system."

D. THE ISSUES

As the two hospitals approached a period of face-to-face negotiations, under circumstances orchestrated by CHPA, the following issues were well known.

DISSIMILAR COMMUNITIES

The marked differences in the peoples of Westhaven and Riviera resulted in civic incompatibility. Few mechanisms existed for communicating; thus, antagonisms tended to accumulate and inflame rather than diffuse.

THE NEW CORPORATION

Although both parties agreed generally that some new organization was necessary, the two communities had different traditions and therefore different attitudes towards its form, particularly on the issue of public vs. private control. Specific legal questions needed examination, since the legal demise of a public entity—Westhaven's district—was a complicated matter.

Then, there was the question of raw control. It was fairly obvious that the two hospitals would have to have precisely balanced influence in the new corporation, at least initially. However, neither the manner nor the timing of transition to a broader representation of all residents of East County was clear. By 1974 Dana had appointed to its board several East County residents who were not from Riviera, in response to Planning Association criticisms of prior years. These persons were insistent on broad geographic representation on the new corporation's board, at an early time. In contrast, Westhaven was constrained by district law which specifies that directors must be residents of the district; thus, Westhaven officials saw a solution coming only through expansion of these boundaries to the entire area.

THE PATIENT CARE MARKET

Both hospitals were in agreement that patients residing in East County should be recaptured, but their strategies differed. Dana had the distinct edge in the patient care market: it had a newer facility which, while not easily accessible by highway transportation, was nearer the area's future population growth. By contrast, Westhaven's existing hospital was located in an inaccessible area which some people feared to enter at night and, by the very nature of a district hospital, its admissions tended to be limited to persons residing within the jurisdiction. Thus, Westhaven's strategy for recapture emphasized retaining patients within the district who were leaving for care elsewhere, notably indigent persons seeking care from the Los Medanos County facility in Ignacio.

This recapturing was a real possibility for Westhaven since the county's hospital was also obsolete, and the county director of medical services, Dr. Ronald Becker—a power in both medical affairs and county politics for 17 years—was urging a new approach. He had obtained federal funds to develop a health maintenance organization and had a contract with the state for service of Medicaid patients by this means of health care delivery. In this plan health care would eventually be purchased from other providers in the county rather than rendered directly by the county hospital at Ignacio. This plan made sense for Los Medanos because of its large geographic area with dispersed population centers. It also avoided the political and economic difficulties which Becker foresaw in attempting to rebuild completely the county hospital.

Late in 1974 the Westhaven board had held private discussions with Becker, centering on the possibility that the county would contract with West-haven hospital for hospitalization of all county patients who lived within the District, and perhaps even those residing elsewhere in East County. Dr. Becker drove a hard bargain: he wanted his medical staff to have full hospital privileges, his teaching programs to be incorporated, and a contract between the district and county wherein county patients would be cared for in the Westhaven Hospital on a per diem cost basis. There was discussion of a separate hospital wing for county patients as an alternative. The Westhaven directors, with obvious influence from the hospital's medical staff, finally concluded Becker's terms were too great a price to pay.

In short, Dana's continued existence without consolidation seemed quite possible, although future expansion was blocked. Westhaven's continued existence on its present site was in clear jeopardy; it needed a new location—with or without Dana. If it did not join with Dana then its future, even in a new location, would depend on its success in capturing new patients.

THE MEDICAL PROFESSION

Physicians had been relatively silent since their 1972 petition, so the nature and strength of their support was not known by early 1975. In Westhaven both generalists and specialists seemed to prefer one facility, assuming it would be at Camp Brendham; they did not care about ownership and management. In Riviera, at least some generalists wanted two hospitals to continue, while the specialists wanted one. As for the type of hospital governance, most preferred Dana's private form while others, like many at Westhaven, did not know or care. However, if public governance meant the introduction of "Becker's type of medicine," Dana's physicians were united in strong opposition.

SITE

Both parties knew the stakes were high: the new hospital would undoubtedly be designated as the single growth institution for the area. In the preceding ten years, two planning agencies had switched positions, first stating that Dana's location was preferred, then settling on Westhaven's.[4]

For Westhaven, there was a legal question relating to site. A location other than Brendham would likely be outside the district boundaries, given the availability of other suitably sized plots. But, could a district providing hospital services locate such services outside its boundaries? At a previous time, in connection with a proposal that the hospital operate an ambulance service, the district's attorney had advised that the hospital could not become involved in providing services outside of the district.[5] Of course, this question could be resolved by an expansion of the district.

CHPA'S CLOUT

Not only had planning agencies changed in recent times but so had planning laws. In 1968 California had passed a franchising law which permitted the State Director of Public Health to issue a license for new hospital construction or expansion only after approval by the relevant comprehensive health planning agency. The Westhaven application had been denied by CHPA under the provisions of this law. Due to a loophole created by an amendment to this law, five hospitals throughout the state applied for an exemption to certificate of need review. Two of these were in the jurisdiction of the Bay Area Comprehensive Health Planning Association, the metropolitan federation of which Los Medanos CHPA was a part. One of these was Westhaven. Westhaven and the other Bay Area hospitals were named defendants in a lawsuit brought by CHPA against the state, filed after an administrative official in the State Department of Public Health had written a letter to both hospitals indicating they could proceed.

This, then, was the situation in the spring of 1975. A court date for the lawsuit had yet to be set, but Westhaven felt that it had the legitimate right to proceed with its planning until a court said otherwise. Bay Area CHPA did not seek an injunction to block further development by Westhaven, believing that the court case would soon come to trial and wishing to proceed cautiously because of out-of-court negotiations with the other named hospital. In short, CHPA's real authority was in a legal cloud which seemed unlikely to lift in the near future.

E.   ROUND ONE OF BARGAINING: MAY 1975 TO
      FEBRUARY 1976

THE NEGOTIATORS

With the momentum now running with CHPA, notwithstanding the question of the agency's authority, Los Medanos CHPA's executive, Joseph Hafey, moved quickly to establish the 3–3–4 member transitional group recommended by the Joint Study Committee. Westhaven's delegation was headed by Daniel Modrow, a stationery salesman and former professional football player who had moved to Westhaven a few years previous and had become associated with the Westhaven Promotion League. Modrow, handsome and gregarious, used his football reputation effectively as a method of attracting attention, although his knowledge of hospital and civic affairs was limited.

Dana's delegation was headed by Ron Coss, chairman and longstanding member of its board of trustees, and an executive with Gow Chemical, Riviera's largest industrial plant. Coss had been chairman of the successful fund raising campaign of 1965 that had secured Dana's existing plant. Another appointee was Charles Eames, M.D., chief of Dana's medical staff and leader of the 1972 physicians' effort to arrange a single hospital.

The four CHPA representatives were in no case prominent civic leaders in East County, reflecting Hafey's view that the merger would not proceed unless the principals of each party were directly to engage the issues that had been surfaced by CHPA.

Hafey also arranged for a consultant to contribute to the effort, another outside party who had professional standing in health care planning and experience with hospital mergers. He was David Starkweather, director of the Graduate Program in Hospital Administration at a nearby university. It was agreed that his fees would be borne equally by the two hospitals and CHPA.

SETTING THE RULES OF PLAY

At its first meeting in early April of 1975 the negotiating group came to quick agreement on several procedural items. Meetings would not be open to the public and the results of deliberations would be withheld from the press.[6] Westhaven's wish to record all discussions was accepted, after much discussion, with the proviso that the expletives-included tapes would be heard only by the four other Westhaven hospital directors. It was understood that members of the group could not commit their institutions on the spot, but instead were to act as negotiators. At Starkweather's urging, it was agreed that neither of the hospitals would meet separately with the consultant unless such a meeting was known and approved by the other party. It was also agreed that the basic outline of a new corporate arrangement would first be proposed by Starkweather, accepted or altered by the committee, and recommended to the hospitals. They would then be asked for an in-principle commitment to the recommended organizational scheme. If they approved, there would follow a second phase of implementation. Finally, it was agreed that the four CHPA members of the committee would remain in the background, not always in attendance, but available for response and reinvolvement at crucial times.

Two key decisions defined the scope of discussions. The first was that negotiations should be limited to matters of corporate organization, avoiding broader aspects of health care planning and, specifically, the matter of site location. Secondly, after reviewing the alternative types of organization identified by the previous committee, it was agreed that the committee had been charged with pursuing either an umbrella corporation or total merger rather than a looser form of association.

THE BECKER ISSUE

At the next and first "guts" meeting, Starkweather sought clarification and agreement on the issues at contest. This effort was quickly interrupted by Dana representatives' claim that Westhaven board members were continuing to meet with Dr. Becker of Los Medanos County on a health maintenance organization contract and that this was contrary to the goal of unification to which both parties were committed. Westhaven's Modrow denied the charge, but Dana's representatives remained suspicious; the newspapers of recent times had been filled with reports of a controversy over Becker's power in the county government, and his contacts with Westhaven had been mentioned. It was then revealed that Modrow's denial had been correct technically: there had been no conversations directly with Westhaven board members—but conversations had been held through an agent of the board, Gregory Fall, its consulting architect for new hospital developments.[7] Fall, present at the negotiating meeting as an observer, admitted to these conversations, stating that they were part of his efforts to develop a total health care system model for East County.

With this admission came a demand from Dana that all future contacts with the county on this matter be made jointly by both hospitals. Starkweather supported this position, believing that folding this aspect of developments into the negotiations added glue to hospital unification efforts. The Westhaven representatives agreed. Yet it became known two weeks later that Fall had met again with Becker, which he explained as a mistake in the scheduling. This precipitated a successful effort by Dana's representatives to have Fall thrown out of the negotiating sessions.[8]

DANA DOCTORS SHOW THEIR HAND

While this was taking place, a letter had been sent by Dana to CHPA, over Dr. Eames' signature as chief of the medical staff, requesting that CHPA's moratorium on expansion at Dana be removed. The letter included statistics on increasing hospital admissions and underscored the frustration of physicians who had come to the area in response to the need for services, only to find insufficient hospital space and no apparent hope of relief.

The June 1975 meeting of CHPA's Health Facilities Committee was packed with Dana physicians, and a single Westhaven hospital director. Dana representatives argued that the earlier moratorium had been a voluntary one, due to Dana's withdrawal of its expansion plans pending unification talks, and that due to complicated adjustment and variance procedures in the certificate of need procedure, Dana could be unfairly frozen to its present capacity if the merger discussions fell apart. The committee eventually voted for Dana's request.

All of this took place outside of the negotiating group, which increased Starkweather's suspicion that it represented a separatists' move on the part of Dana's physicians, possibly supported by the hospital generally. If so, he reasoned, physicians needed to be linked more actively to the merger proceedings; he urged the immediate formation of a joint medical staff group to pursue a common medical staff as an essential parallel to corporate unification.

This became the first item of discussion at the next negotiating session. The committee turned to Dr. Eames for an appraisal of current physician attitude about merger and about forming the recommended subcommittee. He urged that until a new corporation were worked out, there was little sense in their involvement as they would not know what to react to. After this, Eames was relatively quiet as a negotiating team member and subsequently resigned from the committee.

THE SITE

Despite prior agreement to the contrary, discussion of hospital location was pervasive. In early June 1975, following Westhaven's receipt of a state letter granting it leave to proceed with construction, Westhaven officials invited Dana representatives to sit in on their Building Committee deliberations, chaired by architect Fall. Ronald Coss' response was immediate: the Brendham site was beyond Dana's consideration, and therefore it could not participate. Westhaven's representatives countered that Dana's administrator would be welcome to sit in on an informational basis only, with no implications attached. The next meeting of Westhaven's Building Committee was in a few days; Dana's administrator did not attend, claiming a conflict in schedules.

Starkweather calculated that the entire negotiations could break off at this early point, Westhaven was in a huff that Dana would not even attend its planning meetings, even with the understanding that no commitments were implied: its olive branch towards joint planning had been rebuffed. And Dana refused to consider Brendham as even a possible site. Yet, in informal conversations following the meeting, Westhaven's Modrow hinted that Westhaven might be willing to give up its unilateral control over Brendham developments if Dana would accept the site, and a Dana appointee suggested that Dana might accept the Brendham site if it was in control of developments. To Starkweather this evidenced that both parties wished at the least to remain at the negotiating table.

HOSPITAL BOARD SHAKE-UPS

Dana board president Ron Coss was well known not only for his position on the Brendham site question but also for his reservations about collaborating with Westhaven. He had been active in the 1961 medical industrial consortium to defeat the annexation of Riviera to Westhaven's hospital district. However, Coss' hard line position did not enjoy full support of the Dana board. The détente point of view was best expressed by William Forrest, a 45-year old civic affairs enthusiast who owned a small insurance agency in Riviera and was a resident of the small community of Pinewood. Forrest reflected the agricultual East County sentiment on the Dana board, as compared to Coss' Riviera loyalties. At the annual meeting of the Dana Memorial Hospital Corporation, held in late June of 1975, Forrest was nominated from the floor for president. Coss quickly declined renomination and Forrest was elected. Subsequent interpretation of this shift, which had taken most by surprise, was that an agreement had been reached on the part of Dana's conservatives to let the liberals have a try at effecting something worthwhile with Westhaven.

This brought to the fore a new Dana position on the Brendham site: Dana would consider the site if it had been selected from among several options and if its consideration had been made by the new corporation called for by the CHPA report. It subsequently leaked out that this position was stated by Forrest only after he had assembled the entire Dana board in an informal caucus and obtained a 10 to 2 vote of confidence. Forrest's reasoning was that Dana's future ability to obtain donated funds from the community would be lost if the hospital trustees automatically acquiesced to Brendham. But if the Brendham site had been selected by an impartial group, compared to being mandated by Riviera as a condition of proceeding, Dana's leadership might subsequently convince the community of the appropriateness of the move.

At about the same time there was also a reorganization of the Westhaven board: for the first time in two months the board was brought back to full strength and had a new chairman. The board's longstanding chairman, Anthony Luciano, had died. Following the procedure outlined in district law for vacancies such as this, the board solicited applicants for the vacant seat and from nine applicants selected Bill Sora, a landowner and developer prominent in the Westhaven Promotion League. Sora subsequently declined the appointment after he realized it would require divulging his financial holdings and contributions, terming the new state financial disclosure law a complete invasion of personal privacy. In Sora's place the board appointed another applicant who had served a previous six-year term as director, ending in 1972. This person was nominated by Modrow. Modrow was then elected chairman, upon the nomination of another director who was now Westhaven's trustee of longest standing and assumed to be the board's link to the Westhaven Promotion League following Luciano's death.

The way things happened it looked like Modrow's star had risen, that he had been endorsed by Westhaven's subgovernment, and that his line of détente, like Forrest's, had been put to a test and survived. At the next meeting of the negotiating committee, the atmosphere was perceptibly different.

ON WITH THE UMBRELLA CORPORATION:
THE CONSULTANT'S RECOMMENDATIONS

At earlier meetings, Starkweather had reviewed various examples of hospital corporate integrations with the committee. It agreed that several management contract-type integrations did not deal sufficiently with the important question of governance, that a holding company-type arrangement dealt too narrowly with assets to the exclusion of health care delivery questions, and that federation-type combinations which led to certain trade-off agreements between member hospitals might be useful as a first stage, but were insufficient for eventual hospital unification. The committee's preference was for some sort of reorganization that would eventually replace the existing corporate powers while initially preserving their identity and influence. It also expressed interest in pursuing several types of joint powers authorities which Starkweather had sketched out.

Several threads of concern ran throughout these discussions. Must capital and operating funds of the two hospitals be commingled? Should control in a new corporation be based on initial investment or some other measure? Could a public hospital district legitimately transfer its assets to a private corporation? Must existing corporations be abolished? On this last issue, Starkweather obtained a vague agreement that in the long-run, control must pass in total to a new corporation. Modrow granted that this implied the possibility of abandoning the hospital district.

Starkweather's presentation of a written proposal in early August of 1975 occurred against this general background. His report contained three main parts: criteria for any new corporate arrangement, a recommended organization, and mechanisms for transition from the existing to the proposed organization.

Starkweather's four criteria for reorganization were that: 1) initially, control should be evenly distributed between existing hospitals, with appointments from both constituting a controlling proportion of the new corporation's board seats; 2) the new arrangement should incorporate at the outset the influence of elements of East County not properly represented by appointments from the two hospitals, and eventually the board should reflect all geographic areas of East County in proportion to their population; 3) the new corporation should be capable of superseding the existing hospitals, although such should not be the automatic eventuality. Circumstances of the future might make it desirable for one or both existing corporations to continue, particularly in the case of Westhaven district's taxing authority, coupled with the future possibility of expanding its boundaries; and 4) the new corporation's authority should be substantial, defined as the ability to obtain and receive capital monies, purchase and hold title to real assets, plan for comprehensive health services, operate services, enter contracts, recruit and establish a medical staff, and obtain broad citizen input.

Starkweather proposed two new corporations. One would be a private nonprofit entity, operating as a hospital management corporation. The other would be a public corporation, a joint powers authority to be created by any two or more of the five existing governments in the area—the Westhaven Hospital District, the city of Westhaven, the city of Riviera, the city of Pinewood, and the county of Los Medanos. This authority would obtain capital monies through bond issue and own the physical assets of a new hospital.[9] It would lease these facilities for operations to the proposed new management corporation. This operating corporation would assume full responsbility for a new facility and could also run whatever operations might continue at the two existing hospitals, which in Dana's case could be for a substantial time.

Starkweather argued that neither corporate form alone could satisfy all the criteria. In particular, the Westhaven Hospital District could transfer assets only to another public entity. Yet, only a private corporation would have the flexibility to assume responsibility for integrated hospital services on a phased basis, as compared to a sudden death transition. There were several reasons why he felt this gradualism was important. The strongly held but different traditions of hospital governance were simply not going to be readily or immediately abandoned. The broad geographic base of the governing board recommended by the CHPA Study Committee appeared to be the only logical and defensible takeout for this situation. Yet, it would be impossible to achieve this through the joint powers authority alone because substantial portions of East County were not incorporated and therefore its residents would not obtain representation unless Los Medanos County were involved—and the county's involvement was very sticky because of the Riviera doctors' disdain for "Becker medicine."

As for the concerns about commingling of funds, Starkweather recommended full eventual reimbursement to the existing hospitals for whatever initial investments of assets and working capital were provided. He hoped this would quell the arguments that control of the new corporation should be based on initial investment, which would very likely be different between the two hospitals, allowing governance to be based instead on areawide population.

For the joint powers authority, Starkweather suggested a board of seven members, each serving for four years. The number appointed by each government would be in rough proportion to the percent of total East County population represented by it, with the county representing unincorporated areas only and with the city of Westhaven and the Westhaven Hospital District sharing appointments so that there was not overrepresentation of the population within overlapping jurisdictions. For the private corporation, a 14-member board was specified, drawn from four sources whose number of appointments changed over time in order to phase the board from early dominance by the two hospitals to a population proportioned membership:

	Westhaven District	Appointed by: Dana	JPA	New Board
Initial	4	4	2	4
Four years hence	3	3	2	6
Six years hence	2	2	2	8

To obtain areawide geographic representation under this scheme, Stark-weather recommended that East Los Medanos be laid out in six geographic areas of roughly equal population size, using the most recent census data. As each appointment was made, over time, the composition of the total board would be required to contain at least two persons from each of the six geographies.

NEGOTIATORS' REACTIONS

The August 7, 1975 meeting at which the consultant's proposal was discussed was known to be the last in the intense three-month series of negotiations. Vacations were pending, in particular Starkweather's, and the proceedings had become dependent on his guidance.

The general reaction to the reorganization plan was favorable. Dana representatives claimed to understand the proposal and accept it. Westhaven representatives had questions of clarification and expressed several reservations. Modrow continued to feel that the two hospitals would inevitably contribute unequally to the new venture, given the comparative obsolescence of Westhaven's plant compared to Dana's and that Westhaven's larger investment should therefore be matched with increased control.

Westhaven representatives questioned the legality of the plan, particularly as to the extent of permissible delegation by hospital district directors. Starkweather said he had reviewed his plan with legal counsel and was satisfied that it was basically legal. However, it was agreed that direct and formal legal consultation was an important step and that this might be obtained during the summer vacation lull. There was some controversy over how such advice should be obtained. Starkweather urged a single outside party with known expertise on such matters. He suggested two names. This idea was acceptable to the Dana representatives; however, the Westhaven members felt that their district's regular legal counsel had to be used. They cited examples of his general reputation on such matters in addition to his intimate knowledge of the Westhaven situation. Modrow stated that the selection of legal counsel would have to be approved by his full board.

Next, there was a great deal of discussion on Starkweather's plan of phasing control, particularly as regards the change in board composition four years after formation of the new nonprofit corporation. Dana representatives argued that this transition time should be shorter, and Westhaven's that it be longer.

Finally, there was some discussion of Starkweather's suggestion of corporate names: East Los Medanos Health Authority for the joint powers authority and San Benito Regional Hospital for the private nonprofit corporation.[10]

Discussions of names seemed to be a good sign. The meeting adjourned with agreement that each hospital's delegation would recommend Starkweather's plan to their boards for consideration at their August meetings and that each hospital should decide on Starkweather's continued involvement, his having specified that the next level of detail should come only after in-principle agreement to his general proposal. Finally, Westhaven's Modrow again extended an invitation to Dana representatives to participate in Westhaven's continuing hospital planning. This time it seemed possible that this planning might yet end up being a joint endeavor, since Dana would participate if it could do so via the new corporations.

THE BIG LULL

The intended three week break in formal negotiations extended to a six month hiatus during which informal negotiations continued.

The first action was by Dana's board, in late August of 1975. It commented in writing that the study was progressing satisfactorily, urged that specifics be pursued as soon as possible, and requested Starkweather's continued consultation.

The next action was reflected in a letter from Westhaven's Modrow to Starkweather, dated September 3rd. Modrow wrote that the Westhaven board was anxious to continue further consideration and authorized continued consultation. However, the board was not prepared to make any final decision on the program to be adopted, a reluctance based on the fact that three director's terms were about to expire and their continuance or replacement would not be determined before elections in early November. Accordingly, the board suggested waiting to learn the election results before negotiating further.

A PERIOD OF SPECULATION AND REFLECTION

The lull in formal negotiations ran well beyond November, because Westhaven's newly elected trustees did not take office until early January, 1975, with the interim board containing one lame duck trustee. This person was known to be against collaboration with Dana. The two most popular vote-getters were Modrow, returned to office, and Melissa Honor, a 30-year-old black woman who previously had staffed the CHPA Joint Study Committee under Hafey's guidance and had followed through on her intentions to seek a hospital board seat via election when she had not been appointed from among the nine applicants who sought the seat made available by Luciano's death in early 1974. Ms. Honor had campaigned hard and had won widespread support from Westhaven's minority community. Since she had previously worked with CHPA, it was assumed that she held the planning view. In short, the new Westhaven board, coupled with Modrow's pledge to the negotiating committee to lead his board in the direction of collaboration, all boded extremely well for the merger.

Unable to bring the parties to the negotiating table, but authorized to proceed by Westhaven and urged to do so by Dana, Starkweather continued informal contacts. He found widely differing perceptions of the state of merger affairs. Dana's new president, William Forrest, was concerned about his hospital's declining influence with CHPA, as compared to Westhaven's increasing role. CHPA's switch on the hospital location issue now made it appear that Dana was the reluctant party. Forrest counted the votes on the Westhaven board and concluded that beyond Modrow, who was the best thinker, and one other member who would screw Dana, there were three other uncommitted directors, each with long remaining terms of office.

Westhaven's Modrow felt that the long history was one of Westhaven's trying to get together with Dana but Dana's wanting no part of Westhaven's orientation to the minority community, both in its patient services and in its employment policies. Modrow noted that Coss was from Birmingham, Alabama, and that Forrest had also been raised in the South. He felt that if Westhaven could retain sufficient influence, coupled with specific agreements on affirmative action policies, the merger might proceed. Modrow reported that his colleagues were generally opposed to the private nonprofit approach, feeling that Westhaven would put up most of the money with Dana giving little; but he did not close the door on a nonprofit corporation as part of the organizational solution. As for site, Modrow felt it was unfortunate that Westhaven's hospital was in a ghetto where people were reluctant to go, meaning that he did not support those who felt that Westhaven should simply rebuild at its present location. Finally, Modrow felt that residents of the district were apprehensive that there might not be a hospital—that the district would lose one altogether.

Architect Fall's reflection was that the Westhaven board was very used to and enjoyed full immersion in hospital operating details, yet Starkweather's proposal called for substantial delegation of Westhaven's board members' responsibilities. In order for this to work, the directors had to have something left to do. This was why he had pursued the operation of a health maintenance organization and community outreach programs in his contacts of previous months with Dr. Becker, feeling that the district could legitimately remain directly involved in the provision of nonhospital health care services while delegating its hospital responsibilities to other parties. He said that he planned to use his influence with the board to advance this strategy.

At CHPA, Hafey was spending time buttonholing individual Westhaven directors, where he felt lay the key to the merger. He counted two definite yes votes: Modrow's and Honor's. A third vote was a real possibility, given that pressure could be brought to bear through Hafey's contacts with organized labor in Los Medanos. Hafey felt the remaining two votes would be called by the Buffi machine and were unreachable. On the site question, he had heard that one county supervisor owned land near Camp Brendham and that this could ultimately be influential. While Hafey felt that the merger decision would depend on one-on-one attention, he was worried about a general feeling of insecurity and lack of control on the Westhaven board. He did not believe the board understood Starkweather's proposal, which made it difficult for its members to justify the merger to district residents. Hafey concluded that the Westhaven trustees remained suspicious of Dana: to some Westhaven directors Dana's enthusiasm for Starkweather's plan meant only that Dana had figured out how to take advantage of Westhaven.

THE STRANGE PATHWAY BACK TO NEGOTIATIONS

By late January of 1976 it was clear that Westhaven was purposely dragging its feet. Modrow reported that he had yet to decide which members to appoint to a new negotiating team. He also complained of the press of other business, listing 16 meetings between mid-January and mid-March to which he was already committed. Another reason for delay had gone unstated: depositions in the CHPA's lawsuit had been scheduled, and Westhaven's attorney had advised that some break in the legal deadlock might take place by the end of January.

Starkweather knew that Dana was anxious to proceed and that further delays could result in diminished Dana support of the agreements reached in mid-1975. One reason for this was a January 14 newspaper article reporting the Westhaven board's review of a report by architect Fall which included a hospital construction schedule calling for final approval of plans in May, groundbreaking in July, and the completion of construction by November of the following year.[11] Dana took all of this as an act of bad faith. Starkweather called on Westhaven's Modrow to move the questions of corporate legality to the front burner by honoring his previous commitment that the lawyers of both hospitals jointly review Starkweather's plan and render an opinion.[12]

Then Hafey applied his form of pressure: he announced to both parties that a meeting of the full negotiating committee would soon be scheduled.

The letter stating this implied that CHPA might make Starkweather's study public, a possibility Hafey knew the Westhaven directors would not like to see transpire, given its unilateral actions of mid-January to advance a new hospital. The break came in mid-February: Modrow called Starkweather on a Sunday afternoon and asked for an immediate meeting with Hafey, Forrest, and himself. At breakfast the next day, Modrow laid out Westhaven's new posture. First, it wanted to move into immediate and intense negotiations, to last no longer than 45 days, by dividing the committee into subgroups in a manner suggested previously by Starkweather. Second, he wanted the overall negotiating group to be expanded from three to four members from each hospital, to allow Westhaven to involve an additional director. Third, he specified that as an act of good faith CHPA should drop its litigation.

All parties were enthusiastic about the return to negotiations. Forrest reserved judgment on Modrow's plan for breaking the activity into subtasks. Starkweather felt that the 45-day deadline was too ambitious, given the delays that had taken place in obtaining legal opinon and the time it would take to organize and orient new negotiators. Hafey made it clear that the litigation would not be dropped, which did not seem to surprise Modrow.

F. ROUND TWO OF BARGAINING: FEBRUARY—JULY 1976

THE NEGOTIATORS REGIRD

There were significant changes to the negotiating committee. A Westhaven director of longstanding was added, a person reported to be on the fence on the merger matter. For Dana, Dr. Eames resigned, claiming frustration with the whole affair and the wish to spend more time with his family. His replacement was a senior statesman of the Dana medical staff and a longstanding participant and supporter of efforts to improve health care delivery in East County, including hospital unification. For Dana's expansion seat another trustee was named, a person known also to be both influential and undecided on merger.

CHPA's appointment to replace one member was interesting: Zig Wagner, Executive Secretary of the Central Labor Council of Los Medanos County, board member of CHPA, and political activist. Hafey reasoned that Wagner's labor forces might be brought to bear on the situation, particularly in the labor town of Westhaven. Additionally, Wagner's experience in labor negotiations might be useful in the next phase.

In planning for the upcoming meetings, Starkweather reasoned that there had to be some way of involving more Westhaven board members, notwithstanding the law which prohibited attendance of more than two district directors at any nonpublic meeting. Taking his clue from Modrow's request for subgroups, Starkweather proposed five task forces to consist of up to six persons each, appointed jointly by the two hospitals. The topics for consideration were: 1) corporate organization and legality, 2) financing, 3) services and facilities planning, 4) medical staff development, and 5) community relations.

The first meeting, held in late February of 1976, achieved quick agreement to continue private discussions without comment to the press and agreement that both hospitals would instruct their respective attorneys to examine Starkweather's plan and develop a single report. A compromise was developed on the task forces. Westhaven's Modrow had come to the meeting armed with appointments for each group, including all Westhaven trustees, but Forrest was not so prepared. It was agreed that two subcommittees be established, instead of five, to deal with the most pressing matters of corporate legality and facility planning. Dana would appoint its representatives to these two groups within a week.

Shortly after this organizing meeting Forrest contacted Starkweather and reported a lengthy discussion which had been held with Dana's board executive committee. The prevailing opinion was that Westhaven was still stalling, that it was not entering the new negotiations with sincerity, and that because of this two things were necessary: 1) the new corporate arrangement must be developed first so that a new and more broadly based group of persons could substitute for the existing principals, and 2) Westhaven trustees must formally accept in principle the Starkweather proposal, as had Dana. Given these conditions, Forrest was unwilling to appoint Dana's representatives to any subcommittees, despite his previous commitment to do so. This position was subsequently contained in a formal letter from Forrest to Starkweather, with a copy to Modrow and Hafey.

The letter committed to writing the charge of Westhaven's insincerity which risked the very continuance of negotiations, as evidenced by the events of the next meeting. There was a long argument over whether Westhaven should be allowed to continue tape recordings, Dana officials having learned that written transcripts of the tapes were routinely distributed to all Westhaven directors and thus available for leaks. (A compromise was worked out where tape recording would be continued but transcripts would not be distributed). Forrest then reiterated Dana's insistence on formal evidence of commitment from Westhaven, to which Modrow countered with two points: the new Westhaven board did not fully understand Starkweather's proposals; and, of what it did understand, it remained in doubt about its legality.

On Modrow's first point, Starkweather agreed to meet with the full Westhaven board in a working session[13] if Dana would consent to this unilateral relationship, which it did. To preserve parity, it was agreed that Starkweather would also meet with the Dana trustees.

This did nothing to break the deadlock over the appropriate sequence of future actions. At the next meeting Zig Wagner moved quickly into the void, resorting to the techniques of labor-management negotiations where the conflicting parties are placed in separate caucus rooms and a mediator moves between. He won agreement of both sides that, in return for a formal commitment to direction by Westhaven, all issues would be regarded as negotiable, including the question of site. The Starkweather report would be used as the basis for negotiations.

The meeting ended with Modrow's promising to urge this commitment on his board and, significantly, Westhaven's new committee member stating that he would vote for the merger scheme if it was demonstrated to be legally possible.

Starkweather approached the two separate board meetings figuring that 1) the negotiators were barely at the table; and 2) the legality of his proposal might be in doubt since the attorneys appeared to be having trouble coming to agreement. Thus, he was grateful for the delay in scheduled committee proceedings by his separate meetings with the two hospital boards.

ENTER THE LAWYERS

It was the last day of April, 1975 when the negotiators met to receive the lawyers' report—a 30-page brief prepared by the two hospital's legal counsels. Starkweather's objective of a joint report had been achieved, although throughout the meeting it was unclear where Westhaven's attorney stood, having stated that he was the District's legal technician with no wish or authority to involve himself in policy matters.

The brief was in response to eleven questions of which five turned out to be crucial: 1) What were the minimal acts of governance which directors of a hospital district must take directly rather than delegating to a new corporation? 2) Did Starkweather's plan involve a conflict of interest if directors of the existing hospitals were also directors of a corporation with which they contracted? 3) Was the proposed joint powers authority constrained in any way in accomplishing what had been proposed? 4) Were there any limitations on Westhaven, assuming its continuance as a district, in contracting for hospital services rendered outside as well as inside the district? 5) Could the proposed relationship between the joint powers authority and the private management corporation be made legally binding?[14]

The situation, then, was very complex, but the lawyers had reduced the numerous conceivable legal relationships to three plausible ones.[15] Of the three, the negotiating committee was in favor of a joint powers authority-operator plan which evenly balanced initial board powers between the two hospitals, eliminated most problems of delegation to the new corporations, and called for the holding of a license to operate the proposed new hospital by a joint powers authority, leaving dormant the role of hospital operations by the Westhaven District directors. The only possible obstacle the lawyers saw concerned conflict of interest: it could be construed that Westhaven District directors who were likewise serving on the proposed operating corporation's board were in conflict because the corporation's services were being performed for the district.

The attorneys recommended that this question of legal doubt be resolved by state legislative clarification. The attorneys had already assessed such a possibility: legislative relief was quite possible through a special interest bill that might take up to a year to be passed. However, consideration of such a bill would likely bring to the fore a matter of concern that had been lying dormant in the California legislature for some time: the proliferation of joint powers authorities. A view was developing in the legislature that such units of government were beyond the reach of the voters and thus should be limited.[16] For Westhaven-Dana, the solution to one problem might create another, with the wiser course of action perhaps being to let the legislative sleeping dog lie.

The negotiating committee discussed briefly a suggested fourth option: proceed with the private corporation only, as an interim step. The meeting adjourned.

All of this left Starkweather and Hafey on the horns of a dilemma. On the one hand, a new single private corporation seemed to be the only immediate legally clean development. On the other hand, the Westhaven negotiators were now pushing hard for new consideration of expanding the tax district. The dilemma was made more apparent by a widely reported comment in which Westhaven's Modrow advised a Dana trustee that expanding the tax district was the only way to go. This was coupled with another Modrow statement reported in the press, that a final decision on whether Westhaven should merge with Dana should be taken to the voters.

Furthermore, time was now of the greatest essence: Modrow had just written another letter to Starkweather, stating that Westhaven's one year of accreditation was about up and therefore the Westhaven Community Hospital's willingness to extend merger discussions with Dana Memorial Hospital needed clarification. This willingness was predicated on quickly and finally concluding the matter, with Modrow laying out a schedule of meetings which ended one month hence. Also, Modrow called for appointments to the two subcommittees which had previously been agreed upon, but which he knew were objectionable to Forrest.

Forrest still would not appoint to the two task forces. Starkweather did finally obtain his agreement to an investigation of the possibility of expanding the Westhaven district. Forrest had recently discussed this matter informally with civic leaders and had concluded that such was not feasible. Starkweather agreed, but argued that it was essential to go through the process of concluding this with Westhaven officials; otherwise, the district directors were placed in the awkward political position of appearing casually to have abandoned the district approach to hospital ownership and governance.

Starkweather was now forced to consider some new financing exigencies. The bottom had just dropped out of the tax-exempt bond market.[17] He reasoned that potential purchasers of the issues of his recommended joint power authority might question the resources behind it: the authority might be viewed as a novel entity with the purchase price of its bonds increasing to the point of eliminating the advantage of obtaining capital funds in this way.[18]

Worse yet for financing of a new facility, the nongovernment loan market had suddenly dried up in California, where a usury law prohibits lending rates in excess of 10 percent. This had recently limited the flow into the state of private capital funds—monies loaned by lending syndicates, insurance companies, union trust funds, etc.—since with the high interest rates then prevailing these lenders could invest outside of California and make returns in excess of 10 percent.

Starkweather concluded that 1) the money market for hospital construction had suddenly become volatile, unpredictable, and harsh—time was needed for the market to stabilize; and 2) the financing picture remained clouded by the CHPA-Westhaven lawsuit which had yet to be settled and which could become attenuated by appeals.

In his new written proposal to the negotiating committee, fashioned in early May, 1976, the consultant argued for a corporate plan that would make sense to the present situation and preserve as many financing options as possible for the future. Starkweather went on to describe a strictly private corporate solution to the unification effort as inappropriate: it did not respect Westhaven's tradition of hospital governance and was politically unfeasible. And, since the availability of strictly private capital financing was also uncertain, it would be unwise at this time to close the door on the future possibility of district-issued tax-exempt revenue bonds as a way of financing hospital facilities.

Starkweather proposed an interim measure—the establishment of a new private corporation with quasipublic features. The corporation would balance the distribution of control between the existing hospitals, as previously proposed, and there would be proportionate representation of all elements of East County not represented by hospital appointments. This also had been in the previous proposal, but the situation now required that the transition from hospital to areawide influence be incorporated at the outset rather than evolving over time; Starkweather felt that Dana would bolt from any other scheme. Two new provisions were that the new corporation would conduct all of its business as if it were public, adopting in its articles of incorporation all relevant portions of the California law that applied to public bodies, and that the corporation would make full and regular public financial disclosure.

The new enterprise would be called the "Eastern Los Medanos Regional Hospital Consortium" and would have full authority to 1) plan and locate a hospital to serve the area, 2) plan and pursue long-term capital funding, 3) obtain the legislative changes that had been outlined, 4) form a medical staff, and 5) obtain broad citizen participation and understanding. The consortium would receive initial start-up monies from the two existing hospitals, to be paid back over time. It would have freedom of action and discretion in decision making, limited only by the financial commitment to long-term debt, and those things specifically mandated by law to district hospital directors. The consortium would be obligated to report all of its actions to both hospital boards and seek their advice; however, the boards would not have veto authority over its actions. Finally, the entire board membership of the consortium would have to be approved by both boards, as would any replacements in membership. At such time as long-term financing was arranged and legal obstacles to the establishment of a joint power authority were lifted, this corporation would then be modified into the management corporation previously proposed. Any change at that time in its duties or obligations would rest with its incorporators, acting jointly.

The consortium board would consist of two appointments each from Westhaven and Dana, one appointment each by the three cities of Riviera, Westhaven, and Pinewood, and three at-large members to be identified by the initial seven appointees and selected to obtain areawide geographic representation in the manner previously recommended.

In short, the board composition represented a melding of the concepts previously attributed to two corporations, and a direct and early involvement of the three relevant cities as a useful prelude to their subsequent formation of a joint powers authority.

At the next meeting, on May 15, 1976, reactions were clear and direct. Nobody quarrelled with the two new features of publicness. All duties and authorities of the new corporation were acceptable. There was just one objection. It came from the Westhaven delegation: the board composition was overbalanced in Dana's favor, since only two of the ten seats were influenced directly by the district. Dana representatives countered that their hospital was in the same circumstance, to which Westhaven officials said that even if the city of Riviera appointment were tallied to Dana and the city of Westhaven appointment attributed to the district's interests, that left Dana one seat ahead with the Pinewood appointment. Despite this, the meeting ended with both parties agreeing to take Starkweather's proposal to their respective boards.

After the meeting Hafey, Starkweather, and Wagner mused. The air seemed finally to be clear: all peripheral questions had either been negotiated to settlement or provided with a pathway to solution. The two central issues—the same two that had been identified two years previously by the CHPA Joint Study Committee and years before that by various other task forces—had now been reduced to one. On the site issue, Dana had capitulated to Westhaven on the Brendham location. A sense of exchange dictated that Westhaven give something on the other issue, control. One board seat was all that was expected; all else hung in the balance.

In two days Dana officials announced by letter that the new plan was entirely acceptable and urged prompt formation of the new corporation.

ANOTHER LULL

There then followed another lull in negotiations, this one lasting for two months, again due to circumstances within the Westhaven board. For one, an unfortunate series of accidents and illnesses had beset two of its directors; for another, Westhaven's lawyers had entered a plea for summary dismissal of CHPA's lawsuit, and a court hearing first set for early June was postponed a month. A final reason was an internal power shift, centered on the unification issue. Melissa Honor, one of the district's two new directors, had gained new influence and was in a swing vote position. She had previously been informally rejected by the other directors, who often met in private working sessions to which she was seldom invited. Apparently, she threatened her board colleagues with public complaint about this treatment—the last thing they wanted from a black female—and she was subsequently not only included but took a leadership position; her knowledge of health care planning was well above that of any of her colleagues.

During this time Dana's commitment seemed to be fainting away, despite its quick affirmative reply to Starkweather's plan. Forrest was increasingly nervous and angry, as well he might be, facing in late June another annual meeting of the Dana Memorial Hospital Corporation.

THE WESTHAVEN COUNTER

Again, the break came on a weekend, with another telephone call from Modrow to Starkweather requesting that he and Hafey attend a working session of the Westhaven board as soon as possible to discuss some remaining details of Starkweather's proposal. Modrow's manner belied this rather inconsequential purpose, which impression Starkweather passed on to Hafey who interrupted his vacation to join the meeting the following evening. The session was at Modrow's home, where several of the district directors had already been together for awhile when Hafey and Starkweather arrived. They were seated around the kitchen table in a manner that suggested a smoke-filled back room.

Modrow went right to the point. He handed Starkweather and Hafey a three-page letter, accompanied by a 22-page manuscript entitled "Proposal for the Formation of the East Los Medanos County Health Care Federation." The letter stated first that it represented the unanimous position of the Westhaven board. It then went on to say the board found it unable to support the current merger proposal, because: 1) the proposed organization did not assure that people within the present district boundaries were guaranteed an equal voice in the future; 2) the proposal relegated the Westhaven Hospital District to a position of influence not in keeping with the board's interpretation of the peoples' mandate; 3) there were no guarantees that there would be a new facility, nor that it would be built on the Brendham site; 4) there appeared to be significant legal obstacles to the proposed merger, which virtually mandated dissolution of the district; and 5) a joint powers authority/management corporation did not appear to be in the best interests of the district at this time.

The letter went on to state that the Westhaven board continued to subscribe to the goal of comprehensive health care for the entire area and that alternative means existed which recognized the fact that the climate did not currently exist to make a merger workable. The alternative, submitted for review, consideration, and expedient adoption, was for a federation—a formal organization which would span but not replace the two hospitals. The federation would be funded and formed on an equal basis by both facilities, with a nine-member board consisting of two board members and one medical staff member and one community representative from each hospital, and a nonvoting moderator appointed by CHPA. The federation would be a private corporation accountable to the public. The federation's list of responsibilities included 1) the allocation of specialty services between the two hospitals; 2) the development of shared services of benefit to both hospitals; 3) participation in the planning of any expansion or replacement at either facility; 4) development of uniform standards of care; 5) recruitment of new physicians; 6) establishing a framework for a joint medical staff; and 7) the initiation of new programs as deemed appropriate. The list finished with two items which Modrow underscored: 8) establishment of the framework for cooperative efforts toward the ultimate goal of merged facilities; and 9) the fostering of strong local control of East County health programs.

The letter closed with two concessions. Westhaven would open immediate negotiations with Dana and CHPA relative to the possibility of reducing
the number of beds to be built by the district at the Brendham site, leading
to an eventual parity between the two hospitals in the number of beds "to the
satisfaction of all concerned." Further, the district would consider the possibility of a joint application with Dana to CHPA for the total number of beds
needed in the area, estimated to be between 130 and 150 beds.

Modrow asked for both Starkweather's and Hafey's reactions and added
one specific request of each: that Starkweather be the district's representative
in presenting and arguing for the federation proposal with Dana, and that
Hafey, as an expression of confidence, withdraw the CHPA lawsuit.

Both Hafey and Starkweather reacted angrily to what they considered
Westhaven's deceit.[19] It was now clear that during the lull of recent weeks,
due allegedly to circumstances beyond the board's control, Westhaven had
been moving with determination toward what Starkweather termed a different
direction by 180 degrees: preserving two hospitals rather than creating one.
Starkweather was peeved by what he judged to be a lack of confidence, since
the discussion had revealed that Westhaven's new position had been designed
by another consultant, putting the district in the peculiar position of hiring
two advisors to work at cross purposes. He refused to be Westhaven's negotiating agent. Hafey was angry at what he termed blackmail: the condition
that in order to proceed even with this limited proposal the lawsuit would
have to be dropped; he refused.

In response to the question of how the CHPA board would view this
counterproposal, Hafey speculated that it might accept it if there were real
teeth in the federation. Starkweather felt that the federation as currently
described had no teeth and suggested that in order to provide it with such,
a clause be inserted binding both parties to arbitration in case of differences
of opinion on the allocation of services. The board members agreed to this[20]
and subsequently incorporated it in their proposal.

The next day the Westhaven proposal was hand carried to Dana, with
the request that a definite negotiation period be established for a period not
exceeding three weeks, which would result in conclusions.

LOCKED-DOORS NEGOTIATION

The CHPA-Westhaven lawsuit was set for trial on July 14, 1975. The next
and probably final meeting of the negotiating group was set for July 15. The
CHPA membership of the negotiating committee met with Hafey and Starkweather, and it was decided to seek the agreement of both hospital parties
to a locked door negotiating session, to which each party would commit attendance until some sort of solution was agreed. Zig Wagner was asked to
manage the session.

Knowing that the Westhaven counterproposal would be not only unacceptable but offensive to Dana, Wagner felt that the goal for the session should be simply to preserve the status quo, i.e., freeze independent actions of both hospitals and obtain commitments to the continuing engagement of the two parties under guidelines which would seek a compromise between Westhaven's federation and Starkweather's consortium plans.

Melissa Honor headed the Westhaven delegation to the July 15th session. The second representative was the district's other newest director, elected at the same time as Ms. Honor. Westhaven came out of the first caucus with the proposition that it would cease its new hospital activity under terms of a planning freeze of defined length, if CHPA would withdraw its lawsuit without prejudice. Further, Westhaven would take formal and public action committing itself to the "Starkweather concept" with the understanding that six key items remained subject to its final approval: site, working capital and start-up expenses, approval of budgets, approval of board composition, approval of long-term debt, and approval of any by-laws and changes in by-laws of the new corporation.

Dana representatives came out of the first caucus revealing their strategy for the evening: wait and see. The delegation had no specific proposal, stating instead that it fully supported Starkweather's recommendations and would respond to whatever Westhaven proposed anew.

There then followed a long general session, dominated by a replay by Melissa Honor of Westhaven's federation counterplan. She emphasized that any tighter form of unification was not at present possible due to the mistrusts involved; a looser working relationship would allow mutual trust to develop. She also argued that a unified health system for the area could be developed from a two-hospital base: merger of hospitals was not a necessity. Westhaven's other negotiator seemed more conciliatory, stating that Mrs. Honor's comments were not those of Westhaven's trustees but rather her own.

This obvious difference between the two, even to the point of animosity, gave Wagner, Hafey, and Starkweather hope that the federation plan was in fact a minority scheme and that there was still room for a Westhaven decision, albeit split, for hospital unification. Was this why Modrow had switched negotiators?

Then, in another round of caucuses and open sessions, a set of agreements were proposed, and in the absence of direct objection by any party they were recorded as consensus. As the negotiations wore on past midnight it became impossible to hold people to the locked doors commitment. An affirmative vote was never obtained; instead, statements that were agreed to were in fact those to which nobody was in strong objection.

The board of a new federated organization would be composed of six representatives appointed by the two hospitals. These persons would represent both entire hospital service areas. The federation would begin planning on a start from scratch basis with no preconditions as to site or type of delivery system. It was understood that consolidated hospital services were neither mandated nor excluded, but that the planning initiative was placed clearly in the hands of the new federation, as operation of facilities would be in the hands of a successor corporation to the new federation. The federation would be the only group which dealt with CHPA, representing both hospitals. The immediate questions relating to overcrowding at Dana and meeting fire marshall regulations at Westhaven would be the responsibility of the federation. At all stages of the planning process conducted by the federation there would be open public hearings in each city as well as in unincorporated areas. In the event that federation representatives deadlocked on issues, matters would be submitted to binding arbitration, with the arbitrator mutually agreed upon by the federation at the time of its formation. The federation would exist for no more than three years, at which time a new entity would result from areawide elections or a combination of elections and geographic appointments. The method of determining representation would be decided by the federation, with the health system delivery plan submitted to voters for their approval concurrently with the formation of the new organization.

Since these compromises had been recorded in piecemeal fashion, there remained questions of exact phraseology. The locked doors were opened, with the understanding that Wagner would restate the agreements and distribute them immediately to the parties, and that the negotiators would take the statement to their boards for approval by July 25, with a joint public statement. CHPA would call the first organizational meeting of the federation and would continue to meet periodically with the federation members to review progress. It was understood that the negotiating committee had met for the last time.

G. Denouement: July 1976–March 1977

DANA'S RESPONSE

Dana quickly rejected the proposal. At a meeting chaired by newly reelected president Ron Coss, the vote was six against, five for, and one abstention—former president William Forrest.

WESTHAVEN'S REPONSE

Westhaven did not immediately reply, but at its next public board meeting its response became clear. Melissa Honor dominated the meeting. Ignoring entirely the most recent Wagner negotiated plan, she argued that Westhaven had wasted its money and time, that the compromise previously proposed by Westhaven had been rejected by Dana, and that Westhaven should now proceed on its own. Ms. Honor's assertions were aimed as much at her fellow board members as at Dana. She charged her colleagues with having spent $300,000 for hospital architectural consultation without learning how much it would cost to build a new hospital, where the new hospital would be located, what kind of services it would provide, and where the money would come from to build it. She said "the responsibility for our present state of affairs is ultimately ours and, as far as I'm concerned, the buck stops here. We need to shape up or ship out, and the shipping out will come when we are forced to close our doors or run a second-rate facility." Mrs. Honor listed six things the district should do immediately, including a review of the architect's contract and work to date, setting standards for hospital care, withdraw from meddling in administrative matters and focus instead on policy setting and involving the community in the building program. Ms. Honor's swing vote sentiments were consistent with those of her black constituency, which feared discrimination in a hospital run in part by Riviera interests and without the protection of public decision making.

Ms. Honor's assertions acted as a catalyst: the Westhaven board resolved that it would send one final letter containing its sentiment to Dana, stating that if a favorable reply to its earlier counterproposal was not received within one week, by September 29, the district would proceed unilaterally. The vote for a one week ultimatum was 4–0 in favor. Modrow was not at the meeting. Later, he stated publicly that the ultimatum had been a mistake, but that he had signed the tough line letter in the line of duty as president of the board.

This entire discussion seemed well staged for the attending press: there followed immediately a large splash in the newspapers. Copies of the ultimatum letter were sent to the chairman of the CHPA board, the mayors of the cities of Westhaven and Riviera, the chambers of commerce of both cities, and the daily newspapers of all neighboring towns.

The Westhaven directors did not wait for a reply from Dana. In a special meeting on September 26, they voted to proceed with all details of their own hospital project. Architect Fall presented a revised hospital plan for a 78-bed facility requiring 25 percent less square footage than his previous plan. The only board discussion was over the size of the facility, with Melissa Honor wanting a decision on size to be deferred until a study had been made to determine why Westhaven's occupancy rate had been dropping in recent years. However, she was out-voted.

DANA'S RESPONSE TO WESTHAVEN'S RESPONSE

In developing its reply to the Westhaven ultimatum, Dana's new strategy was to appeal directly to CHPA for continued support and assistance in securing approval of Starkweather's proposal. Based on what they called Westhaven's flagrant break of the prior agreement to avoid publicity during negotiations, Dana officials fashioned their own summary of Starkweather's plan for another newspaper splash. In its letter of appeal to CHPA, Dana noted that Westhaven's proposal did not address itself to cost containment since construction estimates ranged from 8 to 12 million dollars, and stressed again that any new hospital should be planned and managed by a regional corporation with input from the entire East County. Dana further charged that the reasons for Westhaven's ultimatum were false: no one had ever seen written evidence that either the Joint Commission on Hospital Accreditation or the state fire marshall would close Westhaven's existing hospital, and it appeared that the installation of fire sprinklers recently voted by the Westhaven board would buy sufficient time for final planning and refinement of Starkweather's plan for a unified hospital.

CHPA'S RESPONSE

CHPA's response had to be developed in the context of widespread doubt about its own future as an agency. The new Health Services Resource and Development Act had been passed by the U.S. Congress, and CHPA was locked into an intense struggle with two other agencies over who would get the franchise to franchise. Further, the executive of the Bay Area CHPA had suddenly resigned, and Joe Hafey had been named his acting replacement.

For official consumption, Hafey fashioned a resolution for his board which stated that CHPA deplored the recent turn of events, reiterated CHPA's position in support of a single hospital for East County, and called for both hospitals to reopen negotiations using Starkweather's report as the basis. The resolution stated that the public should be made aware of the issues through the media, financial institutions, local governments, taxpayers groups, labor and business, etc. Privately, Hafey was investigating ways of taking on the Westhaven Hospital board. He was pursing the possibility of grand jury investigation of the $600,000 of tax funds which the district had spent thus far on hospital planning, including $300,000 in payments to Architect Fall.[21] Hafey was confident that CHPA would win its lawsuit, which decision was soon to be announced.

Events which finally determined the situation unfolded rapidly.

THE JUDGE DECIDES

On October 8, 1976, the court handed down a judgment in favor of Westhaven. Judge Perry concluded that the granting of the exemption was not an act beyond the authority of the State Department of Public Health, noting further that relying upon the state's advice, Westhaven had expended considerable sums of money in preparing lands, etc.

WESTHAVEN WITHDRAWS

On the same day, the chairman of CHPA's Health Facilities Subcommittee received a letter from Westhaven's Modrow stating, in part, that his board had done its utmost to seek a satisfactory compromise, that even during the negotiations it had repeatedly invited Dana representatives to join with it in its hospital planning but had been repulsed, that Westhaven's project was now 20 percent more expensive because of CHPA's interference, and that based on the favorable court decision Westhaven was proceeding with all possible haste towards the construction of a new 78-bed acute hospital.

Many Dana officials attended the next special meeting of CHPA's Health Facilities Subcommittee, but no one was in attendance from Westhaven. Also in attendance was Los Medanos County's medical director, Dr. Becker, a member of the CHPA board of directors. When the staff asked for the sub-committee's endorsement of its stepped up efforts to defeat Westhaven's unilateral action, Becker argued against "any change in the priority of staff attention to the many other important things which CHPA must do."

WESTHAVEN MOVES ON ITS OWN

At the October 28 meeting of the Westhaven board Modrow reported that Riviera was trying to frustrate their plans by hiring a public relations firm to oppose them, and the board contemplated hiring its own public relations firm as a counterforce. Instead of doing this, it voted to form a community advisory team to assist in educating the public on plans for the new hospital, particularly in anticipation of a bond election which would probably be held in March 1977. The advisory team included two former district directors of longstanding, and Bill Sora, civic leader. The board also discussed a proposal by a group of doctors to lease a parcel of Westhaven's Brendham site for a medical practice building. The District's attorney promised to report back to the board soon with a recommendation on how such a facility could be built without having to file a second environmental impact report. Finally, the board voted to retain a financial consultant to advise it on the best method of raising 10.6 million dollars in capital funds.

At its November 1976 meeting the Westhaven directors started an investigation of joint use of their new hospital with Los Medanos County. Directors unanimously approved a proposal made by Dr. Becker for a plan which included attracting new doctors to the area, providing improved hospital services to the community and medical recipients, and obtaining higher occupancy rates. Becker noted that this plan could facilitate construction financing for Westhaven's proposed hospital. The plan would shorten the distance and time needed for indigent patients to travel to the county hospital in Ignacio. All East County residents would be eligible to take advantage of county services offered at the Brendham-site hospital.

At this same meeting the board reviewed its new consultant's advice on methods of hospital financing. All but one scheme required voter approval. The board seemed to favor a complicated tax override measure that would need only a simple majority of voters. It was complicated because funds so provided would be insufficient to finance the total construction; additional bonds would have to be sold. For this, the consultant recommended creating a nonprofit hospital financial corporation, which could sell tax exempt bonds to build the new hospital and lease the completed structure back to the district for operation. The terms of the lease would be set at the amount necessary to retire the bonds. The consultant recommended that the hospital identify five community residents to form the nonprofit corporation. Other financing methods were briefly reviewed and rejected: private financing, because of higher interest rates; general obligation bonds, because they would require a two-thirds voter approval; and a joint powers authority, because the district would have to collaborate with another municipality or the county which would add numerous complications.

CHPA INITIATIVE CRUMBLES

Prior to the November 1976 meeting of the full CHPA board, Hafey's CHPA staff had met with the chambers of commerce of both communities. The Westhaven chamber voted a hands-off policy, as did the Riviera chamber, after some initial expression of interest in assisting CHPA. Its change of mind was apparently based on conversations with both Dana board members and Riviera industry representatives.

Dr. Becker was not present at the November 17 CHPA meeting, but his influence was felt. The board's official action on Hafey's proposed resolution was to take no action. Discussion revealed a new thinking: the action proposed was unrealistic, the staff's anti-Westhaven plan was viewed by some as vindictive, and, importantly, there was no evidence of community support for continuation of CHPA's prior stand. The overall sentiment of the board was that they were "beating a dead horse."

On January 8, 1977, CHPA obtained its reply from the Los Medanos County Grand Jury, which stated that the questions presented related to a superior court decision, state legislation, and the State Department of Public Health, all of which were beyond the scope of authority of the grand jury. It closed the matter.

On March 2, 1977, the citizens of Westhaven Community Hospital District voted the hospital construction tax override by a margin of three to one.

SOME CONSEQUENCES

On July 12, 1979 the new Westhaven Community Hospital, constructed on the Camp Brendham site, opened its doors to patients.

As of December 31, 1979, the capacity and occupancy statistics for Westhaven and Riviera were as shown in the table below.

	Westhaven	Riviera
Number of beds	78	53
Average daily census	60 (est.)	42
Occupancy per tent	76.9 (est.)	79.2

In January 1980, the directors of Westhaven Hospital District and Freemont Hospital District (see fig. 5.1 for location) made the following announcement:

> Westhaven and Freemont Hospitals have recently agreed to a system of shared management, via contracts between each of the two hospital boards and the administrator of the Freemont Hospital. Future possibilities include the establishment of a Joint Powers Agreement between the two hospital districts, and ultimately the establishment of a separate non-profit corporation, with its own board of directors, responsible for administering the joint powers agreement.

H.   EPILOGUE

WHAT MOTIVATES EXCHANGE BEHAVIOR?

Chapters 2 and 3 presented theories of interorganizational dependency, domain consensus, and exchange. There are numerous applications of these in this case, which we believe are straightforward, serving both to validate the concepts and demonstrate their relevance.

In addition, there is the notion of organizational man as a game-playing animal, described by Norton Long:

> . . . the structured group activities that coexist in a particular territorial system can be looked at as games. These games provide the players with a set of goals that give them a sense of success or failure. They provide them determinate roles and calculable strategies and tactics. In addition, they provide the players with an elite and general public that is in varying degrees able to tell the score.

> Far from regarding games as trivial, the writer's position would be that man is both a game-playing and a game-creating animal, that his capacity to create and play games and take them deadly seriously is of the essence, and that it is through games or activities analogous to game-playing that he achieves a satisfactory sense of significance and a meaningful role.

> A final game that does in a significant way integrate all the games in the territorial system is the social game. Success in each of the games can in

varying degrees be cashed in for social acceptance. The custodians of the symbols of top social standing provide goals that in a sense give all the individual games some common denominator of achievement.[22]

Was the whole thing just a game which the parties enjoyed playing without seriously preparing to abandon their original intentions?

In Riviera, where the community power structure was less obvious and more diffuse, those in charge of hospital merger negotiations conducted themselves with well-trained and well-ordered civic behavior, but lacked the necessary base of support when the final plays of the game were called. Industrial leaders in Riviera disliked both the tax district form of hospital sponsorship and the history of hospital governance in Westhaven. Yet, they did not reveal this openly at the outset, leading to considerable gaming within the Dana board and between it and other community leaders.

The Westhaven board seemed in perpetual confusion and internal dissension, unable to make the decisions asked of it. Yet, the basic source of power in Westhaven was known to be well structured and closely held, leading one observer to conclude that Westhaven's behavior was dumb like a fox. It played the game differently than Dana, "more like hit and run guerrilla warfare than Riviera's more predictable battle plan," said Labor Council executive Zig Wagner.

In retrospect, there were all sorts of clues to a strategy of play on Westhaven's part which was remarkably consistent with its original aims: the early discussions with Becker, the several delays in negotiations for reasons beyond their control, the way the district's attorney dragged his feet on the joint legal report and succeeded eventually in being noncommittal on the legality of Starkweather's plan, and Westhaven's continued employment of architect Fall.

CHPA consistently underinterpreted the periodic newspaper reports of Westhaven's separatist actions, assuming them to be exaggerations by the press rather than the reality. CHPA believed that the courts would ultimately confirm its power to declare the outcome. Through all of this, Hafey was described as a political animal who enjoyed this kind of activity.

The role of Starkweather as a consultant/mediator also deserves scrutiny. CHPA's initial supposition was that careful mediation might make the difference. Inherent in Starkweather's involvement for an extended period of time was the risk that he would impose his own outcome preferences on the situation, to the disregard of the values held by the community representatives involved. Starkweather obviously preferred a tight integration. Though this preference was at the outset clearly justified by the report of the CHPA Joint Study Committee which immediately preceded his involvement, it was also true that as time passed on the parties forgot those prior understandings and came to feel that this was an imposition. Melissa Honor, arriving in the thick

of battle at midgame, won Westaven support for her loose federation counterproposal on the argument that Starkweather's merger proposal was a win/
lose situation—that if they accepted one facility, one of the parties would
cease to exist. Starkweather knew he could obtain a federation-type solution
but felt that full unification was the better result, though clearly riskier. Was
this simply his game—the play of which was so enjoyable that he overlooked
some early legal problems with his proposal which broke the momentum at
a crucial juncture and allowed the parties to drift apart? Further, at periodic
junctures in the process it was clear to Starkweather that the parties were
unwilling to negotiate directly with each other without his assistance. This
lead to a dependence on him which was ego-gratifying, but disguised a weakness in the situation. Even Wagner's involvement as a last-ditch negotiator
was due as much to his interest in the application of labor/management
bargaining techniques to a different realm of conflict[23] as it was to his commitment to health care goals in East County.

If the players were not interested in game play, why did they so readily
agree to private negotiating sessions despite the laws governing Westhaven's
decision making, despite its rhetoric about community involvement, and despite CHPA's policies of open deliberations?

Finally, at no time in the long process were the fully defined costs and
benefits of merger an important factor to the contestants. Even though a
sophisticated study had been made of these questions,[24] the study was ignored.

ROLE OF THE PLANNING AGENCY

The first planning agency involved in the two communities was merely a
forum for polite discussions. Then, after reorganization as CHPA, it asserted
itself to the point of setting up a carefully structured negotiation which it
hoped would yield the desired result. Subsequently, CHPA became a participant in this structure, initially by bringing Starkweather into the picture and
then by intruding Wagner. During all of this time CHPA's executive, Joseph
Hafey, was an activist. Even when all these strategies failed, the CHPA staff
actively pursued political and legal action against Westhaven, through attempts to involve the grand jury and efforts to activate community groups
which might oppose Westhaven's actions.

In the end, Hafey could not play out this string, due in part to legal
reversals, and in part to the lack of any broad support for his strategy. In
particular, physician support had withered away; had the doctors actively
supported the merger at the right time, CHPA might well have obtained its
desires. Also, CHPA could not identify any citizen support for its project:
Starkweather's plan was difficult to understand, the East County community
to which it was to apply was fractioned into different subpopulations, and

there were no mechanism readily available for testing public sentiment. Even the organizational viability of CHPA itself was in question, reducing its credibility.

Consideration of hospital merger in East County had started when health planning was a strictly voluntary activity and when the first generation agency had supported the Dana interests. This was perceived by many to have been reversed by the second generation agency, when CHPA endorsed Westhaven's Camp Brendham site. All of this was remembered by the hospital and political interests in East County when the possibility of yet a new third generation planning authority became known.

NOTES

1. The forum role is well described and discussed in an early and classic study by Morris of health planning councils of six communities. Briefly, the planning council serves primarily as a meeting ground for groups and organizations concerned with community policy decisions. It "takes few stands on details, but channelizes the energies, monies, personalities, and enthusiasm of many diverse groups . . . ," by providing 1) a channel for communication; 2) a forum for negotiations; 3) a springboard for leadership; and 4) a means to goal setting. Robert Morris, "Basic Factors in Planning for the Coordination of Health Services— Part I," *American Journal of Public Health*, March 1963, pp. 463–64.

2. Including 24-hour emergency service, enlarged coronary care and intensive care units, improved obstetrics, pediatrics, and surgical services, initiation of psychiatric services, and a hospital-based extended care facility.

3. One of which was headed by the former executive of Bay Area Health Facilities Planning Association, the predecessor organization to CHPA.

4. Of course, at the time the Bay Area Health Facilities Planning Association had designated Dana's site, the Camp Brendham site was not an available option. This did not prevent both hospital groups from complaining that "those planners change their minds; you can't count on them."

5. The legal question seemed to be what constituted "providing service," since clearly a district hospital could contract with a corporation located elsewhere for services to be provided within. Were there certain hospital services which the district could not contract away but were obligated by district law to provide directly?

6. Members of both hospital delegations felt that private negotiations would avoid a repeat of the public spectacles that had taken place at the Joint Study Committee hearings. Nonetheless, Westhaven officials had reservations and asserted that the sessions should remain private only through the first phase, until an organization form was recommended to both boards.

7. Starkweather knew also that Fall's firm had a reputation in some quarters of the state, of presenting boards of small rural hospitals with overly ambitious ideas and plans in order to win a contract. Starkweather knew that when joint planning of a single facility finally got underway, the parties might fall apart over selection of an architect.

8. Even so, the Dana-Becker affair was not over. In subsequent months it was learned that Dana Hospital had cancelled a lease to Los Medanos County of a

building which it owned in the far eastern portion of the County, which lease involved operation by Becker's county hospital medical staff of a primary care clinic to serve poor people, primarily of Spanish surname. Dana replaced the county's operation with its own physician-staffed outpost. Dana was assisted in this development by a consultant who was also one of the four CHPA appointees to the merger negotiating committee.

9. Significantly, a joint powers authority may issue revenue bonds, i.e., bonds to be paid off from the net gain of hospital operation instead of by a general obligation tax, without soliciting approval of voters within the authority's jurisdiction.

10. San Benito is a well known name in East County, referring to an area designated on historic Spanish land grant maps which lies between Westhaven and Riviera. The name had been selected for the new junior college under construction on the Brendham plot.

11. The same newspaper reported that the Westhaven board had settled on an 11 million dollar construction cost limit, but architect Fall was recommending that any bond election to be held should be for authorization of 13 million dollars. It was reported that, despite this discrepancy, the board signed a new contract with Fall, based on a percentage of completed construction costs.

12. The word joint was crucial. Starkweather had been worried that advice rendered by separate attorneys would simply lead to legal adversary. In anticipation of this, he had obtained agreement that if the hospital's separate legal counsels were used they would 1) be guided by questions posed by the joint negotiating committee; 2) be expected to approach the problem from the point of view of the art of the possible rather than to catalog barriers to change; and 3) be expected to render a joint written report.

13. Such nonpublic meetings of all district directors are permitted under California law, given that they generate no decisions.

14. On the fifth issue, the attorneys brought up a question not previously considered by Starkweather: which of the four corporations involved—two existing and two new—should actually hold a new license for hospital operations? Of central concern here was whether a formal lessor/lessee relationship could be struck, presumably with the proposed nonprofit management corporation, with the lessee also the licensee, or whether the lessor should conduct licensed hospital affairs without legal delegation, simply being advised in such operations by the management corporation.

15. Appendix A contains details of the three options outlined by the two attorneys. This appendix will be of interest to those concerned with the public policy and legal aspects of combining a public and private corporation, including questions of dissolution and transfer of assets.

16. This concern was stimulated by a consultant to the legislature who wrote a widely distributed law review article: Taber and Whitacker, *Hastings Law Review*, March, 1972.

17. The reason for this was not New York City's pending bankruptcy, which affected the market later. The problem at this time was twofold. A temporary effect was a decline in the market price of tax-exempt bonds following a time in which they had been artifically inflated by purchases made in the belief that government bonds were recession proof. Then there was a market adjustment to a longer term trend. Tax-exempt bonds were originally issued to finance basic government activities, to be repaid from general taxes. However, more recently they had been used to finance nonessentials such as sports arenas and convention centers, to be retired from revenues derived from such actitivies. These latter were

viewed by investors as being much riskier, thus the prices at which such bonds could be sold had risen sharply.

18. Tax-exempt bonds that have the full backing of an operating government are seen as a better investment than those that do not have such backing. It follows that bonds issued by a district hospital which has obtained voter approval for the issue are preferred over those issued by a joint powers authority (JPA) without such approval. Finally, bonds issued by a JPA that is leasing the facilities back to a governmental unit are preferred over those offered by a JPA that is leasing its facilities to a nongovernmental unit. Unfortunately, the joint powers authority—operator option accepted by the negotiating committee—the one with minimal legal impediments—stood more alone in this regard than the others.

19. The board did not seem surprised at Hafey's and Starkweather's reactions. Nor did Hafey seem surprised at Westhaven's proposal. After the meeting, Hafey reported to Starkweather on a series of discussions he had had with Melissa Honor, from which he had concluded that she was not supporting merger efforts and, in fact, had been the architect of the federation plan.

20. The district directors seemed unconcerned this time whether the hospital district could make such a binding delegation to another entity.

21. These figures had recently come to light in documents which the Westhaven board was obligated to file with Los Medanos County for purposes of setting the annual tax rate of the district.

22. Norton Long, "The Local Community as an Ecology of Games," *American Journal of Sociology*, November 1958, pp. 259–60.

23. There are important differences between the structure for conflict resolution in the labor/management situation and the circumstances of this case. In the former the parties are at contest over features of a legal contract, and this contract defines what the parties may legitimately quarrel over. In the kind of social exchange presented here there is no document which determines what is legitimate strife and what is irrelevant. Under these circumstances the parties can alternate at will between what subjects are negotiable and who should negotiate them, on the one hand, and the actual substance of issues, on the other.

24. E.J. Sondig et al., "A Demand and Cost Analysis of Alternative Strategies for Hospital Development for Eastern Los Medanos County, Working Paper #2, EES Program in Health Care Systems Research, Stanford University, 1973.

APPENDIX A: THREE OPTIONS FOR COMBINING WESTHAVEN
AND DANA HOSPITAL CORPORATIONS

The alternative corporate arrangements outlined by the two attorneys were as follows:

Option 1, Lessee-Operator: The two existing hospitals would create a joint powers authority (JPA) to construct and hold title to a new hospital. The JPA would then lease out the facility to a private, nonprofit operating corporation, with the former in a landlord relationship. This was essentially Starkweather's plan, with the addition of a lessor/lessee contract.

Option 2, District-Operator: This approach would also establish a JPA for financing and ownership, but rather than leasing the new facility to a new corporation, it would be leased back to the Westhaven District, thus avoiding several questions of delegation of authority and conflict of interest by the district directors. In this plan, the Westhaven District would be the licensed operator, but its directors would, in turn, enter a long-term contract with the new nonprofit corporation to furnish administrative personnel and share some of the responsibility for day-to-day operations of the hospital. The directors of the district would continue to function as the new hospital's legal governing body.

Option 3, JPA-Operator: In this approach, a JPA would again be created to finance and hold title but would also operate the hospital directly without establishing a lease-back to Westhaven. In this arrangement the new private corporation would again be the operating entity, performing its functions through a long-term agreement to advise the joint powers authority.

The corporate relationships envisioned in the three proposals are shown in figure 5.2.

The negotiating committee immediately rejected Option 2, District-Operator, on grounds that while it obviously eliminated legal problems for the district, it did so by leaving Westhaven's power so much greater than Dana's that it was unacceptable; even the Westhaven representatives granted this.

Option 1, Lessee-Operator, contained several features that were legally cloudy in respect to California hospital district law. First, a feature of the law appeared to limit lease arrangements to a maximum of 10 years, with some legal confusion as to whether they could be renewed. This provision had originally been inserted in the law to deal with contracts for professional services and not the arrangements envisioned here; yet, the proviso could be interpreted to limit the authority of the JPA to obtain capital financing with more than a ten-year payback, since the state enabling law for JPAs stipulates that they may not exceed whatever authorities are held by the government bodies which create them. If bonds issued by the JPA were limited to ten years it would effectively eliminate such an authority as a useful financing period in excess of ten years, through a JPA. Second, the district hospital law stipulates that only a district board may appoint members to the medical staff, thus eliminating the possibility that a management corporation's board, acting as a lessee with a JPA, could so appoint. The attorneys felt that only if the operating corporation had this authority to appoint could it obtain a hospital license. The law read ambiguously on the question of conflict of interest. The district law seemed to read that conflict existed only if the corporation with which the district was contracting was a profit-making enterprise in which the district directors held a certain percentage of shares; yet, Westhaven's attorney found room to doubt this. As for the location issue, the lawyers agreed that the district law limits hospital activities to within-district territory, but argued that if a JPA was the official sponsor this limitation would be obviated: the governments which created the JPA would not

Figure 5.2   Legal Relationships Between Existing and
New Corporations—Westhaven and Riviera

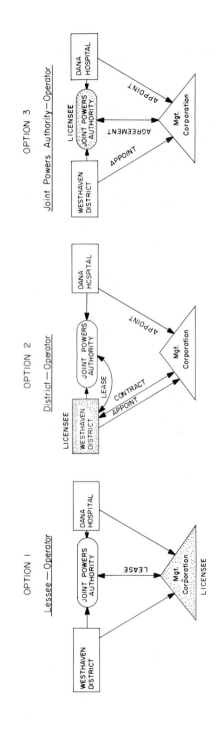

OPTION I

Lessee — Operator

OPTION 2

District — Operator

OPTION 3

Joint Powers Authority — Operator

likely have overlapping boundaries unless the county were involved, and therefore it would be permissible to disregard the district's statutory limitation as long as the facility was to be located within the boundaries of some one of the sponsoring entities.

In Option 3, JPA-Operator, the initial powers balanced evenly between the two hospitals and there were a minimum of legal problems. This scheme eliminated the problems of delegation for the district directors, since the license to operate would be held by the JPA, leaving dormant the role of direct hospital operations on the part of the Westhaven trustees. The only possible obstacle the lawyers saw was concerning conflict of interests, where even if the private corporation were simply to advise the JPA on hospital management, it could be construed that district directors likewise serving on the operating corporation's board were in conflict because the corporation actually served the district, while the JPA acted as a mere conduit. This was admittedly a thin line, when compared to the counterlogic that transferral of authority for new hospital operations from the district to the JPA would break the link between the nonprofit management corporation and the district.

6.
Seattle's Three-Way Merger

Mark L. Secord

Commentaries by Wanda Jones, Robert Dupar,
Ludwig Lobe, and Mark L. Secord

A. INTRODUCTION

This case study[1] covers events that occurred between 1969 and 1976, a period which culminated with the decision by three Seattle hospitals—The Doctors' Hospital, Seattle General Hospital and Swedish Hospital Medical Center—to consolidate their assets into one corporation.

The focus of this case study is on the merger process, with time a critical dimension. Progress toward the decision to merge was highly uneven: at times it lurched forward while at other times it was held up by one conflict or another. One of the key determinants of the rate of progress was the degree to which it was managed; one highlight of the case is the mediating role played by a planning consultant. This person's contribution was both effective and controversial, as discussed in four postcase commentaries. The first of these commentaries is by the consultant, the second by a hospital trustee who figured prominently in the merger proceedings, a regulatory viewpoint, the third, by a member of the Washington State Hospital Commission, and the fourth by the case study author, who interprets the case from the perspective of organization theory.

The consolidation of these three Seattle hospitals is not complete. The chronicle of this case's events concludes with their decision to consolidate. The merging process can be expected to continue for some years into the future.

PERSONS FIGURING PROMINENTLY IN THE CASE

Wayne Chesledon, M.D., Radiologist, Seattle General Hospital

Robert Dupar, President, Seattle General Board of Trustees

Robert Graham, Trustee of Doctors Hospital and Cochairman, Joint Merger Committee

William Hogerty, Executive Director, Puget Sound Health Planning Council

Wanda Jones, Project Director, consulting firm of Gorsline & Associates

Allan Lobb, M.D., Medical Director, Swedish Hospital

Ludwig Lobe, Chairman, Washington State Hospital Commission

Martin Smith, Trustee, Seattle General Hospital

SEQUENCE OF IMPORTANT EVENTS

1968   Seattle General Hospital initiates merger talks with Doctors Hospital.

1970   Maynard Hospital joins Seattle General/Doctors merger talks.

Doctors Hospital and Virginia Mason Hospital agree to consolidate obstetrics services at Doctors and file preliminary application to Puget Sound Health Planning Council (July).

Swedish Medical Center submits a preliminary application to Puget Sound Health Planning Council for expansion of its maternity service (July).

Puget Sound Health Planning Council decides in favor of Doctors/Virginia Mason application (August); Swedish Hospital indicates preliminary support.

1971   Maynard Hospital sold to Seattle General; Seattle General moves to Maynard facilities (April).

1972   Seattle General Hospital begins (again) merger talks with Doctors Hospital (July).

Doctors Hospital presents final proposal for its (consolidated) maternity service to Puget Sound Health Planning Council; Swedish Hospital opposes; Doctors withdraws proposal (September).

1973   Joint Merger Committee established by Seattle General and Doctors Hospitals (February).

Poll of Doctors Hospital physicians favors merger with Seattle General by 93 percent (April).

Swedish Hospital suggests that Puget Sound Health Planning Council convene a group of First Hill hospitals for discussion of coordination and possible merger (June).

Joint Seattle General/Doctors merger committee bogged down; decides to obtain consultation (August).

Gorsline and Associates proposes expanded role of study, from one of facility replacement for Seattle General and Doctors to one of community role; Gorsline recommends affiliation of Seattle General and Doctors with Swedish (November).

1974   Affiliation committee of Seattle General, Doctors and Swedish established; investigation of building sites on Swedish campus.

1975   Affiliation Committee meets with executive of Puget Sound Health Planning Council to discuss pavilion plan; Swedish urges that a decision to merge be made within a few weeks (March).

Doctors Hospital decides to close its obstetrics unit and consolidate with Swedish (April).

Joint Merger Committee calls on consultant Wanda Jones to draft a letter of intent to merge, to be signed by Doctors, Seattle General and Swedish Boards (May).

Robert Dupar proposes holding company idea to Affiliation Committee (June).

Swedish application to Puget Sound Health Planning Council for expansion of maternity service to incorporate Doctors obstetrics volume is approved (August).

Boards of the three hospitals meet jointly for first time (September).

Consultant Jones' merged pavilion facility proposal approved in principle by three hospital boards (October 2).

Corporate merger approved in principle by all three hospital boards; interim planning committee established (October 17).

1976   Architect's estimate of cost of pavilion construction above prior expectations; Swedish announces concern that cost exceeds its debt limit, and proposes remodeling and expansion of existing Swedish facilities as alternative; Dr. Lobb proposes a one-year planning moratorium (February).

Interim Planning Committee proposes financial feasibility study; Swedish approves study but indicates such action does not necessarily mean its endorsement of the pavilion concept (March).

Chairman of Washington State Hospital Commission advises three hospitals that if merger progress is not made, the commission will reopen hearings on their 1976 budgets (April).

Financial consultants conclude that Swedish's debt capacity is sufficient for the merger; Swedish's existing lender agrees to extend loan (September).

Articles of incorporation and by-laws prepared; land purchased for pavilion; architect appointed (by end of year).

1980   Merged hospital pavilion opened (June).

B.   THE FIRST HILL HOSPITAL SITUATION: BACKDROP FOR MERGER

Few cities in the United States concentrate a greater proportion of their health facilities in one small geographical area than does Seattle. First Hill, immediately adjacent to and overlooking downtown Seattle, is the location for six acute care hospitals and a number of related medical facilities, including physician office buildings, clinics, a major cancer research center, a kidney center, and a regional blood bank. These hospitals—Doctors, Seattle General, Cabrini, Swedish, Harborview, and Virginia Mason—are located within a few blocks of one another. A seventh hospital, Providence, lies within one mile of First Hill. A brief profile of each of these hospitals follows.

The Doctors Hospital is a 177-bed facility whose 1940 physical plant is an outmoded structure. Doctors is a private nonprofit corporation governed by a board of trustees with a medical staff composed largely of general practitioners. The obstetrical service and the family practice residency program, the latter initiated in the early 1970s, are especially important to the hospital.

Seattle General Hospital moved to First Hill in 1971 from a site in downtown Seattle, by occupying a facility built and previously occupied by the Maynard Hospital, which closed its doors. Seattle General is a private, nonprofit general hospital with 125 beds, governed by a 24-member board of trustees. Like Doctors, its medical staff is composed for the most part of general practitioners. Seattle General has been plagued by low occupancy for a number of years, with occupancy often falling below 50 percent.

St. Francis Xavier Cabrini Hospital is a Catholic hospital owned and operated by the Sisters of the Sacred Heart. This 219-bed general hospital completed construction of a major physician office building adjacent to the hospital building in 1974. Despite chronic low occupancy, averaging under 50 percent, the hospital remains optimistic about its future as an independent institution.

The Swedish Hospital and Medical Center is the largest health facility on First Hill, comprising 420 beds operated at a high rate of occupancy. The Swedish campus occupies an eight square block site which encompasses two large medical office buildings, the Hutchinson Cancer Research Center, the Northwest Kidney Center, and a surgicenter. The hospital emphasizes secondary and tertiary care, and serves as one of Seattle's important referral centers. About 25 percent of its patients come from outside metropolitan Seattle. Swedish is a private nonprofit institution governed by a nine member board of Trustees comprised mainly of prominent Seattle businessmen.

Virginia Mason Hospital, a 292-bed secondary and tertiary referral center, is linked physically and organizationally to the Mason Clinic, a fee-for-service group of about 100 specialist physicians organized into a partnership. More than 90 percent of the hospital's admissions come from Mason Clinic physicians. The clinic and hospital draw patients from a wide area; about 40 percent of the hospital's patients originate from outside of metropolitan Seattle. Virginia Mason is a private nonprofit corporation governed by a 20-member board of trustees. A number of physicians of the Mason Clinic serve on its board.

Harborview Medical Center, formerly operated by King County, is now one of the University of Washington hospitals. It is licensed for 300 beds, and is the site of Seattle's major trauma center and a regional burn care center serving a four-state area.

Providence Hospital is a 315-bed Catholic hospital located about a mile from First Hill. The Hospital is owned and operated by the Sisters of Providence. Providence offers tertiary as well as secondary services and has recently financed construction of a physicians office building.

Central Seattle has for some time been overbedded in acute care hospital beds. While occupancy rates at the larger hospitals—Swedish, Virginia Mason, Providence and Harborview—have remained consistently high, occupancies at the three smaller hospitals—Cabrini, Doctors and Seattle General—have been lower (see table 6.1).

TABLE 6.1.   Selected Seattle Hospital Occupancy Rates

Hospital	Number of beds	Occupancy, 1972 (%)	Occupancy, 1974 (%)
Cabrini	219	48	45
Doctors	177	76	63
Seattle General	125	56	56
Harborview	300	72	79
Providence	315	80	79
Swedish	420	89	85
Virginia Mason	292	79	82

Source: Puget Sound Health Planning Council, "Hospital Utilization Report, Annual Summary," 1972, 1974.

Compounding the problem of excess beds in the central Seattle area is the development of hospitals located in Seattle's suburbs. Data on regional hospital utilization (Lester Gorsline Associates, 1973) show that the residents of Seattle's growing suburban areas are becoming less and less dependent on the inner-city hospitals. This trend is particularly significant for the small urban hospitals like Doctors and Seattle General that offer secondary level services similar to their suburban hospital counterparts. People in the suburbs continue to travel to central Seattle for most tertiary services (Puget Sound Health Planning Council, 1975).

C. The Merger Process

EARLY MERGER TALKS: DOCTORS AND SEATTLE GENERAL

In the late 1960s the board of trustees of Seattle General Hospital recognized that their hospital had a limited life in its facility on Fifth Avenue in downtown Seattle. The hospital's quarters were cramped and outmoded, medical staff support was waning, many physicians had moved their offices out of the downtown area, and the hospital was losing money. Hospital trustees made the decision to find a new location, possibly merging with another hospital in the Seattle area. Through informal board and medical staff contacts, it was learned that The Doctors Hospital also had concerns about its facility on First Hill, so the two hospitals joined in merger discussions.

The discussions dragged on month after month, and it became clear that Doctors had little real interest in becoming an equal partner with Seattle General in a merger scheme: Doctors was prospering with high occupancy and favorable cash flow, and its board perceived that its medical staff was of higher quality than Seattle General's. To Doctors' decision makers, Seattle General had few assets to bring to a merger.

In 1970 Maynard Hospital joined the Doctors/Seattle General merger discussions. Maynard was a 125-bed hospital owned by the Stewards Foundation and located three blocks from Doctors Hospital on First Hill. Maynard had once been Seattle's leading obstetrical center, but in recent years medical staff support had declined and Maynard was losing money.

Finally, time ran out for Seattle General. Having found a buyer for its Fifth Avenue facility, the hospital had to vacate the site in a few months. Board members initiated separate discussions with Maynard, having become discouraged by the lack of progress in the talks with Doctors. They discovered that officers of the Stewards Foundation were willing to divest themselves of Maynard. Seattle General purchased the facility and moved to its new location in April, 1971.

THE MATERNITY CENTER FIASCO

On July 16, 1970, the Facilities Review Committee of the Puget Sound Health Planning Council faced a critical decision. It had before it two competing proposals for a downtown Seattle maternity center, one from Doctors and the other from Swedish.

Nowhere was the need for consolidation of services more apparent than in obstetrical services on First Hill. Doctors, Swedish, Seattle General, Virginia Mason and Providence hospitals each maintained separate services, and each operated at low efficiency due to small patient volume relative to capacity. The Planning Council was promoting consolidation of maternity services on First Hill.

The proposal from Doctors was prepared in conjunction with Virginia Mason, its neighbor across the street. Over the years the administrations of these two hospitals had built up a close relationship; for some time they had been meeting monthly to investigate possibilities for sharing services. Already the two hospitals shared a common central services department located at Doctors.[2]

Early in 1969 representatives of the boards, medical staffs, and administrations of Doctors and Virginia Mason began a series of monthly meetings to discuss the consolidation of obstetrical services. Both hospitals were interested in establishing a larger and more efficient service, but Doctors' reasons were especially strong: its obstetrics unit was outmoded and nonconforming to building codes, as was the rest of the hospital, and the obstetricians were calling for its replacement. Obstetrics was a very important service to Doctors; though one of the smaller hospitals on First Hill, it ranked second in the number of deliveries among area institutions.

When a well-known San Francisco obstetrician was called to Seattle by Doctors and Virginia Mason to consult for them, his report recommended the consolidation of the two departments. Later in the year the Swedish board announced that it was considering the elimination of its obstetrical service. Doctors and Virginia Mason seized upon this new piece of information, and in February, 1970, discussions were expanded to consider a maternity center large enough for the volume of all central Seattle hospitals.

And so, at its July, 1970 meeting the Facilities Review Committee of the Puget Sound Health Planning Council heard a proposal from Doctors for a six-story, free-standing maternity center located adjacent to its existing physical plant. The facility would be linked by tunnel or bridge to the main hospital and an additional bridge would connect the maternity center to Virginia Mason.

Earlier in 1970, the Doctors proposal had encountered trouble. The Swedish board of trustees' vague statement concerning the possible closure of its obstetrical service was met by an angry blast from its medical staff. The Swedish board and administration then clarified the hospital's position, explaining that Swedish would not necessarily abandon its service, but that First Hill obstetrics was an all or nothing proposition: either Swedish should take over the entire central Seattle obstetrics volume, or it should eliminate its maternity services in favor of some other institution.

Thus, Swedish also prepared a proposal for a maternity center, a 120-bed facility linked to the main hospital. Swedish officials' presentation to the Facilities Review Committee stressed that their institution had become the major community medical center on First Hill and had tremendous potential for the future. Dr. Allan Lobb, Swedish's medical director, expressed his hope that the Medical Center would embrace all of medical care, including obstetrics.

The Facilities Review Committee decided in favor of the Doctors proposal, following the recommendation of the Regional Health Planning Council staff. The committee was impressed by the spirit of cooperation that existed between Doctors and Virginia Mason; in fact, the planning council reasoned that these two neighboring institutions could properly be viewed as one medical center complex. Mr. Robert Thomas, director of the planning council staff, hoped that approval of the Doctors maternity center plan would help pave the way for an eventual merger of Doctors and Virginia Mason.

To the people at Doctors, the favorable decision spelled a new lease on their hospital's life, a raison d'etre. They now saw hope and even a reason for rebuilding the hospital's deteriorating physical plant.

As a first step in making the maternity center a reality, the Health Planning Council solicited the preliminary support of all First Hill hospitals. Swedish, Virginia Mason, Providence and Seattle General all made tentative agreements to support the Doctors maternity center. However, Providence bowed out of the project a short time later, citing its stand on abortions and the distance of the hospital from the proposed maternity center, about one mile, as reasons.

Planning for the maternity center proceeded under the direction of Mr. Ray Zoellick, Associate Director of Doctors, and included the other three hospitals; however, support from Swedish was shaky. Swedish was reluctant to sacrifice its obstetrics service, especially since to do so might result in a corresponding diminution in gynecological surgery activity.

Planning for the maternity center dragged on for nearly two years, during which time the area birth rate dropped steadily and the size of the proposed facility was scaled down. Finally, in the fall of 1972, a two-volume report containing the maternity center proposal was completed, and Doctors brought it to a certificate-of-need hearing of the Health Planning Council.

The hearing was an unexpected disaster for Doctors. Representatives from Swedish spoke in opposition to the proposed maternity center. A statement by Dr. Lobb was particularly damaging to Doctors' case: he argued that it made little sense to build a $7,000,000 facility linked by a bridge to a deteriorating small hospital with a limited future. While he did not directly say so at the hearing, Dr. Lobb believed that Doctors intended in the future to use the maternity center as a wedge to justify building a new hospital, thus perpetuating an institution that should not exist.

Swedish's sudden withdrawal of support abolished the Doctors maternity center plan, which, even with support of all four hospitals, had marginal economic prospects due to the declining birth rate. Doctors immediately withdrew the certificate-of-need application. Its officials felt they had been double-crossed.

DOCTORS/SEATTLE GENERAL MERGER TALKS REKINDLED

Seattle General's move to its new location at the former Maynard Hospital on First Hill was not the panacea expected. The hospital's basic deficiencies remained—lack of programs unique or essential to the community, and insufficient medical staff support. Occupancy remained low, averaging 55 percent in 1972, and the number of obstetrical admissions declined dramatically.

In the summer of 1972 members of the Seattle General board approached members of the Doctors board with the suggestion that joint merger talks be rekindled. Doctors officials agreed to this proposition, even though they were preoccupied with the final stages of planning for their proposed maternity center.

Following the collapse of the Doctors maternity center proposal, merger discussions between the two hospitals became more serious. For one thing, the hospitals' representatives were now more genuinely aware of the limitations imposed on them by certificate-of-need requirements and the local comprehensive health planning agency.[3]

Physician support for the merger was now growing stronger, particularly at Doctors. Dr. Maurice Lawson, a general practitioner and respected member of the Doctors board, polled the Doctors Hospital medical staff during the spring of 1973, seeking their opinion about the proposed merger, and found that 93 percent favored it. Medical staff members felt that the existing facilities, particularly those for surgery and obstetrics, were rapidly becoming unacceptable, and that complete reconstruction of the building was required. The Doctors' representatives in the merger discussions began to feel a greater sense of urgency. At Seattle General a majority of physicians on the staff, including most of the younger doctors, favored merger and joint construction of a new facility. These physicians did not care about site, so long as it was in the vicinity of First Hill. But a vocal minority of Seattle General's physicians was vigorously opposed to the merger, especially if it meant abandoning the hospital's present site.

Early in 1973 a formal Joint Merger Committee was established, representing both boards of trustees, with ten official and three exofficio members. It was led by cochairmen Mr. Robert Graham from Doctors and Mr. Roy Anderson from Seattle General. The contingent from each hospital consisted of the board president, two physicians and two lay members. The administrator of Seattle General and the director and assistant director of Doctors served as exofficio members.

As discussions unfolded, members of the Joint Merger Committee felt that they were developing a working relationship with one another: discussions were cordial, and all felt they shared a strong desire to accomplish the merger. However, this atmosphere tended to mask what was, underneath, a chaotic situation.

The Seattle General Merger Committee members, particularly their outspoken chairman, Mr. Anderson, wanted to focus on the question of facilities; they felt that Doctors' outmoded, nonconforming building, coupled with its small, confining site, precluded development of a shared facility at that location. Instead, they argued, it made sense for Doctors to abandon its site and pool its assets to develop the facility at Seattle General, which had a more modern building and sufficient land. The Seattle General committee members felt committed to their present site, having moved to it only two years previous.

The Doctors, Merger Committee members played down the facility issues, focusing instead on the integration of programs and organizations. Doctors' Merger Committee members favored a two-step process: the two hospitals should first merge organization and assets, and then address the issue of where to locate the new hospital. Even so, Doctors' representatives hoped that ultimately a new hospital would be built on their First Hill site.

At a June, 1973 meeting of the Joint Merger Committee, Mr. Graham and the president of the Doctors board, Mr. Hugh Smith, urged the committee to recommend merger to the boards. But the Seattle General representatives were not ready to merge. Mr. Anderson said that if the merger committee so recommended, it ought to have definite answers for the medical staffs of the two hospitals as to the scope and location of services. Mr. Graham and others attempted several times to move the Joint Merger Committee toward making the merger recommendation, but each time the committee floundered over the unanswered questions of site, facilities and financing. Neither hospital was prepared to sacrifice its independence, yet neither fully understood that as long as they remained separate their futures were very limited.

By August of 1973, the Joint Merger Committee recognized that its discussions were not proceeding, and that the effort of an outside consultant was needed to break the log jam. After investigating several firms, Lester Gorsline and Associates of San Francisco was chosen to study the situation. The Joint Merger Committee believed that the major issues remaining to be resolved were: (1) what the new facility for the consolidated hospital should feature, and (2) where it should be located.

SWEDISH HOSPITAL MAKES A MERGER PROPOSAL

In mid-June 1973, Swedish's Medical Director Allan Lobb made an interesting proposal to Mr. William Hogarty, Executive Director of the Puget Sound Health Planning Council. Dr. Lobb wrote:

> It occurs to us . . . that it would be timely for you to initiate a meeting of principals of at least: The Doctors Hospital, Seattle General, The Swedish Hospital Medical Center and possibly Cabrini, with an eye toward ultimate merger.
>
> Isn't it possible, as a point of departure, to conceive of the following, which is offered as a suggestion?
>
> Ask the joint committee to: 1) Examine First Hill in general, and specifically the entire space bounded by Madison, Boren, Broadway and James Street, approximately 11 blocks, of which the Swedish Hospital Medical Center now owns eight. 2) Jointly recognize the mutual advantages of coordination and integration of hospital services with an eye toward the development of a northwest or community health care center. This could conceivably eliminate such names as the Swedish Hospital Medical Center, The Doctors Hospital, etc.

Mr. Hogarty contacted the board presidents and administrators of Doctors and Seattle General to determine their support for a meeting with Swedish. He found them unwilling to attend such a meeting, but agreeable to a meeting which would include all seven of the First Hill hospitals. This larger meeting was held, but was of little consequence and did not deal with the agenda Dr. Lobb had proposed.

This was not the first time Dr. Lobb had suggested to the Health Planning Council a scenario for the future central Seattle health care system which included a merger of Swedish, Seattle General and Doctors hospitals. In a letter dated November 1971, accompanying a certificate-of-need application for additional beds at Swedish, Dr. Lobb had expressed his view that the small urban hospital is obsolete in today's health care system, and that the assets of Doctors and Seattle General, both financial and staff, might be directed ultimately to the development of a larger hospital complex and referral center—the Swedish Hospital Medical Center.

In the summer of 1973, most of the Joint Merger Committee members considered merger or affiliation with Swedish an unthinkable option. They feared the total loss of their hospitals' identity should they get involved with Swedish. Seattle General and Doctors Hospital officials believed that the powerful medical director of Swedish would be difficult to work with: while they all admired him for his pivotal role in creating the large Swedish institution, many distrusted him. Lingering in the minds of the Doctors Hospital board members was the memory of the defeat of their maternity center proposal, and the feeling that Lobb had never supported the proposal and had waited until the final hearing to torpedo it. Further, they knew that Dr. Lobb preferred to manage the huge Swedish complex without the aid of any assistant administrators. Most on the Joint Merger Committee took a dim view of this unorthodox management style and felt it was indicative of the man's ego.

It was expected that the orientation of Gorsline and Associates would be primarily architectural. The project leader was Ms. Wanda Jones, a graduate of a program in hospital administration and an expert in the areas of health systems planning and organization. After a brief assessment of the situation, Ms. Jones realized that to adhere strictly to the instructions given to her by the Joint Merger Committee would be to provide the two hospitals with only a small portion of the information they would require to make effective decisions about their institutions. The final report (Lester Gorsline Associates, 1973) stated:

> We agreed to evaluate the feasibility of a merger to construct a replacement facility. As a result of our visit, the team concluded that this objective requires re-examination to answer these questions: What will a replacement hospital achieve? To what is the organization committed that requires a hospital for its realization?

> We felt obliged to enlarge our instructions because it quickly became obvious that neither hospital now enjoys what could be called a secure and healthy place in the local hospital system. Only part of this problem can be attributed to obsolete facilities.

Ms. Jones and her staff accordingly engaged in an ambitious study of the Seattle health care system and the possible places of Seattle General and Doctors in it. Their final report identified and evaluated seven alternative futures for the two hospitals. Some of the major findings were:

Community Need for a Replacement Facility:

> Seattle currently has excess capacity in hospitals, concentrated in the smaller facilities. We do not find that there exists a need for a new, freestanding general community hospital in central Seattle.

> There are no known sites in King County that lack hospital services to the degree requiring a new hospital.

> Considering the apparent difficulties [that construction of a replacement facility] present for the satisfaction of community needs, financial feasibility or public agency approval, we find [that it] is not a feasible alternative for further planning.

Physician Support at Doctors and Seattle General:

> The average age of those staff physicians at Doctors Hospital who admitted 20 or more patients in the first six months of 1973 is 51.6 years; at Seattle General the comparable average is 56.7 years.

> Only a few physicians report no additional staff memberships nor any use of other hospitals and so would suffer the greatest loss if these hospitals discontinue operations. The pressure for replacement comes from these physicians, as well as from a much larger group who have multiple staff memberships and admit patients to two or more hospitals.

From the responses to the survey, from the interviews and from our visits to the other hospitals, we must conclude that the current physicians support is marginal to poor in terms of offering future security to a renewed institution.

Financial Feasibility of the Replacement Facility Alternative:

Total project cost (for a replacement facility) could . . . be as much as $16,025,000, or the equivalent of as much as $80,000/bed. This total includes the expenses of parking garages, land acquisition and escalation. The range of possible borrowing, from conservative to an upper limit, is estimated to be $2 to $6 million.

Affiliation with Swedish Hospital:

The alternative of affiliation with a major medical center, specifically Swedish, has several advantages to Doctors and Seattle General, to Swedish and to the local health system. Doctors and Seattle General need the resources to replace their obsolete facilities and remain fiscally solvent; Swedish has the land and supporting services. It recognizes the need for a link with a generalist-oriented support base. Doctors and Seattle General have this generalist orientation. The affiliation of the two organizations (assuming Doctors and Seattle General are one unit) would enhance the likelihood of approval for any new construction expenditures and possibly make capital more readily obtainable.

The conclusions of the Gorsline report came as a shock to the members of the Joint Merger Committee. The committee met in late November, 1973, and held a confused discussion of them. Hugh Smith, President of the Doctors board was bewildered, frustrated and disappointed by the Gorsline recommendations. He and others were distressed that the consultants felt that there was no essential reason for the continued existence of the two hospitals in their present context, and that the replacement option was not feasible. Some committee members questioned the objectivity of the Gorsline consultant.

Most of the Joint Merger Committee members were discouraged, and some repelled, by the recommendation that their hospitals pursue an affiliation with Swedish. Mr. Graham felt that, with Swedish relationships colored by past experience, it would make sense first to investigate a possible tie-in with Virginia Mason, despite the problems that would exist in merging the Mason Clinic group practice physicians with the independent practitioners of Doctors and Seattle General. But Seattle General's Dr. Donald Hall argued that they would have to look beyond the existing image of Swedish and Allan Lobb.

The Joint Merger Committee's November meeting was only the beginning of a long debate about the conclusions of the Gorsline report; the debate ensued not only in the formal atmosphere of subsequent committee meetings, which continued sporadically throughout 1974, but informally among physicians and board members of the two hospitals. More than anything else, the Gorsline report was an educational document; in this regard it was a success. It did not bring the hospitals involved to the brink of merger, as the consultant had hoped, but it did serve to help the leaders of Doctors and Seattle General look beyond their predicament about facilities to the question of their roles in the larger health care system.

MERGER DISCUSSIONS EXPAND TO INCLUDE SWEDISH

Members of the Joint Merger Committee sent out feelers to Swedish and Virginia Mason hospitals to determine their interest, if any, in affiliating with Seattle General and Doctors. The possibility of a tie-in with Virginia Mason was quickly ruled out: everyone involved soon recognized that Virginia Mason was far too dominated by the Mason Clinic group practice specialists to permit integration with hospitals whose medical staffs were composed largely of generalists engaged in independent practice.

An advance party from the Joint Merger Committee determined that Swedish officials were receptive to an affiliation arrangement, not a surprising discovery, given that Dr. Lobb had already proposed such in 1971 and 1973. Swedish recognized that an affiliation or merger with the two small hospitals would help provide a primary care base to feed its tertiary services. The Swedish board also felt that if they could attract Doctors and Seattle General to the Swedish Medical Center campus, they would have clear justification for building additional beds.[4]

The Joint Merger Committee approached the Swedish affiliation gingerly. It attempted to convey to Swedish that they did not come with hat in hand, that there were substantial advantages to Swedish in such an arrangement, and that Doctors and Seattle General had other viable options. By December 1974, the ice was beginning to melt: Doctors, Seattle General and Swedish had held several Affiliation Committee meetings, and they had begun investigating potential building sites on the Swedish campus and the potential for utilizing ancillary services based at Swedish.

The pathway to merger of Seattle General and Doctors and affiliation with Swedish was far from clear. A number of Seattle General Board members, notably Mr. Martin Smith, now Vice-President for Finance of the hospital board, remained staunchly opposed to affiliation with Swedish. This group clung stubbornly to the notion that together Doctors and Seattle General could still go it alone, either by developing the Seattle General site or building a replacement facility elsewhere. However, the members of this anti-affiliation group kept their agenda hidden, preferring to go through the discussions of affiliation with Swedish in the hope that things would go sour eventually. Their sentiments were reinforced by significant opposition to the affiliation from within the Seattle General medical staff. One Seattle General physician reportedly said, "These merger talks have been going on for almost 15 years and we are still hanging in there. I don't see what's to stop us from making

.

it through the next 15." Some general practitioners felt threatened by the specialist-dominated Swedish staff, fearing that they would be handed the dregs of the operating room schedule and lose their independence and identity. A few physicians at Seattle General feared that they would not be accepted on the Swedish staff. One of the more influential physicians opposing integration with Swedish was Dr. Wayne Chesledon, Seattle General's radiologist, who did not foresee a place for himself in the new arrangement.

Despite these rumblings of discontent, talks between the three hospitals continued and the affiliation concept gained momentum. Leadership from Mr. Graham and Dr. Lawson of Doctors Hospital was critical, as was the steady belief in the concept on the part of the Swedish board. By the end of 1974, Doctors officials as well as many of Seattle General's had concluded that they had no alternative but to link themselves to Swedish. The medical staffs of both hospitals favored construction of a pavilion, a separate hospital building located adjacent and connected to the main Swedish facility. The pavilion would permit the two small hospitals to retain something of their identity and preserve the flavor of their prior institutions. Both Seattle General and Doctors officials believed that their hospitals provided patients with warmer, more personal care than did Swedish.

By the Spring of 1975, discussions between Doctors, Seattle General and Swedish were far enough along that the three hospitals felt that it was time formally to let officials from the Puget Sound Health Planning Council in on their plans. The Affiliation Committee invited Mr. Hogarty and two other guests from the Planning Council to its March, 1975, meeting. The purpose of the meeting was to review the affiliation activities to date and to determine the extent of the Planning Council's support.

The ordinary meeting suddenly took a dramatic turn when Dr. Lobb described two decisions to be faced in the near future by Swedish. Current construction of the Swedish tower addition would be topped out on April 8, 1975, and following that date it would be impossible to extend the building upwards without incurring the additional costs of recreating forms, reassembling the crane, etc. If Doctors and Seattle General wished to utilize additional floors built on top of the new tower, the decision to merge should be made in the next two to three weeks. Lobb also reported that Swedish had to decide soon whether or not to use all of the funds borrowed to finance the current construction project, since the amount borrowed exceeded the total cost of the project by approximately $2 million. He suggested that a portion of this money could be used to build a new obstetrical unit at Swedish if Doctors was willing to consolidate its obstetrics at Swedish.

Representatives from Doctors and Seattle General thought it incredible that Dr. Lobb seriously propose they reach decisions to merge their two hospitals, affiliate with Swedish, and locate their facility in several floors atop the Swedish tower all in the space of two or three weeks. Nonetheless, Lobb's proposal to utilize excess borrowed funds to modernize and expand Swedish's obstetrical unit was discussed seriously, and the Affiliation Committee representatives of Doctors agreed to expedite a board decision on the question of whether to terminate Doctor's obstetrical services in favor of consolidation.

The Doctors Hospital board, realizing that its bargaining position vis-a-vis Swedish would never be any stronger and that closure of its existing unit was inevitable, decided in favor of terminating obstetrics upon the completion of the proposed unit at Swedish. During the two-year construction period Swedish obstetricians would utilize Doctors' facilities. Thus their decision was based on a certain quid pro quo.

In taking this decision, Doctors' trustees knew that they had essentially burned a bridge behind them by committing themselves to terminating their maternity services: they had turned their backs on their existing site and deteriorating building. Some form of more comprehensive integration with Swedish was now inevitable.

Swedish's application for certificate of need for a $1.2 million modernization and expansion of its obstetrical unit to accommodate Doctors' volume sailed smoothly by the Health Planning Council at its August 1975 meeting. The Council stated its hope that this step would eventually lead to a total merger of Doctors, Seattle General and Swedish hospitals.

Since the last time Swedish had applied for a certificate of need an additional step in the approval process had been added: the law now required a review of all such certificates by the newly-created Washington State Hospital Commission, to determine the economic desirability and feasibility of the proposed project. The commission was under the dynamic chairmanship of Ludwig Lobe, an accountant by training and a strong consumer advocate. The Hospital Commission strongly endorsed the Swedish proposal, praising it as a step toward lowering the cost of obstetrical care to patients.

REENTER THE CONSULTANT

Doctors was now anxious to reach agreement with Seattle General and Swedish on merger and/or affiliation, having made the obstetrics decision. In May 1975, Doctors officials drafted a letter of intent, the purpose of which was to "outline the proposed program for merger of The Doctors Hospital Association and Seattle General Hospital, and their affiliation with Swedish Hospital Medical Center, or, if that does not prove feasible, merger of The Doctors Hospital with Swedish Hospital Medical Center."

A number of Joint Merger Committee members, especially those from Seattle General Hospital, felt that this document was too vague. They questioned how they could agree to merger and affiliation with Swedish when they hospital. Joint Merger Committee members were further frustrated by their uncertainty about how to implement their plans. In recognition of these elements of uncertainty, the Joint Merger Committee called back Wanda Jones, who had by now left Gorsline and Associates to form her ọwn consulting firm.

Ms. Jones convinced the Joint Merger Committee that merely drafting an improved letter of intent would not be sufficient to bring about the merger decision. She proposed an expanded role for the consultant which included the following: 1) design and organization of the negotiation process, including advice on what decision should be made and a schedule for making those decisions; 2) investigation (or reexamination) of various other alternatives in addition to the proposed affiliation with Swedish; 3) liaison with health planning agencies and other government bodies to ascertain support; 4) coordination of and recommendations concerning financial, legal, organizational and architectural feasibility studies; 5) orientation of the negotiating team and assistance with actual negotiations, acting as an objective outsider in the process; 6) review of existing and potential roles for each provider on the Swedish campus; and 7) in general, provision of the staff support necessary to sustain the momentum of the merger/affiliation process.

Not all of the board members at Seattle General and Doctors were convinced of the necessity to give Ms. Jones such a pervasive role. But the Joint Merger Committee was sufficiently frustrated with the progress of negotiations to date that they agreed to give her a chance to carry on as she had proposed.

One of the dilemmas at this point in the merger process was that the scheme around which the three hospitals had been rallying—an independent pavilion occupied by the merged Seattle General and Doctors organizations and affiliated with Swedish—was probably not financially feasible. The combined assets of Doctors and Seattle General were undoubtedly insufficient to permit them independently to finance the construction of the pavilion; the borrowing power of Swedish would likely have to be brought to bear, and this could be accomplished only if Doctors and Seattle General actually merged with Swedish.

The question was, how to bring this about in such a way as to assure the medical staff and board support from the hospitals involved? The merger issue was particularly touchy at Seattle General where a still strong, persistent faction of board and medical staff members feared being swallowed up by the Swedish monster. The success of the merger process depended upon taking this group into account.

NEW PROPOSAL: A HOLDING COMPANY

During 1974, Seattle General's board and administration underwent key changes in leadership. In January Paul Bliss, the administrator, resigned, leaving his young assistant administrator, Robert Menaul, in the acting administrator's role. In June the Seattle General Board appointed Menaul administrator, recognizing that he was inexperienced, but feeling that it would be inappropriate to recruit a more experienced administrator in view of the likelihood of merger.

In July 1974, the president of Seattle General's board suffered a heart attack, and Robert Dupar, then vice-president, took his place. Mr. Dupar, an independent businessman who had formerly been a key executive of Western International Hotels, brought fresh leadership to the Seattle General contingent of the Affiliation Committee. When he first began attending the merger discussions between the three hospitals, he was dismayed to find that the Seattle General representatives were usually the ones holding up progress. Through the spring of 1975 he gradually assumed the role of the spokesman for the hospital in talks with Doctors and Swedish. Mr. Dupar, with his years of experience in a large corporate organization and his personable style, became one of the prime movers in the three hospitals' joint efforts.

As the three-way discussions continued, the participants gradually realized that their goal of a pavilion hospital was probably not financially feasible if they stopped at affiliation. Then, in June, 1975, Dupar came up with a concept that appealed immediately to many of the Affiliation Committee members: the three hospitals could form a holding company. He outlined his ideas in a letter to the Seattle General board, which explained how Doctors and Seattle General could hitch-hike on the borrowing power of Swedish, as the three hospitals would be merged into one corporation. But there could still be two operating boards and separate medical staffs, which would assure a measure of autonomy for the Doctors/Seattle General unit.[5]

THE DECISION CONFERENCES

One of the first steps that consultant Jones took when she became reinvolved was to lay out a tight schedule for making critical decisions. Her intent was to force the boards of the three hospitals to make the necessary decisions and put an end to the procrastination that had for so long frustrated merger efforts. The conference schedule was as follows:

September 25, 6:00–10:00 p.m.	Background; dinner
September 26, 1:00-6:00 p.m.	Educational conference
October 3, 1:00-6:00 p.m.	"Decision A" conference—facilities
October 17, 1:00-6:00 p.m.	"Decision B" conference—organization

A second feature of Ms. Jones' plan for the management of the merger was the establishment of liaisons with First Hill community groups, the Washington State Hospital Commission, The Puget Sound Health Planning Council, and the city of Seattle. The idea was to keep these parties informed of merger progress, to obtain their support, and to provide them a channel for their input into planning. In the case of the Health Planning Council, a committee was established consisting of Council members and representatives of the three hospitals.

September 25, 1975, was the first occasion on which the total membership of the boards of Seattle General, Doctors and Swedish hospitals had ever met as a group. It was fitting that the meeting was held over cocktails and dinner at Seattle's finest hotel. Although the primary purpose of the evening was social, Ms. Jones had invited a panel of individuals with extensive personal experience in health facility mergers to speak to the assembled board members. The tone of the messages was positive—the panelists spoke enthusiastically and encouragingly about their experiences with mergers. Also present at the meeting were representatives from several other local hospitals, the Health Planning Council, the State Hospital Association, and the Seattle Area Hospital Council.

On the following day an intensive educational conference was held for the benefit of the membership of the three boards. The purpose of the conference was to prepare the board members for the decisions that they were scheduled to make in the next weeks. The same group of merger experts that the previous evening had addressed the dinner meeting of the combined boards now spent an afternoon in dialogue with board members, discussing the alternatives available to them and fielding their questions.

For the most part the discussions were positive; however, several dissonant notes were sounded. Not all of the board members were sold on the idea. Dr. Chesledon, Seattle General's radiologist, proposed that Seattle General and Doctors Hospitals stop short of full merger with Swedish and instead affiliate with the larger institution. (This represented a compromise position by Dr. Chesledon, who had previously been dead set against any form of integration with Swedish.)

The educational conference concluded harmoniously with representatives from the three hospital boards giving different but significant endorsements of the three-way merger. Dr. Lawson, speaking on behalf of Doctors' board, fully supported the merger if it allowed for construction of a separate facility that would permit the flavor of the present institution to continue. Seattle General's Dupar noted that the individual hospitals had to draw a limit on debt service per bed. Speaking for the Swedish board, Mr. Nordstrom cited the very favorable interest rate under which Swedish financed its new addition, noting that it would enjoy extending this rate to the other hospitals in a merged system.

After the conference adjourned, and in preparation for the upcoming October 3rd meeting, Ms. Jones distributed copies of a 50-page report entitled "Decision Report A—Facilities." The report reviewed four alternative facilities concepts: 1) freestanding 150-bed acute care facility, with all major ancillary and support services, independent of the Swedish Hospital; 2) affiliated pavilion hospital, adjoining Swedish, with only basic ancillary and few support services; 3) same as 2) but merger instead of affiliation; and 4) additional bed floors, 150 beds total, to be added to Swedish following merger of Doctors and Swedish Hospital (possibly including merger of Seattle General as well).

The document included an evaluation of these alternatives in light of land and building sites, capital cost, existing services available at Swedish, parking, and financing considerations. By applying these criteria the consultant ruled out alternatives 1 and 2. Her recommendation was for 3, the merged pavilion concept, which combined the features of nonduplication of Swedish's services and financial feasibility.

In effect, the Decision A report was a tightly-written script for the facilities decision meeting. Board members had only to read back the lines of this report at their October 3rd meeting in order to make the decision to proceed with development of the merged pavilion.

Virtually all of the members of the boards at Swedish and Doctors were convinced of the desirability of the new concept. A majority of the 24 Seattle General board members agreed also, but there remained a group of at least six strongly opposed, and several others straddling the fence. President Dupar was not sure who would ultimately side with him in support of merger.

On October 3 the three boards convened to consider the first half of the decision to merge the three hospitals and build a pavilion. Ms. Jones had divided the decision into two parts in order to make the pill easier to swallow for those board members that had difficulty with the concept. Therefore, this first decision conference focused not on the corporate merger itself, but on facilities.

For the most part the Decision A conference proceeded according to plan: the conference participants spoke enthusiastically about the pavilion hospital concept. At one point Mr. Martin Smith of the Seattle General board interjected the suggestion that Doctors and Seattle General abandon merging with Swedish, jointly remodel the existing Seattle General building, and donate the existing Doctors facility to charity. Mr. Smith's proposal sounded incongruous to the other participants—a voice out of the past. Few took it seriously.

The climax of the conference came when each board member was asked to express to the group his position on the issues. Dr. Jack Thomas, Chief of Seattle General's medical staff, spoke enthusiastically for the merged pavilion concept, and in so doing set the tone for the other Seattle General board members. One by one, endorsements came from virtually all members of the three boards.

The boards then met separately, and each of them passed a resolution formally stating their preference for proceeding with the development of a merged pavilion on the Swedish campus.

Subsequent to the Decision A conference, copies of a second consultant's report entitled Decision Report B—Organization, were distributed to all board members. With the primary facilities questions already resolved, this report was designed to assist the boards in reaching agreement on an organizational concept for developing and managing the proposed facility. The report began with a recap of the reasons for merger seen from each of the three hospitals' viewpoints, and provided a common base of knowledge on legal issues, the effects of government regulation and reimbursement policies, capital markets, goals for board and management structure, medical staff organization, the status of present employees at Doctors and Seattle General, and community involvement in the new organization. The report also delineated exactly the decisions that should be made by each board at the next conference; Ms. Jones even included draft resolutions to be passed by each board at the conclusion of the conference. Finally, the report outlined a plan for the period 1975 to 1980, designed to implement the merger.

In contrast to the educational and Decision A conferences, where the people opposed to merger were vocal, the few board members still opposing merger with Swedish were silent at the Decision B conference of October 17th. Most participants felt that they had already made the crucial decisions at the facilities decision conference two weeks before, and they were eager to complete this step in the decision making process. Yet two departures from Ms. Jones' script were proposed. Two members of the Swedish board suggested there be only one medical staff in the new organization. Mr. Graham of Doctors quickly put the idea to rest: as far as a number of members of both of the smaller hospitals' staffs were concerned, merger required a provision for separate medical staffs in the new organization. To do otherwise would destroy the spirit of accommodation that had now developed among the medical staffs. A case in point was Dr. Chesledon, the Seattle General radiologist, whose vocal resistance to merger had been allayed when he was assured of space in the new pavilion, and of the need for a separate radiology service in the proposed pavilion.

The second script change occurred when representatives from Doctors and Seattle General proposed dispensing with the merger between their two hospitals prior to the three-way merger with Swedish. The conference participants agreed with this logic and the boards decided to eliminate the intermediate step. The three hospital boards each passed the resolutions proposed by Ms. Jones, as modified.

The two decision conferences and the resulting board resolutions were major milestones: the three boards had formally agreed in principle to merge with one another and build a pavilion on the Swedish campus to house the primary-care oriented programs of Seattle General and Doctors.

Following the Decision B conference representatives from the three hospitals were selected for membership on an Interim Planning Committee. Mr. Dupar was selected as chairman. Ms. Jones was retained to assist the committee with implementation. The primary tasks facing the Committee were: 1) selection of an architectural scheme for the pavilion hospital which was within cost limitations; 2) initiation of a detailed financial feasibility study of the new facility; and 3) development of specific plans for the new organization. Ms. Jones again laid out a detailed schedule for the committee's activity; if all went according to her plan a final go/no decision on merger and construction could be made by the fall of 1976.

A prominent Seattle architectural firm was selected, and, following an intensive four-week study, the firm provided cost estimates. At the February 1976 meeting of the Interim Planning Committee representatives from the three hospitals were dismayed to learn that the architects pegged the cost of an ideal pavilion at $18 million. The hospitals had expected an estimate of between $8 to $12 million, and all perceived this new cost as out of reach. By trimming the proposal considerably, the architects managed to whittle the cost of the project to $13.6 million.

At this same committee meeting Dr. Lobb startled the representatives from Seattle General and Doctors by announcing that he felt the separate pavilion facility was not financially feasible and that the concept should be abandoned. Lobb pointed to the recent doubling of Swedish's debt, due to the cost of the new addition and the obstetrics remodelling project, and stated that this made Swedish's future cash flow difficult. He suggested an alternative scheme that would add beds on top of the new Swedish tower and remodel two old floors of beds which had been closed earlier. He then proposed that further planning be delayed for about one year until Swedish's financial position stabilized.

A heated discussion followed Dr. Lobb's proposal. Mr. Graham stated that such a plan rendered meaningless the decisions reached in October by all three boards. Representatives from the two smaller hospitals remained convinced of the basic feasibility of the pavilion concept and argued that constructing a pavilion would assure physician support. whereas adding beds to Swedish would not.

Ms. Jones believed that Swedish was seriously underestimating its financial strength; she noted in a letter which followed the meeting that Swedish's debt service coverage ratio would be 2.12 if a $13.6 million pavilion were constructed, providing a comfortable margin over the 1.25–1.5 ratio acceptable to lenders, and that the projected debt/total assets ratio would be less than 50 percent. Furthermore, the pavilion had every potential for becoming a profitable venture in its own right, besides being a substantial user of Swedish ancillary services.

At the March meeting of the Interim Planning Committee Dr. Lobb renewed his objection to proceeding with planning for the pavilion facility. Other committee members were reluctant to postpone planning without concrete evidence of the proposal's unfeasibility. The committee agreed that a detailed financial feasibility study was needed, and recommended to each board that such a study be authorized.

In responding to the Committee's recommendation, Swedish officials made it clear that support of the financial study did not mean that they were necessarily in favor of the pavilion concept. On March 31, President Larson stated in a letter to Laughlin and Dupar that Swedish was withdrawing its support of the concept.

A number of board members of Seattle General and Doctors felt that Swedish had not taken seriously the commitment it had made six months previously, along with their hospitals. Some felt that Swedish had led them down a rosy path, never intending to back the pavilion idea.

The fall of 1975 marked the first time Washington hospitals were required to submit detailed budgets and proposed rates for review by the Washington State Hospital Commission. By law, no hospital could increase any rate without advance approval by the commission. After a number of hospitals had undergone the commission's perusal, it became apparent that the process focussed heavily on each institution's proposed growth and development factor—net income available for future use. In a number of cases the commission cut back a hospital's proposed growth and development factor because it felt that the hospital was seeking to expand in ways inconsistent with recommendations of comprehensive health planning agencies. Further, the commission was attempting to hold most hospitals' growth factors to 3 percent, as a general cost-containment strategy.

The Hospital commission's review of Swedish Hospital's 1976 proposed budget was among the stormiest. The commission debated the appropriateness of Swedish's proposed 7 percent growth factor. Swedish argued that this higher rate was necessary to ensure the financial feasibility of the proposed merger with Seattle General and Doctors Hospital. In the end the commission granted the 7 percent rate, but stipulated that the majority of the resulting capital funds must be used for merger purposes, since it hailed the merger as a significant step in holding down health care costs by reducing excess capacity in the Seattle area.

In March 1976 Ms. Jones met with officials of the hospital commission, including its colorful, consumer-oriented Chairman, Ludwig Lobe, as part of her ongoing effort to keep various public bodies abreast of merger developments. She informed them of the recent letter from the Swedish board to the other merger participants suggesting a one year delay because of concerns over financial feasibility.

Within several weeks Mr. Lobe met with the board presidents and administrators from Seattle General, Doctors and Swedish. He reminded them that the Commission had granted Swedish's 7 percent growth factor on a conditional basis. He told them that if the three hospitals did not begin immediately again making substantial progress toward merger the Commission would reopen its review of their 1976 budgets. Swedish would stand to lose a large portion of its growth and development factor. Mr. Lobe warned that the Commission might begin reviewing the budgets of the three hospitals every six months rather than on an annual basis.

The effect of Commissioner Lobe's interest was quickly to redirect and focus the merger efforts on a determination of financial feasibility. A nationally known accounting firm was retained to conduct the study.

All prior and proposed agreements were held in abeyance for the next five months while the accountants and financiers conducted their analyses. In September 1976 the verdict came in: debt capacity was sufficient for the pavilion-based merger. At about the same time the Interim Planning Committee learned that Swedish's existing lender, an eastern-based insurance company, was willing to extend a new loan without refinancing Swedish's existing debt—a key point for Swedish officials who viewed their existing loan instrument as well structured and favorable.

THE FINAL COMMITMENT

A number of actions were then initiated that, in sum, showed the commitment of all three hospitals to the merger. An attorney was hired to draft articles and by-laws for the new consolidation. He was instructed to design a single corporation with top policy-making board, two operating boards, two medical staffs, and an assistant administrator for all shared hospital services. Swedish officals proceeded to purchase adjacent land necessary to locate the pavilion in an optimal position to the existing main buildings. An architecture firm was retained and directed to proceed with plans and schematic drawings for the pavilion. Finally, officials of all three hospitals participated in a public forum arranged for First Hill residents at which the merger plans were described and comments solicited.

Some actions were not taken; however, the fact that they were deliberately postponed showed both pragmatism and ultimate intent. A management for the new operation was not selected, either from within or from without. New outside board members were not recruited or selected. A new name for the merger was not selected. Yet the path toward finalizing the merger was now free of major obstacles. By the end of 1976 the three Seattle hospitals had indeed committed to merger.

D. THE OUTCOME

On May 4, 1978, papers were signed merging Seattle General Hospital and The Doctors Hospital into Swedish Hospital and Medical Center. From this date until the new pavilion was completed, each of the former facilities was operated as a division of Swedish Hospital and Medical Center. The old boards functioned as division boards (committees) concerned with the continuing performance of the respective hospital organizations.

A new pavilion was under construction next to Swedish Hospital's South Wing. Upon its completion, Seattle General and The Doctors Hospital were to close their doors; thereafter, their patients would be cared for in the new pavilion. Initially, there were to be two medical staffs: one practicing in Swedish and one in the pavilion. In the interim, the present staffs investigated the necessary first steps to merging.

The Pavilion was opened in June 1980. It was immediately successful, as measured by its initial occupancy of 85 to 90 percent. Officials attribute this to a combination of unexpected population growth in the Seattle area and a preference by numerous physicians, including those who previously admitted to Swedish, for the facilities and services of the Pavilion. Robert Dupar reported that "the best candidates from the three hospitals" were selected to head up the various departments, and that the physical facilities were excellent in design and accoutrements. Officials began thinking of adding additional floors to the Pavilion to increase its capacity.

The financing of the Pavilion construction was no particular burden on Swedish: the necessary long-term borrowings were easily secured. At the time the Pavilion was constructed a new parking facility was also built, financed mainly from operating revenues rather than from long-term debt.

After the official merger (May 4, 1978), the boards of Seattle General and Doctors were continued as "operating boards" for what were now called "divisions" of the Swedish Hospital and Medical Center. At the same time a new Pavilion operating board was formed, consisting of 15 persons, 5 from each of the three hospitals. The overall board of trustees for Swedish Hospital and Medical Center began "operating as one group." It consisted of 17 persons, 11 from the Swedish board and 3 each from the Doctors and Seattle General boards.

The former Doctors Hospital was sold to the Virginia Mason Hospital, to which it is contiguous. The building was converted for use in administrative activities and as an outpatient geriatric center. The former Seattle General Hospital was sold to the Fred Hutchinson Cancer Research Center. It is now used for administrative activities, laboratories, and rooming facilities for the families of patients.

The former administrator of Doctors Hospital became the administrator of the new Pavilion, responsible to Dr. Lobb, who continued as overall director of Swedish. The former administrator of Seattle General became an associate director in the new organization, responsible for a number of operations which spanned both the Pavilion and the general Medical Center.

According to most observers and most measures, the merger was a success.

E.   COMMENTARIES

A CONSULTANT'S PERSPECTIVE—
WANDA JONES, M.P.H.[6]

The factors that made the merger happen are obvious, and can serve almost as a checklist against which to test the likelihood of a similar result in other settings. Because of this, the consulting team could be very candid and direct, since few of these factors were unknown or in dispute—their combined meaning needed to be conveyed in an unambiguous manner.

Following is a simplified reconstruction of the situation as it appeared in 1974.

Geography and Population
The hospitals were in the center of a very large urban/suburban/rural complex with water and hills separating the urban core and the suburbs. This meant that valuable urban space would tend to gain business and lose population over the long haul, and that suburbs would eventually seek self-sufficiency in all public services. There was thus no immediate possibility of a resurgence in downtown Seattle of the kind of populations that would support two small hospitals.

Ownership
All merger partners were voluntary nonprofit corporations with local boards. In this sense, they were homogeneous. Differing ownership structures did not bar merger, as they often do in other settings.

Time Pressures
The two small hospitals were both on short time fuses: they had aging buildings, aging medical staffs, and difficulty getting approval for any small moves to help revitalize them. As none of these were self-correcting factors, a large change or closure was inevitable.

Management
The three hospitals had few managers, thus few people with a vested interest in the status quo. In addition, the managers of the two small hospitals did not determine their boards' actions—these had strong internal leadership.

We can conclude that even when chief executive officers do not directly create merger, as is often the case, a merger can still take place if managers' tenure, status, obdurate nature, or historical competitiveness prevent them from barring it.

Governance
All three boards had strong members who accepted their responsibility to find a solution. The two small boards had been meeting together for some time. So, a great deal of the usual preliminary exploration of attitudes and style had already gone on.

Other Parties
There were no obvious contenders for a share of the decision. Civic leaders, community, government, all were willing to stand back while the principals made their own decisions. Often a merger will be hampered by an agency that wants the parties to come to a premature or agency-selected conclusion. The hospitals could have chosen to stop the talks rather than merge under agency interference. This merger benefitted from a well-informed comprehensive health planning agency staff which knew and trusted the consultants and did not feel compelled to coopt the merger discussions. This was particularly unusual since the agency underwent a complete board changeover during the merger, from an 89–749 entity to a 93–641 agency.

One Strong Partner
The merger would not have taken place if one of the partners, Swedish, had not had a well-established role and a base for program continuity—170 MDs in adjacent office buildings, several regional care and research programs, and extensive assets in the form of land and borrowing power. Its role and programs complemented rather than competed with those of the smaller partners.

Positive Outcome
The last significant ingredient in the merger was the fact that it would produce a partial replacement facility benefitting all three parties and acting as a catalyst for all intermediate decisions. Mergers that simply encompass an unchanged set of facilities and programs under a new corporation do not galvanize the parties sufficiently to make real progress after the merger is accomplished.

So, the consultant's task was to make these factors carry their appropriate weight in the discussions and decisions. However, in planning the merger decision process we expected some factors that we did not find but which, by their absence, influenced the way the merger talks progressed:

Other Hospitals
The other hospitals in the immediate vicinity, including another major medical center, did not actively seek inclusion in the merger talks, offer other alternatives, nor protest the creation of a stronger competitor. They could have sought some program consolidation concessions but did not. The merger seemed to make little difference in their collective action on other issues, such as land use planning with the city of Seattle.

External Forces
The only health related public agency that played an active role in the merger was the state rate commission which advised on an issue of budgets in response to a plea for funds needed for the merger. If there had been no rate commission, or no chairman willing to take a direct interest, there would probably have been no outside authority capable of influencing board and management behavior when the going got tough. The hospital board members, while drawn from the community, did not appear to be influenced by civic leaders, either those with political power, money, or old family influence. Barring that, and with a newly reconstructed planning agency, the rate commission took on a role as local system authority when it was needed. We have speculated that had the commission existed earlier, and the planning agency had continuity, the two might well have produced the combined positive and negative incentives necessary to yield a merger a few years earlier.

The Community
We also expected to hear more from the First Hill neighborhood. In fact, its residents did not approach the hospitals after the merger was widely known—we approached them. Their concerns were nonmedical—parking, transportation, and amenities. In a midwestern or eastern city we would have expected requests for specific medical or social services in poor supply—such as psychiatric services; but there were no such requests. Despite hospitals' cost escalation problem, the institutions on First Hill have quite good community acceptance of their value. The First Hill Improvement Association, a small-business oriented organization, was also interested primarily in maintaining commercial frontage and good parking. No one insisted, for example, that the hospitals all coalesce their site development plans—which are only a few blocks apart—and produce some combined service to the community such as an education-community center, senior citizens center, park, day care, or something similar. So, with no outside requests and no advocacy leadership, the merger talks had an internal focus and thus were much easier to manage.

Alternatives
Finally, the merger went the way it did because there were literally few real options other than closure. This is not always the case.

Consultant's Role

The consulting engagement was made easier by the fact that all three hospitals used the same rather than separate consultants. It meant, however, that we had to manage the entire merger process in an up-front manner, when it might have gone more swiftly at times to caucus with one party at a time to deal with its specific concerns.

The up-front method had its good and bad points. It led to a general belief in the integrity of the decision process itself, but the process was not suited to all types of decisions with which the merger partners should have dealt. Following the basic decision to merge and construct the pavilion, the Interim Planning Committee essentially felt that planning was completed—that the task was now an architectural one. The committee could have kept the impetus going, to deal with how a transition would be made to a medical center management structure adequate to oversee the approximately 600 beds and assorted institutes and special facilities. However, the management issue was bound to be a sensitive one, and rather than dealing with it as a problem of the new corporate arrangement, the committee chose to let the matter ride.

The Seattle First Hill case exhibited other universal qualities of merger opportunities. Most of the merger-generating factors were long-standing; they included geography, population, economics, facility design, land use, and other elements characterized by permanence and nonnegotiability. However, to apply the same approach to decision management in even a similar situation would likely be a mistake. The approach we took in this project was tailor-made for the Seattle set of players only—and keeping a good fit was often very difficult. A different set of players might call for a more legalistic approach, or a buy-out approach, or a closed-room negotiating approach, or a civic leader intervener approach.

Further, different roles were needed in each period of the project, and with each group. The roles included 1) health planning consultant, i.e., defining and evaluating alternatives; 2) process consultant; 3) manager of the decision process; 4) medical staff educator; 5) representative of the three hospitals to other consultants; 6) communicator; and 7) staff to the overall decision group, the Interim Planning Committee. All of these roles were planned explicitly for this project alone. Any other situation would need a different process management design.

A TRUSTEE'S PERSPECTIVE—
ROBERT DUPAR

Ten years have passed since we started serious negotiations on merger. It seems like forever, and a bit anticlimactic now that we are straightening out the kinks of working together. The Interim Planning Committee has been dissolved. Representatives from Seattle General and Doctors now sit as full members of the Swedish Board of Trustees. A new operating board, made up of representatives of all three groups, is tackling the problems of the new pavilion.

This merger was brought about by boards of trustees' actions, not through pressure from the medical staffs or administrations. If pressure existed from any source, it was from the public sector. As related by Mark Secord, the Washington State Hospital Commission played a decisive part in holding the negotiations together. But the awakening awareness by the respective boards of trustees to the needs of the community and ways and means to make the health care delivery more economical also played a big role. The boards of trustees evolved from boards of the religious, professional, or ethnic groups that brought the hospitals into being, to groups representing the citizens of our community.

The further we got into our deliberations, the move evident it became that the pavilion concept was the only way we could assure our downtown community a continuing pool of general practitioners. As a matter of fact, the consultants' findings predicted a steady decline of use of Swedish without the pavilion. Their interviews with Seattle General and Doctors physicians found over 90 percent ready to endorse the pavilion concept, or ready to abandon the city for the suburbs were we merely to remodel the older section of Swedish to handle our bed requirements after closing Seattle General and Doctors.

The vast majority of our respective board members hated to see us give up the attempt to continue utilizing our existing facilities. But with the changes in the national controls over health care and the formation of the state and local agencies, we soon could see the handwriting on the wall. How could we risk providing care for our citizens with equipment becoming obsolete and while being denied our requests for certificates of need for new equipment? How were we going to retain and build our medical and hospital staffs with this depreciating situation? A few trustees still feel relocation is a great waste of assets and at least one has resigned over the decision.

What were some of the "high points" of our years of deliberations? I nominate: 1) the unanimous vote of the Seattle General board in favor of the merger, on that 1975 October night when we expected a serious split; 2) Swedish mortgage company's agreement to consider the pavilion construction a separate loan, rather than opening up Swedish's existing favorable mortgage; 3) Ludwig Lobe's timely meeting with the board presidents and hospital administrators, convincing us to get back to the negotiations.

The low points? I would list: 1) the early years of hearing a string of "no progress" reports from the merger committee; 2) the petty squabbles that restrained meaningful negotiations; 3) Doctors, announcement that it was going its own way with a maternity hospital; and 4) the breakdown of negotiations when Swedish announced it could not approve the additional debt load required for the pavilion.

Personalities did enter into our discussions. First, we had to do a much more thorough job of education to keep an outspoken trustee from taking the soap box on a minor point and alienating other members of the board. To keep the personalities from becoming too big a factor, we tried to space the big decisions over the months of meetings. Very few of our meetings were unproductive. In the end, we buried our differences and accepted compromises. We will have stormy sessions in the months to come, but now that we have the experience of working together, I'm sure we can resolve our differences.

What was our consultants' role? Acknowledging the hard work of the team originally put together by Wanda Jones and her company, I would like to dwell on her effect alone. Wanda entered our negotiations in the early stages of national and state agencies' involvement in the control of the health care delivery system, when Doctors' and Seattle General were searching for a way to combine their organizations. The consultant's greatest contribution was in the early education of our boards—organizing our deliberative processes and enrolling other consultants for specific input. But then Wanda did not keep pace with the students, our respective boards and merger committee members. It was fine to start us off step by step, but when our learning curve improved, we were skipping steps, while the consultant wanted us to take each step one at a time, without obvious advantage or benefit. It was as if Wanda felt hurt when we rushed over the agenda, not paying due heed to the hours of work she had put in developing reams of documents for us to read; it must have been an ego deflator to her. When this happened at several meetings, the merger committee felt we could proceed better without our consultant's direction.

Finally, I would like to relate a conversation from our first regular Swedish board meeting after representatives of Doctors and Seattle General joined the board. We were discussing a new fringe benefit for hospital employees. A motion was made and seconded that the benefit be extended to all nonunion personnel, effective June 1st. The question was about to be called when I said, "Does this apply only to the employees on the Swedish Campus, or does it include Doctors and Seattle General division employees too?" I heard a murmur from down the table . . . "That's right!"

In some ways our merger has just begun . . . after ten years!

A REGULATOR'S PERSPECTIVE—
LUDWIG LOBE

At the outset, I must state that the Washington State Hospital Commission's activity in the merger negotiations was intermittent. The commission entered the negotiations when the budget reviews indicated that monies were requested for merger talks and consultants' fees. My perspective on the talks is strictly from the point of view of the hospital commission whose task it is to keep hospital costs from rising inordinately.

From the very beginning, the commission emphasized that the overabundance of hospital beds in certain communities has contributed to high hospital costs. Because of this, the commission takes every opportunity to encourage hospitals to share and/or merge services. Thus, it was only natural to point out to Doctors and Seattle General Hospitals that a merger might well solve their economic problems. As far as Swedish was concerned, a merger with the two others gave it entry to a primary facility, when it had been essentially a tertiary facility. A merger also would combine the obstetrics departments of at least four city hospitals which might minimize or avoid the revenue losses usually incurred by obstetrics services.

The commission's role was essentially that of a catalyst. Whenever conversations and negotiations lagged, it suggested to the boards and administrators that Doctors' and Seattle General Hospitals could not survive much longer unless they made major changes in their physical plants—and equally important—unless they improved their utilization rate. Swedish Hospital was reminded that the commission had placed conditions on its allowed budget increase; namely, the merger. Whenever difficulties arose—and there were many long and short interruptions to the negotiations—the Commission took the initiative to emphasize the need for concerted action, to get the parties together again, to give up some turf, and to consider the benefits which might accrue not only to them but to the community.

The commission appreciated greatly the three boards' patience during the long process. It was gratifying to have the participants repeatedly return to the negotiations and willingly listen to the analysis of merging and the disadvantages of resisting the merger. They never forgot their goal of realizing the financial and professional benefits which a merger might bring.

From the Commission's point of view, the long-range benefits of the merger are obvious: 1) 162 fewer beds in the center of Seattle helps contain costs due to higher occupancy; 2) the merging of duplicate facilities and equipment, which now exist in three plants, into one complex will insure a higher utilization rate of equipment and facilities and better staff use and productivity, and thus contain costs.

The commission's role was purely advisory; it does not have the power to coerce. Its role was that of a catalyst. But, the fact that there was a neutral entity which had no turf to protect and no axe to grind in the negotiations might well have made the difference between success and failure.

F. A Theoretical Perspective—
Mark L. Secord

The Seattle hospital merger situation may be viewed from a number of theoretical perspectives which were introduced in chapters 2 and 3. One is to view the situation as the three hospitals' response to the interdependencies existing between them. From this perspective the key events in the case are the attempts by the two primary care-oriented hospitals and a single tertiary center to gain better control over their uncertain futures by means of a vertical integration: Doctors and Seattle General would obtain access to the resources, especially financial and technological, of the large tertiary center, and Swedish stood to gain a primary care base of patient referrals to its superspecialty services. A high degree of complementarity exists between Swedish and the two smaller hospitals.

A related view of the merger is from the perspective of the three hospitals' responses to changes in their task environments. All three hospitals saw the Health Planning Council, with its certificate-of-need review authority, and the Washington State Hospital Commission, with its power to review and approve rates and budget, as important externalities. Merger was a response to pressures from these social regulators. Swedish, having failed in 1971 to obtain approval for building 150 new beds on its own, saw merger as a way to further its institutional growth. The two smaller hospitals saw merger as a means of survival in an environment which would otherwise eventually force them out of existence.

A third way to view this case is from the perspective of negotiation and exchange, of which many examples exist. One is the obstetrics exchange made between Swedish and Doctors. Both parties viewed this as a quid pro quo: in return for eventually terminating its obstetrics service, Doctors would receive Swedish's patronage until Swedish's new facility was complete.

A fourth view of the merger considers it a complex process of organizational decision making. An adaptation of Thompson and Tuden's (1959) framework can be applied here. In this theory "decision issues always involve two major dimensions: 1) beliefs about cause/effect relations, and 2) preferences regarding possible outcomes" (Thompson, 1967, p. 134). These are the basic variables which the authors put in a matrix to describe four basic types of decision issues faced by complex organizations. This is shown in figure 6.1.

During the period of time included in this study the three Seattle hospitals experienced transition from a cell 4 situation, where there was uncertainty and lack of consensus regarding both factual outcomes and value premises, toward a cell 1 situation, where hospital officials had achieved sufficient understanding and consensus to proceed. What began with almost random merger discussions in 1969 between Doctors and Seattle General

FIGURE 6.1   Four Types of Decision Issues Facing
Complex Organizations

		PREFERENCES REGARDING POSSIBLE OUTCOMES (VALUE PREMISES)	
		Certain (Consensus)	Uncertain (Disagreement)
BELIEFS ABOUT CAUSE/EFFECT RELATIONS (FACTUAL PREMISES)	Certain	CELL # 1 Programming Computation	CELL # 2 Bargaining Persuasion "Politics" Negotiations & Exchange
	Uncertain	CELL # 3 Problem Solving Information Gathering Search for Alternatives	CELL # 4 Chaotic Aimless Conflict

became the determined plan of the Decision A and B conferences. This transition is portrayed graphically in figure 6.2.[7] In the transition to cell 1 the issues facing the participants changed. At times they centered on problems related to uncertainty regarding beliefs about cause/effect relations, as represented by the line in the lower portion of figure 6.2. At other times the decision issues were more involved with uncertainty or lack of consensus regarding outcome preferences, represented by the line in the upper half of figure 6.2.

Thompson and Tuden (1959) assert that each type of decision issue calls for a different strategy. In cell 4 situations where uncertainty exists on both counts, aimless conflict often arises. Participants in the merger process are not coming to grips with the substantive issues facing them.

The most likely action in this situation, we suspect, is the decision not to face the issue. Organizations which appear to be slow to seize opportunities or to

FIGURE 6.2 The Evolution of Merger Consensus:
Seattle General, Doctors, and Swedish Hospitals

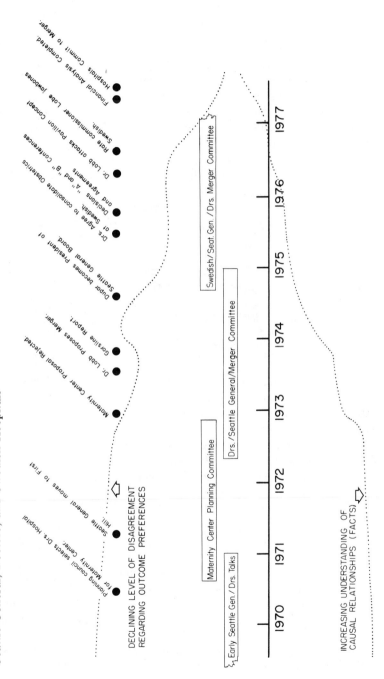

respond to environmental events may, on close inspection, be organizations which contain disagreement as to both preferences and causation. [p. 202]

Seattle General and Doctors began the merger process in cell 4. Their early merger discussions, 1969–73, were characterized by 1) failure to address important issues, e.g., dwindling medical staff support at each hospital; 2) general lack of understanding of the basic cause/effect relationships in the task environment, e.g., the excess capacity in Seattle's general acute hospital beds aggravated by outmigration to suburbs; 3) lack of consensus on preferred outcomes, e.g., each board preferred building a new facility on its own hospital's existing site; and 4) inability to make decisions.

In a word, the situation was chaotic. Each of the two boards operated with a different set of values and a different set of facts. Moreover, the merger process suffered from a lack of leadership and the participants seldom knew which decision strategy to adopt to resolve their differences. It is no wonder that the Joint Merger Committee members grew frustrated with the lack of progress.

In cell 3 the appropriate decision strategy is the problem solving approach. March and Simon (1958) describe this approach as follows:

> In problem-solving, it is assumed that objectives are shared and that the decision problem is to identify a solution that satisfies the shared criteria. Thus, in the problem-solving process the importance of assembling information is stressed, search behavior is increased, and considerable emphasis is placed on evoking new alternatives. [p. 129]

An example of this is the commissioning of Gorsline Associates. The members of the Joint Merger Committee called for the opinion of outside consultants when they recognized that uncertainty and disagreement about facts were preventing further decision making. The Gorsline report substantially reduced the amount of uncertainty regarding the facts; the two hospitals better understood their predicament and the alternatives available to them as a result.

In cell 2, where values are the primary issue, a politically-oriented approach is appropriate. The various involved groups negotiate and exchange, each tugging and pulling in different directions. A bargaining strategy is appropriate, as illustrated in the case when representatives from Seattle General and Doctors took it for granted that they did not share common preferences regarding outcomes (values) with Dr. Lobb and the Swedish board. The two smaller hospitals were interested in taking advantage of the strength of the Swedish organization, but did not want totally to sacrifice their independence and identity. Hence, they attempted to bargain, enticing the large hospital with the promise of additional beds on the Swedish campus and the obstetrics volume from Doctors.

A second strategy of decision making appropriate to a cell 2 situation is that of persuasion. March and Simon (1958) describe this approach as follows: ". . . it is assumed that individual goals may differ within the organization but that the goals need not be taken as fixed. Implicit in the use of persuasion is the belief that *at some level* objectives are shared and that disagreement over subgoals can be mediated by reference to common goals" [p. 129].

The strategy of persuasion was employed continuously throughout the Seattle hospital merger process. One example is Mr. Dupar's attempt to persuade the reluctant members of his board that Seattle General should go along with the merger with Swedish, using the holding company concept as a model that appealed to their desire to keep Seattle General autonomous.

In a cell 1 situation the merger process has evolved to the point where the relevant factual premises are sufficiently understood and there is consensus that merger is the preferred outcome. The strategy for cell 1 is programming—implementation of the merger. The consultant's strategy in the Decision A and B conferences emphasized this. The desired outcomes of the conferences were made explicit in advance, and decisions were made within the context of a highly managed process which left minimal room for either bargaining or searching for additional alternatives. The programming approach was appropriate at this point because the participants had achieved sufficient consensus about the desirability of the merged pavilion alternative. The educational and decision conferences served the purpose of enhancing and crystallizing this consensus.

In summary, the merger process at First Hill was characterized by movement away from the chaos of cell 4 toward cell 1, where the merger could be programmed into reality. This was accomplished by a series of intermediate stops at cells 2 and 3, where consensus on outcome preferences and mutual understanding of the facts was attained. If either type of decision issue had been ignored, merger would not likely have occurred.

A hospital merging is never an orderly, logical decision process. Starkweather (1974) characterized it as halting, often taking 15 to 20 years to evolve, partly explained by a decision strategy inappropriate for the mix of issues the parties face. For example, the parties may be bargaining when they should be using a problem solving approach, i.e., the major decisions relate to uncertainty regarding facts, with outcome preferences of secondary importance. Doctors and Seattle General Hospitals' early merger discussions between 1969 and 1972 were characterized by reliance on a strategy of bargaining and neglected attention to facts. This strategy was inappropriate—the hospitals were bargaining without a basic understanding of the task environment and their organizational strengths and weaknesses.

A second example of an inappropriate decision strategy was the maternity center fiasco. Throughout most of the two-year planning effort Doctors officials adhered to a programming strategy of decision: they remained committed to the basic concept that they had originally proposed to the Planning Council—a freestanding facility with enough capacity to permit consolidation of the bulk of the central Seattle obstetrical services, located on a site adjacent to the existing Doctors facility. They based their planning effort for the maternity center on two crucial assumptions: 1) that the basic features of the proposal made sense from a community health facilities planning perspective—a factual premise—and 2) that sufficient support from other hospitals existed—a value premise. In making and holding to these assumptions Doctors was in effect behaving as if it was in cell 1, where both factual and value premises are certain.

Hindsight permits us to say that neither the facts nor the values bearing on the situation were pinned down. Doctors' decision makers did not deal effectively with three major issues which, in the end, killed the project: the declining birth rate, flaws in the concept of a freestanding obstetrical facility linked by a bridge to a small, deteriorating hospital, and the lack of support from other central Seattle hospitals. If Doctors' officials had abandoned the inappropriate programming decision strategy and adopted a more pragmatic planning approach which recognized uncertainty regarding factual and value premises, they might either have come up with a more widely-accepted scheme or, at least, avoided the unnecessary expenditure of money and energy that the two-year planning effort consumed.

One of the most striking features in the Seattle case is the contrast between the period when the boards of the three hospitals were attempting to manage the process of making merger-related decisions on their own and the period when this was done by a consultant. The time before the entrance of the consultant was characterized by the participants' inability to make decisions, although they expended enormous quantities of time and energy in their attempts, the use of inappropriate strategies of decision, a lack of a sense of timing about decision making, and ambiguity regarding the degree of consensus on the issues. When Ms. Jones became reinvolved in the situation, she essentially took over responsibility for the management of decision making.[8] Some of her techniques were: 1) establishing a schedule for making decisions; 2) breaking the key decision into two parts, focusing first on the facility issues where consensus among the hospitals was the strongest; 3) using Decision Report A and Decision Report B to narrow the field of alternatives to only a few choices; 4) calling for statements of positive interest in merger from key board representatives at the educational conference; and 5) forcing each board member to express his opinion on the merger/facilities issue at the Decision A conference.

The case of the First Hill hospital merger clearly demonstrates the importance of managing the decision process. Without the leadership provided by key board members and by the consultant, the three institutions would likely have floundered indefinitely.

NOTES
1. This case study was written while the author was a student at the University of California, Berkeley, in partial fulfillment of degree requirements for a Master's in Public Health. Upon graduation, Mr. Secord became an Assistant Administrator of the Virginia Mason Hospital, Seattle.
2. Despite these good relations between Doctors and Virginia Mason, neither party professed to have had any interest in merger. Each recognized the difficulty of merging the individual practice generalists of Doctors with the group practice specialists of the Mason Clinic and Virginia Mason Hospital. Administrators from the two institutions focussed their attention on discovering areas where sharing services would be of mutual benefit.
3. The state of Washington was one of the first in the nation to establish a strong certificate-of-need program. The process calls for a review of the certificate-of-need application at the local health planning agency level, with actual approval or disapproval by the state Department of Social and Health Services. The Washington law requires approval for all additions in services and beds, replacement of existing capacity, and capital expenditures over $100,000.
4. At the time Swedish was midway in construction of its new medical/surgical bed tower. A certificate of need had been obtained to replace existing beds, but the planning agency had refused the hospital's request for authority to build 135 new beds.
5. For a more detailed description of the bank holding company concept applied to hospitals, see C.N. Platou and J.A. Rice, "Multi-Hospital Holding Companies," *Harvard Business Review*, May-June 1972.
6. During the earlier time of this case study Ms. Jones was Project Director and Planning Consultant, Lester Gorsline Associates. During the latter time of the study, and subsequently to the present, Ms. Jones is Principal, the H.O.M. Group (Healthcare Organization and Management), San Francisco.
7. Adapted from Thompson and Tuden, (1959). In adapting the original Thompson Tuden decision matrix, I am indebted to Professor Martin Landau, University of California, Berkeley, for ideas. I have also incorporated some of March and Simon's (1958) related concepts.
8. Thompson and Tuden (1959) note that ". . . an important role for administration is to manage the decision process, as distinct from making the decision" (p. 209).

REFERENCES
Lester Gorsline Associates. "Analysis of Alternative Futures, The Doctors and Seattle General Hospitals." Terra Linda, California, November, 1973.
Levine, Sol, and Paul E. White. "Exchange as a Conceptual Framework for the Study of Interorganizational Relationships." *Administrative Science Quarterly*, March 1961.
March, James G., and Herbert A. Simon. *Organizations*. New York: John Wiley and Sons, Inc., 1958.
Puget Sound Health Planning Council. "Hospital Development Guide for the Central Puget Sound Region." Seattle, Washington, 1975.
Simon, Herbert A. *Administrative Behavior*. New York: The Free Press, 1957.
Starkweather, David B. "Health Facility Mergers: Some Conceptualizations." *Medical Care*, Nov.-Dec. 1974.
Thompson, James D. *Organizations in Action*. New York: McGraw-Hill, 1967.
Thompson, James D., and Tuden, Arthur. "Strategies, Structures and Processes of Organizational Decision." In *Comparative Studies in Administration*, ed. by James D. Thompson et al. Pittsburgh: University of Pittsburgh Press, 1959.

7.

A Community Judges a Hospital Consolidation: Davenport, Iowa

Joseph S. Coyne

Commentaries by Anna Jane Stone,
Joseph S. Coyne, and David B. Starkweather

A. INTRODUCTION

This case study represents many instances in which several hospitals in a community have first attempted to proceed simultaneously but independently with renovation and expansion of their facilities, only to be halted by a local health planning agency acting under the authority of its regulatory powers provided by federal or state statute. Typically, these are not final rejections; rather, these planning agencies initiate joint hospital planning efforts by binding the previously autonomous institutions to collaboration.

This case describes how a community's three hospitals committed to such a joint consideration, concluding that merger of two of the hospitals would be advisable. Both hospitals' boards approved this decision in principle. But that was just the beginning; there followed serious disagreement as to how the merger should be implemented. The case focuses on the several seriously debated issues negotiated by the parties. Not surprisingly, we find that the issues express strongly held community values, which come to the fore more obviously in this medium-sized midwestern community than in a larger metropolis.

The information for this case study was obtained through the cooperation of Joseph and Clarice Coyne of Bettendorf, Iowa; Bryan Lovelace of the Illowa Health Planning Council; Jane Robertson of the Illowa Health Systems Agency; Charles Caldwell and Phil Latessa of the Iowa Regional Medical Program; Jack Dumas of Herman Smith and Associates; Edward Motto of the Scott County Medical Society; Paul Hofsted of Mercy Hospital; James Stuhler of St. Luke's Hospital; and Dwight Reigert of Davenport Osteopathic Hospital.

Most Reverend Maurice Dingman, Bishop of Des Moines; former chaplain of Mercy Hospital; chairman of the health affairs committee of the U.S. Catholic Conference

Sister Mary Inviolata Gallager, Sisters of Mercy, Chicago provincial house

William Gluba, Scott County supervisor and leader of the Consumer Coalition for Hospital Choice

William Glynn, Mayor of Bettendorf

Bryan Lovelace, Executive Director of the Illowa Health Planning Council

Monsignor Sebastian Menke, Mercy Hospital board member; member of Special Study Committee; chairman of the two-hospital Consolidated Board

Most Reverend Gerald O'Keefe, Catholic Bishop of Davenport Diocese

Jane Robertson, Executive Director of Illowa Health Systems Agency

Sister Joan Specht, Administrator of Sisters of Mercy, Chicago province

James Stuhler, Administrator of St. Luke's Hospital; president of two-hospital Consolidated Board

Larned Waterman, Vice-president of St. Luke's Hospital board; prominent attorney; member of Illowa Health Planning Council

SEQUENCE OF IMPORTANT EVENTS

1972   Mercy Hospital announces a $13 million expansion plan (December); St. Luke's follows with a $10 million expansion plan.

1973   Scott County Medical Society calls for moratorium on all major hospital construction and proposes consolidation of St. Luke's and Mercy hospital boards (February).

Joint Mercy-St. Luke's Coordinating Committee established (April).

Illowa Health Planning Council disapproves Mercy's expansion plan and recommends negotiations among the three Davenport hospitals (July).

Davenport Osteopathic Hospital announces $1.9 million expansion plan (October).

1974   Davenport Osteopathic Hospital allowed to proceed with $1.9 million expansion (February).

Davenport Osteopathic invited to join the Mercy-St. Luke's Joint Co-ordinating Committee (March).

Iowa Regional Medical Program and the firm of Herman Smith Associates commissioned to study Davenport hospital services; Special Study Committee established to work with the consultants (December).

1975   Consultants' report presented to Illowa Health Planning Council Special Study Committee (December 17) and to the public and the Illowa board (December 23). Recommendation is to consolidate St. Luke's and Mercy Hospital corporations, build a new hospital on Mercy's site, and leave Osteopathic Hospital separate.

St. Luke's raises the question of Mercy's contingent liabilities as a barrier to consolidation; Mercy and St. Luke's boards agree to turn assets over to a new corporation but disagree on board composition (December).

1976   Concerned Citizens for Hospital Choice deliver to Illowa a 2,261-signature petition opposing merger (January).

Plan Development Committee of Illowa Health Planning Council holds public hearing; recommends consolidation (February).

Illowa board approves consultants' recommendation to consolidate St. Luke's and Mercy and states that site should be determined by the new board (February).

Sisters of Mercy provincial house clarifies matter of contingent liabilities and states that it would relinquish its Mercy Hospital assets if such was in the community's best interest (March).

Illowa Health Planning Council reorganized as Illowa Health Systems Agency; Bryan Lovelace replaced by Jane Robertson (July).

Mercy and St. Luke's boards agree in principle to consolidate, with 18 conditions (August).

Osteopathic Hospital expansion and renovation completed (October).

Consolidated Board established, with Monsignor Menke (Mercy board member) as chairman and James Stuhler (St. Luke's Administrator) as president (November).

Womens' Awareness, Inc. proposes to establish an abortion clinic in Davenport (December).

1977   Two hundred fifty members of the Consumer Coalition for Hospital Choice hold a town meeting under the direction of Scott County supervisor William Gluba (January).

The Consolidated Board announces "no decision" on expansion plans and abortion issue; Scott County Medical Society reaffirms support of the consolidation (February).

Illowa HSA board reaffirms support of the consolidation, with a 16–5 vote in favor of consolidation (March).

Seven-member provincial administrative staff of Sisters of Mercy decide to withdraw from the proposed consolidation, giving as their reasons renewed public opposition and the Catholic bishops' proclamation to continue support of Catholic hospitals (March).

Public reacts with amazement (March, April).

1978   St. Luke's and Mercy submit separate applications to Illowa HSA for replacement of facilities (February).

Illowa HSA disapproves both applications, for lack of evidence of interhospital cooperation (March).

Iowa Health Facilities Construction Review Committee tentatively disapproves both applications, but defers action upon request of both hospitals for 30 days in which to develop cooperative plans.

Commissioner of Health, State of Iowa, identifies nine areas of potential changes in both hospitals' applications (April).

St. Luke's and Mercy modify their certificate-of-need applications, incorporating six changes suggested by Health Commissioner (April).

Illowa HSA approves revised application; Iowa Health Facility Construction Review Committee approves revised applications; Iowa Commissioner of Health approves revised applications; HEW approves revised applications (April, May).

B.   BACKGROUND INFORMATION

THE DAVENPORT SETTING

The city of Davenport is located in the central, eastern section of Iowa on two major thoroughfares: the Mississippi River and Interstate 80. Davenport is approximately a three-hour drive from the Iowa capital of Des Moines, to the west, and from Chicago, to the east. Three other cities lie adjacent to Davenport, the four together forming the Quad Cities: Bettendorf and Davenport, Iowa, and Moline and Rock Island, Illinois. The 1970 population of the four was 300,000. The state boundary intersecting the Quad Cities is the Mississippi River.

The four communities frequently raise national interest in their battles against the river's floodwaters. But the people on either side of the Mississippi view themselves as distinct from each other. There are marked differences in the two states' laws and traditions: the Corn State vs. the Land of Lincoln.

POPULATION[1]

In 1970 the population of Davenport was 98,500, having increased by 11 percent over the 1960 population. Scott County, within which Davenport and Bettendorf are located, had a 1970 population of 142,500, of which 97 percent were white. Bettendorf, Iowa had a 1970 population of 22,000, almost twice its 1960 population. This population boom has recently caused the city council to consider limiting growth. According to the Governor's Conference on Iowa in 2000, the Davenport-Bettendorf and surrounding areas will experience a 52 percent growth by the turn of the century—the highest growth rate for any area in Iowa.

Davenport's total land area is 59 square miles with an average population per square mile of 1,666. There is an average density of 314 people per square mile within Scott County, in contrast to the average of 50 people within the state. With a relatively high concentration of people, Davenport has been characterized by the U.S. Census Bureau as 95 percent urban.

ECONOMY

Scott County residents' 1970 median income was $11,000, compared to a state average of $9,000. Their effective 1970 buying income was second among all Iowa counties. Of the 425 industrial firms in the Quad Cities, 35 percent concentrate in the farm implement industry. The employment pool draws from a 30-mile radius and includes over 160,000 people. The retail trade area of the Quad Cities covers a 50-mile radius, as shown in figure 7.1.

EDUCATION

The median years of school completed in Davenport is 12.2—the same for the state. There are two private Catholic colleges in Davenport, both coeducational. The University of Iowa, approximately 60 miles from Davenport, in Iowa City, owns and operates a large medical school and teaching hospital.

DAVENPORT'S HEALTH CARE SYSTEM

Size and Location of Hospitals[2]
The communities of Bettendorf and Davenport are served by three private, acute care facilities, all located within four miles of each other. St. Luke's Hospital, located in east Davenport, has 272 beds. A nonprofit community

FIGURE 7.1   Retail and Wholesale Trade Areas—Quad Cities

EMPLOYMENT MARKET — 30 MILE RADIUS
RETAIL TRADE AREA — 50 MILE RADIUS

Source: Facts on Davenport, Iowa, and the Quad Cities Area.

hospital, it is affiliated with the Episcopal Church. Mercy Hospital in north-west Davenport, founded in 1870, is the largest and oldest of the three, with 282 beds. It is owned and operated by the Sisters of Mercy, whose provincial office is in Chicago.[3] The third hospital, Davenport Osteopathic, also located in northwest Davenport, has 150 beds; it is a locally owned and operated nonprofit hospital established in 1950 by osteopathic physicians.

    The primary service area of the three Davenport hospitals is Scott County: 84 percent of all Davenport hospital discharges in 1975 were residents of Scott County. Included within the secondary service area are two Illinois counties, Rock Island and Henry (see figure 7.2). In 1975, 7 percent of all Davenport Hospital discharges were residents of these two Illinois counties. Within Rock Island County, which includes the Illinois sector of the Quad Cities, four acute care facilities serve the residents of Moline and Rock Island. These hospitals range in size from Illini Hospital's 150 beds in Silvis, to Rock Island Franciscan Medical Center's 383 beds. The former hospital offers mostly secondary care services while the latter offers tertiary services as well. Relative to the Davenport hospitals, the four Illinois hospitals offer a wider range of services and are able to develop these services with greater freedom.[4] Hence, the situation is one of two contiguous health care systems of differing size, service ranges, and regulatory environments.

Hospital Board Compositions and Interests[5]
The working relationships between the three boards of Davenport have increased significantly over the past five years, particularly between Mercy and St. Luke's, clarifying their different operating philosophies.

The 21-member Mercy Hospital board includes a large number of local business people and a small number of Sisters of Mercy physicians. It is described by one of its members as a "determinant board": it makes many decisions, but most are subject to the province's approval. The board president, Paul Hofstad, likens the board members to corporation stockholders who can't make decisions which would change the basic direction of the corporation, like changing from an acute to a chronic hospital or selling assets or going into major debt. The operating philosophy of the Mercy board has been strongly oriented to community needs not necessarily related to financial considerations, as exemplified by its 20-year-old mental health program.

The St. Luke's board includes 20 trustees, 4 senior trustees, and 2 exofficio members. There is one physician among these 26 members. The board president, Henry J. Lischer, is a local bank executive and owner of a drug firm; the board vice-president, Larned Waterman, is a local lawyer. Both men have been consistently committed to developing a financially strong acute care hospital that is accessible to the rapidly increasing population of the area. The authority of the St. Luke's board is more complete than the Mercy board, since there is no governing body beyond the local level.

Davenport Osteopathic Hospital includes three physicians on its eleven-member board. The remaining members are primarily local business men. The board's operating philosphy has been strongly oriented to a teaching program for osteopathic interns, and to providing a wide range of osteopathic services.

Medical Staff Characteristics
There are 139 allopathic and osteopathic physicians with active staff status at one or more of the three Davenport hospitals, representing eighteen spe-

FIGURE 7.2   Basic Service Area, Davenport Hospitals

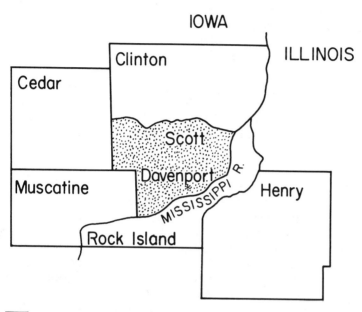

▓ PRIMARY SERVICE AREA

☐ SECONDARY SERVICE AREA

County	Davenport Hospital Discharges (%)	No. of Residents Discharged from Any Hospital	Residents Discharged from a Davenport Hospital Number	Percent
Cedar	1.6	158	30	19.0
Clinton	1.6	792	29	3.7
Henry	1.5	692**	28	4.0
Muscatine	2.7	495	49	9.9
Rock Island	6.3	2,168**	116	5.4
Scott County	84.0*	1,834	1,553*	84.7
TOTAL	97.7	6,139	1,805	

Source: Iowa Hospital Association, Inc., Patient Origin Study, September 2-29, 1973.
* 1,135 patients (61.4% of the total) were Davenport residents.
**Estimate projected from IHA Patient Origin Study during which 1.3% of Iowa's population was hospitalized.

cialties. Sixty-four percent of these are board certified/eligible specialists, compared with the national average of 40 percent. Seventeen percent of these are below age 40, which is significantly below the national average of 39 percent. Eighty-seven percent of these practice in Davenport, 11 percent practice in six neighboring Iowa communities and 2 percent practice in nearly Illinois communities. Sixty percent of this group of doctors practices solo or in two-person professional corporations. There is one group practice of ten physicians in Davenport.

Based on the age of physicians per specialty and the number of persons served per physician, the two specialty areas of greatest need in 1974 were family practice and internal medicine: 55 and 25 doctors were estimated as needed in each of these two areas, respectively. Within these specialty areas, osteopathic physicians were regarded as a key resource. In 1974, osteopathic physicians rendered one-third of the family practice care and one-half of the internal medicine care in Davenport.

According to a survey of medical staff appointments in 1974, 100 (94 percent) of the 106 allopathic physicians had active staff appointments at both Mercy and St. Luke's hospitals. This large number of joint appointments provided for a high degree of unity among the Mercy and St. Luke's medical staff, and created a clear distinction between the allopathic physicians and the 33 osteopathic physicians of the Davenport Osteopathic Hospital. Members of the two groups were also in different physician societies: the Scott County Medical Society and the Scott County Society of Osteopathic Physicians and Surgeons.

C.   Four Key Issues

ISSUE ONE: THE RATIONAL PLANNING VIEW
VS. THE POLITICAL VIEW

Behind the urging of the Scott County Medical Society and several hospital representatives, the three Davenport hospitals retained consultants to study Davenport. After analyzing and projecting hospital activities, the consultants recommended full consolidation of the St. Luke's and Mercy hospitals.

The reactions to this recommendation by various community groups were both dramatic and varied, raising the question of whether this rational planning conclusion had properly acknowledged certain community and political values. The sequence of events that reflect this issue are as follows:

Illowa—The Regional Health Planning Agency
Under the Comprehensive Health Planning Act of 1966, the Illowa Health Planning Council had been given authority to review and comment on all

major health facility and health program expansion projects involving the use of federal funds. Illowa was established in 1974 to serve a five county area including Scott and Muscatine counties in Iowa and Rock Island, Mercer, and Henry counties in Illinois. Any action taken by Illowa was subject to review at the state level by the Iowa Office of Comprehensive Health Planning and the Illinois Health Facilities Planning Board. An appeal procedure existed to accommodate challenges to decisions at the state level.

From 1976 to mid-1976 the executive director of Illowa was Bryan Lovelace, a professional health planner trained at a large midwestern university. During this time Lovelace had become increasingly committed to greater coordination of health care services in the region. His efforts were continuously directed toward making Davenport a regional, secondary health care center.

Mercy Expansion Halted

A consultant's study commissioned by Mercy Hospital concluded that the facility was largely obsolete and inefficient. Based on this report, in December of 1972, Mercy Hospital announced a $13 million renovation and replacement plan.

In response to this announcement, the Scott County Medical Society formed a fifteen-member task force to determine the need for such hospital construction. Both the task force and later the Society passed resolutions early in 1973 calling for a moratorium on all major hospital construction, during which they could assess the need for services and facilities. The Society proposed consolidation of St. Luke's and Mercy governing boards and further suggested the eventual development of a single medical center in Davenport.[7] This proposal laid the foundation for subsequent serious consolidation negotiations.

In July 1973, Mercy submitted its plan to the Illowa Health Planning Council, whose members reviewed and unanimously disapproved it on grounds that it reflected insufficient joint hospital planning among the three Davenport hospitals. Illowa recommended the start of negotiations among the three hospital and physician groups. In this recommendation, Illowa made reference to the firm position taken by the medical society in favor of a merger of St. Luke's and Mercy. Both the decision and recommendation were supported by the Iowa Office of Comprehensive Health Planning.

The Joint Coordinating Committee

Mercy Hospital realized in early 1973 that only through joint hospital planning would it receive Illowa's and the medical society's support for improving its rapidly aging facility. In April 1973 Mercy Hospital, together with St. Luke's, formed a Joint Coordinating Committee, composed of representatives from each of the two hospitals' administrative and medical staffs. Both hospitals agreed to a six-month moratorium on hospital planning while the committee studied alternative forms of interhospital relations. The Committee's initial impact was positive: it provided a means for sharing information among the hospitals and the medical society, it provided informational support for minor renovation projects (e.g., dietary project at Mercy and coronary care project at St. Luke's), it helped guide the development of a joint family practice residency program, and it led actions to improve the coverage and coordination of the two hospitals' emergency rooms. In spite of these accomplishments, the Committee was hampered by general lack of interest among members and a staff too limited to study the major subject of interhospital relations.

The Committee's formal purpose was to consider several alternative corporate forms for reorganizing Davenport's hospital system. In pursuit of this, a task force was appointed to consider the following: 1) superimposed joint advisory board, 2) sharing of personnel, 3) consolidation of certain services, 4) establishing a holding company to provide nonclinical services, 5) a federation-type affiliation, 6) consolidation retaining two plants, and 7) consolidation on one site. The task force appointed legal advisors from Mercy and St. Luke's to aid its study. In May of 1974, these lawyers concluded that consolidation of the two hospitals, as proposed by the medical society, was impossible on account of Mercy Hospital's estimated $39 million contingent liability for expansion and renovation projects at other hospitals owned by the Sisters of Mercy. To relieve Mercy of this liability would require a large number of legal and financial transactions initiated by the provincial office in Chicago. Such transactions appeared both difficult and costly.

Osteopathic Expands

During these early stages of the committee's work, Davenport Osteopathic Hospital obtained permission from Illowa to pursue plans for a $1.9 million renovation and addition. This decision was reversed in early 1974 at the state level, for the same reason that had been applied to Mercy Hospital: insufficient effort to coordinate Davenport hospital developments. On appeal by Davenport Osteopathic, using Iowa's Fair Hearing Process, the state's decision was reversed and Davenport Osteopathic was allowed to proceed.

An important factor influencing final approval was Davenport Osteopathic's role as a trainer of primary care physicians. Since 1968, Davenport Osteopathic had been affiliated with the Kirksville, Missouri, College of Osteopathic Medicine in a clinical clerkship program. The hospital also had an osteopathic internship and residency program. Of those students who had completed the program, about 50 percent had remained in the immediate eastern Iowa or Quad City area. Permission was granted to proceed in recognition of Davenport Osteopathic's need for additional capacity to meet state licensing requirements for approved training programs in family practice and internal medicine,[8] given the critical need for primary care physicians in the Quad City area.

The Committee Grows
Immediately following the approval of Osteopathic's proposal and the committee's initial study, Davenport Osteopathic Hospital and the Osteopathic Society of Physicians and Surgeons were formally invited to join the committee. Aside from the continuing need for joint planning, Mercy and St. Luke's viewed Davenport Osteopathic's success as a potentially positive influence in the committee's efforts to develop coordinated expansion strategies. Davenport Osteopathic accepted this invitation, while stating that it would continue with its approved plan for renovation and expansion.

The Hospital Study
Although the task force of the joint committee had reached the initial conclusion that full consolidation was impossible, its members felt that more intensive study was necessary. The task force had worked on its assignment for more than one year, yet had failed to come up with positive recommendations. In recognition of its limited staff, the task force concluded that outside consultants would be better able to conduct the intensive study called for by the situation.

A similar and concurrent call for outside consultants was voiced by the medical society. Its consolidation proposal had been stamped as impossible, yet its leaders were convinced that not enough had been done to determine if Mercy could be relieved of its financial liability. A major reason for this persistence was the near crisis situation of the Davenport hospitals: utilization had been falling, equipment for many services was inadequate and duplicated, and the necessary approvals for desired improvements were not in sight.

In June 1974, at the medical society's suggestion, the joint committee appointed the Iowa Regional Medical Program (IRMP) to study Davenport's hospital services. The committee felt that IRMP's planning capabilities would be useful, but doubted the agency's capacity to perform the necessary facility or financial analyses. Therefore, upon the suggestion of the Mercy and St. Luke's hospital boards, the committee invited the firm of Herman Smith Associates to help strengthen the consultation.

The Joint Coordinating Committee viewed the two consultants as complementary. Smith Associates had advised numerous hospitals in the region on long-range physical and financial plans. IRMP had been established in 1966 with federal funds to provide assistance to Iowa's health care providers in the development of new and innovative health care programs. These consultants together seemed to satisfy the vastly different interests of the three hospitals' boards, administrations, and medical staffs.

The two organizations presented a prospectus detailing how they would collaborate while retaining separate accountability for specific tasks. In December 1974, IRMP and Smith Associates were retained by the three hospitals to conduct a comprehensive six-month study of hospital services. Although the hospitals financed the expensive study, Illowa was to be the client. The consultants were given complete access to information on all aspects of the hospitals' operations, including governance and financial position. A Special Study Committee consisting of representatives of the three hospitals and the medical society was formed to meet with the consultants and provide progress reports to the client on a monthly basis. Among the members of the Special Study Committee, all except Mercy board members Monsignor Menke and Dean Stichnoth were also members of the Joint Coordinating Committee. The Special Study Committee would be the group to which the consultants' findings initially would be reported; these findings would next be presented to the three hospital boards for their comment and finally to Illowa's Plan Development Committee for a review and recommendation to the full Illowa board.

The Findings

The consultants' report contained five sections. Highlights are as follows:

I. Utilization
   A. Between 1969 and 1974 the number of admissions to Davenport hospitals increased, but the average length of stay declined by one full day (13 percent). These factors in combination kept the occupancy rate of hospitals steady at about 72 percent. However, this stability did not apply evenly to all hospitals.

      1. Utilization of Davenport Osteopathic's services has changed the least, with admissions increasing in proportion to population gain. It had the smallest reduction in average length of stay, possibly because of its teaching role.

      2. Mercy Hospital experienced declines in number of admissions in all major service areas except psychiatric—which showed a substantial increase. However, the drop in average length of stay was only 7.4 percent.

      3. At St. Luke's, the number of admissions rose in all major service areas—even slightly in pediatrics and obstetrics, departments in which both other hospitals showed substantial declines. Yet, St. Luke's average length of stay had dropped 21 percent.

B. While projections through 1985 anticipate further population growth, the projected age distribution of the population, the expected continuing reduction in length of stay, and other factors would inhibit any rise in net inpatient hospital utilization.

C. Based upon these projections, the community would continue to have an excess of beds, and the current utilization problem would be exacerbated. Consolidating Mercy and St. Luke's Hospitals would resolve this problem.

II. Physical Facilities

None of the three hospitals has adequate physical facilities. Substantial improvements will be necessary in order for any one of them to meet 1974 Hill-Burton minimum standards.

A. Davenport Osteopathic Hospital has in progress a construction program that will eliminate significant space deficiencies in both its diagnostic and treatment areas. However, the hospital will still have substantially less than the 800 square feet per bed that represents the national average.

B. Mercy Hospital needs significant renovation and remodeling throughout to modernize its patient care units and environmental systems. It needs new facilities, also, for some diagnostic and treatment services.

C. St. Luke's Hospital has space shortages that hamper major diagnostic and treatment services. Additionally, the space in many of its patient care units is inadequate and several units do not meet Hill-Burton standards.

D. The Davenport Osteopathic site is conveniently accessible and is sufficiently large to accommodate needed future expansion.

E. The Mercy Hospital site, too, is easily accessible and is spacious; it could supply space for a significantly larger facility.

F. The St. Luke's site is accessible but of a size that limits its potential as a site for new construction.

G. Patient care, diagnostic and treatment units are too small at all of the hospitals to be efficient.

III. Financial Considerations

A. Osteopathic Hospital has committed itself to borrow up to what is probably its maximum capacity to finance its expansion and renovation program. For it to consider merger/consolidation would pose almost insurmountable problems, legal and otherwise.[9]

B. Mercy Hospital's financial position is relatively strong, even though over the past five years its net returns on operation have been modest; and, accordingly, it has not accumulated significant reserves to meet prospective long-term needs.

C. St. Luke's Hospital's financial position is strong, reflecting substantial net returns from operation. Accordingly, it has accumulated substantial reserves to meet prospective long-term needs.

D. The financial positions of St. Luke's/Mercy in combination provide a base for development of community health resources well surpassing what either hospital could manage individually.

E. Construction of a new facility on the Mercy site, under a consolidation, would be cheaper by an estimated $7 million—and possibly as much as $14 million—than the alternative of separate developments by the two hospitals.

IV. Physician Attitudes

A. A majority of the allopathic physicians on the active staffs of St. Luke's and Mercy strongly favor a single acute care facility for Davenport.

B. Sixty-five percent of the physicians felt there would be serious shortcomings in the maintenance of three separate hospitals.

C. The allopathic physicians express general dissatisfaction with the present arrangement of services.

D. The allopathic physicians find dissatisfaction with the scope of available services. Examples are pediatric care, particularly neonatology, neurosurgery, and vascular surgery.

E. A substantial majority of allopathic doctors favor a single medical staff for Mercy and St. Luke's.

F. Osteopathic physicians do not in general find dissatisfaction with existing arrangements for hospital services.

G. A majority of osteopathic physicians believe Osteopathic Hospital should continue as an independent operation.

H. Based on responses from both the allopathic and osteopathic physicians, it appears unlikely that a single medical staff for all hospitals operating in Davenport could be achieved in the foreseeable future.

I. Specific problems relating to primary care, public education, research and other areas were not heavily addressed by Davenport physicians. These are problems that must be addressed in the future, after decisions have been made in regard to new arrangements for providing hospital services.

V. Board Member Attitudes

A. With few exceptions the board members of the three hospitals were satisfied with the services offered by their respective hospitals as well as the administrative and financial structures of each.

B. The three-hospital arrangement for the delivery of services was deemed satisfactory by majorities of the St. Luke's and Osteopathic board respondents; 50 percent of the Mercy respondents were dissatisfied. Because of the prevalence of satisfaction, few suggestions were made for substantially revising the organization of hospital services.

1. Most allopathic hospital board members thought efforts should be made to minimize the duplication of hospital services. Most believed this should be done by the Joint Coordinating Committee, not through a reorganization of the hospitals.

2. Some board members suggested changing the hospitals' roles— several proposing that St. Luke's limit itself to acute care and Mercy to chronic care.

3. Only Mercy's board gave any support to formation of a central board of directors—supplementary to the individual hospital boards. The other hospital boards rejected this arrangement, even though their own boards would retain decision-making autonomy.

These conclusions were reached after seven months of data collection, verification, and analysis. The 335-page report was formally presented to the Illowa Special Study Committee on December 17, 1975, and then to the three hospital boards for their comments. Immediately thereafter, on December 23, it was simultaneously released to the press and to the Illowa board.

The report was released to the public before an Illowa board review in an effort to stop rumors that had circulated prior to December 23. These rumors expressed citizens' fears over the consolidation of Mercy and St. Luke's, claiming that merger would restrict their choice of allopathic hospitals and could lead to a disregard of the humanitarian aspects of health care. At the center of these concerns were right to life issues, notably hospital abortion policies. This initial reaction caused Illowa Plan Development Committee member Tom Kalshoven to move that the Illowa board release the report concurrently to the public and the Illowa board.[10] The Illowa board supported Kalshoven's motion.

The Recommendations
The consultants made three major recommendations highlighted in a front page newspaper article:

1) Consolidate the St. Luke's and Mercy Hospitals' corporations, organizational structures, and operations and establish a new corporation for the provision of secondary level hospital services.

2) The new corporation should immediately begin planning a new 400-bed hospital to be constructed on the Mercy site. This addition should adjoin Mercy, which would be remodeled to accommodate 150 beds for use in rehabilitation and psychiatric care.

3) Davenport Osteopathic Hospital should retain its identity as an acute care facility, limited to primary care.

The consultants had considered two other alternatives:

1) Limit allopathic acute care to St. Luke's and long-term, rehabilitative and psychiatric services to Mercy, at separate sites. Osteopathic acute care would remain distinct.

2) Maintain the status quo of all three hospitals and establish a for-profit joint venture corporation to provide central services for the three.

The consultants felt these latter alternatives contained serious deficiencies and gave several reasons for rejecting each:

Alternative 1: Mercy, as a continuing operational entity, would be unlikely to agree to such a radical revision of its role. Administrative and support services could not be unified to a significant degree except under consolidated management. Economies of scale made possible by large scale operations would be lost and hospital costs would likely rise.

Alternative 2: A joint venture corporation would permit economies of large scale operation, but they would be limited to administrative and support activities; direct patient care would be unaffected. Its for-profit status would involve certain shortcomings and could give rise to conflicts of interest.

The consultants felt that only under consolidated management of Mercy and St. Luke's could significant progress be made toward eliminating duplication and establishing the new services needed to make Davenport a regional secondary care center. Their reasons were as follows: 1) more effective utilization of facilities and services, particularly obstetrics, pediatrics, medicine, surgery, administrative support, and ancillary services; 2) more effective planning for future building programs; 3) more effective use of operating funds; 4) more effective use of new medical technology, and the addition of new services and equipment that are too expensive for either hospital to provide alone; 5) more effective recruitment and retention of medical and other personnel; 6) more effective development of medical and other educational programs; and, 7) a higher quality of communitywide patient care.

Illowa's Critique

The Illowa board made its views public in a separate detailed report[11] emphasizing that a newly consolidated board should have full authority to determine such things as building site and number of beds (subject to Illowa's approval). It further indicated that recommendations were not meant to preempt the new board's decision-making ability. The report identified two potential advantages to consolidation: 1) as hospital services improved, more specialized, highly trained personnel would be attracted to the Davenport area, resulting in improved quality of care; 2) with the combined resources of a consolidated hospital, medical education programs as well as continuing education programs for both physicians and paraprofessional employees would be better established and maintained. This would presumably result in more rapid implementation of new research findings in the hospital and would also lead to more direct relations with the tertiary care center in Iowa City.

The Illowa board also noted some potential disadvantages of the consolidation recommendation: 1) the patients, particularly of eastern Davenport and Bettendorf, would suffer a reduction in access; 2) consolidation would reduce hospitals' ability to choose physicians and patients; 3) the new, consolidated hospital could become an impersonal, large bureaucratic organization; 4) Mercy and St. Luke's would lose their identity and support as separate facilities; 5) hospital charges would rise with improved and new services and facility construction.[12] Illowa concluded its critique by indicating that the benefits and losses must be weighed against each other in making a final decision.

Endorsements and Protests

The three major provider groups, the Medical Society, St. Luke's and Mercy, had already developed positions by the time the consultants' and Illowa's reports were released.

Leaders of the Scott County Medical Society had reviewed a preliminary copy of the consultant's report in September 1975, and, following a unanimous vote of the membership, had submitted a statement to Illowa in support of the consolidation. The statement described the consultant's recommendations as a giant step toward the provision of better medical care for their citizens. The society further indicated that it had no preference for site, that the consolidated hospital should have no sectarian ties, and that the new board should be drawn equally from the two existing boards.

In September 1975, the St. Luke's Hospital trustees prepared the following resolution: "The trustees of St. Luke's Hospital stand ready and willing to turn over to the new corporation all of the assets and obligations of St. Luke's Hospital, with no strings attached." The board had its conditions, however: "1) Mercy Hospital be relieved of all contingent liabilities, 2) the new board be composed of at least a majority of St. Luke's Hospital representatives, 3) the new hospital be secular, and 4) the new corporation determine if a single facility would best serve Scott County."[13] The St. Luke's response concluded by emphasizing that if its four conditions could not be met the first alternative suggested by the consultants should be adopted: limit allopathic acute care services to St. Luke's and long-term rehabilitative and psychiatric services to Mercy. The St. Luke's board unanimously rejected the alternative of developing a joint venture corporation for central services.

Mercy Hospital's more guarded position became known in early December. The board stated that a new corporation should be formed and governed by a board equally drawn from the Mercy and St. Luke's boards. The statement criticized the consultants' report for heavy emphasis given to financial considerations, and the lack of justification for the conclusion that St. Luke's financial position was superior to Mercy's. Mercy's statement also claimed that the study failed to provide a comparative analysis of the alternatives which led to selecting consolidation as the recommended course of action. The Mercy statement ended by expressing support for the consultants' recommendations, but cautioning that issues barring consolidation had yet to be resolved.[14]

ISSUE TWO: RELIGION

Ignored by consultants throughout their study, religion became an emotional and widespread issue. There were many public discussions regarding religious differences between St. Luke's and Mercy. As the consultants' recommendations circulated, the conflict lines became more clearly drawn. Of major significance was the differing hospital policies toward abortion. This drew enough public attention to render many of the technically important hospital issues peripheral. Disturbed by this, the Iowa Commissioner of Public Health, Norman Pawlewski, proclaimed: "This is a misuse of religion."[15]

Abortions are prohibited at Mercy Hospital. Catholic hospitals in the U.S. are currently bound by the Code of Canon Law, Canon 2350, stating that those who effectively procure an abortion are by that action excommunicated from the Church.

St. Luke's permits abortions, its trustees having determined from a study that access to abortion services was limited and that some hospital should assume this responsibility. St. Luke's policy is that: 1) no individual is asked to participate in an abortion procedure if it is contrary to the person's moral or ethical code; 2) when a married woman is scheduled for an abortion, it will be necessary for both husband and wife to consent; 3) when a minor is to be admitted for abortion, the consent of the juvenile and both parents is required; 4) if a woman is in the twelfth through twenty-sixth week of pregnancy, the admitting physician must consult with an active member of the obstetric-gynecology service before performing the procedure; 5) in the event an abortion is performed after the twenty-sixth week of pregnancy, the circumstances must be reported in detail to the hospital s tissue committee for a complete investigation and the physician performing such an abortion may be subject to censure by the executive committee.

This policy is more restrictive than that permitted under a U.S. Supreme Court decision that ruled unconstitutional state laws prohibiting abortions. Nevertheless, the policy conflicts with the Catholic code and Mercy's policy. The question of whether a new facility should be a secular institution was thus crucial.

The Physicians' View

The Scott County Medical Society endorsed a recommendation at its October 7, 1975, meeting that the new hospital be fully secular. It indicated that its members acknowledged the important role of religious belief in patient care, but felt that true freedom of religion is achieved in the absence of institutional sectarian ties. The society noted that the new board did not intend to exclude religion, but to be free to recognize all religions equally. The Society also stressed that its recommendation should not be interpreted to mean that physicians were opposed to religion in a hospital.

The Trustee's View

The trustees of St. Luke's and Mercy agreed that the secular missions of the several religious denominations be preserved as much as possible in either new or old facilities operated by the new board. Beyond this, there were differences. Mercy trustees indicated in their resolution of December 3, 1975, that "the new corporation . . . promote operating policies which preserve the dignity of the person and the sacredness of life and which preclude the needless destruction of life." The St. Luke's trustees stated that "St. Luke's and Mercy shall disassociate themselves from their present religious affiliations. The new corporation shall consider those existing apostolic missions and religious rites of both present hospitals and shall determine the extent to which the same may be preserved or recognized by the new corporation."

The Illowa View

Illowa board member Tom Kalshoven moved that the board include the religious issue in its final decision on the consolidation proposal. Further, he urged that Illowa recommend to the Consolidated Board the retention of current St. Luke's and Mercy Hospital's religious identities. This motion was defeated at the February 12, 1976 Illowa board meeting.

Thus, partly by design and partly by default, the key decision-making groups had agreed that the new hospital corporation should be secular in legal form yet responsive to prior religious traditions. But they also passed the hot potato on crucial policy details to the new corporation's board, yet to be formed.

Concerned Citizens Provoke a Public Hearing
In January 1976, a group called the Concerned Citizens for Hospital Choice voiced strong opposition to the recommendations, insisting that a choice of hospitals be maintained. The group circulated petitions of opposition signed by 2,261 Scott County residents and delivered them to Illowa on January 6, 1975. The chief issue was abortion.

The Concerned Citizens also brought the matter of abortions to the attention of the Catholic Bishop of Davenport, the Most Reverend Gerald O'Keefe, urging him to write a letter to various priests in the Diocese on the matter of abortion and its relation to the proposed consolidation. The Bishop did so, and the letter was read to many people attending Sunday masses. The Bishop stated, "To provide better health care is a good thing in itself. However, it should be considered that perhaps the new hospital would be open to abortion. Each of you will have to make up your own conscience as to whether you can support such an institution. . . ."[16] Catholics of Davenport were urged by the Bishop to submit their views to Illowa. Sixty persons did so. As a result, Illowa scheduled a public meeting.

Two hundred persons attended the meeting. Those who presented testimony were extremely critical of the consolidation proposal. Despite the intentions of the committee, most opinions related to the two hospitals' conflicting abortion policies. The Rev. Samuel Vanderfagt of the Christian Reformed Church called for Catholics, Jews, and Protestants to "stand shoulder to shoulder to defeat this costly and unnecessary merger." Robert Ballard, a member of Concerned Citizens, said that constructing a new hospital would cause spiraling patient care costs. Paul Naber of the Scott County Pharmaceutical Association claimed that the discussion of abortion had no place in a discussion of consolidation. And Larned Waterman, prominent lawyer and vice-president of St. Luke's board and an Illowa board member, said that the crucial question remained whether the community would be better served by one vs. two allopathic hospitals—a question he felt the consultants never answered. He also raised the question of how the construction of a new hospital would be financed.

After the speakers finished their presentations, the Plan Development Committee deliberated for less than ten minutes before accepting the consolidation proposal. The vote was unanimous, 8–0, with two abstentions because of potential conflict of interest. The committee deferred any recommendation on two parts of the consultants' recommendations: the construction of a new facility on the Mercy Hospital site and the future role of Davenport Osteopathic Hospital.

The loudest critic of the committee's hasty decision making was Larned Waterman: "That public meeting was nothing more than a hoax perpetrated upon members of the community who are vitally interested in improved health care in Scott County." He said the meeting was "a front to immunize, if possible, criticism about the lack of input from the general public."[17] In a two-page statement to Illowa, Waterman called for rejection by the Illowa board of the committee's recommendation, and the appointment of a new dispassionate and unprejudiced committee.

Another leading critic was the Rev. James Conroy, coordinator of health affairs for the Catholic Diocese of Davenport. He said in a letter to the Illowa board that "public input was treated as a farce; the Committee acted in unseemly haste." "It seems evident," he argued, that "the community will not have enlightened planning but 'pressure' planning . . . The people want the Catholic hospital, and it is a travesty of justice and a gross infringement on the freedom of religion to recommend such a merger."[18] Other criticism came from the executive secretary of the Scott County Medical Society[19] and from Davenport citizens.[20]

In defense of the committee's quick action, its co-chairman, Bruce Shindel, said the committee had enough information from both the consultants and the public to reach a decision. He claimed there was no reason for the committee to delay action "for another year."

The Illowa Board Decision

On February 12, 1976, the Illowa board endorsed the recommendation of the Plan Development Committee. The board also decided that the consultants' second recommendation regarding the future location of facilities should be addressed by the newly consolidated board. The consultants' third recommendation regarding Davenport Osteopathic's role was to be further studied by the Plan Development Committee. Larned Waterman's plea for the appointment of a new Plan Development Committee was not supported by the Illowa board. Instead, Illowa decided that the committee should continue its liaison work by meeting immediately with the hospital's Joint Coordinating Committee. Based on these decisions, the stage swiftly shifted from the board room of Illowa to the hospitals.

ISSUE THREE: FINANCES

In negotiating the consolidation's exact conditions, Mercy and St. Luke's had difficulty accommodating the differences in each hospital's financial status.

These differences involved the legal and financial restrictions of each hospital and the amounts of money each might contribute to the new corporation. Davenport Mercy's assets were committed as partial collateral for construction projects of the Chicago province. In order to relieve Davenport Mercy of this liability, the province would be required to negotiate with all of its lenders for the release and replacement of Davenport Mercy as collateral. St. Luke's, by contrast, was free to turn over its assets to the new corporation without encumbrance. Hence, this difference in the "dowry" each could bring to the consolidation was a major issue. From this derived the question whether control of the new venture should be on the basis of unencumbered asset strength contributed by each, on an equal basis, or on some other formula.

Contingent Liabilities

In a letter to the Illowa board delivered on the day the consultants' report was publicly released, the president of St. Luke's board and the chairman of the hospital's planning task force expressed concern over one serious and fundamental omission in the study: Mercy's contingent liabilities. The two St. Luke's officials argued that these liabilities could be enforced against Mercy of Davenport upon default by any other Mercy hospital within the province, and therefore should be considered a partial liability of Davenport Mercy. They noted that the consultants failed to consider such liabilities in calculating Mercy assets, and that the report contained the same uncertainties that had stood in the way of joint planning since the beginning. Until Illowa received a written confirmation indicating the release of Mercy from the restrictions the St. Luke's officials stated their hospital's intention to proceed immediately along the lines of the consultants' first alternative proposal—to limit allopathic acute care services to St. Luke's Hospital and long-term, rehabilitative and psychiatric services to Mercy Hospital.[21]

St. Luke's officials were becoming impatient. The Mercy provincial office expressed dissatisfaction over the importance attributed to the province's liabilities. According to a representative, Sister Mary Inviolata Gallager, the only contingent liability of Davenport Mercy that had not been released as of March 1976 was collateral for a $3 million loan obtained by the province in 1971 for construction at the St. Joseph Mercy Hospital of Aurora, Illinois. This remaining contingent liability was expected to be cleared soon through negotiations with the insurance company from which the loan had been obtained. The Sister added that the entire province's total long-term debt was approximately $20 million, not $39 million as had been indicated previously. Sister Gallager indicated that the liabilities had been made "the whipping boy of consolidated talks," and that it would be a sacrifice for the province to relinquish its multimillion dollar assets in Mercy Hospital of Davenport, but that it would do so if it was in the community's best interest.

Just as the province officials felt dissatisfied with the continual attention given to the question of contingent liabilities, so were St. Luke's officials irked that the Order had failed to communicate the exact and current status of the liabilities, despite repeated requests. They argued that if the liabilities were not released, St. Luke's and Mercy would become jointly responsible for them as partners of consolidation. Such a case was difficult for St. Luke's officials to accept since the hospital had striven continually for financial strength and wanted to consolidate only if financial improvements could be realized. Even more difficult for St. Luke's was the realization that the provincial office in Chicago was ultimately in control of Davenport Mercy's assets.

Financial Superiority
After release of the hospital study debate continued over the relative financial status of the two hospitals. (See appendix A for audited financial statements.) St. Luke's officials contended that their hospital was in superior financial condition since it had been without long-term debt for two years. Mercy Hospital officials rebutted the St. Luke's claim of financial superiority, citing significant other aspects of Mercy Hospital's management such as operating philosophy, scope of services, and performance.

Despite these circumstances and exchanges, both hospitals agreed to turn over hospital properties to the new corporation. However, the boards disagreed on the composition of a newly consolidated board. The Mercy board had requested in a December 1975 letter to Herman Smith Associates that the new board equally represent the two existing boards, while the St. Luke's board had advocated in a September 1975 letter to IRMP that St. Luke's hold a majority of the new board seats, based on its claimed financial superiority. (This and other issues were detailed in a statement of hospital positions released in March 1976; see app. B.) This difference proved to be a major obstacle in the consolidation talks of early and mid-1976, despite what appeared to many to be financial parity between the two hospitals: the total unrestricted assets which Mercy and St. Luke's reported as of June 30, 1974, were approximately $7 million and $8 million, respectively.

The conflict was resolved, however, when St. Luke's consented in August 1976 to an agreement that the consolidated board have equal representation from both hospitals. One persuasive factor was the medical society's public support of Mercy's claim for equal representation.

ISSUE FOUR: REGIONAL SECONDARY CARE

The original impetus for a study of hospital services in Davenport had come from the Medical Society. The physicians suggested the study as a means of developing solutions to Davenport's health care crisis. Underlying the physicians' suggestion was the motive of upgrading and reorganizing hospital services so that Davenport might achieve the status of a regional care center. This goal gradually became a major rationale for consolidating Mercy and St. Luke's hospitals. No one questioned the worth of upgrading services, but there were other contenders for the regional designation.

Inadequate Facilities and Services
The Davenport Hospital Study confirmed the opinion of the Medical Society that hospital services in the Quad City were in a near crisis situation: ". . . both hospitals will soon reach the critical stage where patient care will deteriorate unless the renovation projects are undertaken." The consultants emphasized two related factors preventing Davenport from achieving the status of a regional secondary care center: a relatively small service area (i.e., 84 percent of the discharges from the three hospitals were residents of Scott County) and three independent hospitals serving the area. Although resources had been gradually developed in Davenport, their distribution among the three hospitals had prevented the necessary coordination for building services and facilities to a self-supporting and high quality level.

Osteopathic Building Progress
While attempts went on to implement the allopathic hospital consolidation proposal, additions to the Davenport Osteopathic Hospital were being made: by October 1976, Osteopathic had added 17 beds to increase its capacity to 150 beds, and had added laboratory and support services to bring the facility up to standards prescribed for approved internships and residencies. Hospital officials boasted that Osteopathic was now the only Iowa Quad City hospital that had an emergency treatment unit in close proximity to intensive care and coronary care units.

Illinois Quad City Hospitals Provide Pressure
The four Illinois Quad City hospitals had implemented informal working agreements to avoid duplication of services and equipment. As a result, these four cross river hospitals had not been subject to sanctions, as had the three Davenport hospitals. The Illinois Quad City hospitals had developed a wide range of secondary and tertiary services which had not been developed in Davenport, including radiation therapy facilities at Moline Lutheran, a burn care unit at Rock Island Franciscan, and neurological services at Moline Public Hospital. In attempting to preserve this competitive edge, an intensive study of the Illinois Quad City hospitals had been initiated by the four hospitals.

Two vs. Three Facilities

A major portion of the conflict which ensued in late 1976 regarding the unification of Mercy and St. Luke's focused on access to health care facilities in the Davenport-Bettendorf area. In view of the area's rapid growth, many persons questioned the feasibility of physically consolidating the facilities of Mercy and St. Luke's, particularly at the Mercy site, since the St. Luke's location was nearer the rapidly growing city of Bettendorf. Alternatively, the consolidation of St. Luke's and Mercy at the St. Luke's site would involve a smaller site, which would severely restrict future expansion of the consolidated facility. Larned Waterman was the chief spokesman for this point of view. His sentiments were echoed by members of the group that previously had argued for the independence of Mercy and St. Luke's because of the abortion issue: the Concerned Citizens. As noted by a physician member of the Mercy and St. Luke's medical staffs and a member of Concerned Citizens: "A merger would reduce accessibility of hospital care to persons in . . . the eastern part of Scott County (who) need a facility as close as St. Luke's; and, those in the western parts of the County should not have to go farther than Mercy for care."[22]

D.   A RESOLUTION

In mid-1976, the Illowa Health Planning Council was reorganized under the authority of the National Health Planning and Resources Development Act (P.L. 93–641) into the Illowa Health Systems Agency (HSA). Bryan Lovelace resigned as director and his assistant, Jane Robertson, became the Illowa director. The new Health Systems Agency was given authority over the same five-county area for which the former Illowa Health Planning Council had been responsible. The degree to which the planning agency's reorganization affected consolidation proceedings was not significant, since composition and authority were relatively unaltered.

On August 3, 1976, the boards of directors of Mercy and St. Luke's hospitals reached an agreement in principle to consolidate based on eighteen conditions. The significant conditions were: each hospital should sever church ties; total control of the hospitals should reside in a local board rather than in either church; the consolidated board should have equal representation from both institutions; a determination of abortion policies at the hospitals should be made; and both hospitals should turn over all their assets to the new organization and become divisions of the new corporation. The Plan Development Committee of Illowa unanimously endorsed this action, as did the Illowa board.

THE CONSOLIDATED BOARD

On November 10, 1976, a Consolidated Board was established with 28 representatives: 14 from the existing boards of each hospital. Monsignor Sebastian Menke of the Mercy board was elected chairman and James Stuhler, St. Luke's administrator, was elected president. The executive committee consisted of the elected officers plus chairpersons of the various committees that were to be established. Articles of incorporation and by-laws under which the new board would operate had yet to be established, but it was agreed that such would be done by March 1977. Stuhler expressed the optimism of the new group when he said: "I think we can accomplish it; it is the beginning of something very significant for health care delivery. It isn't an academic exercise anymore."[23]

The process of forming the new board and electing its officers was severely criticized by the Sisters of Mercy provincial administration. It felt that the process of board formation had been reversed: officers had been decided on before consolidation was finally agreed to. Also, the new board was felt to be acting with authority before actual consolidation. It was also claimed that the new board was made up of wealthy men unconcerned about "the little people in the community."

However, the chairperson of the Mercy board, Sister Mary Josephus Lamansky, publicly supported the merger: she told 60 persons of the Mercy Hospital Nurses Alumnae Association that the best way to provide good quality care at an affordable expense would be through consolidation, even though it would require the sacrifice of other values. Sister Josephus firmly asserted that the abortion policy of the new board had not been resolved.

Relationships were still strained and issues yet to be resolved. Sister M. Marcian of the Sisters of Mercy provincial office noted, "Somehow we don't trust each other. Much of the information given to the public has been misconstrued."

TWO NEW EVENTS

While the new corporation's policies were being developed, two related events were unfolding. One involved a group of local investors that approached Bettendorf Mayor William Glynn, expressing interest in the purchase of undeveloped land in rapidly growing Bettendorf on which to construct a new hospital. In approaching Glynn, the local investors hoped to receive support from the Bettendorf City Council in their bid to win approval for a new hospital proposal to the Illowa HSA. The reaction to this suggestion by Jane Robertson, Illowa director, was that there was no statistical need for another hospital in Scott County.

The second event involved a Florida-based firm, Women's Awareness, Inc., that proposed in late 1976 to open an abortion clinic in the Quad Cities. Local physicians objected to the proposal of a for-profit lay clinic, even though the need for an abortion clinic was recognized and endorsed by some. One doctor noted that "the clinic wouldn't provide 24-hour coverage, and local physicians would be expected to clean up others' mistakes." James Koch, director of the Scott and Rock Island County Medical Society, said the society had been approached by a lawyer representing persons wanting an abortion clinic in the area but that nothing had been formally proposed to the society.

However, Women's Awareness, Inc., had a major selling point: an abortion at St. Luke's cost $400, while the proposed clinic would charge $175, including counseling, medication, laboratory work, birth control information, and a follow-up visit. Further, if the abortion clinic were established in Davenport the major barrier in the consolidation of Mercy and St. Luke's would likely be eliminated.

THE FINAL TRUMP

The opponents of the consolidation recommendation showed renewed strength that snowballed from early 1977 onward. The organizer of this coalition of interest groups was a politically astute Scott County Supervisor, William Gluba. In November 1976 Gluba had resigned his Iowa Senate seat after being elected to the Scott County Board of Supervisors. Gluba quickly became recognized as the final trump card in the effort to stop consolidation, since the consolidated board had established March 1, 1977, as the target date for completing consolidation. Gluba, a Democrat and a Catholic, readily admitted that it would take a miracle to convince the Mercy and St. Luke's boards to cancel consolidation plans.

In developing his coalition, Gluba noted that "I don't care why they oppose the merger; we just want to get them together and effectively turn this thing around."[24] Gluba's Consumer Coalition for Hospital Choice included representatives of organized labor (the Quad City Federation of Labor, Teamsters, and United Auto Workers), both Protestant and Catholic clergymen, representatives of the National Association for Advancement of Colored People, the Knights of Columbus, the Disabled American Veterans, the Diocesan Council of Catholic Women, doctors, nurses, and lawyers.

To demonstrate their genuine support, 250 local citizens braved the bitter cold on January 17, 1977, to attend a Coalition meeting organized by Gluba. In his opening remarks, Gluba claimed a *Quad City Times* editorial exhibited poor taste by alleging that Gluba's intention for calling the Coalition meeting was to offer himself as "a hired gun to turn back the coming of civilization to the range." Gluba responded, denying political motives and claiming the right to call a public meeting and seek public input on a public issue. The Coalition centered its opposition to consolidation on three major points: 1) The consolidation would create a monopolistic situation for the new hospital corporation in Davenport. 2) Applying the evidence accumulated in a comparative study of hospital mergers,[25] the consolidation of Davenport hospitals would result in higher patient costs. 3) The need was great for a hospital with a religious identity.

Among the stop-consolidation strategies discussed at the Coalition meeting was the seeking of a court injunction on antitrust grounds. This tactic was suggested by a local attorney, who also suggested the charge that Illowa HSA members had a conflict of interest with the two hospital boards, and that the Illowa decision in support of the consolidation recommendation gave no weight to public input. Gluba suggested that members of the Knights of Columbus might be effective in picketing and boycotting the services provided by the two hospital boards' members. Gluba also said he had asked that the two hospital boards' voting be made public but had been refused, which he called disgusting.

Gluba invited to the Coalition meeting a distinguished, long-time Davenport citizen: Bishop Maurice Dingman of Des Moines. The former chaplain at Mercy Hospital and Chancellor of the Davenport diocese reminded the attendees of Bishop O'Keefe's pulpit letter, to the effect that to follow the official position of the Church required a Catholic to reject consolidation of St. Luke's and Mercy. Bishop Dingman emphasized that he was making this statement not as a former chaplain or chancellor, but as the chairman of the Health Affairs Committee of the U.S. Catholic Conference. In support of his statement, he quoted Archbishop Bernardin: "The Church should be involved, as it has been traditionally in this country, in the sponsorship of hospitals and other health care facilities. . . . What is needed today more than ever before is an institutional commitment on the part of the Church in the field of health affairs and, in particular, in health care delivery."[26]

The Sunday meeting closed with a singing of "We Shall Overcome," while on stage Bishop Dingman and the Rev. Samuel Vanderjagt, pastor of the Kimberly Village Christian Reformed Church, held up each other's arms in a show of solidarity.

THE CONSOLIDATED BOARD RESPONDS

When the Consolidated Board chairman, Msgr. Sebastian Menke, was asked for his reaction to the Sunday meeting, he reported the Board would "go ahead and get the merger completed." He described the protest effort as late, adding that he honestly didn't think it would get anywhere.

Four days later the Consolidated Board issued a statement that it had not reached a decision regarding two issues raised by Coalition members: 1) whether the two hospitals will be expanded or a single new facility constructed; and 2) if the new corporation will permit abortions. The board responded to the charge that the consolidation would form a monopoly by conceding it would eliminate competition. But it defended the consolidation, noting that the community could no longer afford competition resulting in unnecessary duplication of services and equipment. The board statement further indicated that Osteopathic Hospital represented competition, as did the four Illinois hospitals.

THE MEDICAL SOCIETY AND ILLOWA BOARD REAFFIRMS ITS SUPPORT

In a statement released five days after the Sunday Coalition meeting, the Scott County Medical Society reaffirmed its support of the consolidation. Robert Ketelaar, medical society president, noted that the vast majority of its members supported consolidation. Ketelaar emphasized that consolidation would make optimum use of the currently available services and would eliminate unnecessary duplication. Ketelaar cited an inexorable trend of the federal government toward regionalization as a further reason for consolidation. Ketelaar's statements for the Society were supported by a poll taken of Society members in February 1977. Ninety-one percent of the members contacted supported the consolidation.

In early March 1977, Illowa HSA also reaffirmed its support for consolidation by a 16 to 5 vote of its board.

THE SISTERS WITHDRAW

Ten weeks after the Sunday coalition meeting, the provincial administration of the Sisters of Mercy announced to the Davenport Mercy board of directors that it had decided to reject the proposal to consolidate and to continue Davenport Mercy's separate religious sponsorship. A majority of the Davenport Mercy board approved a resolution accepting the decision of the province with deep regret. The resolution further stated: "We feel the eleventh hour reversal of position has created an environment which will, in our opinion, make it most difficult to reestablish our credibility and integrity in our future interactions with St. Luke's Hospital for the improvement of health care in Scott County."

Sister Joan Specht, provincial administrator, initially claimed that Gluba's Concerned Citizens were not the real cause of the decision by the province's administration. However, Sister Joan admitted that such organized opposition did cause them to look at it again, and that it would have been irresponsible for province officials to ignore recent input from the community. Further, Sister Joan emphasized that Davenport seemed able to sustain two hospitals.

The public received a formal explanation of the Sisters' decision in a full-page press release on March 30, entitled "A Letter to the Davenport Citizens" in which the Sisters explained that they had faced two major dilemmas: 1) the boards of both hospitals believed consolidation was best, yet 12,000 signatures from Davenport citizens said they wanted more than one hospital; 2) the Medical Society had recommended consolidation since 1972, yet the Sisters were committed to the sponsorship of Catholic hospitals. The Sisters closed their statement by proclaiming their decision: "The Sisters of Mercy have decided at this time they can best serve the Davenport community by continued sponsorship of Mercy Hospital. This decision, made in anguish, needs the collaborative support of the doctors and the people of Davenport. We can only beg for this and work toward it."[27]

The specific reasons for this decision were explained in another press release on the day following. Sister Specht said that the seven-member province administrative team made the decision for two reasons, both relating to what she called an evolving consciousness. First, the Sisters admitted that public opposition was a factor because it had become greater than ever before anticipated; it had been clearly missing in early studies, according to the Sisters. Second, the Sisters very seriously heeded the advice of Catholic bishops that all Catholics should continue to support Catholic hospitals. These two reasons made Sister Specht "feel very good about the decision," even though she recognized that this would mean difficulties in future collaborations with St. Luke's.

THE PUBLIC REACTS[28]

The consolidated board reacted to the incredible "pull-out" with the following: "We understand the privilege of the Sisters of Mercy in withdrawing their support for a consolidated hospital unit in our community." James Stuhler, president of the Consolidated Board, expressed the public disbelief of the Sisters' announcement by suggesting the decision was similar to dropping a bomb. Dr. Byron Rovine, consolidated board member, summarized the private feelings of many board members as those of very deep unhappiness and disappointment. Rovine further stated that the withdrawal decision was final, definite, and irrevocable.

Dr. J. H. Sunderbruch, former medical society president, said that he feared the decision would polarize the community along lines many had hoped would never occur. Sunderbruch predicted that the delay in development of Davenport hospital services would cause increased costs and reduced quality of care.

Msgr. Menke, Consolidated Board chairman, reflected on the board's efforts, noting that they felt consolidation was the answer to Davenport health care problems. He identified the next steps as cooperation, which he felt would be supported by the rapport established between the two boards working for a joint goal. Nevertheless, Msgr. Menke felt that cooperation would not be easy since it would have to rely on both boards' good will.

Jane Robertson, executive director of Illowa, candidly expressed the planning agency's feelings, stating that a great injustice had been done to the community by the Sisters of Mercy.

Bishop Gerald O'Keefe, who otherwise had refused comment to the press, said: "I am happy that the Sisters of Mercy have decided to remain in Davenport and continue their apostolate to the sick." He added: "It is my hope that all the people of Davenport will support them in their work."

William Gluba, leader of the Consumer's Coalition, was euphoric. "Frankly, I believe in miracles, along with basic grassroots organizing of a coalition. We're delighted . . . that the hospitals will continue to serve the community as legally separate organizations, and that a monopoly in health care will not be developed in our area." The real triumph of the coalition's efforts, according to Gluba, was that it brought out the importance of Catholic hospitals for the church's mission. In discussing the coalition's future, Gluba said it would continue to encourage both hospital boards to represent the community at large. He predicted that "the day of the elite controlling hospital care is over."

E. THE AFTERMATH

Within the first ten days of February 1978, Mercy and St. Luke's officials submitted separate applications for construction projects to the Illowa H. S. A.[29] The Mercy proposal was for a $27 million, 280-bed replacement facility to be built at its existing site. The St. Luke's application was for a $23 million project that involved reducing hospital bed capacity from 258 to 250 beds, and the establishment of several new programs, including a regional perinatal care unit, an intensive care neonatal unit, a coronary care unit and an ambulatory care program.

These independent and concurrent proposals were received by the general public with enthusiasm, but were viewed skeptically by Illowa's H. S. A. staff. A public hearing was conducted on the Mercy proposal, at which time Mercy's hospital administrator noted that the proposed project would require the hospital to raise its charges by 4.3 percent. Even so, the Illowa review team voted 6 to 1 to recommend approval of the Mercy project to the Illowa board. The Illowa board then responded to the Mercy application with the opinion that cooperation was still lacking between the two hospitals and that the long-run costs would be too great. The board denied approval of the Mercy application by a vote of 14 to 6. The Iowa Health Facilities Construction

Review Committee, a sixteen-member state-level review committee, then considered the Illowa board denial and ruled to postpone a decision on the application until March 30, 1978, in order that the St. Luke's proposal could also be studied.

Meanwhile, with considerable public support, the St. Luke's proposal was presented at a public hearing. The Illowa review team deadlocked on a motion to approve the proposal. Acting upon the suggestion of state planning officials, the administrators of Mercy and St. Luke's met with Illowa planners regarding how the two hospitals could achieve greater cooperation and co-ordination. Despite these initial efforts, the Illowa board voted 14 to 6 against approving the St. Luke's application. Its reason was the lack of tangible evidence of coordination.

Then, on March 30, 1978, the Iowa Health Facilities Construction Review Committee deliberated for eight hours on both applications; it voted 7 to 6 against approval of each hospital's plan. The administrators of the two Davenport hospitals then requested and were granted a 30-day extension to permit them to develop more cooperative plans.

Joint planning between the two hospitals was conducted during April 1978 under the auspices of the previously established Joint Health Services Coordinating Committee. On April 10, the administrators met with the Commissioner of the Iowa Department of Public Health regarding how greater coordination of Davenport's hospital services might be achieved. The commissioner identified nine areas of potential changes to the current applications. The Joint Health Services Coordinating Committee then made changes in each hospital's application, including: 1) reducing the proposed bed size of each facility, from 280 to 265 beds for Mercy and from 245 to 232 beds for St. Luke's; 2) transferring cardiac catheterization services from Mercy to St. Luke's, where all open heart surgery in the Quad Cities is performed; 3) trading off services such that St. Luke's would become the major obstetrical and pediatric center, while Mercy would be designated as the provider of advanced neurologic, psychiatric, and chemical dependency treatment services; 4) sharing physical therapy and recreational therapy services; and 5) establishing an interhospital council for the purpose of minimizing duplication and costs.

Following the formal filing of these changes by the two hospitals, the Scott County Medical Society announced its support for the revised applications. On April 20, 1978, the Illowa board approved the revised applications. On April 27, 1978, the Iowa Health Facility Construction Review Committee unanimously approved each hospital's revised plan. With these approvals, the final necessary endorsements by the Iowa Department of Public Health and the regional Health, Education and Welfare offices were virtually assured.

It seemed that another phase in the slow process of rationalizing hospital services had been taken, a limited but more feasible approach than full merger. Since consolidation was not possible in Davenport, coordination in the context of competition seemed an appropriate solution at the time.

F. COMMENTARIES: WHY THE MERGER FAILED

As the title and introduction to this case point out, much in Davenport's approach to hospital merging has to do with values. The health planners had their values, based on rationalizing the hospital system of Davenport and environs; the allopathic doctors had their values, based on improving the scope and quality of hospital services for them and their patients; the osteopathic doctors had their values, based on protecting their system of practice both in the near future, through hospital replacement, and for the longer run future, through education; Davenport business leaders on the board of St. Luke's had their values, based on prudent fiscal management of the enterprise for which they had accepted trusteeship; the labor unions of Davenport had their values, based on present and future job security and employment opportunity; Mr. Gluba had his values, and organized those of others, based both in his personal political life and in maintaining a political system available for other issues and efforts; and various officials of the Catholic Church had their values, based in religious belief and expressed in numerous ways: public hearings, pulpit letters, coalition politics, and the difficult decisions of the Sisters of Mercy both at the local and provincial level.

There is nothing unusual about varied and conflicting values; organizational change always brings these to the fore. But in Davenport these values seemed very strongly imbedded. A midwestern city, Davenport's population is very substantially white and Anglo-Saxon. Many Davenport families have lived in the community for several generations. Thus, the population tends to fight for traditional values, to cling strongly to religious convictions, and to resist continuously efforts to abolish institutional values established by previous generations. These features explain the strong opposition to consolidation and the reason for success of a grassroots coalition in defeating the proposal to abolish a 100-year-old institution like Mercy Hospital. Below, three students of hospital mergers examine the impact of these cultural, social and political roots in further detail.

THE ROLE OF RELIGION—ANNA JANE STONE

As Joe Coyne's case study reveals, religion was an unanticipated issue which eventually derailed the merger. In today's cost containment hospital environment, mergers like the proposed one in Davenport are sought as a method for eliminating duplication of services. Concomitantly, the role of religion in hospitals is diminishing. The declining importance of charity for support of hospitals, secular staffing, and more pressing demands on religion in other realms such as education all undermine the traditional importance of religion in hospitals.[30] Therefore, as was evident in this case, the continued strength of the religious issue when encountered during a merger negotiation catches planners, consultants, physicians and even board members by surprise.

The role the religious hospital plays as a community symbol, the religious services it offers a patient of its denomination, and the network of social relationships in which it is embedded by virtue of its religious identity, all contribute to the continued vitality of this force. A hospital of a particular religious denomination symbolizes to individuals the presence and strength of their religious community. Since religion imparts a framework of values by which individuals evaluate their own and others' behavior from earliest childhood, it becomes one of the foundations of a maturing personality. Therefore, it is "an essential part of one's self definition . . . and is also intimately related to the individual's need for collective continuity."[31] Because of this entwining of individual personality with religion, a threat to the existence of an institution such as Mercy Hospital, which symbolizes the religion's presence, questions the future continuity of the group and of individuals. Acquiescence to this kind of threat "is a kind of killing of one's progenitors, who still 'live' as long as some symbols of their culture are carried forth."[32]

Because hospitals are in the business of caring for people during the crises of birth, illness, and death, although a secular and nonsecular institution may offer the same medical services, in the mind of the religious individual their services are not identical. A religious hospital is specifically set up to give a certain kind of emotional and ritual support during these crises. In a religiously-oriented institution staff is sensitive to patients' ritual needs. Symbols such as a statue of a madonna or a cross assure acceptance and availability.

In contrast, the patient in a secular institution must actively seek out ritual services and actively reject that which is offensive, such as an abortion service—a difficult thing to do when one is sick, weak and in pain. The staff may be totally unfamiliar with the patient's religious needs, particularly if the religion is in the minority, and may consider them outlandish or frivolous.

Because eliminating the hospital's religious affiliation threatens personal and community survival and also represents loss of an important service for religious people when ill, resistance to such a move is strong if the religious community is strong. In a community with several hospitals of one denomination or in which the religion which originally established the hospital is no longer vital, resistance would probably be less strong than in Davenport. In

Davenport, Mercy was the only Catholic hospital in a strong Catholic community.

Both Davenport allopathic hospitals, by virtue of their religious identities, were embedded in social networks within the community. Although the case does not analyze these networks, it is probable that there was little overlap. Religion locates people sociologically in American society. It works counter to the class system by separating people from one another within a class and by binding them to people in different social classes.[33] Thus an institution with a religious identity has a social identity. The composition of hospital boards, since their members are carefully selected to represent the powerful elements of their constituency, reflect these social identities.

Merger of two institutions with different religious identities, then, tampers with the system of social interactions within a community. It is difficult to ascertain from the case exactly how Davenport's social networks would have been disrupted by the merger. However, one motive for the push for dominance of the consolidated board of the merged institutions by St. Luke's probably was a desire by the social network in which St. Luke's was embedded to establish dominance in the new system of social interactions.

When a religious community is strong and when different social networks support hospitals which are parties to a merger, this case suggests that ignoring the religious issue will not make it disappear. Preferably, mergers between hospitals of the same religious denomination should be sought whenever possible. But when this is impossible, openly facing the issue from the start will perhaps result in creative and acceptable solutions to the problem of merger.

A POLITICAL-ECONOMIC VIEW—JOSEPH S. COYNE

William Gluba, leader of the Consumer Coalition for Hospital Choice, was both a Democrat and a Catholic, as were the majority of those resisting consolidation. Gluba extended the resistance movement to include powerful labor groups, which viewed consolidation as an impediment to economic growth. Both the First District United Auto Workers and Communication Workers of America Local 7117 publicly expressed opposition to consolidation. Since the Quad Cities was the corporate headquarters for three large tractor and farm implement manufacturers (Deere and Co., International Harvester, and Caterpillar Tractor Co.), the United Auto Workers had very strong representation. The local UAW included 20,000 union members, of a total work force of 160,000. Service-oriented labor unions expressing opposition to consolidation were also strong, since 67 percent of the Quad City's work force was involved in nonmanufacturing jobs. The number of Quad City persons working in nonmanufacturing firms had risen 35 percent since 1966, making the Quad Cities both an active industrial and service-oriented center. Hence labor unions' commitment to the protest movement meant a very strong force against consolidation.

Beyond these local pressures, a powerful force against consolidation was the American Catholic Bishops, as represented by the Health Affairs Committee of the U. S. Catholic Conference. This force became readily apparent at the January 1977 consumer coalition meeting, when Bishop Dingman conveyed the views of Archbishop Bernardin, president of the Catholic Bishops: the church is committed to the continued sponsorship of hospitals. The provincial officers were admittedly pressured by this proclamation. To act independently of the Catholic bishops would be to act against the official Catholic position. Thus, the provincial officers came to realize through what was referred to as an evolving consciousness, that consolidation no longer was a suitable alternative.

These socio-political-economic characteristics help explain the final turn of events in Davenport, which to many seemed unexpected. There was in the merger considerations a certain alchemy that brought these factors into dramatic intersection.

A SECOND GUESS ABOUT CORPORATE STRUCTURE—
DAVID B. STARKWEATHER

A full corporate merger was the only form of integration that received serious consideration by Davenport influentials. Although the consultants were charged with providing alternative forms, the other options provided were given little attention by hospital and planning leaders.

Full consolidation was the arrangement that seemed best for medical practice, hospital affairs, and community health care delivery. One large facility would more likely achieve the technical sophistication the doctors were seeking, and full corporate integration was the obvious means to this end. The hospitals placed some importance on the consultants' comments about economies of scale made possible by one facility. From the community's point of view, the advantages of increased technology and lower hospital costs were not markedly offset by reduced access (although there was some concern about this among planners): Davenport was not so large a metropolis that consolidation of facilities would increase travel significantly for anyone.

However, on grounds of organizational politics, community social structure, and community values, some sort of a federation-type integration seemed more plausible, at least at the end. A new corporation with policy and fiscal control might have been acceptable, leaving each hospital corporation to continue as an operating entity on its existing site. This would achieve some gains in technology and economy through the power of the new corporation to achieve trade-offs in hospital services, selective development of specialties, economies in support services, and lower costs of debt capital. In addition to these advantages, the Sisters of Mercy could maintain a separate facility in which they could continue an obstetric service operated under their abortion policies. Further, two continuing hospital operations probably would not incur the opposition of Davenport's labor unions, concerned for future job security and employment. Under these circumstances, Gluba would have found little in the town's grass roots with which to form a coalition capable of upsetting the integration. A final advantage of a federation is the two-stage possibility of developing mutual organizational trust during the first integration so that full physical and corporate consolidation would be possible at the time of a second stage, probably many years hence.

Two other possibilities could achieve more of the advantages of full consolidation than a federation, while preserving identities. Both involve 1) physical consolidation at one site, 2) continuation of prior operations, and 3) formation of a new legal and financial entity.

One is the health park idea. In this integration, both hospitals would relocate to a common site, or one would relocate to the site of the other (in this case, St. Luke's to Mercy, because of St. Luke's smaller plot size). The hospitals would also enter a federation which spans but does not replace prior entities, as described above. The advantage of this scheme is the physical proximity of the hospitals: more efficiencies can be obtained in this arrangement by eliminating duplicating clinical services than in any scheme that leaves the hospitals distant from each other.

The other possibility is a condominium integration.[34] In this arrangement the hospitals would have both unique and shared space. The first type allows each to operate its own facility, typically a patient care wing, and the second allows both hospitals jointly to own a structure containing facilities and services used in common. Such an arrangement would have allowed both Mercy and St. Luke's to effect their different patient care policies, while also obtaining most of the advantages of full merger.

There are other variations. It is tempting to criticize those involved in the thick of Davenport's merger deliberations for not having seen these obvious possibilities more clearly. However, that is not our purpose here. Rather, it is to observe how easily merger discussants can prefocus on one form of integration without giving serious consideration to alternatives. The influentials involved seem to line up for or against a given plan early on, making it difficult to change their positions and seek out other options as circumstances unfold. This is understandable and perhaps even predictable organizational behavior, but not the best reaction to what is inevitably a complicated and changing set of conditions.

NOTES

1. Data for this and the following two sections are derived from three sources: 1) *1970 Census of the Population*, "Characteristics of the Population," vol. 1, part 17, United States Department of Commerce, issued February 1973; 2) *1972 Statistical Profile of Iowa*, Iowa Development Commission, pp. 35–36; 3) *Sales Management*, Sales Management Institute, 1970.
2. *Davenport Hospital Study*, Conducted by Iowa Regional Program and Herman Smith Associates, December 5, 1975.
3. There are 70 Mercy hospitals in the U.S., with approximately 19,000 beds. There are nine provincial offices, each having relative autonomy in its decision making.
4. In November 1975, the Illinois Hospital Association convinced the State Health Facilities Planning Board to assume a more liberal view towards the modernization/expansion projects. The HFPB cannot review projects under $500,000 or 5 percent of a hospital's annual operating income, whichever is less (*The Ryan Advisory*, December 1975, p. 3).
5. *Davenport Hospital Study*, op. cit.
6. Ibid.
7. D. Ramacitti, "Three Hospitals—A Look At The Future," *Quad City Times*, July 14, 1974.
8. Illinois state law mandates that all out-of-state internships must take place at osteopathic hospitals having 150 or more beds.
9. Davenport Osteopathic's outstanding long-term debt was increased to $3 million with the beginning of its building project. Osteopathic received only nominal community contributions and minimal investment income. The hospital's commitment to developing a high-quality internship program represented an additional financial burden.
10. Rick Jost, "Public To Get Report On Merger," *Quad City Times*, December 12, 1974, p. 19.
11. John McCormick, "Rx: Hospital Consolidation? What's At Stake?," *Quad City Times*, March 7, 1976, pp. 1E, 6E, and 7E.
12. Illowa also noted the converse: both institutions will raise rates to pay for new construction needed at both sites.
13. St. Luke's Hospital Board Minutes, September 23, 1975, in *Davenport Hospital Study*, op. cit.
14. Resolution of the Board of Directors, Mercy Hospital, December 3, 1975, in the *Davenport Hospital Study*, op. cit.
15. "Abortion Clouds Real Hospital Issues," *Quad City Times*, March 7, 1976, p. 5E.
16. Rick Jost, "Bishop Questions Merger of Hospitals," *Quad City Times*, January 12, 1976, p. 13.
17. John McCormick, "Hospital Move Blasted," *Quad City Times*, February 11, 1976, p. 1.
18. "Public Ignored," *Quad City Times*, February 12, 1976.
19. "Timing Questioned," *Quad City Times*, February 11, 1976.
20. Elizabeth Coughlin, "Insult to Public," *Quad City Times*, February 13, 1976, p. 7.
21. John McCormick, "Rx: Hospital Consolidation," op. cit., p. 6E.
22. Mike Berry, "Doctor Opposes Merger," *Quad City Times*, April 23, 1976.
23. "Hospital Merger Takes Shape," *Quad City Times*, November 11, 1976, p. 1.

24. Jim Lackey, "Merger Foes Organize," *The Catholic Messenger*, January 21, 1977, p. 3.
25. Thomas Treat, "The Performance of Merging Hospitals," *Medical Care*, March 1976.
26. Jim Lackey, "Merger Foes Organize," op. cit.
27. "Open Letter To The Community . . . To The Citizens Of Davenport," *Quad City Times*, March 30, 1977, p. 15.
28. "Announcement Brings Mixed Reaction," *Quad City Times*, March 31, 1977, p. 4; Rick Jost, "Shock Sets In After Hospital Pact Is Ended," *Quad City Times*, March 29, 1977, p. 9.
29. *Quad City Times*, January 18 to April 28, 1978.
30. Lowell Bellin, "Changing Composition of Voluntary Hospital Boards," *HSMHA Health Reports*, August 1971, pp. 674–81.
31. George De Vos, *Ethnic Identity: Cultural Continuities and Change*, (Palo Alto: Mayfield Publishing, 1975), p. 17.
32. Ibid.
33. Milton M. Gordon, *Assimilation in American Life; the Role of Race, Religion, and National Origins* (New York: Oxford University Press, 1965).
34. Montague Brown and Marc Gelinas, "The Condominium: Time for Application to Health Care Organizations?" *Health Care Management Review*, Summer 1978.

APPENDIX A: FINANCIAL CONDITION OF DAVENPORT HOSPITALS, CIRCA JUNE 1974

Balance Sheets as of:	Osteopathic Hospital Assoc. Nov. 30, 1974	Mercy Hospital June 30, 1974	St. Luke's Hospital June 30, 1974	Combined
	ASSETS			
Unrestricted Current				
Cash	$ 13,999	$ —	$ 21,289	$ 35,288
Investments	—	891,263	$2,521,626*	3,412,889
Receivables				
Patients/and contractual	1,020,120	1,771,395	1,263,097	4,054,612
Less: allowance doubtful accts.	(116,000)	(138,000)	(89,000)	(343,000)
Net patient receivables	904,120	1,633,395	$1,174,097	$ 3,711,612
Other receivables				
Pledge	—	100,000	—	100,000
Other	—	40,361	—	40,361
Total other	—	140,361	—	140,361
Total receivables	904,120	1,773,756	1,174,097	3,851,973

Continued

APPENDIX A.   Continued

Balance Sheets as of:	Osteopathic Hospital Assoc. Nov. 30, 1974	Mercy Hospital June 30, 1974	St. Luke's Hospital June 30, 1974	Combined
Inventories	181,696	192,214	191,377	565,287
Specific purpose assets	8,060	—	—	8,060
Prepaid expenses	22,548	10,513	28,747	61,808
Deferred pension cost	—	—	57,197	57,197
Total current assets	$1,130,423	$2,867,746	$3,994,33	$7,992,502
Unrestricted Fixed				
Land	$ 82,430	$ 216,464	$ 404,666	$ 860,007
Land improvements		156,447		
Buildings	1,608,992	7,027,679	4,998,718	13,635,389
Furniture and equipment	695,744	2,266,520	1,255,116	4,217,380
Automobile and trucks	—	11,617	—	11,617
Construction in progress	50,930	273,780	111,551	436,261
Total	2,438,096	9,952,507	6,770,051	19,160,654
Less: accumulated depreciation	(981,011)	(5,851,073)	(2,621,515)	(9,453,599)
Net property, Plant & Equip.	$1,457,085	$4,101,434	$4,148,536	$ 9,707,055
Total Unrestricted Fund Assets	$2,587,508	$6,969,180	$8,142,869	$17,699,557
Restricted Funds				
Bond and interest sinking fund	$ 237,365	$ —	$ —	$ 237,365
Nurse training act loan assets	—	—	53,759	53,759
Total restricted fund assets	$ 237,365	—	$ 53,759	$ 291,124
Total Assets: Restricted and Unrestricted	$2,824,873	$6,969,180	$8,196,628	$17,990,681

Balance Sheets as of:	Osteopathic Hospital Assoc. Nov. 30, 1974	Mercy Hospital June 30, 1974	St. Luke's Hospital June 30, 1974	Combined
	\multicolumn{4}{c}{*LIABILITIES AND EQUITY*}			
Unrestricted Liabilities				
Current liabilities	$ 629,478	$ 784,728	$ 543,640	$ 1,957,846
Long term debt	1,145,300	—	—	1,145,300
Total liabilities	$1,774,778	$ 784,728	$ 543,640	$ 3,103,146
Unrestricted Equity Funds				
Board designated for property & equip. replacement & additions	—	—	2,521,626	2,521,626
Unrestricted	812,730	6,184,454	5,077,603	12,074,785
Total unrestricted fund balance	$ 812,730	$6,184,452	$7,599,299	$14,596,411
Total Unrestricted Liabilities and Equity Funds	$2,587,508	$6,969,180	$8,142,869	$17,699,557
Restricted Liabilities				
U.S. Government advance	$ —	$ —	$ 50,792	$ 50,792
Other liabilities	150,012	—	—	150,012
Total liabilities	$ 150,012	$ —	$ 50,792	$ 200,804
Restricted Equity Funds				
Nurse training act loan fund	$ —	—	$ 2,967	$ 2,967
Sinking fund balance	87,353	—	—	87,353
Total restricted fund balance	$ 87,353	—	$ 2,967	$ 90,320
Total liabilities and restricted fund balance	$ 237,365		$ 53,759	$ 291,124
Total liabilities and equity: Restricted and Unrestricted	$2,824,873	$6,969,180	$8,196,628	$17,990,681

*Board designated and includes endowment fund balance.
Source: Audited financial statements.

APPENDIX B: THE BOARD POSITIONS

The boards of both Mercy and St. Luke's hospitals have endorsed, in principle, the governance consolidation recommended by the consultants.

Here are the positions taken by the respective boards in relation to that recommendation:

MERCY HOSPITAL

1) That a new corporation should be formed to assume ownership of the assets and liabilities of the two existing hospitals.

2) That the Province (Sisters of Mercy) relieve the present Mercy Hospital of its contingent liabilities.

3) That the new corporation be governed by a board of directors which would be drawn equally from the two existing boards.

4) That the new corporation, recognizing the affiliation of both hospitals with Catholic and Protestant churches, continue to provide strong, aggressive pastoral care services to inpatients of all religious faiths, preserving to the extent possible existing apostolic missions and religious rites.

5) That the new corporation be committed to the development and maintenance of strong "secondary level" patient care services and in so doing maintain those existing services supportive to this concept. That the new corporation recognize the validity of the consultants' recommendation: "To begin planning a new 400-bed hospital to be constructed on the Mercy Hospital site."

ST. LUKE'S HOSPITAL

1) The Mother House of Mercy Hospital, the Province of Chicago, shall relieve Mercy Hospital of all contingent liabilities.

2) The present corporations of St. Luke's and Mercy Hospital will be dissolved and a new corporation will be formed to assume ownership with assets and liabilities of the two existing hospital corporations. The assets will be donated by the two hospitals to the new corporation, without cost to the new corporation.

3) The new corporation shall be governed by a board of directors drawn from the present boards of both hospitals in one of the two following manners:

Appendix B is excerpted from *Quad City Times*, March 7, 1976.

a) Sixty percent of the new board shall be selected by representatives of St. Luke's Hospital; 30 percent shall be selected by representatives of Mercy Hospital; and 10 percent shall be selected from the general community.

b) A majority of the new board shall be selected by representatives of St. Luke's Hospital.

4) All members of the board of directors of the new corporation shall be local residents (although St. Luke's will agree that each group may select a nonresident member who will occupy an exofficio position, with or without voting privileges, depending upon further negotiations).

5) St. Luke's and Mercy Hospitals shall disassociate themselves from their present religious affiliations, with the understanding that the new corporation shall consider those existing apostolic missions and religious rites of both present hospitals and shall determine the extent to which the same may be preserved or recognized by the new corporation.

6) The new corporation, while not committed to a single physical facilities concept, should begin new studies in depth in order to determine whether this concept would best serve the health care needs of patients in Scott County.

8.

Big Merger in Big Government: The Los Angeles County Department of Health Services

Jo Ann P. Johnson

*Commentaries by Liston A. Witherill,
Donald Avant, and Leslie R. Smith*

A. INTRODUCTION

The merger that created the Department of Health Services of Los Angeles County was a massive reorganization by any standards. For example, the departments involved employ a number of persons in excess of the total number of employees of several entire state governments. Its impact was equally pervasive, as were the tensions and conflicts, all heightened by the political context of a very large metropolitan government.

Our case study can examine only a few aspects of this merger process. Those that are highlighted include 1) the clash of professional philosophies of public health, mental health, and somatic medicine, and the impact of these on merger organization; 2) the problems of decentralizing through regionalization while centralizing through merger; 3) the efforts to regionalize by geographies that made sense for health care delivery but did not honor important political subdivisions; 4) the attempts to reorient the merged system towards ambulatory care while basing the reorganization on hospitals oriented towards specialty medical education; 5) the constant search for effective merger managers, with the civil service system operating as a barrier; 6) the intricate time phasing of the merger and the question of whether gradualism was the preferred strategy over sudden-death change; and 7) the constant requirement that agency administrators deal simultaneously with demanding intramerger operational problems and extramerger politics and economics. As this list suggests, the major focus of this case is not on premerger developments, but on postmerger management.

Do the transactions reported in this case really constitute a merger, or are they better seen as a simple government reorganization? Indeed, is the description of this interdepartmental change in a single government appropriate to include in a book about interhospital transactions that otherwise occur among separate or autonomous private entities?

The case has been purposely selected for the features highlighted by these questions. It shows that when the units are as large as those discussed here, much of the merger phenomenon is the same whether the parties participating are drawn from autonomous organizations or from parts of the same entity; likewise, many merger dynamics are similar in government and private enterprise. But we must still consider the importance of professional attitudes and actions even though the professionals are on salary rather than in private practice. Many officials' motives still center on preserving identity and autonomy even though civil service protects their jobs under virtually all consequences. And, the requirements for bartered solutions remain high even though an organizational hierarchy appears able to declare change by fiat.

PERSONS FIGURING PROMINENTLY IN THE CASE

John Affeldt, M.D., Medical Director of Hospitals, County of Los Angeles

Donald Avant, Deputy Director of Organizations/Operations, Department of Health Services

Harry Brickman, M.D., Los Angeles County Director of Mental Health prior to merger; Deputy Director of Department of Health Services after merger

Morrison Chamberlain, Chief Deputy of Department of Health Services as of late 1975

Martin Finn, M.D., Acting Regional Director, San Gabriel Valley Region; then Deputy Director for Community Health Services

Kenneth Hahn, Member, Board of Supervisors, Los Angeles County

Gerald Heidbreder, M.D., Los Angeles County Health Officer prior to merger; Deputy Director of Department of Health Services after merger

I.S. Hollinger, County Administrative Officer at time Department of Health Services created

Harry Hufford, County Administrative Officer at time Department of Health Services recentralized

Peter Schabarum, Member, Board of Supervisors, Los Angeles County

R.J. Schroeder, D.V.M., Los Angeles County Veterinarian prior to merger; Deputy Director of Department of Health Services after merger

Leslie Smith, Acting Regional Director, Coastal Region; then Administrator of Harbor General Hospital; subsequently resigned from county employment

Liston Witherill, Director of Department of Hospitals prior to merger; Director, Department of Health Services after merger

SEQUENCE OF IMPORTANT EVENTS

1963   Los Angeles City Health Department merged into Los Angeles County Health Department.

1966   Los Angeles County Department of Charities divided into two Departments: Public Social Service, Hospitals.

1967   Management audit of Department of Public Health, conducted by County Administrator's office.

Health Services Planning Commission appointed.

1968   American Public Health Association study initiated, as requested by Public Health chief Heidbreder (fall).

1969   Board of Supervisors authorizes comprehensive health care center for Supervisor Hahn's Southeast health district (April).

1970   Health Services Planning Commission Recommends merger of three Departments into new Department of Health Services (January).

Board of Supervisors approves Commission recommendations in principle (February).

Public Health Commission of Los Angeles studies and issues report, *Consumer Need for Neighborhood Health Services* (October).

1971   California legislature passes revision to government code liberalizing qualifications of directors of consolidated health departments (February).

County Veterinarian's office included in proposed merger.

1972   Liston Witherill replaces William Barr as Director of Department of Hospitals (January).

Merger becomes effective (September); Witherill appointed Director of Department of Health Services.

Drs. Brinkman and Heidbreder succeed in revising Department organization to eliminate reporting to medical director of county hospitals (October).

Report of Task Force on delineation of health services regions issued (October).

Deputy Director Avant revises number of recommended regions from seven to five (November).

1973   Board of Supervisors adapts recommendations on designation of regions (January).

Dr. Heidbreder, former Director of Public Health, retires; replaced by Dr. Ralph Sachs, former member of Los Angeles City Health Department and former Assistant Medical Director, County Department of Hospitals.

Witherill issues guidelines for regional organization (January) followed by details by Avant (March).

Martin Finn, M.D. and Leslie Smith appointed acting directors of two pilot regions (March).

Two pilot regions started (June).

Two pilot regions enter Phase II (August).

Selection process for permanent regional directors initiated.

1974   Two pilot regions enter Phase III (February).

Hahn's Comprehensive Health Center opened (March).
"Friends of the Friendless" ambulance chasing scandal revealed.

Conference held to evaluate pilot regions (April).

Permanent regional directors appointed (May to July).

1975   Mistreatment of nursing home patients revealed (February).

Dr. Sachs, Deputy Director of Community Health Services, replaced by Dr. Finn, Acting Director of San Gabriel Valley Region (March).

Board of Supervisors instructs CAO to report in 60 days on feasibility of dividing up Department of Health Services (March).

Board of Supervisors establishes Blue Ribbon committee to study regional boundaries (May).

County Administrative Officer Hufford recommends continuing Department as one unit; approved (June).

County Administrative Officer Hufford recommends recentralization plan to Board of Supervisors (September).

New position of chief deputy filled by Jerry Chamberlain (October).

Public Commission on County Government recommends inprovement of department's management capability (November).

1976   County Administrative Office develops a Health Services Division to monitor the department.

1977   Liston Witherill resigns (April).

County Administrative Officer Hufford recommends continuance of the Department (October).

1978   Morrison Chamberlain appointed Department Director (January).

Morrison Chamberlain resigns (April).

Board of Supervisors creates separate Department of Mental Health (May).

County voters reject plan to alter county charter to provide for an elected county executive and reduction of administrative powers of supervisors.

B.   PRE-EXISTING CONDITIONS: 1916–1969

HEALTH DEPARTMENT MERGER

Between 1916 and 1960 in Los Angeles, there were eighteen identified attempts to merge city and county health functions. The primary issue was usually which government should absorb the other. Secondary issues included governmental simplification, duplication, centralization of staff services, and economy.

In 1963 the Los Angeles City Health Department was merged with the Los Angeles County Health Department. In essence, the city turned over its public health functions to the county on the county's terms. The initiative and decision to do so rested primarily with the city. At the mayor's urging, the Los Angeles City Council voted to make the transfer in order to "correct a tax inequity which had penalized the city since the passage of state legislation in 1935, assigning basic responsibility for public health services to the counties of the state" (Sherwood et al., 1966, p. 10).

Similar consolidations of public health functions had already occurred in San Diego, Oakland, and Sacramento. As mayor of Los Angeles, one of Sam Yorty's 1966 campaign issues had been that of tax inequity suffered by the city. His appointees to the City Board of Health Commission had all made public statements in favor of consolidation, at least in principle. Several reservations expressed by members of the commission were 1) higher quality of care provided by the city health department; 2) services to minorities; and 3) concern with protection of salary, rank, and retirement benefits of city employees. The city administrative officer, C. Erwin Piper, while evidently personally opposed to the merger, supplied the information that the merger would save the city $4 million per year.

An alternative to consolidation would have been a tax subsidy granted to the city by the county. Both Long Beach and Pasadena were granted such subsidies but the Los Angeles County Board of Supervisors refused to grant one to the city of Los Angeles, thus ensuring the consolidation. Supervisors Debs and Bonelli favored the merger on bases of economy and efficiency and the belief that public health functions were countywide activities. Supervisors Hahn and Chace opposed merger. Chace, a former Long Beach mayor, was able to get a tax subsidy for that city. Supervisor Dorn, who had achieved a tax subsidy for Pasadena where he had been mayor, supported the merger when he found support for consolidation high in the rest of his district—the San Fernando Valley.

In Los Angeles, the County Board of Supervisors is composed of five members elected from districts in nonpartisan elections for four year terms. Power is highly centralized in the board and in its appointed County Administrative Officer (CAO), since he supervises departmental budgets and administration.

Other influentials expected to take leadership in such an issue did not do so, notably public health officials. The County Health Officer, Dr. Sutherland, was near retirement. A split in the Los Angeles City Health Department's leadership between the Health Officer and the Deputy Health Officer reduced the department's morale. Health Officer Uhl was opposed to merger but offered little leadership in directing the opposition; to do so would have required him to oppose the City Health Commission. Almost all other employees of the City Health Department opposed the merger.

County Administrative Officer Hollinger had major control in implementing the merger. City employees lost some benefits but gained others, and the larger organization offered greater opportunity for advancement. However, morale dropped among former members of the city department when the merger took place. Most of the complaints concerned the quality of health services and county methods for improving them. An assessment of the differences in quality of services between the two departments had never been made.

TRENDS

National, state, and local conditions contributed to the continuing reorganization of the delivery of health care services in Los Angeles County (Marshall, 1971). Nationally, an increasing demand for health care, accompanied by ever increasing costs, put greater stress upon public medical facilities. This stress accentuated the general economic plight of local governments which resulted in a greater quest for economy and efficiency.

Further, there was a changing pattern of methods of financing health care, with federal and state governments playing a greater role. This was best reflected in Medicare and Medi-Cal programs initiated by national legislation. Local government officials desired to improve their ability to tap these sources of financing for their public health institutions. Further, there existed a belief that it was no longer a question of having or not having a national health insurance program, but only a question of when such a program would come into existence. To take adequate advantage of such a program needed coordinated effort with organizational machinery geared up to respond as soon as the resources became available. A final national trend was a push for comprehensive health services to overcome the inadequacies of existing fragmented programs. Two federal programs reflected this trend: P.L. 89–239, the Heart Disease, Cancer and Stroke Act of 1965 (Regional Medical Programs), and P.L. 89–7491, the Comprehensive Health Planning Act of 1966.

During the late 1960s, task forces studied reorganizational needs at California's state level. In 1970, a recommendation was sent to Governor Ronald Reagan from the Task Force on Organization of Health Programs to create a Department of Health for California which would incorporate functions of the Department of Public Health, Mental Hygiene, and Health Care Services. The Task Force noticed that previous attempted solutions such as campus concept, group practice, manpower innovations, and community health centers had been inadequate or piecemeal attempts to solve a very complex problem. The Task Force opted for a broader, more encompassing solution to the problem, i.e., consolidation. It went on to urge that certain innovations for managing the new department be considered: 1) Selection of a generalist administrator rather than a health professional as department head. 2) Early attention by the director to eliminating unnecessary duplication and overlap. 3) Development of a program management structure and system to help the director coordinate and direct health programs. (Task Force on California's Organization for Health Services, 1970, p. 67)

Local concerns paralleled and reflected these state and national trends, but were accentuated by the growing visibility of county government costs of providing medical care to indigents: taxpayer groups pointed to the fact that the provision of health services used more than one-third of the entire county budget. County officials acknowledged that more state and federal funds were being provided to assist in this financing than had been provided before the amendments to the Social Security Act of the mid-1960s, and they knew that with these new sources also came expectations, mandates, and controls that took discretion and predictability out of local officials' hands. They worried over how big the health care slice of the budget pie might grow due to events beyond their control. Agency reorganization was one way of dealing with these multileveled and multifaceted forces and trends.

The 1963 unification of city and county public health departments did not end the reorganization of Los Angeles health services. In 1966, the Department of Charities was divided into two departments: the Department of Public

Social Service, and the Department of Hospitals, at which time the County Board of Supervisors expressed a desire to review the organization of all the county's health services.

THREE STUDIES

The commissioning of three separate studies of the health care delivery system, all authorized by the Los Angeles County Board of Supervisors, led up to the next reorganization. When Dr. Gerald Heidbreder became the Los Angeles County health officer in the mid-sixties, he requested Hollinger to seek authorization for an American Public Health Association (APHA) study of his department. Since the APHA officially represented public health interests, Hollinger's office viewed such a request self-surviving: the results would only provide the health officer with justification for a larger budget and program expansion.

Instead, in 1966, the CAO made a broader proposal to the Board of Supervisors—first, that a management study of the health department should be conducted by the CAO's office; second, the CAO also somewhat reluctantly recommended that the board authorize the APHA study, and third, that a blue ribbon Health Services Commission be created to study the county's total health care delivery system.

The Management Audit
The 1966–68 management audit of the Health Department, directed by Douglas Steele, chief of CAO's Management Services Division, reflected the CAO's concern for economy and efficiency via tight management control. One result was a recommendation for a reduction in allocated positions. In nursing alone, approximately 60 positions were to be eliminated. An uproar in the health department accompanied the report. Bargaining between the CAO's office and the department finally resulted in a restoration of about one-half of the proposed cuts. However, the department paid for the concession by submitting to a new ongoing management audit system in which actual time involved in various activities would be compared to established standards.

The American Public Health Association Study
The APHA study, funded by the Board of Supervisors in the 1966–67 budget, actually began in the fall of 1968 under the direction of Dr. Malcolm H. Merrill, former California Director of Public Health. Two broad themes were developed by the study group: first, the need for an improved system of delivering personal health services and, second, the need for a massive effort to recapture and preserve the quality of the physical environment (Report of the American Public Health Association, 1970, p. iii).

The APHA study started after the Health Services Commission had been established and given its charge by the CAO. Dr. Merrill or his representative attended and participated in the Health Services Commission deliberations, a move deemed significant by several administrators involved in the county's health care system at that time: the overlap enabled the APHA study group to see the handwriting on the wall, i.e., that a recommendation for a single, consolidated department of health was inevitable.

The APHA study group thus broadened its scope and recognized the interrelationship of all county health services. This resulted in the following broad recommendation: "The County develop a single department for administration of its responsibilities for health services and transfer to this department the functions currently assigned to the Departments of Hospitals, Health, and Mental Health and appropriate health functions of the Department of Public Social Services" (Report of the American Public Health Association, 1970, p. 4). While recommending the creation of a single department of health, the APHA study team, true to its members' public health orientation, expressed concern that the traditional health department's role in preventive and community aspects of health services should not be diluted.

A major additional recommendation called for establishing comprehensive health service centers for the delivery of personal health services. It was anticipated that these decentralized services would be directed by local health officers. Thus, a recommendation was made to strengthen administration at the level of the district health officer to ensure their effective leadership. The study group discouraged the Health Department's past emphasis on strong central administration, insufficiently flexible to meet district needs (Report of the American Public Health Association, 1970, p. 9). It also encouraged community involvement at the district level.

The health officers themselves posed a serious problem in the proposed organization. Few were board certified or had maintained their clinical skills, except in the area of communicable diseases. They lacked status among fellow physicians. Further, their administrative skills had been poorly developed, as major decisions were made at central headquarters. Given this, the APHA recommendation to upgrade the district health officer role was as much an early example of fighting among the departments for power in the new organization as it was genuine professional concern for public health as compared to personal medical treatment.

The Health Services Planning Commission Study
The Health Services Planning Commission membership was selected primarily by the CAO. He appointed 16 members and each supervisor selected one member, for a total of 21. The commission was handicapped for a period by lack of staff support. Then the Department of Hospitals assigned it a staff

member, which gave that department increased influence in the commission's recommendations (Marshall, 1971). The Department of Public Health had also been asked by the CAO for staff contributions but was told the department was too busy.

The Health Services Planning Commission first met in June, 1967. It divided into three task forces, one for the issues of district boundaries and coordination, one to identify overlaps, duplications, and restrictions, and one to deal with the relationships between the private and public health sectors. On September 29, 1969, the Health Services Planning Commission met to review the recommendations of its task forces. All recommendations were unanimously accepted except the one which urged unifying three large existing departments into a new Department of Health Services.

At first, all three departments opposed the consolidation. The Department of Hospitals would have been satisfied with a realignment of functions giving it control of all personal health services. Departments of Public Health and Mental Health strongly opposed the unification, each favoring a coordinated system among the departments in ambulatory health care centers. The CAO staff felt this approach was not viable and pushed for one new health organization. The Departments of Mental Health and Public Health suspected that if they did not capitulate, the CAO would take over the administration of their health programs. "Mistrust between the Department of Health, the Department of Hospitals, and the Department of Mental Health was more than mere organizational conflict. It was also a conflict between different professional orientations and different political philosophies" (Marshall, 1971, p. 874).

The Health Services Planning Commission vote of approval on the merger recommendation had four dissenters. One dissenter expressed concern over the size of the new organization and cited the division of the Department of Charities as an example. CAO Hollinger countered that a dissimilarity of function and not size resulted in the splitting of Charities in 1966.

The remaining three dissenters represented the interest of mental health. Their expressed concern was that the unique blend of clinical and community based mental health services in the county should not be lost through its inclusion in a larger organization. They also pointed out the close relationship between mental health and other community services such as probation and welfare, reflecting a conflict over the philosophy of mental health services delivery. The Department of Mental Health's position, expressed by its director, Dr. Harry Brickman, emphasized prevention and consultation, not direct treatment. The majority of the members of the Health Services Planning Committee felt that mental health programs were definitely health service programs and that, as such, they should be incorporated into the total health care delivery system. Recognizing the intensity of the opposition, however, the Health Services Planning Commission recommended a timetable for phasing in of recommendation #2.

The CAO's office kept the goal of departmental merger alive. It wrote the final report and its representatives met individually with commission members. CAO staff members never brought the commission together again as a group, thus enabling them to deal with any dissension on a one-to-one basis.

An intervening factor occurred which influenced how this phasing in was to be achieved. A Board of Supervisors meeting on April 19, 1969 approved Hahn's request for a comprehensive health care center to be established in the southeast health district at a location in his supervisory district. Hahn's district also included a portion of Watts. Interestingly, Hahn had not discussed his request with the CAO's office prior to this board meeting. The board action on Hahn's request included instructing CAO Hollinger to: "1) budget funds for acquiring land and construction . . . 2) instruct the Chief Administrative Officer, Health Officer, the Directors of Hospitals, Mental Health, and Public Social Services to work together and with all other affected public and private agencies and individuals to identify community health needs and interests as they can be identified and to develop an organizational format for operating comprehensive health care centers" (Los Angeles County Health Services Planning Committee Report, 1970, p. 18).

The Health Services Planning Commission endorsed the board's action of April 15, as an ideal response to fragmentation and duplication in the delivery of personal health services. Recommendation 4 stated the committee's position: "The County should first implement the proposed system in the Southeast Los Angeles area, and in other areas of the County based upon identifiable need, community interest and organizational capacity" (Los Angeles County Health Services Planning Committee Report, 1970, p. 18).

The Health Services Planning Commission then dealt with interdepartmental rivalries by addressing policy and structure. The commission emphasized that four functional methods of delivering health service should be incorporated in the new neighborhood health centers: 1) improving the environment (environmental health); 2) influencing personal and community behavior (health education); 3) improving direct medical care, both preventive and therapeutic (personal health services); and 4) improving services in categorical programs (e.g., mental health and mental retardation).

Further, it concluded that: "it would be better not to turn over administration of personal health services to any of the three existing departments, with their present divided responsibilities and loyalties. It would be better to turn over responsibility to a new organization. This organization would redefine services and operate all health services in a truly comprehensive manner" (Los Angeles County Health Services Planning Committee Report, 1970, p. 15). The Health Services Planning Commission recognized that while the accomplishment of such a major change required time, the board should show immediate support of its goals.

No one seemed to doubt the feasibility of comprehensive health centers. The real question was judged to be whether numerous health centers could be coordinated into an ambulatory care program anchored by a teaching hospital, and without extra cost (Avant, May 11, 1977).

COUNTY MAKES THE MERGER DECISION

In February 1970, the Board of Supervisors took action on the Health Services Commission Report. At that meeting, opposition to the creation of a new department of health services was still being expressed. Dr. Gerald Heidbreder, Los Angeles County Health Officer, and Judge Miller, representing the mental health department's interest, both spoke against the merger. Recognizing a lack of consensus coupled with intense opposition, the board accepted the recommendations in principle only.

SOME COLLABORATION AND SABOTAGE

Many factors interacted to delay any push for the merger. Some were deliberately created by departments, some were coincidental, and others related to county governmental issues that distracted both the Board of Supervisors' and CAO's attention. For example, an Interim Planning Committee was organized consisting of the directors of each of the three departments. Except for the Department of Hospitals, staff support for this committee was not forthcoming.

For the most part, each department continued to go about its own business. However, the Board of Supervisors' April 15, 1969 actions mandated interdepartmental planning in order to achieve Hahn's Comprehensive Health Center. In fact, each department planned independently for what it perceived was needed. When the separate recommendations were presented to the CAO's office, redundancy was rampant: to meet each department's request would have meant substantial additional expenditures with questionable gains. Instead of attempting to develop a coordinated planning effort, the CAO's office readjusted each request. Asked if the departments resented these readjustments, the CAO's office reported that they were relieved at not having to fight it out.

Two pending retirements caused further delay: CAO's L.S. Hollinger, and the Director of the Department of Hospitals, William A. Barr. Barr was scheduled for retirement in January 1972. It had been anticipated that he would be appointed to chair the Interim Planning Committee, a situation greatly feared by the Departments of Mental Health and Public Health. Their fear plus Barr's reluctance to push the issue resulted in inaction.

The Public Health Department's major delaying strategy took the form of a separate study of *Consumer Need for Neighborhood Health Services*, undertaken by the Public Health Commission of the County of Los Angeles, with at least token support from the Board of Supervisors. The Public Health Commission desired to meet with community groups regarding the report of the Health Services Planning Commission. Since neither the APHA study nor the Health Services Planning Commission had involved consumer input, the study was not only appropriate but politically essential, given the mood of consumer advocacy which prevailed at the time.

The Public Health Commission's Report (1970) emphasized continuing functions already under the auspices of Public Health. For example, it emphasized continuous input of consumer needs via health councils which were already established and directed by Health Department personnel. It defined comprehensive health services as a broad spectrum without stressing diagnosis and treatment.

In terms of organization, the report favored decentralization via neighborhood health centers, where it assumed 90 percent of the health needs of a community could be met. This made health centers the hub of the new delivery system, with hospitals serving as referral resources. See figure 8.1 for a diagram of the proposed organization.

The Public Health Commission supported increased interdepartmental efforts: sharing of facilities, joint program planning, unification of data and record systems, etc. However, the commission's opinion was that such activities could be developed through the board's direction without the rigidity of a consolidation.

The Public Health Commission study took six months and was presented to the Board of Supervisors in October 1970. Officials in the CAO's office and the Department of Hospitals viewed it as self serving and without much potential impact on decision making. By contrast, administrators in the Department of Public Health felt it got them back to the bargaining table.

Given the resistance of at least two agencies to consolidation, the County Veterinarian's request to include his organization in the merger came as something of a surprise. Certain changes in veterinary functions led to this request. Traditionally, the County Veterinarian dealt with the care of livestock in an agricultural environment. As Southern California became urbanized, the need refocused on veterinary public health problems such as zoonosis and rabies control: animal diseases which were transmissible to man. The resulting con-

FIGURE 8.1   Organization Proposed by Public Health
Commission of Los Angeles County

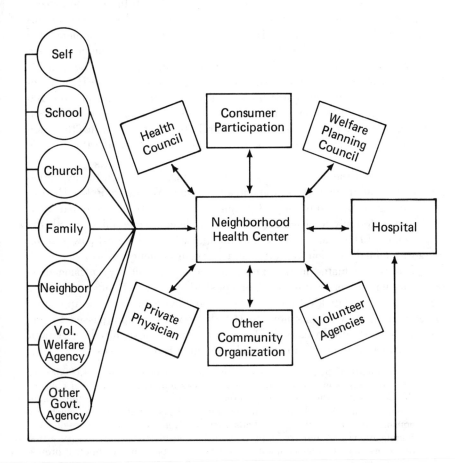

flict over domain between the county health department and veterinarian was
resolved in 1970 when Dr. Aaron, who had been in charge of veterinary public
health in the health department, left and joined the county veterinarian's
office as head of the Division of Veterinary Public Health.

Another change in function had started in the early 1960s, when medical
schools and research-oriented hospitals expanded the use of laboratory animals for research purposes. Establishing guidelines and supervision for the
humane utilization of animals for research purposes became the County Veterinarian's duty. This created an interface between medical schools, hospitals, and the veterinarian.

Yet another interface among these three groups became even more important. The field of comparative medicine was coming into being, a field which studies diseases common to both man and animal. In order to expand his agency's role in this field, the County Veterinarian, Dr. Schroeder, together with the Department of Hospitals proposed the establishment of a Center of Comparative Medicine which would provide the facilities for the study of man-animal diseases. While the primary interface was to be with the Department of Hospitals, recognition was also given to ". . . the Health Department, in that it will materially contributed to the control of over 100 diseases of animals transmissible to man, and the Department of Mental Health in the study of social and behavioral stress on animal health which may demonstrate new approaches to psychological problems" (Schroeder, 1970, p. 1).

The size of the department was also a factor. Even given the expanded roles and the addition of Dr. Aaron and a Division of Veterinary Public Health, the total staff consisted of only 23 people. The small size of the department made any externally imposed restructuring unlikely, while alliance with the Department of Hospitals, perceived as the unit with the greatest power in the merger, enabled the County Veterinarian to gain influence.

During the hiatus in the merger process, one activity envisioned as necessary for merger success was being pushed by the CAO's office. Enabling legislation at the state level was needed if a nonphysician was to be appointed director of the new Department of Health Services. A law passed by the California legislature in early 1971 was a marvel of customized legislation. Section 24306 of the Government Code was modified as follows:

> If the Board of Supervisors in counties having a population of 4,000,000 or more persons, consolidates two or more offices pursuant to statute or charter, the occupant of the consolidated office need not possess any of the qualifications required of the occupant of any of the separate offices which are consolidated if . . . the board finds that sufficient personnel possessing the qualifications required are employees in the consolidated office to assure that decisions made by the occupant of the office are based upon competent professional advice.

Once the state code was changed and necessary county ordinances modified, the process of hiring the chief administrator for the new department got underway. Recruitment was primarily by invitation. The CAO anticipated that the merger would take place on March 1, 1972, the date the state legislative change became effective, and that the position would be filled by that date.

THE MERGER TAKES EFFECT

The merger, delayed over selection of the individual to head the new department, became a reality on September 1, 1972. Liston A. Witherill was appointed to the position, effective September 1, 1972. Witherill had just replaced Barr, who had retired in January, 1972, as director of the Department of Hospitals. Prior to that, since 1965, he had been administrator of the county's 2,200-bed Los Angeles County-University of Southern California (LAC-USC) Medical Center. He was well known to the CAO's office, having started there as a trainee in 1948, having become chief of the budget division in 1955, and then having moved into hospital administration in 1956 as assistant administrator at the gargantuan Big House. To the Departments of Public and Mental Health, Witherill's appointment materialized their worst fear: indeed, the Department of Hospitals was in the driver's seat.

D.   Dynamics of Implementation: 1972 to mid–1975

WITHERILL'S ORGANIZATIONAL PLAN

Witherhill quickly developed a plan for the top level of his organization which the new CAO, Arthur G. Will, presented to the Board of Supervisors. Will's letter to the board stated that the organization's necessary support staff would be drawn largely from Department of Health Services' existing staff (Will, November 16, 1972). In fact, however, Witherill drew staff members largely from the former Department of Hospitals—people whom the director knew and had worked effectively with before. These appointments further enhanced the fears of the Departments of Mental Health and Public Health. However, Witherill took one action designed to minimize the continuing fears of the two departments: he appointed both of their departmental heads as deputy directors, reporting directly to him.

Donald Avant, deputy director of organization/operations, had recommended that the department heads of mental health and community health report to Dr. Affeldt, medical director of the county's five hospitals. However, Dr. Brickman from the old Department of Mental Health brought pressure to bear via state legislatures and the local Mental Health Association, reinforcing Witherill's decision initially to give all three physicians equal positions as deputy directors.

From the very beginning, Witherill reassigned existing staff instead of hiring additional persons. All the recommended new positions for the central staff were offset by the deletion of existing positions in the prior departments.

In the organizational structure proposed to the board (see figure 8.2), Witherill continued to serve as the Director of Hospitals. Actually, no such position continued to exist. While other departmental directors became deputy directors, Witherill did not develop this role for the Department of Hospitals. These factors probably influenced his decision: 1) the deputy director positions for mental health and community health were established in part to overcome resistance to the merger, an unnecessary precaution for the Department of Hospitals; and 2) hospitals already operated under a decentralized form of organization, which enabled Witherill simply to group them into five hospital service units, reducing the number of individuals reporting directly to him (see fig. 8.2). He could thus set the stage for a smoother transfer later when the county was regionalized, at which time each hospital administrator would report to his regional director. A deputy director of hospitals would be one more individual concerned with loss of domain.

In the proposed organization, the County Veterinarian, Dr. Schroeder, became a deputy director right along with Dr. Brickman from mental health and Dr. Heidbreder from public health—henceforth to enjoy a peer relationship with heads of much larger and more influential units. Dr. Schroeder played an important role during the early stages of merger implementation. The Departments of Mental Health and Public Health remained antagonistic and fearful of anyone coming from the Department of Hospitals. Perceived as neutral, Schroeder was appointed to chair several high-level administrative committees.

Schroeder's request to be included in the merger paid off in another way. Whereas the deputy directors of mental health and public health were destined to lose line authority when all regions became operational—to become staff advisors instead—the County Veterinarian was scheduled to retain his line of authority. This was justified on the basis that the department was small and highly specialized.

Dr. Heidbreder, former Director of Public Health, retired and was replaced in early 1973 by Dr. Ralph Sachs as deputy director for Community Health Services. Dr. Sachs, previously an administrator in the Los Angeles City Health Department prior to its 1963 merger with the County Health Department, presented an ideal candidate for the vacated position: he knew first-hand what the future held for Community Health Services, he had worked well with people in the Department of Hospitals, and he was nearing retirement age.

In September 1972, Witherill appointed Dr. Stella Soroker of Community Health Services to head up the establishment of a task force to make recommendations on the delineation of health service regions. The Task Force's report was due by October 20, 1972, a deadline which precluded any new analysis, or even new designs. Only a short time was provided for its work because a push was on to speed up merger implementation. Also, considerable work on the study had already been done by the Department of Hospitals staff prior to the merger. Some speculated that the Task Force was a sop to participative decision making; that Deputy Director Avant already knew what regions he wanted.

The Task Force held only three meetings, at the first of which Donald Avant, deputy director for organization/operations, set the guidelines: 1) the

FIGURE 8.2 Organization Chart of Los Angeles
Department of Health Services

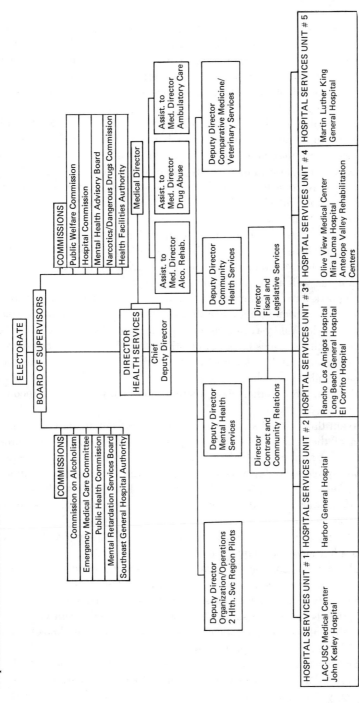

ELECTORATE

BOARD OF SUPERVISORS

COMMISSIONS
Commission on Alcoholism
Emergency Medical Care Committee
Public Health Commission
Mental Retardation Services Board
Southeast General Hospital Authority

COMMISSIONS
Public Welfare Commission
Hospital Commission
Mental Health Advisory Board
Narcotics/Dangerous Drugs Commission
Health Facilities Authority

DIRECTOR
HEALTH SERVICES

Chief
Deputy Director

Medical Director

Assist. to
Med. Director
Alco. Rehab.

Assist. to
Med. Director
Drug Abuse

Assist. to
Med. Director
Ambulatory Care

Deputy Director
Organization/Operations
2 Hlth. Svc Region Pilots

Deputy Director
Mental Health
Services

Deputy Director
Community
Health Services

Deputy Director
Comparative Medicine/
Veterinary Services

Director
Contract and
Community Relations

Director
Fiscal and
Legislative Services

HOSPITAL SERVICES UNIT # 1
LAC-USC Medical Center
John Kesley Hospital

HOSPITAL SERVICES UNIT # 2
Harbor General Hospital

HOSPITAL SERVICES UNIT # 3*
Rancho Los Amigos Hospital
Long Beach General Hospital
El Corrito Hospital

HOSPITAL SERVICES UNIT # 4
Olive View Medical Center
Mira Loma Hospital
Antelope Valley Rehabilitation
Centers

HOSPITAL SERVICES UNIT # 5
Martin Luther King
General Hospital

*Administrator of each Hospital Services Unit will be the present Administrator of the major County Hospital in the Hospital Service Unit.

Health Services Commission Report was to serve as a guide; 2) regions should be relatively self-sufficient and encompass a full range of health services; 3) the regions should not number fewer than five nor more than ten; and 4) two regions were to be selected as pilots. Pilot regions were specified because no detailed advanced planning had been done to allow implementation of the regional concept in one shot.

On October 18, 1972, Dr. Soroker presented the Task Force's recommendations to Avant. Her report noted that a diversity of points of view among task force members had made consensus difficult. The point of greatest conflict had to do with the various geographies that had defined the former departments' relationships with the community. The only expedient and acceptable manner in which the task force could divide the county was by former public health districts. A region was to be delineated by two or more contiguous districts, since 1) many local and state agencies knew and accepted health districts; 2) most statistical reporting systems were established along health district boundaries; and 3) changing boundaries would create community as well as administrative confusion.

The task force recommended creating seven regions, each encompassing three to five former public health districts. It had no difficulty in selecting the San Gabriel Valley region as one of the two pilot regions, as it lacked organized health services (a condition stipulated by the Health Services Planning Commission and endorsed by the Board of Supervisors). But the task force was divided over whether to recommend the Coastal region or the South/Central region for the other pilot program, and finally decided to recommend the latter.

Avant then played an influential role in determining both the final composition of the regions and the selection of pilot areas. On November 22, 1972, he sent a memo to Witherill regarding Dr. Soroker's report. Avant felt that the Antelope Valley was not large enough to merit designation as a separate region. Avant also felt that the West Los Angeles, Hollywood, and Santa Monica area should not be designated a separate region, since two of the health districts in that region provided 16 percent to 18 percent of LAC-USC inpatient admissions, and the Medical Center's director feared the drop in admissions subsequent to the separation of this region would harm medical education. While for years county hospital administrators had expressed the need to reduce the size of the LAC-USC Medical Center, when an opportunity existed for doing so, the effort was blocked. U.S.C. medical school officials raised the same objection later when the San Gabriel Valley Region, the only one without a county hospital, explored methods of contracting with local hospitals to provide services.

These changes left the county divided into five regions which Avant recommended as being consistent with providing a sound basis for unification and quality care within the department (Avant, November 22, 1972, p. 2).

Four of the regions were structured around existing county hospitals, since the task force knew that enough private practicing doctors and hospitals considered county patients undesireable to require that county operated facilities be available. Affiliation with medical schools was the best available method of assuring quality medical care, and the hospitals in the two medical schools, USC and UCLA, were well established. In addition, hospitals represented the department's major resource—80 percent of its budget, personnel, and skills.

On January 23, 1973, the Board of Supervisors approved the regional designations. The five regions did not fall completely within any supervisorial district; however, the San Gabriel Valley region was predominantly in the First District of Supervisor Peter Schabarum and the San Fernando Valley region was predominantly in the Fifth District. Figures 8.3 and 8.4 show the relationship between health services and supervisory districts.

FIGURE 8.3   Supervisorial Districts, Los Angeles County

FIGURE 8.4   Health Services Regions and Supervisorial
Districts, Los Angeles County

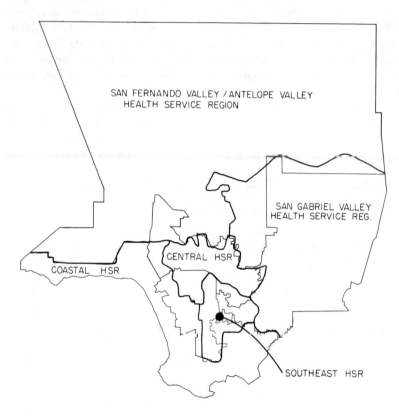

Figure 8.4 is reprinted with the permission of the Los Angeles County
Department of Health Services.

Avant recommended Southeast and San Gabriel for pilot regions. Witherill chose San Gabriel and Coastal. Coastal was chosen by a process of
elimination: Central was too big; San Fernando/Antelope was inappropriate
because Olive View Hospital had been demolished by an earthquake; and in
Southeast the King Hospital was new and had many start-up problems to
solve.

DECENTRALIZATION

Witherill's guidelines for regional organization, issued in early January 1973,
flowed from the earlier recommendations of the Health Services Planning

Commission for regional unification of all health services. Witherill opted for geographic decentralization for several reasons: to develop a responsive health care delivery system by providing care where it was needed, and to monitor need by delegating organizational decisions as close to the consumer as possible. Geography was the chosen form of decentralization because Los Angeles' dispersed population tended to identify with particular areas.

Health service regions were designated to serve as the basic organization through which the Department of Health Services was to discharge the bulk of its health service activities. Regions were to be divided into districts. Each district was to contain a comprehensive ambulatory care program along with a network of neighborhood health centers which would make extensive use of paraprofessionals.

Witherill developed a job description for the position of regional director, making the position that of a deputy director, who should be autonomous in matters of budgeting, personnel, and program planning (Witherill, 1973, pp. 2, 3). There was a salary differential between the directorship of the three larger regions and the two smaller ones.

Each region that contained a county hospital was to select a regional medical director, assumed to be the hospital's medical director. In the San Gabriel Valley, the positions of regional director and regional medical director were combined into one, to be held by a physician.

Avant added details to Witherill's broad guidelines for regional development. In a memo issued in March 1973, titled "Identification of Functions to be Regionalized and Functions to be Centralized," he emphasized that nonregionalized functions would be exceptions to the general policy to regionalize.

Only those functions which had an ongoing need for central coordination would remain at the central office: coordination of the alcoholism and drug abuse programs, contract negotiations, negotiations with the state, etc.

An early exception to the rule was Rancho Los Amigos Hospital, a specialized rehabilitation facility. Eugene Erickson, the hospital administrator, wanted to maintain relationship with Witherill. His reason for not regionalizing Rancho was "the total orientation of the hospital to countywide programs not serving any one region in particular." Many felt this argument was weak, as other specialty programs were not excluded. It was recognized that Erickson's personality influenced the decision not to regionalize Rancho.

THE EXPERIMENTAL REGIONS

Avant planned implementation of the two pilot regions to occur in three stages. During Phase I, June 1 to August 8, 1973, regions would develop their new administrative organizations and cast aside their old reporting relationships: all health service units within a region would report to the regional director instead of to deputy directors of Community Health Services, Mental Health Services, and the hospital administrators. This phase was not to involve any physical relocation of personnel, but was to focus upon reassigning control over programs.

Phase II, expected to last six months, consisted of reorganizing services in the region to provide greater focus on the delivery of personal health services in ambulatory settings.

Avant considered that entering Phase III was "passing the point of no return." This final stage involved the reassignment and relocation of personnel formerly located in the headquarters office for Community Health Services and Mental Health Services. Success of this phase rested upon the activation of and space available in all five regions.

Avant clarified that no attempt would be made to represent every discipline on either the departmental or regional central staffs, presenting a severe threat to the several disciplines of public health, which for years had operated with a very strong bureau system (a functional-type management structure in which several deputy public health directors are each given substantial line authority for operations in various districts of the public health specialties of nursing, environmental sanitation, epidemiology, laboratory services, etc.).

This only contributed further to the general anxiety of central staff personnel in Community Health and Mental Health. Many knew they would be reallocated to a region, but the region and function remained a mystery, as did the timing of the change.

Effective March 15, 1973, acting regional directors were appointed for the two pilot regions. Martin Finn, M.D., was appointed acting regional director for the San Gabriel Valley Region. He had previously been the health officer of a district within the new region. Leslie R. Smith, the newly appointed acting director of the Coastal region had been administrator of the LAC-USC Medical Center. Both appointments were temporary because the full civil service recruitment and appointment procedures of the county's Personnel Department had not been followed; this procedure allowed regional experimentation to start, and provided Witherill with wider discretion in making the initial appointments.

While official statements downplayed any competition between the two regions, unofficial comparisons were constantly being drawn. Smith, an experienced administrator from a complex medical center, was perceived as having an edge over Dr. Finn. He had worked closely with Witherill and was perceived as knowing the rules of the game. Finn, on the other hand, had operated in the bureau structure of the old Department of Public Health. His first regional organizational plan incorporated the bureau approach, designating regional central staff representation for most disciplines. Witherill and

Avant's rejection of the plan indicated the limits of Finn's decision-making parameters.

The regional central staffs started small and remained small. In San Gabriel Valley, Jesus Ramirez was named acting administrative deputy to Dr. Finn, and Mrs. Eunice Hankins as acting director, Community Development and Education. Ramirez' previous experience had been in county personnel services; Hankins' background was in health education. These two, along with Dr. Finn, constituted the central staff of the region; though other assistants were added later, they remained the policy-making group for the region.

Smith's Coastal region staff was also small. Since his region included Harbor General Hospital, Dr. Bill Swanson, its medical director, became medical director for the region. Roy Fleishman was brought in to administer budget and legislative aspects. Roy had previously been in the CAO's office. Joel Prell from the old Department of Hospitals central staff joined Smith as a planning specialist.

The difference in the personnel of the two regional staffs reflected variations in their resources and settings, as well as differences in approach. The Coastal region had a management orientation emphasizing planning, budgeting, and controlling. The Coastal region contained two county hospitals, three and one-half mental health regions, six public health districts, and UCLA Medical Center. These resources enabled Smith to build his structure for providing services around medical expertise available in abundance in the county hospitals. By contrast, the San Gabriel Valley region lacked a county hospital, contained only one and one-half mental health regions, and had six public health districts. Lacking hospital resources, Finn had to focus his restructuring around existing community and mental health resources. In this, Eunice Hankins' orientation toward community involvement played a key role.

San Gabriel Valley Region

One of Dr. Finn's major strategies was to upgrade the clinical skills of physicians in district health officer positions. Finn himself had been an unusual district officer in that he had maintained his clinical activity and skills. Many of the district health officers in the region were nearing retirement; Finn replaced each with a clinically-oriented, often board qualified specialist, who could obtain staff privileges at LAC-USC Medical Center. These physicians then served as consultants in their specialty to other regional clinicians.

To underscore the change from an administrative to clinical emphasis, the title of district health officer was changed to chief physician. Thirty percent of a chief physician's time was to be spent in clinics providing direct services, 30 percent in managing the district, 30 percent in tying regional programs and the LAC-USC Medical Center resources together, and

10 percent in maintaining and improving professional skills and setting standards. A district manager was provided to support the chief physician in his administrative responsibilities.

Most planning in the San Gabriel Valley Region was done by task forces, partly in response to a push from Avant's office to use the task force approach in problem solving. Finn's regional staff mildly resented this prescription, but it was nonetheless followed. A particularly sensitive area was the future role of the public health nurse, so nursing task forces were established to study 1) nursing home visits and 2) the expanded role of the nurse. Home visits, the traditional modality of public health nursing, was under scrutiny because of the cost of home visits compared to patient care in a clinic setting.

The Nursing Home Visit Task Force re-emphasized the importance of the public health nurse role and objected to further reductions in home visiting time. (At the time, one-fourth of a nurse's time was spent in home visits.) Finn, previously a strong supporter of nursing home visits, now found himself on the other side of the fence with pressures from Witherill and Avant to develop ambulatory health care utilizing available personnel.

The district nursing directors objected strongly enough to petition Witherill for a meeting. He did not state that home visits were to be eliminated, but that there had to be a switch to include sick care/ambulatory care. Witherill challenged the community nursing directors to find a more economical method of providing traditional public health nursing. He emphasized that they had entered an era of accountability.

Mental health nursing personnel were equally concerned about the emphasis upon ambulatory care. Their old department's philosophy had been towards consultation and prevention; however, they had already moved to providing emergency psychiatric services. One of Dr. Finn's objectives during Phase I was to merge mental health services with an ambulatory care program at the La Puente Center. Since the mental health nurses' only designation was that of public health nurse, they feared being used to provide other than mental health care. In August, 1973, their title and job descriptions were changed as part of a strategy to protect their role: their positions were retitled 1) assistant mental health counselor, R.N.; 2) mental health counselor, R.N.; 3) senior mental health counselor, R.N.; and 4) principal nurse (one position in the county).

Dr. Finn's actions generated more fear and resistance among his region's personnel than did Smith's, at least during the pilot phase. Having fewer resources, Finn immediately had to restructure community health and mental health.

Phase I began June 1 and ended August 8, 1973. During this period, Dr. Finn followed Witherill and Avant's instructions for revamping the reporting system within the region—a change which upset several disciplines, especially nurses and sanitarians in community health and personnel in mental health. Reports and requests were now to be channeled to Dr. Finn rather than the central office of public health bureaus, or Dr. Brickman in the case of mental health. For a while, a dual reporting system existed in which the bureaus and Brickman received the same communiques as Finn.

Dr. Finn desired to have the sanitarians report to Ramirez, his administrative assistant—a situation to which the sanitarians objected, complaining that Ramirez lacked knowledge of their field of practice. Finn acquiesced: he chose one sanitarian in the region to serve as chief and had all others report to him; then he reported to Ramirez. Since the role of the sanitarians did not involve direct personal health services, some were physically relocated away from health centers to make more room for new ambulatory health care programs. Sanitarians did not exhibit much anxiety over these changes; many of their functions were mandated by law.

During Phase II (August 8 through December 31, 1973), the San Gabriel Valley region emphasized developing and implementing a procedure for community input at both the district and regional levels. The relationship Dr. Finn built in his region with various communities played a critical role later when he took the examination for a permanent position as regional director and was not ranked high on the eligibility list. His popularity in the region, as evidence by community support, contributed to Witherill's decision in the summer of 1974 to reappoint Finn as acting director rather than someone else from the county eligibility list.

Also, the county supervisor of the First District, in which the San Gabriel region was primarily located, took an active role in health care activities. Supervisor Schabarum appointed a full-time assistant, Tom Hibbard, to monitor the health care situation. Hibbard had previously served as a health educator and community organizer with Dr. Finn in the El Monte Health District, and this relationship proved beneficial. If regional staff were frustrated at the departmental level, they could seek help from Schabarum. Members of the departmental central staff complained that Schabarum acted too much like an administrator and not a policy maker; he should not have interfered with administrative decisions. Schabarum's support for Dr. Finn undoubtedly influenced Witherill to reappoint Finn.

In summary, because of its lack of both county and private health resources, San Gabriel Valley was viewed by many as the proof of the merger pudding. Dr. Finn had few administrative credentials for the job, but enjoyed respect as a public health physician and practicing clinician. He successfully handled a number of severe organizational changes involving role definitions and restructuring authority and accountability. He was aided by community and political support, both in running the region and being sustained in office beyond the trial period of reorganization.

Coastal Region

Leslie Smith did indeed have a clearer idea of what the department expected
of him. He never attempted to duplicate a bureau form of structure at the
regional level; instead, he conceptualized decentralization as a three-dimensional structure of programs, resources, and geography.

His approach to program management was particularly important. The
region's major resource was the clinical departments of Harbor General Hospital, yet these departments were organized along the traditional clinical specialty lines of medicine, surgery, pediatrics, etc. Smith altered this structure
and introduced ten programs: 1) adult medicine and surgery, 2) child and
adolescent, 3) maternal, 4) mental health, 5) substance abuse, 6) geriatric, 7)
preventive health, 8) dental, 9) intermediate and long-term disorders, and 10)
emergency care.

Program planning committees were established for each, with a department chief from Harbor General serving as chairperson. In this way the
traditional categories were redrawn in terms of programs. Clinical services
to each of the district health officers were then decentralized, while coordination of clinical care remained the continuing responsibility of the program
chairpersons from Harbor General Hospital.

Reorganization in the Coastal region directly affected functions and
personnel from the old Department of Hospitals (considered inviolate by many),
in contrast to the focus on public health and mental health functions in the
San Gabriel Valley region.

Regional resources, which comprised Smith's second axis, were grouped
as follows: 1) community relations, 2) planning and evaluation, 3) administrative services, 4) regional medical center, and 5) regional specialized hospital.
The committees dealing with each of these were not established along functional lines in accord with Smith's strategy to incorporate the various disciplines into committees dealing with either programs or resources. In both
cases traditional public health bureau identification was broken. To emphasize
this break, Smith excluded regional nursing directors from attending monthly
bureau meetings held countywide. Smith's plan also mitigated the effects of
clinical overspecialization that had built up at Harbor General Hospital.

The third axis of Smith's grid was geographic decentralization. Six districts were delineated, then five. The committees relating to these districts
were community health service councils, composed of 51 percent or more
consumers. Members of the district councils were to be represented on a
regional council similarly composed.

Obviously, potential conflict existed where the three axes crossed, and
the use of a large number of committees risked confusion. Yet, Smith had a
reputation as a firm decision maker; he was prepared to resolve conflict
between programs, resources, and geographies at the central regional level.

In summary, while Smith introduced change in his region, old departments displayed less resistance and exhibited less anxiety over the change. To be sure, much of the change had not yet filtered down to the operating levels. For example, community health district nursing directors were offended at being excluded from the department's nursing bureau meetings, but the public health nurses' role in home visiting had not been attacked. Further, Smith already had personal health care-oriented medical and paraprofessional personnel available in the hospitals which he could transfer to clinical programs set up in the five districts; he did not have to reallocate traditionally preventive-oriented personnel to direct care to the degree that Finn was required to do.

Everyone lauded Smith's ability as a regional director; no one doubted that following the civil service examination in the spring of 1973 he would become the permanent regional director.

DEPARTMENTAL CENTRAL STAFF

While regionalization was in process, changes were also occurring at the departmental level. The departmental central staff had been enlarged, a situation which Eugene Erickson, administrator of Rancho Los Amigos Hospital, called to Witherill's attention: "You talk about decentralization of Health Services Department, and we feel you mean it. Yet, at the same time regions are being developed there has been a proliferation of central administrative staff" (Erickson, Nov. 23, 1973).

Part of the central staff's enlargement was due to the decentralizing of other county departments' activities. The CAO's office assigned a person to work directly with Witherill and located him at the department's offices. It was unclear exactly what this relationship was to be like; the impression was that it would be one of consultation and coordination. Certainly, the CAO representative would be concerned with fiscal matters. The Department of Health Services was the largest element in the county budget; the CAO was not about to let the department get beyond his office's close scrutiny.

Another expansion of the central staff included personnel activities. Robert Banning, from the Los Angeles County Department of Personnel, viewed decentralization as a means of obtaining whatever functions he could get for the Department of Health Services from the Department of Personnel. Banning had a line relationship to Witherill and a staff relationship to the Department of Personnel. As of spring 1974, employee relation activities had been relocated to the Department of Health Services, consisting of one team sufficient to deal with the eleven collective bargaining units the department faced. However, areas of testing and training had not been transferred to the department; these activities were dispersed in the Department of Personnel and no one in that agency wished to decrease their domain. Banning predicted he would need additional personnel to deal with communication problems.

Bonnie Norman, former director of nurses at El Cerrito Hospital in Long Beach with a master's degree in public administration, was also brought on the central staff in the spring of 1973. Her appointment to the role of nursing programs coordinator was made despite Witherill's and Avant's statements that representatives of specific disciplines were not desired on the central staff. Mrs. Norman's position in the department gave her power: she reported directly to Dr. Affeldt, who reported to Witherill.

Appointed to help bring nursing into line with the new focus on ambulatory sick care, Mrs. Norman perceived her role as that of a change agent: her educational preparation in both nursing and public administration enabled her to see issues from both sides, and her low-key personality enabled her to serve as an effective liaison between the central office and nursing administrators in hospital, community, and mental health settings.

Conflict resided on the departmental level just as it did on the regional level. One triangle of strain existed among Drs. Affeldt, Brickman, and Sachs; their traditional professional domains were still evident. Witherill had assigned programs in alcoholism and drug abuse to Dr. Affeldt, yet many aspects of these programs had previously been divided among hospitals, community health, and mental health. The organization solution to this general conflict seemed to be the retirements of Brickman and Sachs, at which time their positions would be downgraded to staff positions. However, this time had yet to come.

In preparation for total regionalization, certain central administrative positions in community health and mental health were designated as BAT #1's, budgeted positions available for transfer; and BAT #2's, positions to be phased out. There were more #1 positions in community health than in mental health, as the latter was already regionalized. Many of these changes awaited total regionalization; thus the anxiety and uncertainty that had characterized the central office continued for some time.

These and other central office developments formed the basis of Erickson's plea for more decision-making authority at the operating level. He defined decentralization as "the systematic and consistent delegation of authority to the levels where the work is performed" (Erickson, 1973). He felt the department's central office should be concerned primarily with planning and controlling, and the regions should be concerned almost exclusively with organizing and leading.

Organizational parameters were indeed being set at the departmental level. Donald Avant's office of organization/operations was charged with implementing the merger in respect to regionalization.

REGIONALIZATION ONE YEAR LATER

It was now summer, 1974—two years since the merger and one year since the pilot regions had been started. Regionalization had not gone smoothly in either experimental unit. Little had been heard about Supervisor Hahn's comprehensive health center in the Southeast District, although it was now open and running. Since the center was not in a pilot region, planning for it had remained a central office activity. Implementation of the center had not served as the transitional avenue for the merger that the Health Services Planning Commission had envisioned.

A conference was held to enable the pilot regions' experiences to be shared before the other three regions were activated. Dr. Finn presented a paper entitled "Administrative Pitfalls in Regionalization" that he had experienced in San Gabriel Valley. Many of the problems Finn delineated referred to lack of guidance and/or support from the departmental staff: inadequate lead time for planning, lack of a unified approach to pilot region planning (which was deliberate), lack of support from central staff personnel in defining regional positions, and absence of established criteria for evaluating the regions. Finn seemed to waver ambivalently between the wish for greater guidance and a call for greater autonomy.

It was now time to select permanent regional directors. Defining the process itself was very time consuming. It took the Los Angeles County Department of Personnel six months to solve two issues concerning the selection procedure: 1) should one or five examinations be administered? and 2) should there be one level of position or two, as Witherill had originally established? The department decided to administer one examination and establish only one level of position, the latter partly because Finn had consistently argued that having fewer resources made his task more difficult, not less.

Of the 120 applicants, about 40 were physicians. A board of screeners reduced the number of acceptable applicants, some of whom appealed their rejection, which created further delay. Finally, in the spring of 1974, interviews were held to establish an eligibility list. Then, after a further delay, appointments were announced one at a time during the summer. During much of this time, pilot regions' personnel felt in limbo. As the authority of the acting directors was uncertain, new changes were not pushed.

A completely unexpected event caused further delay, affecting the final choice. The *Los Angeles Times* exposed an illegal ambulance chasing ring at the LAC-USC Medical Center which had been recruiting hospitalized patients for lawyers. According to the news articles, medical center administrators had been aware of the Friends of the Friendless operation, but had not intervened due to legal advice (which turned out to be wrong) that while such was unethical, it was not illegal. Also, pressure had been exerted from a Board of Supervisors member's assistant not to push for an investigation (*Los Angeles Times*, March 19-23, 26, 1974).

Leslie Smith had been the administrator at the Medical Center when some of the activities occurred. Witherill, under tremendous pressure to take disciplinary action against administrators who had allowed the operation to continue, demoted Smith from acting regional director of the Coastal region to administrator of Harbor General Hospital. Departmental personnel perceived this as only a temporary setback, as Smith was considered an able regional director. Soon afterward, Donald Avant, who had been deputy director of organization/operations, was appointed regional director of the Coastal region. Smith resigned from county services and took a position as a hospital administrator in a local community hospital.

The next permanent appointment as regional director was for the Central region. Dr. Tranquada, who had been the medical director at LAC-USC Medical Center, was named. Dr. Finn was continued as an acting director at San Gabriel Valley. In the Southeast region, the medical director of the Martin Luther King Hospital, Dr. Phil Smith, was appointed acting director for the region. Then in late July, 1974, Doris Harris, M.D., formerly of community health, was appointed acting director of the San Fernando Valley region.

The fact that four of the five regional directors were physicians was contrary to most people's expectations: from the time of Witherill's original appointment the emphasis had seemed to be upon nonmedical administrative leadership. The administrators who had been most criticized for allowing the Friends of the Friendless operation to continue were nonmedical types—a definite setback for this kind of leadership in the county's health care system. That Witherill's ability to avoid using individuals ranked high on the Personnel Department's eligibility list was demonstrated by his appointing three acting directors instead of selecting them from the list.

E.   A PERIOD OF STABILIZATION:
     MID-1975 THROUGH 1976

REASSESSMENT OF DECENTRALIZATION

On September 3, 1975, four years after the consolidation had been made official, Harry Hufford, new (as of January) Los Angeles County CAO, recommended to the board of supervisors that departmental planning and staff activities be centralized at the agency level. Hufford recognized in the letter that while decentralization of these activities was valid, it was too costly; recentralization would reduce overlap and duplication. He wrote that the role of the regional directors and their staffs should be to supervise and monitor all field operations (Hufford, September 3, 1975).

This shift reflected the many ways in which the decentralization designed to implement the merger had failed to go according to plan. The two pilot regions had now existed for over two years; the other three for only one year. Many organizational changes had occurred. Regional boundaries were being restudied by a blue ribbon committee appointed by the board of supervisors. Activities orginally assigned to the regions such as planning and staffing were being recentralized. The role of the regional director and his/her staff had not yet been finalized, but appeared to be moving towards one of supervision and control. The CAO's office was exerting pressure to keep regional staffs small.

The title of regional director was changed to that of deputy director. The meaning of this was unclear, but one administrator stated it was a step toward making the position one of mere coordination. It was also obviously a way to prevent regional directors from establishing too strong an identity and power base in their locales. Yet, personnel in the regions continued to expect their director to fight for their regional needs—an advocacy role that was inconsistent, to a degree, with the emerging concept.

Of the five regional directors appointed in mid-1974, only one remained in office as of January 1976—Dr. Harris in San Fernando Valley. Dr. Smith, Acting Director of the Southeast region, left to resume private practice; he was replaced by Melvin Fleming, hospital administrator of Martin Luther King Hospital in the Southeast region. Dr. Finn, Acting Director of the San Gabriel region was replaced by Alvin Karp, also a hospital administrator from another region. Dr. Finn took the role of medical director for the San Gabriel region, and then became Deputy Director of Preventive Health in the central administration—the old county public health director's position. Dr. Tranquada, Director of the Central region, left the department in late 1975 to become Associate Dean of the UCLA Medical School.

Several factors led to such a high turnover rate: the change away from an autonomous role that included planning and programming to one of day-to-day supervision and control only; size restrictions the CAO had imposed on regional staffs; and intervention in regional activities by some members of the Board of Supervisors.

The re-examination of regional boundaries was a partial consequence of decisions made in the early stages of regionalization due to community pressure. Citizens of the Bellflower-Whittier area had refused to be part of the Southeast region because the primary hospital was Martin Luther King, a black-oriented facility. So, Bellflower was assigned to the Coastal region and Whittier to San Gabriel. This left the Southeast region the smallest in terms of area and population. Concern now existed that the regions should have approximately equal population, in anticipation of federal health dollars allocated on the basis of population size.

There were still more racial demographics in the issue of regional boundaries. With only black communities identifying with Martin Luther King Hospital, should black areas contiguous to the Southeast region be realigned to that region? If so, this would greatly decrease the black population in other regions, resulting in the majority of the black community of Los Angeles comprising one region.

Finally, political pressure had grown to have the five regional boundaries correspond exactly to supervisorial districts. This was intentionally avoided originally, hoping to decrease supervisorial intervention in regional affairs. However, each supervisor had kept in close touch with the major hospital in his area, bypassing both Department Director Witherill and the regional director. Early interventions by Supervisor Schabarum in the San Gabriel region had seemed beneficial, but his subsequent activity resulted in communication and authority problems between Finn and the department which Finn later felt had been disfunctional.

As of early 1976, the resolution of regional boundary conflicts remained unclear. The Board of Supervisor's special committee was still holding community hearings. The Public Commission on County Government recommended that regional boundaries remain unchanged until after the new Health Services Agency mandated by P.L. 93–641 had been designated and implemented for Los Angeles County, thus enabling health planners to have input into the decision.

The pilot regions had been conceived as a rational method for implementing the decentralization plan that would minimize disruption of services. Later assessment showed that another consequence had occurred: phasing in of only two regions had allowed old organizational identities to continue in nonpilot regions. By the end of 1976 the old lines between hospitals, public health, and mental health had far from disappeared and still influenced operations, in part because of the extended period of coexistence of two forms of organization (Public Commission on County Government, 1975).

CONTINUANCE OF THE MERGER?

Three Crises
Various crises such as the ambulance chasing ring at the LAC-USC Medical Center had presented a real threat to the department. Another scandal erupted early in 1975 upon the discovery that some private nursing homes were mistreating patients and failing to maintain sanitary conditions. The department came under fire because of its role as a delegate of the state in inspection and regulation of nursing homes. As with the Friends of the Friendless crisis, various leaders were demoted. The director of the Health Facilities Division was fired, later to be reinstated as an assistant hospital administrator after an

appeal. Dr. Sachs, Deputy Director of Community Health Services, was demoted and replaced by Dr. Finn.

This second round of demotions had pervasive consequences. Administrators at all levels of the organization learned that if things got difficult, they would be without support. Witherill had demonstrated that he alone would not take responsibility for and absorb the political onslaught for these departmental actions, and in so doing, lost the respect of some of his subordinates. An unwritten modus operandi developed: follow policy exactly, no matter how impractical, and protect yourself. For instance, one regional director forwarded every reasonable budget request submitted, thus abandoning regional priority setting.

The above policy flowed in part from yet another crisis: the interns and residents at the Martin Luther King Hospital struck over inadequate facilities and support staff. During the strike, Supervisor Hahn (whose interest in the hospital was such that some called it Hahn's living memorial), asked the regional director of Southeast if he had included the interns' and residents' requests in his regional budget. The answer was no, that the regional director saw no hope for receiving such a budget. The Board of Supervisors subsequently awarded supplemental funds to alleviate the problems highlighted, to be controlled by a representative group of the interns and residents of Los Angeles County. Undoubtedly, such funds would not have been forthcoming without a strike; the Southeast regional director was essentially correct, but the turn of events placed the Department's medical administrators in the peculiar position of seeking approval for needed equipment from their own employees.

New CAO Recentralizes the Departments
These continuing crises disenchanted some members of the Board of Supervisors. On March 25, 1975, with the support of his board colleagues, Supervisor Hahn instructed the CAO to report in 60 days on the feasibility of dividing the Department of Health Services back into its original departments. CAO Hufford responded, on May 22, 1975, in a "Report Regarding the Department of Health Services," which indicated that while the crises had certainly raised concern about the department's managerial effectiveness and total size, they were not in general directly related to its primary mission— the delivery of direct and curative health services (Hufford, May 1975). The CAO's report analyzed five alternative organizational strategies, but concluded that it remain one department. Hufford recommended various strategies to make the $550 million department more manageable: 1) transfer selected departmental support functions to other government units; 2) restructure top level organization for more effective management; 3) review concept and implementation of decentralized regional organization; 4) examine

the effectiveness of preventive public health and mental health programs to ensure proper emphasis within the department; and 5) unify numerous advisory commissions.

In September 1975, CAO Hufford followed his report with a set of recommendations to the Board of Supervisors entitled "Top Management Reorganization of the Department of Health Services." The main thrust was to recentralize planning and staff work. In Hubbard's view, the plan would: 1) remove an entire organizational layer of staff personnel by centralizing the major staff work; 2) result in tighter control over the performance of hospitals and health centers; 3) reduce the number and scope of top management positions; 4) provide more specific identification of responsibility for actions and activities of the department; and 5) produce an immediate cost savings (Hufford, September 1975).

Also, two new deputy director positions were created, one for planning and one for administration. These two positions were classified below that of the regional deputy directors, thus precluding regional heads from competing for either new position. Hufford's report set the role of a regional deputy to be supervision and monitoring of all field operations.

Finally, Hufford imposed new reporting relationships (see fig. 8.5). Traditionally, hospital administrators of major county facilities had enjoyed great autonomy. Hufford's new reporting system indicated clearly that the deputy director of each region was the hospital administrator's administrator.

In October 1975, the position of Chief Deputy was filled by Jerry Chamberlain, a retired Air Force colonel with 25 years experience in hospital administration. He replaced the term "centralization" with "standardization." Chamberlain's standardization was consistent with the CAO's goal of central control. He put together a department policy book, the scope of which ranged from policies on capping (soliciting business for attorneys), to contacts with members of the Board of Supervisors, to flying flags at half-staff.

An Independent Study

In late 1975, the Public Commission on County Government, an independent body created pursuant to a foundation grant to the Los Angeles County Bar Association, studied the Department of Health Services. This commission also noted the crisis the department had faced, but went on to recognize that "in merger the resulting point of control acts as a lightning rod for public and press attention formerly dispersed among the constituent agencies" (Public Commission on County Government, 1975, p. 2). The report's thesis was to wait and see.

The commission felt that the administrative problems facing the department were due to some extent to limited resources allocated for administrative purposes. The commission's study found a relatively low ratio of top

FIGURE 8.5   Reporting Relationships of Department of
Health Services—Los Angeles County

MEDICAL DIRECTOR
Preventive health consultation
Mental health consultation
Comparative medicine and
  veterinary services
Malpractice
Allied health
Developmental disabilities
Quality assurance
Drug abuse
Alcohol abuse
DEPUTY DIRECTOR, H.S. COASTAL
  REGION
Harbor Hospital
Long Beach Hospital
Six district health centers
Four mental health centers
DEPUTY DIRECTOR, H.S.
  SOUTHEAST REGION
King Hospital
Two comprehensive health
  centers
Four district health centers
Two mental health centers
Public health pharmacy
DEPUTY DIRECTOR, H.S. SAN
  GABRIEL REGION
One comprehensive health center
Five district health centers
Rancho Los Amigos Hospital
One mental health center
Public health laboratory

DEPUTY DIRECTOR, H.S. CENTRAL
  REGION
LAC/USC Medical Center
Five district health centers
One comprehensive health center
Two mental health centers
Crippled children services
DEPUTY DIRECTOR, H.S. S.F./A.V.
  REGION
Olive View Hospital
North County Hospital
Four district health centers
Three mental health centers
Two A.V. rehab. centers
DEPUTY DIRECTOR, H.S. PLANS
  AND PROGRAMS
Facility management
Plans and programs
Community relations—
  emergency service
Systems management
* Health facilities
* Environmental management
DEPUTY DIRECTOR, H.S.
  ADMINISTRATION
HQ administrative services
Contract management
Financial management
Personnel management
Legislation and governmental
  programs
Bureau of resources and
  collections

*Special reporting line to Chief Deputy Director

Figure 8.5 is reprinted with the permission of the Los Angeles County Department of
Health Services.

management personnel per 100 employees; in fact, the Department of Health Services had a .5 ratio of top management staff to total staff per 100 employees, while the County's Department of Public Social Service had a 3.3 ratio.

The commission's report also noted that of twenty departmental positions generally regarded as influential, only four were filled by incumbents who had been in the position for more than twelve months. As in the regions, central staff positions had undergone rapid turnover.

The Merger is Confirmed
By the end of 1975, the recurring question of the department's viability appeared to have been laid to rest. The CAO's report of May 1975 had supported the continuation of a single department, and his reorganization of September 1975 seemed to have secured its future.

F.   THE DEPARTMENT AND THE COUNTY AFTER 1975

Intradepartment reorganizing continued. The structure and authority of the central office re-emerged. The fate of the regions became uncertain; they seemed destined to become more standardized with decidedly less autonomy than originally planned.

Even after Brickman's departure, mental health remained a separate identity, barely integrated into the new department, partially because mental health centers were physically separated from other health facilities in most regions. Further, the Mental Health Advisory Board still opposed the merger. Mental health services continued to have an outside source of funding and vastly different regulations, due to the state's Short-Doyle Act. In regions where new comprehensive health centers had been constructed, notably in the Southeast, public health, mental health, and sick care were fully integrated.

Community health likewise underwent changes. Dr. Finn recognized that his role was staff rather than line. He too became housed in the central departmental office, where initially he shared a secretary with the acting deputy director of mental health. Finn felt that there was renewed interest on the part of the Board of Supervisors in communicable diseases, especially TB and VD; he emphasized these in his program planning.

One of the department's major continuing problems was the number of separate committees and commissions—twelve in all—to which it was required to relate, whose members were appointed by the Board of Supervisors and who each displayed narrow programmatic interest.

The CAO's office continued to play a major role in decisions affecting the Department of Health Services by developing a Health Services Division to bring together monitoring activities dispersed throughout his offices.

All of these conditions prevailed from late 1975 to early 1977, when a series of events took place which altered the very fundamentals of the department.

In April 1977, Liston Witherill resigned as Director of Health Services to take a private consulting position in health services management, one that he said offered him new opportunities and an improved salary. Upon resigning, Witherill told the Board of Supervisors that merger had resulted in an increase in service for health dollars spent (Bernstein, *Los Angeles Times*, April 4, 1977).

> Witherill's resignation and defense of the merger were accepted by two of his bosses—Supervisors Baxter Ward and Kenneth Hahn. Ward, chairman of the health services department for the supervisors, lauded Witherill's services. "He has been subjected to criticisms galore," Ward said, "but he has managed to maintain his direction and provide the services that are required. There might still be a question as to whether health services are simply too large but there has been no question as to Mr. Witherill's ability to conduct his assignment." Hahn also praised Witherill for an outstanding job "in one of the most difficult administrative positions in California."

One week after Witherill's announcement, the Board of Supervisors took what was reported as the first tentative steps toward breaking up the Department of Health Services (annual budget of $721 million; 25,000 employees). As reported in the *Los Angeles Herald-Examiner*, April 11, 1977:

> After rejecting a motion from Supervisor Kenneth Hahn for immediate division of the giant health department, the board called for a comprehensive study by Chief Administrative Officer Harry Hufford to be presented by Sept. 1. The board asked Hufford to analyze three options. One option would be to leave things as they are, with one department incorporating all services. Another, supported by Hahn, would be to return things to the way they were before Sept. 1, 1972, with four departments. The third option, supported by Supervisor Peter Schabarum, would break the present department into two—hospitals and public health services.

On July 11, 1977, John Affeldt resigned to become head of the Joint Commission on Accreditation of Hospitals. It was reported that he had no particular interest in assuming the department's directorship.

In October 1977, CAO Hufford submitted to the Board of Supervisors a 36-page report (Hufford, 1977) detailing the advantages and disadvantages of the three options specified by the Board, as well as a fourth: separating the planning, contract management, program development, monitoring and evaluation of mental health, alcohol, and drug abuse into a separate department.

Hufford's principal recommendations were as follows:

> This field survey has disclosed that almost without exception, health care professionals, health consumer organizations, and independent advisory groups

agree that the Department of Health Services should be retained as a single, integrated, comprehensive health delivery system. Only two bodies—the County Mental Health Advisory Board and the Southern California Public health Association—favor splitting the current department. Further, the principles and recommendations as they relate to delivery of comprehensive care which are expressed in the "Los Angeles County Health Service Planning Committee Report on the Study of Health Services" (Bauer Report) that led to the present merged department, effective September, 1972, are still appropriate.

Rather than from any fault inherent in the concept of an integrated Department of Health Services, our findings indicate a number of serious problems which bear on whether or not the department should be continued or separated into smaller units. The basic findings of our study indicate that the problems encountered by the department developed from:

A. Our attempts to implement the merger too broadly and too fast.

B. The dominance of acute-care programs over preventive and mental health programs.

C. Inadequate styles of management, organizational planning, financial management, policy oversight, and poor communications throughout the system.

D. The involvement of numerous commissions and community groups in planning and program development that have created conflicting pressures for resource allocations and program priorities.

The principal focus of change has to be on effecting organizational improvements and therefore, the Department should continue its thrust to:

1. Insure adequate public participation in decision making in each major program area.

2. Develop proposals to improve and better define the proper roles of the citizens' advisory commissions.

3. Update the long-range plans for the delivery of health care services, weighing improvements to the health care system against the taxpayer's ability to provide financial support.

4. Improve the financial forecasting and financial management.

5. Restructure the Department's financial management efforts to provide greater centralized information and control.

6. Create a more effective top management structure which can more effectively deal with operational problems and strategic or long-range planning considerations.

7. Improve lines of authority within the Department, which will identify responsibility for planning and operations and hold managers responsible for results.

Your Board deferred action on recruiting a permanent Director for the Department of Health Services until a full analysis was made of how to organize the county health service delivery system. With the adoption of this report and its recommendations to continue with one Department of Health Services, I recommend your board take the necessary action to recruit a permanent Director for the Department of Health Services.

In January 1978, Witherill was replaced by Morrison Chamberlain, former chief deputy of the Department of Health Services.

In April 1978, Morrison Chamberlain shocked county officials by his sudden resignation. He likened the county's health care system to a tin lizzie. As reported by Keppel in the *Los Angeles Times*, April 5, 1978:

> "If you maintain it well," Chamberlain told reporters, using the tin lizzie analogy, "it will keep on running. But it will only go so far, so fast." The massive County-USC Medical Center is half a century old, he noted, far past its prime.
>
> And Chamberlain complained that county government lacks the "ability for clear, quick, decisive decision-making that can be implemented. I work for five supervisors," he said and complained that an aide to one supervisor had attempted to interfere with his administration of the health program. . . .
>
> In discussing the lack of decision-making at the county level, Chamberlain cited the failure over the past 2½ years to appoint a chief deputy director of the department in charge of mental health. And, when asked what was the last straw that led him to quit, Chamberlain claimed that it was interference from a deputy to Supervisor Pete Schabarum, Thomas Hibbard, who specializes in health matters. . . . Hibbard borrowed a nurse from Chamberlain's department ("not an unusual thing," Chamberlain noted), called him on the telephone "three to five times a day" and then posed "the same question he asked me to five other people in the department." Chamberlain also said Hibbard threatened to go to the Board of Supervisors if Chamberlain did not do his bidding. "I basically don't need a health care educator (Hibbard) and a nurse to advise me on running a health system for which I have some national recognition," Chamberlain said.
>
> Asked for comment, Hibbard expressed surprise.
>
> Chamberlain praised Hibbard's boss, calling Schabarum "a fine man" for whom he can work with in agreement or disagreement. . . .
>
> Chamberlain said he had previously discussed his problems over Hibbard with Schabarum and again before both men on Monday. But he stressed that factor as incidental to his basic dissatisfaction with the way public health is organized today. Some of its problems have been akin to those plaguing the state's massive Department of Health which was created by a similar organization about the same time.

One week after Chamberlain's resignation the Board of Supervisors instructed CAO Hufford to prepare ordinances to separate mental health functions from the Department of Health Services. By the end of May 1978, Hufford (1978) submitted the following plan, which was approved immediately:

> It is recommended that the Department of Mental Health be re-established with a structure in which it would:
>
> —Directly operate outpatient and day care clinical treatment services through the twelve regional mental health centers;

—utilize the facilities and resources of the Department of Health Services for inpatient psychiatric services, through purchase of service agreements.

—and finally, would contract with the state hospital system and private psychiatric facilities for services.

We propose to retain the working relationship with the Department of Health Services in the delivery of hospital-based inpatient and outpatient services. This will amount to a contract arrangement which will avoid a myriad of logistical problems associated with the hospital-based support of inpatient services and the complexity of working out effective relationships with the involved medical schools.

A long-time staff person in mental health said that this abrupt change was due to a number of conditions that had built up over time. Mental health had lost its voice in the Department of Health Services: a permanent deputy director for mental health had never been appointed since Brinkman's resignation; the department's leadership was clinically oriented and treated mental health with benign neglect. Mental health officials had no direct control over services in the regions. Further, in the years which had intervened since the department's creation, the state mental hospital system had cranked down in favor of local services, and the county mental health officials had found themselves unable to respond properly.

In September 1978, Donald Avant resigned, feeling that he had "played out his hand in reorganization," and wanting to avoid "becoming a relic." He felt that the department had moved away from its original concepts, particularly in the CAO imposed, highly centralized controls. To Avant this represented the county's inability to accept decentralization. "Nobody was prepared to experiment any longer on that scale" (Avant, 1979).

In November 1978, county voters had the opportunity to approve a charter amendment put forth by the Public Commission on County Government. A *Los Angeles Times* article by O'Reilly, October 15, 1978, summarized the history and details of the proposal. Excerpts follow:

Proposed County Charter Amendment C would give the county something it never has had before—an executive elected by all the voters who would have sole responsibility for administration of the county government.

The present board administers the county indirectly through an appointed chief administrative officer and directly through a system which names each supervisor as chairman of about one fifth of the county's 58 departments. In addition, each supervisor is free to give orders to any department head about services in his own district. Under the proposed change, the elected county executive would take over all administrative duties, hire and fire department heads and issue all the orders.

The proposal was placed on the ballot by a 3–2 vote of the present Board of Supervisors. Why would three supervisors vote for a measure that would strip them of many of their powers? At least two of them, Supervisors Kenneth Hahn and Pete Schabarum, would like to run for the powerful new office of county executive, if it is created. . . .

As Hahn, a supervisor for 25 years, put it: "After I became a supervisor I found out the five supervisors were making the law, then we turned around and administered the laws we passed. Then I found out we were the quasi-judicial body and if the people didn't like the laws we made they could appeal to us to modify them."

. . . A study published in 1976 by the Public Commission on County Government found that the supervisors consistently budgeted more money for many departments than recommended by the chief administration officer. And for those departments where the rule was to divide the spending equally among the supervisorial district, such as roads and flood control, the budgets had more than doubled in three years.

On November 7, 1978, Proposition C was submitted to the voters, and failed to pass.

G.   COMMENTARIES

Two persons influential in developing and implementing the Department of Health Services critiqued the case: L.A. Witherill, Director of Health Services, and Donald Avant, Deputy Director, Coastal Region (originally, Deputy Director of Organizations/Operations). Excerpts of their comments, presented here exactly as stated in letters solicited by David Starkweather in late 1977, add breadth to Jo Ann Johnson's case study. They are followed by Regional Director Leslie R. Smith's comments and by some theoretical observations by the case study author.

[PLANNING]

> *Avant*: Not long after we were into the merger/regionalization, comments were made by various staff that we really didn't know what we were doing and more time should have been devoted to planning the organization. . . . Development of the Department could have proceeded from any one of several different approaches: paper planning models, gradualism, pilots, etc. The choice we made to use a pilot type approach to developing the Department was made for reasons of strategy and equitableness. . . . Development of a detailed organizational plan prior to implementation ran the distinct risk of a plan never to be implemented. . . . A public merger of the complexity and size of Los Angeles County health services had never before been attempted. The status quo was being threatened in health, mental health, and hospitals. . . . Clearly from a strategy point of view, the merger represented one of those rare cases in which too much information could be damaging.

> Gradualism, as an implementation approach to the merger, was reasonable but not racy enough to catch on. Some Bauer Committee members and others connected with the merger had hyped themselves with such a large dose of merger mania that the building block approach was seen as reactionary foot dragging. . . . The chosen approach, in my view, represented a balance between the Board's felt need for action and the necessary tentativeness required

to establish a departmental position that all would have their say as the facts became available from our pilots. To those with an interest in doing something new, this approach implied a call for reasonableness, a way of avoiding interminable discussions about a detailed and hypothetical plan which was without a precedent in practical operating experience. I quickly admit that for smaller, less complex and nonpublic mergers, our approach might not be appropriate. . . . Finally, the choice of strategies also reflected . . . the experience and training of the key staff involved with the early portion of the merger/regionalization. . . . We were operational people who intuitively knew that in a fluid situation complicated planning schemes rarely get anywhere. . . . We could not spend much time jawboning the subject of merger.

In the merger of a large complex organization, there is a definite need for a small central staff to devote a major part of their time to the problems of the merger . . . [but] I was drawn off to other tangential problems . . . to the detriment of the merger process itself. Although everyone necessarily gets into the act in the merger process, there needs to be one small clearing house through which all proposals are analyzed before action is taken. For example, the medical director's office more or less grew independent of any overall departmental considerations. Also, the development of the regions was left primarily in the hands of acting regional directors. If I were doing it again . . . there would be a much more strict protocol to follow prior to initiating any action with regard to the merger.

[ACUTE CARE, AMBULATORY CARE, AND PREVENTIVE CARE]

Witherill: It is true that at the start we emphasized personal care (ambulatory care), but I have to now admit that I missed the key importance of preventive services such as tuberculosis, V.D., and immunization. Now this is fully recognized. . . . The preventive services are protected.

Avant: In looking back, I don't believe that we completely appreciated the need for quick and significant successes. The Board, the public, and the staff anticipated that the merger would bring comprehensive ambulatory care centers with improved efficiency. . . . The merger did improve ambulatory care in certain parts of the County, but the improvement was uneven and not significant enough to capture the imagination of the Board and departmental staff.

[REGIONS]

Witherill: On the matter of the initial health services regions, my personal choice would have been to go with more regions, but we did not have enough dollars for administration. On hindsight, it was very bad to go with five—the same number as the Supervisors of the Board. Secondly, if I had it to do over again, I would start all five regions at once. The reason for starting two pilots was that I was worried that we would have a massive public health and mental health revolt if we took the whole shot at one time. In retrospect, the anxiety of those not involved in the pilot regions was so great that we might just as well have started all five of them at the same time.

Avant: The concept of a regionwide director as a more or less freestanding entity in each region was one of two concepts considered early in regionalization. Thought was given to converting the hospital administrator at the major teaching hospitals in each region (excluding, of course, San Gabriel) into a regional director. . . . But the idea never got anywhere because there was definitely a fear that the merger would be characterized as a hospital takeover. . . . Five years later we are now seriously considering implementation of this concept since the idea of a freestanding regional director has been viewed by various people in the County as an unnecessary additional layer of bureaucracy.

The important point about the selection of Finn and Smith was the obvious difference in their backgrounds. Since we were embarking on a pilot program as a means of getting into regionalization we decided that we might as well experiment with different kinds of leadership. There was a prevailing anxiety at the time that the merger and regionalization might turn out to be a full employment act for administration-type personnel; . . . to dampen this problem, a definite effort was made to get physicians involved in the overall administrative process of the Department.

There were some comments flowing around that we were setting up the San Gabriel Region for failure because an appointment of a slick sheet administrator was not made. . . . We weren't sure what kind of person might work out well as a regional director. . . . It doesn't make much difference whether a physician or a nonphysician is the head of a region as long as the regional organization reflects certain changes to accommodate the different types of leadership.

[CENTRALIZATION VS. DECENTRALIZATION]

Witherill: The principal reason for taking more control downtown was our terrible money crunch and the fact that operating units were overspending their budgets. In the last 18 months, we have had to make workforce reduction of 1500 positions. This could not have been done without central control. I expect that control will be decentralized late this spring well beyond any previous decentralization levels.

On the issue of central staff versus regional staff, I personally expect this kind of tug of war to go on for all time and believe that when it is kept inbounds, it is healthy and produces the proper balance.

Avant: The implication that the merger was a form of centralization is, in my opnion, misleading. I don't consider fragmentation, which was the state of affairs with County health programs prior to the merger, a form of decentralization. . . . [which] implies some type of rational organization. . . . As to the regions, the philosophy in the early stages of the merger was to decentralize the administrative and clinical programs to the greatest extent possible and leave the central staff with a monitoring, guideline-developing, and liaison function.

Witherill: On the matter of the CAO budget staff being housed in our offices, this was a noble experiment that failed. We did the same thing with Personnel. The concept was that we would accomplish more if there were interaction between our staff and that of the CAO and Department of Personnel by physically locating them in the same structure. There was frankly too much paranoia on the part of the central CAO and Department of Personnel. They worried about their staff being co-opted by us.

[POLITICS]

Witherill: On the comment that I did not take responsibility for such matters as Friends of the Friendless, nursing home scandals, etc., and was willing to have others take the political flack, I will try to not be too overly sensitive to that comment. I realize staff that had not performed properly and got caught in the situations and thus suffered transfers, demotions, etc., feel that I did not do all I could to protect them (although some of my bosses wanted much more severe discipline than I gave them). Perhaps I could have done more for them, but I can tell you that the price I paid personally was large. Aside from taking pressure and political flack that others in the organization have no real feel for, I did not receive a salary increase for a number of years. . . . I was appalled at the findings of the nursing homes scandals. In short, our people had not been doing their jobs and patients' lives were put in jeopardy. Therefore, very stringent action was taken both in discipline and in terms of changing our policy on inspection from one of education to one of enforcement.

Avant: The Public Commission on County Government was created to study the need for a mayor of the County and this group subsequently became the public agent which tried to convince the electorate that the mayor was, indeed, a necessary ingredient in County government. The staff members of the Commission with whom I talked felt that the merger had never been given a chance to work because of the lack of an elected official who could work on an equal basis with the Board of Supervisors. Prior to the formation of the Commission, the Department had become something of a political football and List Witherill serving in a Civil Service capacity could do little to stabilize the situation. . . .

[COSTS]

Avant: One element left out of the implementation strategy, which I believe to be important, concerns the question of the cost of the entire ambulatory care project. We had two main guidelines to follow: increase patient access to health care through a network of ambulatory care centers and don't increase net County costs. What we needed but did not have was a hard-nosed financial feasibility study that explored the potential for funding from Federal funds and the availability of existing hospital staff for reassignment into ambulatory care centers without the availability of front end money. The use of an outside consultant for exploration of this fundamental problem prior to the merger would have done a great deal to get expectations back into line.

As to the issue of increased efficiency, we never defined the parameters of efficiency prior to the merger; therefore, we had difficulty showing where we had actually improved. By not having identifiable success targets within our overall strategy, I don't believe we got the maximum benefit from the honeymoon period that followed the date of merger. I don't want to give the impression that we have not made progress. For instance, two new ambulatory care centers are scheduled, beyond the Southeast Center, to open in the near future. Economies have been effected but the entire five years of merger have been a grinding activity which has had a tendency to obscure the progress.

[THE FUTURE]

Witherill: I guess I agree with you, Dave, that the merger will take 10–20 years to really be effective. I would add another dimension; I don't think that an effective operation will come until all of the principals at the top positions that were involved in the merger are gone. As you may know, I am leaving June 1st so maybe the merger will go faster and better.

COMMENTS BY LESLIE R. SMITH

It's my belief that the challenges which faced Los Angeles County in its effort to coordinate health services by a major reorganization were substantially beyond the capability of the bureaucracy above the level of the Acting Regional Directors, myself, and Martin Finn. Kingdon (1973), one of the earliest authors on matrix organization, indicates that traditional bureaucracy does not work at the level of complexity and uncertainty of organizations such as ours. Kingdon's alternative form was put into the design of the Coastal Region management structure.

Factors which favored the probability of success for the proposed matrix organization included: 1) success of a two-dimensional form in the L.A. County teaching hospitals, UCLA-Harbor and USC Medical Center, from 1966–72; 2) adaptability of matrix theory of organization to geographic decentralization. The principal weakness of this was its threat to the traditional patterns of authority in Los Angeles County government and its many central staff developments.

Two dimensions of the organization developed easily—administrative and professional. The third dimension, that of the many communities within the region, followed naturally the charge to identify and respond to local priorities within the large region.

Factors which favored the probability of success for this revision of the matrix form included: 1) a strong administrative structure which could deal effectively with the traditional County organization, providing staff direction, support and analysis; 2) an effective professional component capable of providing primary, secondary and tertiary levels of health care in ambulatory care centers or medical centers, and a program-oriented professional staff; 3) an ombudsman-like role for district staff to represent priorities within communities.

This three-dimensional matrix took the pilot region a year to develop, and by March, 1974, it was submitted to Witherill for approval. It was not accepted and the pilot region reverted to the traditional bureaucratic form. The organization might have been approved had Witherill more experience as a chief executive officer in a teaching hospital (he had served only six months, not the several years Johnson describes), or had the other components of the County's or Witherill's bureaucracy not been threatened by it. This lack of support was my principal reason for leaving the L.A. County of Health Services for the private sector, as has been done since by many of my former colleagues.

The results could have been anticipated. Bureaucratic regression occurred instead of adaptation. This is evidenced by the 1979 status of the Agency. Mental health has been returned to departmental status, and the organization faces major problems in holding public health services together with personal health care services. Who is to say today which is a better organization. We only know that the traditional bureaucratic structure has not succeeded in integrating the three major services in a regional pattern.

SOME THEORIES—JO ANN P. JOHNSON

Determinants of Retained Integrity
In the summer of 1974 the Department of Health Services achieved what Avant (1973) termed the point of no return with the appointments of all five regional directors. Yet subsequent scandals resulted in questions being raised about the size and control of the Department. These were settled in late 1975 through assurances by the county administrative officer of the continued desirability of one department, coupled with strategies for tighter controls. The Department of Health Services has now achieved what Mosher (1967) referred to as structural effectiveness. Even though early in the merger process the prior existing departments officially ceased to exist, their organizational identities remained; organizational death (Kaufman, 1971) had not occurred for them until many years after official consolidation.

Humpal (1968) proposes analyzing a merger by the degree of organizational integrity each merging organization retains. By this guide the County Veterinarian ranks highest, followed by the Department of Hospitals. The Department of Mental Health did not fare as well, and Public Health retained the least.

The County Veterinarian Department was small, and although its role was changing, its functions were clear relative to the other departments. In the new department it remained centralized and fairly autonomous. What little the County Veterinarian's department surrendered in terms of autonomy, it more than gained in terms of increased influence. The old Department of Hospitals experienced little loss of organizational integrity because it was already organized to deliver personal health services, the main goal of the new department. The old Department of Mental Health experienced less loss of organizational integrity than the old Department of Public Health because it was already regionalized when the merger occurred. Yet its loss of integrity at the departmental level was substantial, as it was forced to change its focus from preventive/consultative services to more direct personal health care. The old Department of Public Health suffered the greatest loss because its bureau structure had been attacked. And it too was forced to change its focus from prevention to curative services.

The Political Environment
As Mosher's (1967) analysis of other governmental reorganizations concludes, political considerations condition important decision making even on matters of internal organization and procedure. Several examples of this are evident in this case: 1) Brickman's influence through the mental health associations to obtain a direct relationship to Witherill; 2) community pressure leading to realignment of regional boundaries; 3) Smith's demotion and transfer from acting regional director of the Coastal region to director of Harbor General Hospital because he had been director at USC-LAC Hospital during the time of the Friends of the Friendless operation; 4) the initial firing of the director of the Health Facilities division and the demotion of the Director of Community Health Services because of inadequacies found in care being rendered in nursing homes; and 5) the funds placed under the control of interns and residents following their strike.

Independent Studies
Mosher also found that formal studies preceded all the reorganizations he had analyzed, and that these studies played a major role in the decision to reorganize. In this case, it would appear the Report of the Health Services Planning Commission played just such a role. Yet, Marshall's (1971) analysis suggests another motive: staff from the CAO's office had criticized the study by the Public Health Commission on *Consumers' Need for Neighborhood Health Services* as being self-serving of Public Health Department interests. Control of the Health Services Planning Commission by the CAO made its report subject to the same criticism. According to Marshall, 16 out of a total of 21 members of the Commission were appointed by the CAO. The final report was prepared by the CAO's staff. After the report was finished, CAO staff met with members of the Commission on an individual basis and never reconvened the entire committee to review the report. Any member's differences were dealt with individually, thereby avoiding the sharing of common

concerns by Commission members. To generalize from these examples, are any independent studies truly objective? The orientation—indeed, the conclusions—of most independent task forces can be predicted by who is appointed.

The Meaning of Policy

Mosher (1967) identified shifts in policy direction as a common motive for reorganization, and so it was in this case study. The development of ambulatory health care was the hub around which the merger turned. Decisions were evaluated by how they contributed to this goal. An early given was that the Department of Health Services would not hire additional personnel but would reallocate personnel already on the payroll. Reallocation of personnel requires trade-off: something must be given up to obtain gains elsewhere. The San Gabriel Valley Region experienced the greatest disruption due to reallocation of personnel for ambulatory health care services. . . .

Mosher (1967) also found that the greatest amount of tension in the reorganizations he studied was generated over issues of purpose. The continued rivalry exhibited by the old Departments of Hospitals, Mental Health, and Public Health supports Mosher's findings. This rivalry coupled with the resistance of the old Departments of Public Health and Mental Health to shift in purpose were organizationally costly to the Department of Health Services. Overcoming factors such as these is one reason why Starkweather (1970) predicts that it takes 15 to 20 years before all stages of a merger are fully evolved.

Organizational Development

Early participation in the decision-making process concerning proposed change is a popular change strategy. Blumberg and Wiener (1971) proposed that the utilization of selected social intervention techniques could reduce some of the costs of change. Similarly, Mosher (1967) hypothesized that if persons whose behaviors are expected to change were involved in the decision-making process, future relationships would be more effective. However, Mosher's data did not support his hypothesis.

In the early decision making about this merger, participation of those affected was given only token attention. The interim planning committee was never operationalized. Neither was there cooperative effort for the planning of Hahn's requested comprehensive health care center. It was not until the merger was a fact that a participation strategy was really used, when members from various departments began serving on joint committees. The specific form of participation advocated by the central staff of the Department was task forces. An advantage of the task force approach was that members were hand-picked by the central staffs of either the department or the region, and the task forces were chartered for a limited time only. Many of the task forces were interdisciplinary, thus purposefully disruptive of previous functional relationships. The task forces made recommendations to the central staff of the department or region, not final decisions. . . .

Decision Makers' Qualifications

At the Departmental level, the majority of decision-making personnel were educated as administrators and did not come with previous backgrounds in medicine or allied health fields. Avant and Witherill are chief examples. The Coastal Region central staff followed the same pattern. In the San Gabriel Region, the acting director was a physician and one of his central staff members a health educator. However, the buttressing of these persons with nonmedical administrative assistants indicated a greater role in decision making for lay administrators.

It is not surprising, then, that the shift in major influence, after merger as compared to before, was towards those decisions preferred by administrators without backgrounds in medicine or allied health sciences: efficiency over effectiveness. The two crises and the appointment of four physician-administrators as regional directors did not alter this basic imprint. By winter, 1975, it was evident that nonphysician administrators were still acting as the primary decision makers: the appointment of Chamberlain as Chief Deputy Director of the Department, and the replacement of three of the original physician regional directors with hospital administrator types. From the beginning, the county administrative officer had desired lay administrative leadership for the new department. This began with Witherill's appointment as director and permeated downward. The CAO wanted people skilled in administration without divided loyalties to professional values. Given both the strength and wide divergence in professional goals and orientations, a top administration of dispassionate laymen—professionals only in management—was essential to making the merger work.

Centralization vs. Decentralization

Kaufman (1969, 1973) and Hirsch (1970) both prophesy a continuous shift between periods of centralization and decentralization. The merger which created the Department of Health Services was an act of centralization. Following this, both policy and major management decisions were located at the Departmental level. For example, a major policy decision was the mandate to develop and deliver ambulatory health care services. Several major management decisions were: (1) personnel reallocated without creating new positions, and (2) no attempt to represent all functional specialties at either the departmental or regional level.

Centralization of both policy and management decisions during the early phases of the merger appears necessary: "A single organization always seeks a way to concentrate on a single goal, or order multiple goals by a priority system so that conflict is eliminated" (Litwak, 1970, p. 184). However, as the merger evolved, the tug for control of decision making between the central staff and the emerging regional staffs increased. This conflict was reminiscent of the tension between the original merged Department of Hospitals, Public Health, and Mental Health. As put by Newgarden and Mars (1971) "Conflict is not eliminated, it just shifts from interorganizational to intraorganizational." The development of standardized procedures by Chief Deputy Chamberlain reinforced the concept of uniformity throughout the Department. CAO Hufford's letters to the Board of Supervisors in late 1975 recommended that planning and staff activities be centralized at the departmental level, thus greatly reducing the decision-making boundaries of regional directors to ones involving day-to-day supervision and control. By the end of 1976, regionalization looked more and more like "organization by area" (Kaufman, 1969): Activities may be decentralized but decision making remains centrally controlled.

Our conclusion from this case is that true decentralization, with emphasis on both local activity and local decision making, is ideal but extremely costly from an administrative viewpoint. The fluctuations in the Department of Health Services supports Kaufman's conclusion that the variables of centralization/decentralization are always in conflict and that a strong move in either direction will activate a counterreaction.

REFERENCES

American Public Health Association, County of Los Angeles. "Consumers' Need for Neighborhood Health Services." Los Angeles: American Public Health Commission, 1970.
Avant, D.W. "Identification of Functions To Be Regionalized and Functions To Be Centralized." Memo addressed to L.A. Witherill, director, Department of Health Services. Los Angeles, Calif., March 14, 1973. Reproduced.
_____. Memorandum to L.A. Witherill, in response to inquiry from D. Starkweather, May 11, 1977.
_____. Personal communication with D. Starkweather, November 21, 1979.
_____. "Regional Boundaries." Memo addressed to L.A. Witherill, director, Department of Health Services. Los Angeles, Calif., November 22, 1972. Reproduced.
Bernstein, Sid. "County Health Director Resigns: Witherill Surprises Officials, Joins New York Firm." Los Angeles Times, April 4, 1977.
Blumberg, A., and Wiener, W. "One from Two: Facilitating an Organizational Merger." Journal of Applied Behavioral Science, 7(1) (1966): 87–107.
Blumberg, M.S. "Changing Times Spur Hospital Mergers." Modern Hospital, 107: 83–84, 1966.

Consumer Need for Neighborhood Health Services. Los Angeles County Public Health Commission, Los Angeles, 1970.

Daggett, E.L. "Los Angeles County's New Health Services Super-Agency." *California Health*, 30(9) (1973): 9–11.

Epstein, M. "Study of Health Services Merger—Your Request for Comments." Memorandum to L.A. Witherill, in response to inquiry from D. Starkweather, Nov. 2, 1976.

Erickson, E.R. Decentralization of the Department of Health Services. Letter sent to L.A. Witherill, director, Department of Health Services. Los Angeles, Calif., November 23, 1973. (Reproduced)

Harmon, M.M. The consolidation of the Los Angeles City and County Health Department: A case study. Unpublished Ph.D. dissertation, University of Southern California, 1968.

Hirsch, W.Z. Giant government and centralized power. In W.Z. Hirsch & S. Sonenblum (eds.), *Governing urban America in the 1970's*. New York: Praeger Publishers, 1970.

Hufford, Harry. Establishment of the Department of Health Services. Memo addressed to the Honorable Board of Supervisors, Los Angeles, May 31. (Reproduced), 1978.

————. Organization of County Health Services. Memo addressed to Honorable Board of Supervisors, Los Angeles, October 18 (Reproduced), 1977.

————. Report regarding the Department of Health Services. Report addressed to the Honorable Board of Supervisors, Los Angeles, May 22. (Reproduced), 1975.

————. The top management reorganization of the Department of Health Services. Memo addressed to the Honorable Board of Supervisors, Los Angeles, September 3. (Reproduced), 1975.

Humpal, J.J. "The Study of Mergers: Notes Toward a Theory and Conceptual Framework." A work paper prepared at a Behavioral Science Organization Workshop, University of Chicago, December 6, 1968.

Kaufman, H. "Administrative Decentralization and Political Power." *Public Administration Review* 29 (1969): 3–15.

Kaufman, J. *The Limits of Organizational Change*. University of Alabama Press, 1971.

Keppel, Bruce. "Chamberlain Hits Archaic Care: County Health System Called a 'Tin Lizzie.' " *Los Angeles Times*, April 5, 1978.

Kingdon, D.R. *Matrix Organization: Managing Information Technologies*. London: Tavistock, 1973.

Litwat, E. "Towards the Theory and Practice of Coordination between Formal Organizations." In *Organizations and Clients*, ed. by W.R. Rosengren & M. Lefton. Columbus, Ohio: Charles E. Merrill, 1970.

Los Angeles County Health Services Planning Committee. *Los Angeles County Health Services Planning Committee Report on the Study of Health Services in the County of Los Angeles*. Los Angeles: Health Services Planning Committee, 1970.

Los Angeles Times. Series of 1974 articles on so-called "ambulance chasing ring" at LAC/USC Medical Center: March 19, Pt. I, pp. 3, 22, 23, 24; March 20, Pt. I, p. 22; March 22, Pt. I, pp. 1, 20; March 23, Pt. I, pp. 1, 20, 21, 22; March 26, Pt. I, p. 22.

Marshall, D.R. "Attempting a Merger: Reorganizing Health Services in Los Angeles County." *Health Services Mental Health Agency Health Reports* 86 (1971): 867–78.

"Master Plan for Health Services—Phase IIA: Study of Health Care Needs." Los Angeles: Los Angeles County Hospital Commission, 1973. Mimeographed.

Mosher, F.C., ed. *Governmental Reorganizations: Cases and Commentary.* Indianapolis: Bobbs-Merrill, 1967.

Newgarden, D. & Mars, D. "Interorganizational Relations: State of the Art." A work paper prepared in the School of Public Administration, University of Southern California, 1971. Reproduced.

O'Reilly, R. "County Executive: Important Charter Measure Buried in Ballot." *Los Angeles Times,* October 15, 1978.

Public Commission on County Government, 1975. Public Commission Staff Working Paper. "The Los Angeles County Department of Health Services," November. Report of the Commission, Los Angeles.

Schroeder, R.J. Center of Comparative Medicine, Los Angeles County. Paper stating the need to establish a Center of Comparative Medicine. Downey, Calif.: (n.n.), (n.d.). Reproduced.

Sherwood, F.P.; Harmon, M.; and Cloner, A. *The Inherited Decision: Health Consolidation in Metropolitan Los Angeles.* Monograph. Los Angeles: University of Southern California, School of Public Administration, 1966.

Starkweather, D.B. "Health Facilities Merger: Some Conceptualizations." *Medical Care* 9(1971): 468–78.

Task Force on California's Organization for Health Services. "A Department of Health for California." Report to the Human Relations Agency. Sacramento, Calif.: State Printing Office, 1970.

Will, A.G. "Recommended Top Management Organization for the Department of Health Services." Memo addressed to the Honorable Board of Supervisors, Los Angeles, November 16, 1972. Reproduced.

Witherill, L.A. Letter to D. Starkweather, April 13, 1977.

————. "Regional Organization." Memo to Group II staff meeting participants. Los Angeles, January 2, 1973. Reproduced.

9.

A 90-Day Merger? The Medical Center Hospitals of Norfolk, Virginia

David B. Starkweather

With Leonard Dougherty[1]

A. INTRODUCTION

The consolidation reported in this case transpired in three months—a marked contrast to the fifteen to twenty year duration that characterizes many hospital integrations.[2] The merger moved quickly because Norfolk's community has unusually strong and effective links, primarily informal, between leaders of the hospital, medical and civic establishments. What had been achieved formally and legally in three months was, in another view, an expression of longer-term relations among elites who, as one leader noted, "had known each other since grammar school." This case thus highlights the interplay between formal and informal structures, and between medical institutions and those of the larger community.

More unusual than the interhospital dynamics is the merging and "unmerging" that went on within the community of medical practitioners, both preceding and paralleling the hospital developments. An understanding of the hospital dynamics in this case requires understanding the reorganization of medical practice. Indeed, these two evolutions are deeply entwined. We have, then, not two mergers but six or seven corporate fusions and fissions, each stimulating others and being stimulated by others, with much overlap in leadership.

This case study was written while the principal author was visiting professor at the Department of Hospitals and Health Administration, Medical College of Virginia, Virginia Commonwealth University. The author is indebted to Professor Lawrence Prybil and other officials of the university for providing the time to conduct the study.

SIX CASES

Some of the names in this case are fictitious.

Barton "Sox" Baldwin, President of Leigh Memorial Hospital at time of merger; second president of Medical Center Hospitals

Eleanor Bradshaw, President, Board of Trustees, Children's Hospital of the King's Daughters

William P. "Billy" Dickson, Trustee of Norfolk General Hospital, first president of Medical Center Hospitals; partner in the firm of Wilcox, Savage, Lawrence, Dickson, and Spindle

Phillip Drager, M.D., Urologist; partner in Doctors' Clinic Company; partner in Tidewater Surgical Partnership; president-elect (1976) of Medical Center Hospital Medical staff

Alan Hofheimer, Trustee of Leigh Memorial Hospital for 30 years; senior partner of law firm of Hofheimer, Nusbaum, and McPhail; personal friend of Charles Kaufman

Charles Kaufman, Trustee of Norfolk General Hospital for 48 years; trustee of Medical Center Hospitals; chairman, Norfolk Redevelopment Authority; senior partner in the law firm of Kaufman, Oberndorfer, and Spainhour

Michael Madden, appointed administrator of Leigh Memorial Division (following Oliver) in 1974; administrator of Norfolk General Division, 1976 (succeeding Neil)

Robert McAlpine, M.D., cofounder, Payne Surgical Group; managing partner, Doctors' Clinic Company

Richard Magraw, M.D., President, Norfolk Area Medical Education Authority (became Eastern Virginia Medical Authority in June 1975)

Glenn Mitchell, Administrator, Norfolk General Hospital, 1971–72; executive director, Medical Center Hospitals, from 1972

Robert Neal, Jr., Associate Administrator of Norfolk General Hospital prior to merger; administrator of Norfolk General Division at time of merger (succeeding Mitchell); corporate director of shared services, Medical Center Hospitals, 1976

Warren Oliver, Administrator of Leigh Memorial Hospital prior to merger; administrator of Leigh Memorial Division after merger; then Medical Center Hospital first corporate director of finance; resigned in 1975

Robert L. Payne, Jr., M.D., Chairman, Norfolk Area Medical Education Authority (became Eastern Virginia Medical Authority in June 1975); co-founder of Payne Surgical Group

Toy Savage, Chairman of the Mayor's Study Committee that established the Norfolk Area Medical Education Authority, and vice-chairman of the Authority; trustee and former president, Norfolk General Hospital; partner in the law firm of Wilcox, Savage, Lawrence, Dickson, and Spindle

E. Todd Wheeler, Consultant to Joint Planning Committee

Wendell Winn, President of Norfolk General Hospital at time of merger; trustee of Medical Center Hospitals

B. PRE-EXISTING CONDITIONS

PHYSICAL LOCATION

Both merging hospitals, Norfolk General and Leigh Memorial, are located in Norfolk, Virginia, separated by less than a mile. Their neighborhood, immediately adjacent to the commercial center of Norfolk, was originally a fashionable district called Ghent which subsequently declined and is currently being revitalized under urban renewal programs.

The city of Norfolk has a population of approximately 300,000 people. The greater Tidewater area, including Norfolk, Virginia Beach, Chesapeake, Suffolk, Portsmouth, Hampton, and Newport News, has a population of approximately 1.3 million. The city of Norfolk is surrounded by Virginia Beach to the east, Chesapeake to the southeast, and Portsmouth to the southwest. To the north and west are the waters of Chesapeake Bay. Thus, Norfolk cannot expand. Further, with the exception of one small industrial park, it has little undeveloped land within its city limits for new industrial, commercial, or civic ventures. This makes redevelopment activity of particular importance to civic change.

ECONOMICS

One reason for the land shortage is the large amount owned by the federal government for the U.S. Navy. A prevailing local saying is that if the Navy were to hang up the "closed sign," Norfolk would cease. Much of the city's economy is directly or indirectly related to the Navy; 56 percent of all personal income in the Tidewater area comes directly from the government payroll. In the 1960s Norfolk made efforts to reduce its dependency on the Navy by encouraging new light industry. At the same time, the Vietnam War saw a large number of Navy ships and men moved from the East Coast to the West.

However, starting in 1970 and continuing for the next two years, with the war slowing down and the Navy reorganizing and closing bases elsewhere, 46,000 Navy men were transferred back to Norfolk, representing a total population increase in the Tidewater area of over 103,000 people, or 10 percent.

In brief, the federal payroll continues to dominate the area's economy.

POPULATION

Norfolk is 60 percent white and 30 percent black. The next largest minority group, virtually unrecognized, is Filipino.

POLITICS

The white leadership of Norfolk has been stable, reflecting the dominance of old line families. Roy Martin was mayor from 1962–1974, and before him Fred Duckworth for 16 years. The established families are always behind the scenes and sometimes in public office, appointed or elected. In recent years, the black minority has obtained some political visibility and influence, including the vice-mayor's office since 1972.

Relations between the several Tidewater cities are generally strained and often bitter, as could be predicted from their origins. Because of their water-locked locations, the cities of Norfolk and Portsmouth initiated efforts to annex lands to the west and south. Norfolk, in particular, sought not only land but also additional tax base to support services to its growing urban population. Virginia Beach, Chesapeake, and Suffolk were quickly incorporated to block these annexation moves. As a result, their land area grew to number them among the largest U.S. cities.

HOSPITALS AND DOCTORS

As of 1972, there were six acute care hospitals in Norfolk: the two involved in merger, Norfolk General and Leigh Memorial, Children's Hospital of the King's Daughters, De Paul, Norfolk Community, and a U.S. Public Health Service hospital.

Norfolk General was the largest: a 733-bed not-for-profit hospital providing specialized referral services to the Tidewater area and serving as a general hospital for Norfolk's core city population. Approximately 85 percent of its patients are private paying; 15 percent are poor, mostly blacks, whose care is financed by Medicaid and by the private-paying patients. It is the prime teaching hospital for a new medical school established in 1964. Norfolk General was founded in 1888 as the Retreat for the Sick by the members of the Women's Christian Association concerned for the plight of the sick due to the depression brought on by the Civil War and yellow fever epidemics.

By the turn of the century, the hospital had moved to its present location, expanded from 25 to 100 beds, and been renamed the Norfolk Protestant Hospital. Shortly after a rebuilding in 1903, a fire destroyed most of the new structure. Reconstruction and further expansion began in 1909. Norfolk General became the hospital's new name in 1936, acknowledging the institution's policy of rendering care without regard to nationality or creed. Starting in the early 1940s, several expansions of both size and service brought the hospital to its current position as a major regional referral center.

Leigh Memorial, a 167-bed hospital with a medical staff composed primarily of general practitioners, was founded in 1903 by Dr. Southgate Leigh, a prominent physician in the Norfolk community, in honor of his aunt who had raised him from early childhood after the death of his parents. The 35-bed private Sarah Leigh Hospital was reorganized in 1936 upon Dr. Leigh's death and in view of the hospital's financial plight due to the Depression. It became a nonprofit insitution under the name Leigh Memorial Hospital, in memory of its founder. A major expansion program was undertaken in 1940, and again in 1944, raising the total number of beds to 167.

The Children's Hospital of the King's Daughters, an 88-bed pediatrics hospital, is located immediately adjacent to Norfolk General from which it purchases some of its support services: radiology, respiratory therapy, operating rooms, recovery, ekg, food service, central supply, and some laboratory and pharmacy. Like many pediatric hospitals, it is a favorite charity in the Tidewater area. The King's Daughters, a 1500-member organization of civic-minded women founded in 1896, take great pride in the hospital, conduct successful fundraising in its behalf, and generally wish to protect it from the larger sweep of health care and civic dynamics. The hospital serves patients from all walks of life, but the King's Daughters is comprised of middle and upper class whites.

De Paul is a Catholic hospital of 349 beds, providing general acute care services, with a medical staff of both specialists and generalists, but primarily the former. The hospital also operates a school of nursing, and enjoys a sound community reputation and support.

The 192-bed Norfolk Community Hospital was founded in 1915 as the Tidewater Colored Hospital. It was rebuilt, relocated, and renamed in 1939, growing to its present size through a series of subsequent expansions. It sponsors a school of nurse anesthetists, and affiliates with three colleges for clinical instruction in nursing. Its residency affiliation is with Howard University College of Medicine.

The 210-bed U.S. Public Health Service Hospital was scheduled for closure in 1974, as were most of the nation's USPHS facilities, but was continued in operation due to the national efforts of community and employee groups which were reflected in congressional pressure.

Of the 830 actively practicing doctors in the Tidewater area, 450 of which are in Norfolk, specialists outnumber generalists three to one. Although over 700 doctors hold medical staff privileges at one or more of the four hospitals in Norfolk a much smaller number constitute the active users at each. At Norfolk General, 73 physicians admit 50 percent of the Hospital's patients; at Leigh Memorial the comparable figure is 12.

MEDICAL EDUCATION

Formed in 1964 first as the Norfolk Area Medical Education Authority and then reorganized as the Eastern Virginia Medical Authority, this unusual public entity is supported by limited tax funds from the Commonwealth of Virginia and from the cities of Norfolk, Virginia Beach, Portsmouth, Suffolk, Chesapeake, and Hampton. It has a special obligation to provide medical, nursing, and other health sciences education for the residents of the Tidewater area. A "school without walls," its core faculty is minimal, it uses practitioners as faculty, primarily, and it has deliberately chosen to use community facilities rather than developing its own clinical education facilities.[3]

Figure 9.1 is a map showing both the geography of the Tidewater area and the location of hospitals.

C.   A BRIEF HISTORY OF MERGER EVENTS

In 1970 some doctors practicing actively at Norfolk General decided to relocate their practices to a 27-acre parcel of land they had bought, 8 miles east of the hospital near the Virginia Beach city limit in a suburban growth area of Norfolk known as Kempsville. These physicians wished to relocate primarily because of their dissatisfaction with the limited and inflexible space in the Medical Tower, a high-rise office building located immediately adjacent to Norfolk General and owned in part by some of the seventy physicians who had decided to relocate.

Fifteen of the relocating doctors were members of two group practices, one in surgery, known as the Payne group, and the other in internal medicine, known as the Franklin group. Both groups had expanded in recent times and wished to continue to do so. These fifteen were the original purchasers of the land, having formed themselves into a new partnership called the Doctors' Clinic Company.

In 1971 these doctors, along with others, approached Norfolk General and asked it to build a satellite hospital on or near their plot in Kempsville. The idea was plausible: Norfolk's population was drifting in the direction of Kempsville, the 35 physicians represented a good mix of highly qualified practitioners, a satellite could block a proprietary corporation from construct-

FIGURE 9.1 Location of Hospitals, Tidewater Area

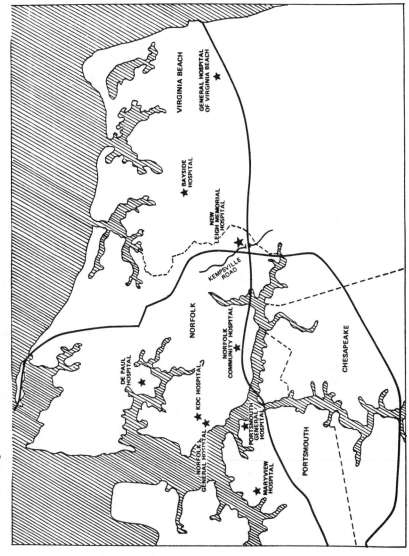

ing a hospital on or near the same site, and Norfolk General might be better off decentralized—some considered its present complement of 730 beds too large. Norfolk General's new administrator, Glenn Mitchell, favored the proposal; he saw the value of a hospital system consisting of urban and suburban facilities, similar to the Fairview Plan, a hospital group in Minneapolis.[4] But most of Norfolk General's Board opposed the proposal: the vote was unanimous against, with one abstention.

Two other important changes were simultaneously being debated in the Norfolk hospital and medical community. One was at Leigh Memorial Hospital where a consultant was advising this small hospital's board on its future role. Gordon Frieson and Associates found an institution that had changed little in recent years, had a reputation for adequate service, had a large medical staff but a small number of older active admitters, and was governed by a watchful board which had shepherded the hospital's finances into a prudent reserve of two million dollars with no long-term debts.

Frieson recommended that Leigh Memorial abandon its present site and move either to the Kempsville area or to Chesapeake, Norfolk's adjacent rural city to the south. The consultant's choice of Kempsville preceded the Doctors' Clinic Company purchase of 27 acres; such had not been contemplated at the time.

The second dynamic centered on medical education. The early 1960s had been a time of national concern for the production of sufficient physicians for an expanding population, and there was federal money available for the construction of new medical schools. In Virginia, pressure grew to establish a third medical school to augment the two already located at the University of Virginia, Charlottesville, in the west, and at the Medical College of Virginia in Richmond, in the center of the state. The Tidewater area was the logical place for a new school because of its eastern geography and its dramatic population increase of recent years, constituting 26 percent of Virginia's people by 1970. A Carnegie Foundation survey had established that Tidewater was the largest urban population in the U.S. without a medical school.

To advance these ends, the Eastern Virginia Medical Authority (EVMA) had been formed in 1964, through state enabling legislation. This public authority was supported by an allocation from the city of Norfolk, a federal government grant, foundation gifts, and significant local donations.

In forming the authority, local and state leaders had benefitted from the services of Dr. Vernon Wilson, Dean of the University of Kansas Medical School and a person familiar with federal government policies and sources of funding for medical education. Wilson consulted many parties in Norfolk, including those connected with Leigh Memorial who were involved in its deliberations of future location and role. In mid-1969 he presented a plan calling for the construction of a new 400-bed hospital on the Norfolk General site to be owned by Leigh Memorial. Two hundred would be teaching beds financed by a federal grant obtained by the authority, and 200 would be community beds financed by Leigh. This plan was well received by the Norfolk General board and medical staff and well publicized in the area's newspapers.

To advance the plan, Norfolk General, Leigh Memorial, Children's Hospital of the King's Daughters (located immediately adjacent to Norfolk General), and the Eastern Virginia Medical Authority formed a joint planning committee and hired the consulting firm of E. Todd Wheeler, Perkins, and Will to analyze the feasibility of Wilson's plan with respect to site layout and physical plant development. A plot plan of the Norfolk General campus is shown in figure 9.2. Todd Wheeler was instructed to develop the firm's recommendations in such a way that the three hospitals involved would not lose their identity—they must be continued as autonomous institutions. This led to a plan for developing separate facilities in close proximity, with a shared services corporation to conduct certain activities which they could best undertake in common.

Toy Savage, trustee of Norfolk General and member of the joint committee, posed numerous questions on Wheeler's plan which revealed both its political acceptability and its organizational impracticality. Savage recalled the southern gentlemen's appraisal of his hound: "He is a good-lookin' dog, but he won't hunt." Others agreed with this sentiment and the report was returned to the consultant. Released of the stipulation that all three hospitals retain their identity, Wheeler quickly replied with a one-page recommendation: merge all three hospitals.

There was another reason for Wheeler's switch. In early 1971 Robert Manning, new dean of EVMA's medical school, arrived to take up his duties. Assessing the hospital situation anew and aware of his school's unusual public sponsorship, he announced that EVMA was no longer interested in obtaining financing for or using 200 designated beds at a new Leigh Memorial hospital; instead, it would seek affiliations with numerous Tidewater hospitals for its teaching programs.

The next important event occurred within the next month, in late May of 1972, when, under the leadership of Wendell Winn, president of Norfolk General, and Barton "Sox" Baldwin, president of Leigh Memorial, a one-day retreat was held for five trustees each, the presidents of the medical staffs, and the administrators of their two hospitals and the Children's Hospital of the King's Daughters. Medical school officials were not invited. It was agreed that all conversations were off the record and no minutes would be recorded.

For most of the day at the White Heron Inn, a lovely seaside resort, a series of presentations and discussions explored how the three hospitals could best serve the community. Late in the day these general conversations

FIGURE 9.2   Norfolk General Hospital Complex

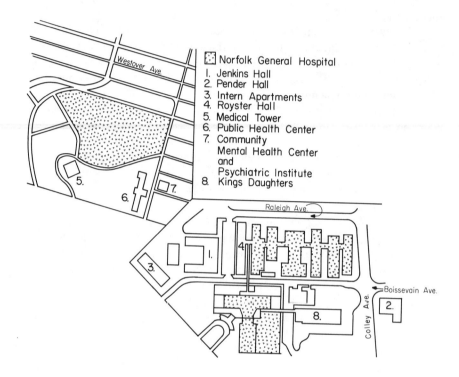

Norfolk General Hospital
1. Jenkins Hall
2. Pender Hall
3. Intern Apartments
4. Royster Hall
5. Medical Tower
6. Public Health Center
7. Community
   Mental Health Center
   and
   Psychiatric Institute
8. Kings Daughters

were interrupted by a memorable 15-minute speech by Charles Kaufman, a respected and influential Norfolk General trustee for forty-eight years. In his dramatic speech Kaufman carefully outlined the logic and advantages of full merger for each of the three hospitals. He spoke of the need for the three boards of trustees to do what was best for the entire community, and indicated that he would resign from Norfolk General's board if it would help the institutions serve the Tidewater area. Following his erudite and convincing talk, the president of the King's Daughters reported that her board wished the Children's Hospital to remain an autonomous and free-standing institution. Mildred Godwin suggested that her hospital's delegation leave the meeting, at which Kaufman invited the ladies to adjourn for sherry and rejoin the gentlemen later for dinner.

Upon this exodus the merger idea, now involving Norfolk General and Leigh Memorial, was put to a straw vote. Every person present voted in favor. It was then quickly decided that the new corporation should contain a board composed of all trustees of existing hospitals, yielding 103 seats distributed approximately equally between the two institutions. An executive committee of thirty-three members, formed with similar parity, would play a prominent role in governance. Billy Dickson, president-elect of Norfolk General, would be the first president of the merged corporation, followed by Sox Baldwin, current president of Leigh.

A satellite facility of 200 beds to be called Leigh Memorial Division would be built in Kempsville, and two hundred beds would be added to those of Norfolk General's at its existing site. Three attorneys, Kaufman and Savage of the Norfolk General Board and Alan Hofheimer of the Leigh Board, were assigned the responsibility of legally accomplishing the merger. Finally, it was determined that an administration should be formed to consist of a chief executive officer and administrators for the two exisiting and future hospitals.

The plan was quickly ratified by the executive committees and full boards of both hospitals. By late October the necessary documents had been drawn up by Kaufman, Savage, and Hofheimer, and the merger was officially and unanimously approved by both hospital boards.

A summary of merger events is shown in diagrammatic form in figure 9.3.

D.   ENABLING FACTORS: A LONGER HISTORY— TO MAY 1972

Outwardly, the merger took place in three months; there was no protracted bargaining, a minimum of outside consultation, and little of the institutional posturing that typically takes place. Issues which could be predicted to have been thrown in the way were not, or were overcome with amazing deftness.

COMMUNITY INFLUENTIALS

This can only be explained as the calculated result of a small group of civic-minded elites whose personal and business relations with each other were so strong and whose influence in civic affairs so pervasive that they could vir-

FIGURE 9.3   Sequence of Major Events Creating Medical Center Hospitals

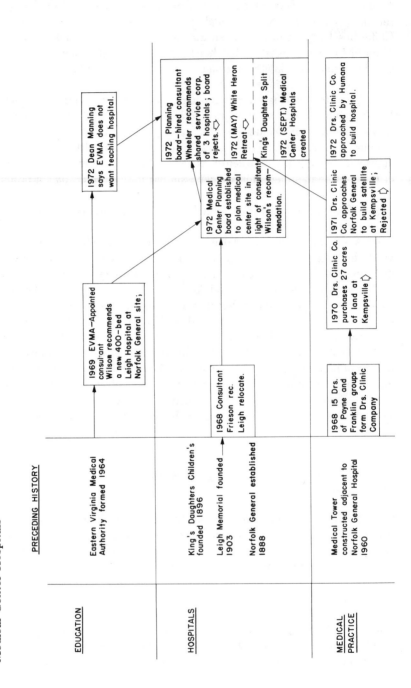

tually declare the results. Members of this group enjoyed political and economic power in Norfolk and in Virginia; they were clearly the civic leaders whether or not they held public offices. They shared a keen desire for community betterment.

Members of this group had for years been prominent on the boards of the two hospitals. While each was loyal to his own institution, they were "all in one family," as stated by one of the group's members. Looking back on it three years later, he said, "It didn't make much difference what board you were on; now, everyone's forgotten."

Unlike the elites of many communities, these individuals were active in hospital affairs and the group contained a few physicians. So, it was relatively easy both to guide the course of hospital affairs and to link these designs to the activities and interests of the medical profession. Members of this "southern family," as one of its members called it, dedicated immense amounts of time to hospital and medical affairs, grappling with issues and decisions with thoroughness and finesse.

The work location for several persons of the group—specifically two law firms—is at the top of Norfolk's tallest building, the Virginia National Bank Building. These attorneys are prominent in Norfolk General's governing board. Other attorneys identified with Leigh Memorial's board are located atop a second nearby office building.

Charles Kaufman, 76 at the time of the merger, is senior partner of Kaufman, Oberndorfer, and Spainhour.[5] While he was not involved in all features of the merger, most people agree that without him it would not have come about. Kaufman was widely known as "Mr. Norfolk General" for his 48 years of active leadership on its board. To others he was known as "Mr. Norfolk," due to his involvement in many civic efforts, most notably as chairman for 27 years of the Norfolk Redevelopment Authority. With Norfolk's land scarcity, the Redevelopment Authority was a prime instrument of community power and change.

Given all of this, Kaufman certainly could have blocked the merger or vetoed any portion of it. But he favored it. He was proud of Norfolk General's charity activity, feeling that this was an obligation of any community hospital. However, he worried that the hospital's close affiliation with the new medical school would bring an even higher volume of patients without ability to pay, to the point of jeopardizing the financial viability of Norfolk General.[6] Leigh Memorial, also a community hospital, rendered no charity care. It was well off financially. Kaufman calculated that through merger, Leigh's paying patients would help to pay for the indigent load borne by Norfolk General. Finally, Kaufman calculated that a merger was now possible from the doctors' point of view: the hostility between the two hospitals' medical staffs that had blocked a merger eighteen years previous seemed now to be much reduced.

Kaufman operated as an informal broker before, during, and after the White Heron meeting. Kaufman's sense of civic fairness and institutional parity led him to reject the idea that Norfolk General should obtain a share of power in the merger proportionate to its size. Thus, the board of the new venture should contain all trustees of both merging hospitals, approximately 50 in each; it was assumed that whatever unwieldiness this caused could be worked out later. Likewise, he insisted on parity of membership on the executive committee of the merged corporation, as well as in the new medical staff leadership. With Mr. Norfolk General urging this, who might complain?

Kaufman also knew the limits of his influence. The leaders of King's Daughters had indicated to him privately the position they would take at the upcoming White Heron retreat. So, when the King's Daughters trustees attending the White Heron retreat indicated that they wanted to remain independent, Kaufman accepted this in a way that those attending later described as "utter cool"; he knew that the merger he and others had put on track should not risk being derailed by efforts to convince a reluctant group to join.[7]

It was the same well-honed sense of institutional personality that led Kaufman to conclude that the leaders of Leigh Memorial would have bolted from the merger had they been held to the Norfolk General site, as had originally been proposed by consultant Wilson in order to accommodate the new medical school. Kaufman judged that this arrangement would put Leigh Memorial too close to both Norfolk General and the medical school—so close that Leigh leaders would calculate their eventual loss of identity. Thus, the Kempsville site, or some other, made sense.

In the same tall office building that houses the law firm of Kaufman, Oberndorfer, and Spainhour is the law firm of Wilcox, Savage, Lawrence, Dickson, and Spindle. Two of its senior partners are Toy Savage and Billy Dickson. Savage is of an old Virginia family, educated at the University of Virginia and the University of Virginia Law School. In 1963 he had been appointed by Norfolk Mayor Roy Martin to be chairman of a Medical School Study Committee, which committee subsequently obtained from the state legislature the enabling legislation to establish the Eastern Virginia Medical Authority. From 1964 to 1966 he had been vice-president of the new Authority, but then resigned from its board because he was in line to become president of the Norfolk General board of trustees: "The doctors felt more comfortable with me not simultaneously an officer of both organizations." Well before the White Heron meeting Savage had seen the advantages of the Kempsville development, both for Norfolk General and for Leigh Memorial. He saw Leigh struggling over its long-run future plans while in the short run it faced possible disaccreditation. Leigh was financially sound but too small to survive on its own and unable to grow due to its location, site, and medical staff.

Billy (William Petty) Dickson was born in Norfolk in 1915 and, like

Savage, educated at the University of Virginia. He was a decorated naval officer of World War II. Active in legal association affairs, Dickson served as president of the Virginia Bar Association in 1960 and was a member of the American Bar Association's house of delegates. His involvement in health affairs included membership on the board of Blue Shield of Virginia and chairmanship of the board of Blue Cross of Virginia, in 1974. Dickson was prominent in democratic politics in Norfolk and Virginia, having helped put William Spong into a U.S. Senate seat in 1966. Dickson was blunt and direct where Savage was diplomatic and quietly persuasive. It was a natural thing, then, for these law firm partners to divide up this job of civic rearrangement along lines whereby "Dickson would handle the personalities, Savage the legals."

Therefore, it was Savage who had stimulated an informal planning committee composed of representatives of Norfolk General, Leigh Memorial, EVMA and Norfolk's Public Health Department that hired Todd Wheeler to examine the situation.[8] It was Savage who later saw that Wheeler's recommendations were institutionally unworkable. And it was Savage who later arranged for Norfolk General to become the successor corporation in the two-hospital merger. Having been president-elect of Norfolk General, Dickson became the first president of the merger, and used that office to take on the job of unifying the two medical staffs.

Another civic-minded elite was Wendall Winn, president of Norfolk General at the time of the White Heron meeting. Winn viewed himself as a "low profile leader," accomplishing his results through informal conversations and meetings with other leaders and by asking questions. He contrasted himself to Billy Dickson, whom he characterized as a "hard-nosed person who pulls no punches." To Winn, civic leadership needs different types of people, and one of his jobs was "to keep all these types on board."

Winn's grandfather had started the Winn Nursery in 1885, his father had continued it in 1922, Wendell assumed it in 1945, and his son was now involved. The Winn Nursery employed approximately 100 persons. Educated in architecture at Virginia Polytechnic Institute, Winn was a member of Norfolk's Planning Commission for eighteen years and its chairman for twelve. Mayor Martin was a personal friend.

The three Norfolk public offices most influential in its post-World War II urban development were Duckworth's and Martin's office of Mayor, Winn's office of Planning Commission chairman, and Kaufman's office as president of the Norfolk Redevelopment Authority. The list of civic projects planned and implemented primarily through these three offices was long: new highways, public housing, downtown redevelopment, neighborhood conservation, new public utility districts, model cities projects, juvenile court building, public health department, mental health institute, rehabilitation center, etc.

A fifth influential was Sox Baldwin, also born in Norfolk in 1915—an insurance company president, member of a Virginia first family, brother of a former governor of the state, and an indefatigable worker on behalf of communitywide harmony. He understood the informal leadership system; in his own words, he knew them all from grammar school. In the words of another, "If Kaufman and Hofheimer were the godfathers, Winn and Sox were the two who made it happen."

As president of Leigh Memorial's board, Baldwin had privately concluded that his hospital was "going nowhere on its own," having been helped to this conclusion by Glenn Mitchell, Norfolk General's new administrator, in informal conversations conducted while both were attending an out-of-town Blue Cross conference. He also knew that Norfolk General leaders had become increasingly worried in recent times about their institution becoming a hard-core inner city hospital, overwhelmed by the problems of serving a poor constituency.[9] Baldwin had studied the proposal for Leigh to relocate to the Norfolk General site and concluded that it was "too much in one place." Wheeler's data on current and future geographic origins of hospitalized patients highlighted the out-migration from downtown Norfolk.[10]

So, when Norfolk General's president Winn talked informally with Baldwin about the two hospitals collaborating in some way, Baldwin felt Leigh was compelled to do so. Winn asked Baldwin to discuss the matter with some leaders of Norfolk General.

A lunch was arranged for Baldwin and Kaufman, attended by Dickson and Savage. As Baldwin recalled it later, they talked generally of the institutions' problems and "did some negotiating." Baldwin said Leigh's name had to be preserved; if it were dropped, the resistance of other Leigh board members could not be overcome. Kaufman agreed that this was appropriate; the merger could have a new name with both prior hospitals continuing as divisions. Baldwin made it clear to Kaufman that Leigh's finances were strong and thus Leigh was not in a hat in hand position, available for Norfolk General to swallow up. Soon thereafter, Kaufman also lunched with his old friend, Alan Hofheimer, thirty-year trustee and former president of Leigh Memorial. They discussed the need to preserve Leigh's identity. Kaufman stressed that Leigh could do better by collaborating with Norfolk General than by continuing as a separate hospital.

This conversation was but a short time before the White Heron retreat. The first person to congratulate Kaufman after his speech at the retreat was Alan Hofheimer.

THE MEDICAL INFLUENTIALS

Actions of another group of elites—those leading the medical community—combined with Norfolk's "southern family" and those of the King's Daughters to yield the White Heron results. The physician most active in envisioning and bringing about the Eastern Virginia Medical Authority was Mason Andrews. Trained at Johns Hopkins in obstetrics and gynecology, Andrews had formerly been president of the medical staff of Norfolk General. Aside from his credentials in clinical medicine, Andrews was well connected to Norfolk's network of influentials, having worked for years with Toy Savage and colleagues in "scrambles with the state legislature" to bring about the necessary enabling legislation for the unusual medical school to be sponsored by an independent public authority.

Another influential physician was Robert L. Payne, Jr. He became chairman of the Medical Education Authority in 1974. (Toy Savage was his vice-chairman.) Robert L. Payne, Jr. is the fifth generation of Paynes to practice medicine and surgery. About the time of Robert L., Sr.'s retirement in the early 1950s the family was joined by Dr. Robert McAlpine, and shortly after that the two began expanding their partnership. It numbered five surgeons by 1972. The group's legal name was the Norfolk Surgical Group, Ltd., but was known locally as the Payne Group. Referring physicians held its members in high professional regard.

A group of internists who referred patients to the Payne group had been organized shortly after World War II when Dr. John Franklin joined Dr. Walter Martin, former president of the American Medical Association. They too began adding partners and by 1972 numbered six physicians. The Franklin Group also enjoyed influence in the medical community, for reasons similar to those of the Payne Group. In combination, the Payne and Franklin group members admitted 10 percent of Norfolk General's patients.

In 1960, Doctors Payne and McAlpine had joined with 70 other physicians in development and ownership of the Medical Tower, an 81-suite building immediately contiguous to Norfolk General on land cleared by the Redevelopment Authority for urban renewal. All members of both the Payne and Franklin groups were tenants in the Medical Tower. Other owners or renters, mostly specialists, were in individual practice or small partnerships. One of these small partnerships was a three-doctor family of urologists, the Dragers.

In 1970 the Tower was the same physical size it had been at the time of construction, despite the expansion of most of the groups who owned or leased space therein. No other large medical office buildings had been built in Norfolk in the interim, despite its population growth and influx of physicians. Dr. McAlpine attributed this slow development to a combination of turmoil and uncertainty about medical school developments, and the absence of available land other than that within designated redevelopment areas. There were also shortcomings in the management of the Medical Tower; one knowledgable observer reported that it was "operated by an anarchic organization."

REORGANIZATION OF MEDICAL PRACTICE

In the late 1960s, national discussion of the health maintenance organization idea was beginning. It seemed to the leaders of the Payne and Franklin groups, plus others, that group practice was the way of the future and that their two established single-specialty groups might form the basis of a single multispecialty group, along the lines of the Oschner Clinic in New Orleans.[11] Some among these physicians also saw such a development as the basis of prepayment, were the health maintenance organization idea to become pervasive; others saw in it the development of a critical mass in the private practicing medical community sufficient to prevent domination by the emerging medical school.

Under the leadership of McAlpine of the Payne surgical group and Dr. Cecil Chapman of the Franklin medical group, a new partnership consisting of the fifteen full partners of both groups was formed in 1968 for the purpose of exploring and developing this concept. The Doctors' Clinic Company did not replace the existing groups, although this was discussed as a future possibility. Consistent with its purpose of investigation and development, this new corporation arranged for visits of its members to the Oschner Clinic and several others and contracted for the development services of Ellerbe and Associates, the Minnesota-based firm that had built the famous Mayo Brothers' Clinic. The Oschner concept under which it was planning called for a hospital to be closely tied to medical practice. Thus, the physicians also conducted an extensive search for new land for this promising venture. It could find none near Norfolk General but did locate substantial acreage eight miles east of downtown Norfolk within the city limits and in a high-growth suburban area near the Virginia Beach line. In 1970, the Doctors' Clinic Company bought 27 acres for $27,000.00 per acre. The favorable financing arrangement called for $125,000.00 in cash down payment, which the members of the corporation shared directly and immediately, and ten-year pay back of the remaining amount, scheduled with a balloon payment at the end.

By now, however, thinking about new forms of medical practice had changed: the physicians had concluded that, for two reasons, an Oschner-type development was not feasible. It was much more difficult to form a new group out of prior groups than to do so de novo; established income level and income sharing arrangements were difficult to accommodate in whatever take-out arrangements were devised. Further, the surgical specialists who had recently entered into the development—in particular urologists and orthopedists—were now worried that the new corporation would not provide sufficient referrals for them; they currently drew from all over the Tidewater area. In short, for different reasons, the several prior individual and group practitioners could or would not commit to a single multispecialty organization.

This was not a genuine merger failure, for, though no integration of medical practices had been achieved, developments in corporate medicine continued along different pathways.

DOCTORS-HOSPITALS RAPPROCHEMENT

Interest of the Doctors' Clinic Company now turned to office building construction,[12] and with this came a new consulting firm, Erdman and Associates, specialists in turn-key medical facility developments.[13]

The Doctors' Clinic Company took in ten additional owners, comprising three prior group practices in urology, orthopedics, and plastic surgery. The urology group consisted of the brothers Phillip and Morton Drager, Jr., successors in a former three-man group that had included their urologist father, Morton Drager, Sr. The three groups of surgical specialists entered the partnership without abandoning their offices at the Medical Tower and elsewhere.[14]

When this expanded group of physicians inevitably sought hospital facilities, it turned in April of 1971 to the board of Norfolk General. President Winn acted quickly to arrange a meeting between the hospital's executive committee and company officials. Dr. McAlpine was the company's discussant, since he was its managing partner.

Shortly after the meeting, Norfolk General advised Doctors' Clinic that it would not build a satellite hospital on the Kempsville site. This reply reflected a strong opinion within Norfolk's executive committee as to the likelihood that such could be financed and the appropriateness of the long-term debt that would have to be assumed.

Newly arrived administrator Glenn Mitchell had presented a neutral memo which outlined fourteen pros and fourteen cons of such a move. The

Pro	*Con*
1) Relieve high occupancy at Norfolk General, thus assisting medical school relations.	1) Possible loss of united support for medical school.
2) Better geographic distribution of beds in community.	2) Norfolk General would be seen as bailing out of its inner-city constituency, spending money on a plush suburban hospital while ignoring Norfolk General's pressing needs.
3) Financially advantageous to Norfolk General because Payne-Franklin groups would attract many other doctors.	3) Financial success of the satellite would depend on community acceptance of the Payne and Franklin group practice approach.
4) Eliminate costs of duplication if a competing hospital developed instead.	4) Even though shared services would be maximized, there would be some duplication of services.

5) Keep Payne-Franklin doctors from drifting away from Norfolk General.

5) Norfolk General would be seen as supporting the Payne-Franklin doctors at the expense of other medical staff members. Payne-Franklin doctors could control the satellite to the exclusion of others.

6) Potential for developing new capitation-based methods of health care delivery.

6) Resistance from other Tidewater hospitals, fearing Norfolk General's aggressiveness.

Most of Norfolk General's board opposed the proposal, though all were concerned that if Norfolk General did not build at Kempsville a new competing hospital might be built instead. Charles Kaufman, board member of longest standing, led the opposition. Kaufman cherished the dream that Norfolk General should be the dominant specialty and referral hospital for Tidewater, probably in excess of 1,000 beds. This plan would divert the hospital from that goal, which was achievable only through building up the hospital-medical school relationship at the downtown Norfolk General site. More importantly, he worried that the board would be accused of favoring one group within the medical staff—those that had bought the Kempsville property and stood most to gain by the satellite—over others. When the president of the hospital, Wendell Winn, called for a vote, the decision against was unanimous with one abstention. Toy Savage abstained, avoiding a possible conflict of interest arising from his position as attorney for the Doctors' Clinic Company.

Winn seemed to favor the plan, given his initial response to the physicians from Kempsville; but, as presiding officer, he had not voted. Nor had he revealed his opinion in the discussion, demonstrating his deep respect for Kaufman.

It was now mid-1971. The company had previously been approached by Humana officials, an investor-owned hospital corporation referred to the Doctors' Clinic Company by one of the consultants of Frieson and Associates who had been advising Leigh Memorial on its possible futures.[15] Humana now proposed to construct a hospital on the company's 27-acre plot, and outlined three ways of proceeding: 1) construction, ownership, and operation by Humana; 2) construction by Humana, ownership by Doctors' Clinic Company, management by Humana; and 3) construction, initial ownership and operation by Humana, followed by turnover to the physicians at some specified future time.

While there was considerable joint planning with Humana, the physicians of the Doctors' Clinic Company had reservations, for multiple reasons: worry about the quality of and control over pathology and radiology under an arrangement with Humana, general unfamiliarity with the company coupled with concern for its profit motivations, and a wish to remain related to Norfolk General.[16] Yet, Humana's was a very favorable and flexible offer, and its wooing was intense.

SUMMARY

By mid-1971, the constellation of influentials in Norfolk had moved hospital developments to the point where Norfolk General's and Leigh Memorial's futures seemed logically (and to some, even inevitably) entwined. Progressive elements in the medical community had both fostered medical education in the Norfolk area and advanced future-oriented forms of community medical practice. The second had evolved to medical office and hospital development, which at this juncture offered both an opportunity for Norfolk General and Leigh Memorial interests and a threat to both if seized by outsiders by default. Though physicians in the Doctors' Clinic Company had failed to unify for professional practice, their land holdings put them in a powerful bargaining position relative to all forms of medical practice and health facility developments. The general shortage of land in Norfolk and Kempsville's prime location vis-a-vis population shifts guaranteed this leverage.

The links between these various foci of influence and leadership were unusually strong, based as much in the social structure of Norfolk as in formal institutional arrangements. These relations ran thick between leaders of Norfolk General, Leigh Memorial, the Eastern Virginia Medical Authority, and the medical practice community. Relations ran thinner between all of these and the King's Daughters. Yet, the King's Daughters' Hospital was located on the Norfolk General site and dependent on it for certain essential services.

The White Heron meeting of May 1972 was clearly not an act of inter-organizational serendipity, but a planned convergence of carefully selected institutional and community influentials drawn together to grapple with the problems and the potential payoffs of a series of investments in health facility and service developments that had long-run implications for hospitals, doctors, patients, and, indeed, the entire Tidewater community. Yet, the outcome of the retreat was by no means clear in advance; if it had been there would have been no need for such a meeting—the actions of Charles Kaufman and Mildred Godwin made that apparent.

E.   Dynamics of Iimplementation: May 1972–1976

IMPLEMENTING THE WHITE HERON ACCORDS

The May 22, 1972, commitments and decisions were made with a view of work yet to be accomplished rather than as a confirmation of work already done. There were some sticky problems: 1) the unification of two very different medical staffs possessed of accumulated years of mutual distrust; 2) the financing of the new venture, including land acquisition; 3) guidance of the plan through the certificate-of-need process, complicated by the immature state of franchising legislation and the politics of local comprehensive health planning; 4) the state of the corporate administration of a new enterprise composed of very different parts; 5) the future of the Doctors' Clinic Company; and 6) the loose end created by the King's Daughters' actions.

Each of these issues constitutes a pathway of events which began to unfold with the White Heron decisions and tracked through a time period beginning in 1972 and continuing through 1976. Most of these were not finally resolved during this extended period of merger implementation. With basic merger decisions having been made with seeming greater speed and ease than is usually the case, there followed a period of implementation which, conversely, was more protracted. By 1976, the merger had not yet progressed to a full and final integration. The new hospital at Kempsville, representing the combination of Leigh Memorial's merger take-out and Norfolk General's bold thrust out from its inner city, had yet to be opened. In the meantime, the merger's new management had to deal both with continuing political, environmental, and developmental strategies as well as day-to-day exigencies of running two hospitals each with different but significant operating problems.

In general, this long implementation phase consisted of two subperiods: a time immediately after the White Heron meeting when short-range activities were undertaken, and a time after that when longer-run issues resurfaced or emerged for the first time. The description of these six streams of events will be sequenced in the order indicated above; in fact, there was much overlap and simultaneous activity, as shown in figure 9.4.

MEDICAL STAFF UNIFICATION

In their approval of the White Heron recommendations, the boards stipulated that the medical staffs had six months to integrate by abolishing their prior organizations in favor of a new set of by-laws. The boards were aware of various charges of relatively inferior medical care at one hospital or the other, depending upon the specialty under discussion and the parties making the charge. Key board members and medical staff leaders felt that the only way to deal with this circumstance was to unify the medical staffs completely.

In this the actions and sentiments of Billy Dickson, soon to assume presidency to the merged 103-man board of trustees, were instrumental. As a personality, Dickson was "rough as a cob, and disliked doctors." His philosophy on the medical staff was summarized by his statement: "There's no sense in merging hospitals if you don't merge medical staffs." Dickson felt that the reorganization would have to be bulldogged through, particularly with the more numerous and more specialized Norfolk General physicians who tended to patronize the Leigh generalist-oriented staff. Dickson felt that Leigh medical staff members had to enter the merger as equals. He also felt that a strong medical staff executive committee would be needed.

Dickson's assertive use of his position, his personality, and his opinions

FIGURE 9.4   Sequence of Major Events in Merger
Creating Norfolk Medical Center Hospitals

	1972	1973	1974	1975	1976
Medical Staff Unification	Difficulty in finding acceptable officers; Billy Dickson steps in.	New by-laws approved, including medical board and executive committee, after grandfather clause inserted.	Eight-man executive committee assumes major policy role.	Reorganization proposed by president-elect Drager.	Mitchell brings in consultant on medical staff organization; prior organization preserved.
Finance and Land for Medical Center Hospitals	Medical Center Hospitals formed. Split in board over philosophy of financial operations and financing of Kempsville satellite.	Problems in financial operations. Twenty-two acres bought at Kempsville, ten from Doctors' Clinic Company.	Friction between Medical Center Hospitals and Doctors' Clinic Company over common developments at Kempsville.	Booz, Allen, Hamilton recommends $21 million bond issue for Kempsville. Medical Center Hospitals takes over surgi-center development.	Surgi-center opened at Kempsville. Construction of Kempsville satellite hospital progresses.
Certificate of Need	Tidewater Health Planning Agency attacks merger; proposes to cut MCH's certificate of need from 256 to 175.	Under new state law, 256 beds requested for MCH; approved by State Director of Public Health.	Certificate of need granted to Tidewater Ambulatory for surgi-center.	Chesapeake Authority Hospital opens, drawing patients from Leigh Memorial Division.	
Management	Employee morale problems, particularly at Leigh Memorial Division.	Various reorganizations of operating departments.	Corporate office of finance established. Oliver becomes first finance director, then resigns. Madden comes to Leigh Memorial Division.	Corporate office of personnel established, including labor relation's division.	Top management reorganization: Norfolk General Division's Neal becomes Corporate Director of Planning; Madden takes over Norfolk General.
Various Physician Corporations	Doctors' Clinic Company approaches Medical Center Hospitals to build a Kempsville satellite.	Doctors' Clinic Company expands partnership. Norfolk Diagnostic Clinic formed. Tidewater Ambulatory Surgery formed.	Tidewater Ambulatory forms nonprofit corporation to operate surgi-center.	Hague Medical Tower established, near Norfolk General Division.	Construction of Doctors' Clinic Company office building completed.
King's Daughters	Attend White Heron meeting; decline merger.		Fund raising started for new hospital.	$5 million received in pledges; but construction costs increased.	Proposal for area-wide maternal and child center, to be located at King's Daughters. Baldwin's plan for new Federation rebuffed.

seemed destined to set up severe hospital-physician abrasion. He took a personal and active role in all important medical staff discussions, which on subsequent account amounted to "one-third of his waking hours" over the next two years. Early on he developed excellent relationships with physician leaders and eventually became the "hero of the medical staffs" for bringing the two groups to an effective integration.

Another active participant, Administrator Glenn Mitchell, was anxious to fashion the proper relationship between the new medical staff organization and several other elements of the merger simultaneously evolving: the structure of the hospital board, the relationship of the medical staff to the medical school, and the touchy matter of contractual relationships between the hospitals and their radiologists and pathologists.

Mitchell also recognized the potential awkwardness of conducting medical staff affairs in the merged situation. It would require new teaching programs, appointment of new full-time physicians, and quality review mechanisms. The problem was to combine the institutional arrangements necessary for teaching and supervision of quality with the open medical staff philosophies and arrangements of two community hospitals.

Dickson viewed the job of unifying the medical staffs to be one of dealing with personalities and melding power centers. To Mitchell it was more a question of establishing a leadership structure that could effectively handle the variety of functions incumbent on a medical staff in the new situation. To the Leigh medical staff leaders it was a question of coming into the merger with parity. To private practitioners of both hospitals it was a question of building some safeguards against medical school domination. And, to the medical school, it was a question of maintaining access to hospital facilities for teaching, without constructing its own institution and without control of medical affairs in someone else's hospital.[17]

What emerged was something of a parallel to the new hospital board structure: a medical board consisting of twenty-nine physicians, including members of the medical school faculty and private practicing physicians. Private practicing physicians elected by the medical staff would have one full vote each, while hospital-based specialists and educators provided for in the by-laws would have one-half vote each. This arrangement guaranteed that all clinical specialities would be represented and also provided for a check against domination of medical staff affairs by any one block, whether it be Norfolk General vs. Leigh or educators vs. practitioners.

With a medical board of this size it was obvious that a smaller executive group was needed. Two executive committees for the two hospitals was rejected because some felt that the Joint Commission on Accreditation of Hospitals would insist upon one executive committee, and because many argued that two executive committees would perpetuate two hospitals. Next consid-

ered was an executive committee to consist of four officers—president, president-elect, past president, secretary-treasurer—and three physicians
appointed by the president of the medical staff to oversee three broad activities: medical education, interdepartmental cooperation, and patient care.
These three would focus on these functions, one appointed for each, but they
would also be at-large members with views that would cut across specialty
and departmental lines.

This unusual arrangement satisfied the medical school Dean Manning,
who felt that by maintaining an open medical staff, his faculty members, who
were mostly practitioners, could obtain sufficient access to hospital services.[18]
Also, a system had been operating for several years where directors of education for several specialities were appointed by the hospital upon recommendation of the medical staff. It was agreed that the nominations to such
positions would in the future be made by committees jointly appointed by the
medical school and the hospital. Such positions were obviously important to
the medical school, although the individuals who held them would not necessarily be chairmen of the relevant medical school departments because the
school's teaching activities were located in numerous facilities throughout the
Tidewater area. In short, although unusually loose by traditional standards of
medical school organization, the proposed medical staff was in keeping with
the philosophy and circumstances of the Eastern Virginia Medical Authority.

These plans almost went awry when it came to the actual appointments
of executive committee members: the joint medical staff committee could
not come up with a slate of officers acceptable to the two medical staffs. Dr.
Kruger, president of the Norfolk General medical staff at the time, was acceptable to the Leigh medical staff leadership, but the Leigh candidate who
would be his successor in an alternating arrangement was unacceptable to
the Norfolk General medical leadership. The committee voted to disband as
a result of this deadlock.

At this point Billy Dickson applied pressure and personally intervened.
Feeling that the board "must let the physicians know we are firm," he insisted
that the joint medical staff committee keep meeting until it had done its job.
He informally negotiated with representatives of several influence centers
within the medical community, notably the Payne surgical group and the
Drager brothers—two articulate and outspoken urologists who spoke for a
larger group of surgical subspecialists. The committee arranged that Norfolk
General's Dr. Kruger would remain as chief of staff for another year, since
his term of office would otherwise be short due to timing of the merger. He
would be succeeded by Desmond Hayes, a previous chief of Leigh's medical
staff, who was willing to serve in the new role, and was respected by Leigh's
doctors for his prior efforts to assure the quality of medical practice at the
hospital. Ironically, Dr. Hayes had been president of the Leigh medical staff

despite the fact that he admitted very few patients to that hospital; he used Norfolk General instead.

The new medical by-laws, now a mere seventy-two pages in length, coupled with a slate of officers, was then forwarded to and approved by both hospital medical staff executive committees and submitted to the full medical staffs of both hospitals, meeting jointly.

Dr. Robert Morton, long-time "speaker of the medical society," conducted the four-hour meeting. In a tour de force of parliamentary practice and statesmanship, he led the discussion through numerous issues, satisfied dissidents, and preserved a quorum. At 12:30 A.M. he obtained approval. This came after some grandfather clause additions had been written in to protect current medical staff members during the transition.[19] Also, the executive committee was expanded to an eighth member, a chief of some clinical department to be selected by his fellow chiefs.

FINANCING THE NEW VENTURE

It turned out to be relatively easy to fold Leigh Memorial's assets into the merger. Kaufman, Savage and Hofheimer quickly concluded that the Leigh corporation should cease to exist and the Norfolk General corporation become the legal vehicle for the merger. Norfolk General's articles of incorporation were modified to change its name to Medical Center Hospitals, to increase its board, to stipulate that Norfolk General's officers would become Medical Center's first officers, and to provide by-laws for the new corporation derived from the old.

Leigh Memorial's unencumbered assets amounted to $5,200,000. Its physical plant was sold to EVMA for $2,125,000, and in turn leased to the new Medical Center Hospitals for $200,000, annually for the ensuing five years. This arrangement allowed EVMA to obtain title to some physical facilities that it needed, notably a student dormitory.[20] Leigh Memorial's $5,200,000 of balance sheet reserves reflected the hospital's sound financial operations at the time of dissolution. In 1971 it had a net operating gain of $375,000 (8.5 percent). It had working capital in the amount of $675,000, after having purchased $130,000 of equipment and $450,000 of securities.

Norfolk General's financial dowry was equally impressive. It too had no long-term debt, and a building fund reserve of $6,000,000. Norfolk General had a net income of $1,600,000, in 1971 (7 percent), plus $885,000, in reimbursed depreciation, after it had allocated $2,000,000, to building and plant funds. It had increased its working capital by $750,000, to handle an increasing accounts receivable, now over $6,000,000 with $1,400,000, in uncollectables.

These sound financial conditions reflected a custom of hospital economics which prevails in Virginia: the financing of both government and private hospitals should be on a pay-as-you-go basis. This makes private philanthropy and long-term capital financing from operations crucial, as compared to borrowing.

These different methods of financing capital development were now put to a test. The Doctors' Clinic Company still had reservations about Humana as a hospital partner. In mid-1972, officials of the company came to Medical Center Hospitals to see if it would build a satellite at Kempsville. They had been rejected by the previous Norfolk General. Many of the personalities were the same. Yet, some of the intervening conversations at the White Heron had led them to believe that construction by Medical Center Hospitals was a possibility. Kempsville had been mentioned as a possible site for a new Leigh Memorial Division of Medical Center Hospitals. The doctors knew that Glenn Mitchell was strongly in favor, and he had now been in the administratorship long enough to be persuasive with the new board—more so than he had been able to be with the old board just after his arrival in Norfolk.

Discussion of the proposal led to a serious split in the new hospital executive committee over financial management and development. The differences were rooted deeply in concerns and philosophies on the part of several directors of both prior hospitals about the nature of hospital financing and motivations for hospital efficiency.

While most supported Virginia's tradition of pay-as-you-go capital financing and private philanthropy, some reasoned that such a strategy would be insufficient for Medical Center Hospital's future: old Norfolk downtown interests might not give for an edge-of-town development, and the new population in Kempsville was not likely to support an unknown. Further, the new medical school had been started in large part by private gifts and pledges totalling $17 million, which might otherwise have been given in some proportion to advance Medical Center Hospitals' plans.

Another philosophical rub was over financial operations. In one view, Leigh Memorial's board and management had been appropriately prudent, resulting in a most favorable balance sheet. In another view, those running Leigh had been tight-fisted to the point of choking off essential venture development, as had taken place at Norfolk General, leaving a small hospital that until the merger had been in stagnation.

Alan Hofheimer, 70, senior partner of the law firm of Hofheimer, Nusbaum, and McPhaul, close professional colleague and personal friend of Kaufman and Dickson, and 30-year member of the Leigh Memorial board, reflected the conservative approach to the future. He had been president of Leigh in the early 1960s, and had been on its board's executive committee for the entire 30 years of his trusteeship. Prior to the merger, Hofheimer had represented the Leigh board element opposing merger with Norfolk General but had been won over by Sox Baldwin and Charles Kaufman. His reservations related directly to finance. Admittedly, Norfolk General was now in good financial shape, and had been for some time (since 1960), although its rising accounts receivable coupled with growing proportion of nonpay or part-pay patients concerned him. But in years past Norfolk General had lost money regularly. Eighteen years prior there had been informal merger discussions, but the then president of Leigh had resisted it because Norfolk General was so often in the red. Hofheimer remembered all of this, and was now worried that Norfolk might return to deficit conditions, consuming Leigh in the process.

Further, Hofheimer and several others thought Norfolk General rendered excellent patient care but at too high a cost. In this he was complaining less about Norfolk General and more about hospital economics generally, which in his view lacked efficiency incentives: "The more you charge and the more you build, the more you get back from Blue Cross." This view was shared by Hofheimer's friend, Charles Kaufman; they discussed these matters frequently and agreed on approaches to future financing. To them, the merger ran the risk of losing a sense of proportion. They wanted to build a hospital at Kempsville smaller than that proposed to avoid incurring the large long-term debt under consideration. They felt the needed capital funds should be raised from donations, thus reducing the costs of borrowed money; financing should be accomplished by philanthropy, not by government subsidy or borrowings.[21]

As it turned out, their view lost out to a more venturesome philosophy; the executive committee decided to proceed with the Kempsville satellite. As events unfolded and financial plans approached reality, two or three conservative directors resigned in protest. Although neither Hofheimer nor Kaufman was among them, neither was continued on Medical Center Hospital's board executive committee at the time it was reduced from 33 to 13 members— thus ending for the two a combined total of 79 years of that kind of hospital involvement and influence.

As for the Kempsville development, officials of Medical Center Hospitals countered Doctors' Clinic Company with an offer to buy all of the partnership's 27 acres of land, with commitments of continuation of the company's plans for a medical office building. Dr. McAlpine and his colleagues refused this offer, based less on price and more on their belief that a medical practice facility should not be built on hospital land, due both to tax complications for both parties and a wish not to be bound so closely to future hospital developments. The company suggested that, instead, Medical Center Hospitals seek the purchase of adjacent land, since the land available was inadequate for full hospital developments; if not enough land for full hospital developments could be obtained, the company would then sell some of its land. Twelve additional acres of land could be bought for $35,000 per acre, and it was purchased after commitments had been obtained from Doctors' Company for the sale of 10 acres at the same price.[22] The transactions were agreed to, conditioned only by the obligations of Medical Center Hospitals to start hospital construction in 24 months and to refrain from building any doctors' offices for at least 25 years. The two sales netted 22 acres for the Hospital and 17 for Doctors' Clinic Company.

These agreements were struck in August of 1972, at which time the parties agreed to certain collaborations: 1) the entire acreage would be jointly master planned, through common use of a single consultant (Perkins and Will); 2) architecture of hospital and doctors' office building would be coordinated; 3) the doctors' office building would include optometrist, prosthetic shop, surgicenter, diagnostic screening center, and some laboratory, EKG facilities, and x-ray facilities; 4) the doctors' office building might also include nonmedical services such as drugstore, lunch facilities, branch bank, and overnight accommodations for out-of-town patients and relatives; 5) though the Doctors' Company would construct and own the office facility, it would do so on an open medical staff basis and would commit to building whatever doctors' offices were needed for the hospital, up to a maximum of 125 suites.

Next came long-term financing both for land purchase and hospital construction. The usual patient utilization studies had already been done by consultant Wheeler; they justified a 200-bed general hospital without pediatrics or obstetrics. But financial capacity to borrow funds needed to be validated by independent authorities. After successful operating years of 1972, 1973, and 1974, in March of 1975 the firm of Booz, Allen and Hamilton endorsed Medical Center Hospitals for $21,500,000 of tax-exempt revenue bonds. Their final report read, in part:

It can be concluded that the project is financially feasible in that:

—Medical Center Hospitals has shown operating surpluses each year since incorporation and these have been supplemented by substantial non-operating revenues.

—Utilization is conservatively projected.

—Cash flow projections indicate sufficient balances in the critical years with improvement each year thereafter.

—Medical Center Hospitals has substantial equity reserves.

—Medical Center Hospitals appears to be well-managed.[23]

The choice of long-term financing, a tax-exempt bond issue rated AA by Standard and Poors as well as Moody's,[24] reflected the history of relationships surrounding the two-hospital developments in Norfolk. The issuing agency was the Industrial Development Authority of the City of Norfolk, a conduit type of agency that had been set up many years previous to finance public service facilities, including the airport, and industrial park, port cargo handling facilities, and an expansion of DePaul Hospital. Charles Kaufman had been instrumental in establishing the authority although in this instance he opposed its use because he was opposed to the level of debt financing involved.

The loan terms were typical of lease back arrangements of such authorities: the 15-year lease struck between the authority, owner of the proposed facility, and Medical Center Hospitals could be expanded with the issuance of new bonds, essentially permitting refinancing. Significantly, the lease agreement gave Medical Center Hospitals an option to purchase title to the facilities at any time prior to full bond retirement, at an amount equal to the remaining debt, or to purchase the facilities at the expiration of bonds and lease for one dollar.

In summary, the controversial decision to build a satellite hospital at Kempsville was made, sufficient land and capital financing was secured, and in the process the merged corporation's strong financial operation was tested and validated. The process had evoked some important organizational changes. For one, Medical Center Hospital's contiguous land arrangement with Doctors' Clinic Company destined the two to an interdependent future. For another, the process had caused a stress in the otherwise smooth relationships among the Norfolk leaders who had controlled Leigh and Norfolk General and continued to control Medical Center Hospitals. Partly because of this and partly due to natural evolution, some new leaders had taken over.

GETTING A CERTIFICATE OF NEED

The merger next faced the scrutiny of comprehensive health planning agencies. With this came the necessity to deal with the political turbulence between Tidewater's governments (which appointed members of the regional planning agency's board) as well as the suspicions of the area's other hospitals.

Although the regional planning body had not initially been concerned or involved with the merger, it now attacked the plan in response to the coincident applications from four hospitals, of which Medical Center Hospitals was one, for expansion approvals. Medical Center's original application was for 200 replacement and expansion beds for the Leigh Division, at the Kempsville location, and 200 additional beds to be added to the former Norfolk General plant. If approved, Medical Center Hospitals would net 233 additional beds, 933 at the Norfolk General Division and 200 at the new satelite in Kempsville. At the same time the Humana Corporation, now focused at a new site in Virginia Beach, was seeking approval for a 250-bed hospital, and the General Hospital of Virginia Beach was seeking approval for

76 additional beds. Finally, the Chesapeake Hospital Authority was seeking approval for 35 beds, to be added to 106 beds for which it already had grandfather clause endorsement but which it had not yet constructed.[25]

In addition to the planning agency's concern for sudden bed expansion in the Tidewater Area, its executive director was miffed that he had not been consulted on Medical Center's plans; he had been advised of them only the night before a scheduled press announcement. Medical Center did not plan this strategy; rather it resulted from the speed of events which flowed from the White Heron agreements.

Faced with the sudden prospects of 700 new beds in Tidewater, and a hostile planning agency, Medical Center Hospitals officials modified their application to delete the addition of new beds to the community. The revised application requested a certificate of need for 256 new beds while closing 167 at Leigh Memorial and 89 at Norfolk General.

A tentative counter plan was then offered by the planning agency: Medical Center Hospitals would be granted a certificate of need for 350 beds and the Chesapeake Hospital Authority would receive none. This would be in lieu of both Medical Center Hospital's application for its 256-bed Kempsville satellite and Chesapeake's plan for a 141-bed facility. This would avoid granting a certificate of need to a wholly new facility in Chesapeake, and would "premerge" the Chesapeake and Medical Center Hospitals operations before Chesapeake became an autonomous entity. However, the plan nullified the Kempsville development, leaving Chesapeake as the take-out for the former Leigh Memorial and leaving the physicians of the Doctors' Clinic Company without a hospital immediately at hand.

The Tidewater planning agency's response was stimulated in part by the threat of a law suit filed by the Humana Corporation, charging the planning agency with illegal restraint of trade in favor of Medical Center Hospitals' proposed satellite at Kempsville: allowing a hospital already dominant in the marketplace to expand, rather than allowing market entry of a new competitor. Medical Center Hospital officials saw the planning agency's counterproposal as a yielding to this threat.

Medical Center leaders backed away from the agency's counter, arguing that its solution simply granted their hospital's proposed bed allocation to other hospitals.[26] They were particularly peeved at the agency's willingness to let Humana proceed, given that it would be contructing a new hospital and that its proposed location was near the Kempsville site. As for the Chesapeake connection, both Medical Center Hospitals and the Chesapeake Hospital Authority officials rejected the planning agency's idea, for different reasons. Administrator Mitchell worried that there were too few doctors in Chesapeake to sustain the size hospital proposed by the planning agency, as compared to the circumstance at Kempsville where a well-rounded mix of competent physicians was virtually assured. Chesapeake Hospital officials had planned for their hospital for years, and simply wanted to run their own institution.

The planning agency had no authority to impose its plan on Medical Center Hospitals and the Chesapeake Hospital Authority, so it reverted to another set of actions it believed to be within its authority to take. It applied a proportional reduction of approximately 30 percent to all requests: Medical Center Hospitals from 256 to 175, Humana from 250 to 175, General Hospital of Virginia Beach from 76 to 54, and Chesapeake from 35 to 25. All of this was duly recommended by the Tidewater B agency to the state-level A-agency, where final authority rested according to federal government procedures.

At this point the Commonwealth of Virginia passed a certificate-of-need law modifying the federal guidelines, establishing new procedures of due process, and granting authority to the State Commissioner of Health to reinforce the certificate-of-need process by granting or withholding hospital licenses for any proposed changes in any hospital's bed complement. Medical Center Hospitals then re-entered its request for 256 beds, as did the General Hospital of Virginia Beach for its 54, and Chesapeake for 35. Humana made no reapplication, but instead applied to the federal government for an exemption to the entire process on the grounds that it had started its construction of a 250-bed hospital prior to the effective date of the laws requiring a certificate of need. This exemption was granted; and Humana continued with its construction.

The State Commissioner of Health, acting under his new authorities, then issued approvals to all three applicants for the bed constructions they originally had requested, instead of the planning agency's proposed 30 percent cuts. He had legal reasons for overruling the B agency: the Tidewater agency had no authority to modify applicants' proposals; it could only accept or reject them.[27]

THE DOCTORS' CLINIC COMPANY REVISITED

Originally, the Kempsville-oriented physicians were interested in new forms of medical care organization and delivery, but their efforts subsequently turned to land and building development. In mid-1973 they made an effort to return to some of the original ideas. With an eye on some developments in the American Academy of Internal Medicine concerning future certification of subspecialists, leaders of the Franklin group of internists envisioned the formation of a unispecialty clinic. They envisioned adding a number of medical subspecialists to their present cadre of general internists, to reflect the six subspecialty boards being established by the Academy. In order to do this they needed additional space and a complete laboratory. The six members of the Franklin group joined with three members of a smaller partnership of internists and three solo practitioners to form a new corporation called the Norfolk Diagnostic Clinic. This new organization, a merger and expansion of two previous entities, then leased space from the Doctors' Clinic Company and both outfitted its members' practicing suites and constructed laboratory and radiology facilities. It was understood that the lab and x-ray facilities would be sized to serve only the members of the new group practice and not be expanded to compete generally with Medical Center Hospitals' Services.

Thus, the Doctors' Clinic Company, itself a spin-off from the Medical Tower corporation with several physicians in ownership of both, now had its own corporate spin-off, some members of which were partners or stockholders in all three enterprises.

Some surgeons also looked ahead to new developments in the delivery of care. Reflecting an initial wave of interest in freestanding surgicenters, 15 surgical specialists decided in mid-1973 to construct an ambulatory surgical facility adjacent to the planned doctors' office building. The initial leader in the development was urologist Phillip Drager. The group was encouraged in the idea by officials of Virginia's Blue Shield, who saw in the come-and-go surgery facility a less expensive alternative to hospitalization for surgery.

These 15 surgeons formed the Tidewater Ambulatory Surgical Partnership, Ltd. Each physician provided startup funds, and a line of credit was established with a bank for borrowed capital sufficient to build the surgicenter.

This further complicated the already complex set of overlapping directorates, which some claimed were related and others claimed were derived from unrelated happenstances. A diagram of these overlaps is shown in fig. 9.5.

Implementing the surgicenter then became complicated by two issues showing the intersection of hospital and physician concerns. One issue was whether the surgicenter should be available to all surgeons on Medical Center Hospitals' medical staff, or be limited to members of the Tidewater Ambulatory Partnership. The other issue was whether the surgicenter should be profit or nonprofit. These two issues were related.

Both stemmed from an August 1972 memorandum of agreement between the Doctors' Clinic Company and the hospital concerning coordinated development of the Kempsville land. Hospital officials thought that the agreement was clear that the surgicenter development should be available to any and all surgeons on the medical staff who wish to operate in the ambulatory surgical center. The interested surgeons felt that limiting access to a smaller number of doctors was essential to quality control, especially at this time of early development of a new service for which professional standards and guidelines had yet to be developed. Hospital officials felt there was sufficient quality control built into the medical staff credentials process, and that the hospital could not associate so intimately with a privately held activity whose

FIGURE 9.5   The Relationship of Physician Corporations

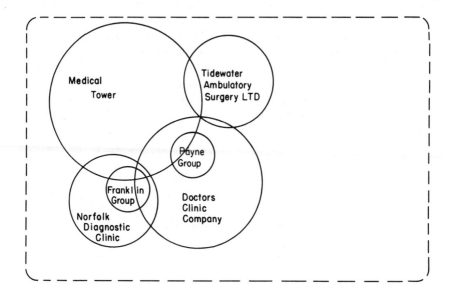

operation would be contrary to the open medical staff policy that had been hammered out so carefully at the time the medical school had started. Members of the Tidewater Ambulatory Surgery soon came to recognize and support this view.

Concerning the second issue, profit vs. nonprofit, serveral Tidewater Ambulatory physicians felt that the hospital's insistence on nonprofit operations was part of a strategy for the hospital to take over the surgicenter development, since only with a for-profit corporation could the original founders obtain any return on their investment. However, a number of hospital board members worried that the Tidewater Ambulatory Surgery development could work at cross-purposes to the hospital, while others felt that the surgicenter should be a hospital activity.

Medical Center Hospitals had limited leverage in the situation: Doctors' Clinic Company owned the land and building, and Tidewater Ambulatory Partnership held a certificate of need for the surgicenter that had been granted enthusiastically by local and state hospitals' agencies. Further, it appeared that the hospital would have trouble obtaining anesthesiologists for the facility if the hospital prevailed in a bitter showdown.

At this point, new complications arose that eventually resolved these issues. First, the "malpractice crisis" hit. Tidewater Ambulatory Surgery officials did not know if malpractice insurance could be obtained or affordable. By contrast, Medical Center Hospitals could fold the surgicenter insurance into its general malpractice policy. Secondly, reimbursement to the proposed surgicenter corporation from Virginia's Blues plans now seemed complicated: Blue Cross had no mechanism for dealing with nonhospital facilities, and Blue Shield reimbursed only for physicians' services, not institutional operations.

These circumstances convinced some Tidewater Ambulatory surgeons that they were "doctors first and businessmen second" and had gotten themselves into an activity foreign to their backgrounds and skills. Some realized that they never had wanted the development to be at cross-purposes to the hospital. Some felt that the opportunity for national innovation and recognition had now passed, due to the protracted development time. Others had simply become fatigued by the attentuated efforts.

So, for the price of certain of its development costs, Tidewater Ambulatory Surgery Partnership, Inc., yielded to a Medical Center Hospitals' proposal to take over the space lease from Doctors' Clinic Company and complete the surgicenter.

This was an attractive offer to the Doctors' Clinic Company, which was having trouble obtaining financing for its building: investors wanted tangible evidence of full occupancy. The hospital would be a new tenant for not only the surgicenter but other proposed activities; part of its renal dialysis and radiology services.[28]

Tidewater Ambulatory Surgery Partnership withdrew from further development, and subsequently liquidated its assets through distributions to its founders. Medical Center Hospitals then assumed planning of the surgicenter, modified the space plans to meet more recently established state building code requirements, and proceeded with construction of the leasehold. In September of 1976, four years after the original idea had been conceived by Dr. Drager and colleagues, Medical Center Hospitals' surgicenter started operations on an open staff basis, after a large open house to which many interested parties were invited and at which a good time was had by all.

A medical office development near Norfolk General showed still another aspect of the dynamics of surgical practices vis-a-vis hospital facilities. The situation now was that two of the former founders of Tidewater Ambulatory Surgical Partnership held interest in the Doctors' Clinic Company, and took up offices in its Kempsville building. Others worried that their service and referral bases might be too restricted if they concentrated their practices at Kempsville Hospital. More important, these specialists saw Kempsville Hospital as a small general facility, while Norfolk General was clearly destined to remain the large tertiary facility for the community. For these reasons, an office site near Norfolk General was preferred.

In 1967, Phillip and Morton Drager had bought a plot of land near

Norfolk General. Approximately 10 years later, a seven-doctor partnership named Drager-Williams-Prybil Associates, Ltd., developed this land into a new 10-suite office building called the Hague Medical Center, which was occupied in 1978. It contained office suites and an in-and-out surgical facility.

ADMINISTRATION OF THE MERGER

This perception of management problems, successes, and strategies is primarily that of Medical Center Hospital's chief executive, Glenn Mitchell. Mitchell was involved in most events preceding the actual merger, as administrator of Norfolk General, and continued as Executive Director of the merged organization. He thus knew the historical circumstances to which he must fashion his management of the new venture. And, he placed his own stamp on the new venture, rooted in his well-honed management philosophy.

Mitchell's Style

Mitchell came into the merger with a philosophy that opposed large corporate organization. This was based on both his prior administrative experience elsewhere and a selective review of the organization of other hospital mergers about the country.

Previously in his career, Mitchell had been in the administration of the John Hopkins University Hospital which, though claiming to be decentralized in its management, had a top administration with ten assistant administrators and numerous others reporting to the chief executive. Mitchell observed that middle managers and supervisors throughout the hospital naturally leaned on the administrative staff, feeling somehow that they must "touch base" on all decisions. The administration became out of touch with the feel of the organization and it coordinated the hospital's many activities only with great difficulty. Mitchell recalled, "If something went wrong, there was always someone else to point the finger at." A successful unionization effort made an indelible impression on Mitchell: he had thought, as had his fellow administrators, that there was general satisfaction and job security on the part of hospital employees, yet the hospital was "smashed by the unions" when organizers fanned the flames of job insecurity.

In response to this, when Mitchell came to Norfolk General he managed the 730-bed hospital with only himself and three assistants. As the merger was unfolding in Norfolk, Mitchell and his colleagues visited the Samaritan Health Services of Arizona at a time when criticism was running high of its large and visible corporate management.

For these several reasons, then, Mitchell fashioned a low profile corporate management, designed to locate as much authority as possible with the two division administrators and avoid a "third organization." This management approach, while remaining basically intact for the several years ensuing from the merger, met a variety of challenges that required adjustments towards greater centralization.

Corporate Finance

Mitchell's biggest integration problem was financial, as the technical problems of financial management were linked to the personalities of existing administrators. Specifically, Warren Oliver, administrator of Leigh Memorial at the time of the merger, chose to concentrate on the accounting and operational aspects of rate setting, cost accounting, and bill collections. Oliver was generally conservative, authorizing equipment purchases only after very careful study, particularly where such involved pressure by or service to physicians. By contrast, the prevailing financial policy at Norfolk General had been to support physician requests for new developments, whenever possible, feeling that this was both in the best interests of medicine and the hospital's future. Oliver was a solo decision maker whose management philosophy dictated that he know the details of issues he decided and of activities he directed.

While it seemed that Oliver was better suited for a small hospital operation than a large, some members of the Leigh Memorial board supported his point of view. After merger, many felt his skills to be in particular need. In the words of administrator Mitchell, the day-to-day business operations of Medical Center Hospitals had suddenly "gone to hell" when, during a transition in computer operations, an electronic record file representing five days of accounts renewables was irretrievably botched; in a financial operation the size of Medical Center Hospitals, this constituted a loss of approximately $750,000.

For these many reasons, the immediate mingling of the two hospitals' financial operations at the time of legal merger would have offended many influentials from Leigh and some from Norfolk General. As time passed, no improvements were seen in financial results—not surprising since no basic management changes had been made. In particular, neither of the two hospital administrators effectively communicated or collaborated. Mitchell finally intervened, meeting directly with the two hospital administrators and then the two controllers, and imposing his solution: a new corporatewide director of finance.

Mitchell was not surprised when Oliver, who had continued in the position of Administrator of the Leigh Memorial Division, the postmerger counterpart of his previous administratorship, applied for the position. Yet, Oliver knew that he would have great difficulty in obtaining the loyalty of the Norfolk General physicians who would constitute the bulk of the medical staff of the new Leigh Memorial Division at Kempsville.

The reorganization did not work. Oliver's skills matched the financial management needs of a single 167-bed hospital, not those of a 900-bed, multifacility corporation. Both Mitchell and Oliver had tried hard for an adjustment, and an accommodation had been achieved, Yet, a year later Warren had an opportunity to become a chief executive officer of a newly developing hospital in South Carolina, and left Medical Center Hospitals.

Personnel

Employee reactions to the merger had been varied, depending on location and level. At Leigh Memorial, in the earliest stages, rank and file employees felt betrayed by their board and administration superiors, who neglected to consult or advise them about the possibility of full merger as opposed to the "promised" federation plan retaining Leigh's autonomy. Not one month before the White Heron meeting, Sox Baldwin, then president of Leigh, had indicated to hospital employees that there would be no loss of job autonomy in the new venture. Early reorganizations confirmed employee's predictions that Norfolk General would absorb Leigh employees. Leigh department heads and supervisors felt that their Norfolk General counterparts would be selected to run integrated operations.

Norfolk General employees, more curious than worried or fearful, wondered why their hospital had merged with another one so dissimilar. There was more employee turnover at Norfolk General, so this curiosity was based in part on ignorance. By contrast, the Leigh employees were a more stable group, and their smaller numbers allowed for quick communication of fact or rumor.

The reactions among Norfolk General department heads varied. Some saw the Leigh acquisition as an opportunity to enlarge their domains; indeed, some were subsequently successful in doing so. A few showed concern over job security; but there were no strong feelings about not having been consulted, as there were at Leigh.

Most of these initial perceptions changed when it was later decided and announced that improvements in facilities and bed expansion at Norfolk General would be delayed or cancelled in favor of the Kempsville development. To Leigh employees, both salaried and hourly, a new Leigh Memorial seemed like the take-out they had originally understood, complete with job security. Now resentment set in at Norfolk General. The merger was seen as having provided a new generation of facilities for Leigh, based on Norfolk General's strength, that otherwise would have come to Norfolk General. There was even a medical staff petition demanding that certain older buildings at Norfolk General be replaced before monies be spent at Kempsville.

Against this backdrop, and consistent with his low profile philosophy, Mitchell concluded that two separate personnel activities should be maintained for Norfolk General and Leigh Memorial, coordinated through common policy. But the plan did not work. Common policies were slow to develop and to be executed. The administrators of both hospitals remained involved in the details of personnel administration based on prior policies and procedures rather than developing new strategies for current and future realities. In addition, the separate personnel departments remained less effective than Mitchell had hoped or expected.

Again, the situation reflected the hospitals' long histories and basic differences. The small Leigh Memorial was known for its friendly atmosphere,[29] carefully nurtured by the hospital leadership and aided by an employed staff with low turnover and an administrator who kept close to detailed events. To Leigh Division's Oliver, a personnel department was necessary only for clerical processing. The much larger Norfolk General, with its high employee turnover, had lost the sense of an employee family. Norfolk General's personnel department prior to the merger was also underdeveloped because of Mitchell's predecessor's management philosophy, which was akin to Oliver's. These two situations, then, led not only to markedly different personnel policies between the hospitals but also to widely varying personnel decision-making within each hospital. Both administrators preferred this, since, between 1973 and 1975, they rebuffed three proposals by the two divisions' personnel directors for unified personnel policies and function.

Further differences existed between the racial composition of the two staffs. While the proportion of black rank and file employees was about the same at both—36 percent at Leigh and 40 percent at Norfolk—Leigh had no black supervisors while 25 percent of those at Norfolk General were black. Yet, the two hospitals were less than a mile apart and both shared the inner-city employment market. In 1972, Norfolk General had been charged successfully by the Equal Employment Opportunity Commission with discriminatory employment practices.

Mitchell was deeply committed to advancing employment opportunities and the general human condition of racial minorities. He attributed the successes in union recognition at his previous employment to a top management that had grown out of touch with the rank and file.

So, in early 1975, Mitchell made a big change: he brought in a new personnel director at the corporation level and established four assistant personnel director positions for 1) wage and salary administration, 2) labor relations, 3) employee relations, and 4) education and training. Mitchell saw the employee relations division as an employee advocate. The number of positions in personnel administration jumped from seven (four at Norfolk General and three at Leigh, all primarily clerks) to twenty-four. All wages and salaries were quickly standardized. A grievance procedure which Mitchell had developed for Norfolk General prior to the merger was strengthened and used widely as the vehicle for handling employee concerns relating to merger insecurity and other matters. This became Mitchell's major instrument for keeping in contact with and measuring the pulse of his new, larger and more diverse employee organization.

After this, suspicion and anxiety seemed to reduce, notably at the Leigh Division, where it had been highest. Yet, by 1976, the merger was four years old and the Kempsville satellite not yet on line. Inevitably, employees' perceptions reflected this continuing uncertainty.

Reorganizing without Centralizing
A different adjustment was made with another group of departments: materials management, industrial engineering, and public relations. Each of these operations was unified by making one of the hospital operations the responsibility of the appropriate department head and general administration of the other. In the case of materials management, supervision of mergerwide activities was placed at Leigh. For the others, it was placed at Norfolk General. Neither the industrial engineering nor public relations groups liked this arrangement, preferring instead the "clout of the corporate office."

Integration took still another pathway in the case of dietary services. Prior to the merger, Norfolk General had arranged a management contract for complete operation of its food services, while Leigh Memorial had its own dietary operation. At about the time of the merger, the manager assigned to Norfolk General by the food contractor resigned, for reasons unrelated to the integration. When Mitchell modified the contract to have food services provided for both divisions, he unified the supervision of the contractor by assigning that duty to the Norfolk General administrator.

In summary, a number of operational integrations had been accomplished using management devices other than direct and complete centralization and operation by corporatewide executives. In only two cases, finance and personnel, were new and large centralized offices established—two functions which any manager would say are crucial to effective control.

Professional Services
Developments differed in several hospital-based services, depending on the relationship of these activities to the medical staff, the medical school, and the entire medical community of Norfolk. In both pathology and radiology, reorganization took place through a series of events not entirely planned or anticipated by top administration, despite Mitchell's efforts to maximize his influence at the time of the merger. Of the three board committees set up for finance, building, and professional relations, Mitchell purposely downgraded the last of these through his influence over committee appointments and through studied managerial avoidance, believing that the sensitive features

of contractual relationships with professionals were best handled by the chief executive.

For laboratory services, a partial integration had occurred at the time the hospital merger took place: the larger pathology partnership under contract with Norfolk General absorbed the pathologist on contract to Leigh Memorial. This was acceptable to both medical staffs. Then, in early 1973 the senior pathologist of the group came to the Norfolk General administration and said that an integration of the two hospitals' laboratory operations could and should be done promptly. He was authorized to proceed, and in a week's time the Leigh hospital laboratory was drastically reorganized through changes which required dismissing several technicians and accepting the resignation of others. These changes reverberated throughout the employed ranks of Leigh Memorial, confirming the worst fears of job insecurity which were abounding at this early stage of the merger.

Though the chief pathologist's reorganization was abruptly executed, it was essentially correct: it allowed the advantages of technology previously applied to Norfolk General's large operation to be extended to Leigh's small operation. Several Leigh technologists were replaced by machines. The blood bank operation was centralized at Norfolk General and several test procedures were relocated to Norfolk General, with frequent pick-up and delivery service to Leigh Memorial.

In radiology, Medical Center Hospitals inherited two separate contracts, one from Leigh Memorial and the other from Norfolk General. Mitchell realized early on that he would have to deal with this situation, since the Board had mandated one medical staff and since it seemed logical and practical for there to be one contract with one radiology group. The radiologists from the two former hospitals respected each other but were not likely to enter into a single contract without considerable mutual adjustment. Mitchell was greatly relieved when the chief of Leigh's radiology department agreed that he would like to retire from practice and yield to the other group. One other radiologist practicing with him transferred his practice to the former Norfolk General Hospital group for three years, and then became the director of radiology at the new Chesapeake Hospital.

However, this did not end the problems in the department of radiology, since there had always been concern from physicians, the board, and patients about the services provided by the radiology group that now inherited the Medical Center Hospitals' contract. In addition, the chief radiologist held views on medical education that did not put him in favor with EVMA medical school officials as the school's faculty head in radiology.

Many discussions and negotiations were held between Mitchell's staff, medical staff committees, and the radiologists about the performance of the department, which did not result in basic change. Then, late one afternoon in early 1976 at a medical staff executive committee meeting, Mitchell informed the committee that he was going to seek board approval for cancelling the radiology contract. He asked specifically that the medical staff leaders refuse to endorse this action, but indicated that it was being taken because of insufficient service and lack of management ability on the part of the contractees. The next morning he took his plan to the board executive committee, which concurred, after which he summoned all the radiologists and announced that the contract was being terminated.

Despite a certain amount of "back bench sniping," Mitchell was supported and confirmed in this action. A reorganization of the radiology group yielded first a new chief, then a new contract, which resulted in a department well supported by the other members of the Medical Center Hospitals' organization.

Both the problem and the solution confirmed Mitchell's philosophy that "in situations like this it is sometimes necessary to perform surgery rather than to use more conservative methods of treatment." To him, the events had confirmed the advantages of having professional service contracts dealt with by the administrative staff of the hospital rather than by a committee of the board. In the shared and perhaps blurred leadership context of a large merged teaching hospital, some one official had to be in the position to take decisive action.

Top Administration as of 1976

Mitchell's top management of mid-1976 showed his recognition of both past history and current operating exigencies. The administrator of the Norfolk General division was Robert Neal, 55, former controller of Norfolk General. Michael Madden, 33, was the newcomer. Appointed in mid-1974 to replace Oliver as administrator of the Leigh Division, Madden brought experience gained at the University of Michigan Hospital in union campaigns and negotiations, hospital-medical school relations, and ambulatory care arrangements.

Mitchell regarded these two and the directors of finance and personnel as his "trust of equals": each person prepared to take on individual and group responsibility so that any corporate officer could run things for the medical center.

Events in the latter half of 1976 proved the wisdom of Mitchell's philosophy of management development. When he suffered a heart attack, taking him out of action for a time, the board reviewed its top management—in particular, the situation at the large Norfolk General Division. Its administrator, Robert Neal, had also been ill some two years previous. The boards' executive committee declared a three-person reorganization in which Neal became the Director of Shared Services (a new corporate-level position), an associate administrator of the Norfolk General became administrator of the

Leigh Memorial Division, and Leigh Division's Michael Madden became administrator of Norfolk General Division. Mitchell returned to full-time duties with the feeling that, had he not been ill, he would have prevented or modified this reorganization.

A Reflection

Mitchell's reflections on his six years of hospital integration are that if he were to do it over again, he would "do more drastic surgery, particularly in finance." Further, he would de-emphasize the "myth of parity" between institutions, which was designed into the corporate structure and thus maintained by many people: "I would be more honest about de facto takeover."

Mitchell believes that further centralizations in management and operations will have to be made, due partly to the advantages of running certain departments as one in order to avoid the inefficiencies of the small Leigh operations, be it a few blocks or a few miles away, and due partly to pressures from the Leigh Division for the corporation to take over supervision of certain activities "to protect them from Norfolk General." Mitchell believes that the trend toward centralization will plateau at a point where patient care operations—nursing, pharmacy, social work, etc.—remain the responsibility of the separate divisions under their administrators, while business and institutional support services will come under direct corporate development and control. He believes this is appropriate for Medical Center Hospitals, as well as the centralizing of the second group of activities to allow for their marketing to other organizations through contract arrangements.

Mitchell's view of future merger dynamics combines his professional and personal assessment. As a manager of health care, he believes that Medical Center Hospitals should merge with still more institutions, or link to them in other ways, despite the growing resistance in the Tidewater area to his "corporate giant." Revealing his personal fatigue and sense of family sacrifice, Mitchell says "no more mergers".

MEDICAL STAFF REORGANIZATION

Aside from the many events flowing from the establishment of the Doctors' Clinic Company, by 1976 the Norfolk medical community had changed substantially from what it had been at the time of merger. Many former Leigh Memorial doctors, having relocated their hospital practice to the new Chesapeake hospital, no longer felt a part of the Kempsville satellite. Developments in medical education had been different than expected. For one thing, in 1975 the EVMA had broadened its government sponsorship to include the cities of Virginia Beach, Portsmouth, Suffolk, Chesapeake, and Hampton. For another, the Authority's energetic executive, Dr. Richard Magraw, viewed it as a reorganizing instrument for patient care delivery as well as medical education, considering it the Authority's opportunity and responsibility to undertake those activities the private medical community was not performing, thereby challenging it to change. As an example, the Authority continued operating a large community mental health center, to the growing consternation of some private practicing psychiatrists.

All of this heightened the fear of medical school takeover for at least some members of the private practicing community, notably those in specialties and subspecialties most likely to be assumed by medical educators. These fears were augmented by the widespread discussions of increased federal and state government control of medical practice.

Urologist Morton Drager held some of these views, and began active discussion of a new medical staff organization after being chosen president-elect of the medical staff. Viewing the situation both as a practitioner and a professor of urology, he noted that the medical staff's 29-man medical board had become a rubber stamp body to the smaller 8-man executive committee, and that in this process the various clinical specialities had lost their representation to the functionally organized executive committee. Further, he felt that the two groups created an unnecessarily cumbersome decision making process for the medical staff. Drager proposed cochairmen for the important Medical Staff Patient Care Committee, one for the Norfolk General division and one for the Leigh division, each of whom would be responsible for the care in his division. The Patient Care Committee would be organized to represent the specialties practicing in each division. Drager felt this would both return proper influence to the various clinical groups, and, for the hospital at Kempsville, maintain proper control for physicians practicing there.

Mitchell was not in favor of the traditional pattern of specialty department strength, arguing with Drager that if the medical school were to gain dominance it would be via the various clinical departments. Mitchell reasoned that the existing organization, which allowed the president of the medical staff to appoint physicians he wanted to the medical staff executive committee, avoided this risk. Mitchell granted that the medical board's role had diminished and suggested that its policy making activity be expanded, leaving operational responsibilities to the executive committee. Mitchell felt that Drager's plan could lead to regular policy fights between the two divisions, and could even be the forerunner of two separate medical staffs.

Mitchell's initial strategy was that the institution should propose a revised medical staff organization. As a part of this plan, the medical staff and administration obtained the consulting services of an outside physician known to Dr. Drager and known for his judgement in such matters. In August 1976,

Dr. William Robinson, Director of Medical Affairs of the Swedish Medical Center in Denver, Colorado, came to Norfolk for two days of consultation. His summary of physician perceptions of the relationship of Leigh Memorial and Norfolk General Divisions was insightful.

> Concern appears to vary considerably in intensity, depending upon 1) awareness of what is going on outside of one's own practice, 2) the degree of comparative "loyalty" or "affection" for one facility or the other, 3) the degree to which contemplating the uncertainties of a new, more remote facility causes alarm, 4) the likelihood of being forced to make a choice of continuing practice in an established, downtown tertiary, academically oriented, prestigious hospital, or contemplating practice in a brand-new facility serving a rapidly growing suburban, probably affluent, area. Although the medical staff bylaws clearly provide for a single medical staff organization, I didn't sense as much "oneness" as I might have expected; there seemed to be more references to "here" and to "there" rather than to "us." And again, in spite of single medical staff organization and the single governing board—with resultant opportunity for consensus on community-wide health care policies—I nevertheless heard opinions and conversations more reminiscent of two autonomous hospitals.
>
> I encountered a strong commitment to . . . the graduate education of residents. In spite of an intimate relationship with a medical school, there was little, if any, evidence of conflict of the so-called town-gown variety. There was certainly little suggestion of disharmony, and one might conjecture that this happy state is related to the fact that school and hospital are both operating out of the private sector of the economy.

Dr. Robinson did not endorse president-elect Drager's idea of Patient Care Committee cochairmen. However, he did acknowledge the confusion and overlap between the 29-man medical board and the 8-man executive committee.

> I believe I would "write out" either the executive committee or the medical board as they currently exist. The medical board includes the input of the faculty directors, but this could also be provided at the executive committee level. These faculty members do not appear to demand unreasonable representation and there seems to be no apparent reason why they should all sit ex-officio on a top level committee. If they are particularly effective leaders, they might even welcome election by the attendings, to represent the attendings!

On Drager's ideas about stronger specialty organization of the medical staff, consultant Robinson remarked: "Apportioning group representation on the basis of clinical activity is an objective method. Small groups with relatively little activity can sometimes gain representation by banding together, viz: ophthalmology, otolaryngology. . . ."

Dr. Robinson's report closed with some technical recommendations about length of tenure of medical staff offices, privileges associated with different classes of membership, and the conduct of medical audits. In the main, the report confirmed the design of medical staff organization developed four years previous by Mitchell, Dickson and the then medical staff leadership. It also achieved Dr. Drager's wish to simplify the medical staff's decision making, since the medical staff and hospital subsequently abolished the medical board.

The original Medical Center Planning Board—the multiagency group that had hired Todd Wheeler—was still meeting. Since the White Heron decisions this group had continued to serve as a forum for communications among the institutions located on the Norfolk General campus and had also undertaken certain projects common to all, notably joint parking and the construction of a new power plant. Nonetheless, Sox Baldwin noted, their procedures were breaking down. Baldwin perceived the destinies of Norfolk General Division and EVMA as inextricably entwined, but the physicians and administration did not. Likewise, Baldwin saw the King's Daughters' Children's Hospital as dependent on Medical Center Hospitals, but its board and medical staff did not. Futher, complications and delays in joint decision making over the location of the power plant had demonstrated to Baldwin the need for a new authority for making decisions that would be binding on all parties.

Two related pending issues seemed to warrant a new corporate structure. One was the King's Daughters' future hospital, the other the designation of a "level-three" tertiary maternal and child health center for the Tidewater area. A successful fund raising campaign at King's Daughters' had obtained five million dollars in pledges and donations for a new building, but the King's Daughters' board now realized that a new plant would cost much more, probably in the order of eleven to thirteen million. Board officials were pursuing a tax-exempt bond issue to raise the rest, but some "hard money boys," to use Baldwin's term, doubted that the financial ratings for such an issue would be very high, making the sale of such issues doubtful. Some combination of Medical Center Hospitals and King's Daughters' Hospital might yield a debt retirement capacity that would solve this problem.

That this thought could be entertained by the leaders of King's Daughters, in the face of their White Heron meeting actions, was witness to a new realization on their part that Children's was not a complete hospital, but dependent on Medical Center Hospitals for numerous essential professional and support services. To add these to the King's Daughters' reconstruction would drive the cost even higher. Further, the hospital now had seven EVMA doctors running its professional services; it did not hire the physicians directly but contracted with the Authority for their services—another dependency. King's Daughters' president, Eleanor Bradshaw, wondered about the future: "We may find ourselves merged without knowing it. There's a difference between independence and autonomy; we can't be independent."

One reason the King's Daughters' construction price tag had gone up was a proposal from the obstetricians of the Tidewater area seeking to obtain designation of the area's tertiary maternal and child care center. The area had now been redefined: the cities of Hampton and Newport News, across the James River to the north, had been added to the Health Systems Agency, which in early 1966 had been designated to succeed the Tidewater Comprehensive Health Planning Agency. Riverside Hospital in Newport News was known to be seeking the designation as the tertiary neonatal unit for the region. Norfolk's maternity business was split between Medical Center Hospitals' Norfolk General Division and De Paul Hospital and Norfolk Community Hospital: 2300, 2200, and 650 deliveries, respectively.[30] Thus, no hospital clearly justified the designation on its own. The obstetricians at De Paul did not want to come "hat in hand" to Medical Center Hospitals: the competition between De Paul and Norfolk General had been longstanding. Instead, the obstetricians from De Paul and Medical Center Hospitals came to King's Daughters' Hospital with a proposal for a complete maternity and neonatal intensive care service, to be operated by King's Daughters. Medical Center Hospitals had just received a consultant's report that recommended expanding its obstetrics service. The obstetrician's proposal made sense since the planned reconstruction of King's Daughters called for a physical connection to the Norfolk General Division of Medical Center Hospitals; thus the only remaining question in the proposal for joint development of King's Daughters and Medical Center Hospitals was the question of who would finance and administer the center. Whether it sat on one side or the other of a bridge spanning two buildings seemed to matter little. For this reason some Medical Center Hospitals' Norfolk General Division obstetricians were willing to "abandon their institution" in support of a scheme that would tie De Paul's and Norfolk General's obstetricians into a critical mass sufficient to obtain the single available tertiary designation for the area.

In short, Sox Baldwin saw in a revised Medical Center Planning Board a decision making body that could help resolve issues like the organizational, financial, and space implications of the proposed maternal and child center.

After members of the Planning Board learned of an umbrella corporation that had been established for a similar situation in Pittsburg, they devised and circulated a plan for an organization in Norfolk. An executive committee of the Planning Board would consist of seven members and three alternates: two each from the boards of Medical Center Hospitals, King's Daughters, and EVMA, and a chairman. Decisions of the executive committee would be binding on all parties.

However, Baldwin's plans for a more integrated and more powerful decision making body were frustrated. The potential parties were interested, but insufficiently desperate. Medical Center Hospitals, the giant in the proposed federation, was indisposed to dilute its decision making base: its executive committee failed to endorse the Planning Board's proposal. EVMA officials concluded that their public status prohibited them from subordinating their decision making responsibility to a private body. Officials of the King's Daughters obtained consultation from a national accounting firm which indicated that its requirements for a capital loan for hospital reconstruction were feasible—or at least sufficient for what it had planned prior to the neonatal center proposal.

So, two more hospital rationalizations were approached but, at the last, abandoned: Baldwin's plan to fold two more organizations into common decision making, and the obstetricians' plan to consolidate maternity services.[31]

STATUS OF THE MERGER AFTER FIVE YEARS

Indeed, this turn of events seemed to characterize the Medical Center Hospitals merger at the late 1977 juncture in its history. A new balance seemed to have been struck between the hospital and medical establishments over not only land and financial developments but also, more importantly, over the proprieties of organized behavior.

The relations between practicing physicians and medical educators, in which Medical Center Hospitals was at the crossroads, were sometimes rough but still developing; they now centered on the medical school's need to develop its core full-time faculty, the consequent relationships with numerous health services delivery organizations in the Tidewater area, and the transition in EVMA leadership due to Dr. Magraw's resignation.

While Leigh Memorial had yet to get its new hospital, the new satellite was scheduled for opening soon, in November 1977.[32] The old Leigh Hospital was being considered for use by some community groups as a school for handicapped persons, or perhaps a dormitory.

The King's Daughters proceeded with a new 128-bed hospital, constructed by a design-build contractor and scheduled for completion in early 1979. While the hospital would continue to obtain some support services from Medical Center Hospitals, the King's Daughters designed the new hospital for their own conduct of several professional services previously secured from their giant neighbor. Mitchell described the new hospital as "physically more integrated, organizationally more independent."

For the Norfolk General Division, the board of Medical Center Hospitals initiated a successful $10 million fund raising campaign to build a new 7-story wing to replace 180 obsolete beds and related services. Contrary to prior experience, this plan breezed through the certificate-of-need process: the local HSA board approved the application unanimously and the State Commissioner of Health granted a certificate of need. Medical Center Hospitals' Board decided to name the new facility the Charles Kaufman Pavilion.

While Medical Center Hospitals was effectively managed, the management was still dealing with the full ramifications of the original merger and thus was indisposed to plow into another major new integration. Stated Mitchell:

> As I look at our community I think the possibility of merger with other area hospitals is not very good. We try to be nice guys but are generally regarded as the Norfolk big guy. Others don't seem very anxious to talk about taking us over—or joining us—or being taken over. It seems to me that we are having, and will have, better results in discussions with smaller neighbors who are more distant from us but within our service area and conceivably with large institutions outside our region.[33]

The "southern family" leadership of Norfolk was still in charge, even after the political and economic turmoil of urban governance of the early and mid-70s.

In short, though it had been over five years since the White Heron meeting, the organizational dust had yet to settle fully. The key parties were satisfied that the right decisions had been made, but sobered by the many consequences thereof. While all medical institutions were facing a harsh environment, no single hospital's plight was desperate. After so many dramatic changes, why not some gradualism for a while?

F. DISCUSSION

As this case makes obvious, the community of Norfolk is socially and institutionally tight, with leaders highly committed and involved in hospital and medical affairs. The mystery lies in just how this informal guidance system actually works: what institutional and personal roles, both public and private, does it require?

One useful game board was the Medical Center Planning Board, which had already been functioning for several months by the time of the White Heron meeting. Its peculiar structure and role was particularly rational to the situation. It enjoyed no delegated authorities from its participating institutions, nor any legal or financial standing of its own. Even after years of useful functioning, these were denied it by its sponsors. Yet, it had guided the participating institutions through two consultations costing in excess of one quarter million dollars, had arranged for several shared facilities and services, and was generally cognizant of most problems and potentials. The Planning Board made no pretense of being a power unto itself, even granting Sox Baldwin's 1976 attempt. Rather, it acted as a forum for communications between powers and an intelligence agency for the established institutions.[34] In this role, it exercised influence by focussing on space on the Medical Center campus—space already occupied by Norfolk General, King's Daughters, Norfolk City Public Health Department, and Eastern Virginia Medical

Authority. The Board's activities seemed, on the one hand, to stimulate the participating institutions to deal with requisite organizational issues and, on the other hand, to serve as a game board where influentials could interact on various specific and immediate matters while they were otherwise engaged in larger and longer run politics. The Board was a worthwhile and important vehicle for achieving domain consensus among the parties.

Another essential vehicle was that of several "boundary persons." Though a clear community power structure existed in Norfolk, it was not homogeneous nor without its factions (a fact easy for outsiders to overlook). The best example of a boundary person is Sox Baldwin. He characterized himself as an emissary in the community. Baldwin's influence was based less on that which he held as a person and more on what he gained as a broker of power. Since he was younger than Hofheimer or Kaufman he did not enjoy all of their old-line status. But he did understand their modus operandi, had the vision to see the possibilities of well-connected new arrangements, and was willing to work tirelessly in behalf of improved communications. With our increasing tendency to view organizations—indeed, much of society—in terms of power relations and power plays, it is easy to overlook the essential roles of integrators and communicators.

It is also easy to reach for "insightful" explanations of events rooted in the history or culture or sociology or a situation—and overlook the direct and obvious impact of personalities. Social scientists tend to downplay the "great man" theory, partly because so little can be said by way of useful and valid generalization about the uniqueness of leadership. Of the many effective Norfolk leaders, one was Kaufman, the epitome of the "superb politician" as described by James Thompson.[35] Another was Mitchell, representing in one person the leadership requirements outlined by Etzioni in his insightful paper, "Dual Leadership in Complex Organizations."[36] The expressive leader in Mitchell kept human considerations and personal concern as an essential component of his administration—at times under circumstances that would divert most chief executives from such concerns. Yet, he was also the instrumental leader, concerned with production when the circumstances required. The different leaderships of Kaufman and Mitchell were complementary: Kaufman could alter institutional patterns in the community in ways unavailable to Mitchell, while Mitchell could make an institution effective in ways unknown to Kaufman. The two enjoyed great mutual respect.

Though this case has highlighted the sociological and managerial aspects of the several mergers in Norfolk, the situation could readily be seen as a set of economic considerations: the financial outlook for Leigh Memorial as an autonomous hospital; the estimate by the King's Daughters that their hospital could generate more philanthropy as a small childrens' hospital than as part of a corporate giant; the restrictions in hospital reimbursement which caused Norfolk General—an inner city hospital—to be interested in the greener pastures of Kempsville; the differences in economic philosophy which divided the Medical Center Hospitals executive committee over financing the Kempsville satellite; the several corporate developments among physicians; and the changes in financing of medical education that caused EVMA officials to approach their task in a manner unusually sympathetic with community medical and hospital interests.

Yet, there was much more than economic self-interest at stake. Those who engineered the merger were unquestionably the medical and civic establishment, whose power was seldom challenged. This gave them many opportunities to choose who should gain. Some tussles hinted of self-interest, either personal or corporate, but the fundamental motivation of the key parties remained the community good. Their time, talent, and commitment to this end was a remarkable example of hospital trusteeship at its best.

Beyond all the details of this complicated merger, this important fact stands out as an example to others who might undertake such bold and important changes.

NOTES

1. MHA, Virginia Commonwealth University, 1977; former Personnel Specialist, Medical Center Hospitals of Norfolk; former Consultant with Health Planning Associates of Tucson, Arizona. Leonard Dougherty is currently Associate Administrator of the Children's Hospital of the King's Daughters in Norfolk, Virginia.
2. Technically, the integration described in this case study is not a consolidation but a merger. In a merger one of the prior corporations survives.
3. For consistency in presentation, the name Eastern Virginia Medical Authority (EVMA) has been used throughout this case. Though founded primarily as an educational entity, the name and charter were purposely designed to include medical care delivery activities as well. To EVMA leaders, this meant using the Authority to develop new health care programs, fill gaps in health care services, etc.
4. For details see C.N. Platua and J.S. Rice, "Multi-Hospital Holding Companies," *Harvard Business Review*, May-June, 1972; C.N. Platua et al., "The Consecutor Theory of Hospital Development: An Examination of the Multi-Unit System of the Fairview Hospitals," *Hospital Administration*, Spring, 1973; and Edin Trevelyan and A. Corlis, "Fairview Community Hospitals," Intercollegiate Case #4–374–001, Harvard Business School, 1973.
5. One of the law firms located on the top floor of the Virginia National Bank Building.
6. However, Kaufman strongly supported medical school development.
7. Kaufman's logic here was that if the King's Daughters' Hospital were merged it would lose both its strong volunteer effort—important in the care of children—and its successful fund raising. For Norfolk General to take on King's Daughters' Hospital charity load and in the process lose that organization's private fund raising capacity did not seem logical. Thus, for the same reasons that a Norfolk

General-Leigh Memorial merger seemed appropriate, this one seemed inappropriate.

8. It is revealing of Savage's style that three years later, two other persons thought they had initiated this endeavor.

9. The local phrase for this condition was the "MCV syndrome," referring to the plight of the Medical College of Virginia Hospital in Richmond, serving the poor of that city with dwindling resources and an obsolete physical plant requiring 120 million dollars to replace.

10. Baldwin and his colleagues were also considering another alternative: to relocate Leigh Memorial south to the city of Chesapeake. Representatives of the government of Chesapeake had approached the Leigh Board with an offer of 400 acres of donated land and a substantial contribution towards construction of a new hospital. Moreover, Dr. Jennings, the most active user of Leigh Memorial and responsible for 30 percent of its admissions, practiced in Chesapeake and was anxious to have a hospital there. Yet, the Board was not disposed to this offer; relations with Chesapeake had never been good, and Baldwin had reason to believe the city would eventually take over Leigh if it were relocated there. And, aside from Dr. Jennings, most physicians of the Leigh staff were Norfolk-oriented.

11. The Oschner Clinic was taken as the prototype, but there are several across the country, including the Louisville Clinic in Kentucky, the Cleveland Clinic, the Virginia Mason Clinic in Seattle, etc. They are characterized by large, multi-specialty composition; fee-for-service income from patients referred from throughout the region in which they are located; tight financial as well as professional ties among group members; ownership of practicing facilities and support services by the partnership; and either ownership or essential control of a hospital.

12. The Doctors' Clinic Company was formed as a business partnership, not a professional partnership.

13. A type of firm which goes beyond consultation in one function and contracts to perform all corporate, financial, design, and construction services, resulting in a complete building ready for occupancy and operation.

14. These were not the only physicians with multiple locations. Many surgical specialty groups, including plastic, orthopedic, and pediatric, had multiple offices near the Norfolk General and DePaul Hospitals, and in the communities of Chesapeake, Virginia Beach, etc.

15. A proposal was also made by the Hospital Corporation of America.

16. Another intepretation of Doctors' Company's traffic with Humana was that it was never a first option for the physicians involved, but instead part of a "Norfolk General strategy": increase the pressure on Norfolk General to build a satellite at Kempsville and hold a take-out option if Norfolk General did not respond.

17. Given this, why were the community physicians still so guarded? Dr. Howard Kruger, long-time general practitioner of Norfolk General, teacher of family practice in the medical school, and tireless worker in behalf of the merger, felt that a core city tertiary hospital demands a strong teaching program in order to provide medical care, and that this in turn leads to faculty dominance. He and his colleagues understood and even accepted this but feared simply that there would be no room for private doctors, particularly general practitioners, to admit and follow patients.

18. The unusual nature of EVMA is shown by this posture; ordinarily, medical school faculties want closed medical staffs. Medical School-Hospital relations had already been hammered out prior to the merger and expressed in a document

known generally as "the McAlpine Report," named for the chairman of the ad hoc committee. After the usual phraseology about EVMA responsibility for education and Norfolk General responsibility for patient care, the report contained these significant phrases: "It should be made clear that participation [by community physicians] in the medical student program of EVMA is not a requirement for [hospital] appointment. . . . The Norfolk General Hospital may suggest to EVMA certain individuals for appointment to the EVMA faculty, [and vice versa]. On occasions it is expected that Norfolk General Hospital and EVMA will form joint search committees. . . . A full-time faculty member shall limit his practice to physician-referred patients. Certain full-time faculty members may have to be exempted from this limitation as it is anticipated that Norfolk General Hospital and EVMA will jointly establish family practice programs. . . . A full-time faculty member will derive the greater percentage of his income from EVMA." (pp. 2, 3)

19. Earlier the new hospital board had established a policy that privileges in the new medical staff would be based on training and experience. All doctors were to be grandfathered into medical staff membership, but not into practicing privileges. This latter was the concern of some Norfolk General and Leigh doctors.

20. The health planning agency did not like this arrangement seeing in the sale/lease-back arrangement some kind of collusion. Some private physicians also saw in it the beginning of medical school takeover.

21. Specifically, Kaufman and Hofheimer proposed 1) full use of both hospitals' building fund reserves, 2) a gift campaign of three to five million dollars, 3) construction in three stages spaced five years apart instead of all at once, and 4) use of expensive long-term debt only to round out the project. In this way the debt burden would be in the range of seven million dollars rather than the estimated amount of three times that much.

22. To some this seemed like undue entrepreneurship on the part of Doctors' Clinic Company: they should have sold to Medical Center Hospitals for their per acre cost of $27,000. To others, the Company's loyalty to Medical Center Hospitals had been demonstrated: they had turned down Humana's offer of $50,000 per acre. The administration and board of Medical Center Hospitals agreed that the $35,000 per acre was a reasonable price.

23. "Final Report: A Study of the Financial Feasibility of Constructing the New Leigh Memorial Hospital, Medical Center Hospitals," Booz, Allen, Hamilton, Inc., March 21, 1975.

24. Reflecting the strong financial positions of both the prior hospitals and Medical Center Hospitals since its inception, the AA rating was only the seventh for a U.S. hospital.

25. The Chesapeake application represented the aftermath of discussions between Leigh Memorial and Chesapeake City officials, which ended in naught. After Leigh trustees decided not to relocate their hospital to Chesapeake, a Dr. Jennings, Leigh's most active hospital admitter, spearheaded the organization of a new hospital for Chesapeake.

26. To Medical Center Hospital officials this was small thanks from CHP for having merged two hospitals—a move which the Tidewater Agency should reward because it reduced independent hospital construction and autonomy. Yet, some CHP officials saw the merger as having stimulated the bed expansion proposals from other hospitals, whose leaders were suddenly worried about Medical Center Hospitals' potential domination.

27. The bed counts approved by the Commissioner were the ones eventually con-

structed by the three hospitals, except that Chesapeake subsequently applied for and was granted authorization for 69 additional beds, bringing its total from 141 (106 plus 35) to 210.

28. The dilemma for Doctors' Clinic Company was that it needed the rental occupancy proposed by the hospital, but this occupancy in turn complicated its efforts to secure financing for building construction. The Company was seeking a loan guarantee from the Small Business Administration. The maximum loan was for $5 million. Aside from the Company's need for more than $5 million, the proposed lease to Medical Center Hospitals was judged by the SBA to disqualify the loan, because the Medical Center Hospitals was a nonprofit corporation the activities of which would not contribute to the SBA's goals of stimulating small business entrepreneurship, and because Medical Center Hospital's debt would have to be counted as a debt of the proposed lender, Doctors' Clinic Company—enormously complicating the whole financial affair. For these reasons and others Doctors' Clinic Company abandoned its pursuit of SBA money and obtained instead a regular commercial loan from an insurance company. This was possible because Medical Center Hospitals, along with several new physician tenants, increased the percentage of total leased space to a loanable proportion. By the time the building was completed all space was rented.

29. When new stationery was printed for the Medical Center Hospitals, Leigh's prior masthead slogan of "the friendly hospital" was dropped because to continue it would make the Norfolk General Division, by comparison, seem unfriendly.

30. Riverside Hospital delivered 2,500 babies.

31. This illustrates the ripple effect of hospital mergers. Had King's Daughters come into the Leigh-Norfolk General consolidation in 1972, the maternity consolidation would undoubtedly have taken place in 1976. Since it did not, the King's Daughters now seemed more determined than before to maintain their identity relative to Medical Center Hospitals. Higher capital costs was one price for independence.

32. The new Leigh Memorial Division did in fact open in November 1977, and its occupancy rose steadily after opening. The satellite was carefully designed to obtain the advantages of its multihospital corporate setting. At a speech delivered in August 1978, Mitchell provided the following summary: "The Leigh Memorial Division has been built as an all single room hospital and is completely coordinated with the downtown Norfolk General Division. In explaining this we often describe those services which the Leigh Memorial does not have rather than what it does have. It was built without a kitchen and uses a preplated frozen food concept with all food prepared at Norfolk General; the switchboard for both complexes is located downtown where all telephone operations and paging originate; the Leigh building is monitored at the power plant at the Norfolk General location. Some of the services at the Leigh are provided by departments administratively responsible to the Norfolk General administrative staff. These include laboratory, maintenance, security, cardiac diagnostic laboratory and respiratory therapy. The Leigh has no psychiatry, pediatrics, obstetrics, nor such specialized services as CAT scanning, open heart surgery, kidney transplants, radiation oncology and intercranial neurosurgery. In almost all medical and surgical departments there are programmed limitations on capabilities of the Leigh Memorial with the requirement that patients receiving highly specialized services be provided care at the Norfolk General. We have continually resisted efforts of the Medical Staff using the Leigh to increase its medical capabilities and recognize that this pressure will always be with us.

. . . Medical Center Hospitals is now organized with five divisions—two hospital divisions and divisions of Finance, Personnel and Support Services. Support Services consists of Materials Management, Printing, Medical Photography, Audiovisual, Development, Marketing and Public Relations. Two new corporations are being established subservient to the Medical Center Hospitals Corporation. One is a Research Corporation which we plan to use for research in hospital operations and activities and the second being formed is a for-profit corporation to provide reference laboratory and other services to other hospitals, physicians' offices and health care institutions. In addition to these, we participate like almost all other hospitals today in some community-shared activities: data center, laundry, purchasing, training, and as a participant in the Voluntary Hospitals of America."

33. Glenn R. Mitchell, "Medical Center Hospitals—A 90 Day Merger," Multihospital Systems/University Teaching Hospital Conference, August 21, 22, 1978, pp, 6, 7.
34. Actually there were two organizations. The Medical Center Planning Board had been in existence since well before the White Heron retreat. The Policy and Planning Committee of the Board, a de facto executive committee and its strongest element, was composed of equal representation from Medical Center Hospitals, King's Daughters, and EVMA.
35. James Thompson, *Organizations in Action* (New York: McGraw-Hill, 1967, p. 105).
36. Amitai Etzioni, "Dual Leadership in Complex Organization," *American Sociological Review*, October 1965, pp. 688-98.

PART III.

The Ramifications

Introduction

The chapters of this part correspond roughly to the audiences for which this book is designed: those concerned with the development of policies and plans about health care organization will be most interested in chapter 10, social scientists in chapter 11, and managers in chapter 12. In a way, these divisions are dysfunctional; each of these parties ought to be interested in the other realms. Yet, this organization does provide for some selectivity.

Cross-case comparison is often proposed as a useful analytic device yet seldom actually carried out. The approach here will be to concentrate on different facts of the six cases, noting similarities and differences. The context for doing this will be the assumptions of chapter 2 and the propositions of chapter 3. The attempt will be to determine whether these assumptions and propositions bear the test of application to the cases, and to offer discussion and comment.

The format of Part III roughly corresponds to the model of the merging process outlined in the beginning of chapter 3 and summarized in table 3.1 and figure 3.1. Chapter 10 deals generally with the first two stages, pre-existing conditions and enabling forces. Chapter 11 deals with the second and third stages of the merging process, enabling forces and dynamics of implementation. Chapter 12 deals with the latter stages of the process, dynamics of implementation and stabilization. The overlaps between stages and chapters are unavoidable and intentional. Chapter 13 is a brief summary comment.

The chapters of Part III include two reference systems, one to the propositions stated in chapter 3, the other to the relevant sections of cases in chapters 4 through 9. These references are placed in parentheses in the running text, at points which should help the reader refer to these previous portions of the book.

10.
Mergers and Public Policy

This chapter deals with those propositions of chapter 3 that focus on the conditions preceding mergers and the factors either facilitating or preventing them. There is also further discussion of the issues introduced in chapter 1 having to do with the place of hospital mergers in medical care reorganization and some of the advantages and drawbacks of hospital consolidations of different types. Evidence is drawn from our six case studies, where relevant.

During this pre-existing stage options are greatest for public policy to impact on the merger phenomenon. Therefore, the chapter starts with an historical review of germane federal legislation and concludes with an outline of potential new government policies at federal, state and local levels.

A. MERGERS AND NATIONAL LEGISLATION:
   A BRIEF HISTORY

Proposition 1b (chap. 3, B) asserts that economics affects merger activity in two stages: availability of capital monies and manner of distribution. The proposition goes on to state that the first is a necessary but insufficient condition, while the second is a reflection of public policy rather than market behavior. We need to look at national policy in the light of its impact on the distribution of capital monies and thus on hospital mergers.

It is often said that federal policy in respect to the organization and distribution of hospital services started in 1946 with the passage of the Hill-Burton Act. That law made explicit the desirability of linking hospitals to each other—the notion underlying the merging phenomenon. This assumption threaded its way through over three subsequent decades of national policy formulation. The most recent relevant law, the National Health Resources and Development Act, specifies as one of ten national health goals the development of multi-institutional systems for coordinating and consolidating institutional health services. Unfortunately, while the linking goal has become clearer over time, the implementation strategies have become weaker, more confused, and less effective.

The 1946 National Hospital Survey and Construction Act (Hill-Burton) called for the establishment of functional relationships among hospitals, patterned around Joseph Mountin's (1945) well-publicized, three-tier hierarchy of hospitals. It was left to the states to come up with specific plans for advancing this or other regionalized networks, with the stipulation that no federal funds would flow until such plans were established. The states then proceeded to honor the state plan proviso in letter but not spirit, but the federal government granted funds anyway (Roemer and Morris, 1959). Construction grants then started flowing to a variety of health facilities. Through numerous amendments to the law, the priorities changed over time—rural hospitals, specialized hospitals, public health centers, modernization of inner-city hospitals, ambulatory care facilities, etc.—but at no time were any teeth put into the functional relationships proviso. The Hill-Burton Act became a program whose implementation ran contrary to one of its main goals: the flow of capital monies served to fractionalize the health care system rather than to advance linking among hospitals.

The Act never gave government officials direct franchising authority in a way that would lead to hospital linking; nor did those responsible for implementing the law seize opportunities to foster such through indirect means. One opportunity was more aggressively to enforce the requirement for state plans. Another was to put higher priority on grants to facilities that showed effective linking; this was seldom done. Another was to use the leverage of federal grants to influence capital funds flowing from other sources. Several other opportunities were missed.

Legislation of 1964 establishing construction and expansion funds for medical schools was the next federal law that might have had impact. This legislation was a response to concerns at the time about an insufficiency of doctors. Part of these funds went to the construction of new university teaching hospitals. These same hospitals were also highly complex and expensive treatment facilities, and could have been developed in a way that made clearer their availability as tertiary centers in regionalized health care delivery systems. To be sure, all academic health centers serve in this capacity to some degree. But it is also true that there exist excellent referral hospitals in many communities that are insufficiently used for medical education, and there are many communities with service and facility duplication between university-controlled and community-controlled hospitals. The distribution of funds for teaching hospitals under the act could have included priorities to enhance town-gown links.

The year 1965 yielded a bumper crop of health care bills. Title 18 and Title 19 amendments to the Social Security Act established Medicare and Medicaid, but they said virtually nothing about the organization of health care enterprises into a system. Yet, Medicare and Medicaid did have their influence on the merging phenomenon, primarily by defining reasonable reimbursement relating to depreciation costs and interest on capital debt. In the for-profit section of the hospital field, investors and managers saw in these provisions the opportunity for a guaranteed floor of return on borrowed and invested monies. An industry that previously had seemed too risky suddenly seemed less so. The Social Security Act amendments fueled a total reorganization among for-profit hospitals that saw "mom and pop" owners bought out by new investor-owned corporations. Then, many of these corporations merged (chap. 1, B), creating a highly concentrated industry. This showed the influence of federal policy on hospital mergers through its policies on capital money reimbursements. Yet, the links created did not in this instance represent functional relations in terms of health care delivery.

Another effect of the Medicare and Medicaid laws was quite the opposite. The same guaranteed floor served to prop up many not-for-profit hospitals that otherwise would have been forced to close or merge. Williams (1976) cites this as a main contributor to New York City's subsequent hospital problems: "The record shows Medicaid reimbursement became the main financial underpinning for the continued existence of inadequate and redundant institutions which offered the most limited kind of inpatient services" (p. 4).

The second major piece of 1965 legislation was the Heart, Cancer, Stroke (Regional Medical Programs) Act, designed to establish regional networks of preventive, diagnostic, and treatment services. As envisioned by the DeBakey Commission that originally proposed the legislation, these networks would close the gap between medical knowledge and the 300,000 annual preventable deaths caused by the three dread killers. These networks were never funded by Congress, due in part to their high cost and in part to a clause that the American Medical Association successfully injected into the Act stipulating that no funds would be used to alter the existing pattern of U.S. medical care delivery. For the next ten years the Heart, Cancer, Stroke Act funded primarily physicians' continuing education, ignoring interhospital relationships.[1] What started out as a piece of legislation designed specifically to advance linking failed completely—a classic case of goal displacement. The program was quietly passed into oblivion in 1974 when Congress voted to merge it and several other laws relating to health care delivery into the National Health Services Resource and Development Act.

The third 1965 legislation of national significance in the health field was the Comprehensive Health Planning Act. This Partnership for Health Act (i.e, partnership between government and private medicine) established local and state health planning agencies across the nation. The local agencies were responsible to the state ones, and both operated under federal guidelines. Expected to plan comprehensively for health, these agencies soon became enmeshed almost entirely in questions of medical care delivery in response to various mandates subsequently given the agencies to review and comment on hospital capital projects, and grant certificates of need accordingly. There was a good deal of confusion about what authorities were actually contained in the review and comment proviso; in some states it meant little while in others, where enhanced by further enabling legislation, it amounted to strict franchising. Regardless of authority, each local health planning agency was obligated to come up with a plan that would become the basis of its review and comment activity. This requirement was similar to the Hill-Burton one of twenty years previous, but now it was directed at local as well as state agencies. However, the impact was about the same: the resulting plans were general to the point of uselessness. Whenever the plans spoke to linking among, which was rare, their loopholes were readily apparent.

The Health Services Resources and Development Act of 1975 was designed to remedy the problems of insufficient or unclear authority of comprehensive health planning agencies, to tie in the previous federal initiatives in hospital construction grants and regional medical programs, and to establish tighter controls on health care costs through reorganized health care delivery. Not only did the law include specific language on ten national priorities—an unusual feature in itself—but it further required the Secretary of HEW to issue guidelines and criteria for plan development by local health systems agencies and to approve directly such individual plans before any agency became fully operative. Two of the ten priorities were: 1) development of multi-unit systems for coordination and consolidation of institutional health services; and 2) development by health service institutions of the capacity to provide various levels of care on a geographically integrated basis.

If ever there was an opportunity not only to correct prior shortcomings but forcefully to implement national health policy, this was it. No longer was government action limited to projects which it funded directly, as with Hill-Burton. No longer could the worthwhile goals of expanded medical education divert needed changes in health care delivery systems, as they had in the Regional Medical Programs Act. No longer would Medicare and Medicaid reimbursement practices thwart integration, because the authority of Health Systems Agencies over capital construction was now very clear. No longer were the franchising authorities of Health Systems Agencies clouded by the vagueness of review and comment language, as they had been in the Comprehensive Health Planning Act. In brief, there was now a declared national policy and a clear pathway of implementation that started with mandated action by the Secretary of HEW and continued with decision making by local and state agencies that were duly funded and authorized. Incredibly, action on the ten goals of the National Health Services Resources and Development Act seem scheduled for frustration and perhaps failure.

In the first place, the law permits health systems agencies to be formed and operate without specifically advancing all the goals contained in the act. In the second place, initial guidelines developed by the Secretary of HEW for implementation by local health systems agencies bear no particular reference to the ten priorities written into the law. In the third place, it has been established in the courts that the act's ten priorities do not constitute a sufficient basis for decision making by local health systems agencies in certificate-of-need actions.[2] In the main, the ten priorities seem almost to have been forgotten, and the linking assumption destined to another era of damnation by faint praise.

In mid-1978 Senator Schweiker, a U.S. Congressman prominent to health care legislation and later appointed Secretary of Health and Human Services, summarized the federal government's efforts to encourage multi-institutional arrangements.

> On the current scene, there is some discussion by people in government of encouraging multi-institutional arrangements by changing the tax code. In addition to that, both the Talmadge and Rogers cost containment bills would offer financial incentives for hospital consolidation. . . .
>
> All in all, though, federal law contains very few incentives, and many more disincentives, and there aren't many detailed proposals floating around on what the government's position ought to be. The subject is wide open and begs for decisions. [Schweiker, 1978, pp. 4, 5]

B.   A RECONSIDERATION: FIVE VIEWS

These six legislations, spanning a thirty year period, had many virtues. But in respect to linking among hospitals they can be described as either a series of missed opportunities or a series of intentional oversights. Why the failure of implementation?

Our assumption thus far has been that the linking together of hospitals is an appropriate goal for the U.S. health care system, and therefore the long if not thin thread of legislative development is in the public interest. However, a number of facts presented in chapter 1, H, force us to question and rethink this assumption. Reflecting on both our propositions of Part I and our case studies of Part II, we will explore five contrasting views of mergers, views that reveal the flaws as well as the strengths of hospital consolidations.

MERGERS AS INEFFICIENT?

In chapter 1 (fig. 1.1) the dual objectives of efficiency and effectiveness in health care reorganization were discussed. Combinations among health service organizations were seen as ways of advancing both, because they capture economies of scale—efficiency—and because they form the critical mass necessary for extending new services to new populations—effectiveness. Further, in an era of excess hospital capacity in many communities, mergers obtain these gains in inputs and outputs without increasing total bed capacity (chap. 1, G).

The Evidence
Unfortunately, several facts point to the contrary, particularly as regards efficiency: newly formed mergers usually experience an increase in unit costs, lasting for a substantial time after their formation (chap. 1, G). Only in selected small and rural hospitals where potential returns to scale are the greatest might there be immediate efficiencies. The researchers who have obtained these results offer some speculation as to the reasons: inordinate system set-up costs, and costs associated with overcoming organizational resistance to change. The time period associated with these cost overruns obviously varies across mergers (Money et al., 1976).

> The systems organized after 1966 (younger) perceived themselves to be less successful in accomplishing system goals, to have higher levels of role ambiguity, and to have higher levels of role conflict than the pre-1967 multiple-hospital systems. The younger systems were also found to be significantly less flexible and less able to respond to different environmental demands than older systems. Finally, the younger systems were perceived to be less capable of training and developing internal personnel, less able to attract outside personnel, and to have lower levels of job satisfaction than the older systems in the study.

> The overall pattern of results suggests that large size and elaborate structure are not necessarily advantageous to multi-hospital systems; and that, when a new multi-unit system is created by merger, negative organizational side effects may be expected for the first five to 10 years. (pp. 56, 58)

The soft data from three of our case studies (mergers that went beyond the initial stages of integration), revealing the nature and depth of organizational trauma, confirm this phenomenon. While the cost impact of this trauma was not determined, the indication is that the adjustment period lasted or could be predicted to last at least ten years.

At Palo Alto-Stanford, the merger was still in adjustment in 1968 when one owner purchased the equity of the other—nine years after the time of initial integration in 1959 (chap. 4, E). During this stabilization period much effort was spent trying to integrate services previously duplicated for reasons of professional politics: two radiology and pathology departments (chap. 4, C, D, E), and two medical staffs (chap. 4, E). These were constant and heavy organizational drains. Even after this nine year period, Stanford's 1968 acquisition of the total corporation ushered in another era of stress (chap. 4, apps. A, B) as the enterprise initially set up to be relatively independent of its two former owners was now destined to be controlled entirely by one of them. The Palo Alto-Stanford case shows some direct evidence of high adjustment and stabilization costs: the need for rate increases above the community norm, in 1960 (chap. 4, D), and the requirement of capital cost payback by one owner because the other owner had so stipulated (chap. 4, C). To be sure, these and other inefficiencies could have been associated with increases in services and in quality of care—mergers centering on medical education typically offer these advantages. It is very difficult to separate these kinds of costs.

At Norfolk, little was said about operating efficiencies as a rationale for the merger. Some officials at Leigh Memorial complained about the inefficiency of Norfolk General, but this was not crucial to the merger dynamics. However, there was a good deal of controversy over capital monies: the concern that Leigh Memorial's debt-free assets would become lost in the integration, and the concern of fiscal conservatives on the merged board over what they considered reckless borrowing in order to finance the Kempsville satellite (chap. 9, E). Again, the adjustment period seemed attenuated. Almost five years after the initial merger the Kempsville facility had yet to be opened. The delay was due to postmerger financial operations that made capital borrowing difficult, and to complications in obtaining necessary certificates of need (chap. 9, E). In addition, the general practice-oriented doctors and employees of small Leigh Memorial were still in a state of anxiety, looking to the new Kempsville facility as their salvation in the merger, while some specialty-oriented doctors and employees of Norfolk General viewed the satellite development as potentially draining off resources that might otherwise go to their main hospital; and the physicians of the Doctors' Clinic Company who had earlier migrated to Kempsville had different views of the satellite development than those primarily associated with Norfolk General (chap. 9, E).

At Los Angeles County, efficiency was the overriding rationale for the merger: county officials had become increasingly concerned over the post-Medicaid cost squeeze on county governments in California, as well as over the increasing burden of health care costs on total county revenues (chap. 8, B). To be sure, the Health Services Planning Commission report and the Public Health Commission report also justified the merger on grounds of reform in health care delivery (chap. 8, C). But, as the merger unfolded, the rationale for changes in delivery of services receded in importance relative to cost considerations. Two examples of this are the slow development of the experimental primary health care centers (chap. 8, C, D), and the cost criteria used to settle the dispute over home visits by public health nurses (chap. 8, D). Two years into the merger the regionalization plan—the cornerstone of both efficiency and effectiveness reforms—was bogged down in bureaucratic delay and interprofessional rivalry (chap. 8, D). Four years into the reorganization the very continuance of the merger was in jeopardy, with the county administrative officer intervening and reversing the regionalization plan in favor of centralized cost controls (chap. 8, E). The case closes on a note of continued questioning and criticism by some county supervisors, including a study and report on possible demerger and separation of mental health activities into an independent department (chap. 8, E). Again, we have no direct evidence of increased adjustment costs, but strong inference that such is the case by the extreme concern of top county executives for cost considerations. And, organizational trauma, particularly among physician groups, showed no signs of abating by the close of the case. Could this continue to impact the merger for some years to come?

There is a pattern in our three case study mergers: (1) unexpected cost overruns, (2) accentuated organizational stress, and (3) focus of this stress in professional groups. We can conclude that the cost-related adjustment period hypothesized by the A.H.A.-Northwestern researchers (chap. 1, H) will be roughly the same length of time as the organizationally related stabilization period proposed in chapter 3, and that these periods will last until "all significant power and identity of one or more of the organizational contestants are submerged and a new order is established and commonly recognized" (chap. 3, D). These cases indicate that eight to ten years can be expected, and longer times for some mergers.[3]

Policy and Managerial Dilemmas
Numerous experts suggest a policy of slow growth of multihospital systems through merger, in order to avoid at least some of the adjustment costs of organizational change (chap. 1, D). We shall call this planned gradualism. Gradualism is recommended both to mitigate costs associated with change and avoid the creation of nonrational systems that might result from opportunistic development. As stated by Cooney (1975):

> In this area of system acquisition and growth strategy development, the non-selective acquisition of numerous hospitals over short periods will have long-run dysfunctional consequences for the system. It is apparent that management could be less able to react immediately to required service changes in many hospitals, that problems with staff development would have less time devoted to their solution, and that the rapid acquisition of hospitals with limited resources to contribute to the system might have an unfavorable effect on the entire system. [Vol. 1, p. 7]

The dilemma is that hospitals are often propelled into merger when organizational strife is high. Proposition 5 asserts that mergers are more likely to occur when all potential merger parties face crises in their respective organizations (chap. 3, B). The analysis of cases presented in chapter 11, B indicates that this is true. Seizing the merger potential that lies in mutual crises—a temptation for planners and regulators, and perhaps a necessity—can lead to an extended period of higher costs, and perhaps even to a nonrational system. Neither are good results.

Another way out of this dilemma is to avoid the negative consequences of postmerger strife by designing looser forms of integration. As put by one merger manager: "Set up the umbrella and do nothing for five years."[4] Of course to do absolutely nothing is to change nothing; what he probably meant is to integrate only those hospital activities that either 1) do not create substantial strife, or 2) are easily controlled by top management. This is the strategy used by a great many institutions, as revealed by surveys of the American Hospital Association (1977) and discussed in chapter 1, I.

The strategy is shown in figure 10.1. The horizontal axis shows different categories of hospital activity; the vertical axis shows frequency of sharing among hospitals. The problem is that the high frequency integrations, those on the left side of the figure, are of little economic consequence: their integration avoids strife but also avoids the opportunity for real gain.[5] The services in which substantial economies can be realized are those on the right side of the figure: services controlled or strongly influenced by professionals and beyond the reach of ordinary managerial discipline. Further, as discussed in the Assumption of Conduct (chap. 2, C), these looser forms can be viewed either as transitional steps between strictly limited and more complete forms— a multistage policy of gradualism in which middle range relationships are taken as means to a more distant end—or as alternatives to complete integration, not transitional steps but ends in themselves. In the second instance the risk is that the integration is rationalized as beneficial but is of no real consequence.

FIGURE 10.1   Frequency of Hospital Sharings, by Type of Activity

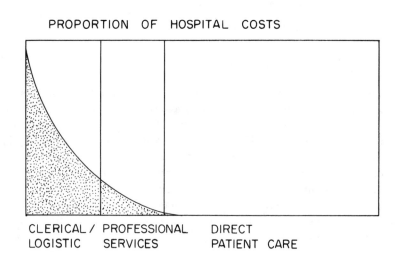

In making the decisions that yield one or the other of these results, planners and regulators must make a calculation that our propositions and cases indicate is most difficult: assess the degree of future organizational strife. Consequences are likely to be unanticipated (see Propositions 9d and 22c) and competent planners can err in judging or predicting events (chap. 5, H). The second dilemma, then, lies in the conflict between the safety of planned gradualism at the risk of low ultimate gain, and the virtual assurance that an initally tight integration will incur high adjustment costs, perhaps for a period of time beyond the tolerance of those responsible for the merger.

Reducing Adjustment Costs
One way of reducing adjustment costs is to deal explicitly with those stemming from interpersonal and intergroup behavior. It is theoretically possible to reduce these by investing in the application of behavioral science techniques aimed at either mitigating organizational conflict or turning it to constructive ends. These possibilities are discussed in chapter 12 dealing with the implementation stage of mergers. At this point we need simply note that 1) none of the merger planners or managers in our cases deployed these interventions to any serious extent; 2) the evidence from the literature is vague and inconclusive as to the real effects; and 3) the use of management initiated interventions in hospitals is effectively limited to those realms clearly within the control of top administrators (Weisbord, 1976). Thus there are practical limits to efforts to reduce the behavioral component of total adjustment costs, leading Money et al. (1976) to state the following:

> It is possible . . . that the technological-economic benefits of merger are greatest when the size of the final entity is relatively large, but the benefits in the human and professional advantages peak at a somewhat smaller . . . size, and thereafter decline. Should this prove to be the case, it would suggest that labor-intensive and professional organizations should undertake only mergers that combine small units into moderate-sized final entities, rather than those mergers that combine moderate-sized units into very large final organizations. [p. 58]

Another type of cost, termed prospective by Treat (chap. 1, G) and called hidden costs in the business world, includes the salary cost of suitable replacement managers, specialization of management, wage and fringe benefit costs associated with bringing all employees up to the highest common denominator, possible costs of unionization, costs of mechanization that need to be undertaken, etc. These are all modernization costs, since they are one-time catch-up payments for various forms of obsolescence that can no longer be tolerated if the merged enterprise is to survive and thrive. It is difficult to see how several of these costs can be avoided, although a new merger management can avoid indulging in corporate excesses unrelated to survival or enhancement of quality.

A third kind of adjustment cost, revealed by Newmann's examination of the Samaritan Health Service (chap. 1, H) is usually termed equity costs. In the business world this is called the Penn Central phenomenon: big corporations become the target for those who say it is their duty to take on the losers. In the health field the arguments for equity often win out over decisions to close small, inefficient and remote hospitals at the margin of existence. These decisions burden the larger and more efficient hospitals of a merger, inflating the costs of operation for the total enterprise above what they would otherwise be.

Little evidence of this kind of cost exists in our cases, selected as total fusion type integrations that eliminated most of these continuing expenses.[6] But, such costs are common in management contract and umbrella type integrations and can usually be reduced by closing marginal operations and eliminating local services. However, such decisions are seldom made solely on the criterion of efficiency, which is as it should be.

To summarize, the evidence from our case studies validates the research of others concerning adjustment costs, indicating that the period of adjustment is likely to be longer than most care to admit. Analysis of the cases indicates that behavioral costs can be controlled only to a limited degree because they are centered in those realms of hospital operations only nominally within management's purview, that prospective costs are difficult to avoid except to the extent that they constitute inappropriate frills, and that equity costs are sometimes substantial but are usually accepted on grounds other than operating efficiency.

Some Key Efficiency Variables

Despite these apparent uncontrollables, several factors influencing merger efficiency are within the discretion and control of policy makers and managers. One is timing. A fast rate of change accentuates behavioral costs, and perhaps others. Even though many consolidations result from opportunities seized that may not recur, there often remain choices as to the speed of integration. We can distinguish between rate of merger and rate of absorption: the first applies externally to new institutions entering a merged system and the second to the internal changes within already consolidated hospitals. The two are related, depending on the type of integration. In looser forms of integration the merger rate will have less effect on the behaviorally-oriented absorption rate than in tighter forms, namely mergers and consolidations, where the impact will be greater. This is for reasons generally associated with Propositions 19 through 23 (chap. 3, C, D). The direction of influence can go both ways: merged hospitals with many absorption problems will divert merger planners and managers from pursuing new mergers. There is some evidence of this in the Norfolk case, as revealed by administrator Mitchell's reflections on six years of management of the merging process (chap. 9, E). Conversely, a high rate of new mergers can divert top administrators from managing the process of absorption within those hospitals already folded in.

A second variable influencing adjustment costs is the degree of organizational control available to merger managers. The typology of integrations presented in chapter 1 (table 1.3) shows that the services combined in looser forms are often limited to support, logistic, and administrative activities; umbrella-type integrations often involve professional services; and, only complete mergers or consolidations involve all of these as well as direct patient care operations. The table also shows that each of these forms is associated with increasingly severe and pervasive organizational impact. The reason, again, runs to the nature of hospital operations: doctors are vitally concerned with professional services and patient care operations; they are thus involved and influential, yet remain insulated from strict organizational discipline due to the nature of the medical staff structure.

The third variable affecting adjustment costs is physical location. The same table in chapter 1 also indicates that looser forms of integration are usually associated with wider geographic dispersion of hospitals and with peripheral support functions. In these situations the behavioral costs of adjustment are minimal. Problems in management control are those of communication and coordination over great distances. Some merger managers argue that for this reason multihospital systems should be confined to single regions.[7] Others, notably those involved in for-profit corporations, argue that the advantages of centralizing certain administrative functions—finance, computer services, planning and development, capital formation, etc.—across many hospitals and regions of a nationwide system offset the disadvantages of distance, once that distance exceeds a single community.[8]

Either way, the effect of geography is less in these integrations than in tight ones where physical integration of facilities forces the new organization to face all the behavioral dimensions of redundancy, pluralistic ignorance, false fate assessments, and unanticipated consequences discussed in connection with Propositions 21 and 22 (chap. 3, C).

Several of our case studies illustrate these three summary factors. Palo Alto-Stanford underwent virtually complete physical integration, but no total organizational fusion—a peculiar reversal of the usual tight merger. The sustained period of strife that followed the merger would undoubtedly have been shortened had the merger architects bit the bullet at the outset on a unified medical staff and single departments for each of the hospital-based professional services (chap. 4, D). They calculated that the merger could not proceed under these circumstances. They were probably correct, but the organizational costs of that decision were very high, and much higher than they had anticipated. At Norfolk, the more typical sequence of total corporate merger followed by planned physical change took place. The acquired hospital, Leigh Memorial, underwent the intended move to a new location rather than becoming absorbed by the giant Norfolk General. At least this was Leigh Memorial's perception (chap. 9, E), acknowledged early in the merger negotiations when leaders rejected a plan to relocate Leigh Memorial to a site physically contiguous to Norfolk General (chap. 9, D). Thus, by skirting the issue of physical integration the White Heron accords were accepted with remarkable speed, and the merger progressed to the implementation and stabilization periods at a much faster rate and lower level of adjustment cost than at Palo Alto-Stanford. The merged/pavilion solution (chap. 6, C) was Seattle's similar arrangement.

In all three cases, the merger planners deferred several organizational problems in order to obtain a merger. This deferred giving or problem liening made the subsequent stages of merger implementation difficult and protracted. As further illustration of this, in our two nonmerger cases, Westhaven/Riviera and Davenport, the planners and decision makers seemed to lack the choice to defer or not: to merge organizationally meant to fuse physically. In both cases the price was too high. At Westhaven/Riviera, Dana Memorial's insistence on a single-site merger was unacceptable to Westhaven, and Westhaven's last minute federation plan was unacceptable to Dana (chap. 5, F,). In Davenport, the prospect of physical integration caused Mercy Hospital's provincial house to turn away from the merger in order to protect its right-to-life policies (chap. 7, D).

In short, our case studies of both successful and unsuccessful mergers show the subtle trade-off that merger designers must make between immediate organizational fusion and future organizational problems.

There is an important ramification of this for national, state, and local policy makers: the kinds of integrations that make a substantial difference in health care costs and health care delivery are the very ones whose gains will not be realized for a decade or more. Are policy makers willing to wait this long to realize benefits? The discontinuities across time are so great that the planning intelligence necessary to deal with these long-run subtleties of linking is likely to be missing; the nation's policy development and implementation are simply insufficient.

CRITICAL MASS FOR WHAT?

Chapter 1 (fig. 1.1) presented the long-run rationale for many hospital mergers: horizontal combinations create the critical mass necessary to achieve vertically linked services. A standard rhetoric supports this: the ultimate goal is outreach services, satellite clinics, ambulatory care development, health maintenance organization, formation of group practices, etc.[9]

Unfortunately, results thus far have fallen short of these aspirations, particularly in horizontal mergers that have created multihospital systems spanning different communities and regions. Two experienced merger managers, Robert Sigmond and Edward Connors, have carefully analyzed this shortfall as well as directions to be established for the future. Sigmond (1978) writes:

> Some may be disappointed that I don't see the future of multihospital corporations in terms of simply perfecting business-like support systems within the multihospital corporation, taking an essentially neutral role in terms of community health systems development—leaving that up to the HSA's or some other agency. Well, I just don't think that the social and community responsibility of a multihospital system can be less than the community and social responsibility of a single hospital. There has to be a multiplier effect—not a neuter effect; otherwise multihospital systems will not be able to justify support from society. Very few multihospital systems have begun to face this kind of issue as yet.
>
> The nation is inevitably moving toward comprehensive community health delivery systems—tortuously, painfully, but inevitably. Multihospital systems can facilitate this process, they can smooth the way, lead the way, by formulating their missions in terms of community health delivery systems. The opportunity is great. But if multihospital systems attempt to compete with evolving comprehensive community health systems—to present a choice between highly structured hospital support systems and less structured community systems—they may achieve some short term gains, and they will create much turmoil, but they will eventually inevitably lose out. . . .
>
> Multihospital systems can take the lead, and can succeed, but only based on a clear understanding of individual hospital development, their hang-ups and their important assets and resources. The transition that is required in the decades ahead will be much easier for hospitals which can associate themselves with forward looking multihospital systems. The challenge facing multihospital systems, then, is how to demonstrate to most hospitals that the multihospital system is the safest vehicle for traveling this treacherous road to the future [pp. 1–13]

Connors (1978) draws even more distinctly the difference between Sigmond's systems efficiency and community effectiveness goals, by specifying two models of behavior:

Efficiency Model

1) View oneself as a model of efficiency.
2) Apply latest business techniques to current operations.
3) Work hard on productivity indices and performance measures.
4) Optimize economies of scale in such endeavors as purchasing, cash management and capital financing.
5) Avoid ventures with high financial risk such as ambulatory care or long term care.
6) Devote political effort to maintaining status quo with regard to reimbursement and regulation.

7) Build better mousetrap in order to out-compete the neighboring hospitals. Place high value on market penetration.

8) Allow government—or someone else—to care for the poor and near poor.

9) Be sanguine or unconcerned about unmet needs in the communities being served.

10) Work harder on optimizing reimbursement than on containing costs.

11) Be in the vanguard of technological diffusion because the latest equipment is likely to enhance the competitive edge.

Change Agent Model

1) View oneself as a vehicle to bring fundamental change in the delivery of health services.

2) Work actively to achieve a coordinated, comprehensive plan of services for all communities in which we serve.

3) Move in the direction of developing ambulatory care centers with heavy emphasis on primary care, prevention and health education.

4) Convert excess bed capacity to ambulatory and long term care services and to centers of health rather than treatment of illness.

5) Be open to linkages with other providers in order to achieve comprehensiveness and continuity of care at local levels.

6) Be less concerned about maintaining the current number of beds and more concerned about providing the appropriate number of beds and services.

7) Acknowledge that there are problems of costs quality and access and design specific goals and programs to deal with these problems.

8) Be sure that current and future utilization rates can stand the test of professional scrutiny and that variations are defensible.

9) Actively work to eliminate the injustices that can be found in all of our communities.

10) Attempt to inculcate compassion and caring into the fiber and fabric of the organization. Try to be a value-oriented enterprise even though those values may be working against the grain of some of our historical patterns. [pp. 4, 5]

Connor's and Sigmond's suggestions on how merged systems can achieve community health delivery system goals emphasize corporate mission and governance. Connors writes of the problems of achieving clarity of purpose and goals: "Many multi-hospital organizations seem to have evolved or emerged without the fundamental building block of clarity of purposes. [They have] rush[ed] toward expansion and uncritical adoption of marketing techniques without a clear product to be marketed; and, the desire by many to achieve a competitive edge seem to be an all-too-common symptom" (p. 3). Sigmond discusses missions: ". . . there are only a few multihospital corporations which will not require a thorough revision of the corporate mission statement, based on an intensive and extensive planning process. Only through such a process will most multihospital corporations achieve a corporate understanding and commitment to the role of each of its hospitals as the key organization component for health services delivery in its own community" (p. 15).

Both experts then discuss governance. Connors writes:

What sufficed for governance prior to the mid 60's is proving to be insufficient for the multi-hospital system, particularly the horizontally integrated system. Some seem to have rejected the value of local governance and citizen involvement in the policy issues of the organization. The rationale, although implicit, seems to be that local decision making is likely to get in the way of corporate wide authority and need for responsiveness, and that, further, the voice of the citizen can appropriately be heard in such arenas as HSA, certificate of need, rate setting or prospective budget review, etc. This point of view is banking heavily on the abilities of the professional health executive and physician for important governance decisions. Others, including our own system, are attempting to build a model of shared governance through achieving a balance between local initiative, responsibility and systemwide responsibility and opportunity. [p. 5]

Sigmond states:

We know . . . little about governance—how it works, how it can be strengthened, and what its potential is—either in individual hospitals or multihospital systems. Governance structure of multihospital systems should be designed primarily to strengthen individual hospital governance and to stimulate continuous constructive and creative tension between the governance of the individual hospital and its community delivery system as well as between the governance of the individual hospital and the multihospital system. Among other things, this will require new definitions of appropriate balance between inside and outside directors on multihospital system governing boards. . . .

What do we really mean by governance responsibilities and how are they to be differentiated from management responsibilities?

Will strengthened governance of multi-hospital systems more likely be creditable to citizens served, to owners/sponsors, to government, or to external agencies?

Should trusteeship remain a voluntary unpaid function? Can trustees devote sufficient time to become knowledgeable about the issues?

Does the professional manager and physician have a role in trusteeship?

What governance approach is likely to achieve the "change agent model" previously enumerated? [pp. 14–15]

All these suggestions by Connors and Sigmond are designed for voluntary action by the leaders of multihospital systems as private corporations. Another approach emphasizes government regulation, primarily franchising, as the mode of intervention and change. This approach will be discussed in section C of this chapter, "Some Policy Options."

MERGERS AS TECHNOLOGY TRAPS?

Propositions 2a, b, and c (chap. 3, B) highlight the central role of technology in stimulating mergers. They assert that mergers will take place when the technological gap between hospitals is wide, that the diffusion of technology is from tertiary to primary care institutions, and that the effect of technology on merger dynamics is described by a lower level institution seeking an asset held by a higher level hospital. They identify three different types of assets: "direct technology" possessed by large tertiary hospitals, "referred technology" possessed by medium-sized secondary hospitals, and "reflex technology" possessed by small general or primary care facilities.[10]

The desire to capture medical technology was part of the merger motivation in all our cases, and in most, the reach was from institutions lower on the technology hierarchy towards those at higher levels. In Westhaven/Riviera, two reflex technology hospitals thought merger would provide new services and facilities that would attract needed doctors (chap. 5, C). In Davenport, the striving for referred technology was expressed as the goal of becoming a regional care center (chap. 7, C). In both Seattle and Norfolk the leaders of the smaller, general practice-oriented hospitals understood the problems their institutions had as reflex technology facilities, and that they could be solved by linking to a direct technology center (chap. 6, C; chap. 9, D). Certainly the medical sophisticates in Palo Alto saw in merger with Stanford the solution to their problem of a technically obsolete hospital (chap. 4, B). And, in Los Angeles, the reorganization was seen in part by the Health Services Planning Commission as a way of tapping the medical expertise of the Department of Hospitals to the benefit of a regionalized system of outreach services (chap. 8, C).

In short, technological striving is a strong merger motivation partly because technology is a key organizational resource for hospitals, and partly because of the pervasiveness of technology as a cultural value in American life: community elites accomplish good things by advancing cultural values.

Yet, is technology that worthwhile? Its value is being challenged increasingly, from many different sources (Fuchs, 1975; Illich, 1976; Lalonde, 1974). The challenge is aimed primarily at the decreasing contribution of medical technology, at the margin, to health status. Even as a cost containment strategy, a prominent health care official places control of technology as an important mechanism (McNerney, 1980).

Hospital mergers help capture technology. They yield large volumes of patients that permit the development and use of sophisticated treatment programs that cannot be supported in smaller hospitals, and they provide sufficient numbers of cases to keep specialists at high performance levels. Yet, Homer and Smith (1975) state that:

Fewer larger sized institutions seem to serve the interests of the "professional monopolists"; the commitment to further specialization and to high technology medicine has been served by consolidation, and the professional monopolists would seem to have a far greater degree of insulation from the sometimes countervailing pressures of the hospital boards today than they did 15 years ago. In increasing the number of full time medical staff and creating physician office buildings adjoining new hospitals, it is not entirely clear who has co-opted whom. . . . It is not easy to separate out what is managerial or medical technology used to legitimize class interests while masquerading as science and what is closer to means for reaching commonly shared goals. [pp. 10, 11]

Are mergers creating technology traps that will render health care organizations incapable of advancing larger goals of health care reform? Are two of the goals of the National Health Services Resources and Development Act calling for the consolidation and improved quality of institutional health services inconsistent with two others aiming to develop primary care services for medically underserved populations, and to promote activities to prevent disease?

The answer seems to lie in channelling medical technology to serve new ends. In this lies the question whether merged hospitals are captured by the technology they usually obtain, or, instead, can use their greater organizational power to rechannel the many worthwhile applications of modern science.

MERGERS AS MONOPOLIES?

Mergers create dominance in a local health delivery community. Because of this, Cooney and Alexander have suggested (chap. 1, G) that merged corporations, especially those operating multiple units in a community or area, act as planners, allocators, and distributors of services—a bold proposal, given that most merged corporations are private enterprises and would be usurping what is now considered a government function. Yet, it has a degree of practicality; thus far health systems agencies have been insufficient to the task. This point has been stressed by investigators of the Harvard Center for Community Health and Medical Care, in response to a commission by HEW officials to clarify the issues surrounding the linking of health planning to regulation. Their report (Bauer, 1978) states in part:

The Planning Act excludes from the purview of the agencies it creates most of the key elements that currently determine the way the U.S. health system actually operates. Physicians and other health professionals continue to function just as autonomously as before, the basic way the operation is financed continues unchanged, and the new review and regulatory functions prescribed by the Act are for the most part simply superimposed on a highly complicated existing federal, state, and local regulatory function, not integrated with it. [p. 2]

> Hospital consortia designed to promote multi-institutional networks should be encouraged. Insofar as they assume responsibilities for working out detailed arrangements . . . , the burden on the HSA's and state regulatory agencies is lightened [p. 10]

The same line has been taken by a former HEW official, the administrator of the Health Resources Administration. In a policy speech delivered to a group of multihospital systems executives, Henry Foley (1978) said:

> Given the situation hospitals face today, and the projections for the future, there is little doubt that the days of the independent, autonomous community hospitals are numbered . . . the independent, free standing hospital may simply be too small too make effective use of the management, technical, and legal talents required for effective operations. . .Through a dominant role in the health care market, the multi-institutional system has the potential resource and power base to design the scope, quantity, quality, and distribution of services provided to the community and at the same time eliminate duplication of facilities and services.

> Despite the many advantages we see favoring the cooperative venture for hospitals, there are also some problems. . . . The consumer may present a barrier in the development of multihospital systems. During the initial stage of development, the hospital system may experience adverse community reaction because of the possibility of losing customary kinds of care. . . . Since a community generally maintains loyalty to its local health care institution, the multi-hospital system sometimes has a negative political impact; community involvement becomes a problem. [pp. 3, 5]

This brings us to the question of who is the primary beneficiary of merged operations—hospitals as enterprises, doctors as medical staff members, patients as consumers, or the community-at-large. Cooney and Alexander (1975) state that multihospital systems do not act as monopolists (Pt. I, p. 3), but by their own admission, the evidence for this conclusion is scanty. The opposite possibility exists: mergers represent purposeful attempts by corporations to control the health care marketplace in order better to gain from those who must use their services.

At the same conference to which Foley made his remarks, U.S. Senator Robert Schweiker (1978) also commented on these ideas from what he called a political perspective:

> Should the government encourage multi-institutional arrangements? From a public policy perspective I think there are pros and cons. . . . The arguments that consolidation will advance these important government policies are so convincing that it's hard to find significant resistance to the trend in professional health circles.

> My first concern is that, along with all the benefits of consolidation, will come the dangers of monopoly power. . . . Will [decision makers] use [their power] to exclude competitors? Will they resist innovation in the health care delivery system, innovations like HMOs?

My second concern grows out of the first: multi-hospital arrangements may be a surrender to government regulation. They seem to be caused partly by the need to cope with regulation. And . . . they will probably spawn even more regulation, . . . because hospital concentrations—or some forms of them— will have too much power—political and economic—to operate without public safeguards.

Thirdly, I have a number of concerns from the perspective of the patient. Less competition may lead to diminished services. Will powerful multi-hospital systems be responsive to patient complaints? . . . Patient access to care may be adversely affected. . . . I see few consumer safeguards in these new concentrations of power.

Fourth, moving beyond the individual patient perspective, I am concerned about safeguards to local interests as larger, more concentrated systems are developed. . . . Will the differing needs of individual communities be overshadowed by the broader demands of larger systems?

My fifth area of concern is what impact consolidation will have on the physician community. As I said, it will probably increase the leverage of administrators and trustees. Will this cause physicians to close their ranks, too—to integrate, or even unionize, themselves?

Finally, along with positive effects on federal health policy, I can think of some potential negative effects stemming from the multi-hospital trend. Will these new systems coordinate their efforts with health planning mandates, or overpower them? Will the temptation for larger systems to acquire new technology frustrate health planning and cost containment objectives in the long run? And will the tendency to specialize that is inherent in consolidation frustrate federal efforts to promote primary care and family medicine? (p. 3)

The different points of view expressed at this conference led to a follow up statement by the president of the National Council of Community Hospitals. In something of the same vein as Schweiker's remarks, John Horty (1978) wrote an "unabashedly partisan rebuttal" to those rendered by Foley. Excerpts are as follows:

Dr. Foley informs us that the community hospital is dead as a dodo, and that it will be replaced with multi-hospital systems. Unfortunately, in his remarks Dr. Foley exhibits a tremendous bias for bigness and an astonishing lack of doubt that his premise about multi-hospital systems might possibly be incorrect. . . .

Dr. Foley's remarks will bring tears of joy and nostalgia to the managers of such paragons of efficiency as the United States Postal Service, the Penn Central Railroad, not to speak of HEW itself. For each was created on the basis of studies that demonstrated its tremendous potential for efficiency. Bigness can bring efficiency. But it can also bring bankruptcy, either financial or innovative.

Dr. Foley . . . equates "community hospital" with smallness, inefficiency, and ineffectiveness. In truth, the crux of a community hospital is not size, it is that it is rooted in its community, is locally operated, and locally controlled. . . .

It is easier for large institutions to resist HEW. But, it is also easier for HEW to control large institutions. The bureaucrat's life is simplified if he has fewer units to deal with. Freedom and diversity are messy. A host of individual hospitals with varying relationships between each other is difficult for the bureaucratic planner to get his tentacles around. Such a system cannot be charted and categorized and pigeonholed. Because it can't, it must, therefore, be inefficient. . . .

Dr. Foley notes the need for competition between health care units—a goal I enthusiastically share—but he assumes that competition can only be effective between large units. Yet, government planning policy is to abort competition by promoting an oligopoly. I would think government policy would be— or certainly should be—to maximize the number of competing units—not rationalize the few. [pp. 5, 6]

Horty's last comment is at the crux of it: should national policy be further to encourage hospital combinations and even count on such systems to function as planners and allocators in the public interest, substituting for government; or, should national policy be to prevent the various kinds of expolitations outlined by Schweiker and Horty, by maintaining or increasing free competition among community hospitals? If the latter, the way to do so would be to vigorously apply antitrust laws.

Havighurst (1970) asserts that legislatively and professionally conceived trade restraints have prevented the market place from functioning with close to its potential effectiveness, and that restoration of the market regime offers the best hope for solving the nation's health delivery problems. As part of this return, vigorous antitrust enforcement is needed. Regulatory type controls are also needed, according to Havighurst, but should be supplementary and temporary only. Havighurst traces the cause of current dysfunctional regulation in the health field to the medical profession, which he believes has used the guise of quality control and the prevention of unethical practice as a device to suppress competition. Yet it seems unfair to expect the organized profession to have acted against its self-interest. Rather, the fault, he states, lies with well-meaning policy makers who turned many trade restraints into positive laws.

Havighurst worries about the possibility of natural monopolies developing by and among hospitals were various current regulatory controls to be lifted. "That hospitals may sometimes enjoy a natural monopoly seems clear. Scale economies are thought to be substantial up to 250 beds. If two competitors were to exist in a natural monopoly area, in free market theory one of them would eventually drive the other out, barring collusion. One would get a size edge, would be able to lower costs, and would set prices unbearable to the other." In his view, many hospitals have substantial monopoly power. He also admits that the natural monopoly theory does not fully apply to hospitals because most are nonprofit institutions and many of the normal economic assumptions do not hold.

Where the profits in nonprofit hospitals go is open to wide conjecture. Some economists believe that these gains go into status and prestige seeking medical gadgetry and new services that are more than sufficient for the tasks at hand (Lee, 1971). Another view holds that nonprofit hospitals are started by two groups, doctors and trustees, with residual profits from the enterprise going to the doctors since trustees are not equity holders. According to Pauley and Redisch (1973), trustees merely legitimize the hospital to the local community. To Buchanan and Lindsay (1970), this arrangement sets up continuing conflict between medical and administrative personnel. Administrative staff are the trustee's agents, but the medical staff usually holds all the aces and has no incentive to keep hospital costs down. Indeed, it wants high cost equipment and extra staff so that its members can economize on their own time. This leads to general slack and inefficiency. Yet another model emphasizes the distinctive behavior of profit and nonprofit hospitals. Directors of profit-making firms use profits as their measure of management success. In nonprofit firms, owners do not seek additions to wealth, hence managers can pursue policies and practices deviating from profit maximization with fewer consequences (Clarkson, 1972).

All of this is generally an unsettled question, with most analysts and theorists failing to come up with complete models that encompass the behaviors and motivations of trustees, doctors, administrators, and customers (Jacobs, 1974).

Havighurst would not only transform the U.S. health care system to more open market structures, but as a part of this restructuring, would put hospitals on a for-profit basis. His prime tool against the natural monopoly problem would be trustbusting (1970, p. 794).

Current thinking about hospital integrations runs precisely opposite to that highlighted by antitrust laws. This thinking, coupled with the national health policy declared in the Health Services Resource and Development Act, and with the existence of health systems agencies that generally go about encouraging integration in the field, all suggest that government action has pre-empted antitrust application to hospitals.

This is not so. The fact that health systems agencies write plans encouraging hospital integrations is insufficient to avoid antitrust (Starkweather et al., 1979). We will discuss the relationship between trustbusting and regulation in section C.

MERGERS AS INDUSTRY RESTRUCTURING

Industry regulation and industry concentration go hand in hand—regulation raises barriers to market entry, thus reducing the number of small, new firms; yet, established firms often seek regulation (while at the same time espousing free competition) as a protection against unwanted new competitors. Whatever the cause/effect relationship, the advantages of regulated markets always go to the bigger firms.

In most communities some sort of an equilibrium is struck between the forces of competition among several or many hospitals and dominance by a few. Our discussion in connection with Propositions 1 through 3 (chap. 3, B) indicates that this equilibrium constantly changes, moving generally towards greater concentration of power.

Proposition 4a (chap. 3, B) states that mergers will take place in communities where a sufficient number of hospitals permits dominance by a few without eliminating competition. Proposition 4b states that mergers are, therefore, more likely in larger cities and metropolitan areas than in small cities and rural areas. Propositions 11a through d (chap. 3, B) deal with the relationship of institutional power, complementarity, and ability of hospitals to survive independently of merger. Specifically, these propositions state that merger between hospitals of balanced power is a function of their complementarity, that where they are of balanced power and low complementarity few mergers will transpire unless continuance of one or more is threatened, and if continuance is threatened merger will likely result even though complementarity is low and power is imbalanced. Hospitals with low continuance will first vigorously pursue support as autonomous institutions, and not until this possibility has been exhausted will they enter merger.

If these propositions are true because of the interplay of competition and dominance, then much can be said about the future evolution of the hospital industry. Further, if the conditions outlined in Propositions 11 and 13 are the ones that modulate competition (no merger) and dominance (merger), we are a long way toward being able to predict and plan mergers, since the variables included in these propositions are measurable.

Our cases seem to confirm these hypotheses. At Palo Alto-Stanford the merger led to dominance, first of the midpeninsula hospital market and then, potentially, of the medical practice community by the medical school faculty (chap. 4, E). This situation led to efforts by the 150-doctor Palo Alto Medical Clinic to construct its own hospital (chap. 4, E). Failing in this, many community physicians reoriented to a new hospital in a nearby community that had emerged as an alternate. This was a competitive hospital, as illustrated by its acquisition of Palo Alto-Stanford's prized but controversial pathologist (chap. 4, E). In this instance, a hospital merger stimulated several competitive developments.[11]

The premerger circumstances at Palo Alto-Stanford fit Proposition 11a: 1) the two institutions were of relatively balanced power, i.e., similarly sized hospitals each with capable medical staffs and both backed by owners (university, city) with strong financial capacity; 2) there was complementarity, wherein Stanford needed Palo Alto's patients and Palo Alto desired Stanford's super-specialization, and both needed their combined capital asset strength; and 3) both parties were capable of independent survival. Thus, the Palo Alto-Stanford merger was based primarily on complementarity.

Unlike Palo Alto-Stanford, the merger in Seattle took place and still left several competing institutions. Consultant Jones notes in her summary comment to the case study that no opposition nor alternative plans came forth from these other hospitals (chap. 6, D). This merger fits Propositions 11c and 11d: both small hospitals in the Seattle case had previously attempted independent survival—Doctors' through purchase of Maynard Hospital and physical relocation, and Seattle General through investments in a family practice residency and primary care programs (chap. 6, B). Leaders of both hospitals subsequently concluded that these efforts were insufficient, and turned reluctantly to the giant Swedish, recognizing that this was like "two guppies approaching a whale." Doctors' and Seattle General officials nonetheless obtained a modest degree of autonomous survival in the merged-pavilion settlement (chap. 6, C). Complementarity was low between Doctors' and Swedish: they were similar in their size, location, and nature of medical staffs. Nonetheless, they merged because their separate survivals had been threatened. Comparing these two to Swedish, there was high complementarity and obvious imbalance of power between the whale and the guppies. Yet, without this merger the Doctors'-Seattle General combination faced an uncertain future. We can call this a merger based primarily on survival, with complementarity as a supportive factor.

The Norfolk situation is very similar to the Seattle one in respect to both sets of propositions: 1) merger could take place without eliminating competitive hospitals (chap. 9, B); 2) there was a very real threat to Leigh Memorial as a separate hospital; 3) Leigh Memorial first pursued survival independent of merger by investigating relocation to Chesapeake (chap. 9, C); and 4) a take-over consolidation then transpired with Norfolk General. Again a modest degree of continuance was negotiated for Leigh, in the Kempsville satellite plan (chap. 9, C, D). In further support of Proposition 11d, we note the King's Daughters' decline of merger, based on its leaders' assessment that funds could be obtained for reconstruction as an independent entity (chap. 9, B, E).

Our fourth successful merger, Los Angeles County, might be considered irrelevant to these propositions: forces of competition vs. dominance do not apply to a government enterprise since government has a monopoly, and forces working for or against institutional autonomy do not hold since the agencies involved are all parts of a single larger public entity. Even so, the strivings for independent continuance ran strongly through the entire Los Angeles merging process (chap. 8, D), complementarity of functions was important to the original merger rationale (chap. 8, C), and relative power between the departments of hospitals, public health, and mental health was of great concern to the key parties (chap. 8, D).

Our two nonmerger cases also support these several propositions. A merger of Westhaven's and Riviera's hospitals would have eliminated all hospital competition in the region. Dominance by one hospital or another was the hottest issue in the case, with the entire merger at one point hanging in the balance of a single board position (chap. 5, F). The hospital under the greatest threat of survival, Westhaven, vigorously pursued its independent continuance, even while simultaneously pursuing merger, and in its final calculation decided to go it alone, banking strongly on 1) its tax base support for capital funds; 2) an arrangement with Los Medanos County for additional patients; and 3) the knowledge that legal barriers had been eliminated (chap. 5, F). Thus, while the two hospitals were of balanced power and low complementarity (Proposition 11b), and in a community where the intervention of a third party was undoubtedly necessary (though not sufficient) for achievement of merger (Proposition 13b), survival of neither party was threatened sufficiently to drive it to full integration (Proposition 11b).

In Davenport, the merger of St. Luke's and Mercy would have eliminated allopathic hospital competition in the community. Both parties were capable of independent survival—Mercy with backing from its religious order, and St. Luke's with its strong financial position and occupancy (chap. 7, C). The units were of relatively balanced power, and while the planning agency's intervention was initially strong, it lacked effective follow through (chap. 7, E). Neither party could supply an essential lack of the other; i.e., there was no obvious complementarity.

Some Likely Changes

Drawing on our several propositions and review of cases, three types of future mergers can be distinguished. One type is the specialty referral merger, best illustrated by hospital integrations motivated by the needs of medical education. Medical schools expand their teaching realms and obtain referrals, while community hospitals (governmental or nongovernmental) obtain access to high specialization and technology in personnel and equipment. These mergers change market structure by creating fewer enterprises that tend to dominate. There are examples of this kind of merger rationale among our cases: Palo Alto-Stanford's three legged stool philosophy (chap. 4, C), the importance of Norfolk's Medical Center Hospital to the emerging medical school in the Tidewater area, and the wish of Medical Center Hospitals' officials to develop a satellite in Kempsville before a competing proprietary hospital did so (chap. 9, D). This type of merger is likely in the future because of the decline in federal and state funding for medical education, with the consequence that medical schools can no longer depend as much on their own teaching hospitals and must instead develop new arrangements with community hospitals in the area or region.

The second type is the closure/survival merger. The prime motivation here is survival of at least the parts of one or more hospitals that are in economic jeopardy. Mergers of this type are often whale-guppy ones. The effect on industry structure is further concentration, obviously, but not the domination often obtained in the first type. Rather, the whale institutions keep going largely as before, while the guppy institutions are absorbed. Examples of this type include the merger in Seattle of Swedish Medical Center and two small general practice hospitals, and Westhaven-Riviera. This second example points up that closure/survival type mergers need not be of whale-guppy proportions; they may be of guppy-guppy proportions, but not likely whale-whale. Closure/survival mergers are becoming more common, since they are associated with harsh economic times for hospitals.[12] This type will continue to dominate until the basic health economy changes.

The third kind of merger is the utility-status or franchise-motivated type. This type is associated with the combined circumstances of excess hospital capacity and strict certificate-of-need regulation. Certain hospitals want and need to change, but cannot do so through internal growth because franchises cannot be obtained; merger becomes the best alternate strategy. Weak hospitals enter these mergers because it is their only hope of survival. Stronger hospitals do so for either/both of two reasons: 1) to acquire another institution's license in order to eliminate duplication, 2) to obtain a franchised bed and services capacity without having to seek new certificates of need. In either case, the acquired institution is eventually converted to different uses or removed from the licensing roles, with the existing bed franchise now held by the acquiring corporation.

There were hints of this third kind of merger motivation in three of our cases: Norfolk, in its numbers game with the Tidewater health planning agency and the proprietary hospitals (chap. 9, E); Westhaven-Riviera, during the time Westhaven offered to build at Brendham while stipulating a reduced bed franchise for the total area (chap. 5, E); and Seattle, in respect to Swedish's strategy on maternity bed certificates (chap. 6, C) and as regards the two smaller hospitals generally. We can expect more of this kind of merger in the future, assuming the circumstances of excess capacity and certificate of need.

These three types have different impacts on industry structure. In respect to allocation of capital, specialty referral mergers may involve net additions of capital, while survival/closure ones do not, and utility status mergers may reduce capital investments. Unlike the latter two types, specialty referral mergers are not likely to call for internal redistributions of capital, i.e., subsequent reallocations within the merged corporation.

These latter two types also have different impacts on the regionalization of health care delivery. Specialty referral mergers can enhance regionalization of services while survival/closure mergers will likely not. Utility status mergers can enhance regionalized services since the merged corporations are motivated to rationalize services previously unrationalized.

Beyond these changes there is a second order impact of mergers on the structure of the industry—a ripple effect. Since mergers establish a new mix of dominant and dependent hospitals in communities, nonmerged hospitals react, developing new strategies, undertaking new plans, and entering new interhospital negotiations. We have several examples of this in our cases: Davenport's osteopathic hospital moves (chap. 7, C) and the several pursuits of certificates of need in the Norfolk area following the Norfolk General-Leigh Memorial consolidation (chap. 9, E). The best example of the ripple effect is in Seattle, involving events that followed those reported in Secord's case study. When officials of Virginia Mason Hospital, another hospital on First Hill, became worried about their institution's referral base, they established a network of existing small rural hospitals throughout the state of Washington. Then, Virginia Mason acquired the old Doctors' Hospital facility. Both moves seemed calculated better to position Virginia Mason vis-a-vis the consolidated Swedish.

Thus, a long-term consequence of one merger in a community or region is likely to be other integrations. Often, the motives for these integrations are competitive. This is the way the highly decentralized hospital field moves from competition among hospitals to competition among hospital systems. Along the way virtually all interhospital relationships are revised.

These three types of mergers are not pure nor mutually exclusive; there are elements of two or more types in each of several of our case study mergers, as there are in the universe of hospital combinations which our cases represent. Each type represents hospitals' typical responses to circumstances in which they find themselves, illustrating the impact of socioeconomic environments on organizations.

C.   Some Policy Options

Hospital mergers can be stimulated or guided in a variety of ways. One can classify these by level: 1) federal; 2) state; 3) local; and 4) consumers. Further, the variety of possible initiatives also number four: 1) use of reimbursement economics; 2) use of utility regulation; 3) use of planning and education; and 4) stimulation of free market behavior.

The combination of these two categorizations provides us with the framework shown in figure 10.2, and leads us to a discussion of the following four possibilities.

FIGURE 10.2   Some Different Policy Interventions

	LEVEL			
POLICY INTERVENTIONS	FEDERAL	STATE	LOCAL	CONSUMER
Reimbursement Economics	Capital Control Operations			
Utility Regulation		Franchising with Guarantees to Serve Internal Cross-Subsidies		
Planning and Education			HSA Plan Development Trustee Development	
Free-market Behavior				Antitrust Laws The Invisible Hand

FEDERAL GOVERNMENT REIMBURSEMENT
AS A REGULATORY TOOL

This strategy assumes the power of money as a controlling factor residing primarily at the federal level because of Medicare and Medicaid reimbursement leverages. In mid-1978 the administrator of the Health Care Financing Administration hinted that changes in federal policy toward hospital integrations were being considered (Foley, 1978).

> While P.L. 93–641 provides the mandate for innovation, particularly in terms of systems development, financing for the development of multi-institutional systems has not yet been made available. (p. 10)

Federal intervention can take two pathways: control of capital, and thus strategic factors about hospital merger decisions, or control of working funds, and thus operational aspects of hospital affairs. The first of these would be most influential during the initial stages of the merging process, while the latter would apply more to the follow-on stages.[13]

Boston and Edwards (1974) propose a new use of capital reimbursement as a stimulus. They point out that funds invested in merged projects earn no return under current regulations, thus discouraging hospitals from so committing. They suggest that capital could be loaned for mergers and other integrations expected to result in operating economies, with part of the savings resulting therefrom to be used as repayment. The adjustment costs discussed previously (section B.1) pose a problem with this proposal, as economies of scale are not realized for perhaps ten years postmerger. Even so, the strategy could be used to fund portions of consolidations where the sponsors could engineer savings in the shorter run, thus acting as a stimulus for management more effectively to control the costs of transition.

Another plan, offered by Malm (1977), would reward merged systems that can document a record of operational savings with low interest loans for justified expansion or replacement projects. "(This) would help considerably to shorten the length of time that is required for a new system to achieve cost savings . . . and to develop financial strength" (p. 67).

There are several possible sources of these capital investment monies. One is direct loans or loan guarantees from the federal government, issued in a manner similar to loan programs available in the past and currently for various health facilities constructions.[14] A modification would operate either/ both loans and loan guarantees out of a special revolving fund created for the purpose of encouraging and bankrolling integrations. Boston and Edwards describe a federal agency, with an independent advisory committee, that would supervise the fund and make the evaluations necessary for disbursements. Their recommended criteria are 1) rate of return offered by the project, 2) quality and comprehensiveness of care to be offered by the merger, 3) the ability of the institution to implement its plans, and 4) the realism of the projected savings (p. 45). Funds for such projects would be derived by some combination of an initial working capital grant to the revolving fund, loan repayments, and portions of savings obtained that would otherwise have been incurred by hospitals and reimbursed by government. In this way the desired industry restructuring and efficiencies would be stimulated, resulting in social savings.

Funds created for the purpose of stimulating merger activity could also be used for buying up excess hospital beds; the two purposes and activities are closely related.[15] Malm (1977) has suggested that such pools could also be set up by private banks and other financial institutions, through the formation of lending consortia.[16]

Use of loan funds of this sort would respond to an objection voiced about many mergers: one or more parties to merger complain that capital monies secured in one community (from donations, taxation, or hospital operations) and intended for use in a certain facility in that community are diverted elsewhere through merger.[17] There were hints of this in three of our cases. In Seattle, Swedish officials did not want their hospital's debt capacity used for construction of Doctors' and Seattle General's pavilion (chap. 6, C). In Davenport, misunderstandings and strife arose over whether Mercy Hospital's assets were pledged for mortgages obtained by the provincial house for other hospitals (chap. 7, C). The most dramatic example is in the Westhaven-Riviera case: Westhaven officials could not see their tax district resources diverted to out-of-district and private uses; indeed, they challenged the legality of such a plan. Dana Hospital officials did not think they could sell the community, meaning all those who had given money for the existing hospital, on merger if it meant eventual relocation five miles away (chap. 5, D, E).

These objections would be partially overcome were merger financing and/or closing costs derived from funds located outside local communities, as in most debt situations. Optimal use of funds is obtained when capital costs, obtained from whatever sources, are spread across all units in a corporate merger, ensuring that all units in the system[18] will enjoy the benefits of pooling capital costs in a merger. Where capital is obtained from debt, usually the total system is committed to the liability. Even so, this is a bitter merger pill for many merger candidates to swallow: inevitably, the stronger and larger units in mergers feel they are giving up financial leverage in the money markets in order to support the weak—perhaps even the bankrupt. The advantages to them of a larger referral base and the opportunity to reach new people in more effective ways are neither measurable nor obvious.[19]

The second source of federal level economic influence is operating reimbursements. It is often stated that federal (Medicare) reimbursement policy discourages the development of mergers and multiunit hospital systems by its insistence on individual hospital cost submissions: the so-called individual provider number proviso (Malm, 1977). Vraciu and Zuckerman (1978) offer this illustration:

> Medicare limits its liability to hospitals for routine service costs . . . to a particular hospital's relationship to a "peer group" determined by hospital bed size and location. Hospitals above the 80th percentile of their peer group are reimbursed at the 80th percentile. A single hospital within a multiple hospital system may offer a more sophisticated set of services and treat a more complex case mix than independent hospitals of the same size simply because of its ties with other hospitals in the system. Consequently, a hospital in a multiple hospital system may lie at the high end of the distribution and get penalized. [p. 16][20]

Yet, the same policies can provide the opposite motivation. Stromberg (1978) has reported two mergers that were sparked by the same limits Vraciu and Zuckerman claim are barriers. Since the peer groups for which 80th percentile reimbursement limits are set are based in part on bed size, and since higher bed count groups are allowed higher ceilings, a provider can obtain additional reimbursement by upgrading to a larger bed size peer group. One way to do this is through a merger that will obtain a single provider number associated with a larger number of beds—though the actual number of beds is unchanged.

The rationale for current federal policy is provided by Diamond (1978), an official of the Health Care Financing Administration.

> If a merger is a merger in name only, or if the formation of a multi-hospital organization consists merely of creating an umbrella organization over existing hospitals that continue to operate the same way, the superstructure may be a cost inducer rather than a cost saver. In our programs we directly address this issue. . . .
>
> Our current provider certification rules include criteria for determining whether multiple facilities should be considered as single or multiple entities for HCFA program purposes. In order for an entity with multiple components to be treated as a single hospital, the hospital must (1) be subject to the control and direction of one governing body; (2) have a single chief medical officer who reports to the governing body and is responsible for all medical staff activities in all components, (3) demonstrate a total integration of the medical staff by credentialing them without limitation to all components and by having committees that are responsible for their specific areas of concern in all components of the hospital, and (4) have a single executive officer through whom all administrative authority flows and who exercises administrative control of all components.
>
> If the formation of the multi-hospital organization is merely to make easier the raising of capital for merger, acquisition, building or expansion activities, that motivation may not be one to reduce cost but may be a cost inducer. In such a case, there will be an incentive to put the capital to use without substantial risk under cost reimbursement formulas which have relatively liberal depreciation, interest, and other provisions and which many people view as inflationary in nature. [p. 8]

Aside from the question of pseudomerger stressed by Diamond, the individual provider number proviso is a barrier to the commingling of operating funds. This issue is usually strongest in mergers serving a defined region. Those from stronger hospitals often oppose commingling with the same argument applied to operating funds as has been stated about capital funds: "Why should our hospital be bled for the gain of some other hospital? We did not enter this merger to be disadvantaged like that." An objection may also come from smaller, less specialized units: "Why should we be hit (through cost spreading) with those tertiary costs of specialization and teaching that we don't need?"

At issue here is the question of cross-subsidization. The optimal use of capital and operating funds—putting them to use where the greatest need or yield exists—will come with elimination of individual provider numbers that force segregation of funds by requiring separate revenue and cost reports.[21]

With this elimination comes the claim that patients of one facility in a merger are, in some way, subsidizing the care of those in another.

This is not corrected by establishing different rates for different costs at each facility, because most hospitalized patients pay for their care through insurance premiums that spread all costs or charges across all insured patients of the same premium group. So, patients are not likely to know or feel the dollar effect of funds commingling.

The effect is more apparent to providers, in respect to the opportunity to develop new facilities and services. The best example is in the treatment of depreciation. Generally speaking, this is a recognized cost of operation and is reimbursed by governments for Medicare and Medicaid patients, by most Blues which reimburse on the basis of costs, and by indemnity insurance carriers and individual paying patients who pay billed rates that are usually calculated to include such costs. Thus a stream of reimbursed funds flows to each hospital, based roughly on the amount and age of its fixed assets. Unlike other operating reimbursements that are passed through the hospital's operation as payroll and supplies, etc., depreciation funds are retained by the hospital and may be used for some combination of 1) build up of working capital, 2) purchase of new equipment, 3) reserve for future building or equipment needs. Thus, depreciation monies become the major source of discretionary funds for new developments. Each hospital in a merger identified by a separate provider number earns these funds, based on the book value of its fixed assets. Typically, there are widely varying flows between hospitals due to their different sizes, relative plant obsolescence, method of depreciation scheduling, etc. If there is only one provider number for the entire merger these deprecation streams can be commingled, and, at the discretion of those who manage the merged corporation, diverted from the facility that earned them to various uses elsewhere.

An example is the small general practice hospital linked to a large tertiary facility through merger. Without merger, this hospital is in financial jeopardy (chap. 1, C), or cannot deliver the quality and scope of care made possible with merger. But achieving these gains through merger may require diverting funds from elsewhere in the corporation. Conversely, the larger, specialized hospital may need the feeder system provided by the referral of patients from the smaller facility in order to obtain sufficient volume to develop or maintain its specialized services. This kind of cross-institutional exchange is enhanced by merger; the appropriateness and necessity of cross-institutional financing follows.

This view suggests a revision of federal policy, in the form of an addition to Diamond's four criteria described above aimed at recognizing real mergers: single provider numbers should also be allowed for those looser forms of integration, notably umbrella corporations (chap. 1, I), where the integration enhances the regionalization of medical care delivery at a local or area level. Such integrations could readily be distinguished from far flung ones by requiring documentation of the amount of patient care traffic between facilities. Proportions of total number of patients, measured separately for inpatients and outpatients, could be established as qualifying criteria. Such a policy would have the long-term effect of encouraging mergers that are of greater public benefit and discouraging those that either have no potential for this eventuality or are, as Diamond has stated, cost inducers.

The provider number policy is only one form of reimbursement proviso that could be altered in order to provide incentives for certain kinds of mergers. Another would be aimed at controlling the high start-up, transition, or adjustment costs already highlighted (chap. 1, H; chap. 10, B), or separating the costs commensurate with service or quality improvements from those resulting solely from reorganization.[22] This requires establishing comparables for each facility in a new merger, a job that has already been done for purposes of research (chap. 1, H and note 12) and could be done for purposes of reimbursement. Reimbursement relative to the comparables could then be put on an incentive system, in a manner similar to the several proposals for incentive reimbursement to hospitals generally, based on peer grouping. Three possibilities follow:

1) As with some state level rate review procedures, reimbursement for a series of departmental operations could be pegged at the mean unit cost, or some reasonable range of unit costs, for groups of hospitals that included merged ones. The merged hospitals would then gain part or all the difference if their operations were more efficient. The department-by-department approach has the advantage of identifying activities specifically enough to allow vague benefits such as quality enhancement to be isolated for special examination.

2) By using the cost cap method of limiting reimbursement, merged hospitals could be reimbursed only up to the caps set for the pre-merger hospitals, plus adjustments for production factor price rises, etc., according to their comparable group. This would allow more flexibility for merger managers than the departmental review method. However, it is negative regulation; much preferred would be a reimbursement system that also builds in rewards for beating the cost caps.

3) The above two systems could be modified in order to recognize some amount of adjustment cost of a new merger. Reimbursement at above-comparable levels could be authorized for defined percentages and for defined periods of time. If a merged corporation was incorporating different hospitals at different times, each facility could be

identified with a different period, in a manner analogous to a corporation's fixed assets on various schedules of depreciation. Above-average reimbursements could be authorized for certain lengths of time, as could below-average amounts, in recognition of the efficiencies eventually to be gained through merger. Once again, both reimbursement levels could have incentives built in for beating prospectively set targets, as well as penalties for excesses. Any multiyear reimbursement provisos would have to contain inflation adjustments.

These are but a few of the possibilities designed to modify a reimbursement system characterized by Vraciu and Zuckerman (1979) as one in which "the short-run considerations of a third party attempting to minimize its cash outflows may be perpetuating long run system costs associated with overbedding and duplication of services" (p. 18). Our thesis is that policies concerning both capital and operating reimbursements can encourage integrations among hospitals, that such provisos can discriminate between types appropriate for one setting but not for another, and that incentives should be built into the reimbursement policies to stimulate merger managers to take the greatest possible advantage of the many options available to them.

STATE-LEVEL UTILITY STATUS AS A REGULATORY CONTROL

Since hospitals are clothed with the public interest, they are candidates for regulation as public utilities, probably by commissions established by state legislatures (Priest, 1970). Many prefer state level to federal regulation (Somers, 1972); it is closer to home, and can recognize circumstances that vary across states. Many states have recently established rate review or rate setting commissions seen as forerunners of more complete utility-type commissions.

Public utility commissions typically perform three functions: 1) maintenance of safety in the regulated industry, 2) control of quality, and 3) control of market entry and exit. Each of these is already imposed on hospitals in one way or another: maintenance of safety by state government licensure and local government inspections for fire protection, sanitation, etc., quality control by federal government insistence on accreditation as a condition of reimbursement, and certificate-of-need laws at both state and federal levels relating to franchising hospital beds and services. This being so, what would be different or new about state level utility regulation?

For one thing, regulation that is now fragmented and dispersed among dozens of government agencies could be brought together into a single entity. This would presumably yield an economy in the cost of regulation, but more important could lead to a new consistency in control. For another thing, state level utility commissions often develop highly qualified staffs serving well-qualified commissioners, while most of the regulatory agencies on the current hospital landscape are poorly equipped for the tasks put upon them.

Beyond these process-type considerations, two related features of utility-type regulation important to mergers differ structurally from other types of regulation. One relates to guarantee-to-serve provisos, the other to what we have already called internal cross-subsidization.

When franchises are granted to public utilities, the private corporation assumes an obligation to provide all customers in a defined geographic area with a uniform level of service. For example, a telephone line may be expensive to run to a remotely located customer, but that does not excuse the telephone company from the obligation to serve that customer. The analogy to health care delivery is obvious.

Each franchised company, then, has some areas that are expensive to serve, and other areas that can be served efficiently. The former are usually sparsely and the latter densely populated. If rates are set at levels below costs for the first set of customers and above costs for the second, the result is internal subsidization of the first group of customers by the second. This is generally the practice in utility regulation, and distinguishes this form of social control from other forms in which the subsidization of difficult to reach or high-cost customers comes from external sources such as government grants (Posner, 1971). In both internal and external subsidization there is redistribution of the cost burden of service; in the former it is done through rate regulation and in the latter through taxation. This means that rate calculation is a crucial activity in utility-type regulation; for hospitals, this feature would differ from the present dispersed pattern of control that generally uses cost reimbursement as the economic leverage.

Two technical aspects of state-level utility regulation have particular relevance to hospital mergers: 1) what corporate entity is to be licensed, and 2) when should franchising or refranchising be considered?

The unit to which a state grants a license is the unit to which it looks for performance and accountability. When an integration occurs, and depending on the type, the state may license the new corporation or license each of the separate facilities that have entered the consolidation. In hospital integrations, the license often remains with the separate facilities, since a hospital license requires an organized medical staff, and other professionals, while several loose forms of hospital integration do not reorganize medical staffs (chap. 1, J) and even in full corporate mergers there will often remain separate medical staffs tied to existing facilities (chap. 4, C). Yet, a newly merged corporation is likely to be capable of fulfilling the obligations of a regulated utility, notably those relating to an assurance of service to all persons in a geographically defined area. It follows that the merged corporation should become the licensee, which would give it the flexibility to make the shifts in both finances and services implicit in the concept of internal cross-subsidization. In the hospital field, a corporation could not perform as a utility without integration of its medical as well as administrative components. Here is the rub, yet also the opportunity.

The theory and practice of utilities assumes control exists not only of market entry but also of market exit. In order to maintain public service, utilities may not abandon service at whim, or even with good economic justification. Particularly in transportation, commissions commonly require continuation of service despite pleadings by the carrier to abandon. In the extreme case of bankruptcy, there are usually provisions of temporary operation by the commission or by operators designated by the commission until a satisfactory new franchisee comes forth or can be located. Indeed, the likelihood of such failures often stimulate mergers.

Whenever there is a sale of a company in a regulated industry the commission has the option of withholding or granting a new franchise; it insists on this in order to be sure the new owner is capable of public service. All parties know this in advance, sales are usually made conditional on it, and refranchising provides opportunities more frequently than would otherwise obtain for public intervention in the conduct between private corporations serving the public.

Again, the parallels to hospital mergers are obvious: the use of market exit as well as market entry controls, coupled with refranchising provisos at time of corporate changes in ownership, could be strong public policy leverages. Specifically, franchises or refranchises could be granted only to mergers prepared to undertake certain needed services in a given area or region. Such services could be determined well in advance through effective planning by health planning agencies or by the utility commission, and known to all parties of interest. Some examples of such merger follow:

1) Franchise mergers that are committed to effectiveness-type changes as well as efficiency-type gains as a simultaneous rather than sequential development. This is often the difference between horizontal and vertical integrations (chap. 1, I), and the specialty referral and closure/survival mergers discussed previously in this chapter. From a public policy point of view this has the appeal of enhancing the role corporate reorganization plays in improving local or regional health care delivery systems.

2) Franchise mergers that are committed to redistribution or regionalization of scarce medical personnel, and demonstrate the capacity to do such.

3) Franchise mergers that are committed to reducing excess bed capacity, or are committed to redistributing bed capacity to provide the proper hierarchy of dispersed general hospital beds and concentrated tertiary service beds, and the proper mix of acute, subacute, and ambulatory care services.

4) Franchise mergers that are committed to channeling technology to increase access to medical care by underserved persons, or to advancing the health status of persons in the area of service.

As an example, several of these options could be applied to integration between large referral hospitals, typically in cities, and small hospitals, typically in rural areas (i.e., specialty referral type). As we have noted, political equity often dictates that small rural hospitals be continued as autonomous institutions, while rational health care planning often concludes that these facilities should either 1) be closed, 2) be closed in favor of ambulatory care services, or 3) be continued only as part of a hierarchy of functionally linked hospitals. Again, those who regulate via the utility approach can choose either 1) to franchise a nonregionalized hospital merger and let a hospital destined for a marginal future (in quality and efficiency) cease for lack of external support; or 2) to franchise a regionalized hospital merger with enough beds to serve the region but with certain agreements that the merged corporation would redistribute the total bed complement into a functional hierarchy. In another case the best choice might be to franchise a regionalized-type merger with a reduced total bed capacity, knowing that such would lead to expansions in certain locations where population growth and technological capacity warrant, and conversions to nonhospital substitutes in other locations where hospital operations are no longer warranted.

One questions whether hospital corporations could or would come forth with the commitments called for in situations like this. Certainly their capacity to respond would show great variation. Yet, the power of the utility approach is that rates can be set to make such possible: the inducements can be provided. More basic questions are those of underlying social philosophy: where should the burden of costs rest, and how resources should be redistributed.

LOCAL EFFORTS

It is always tempting to assign opportunities or responsibility for important change to higher levels of government, when in fact change is usually rooted in the local situation. We have chronicled the long-run failure of federal laws to achieve a regionalization of hospitals and other providers, and the more recent shortcomings in implementation of the goals of the National Health Resources and Development Act relating to hospital integrations. And, we have asserted the meaninglessness of the linking assumption without the capacity to implement it at the local level.

All of these suggest the indispensability of local strength in matters of health care reorganization. Two broad options exist for local development: (1) further development of health system agency (HSA) planning and regulating capacity, and (2) further development of hospital governance capacity. They conflict, to a degree, because powers vested in HSAs are generally those previously vested in hospital boards, and the strengthening of HSAs is seen as the weakening of hospital boards (Starkweather, 1975). The notion that both should be strong and effective—indeed, synergistic—is an attractive one.

The HSA pathway of policy development on hospital mergers rests largely in the development of local health systems plans, as mandated by the law that created the agencies. These plans could contain specific provisos about hospital closures, mergers, and other integrations, to the point of naming specific hospitals, services, and geographies.[23] The challenge seems to be to develop enough sophistication in HSAs to ensure that such provisos constitute real targets for action rather than vague generalities or "wish" lists.

One example of the required planning sophistication is the two stage/ one stage strategy discussed previously in this chapter: the safety of planned gradualism, with the possibility of lower ultimate gain, vs. the likelihood of initial high integration costs, in behalf of a more worthwhile end result. Another example is the analysis of industry structure that would be effected by merger, also discussed previously in this chapter (sec. B).

Even granting the difficulty HSAs have in dealing with these subtleties, accomplishment is more likely at this lower level than at higher levels, and argues for a strong local approach to the merging phenomenon.

The other approach is to strengthen hospital boards' ability to discern and deal with the potentials of merging. This approach, generally associated with the virtues of volunteerism, is espoused by hospital organizations. An editorial note appearing in *Hospitals* (1974), the official journal of the American Hospital Association, states that many voluntary community hospitals, faced with duplication and fractionalization of their services, are now willing to share their trusteeship with like community institutions (p. 39). An experienced merger administrator, Donald Rosenberger (1966), has stated:

> Hospital mergers result when civic leadership and hospital trustees and physicians reach a consensus that better hospital care can be achieved through coordination of existing programs and the consolidation of community resources. If, as is the usual case, the trustees represent the strongest civic leadership, they can be expected to recognize the need to reconcile differing interests for the sake of broader needs of the community. [pp. 86, 87]

Another administrator experienced in mergers, Robert Sigmond (1978), believes that development of hospital governance is one of the most important challenges of the multihospital system trend. He suggests that there is a dynamic, beneficial tension between local hospital and system boards (which assumes that local boards should be preserved in mergers). Further, he suggests a new balance of inside and outside directors to provide for both a strengthening of boards and a balancing of local parochialism where only inside directors are seated. To some these expressions seem naive or self-serving; to others they represent a firm conviction that local hospital trusteeship is the bedrock of a hospital system that would otherwise become unstable.

Our cases are instructive. In two, Palo Alto-Stanford and Norfolk, the trustees were entirely capable of identifying and working toward the total community betterment (chap. 4, C; chap. 9, F). In another, Westhaven-Riviera, the trustees had difficulties seeing their way to the larger good, based seemingly in both their lack of knowledge and their institutional values (chap. 5, E). The trustees of the three hospitals in Seattle were between these extremes: their latent sense of total community trusteeship needed development and guidance, which was provided in part by a consultant (chap. 6, C).

Many planners believe that education would make a difference: education leads to changes in outlook which in turn lead to behavior modification. This possibility suggests an avenue of development that moderates between the two extremes of emphasis on HSA regulation—that hospitals must be forced into integrations that better serve a community, and that hospital trustees hold the community in trust as well as their individual institutions. This middle strategy calls for HSAs to provide the forum for both education of and discussions between hospital trustees on the advantages and disadvantages of merger or other forms of integration. Board members and staffs of HSA's would also benefit, since they are often ignorant of the realities of institutional survival which hospital directors must address. This simple suggestion is neither new nor dramatic. (It is the main recommendation stemming from Morris' (1963) early and excellent study of interhospital relations in the context of community planning agencies.) It is perhaps surprising that such is not routine planning agency and trustee behavior; yet, the political dynamics between regulators and regulatees render this an unusual occurrence: the prevailing mood is one of mutual mistrust.

The challenge seems to be to create, inform, and maintain the forum for discussion. This is one way of enhancing local strength and ability to deal intelligently with the hospital merging phenomenon.

THE OPTION OF CONSUMER CHOICE IN A FREE MARKET

We have described previously in this chapter (sec. B) the differing views on whether hospital combinations advance the public interest or result in undue private gain at consumers' expense. Increasing consumers' options would require shifting the hospital industry away from government regulation and towards a free market economy where competition and choice could flourish. One instrument of national policy and procedure for doing such is trustbusting.

Three federal antitrust laws might be applied to hospital mergers: the Sherman Anti-Trust Act, the Clayton Act, and the Federal Trade Commission Act. Two features of these laws run contrary to the common impression. One is that they are not confined to for-profit corporations; the other is that their definition of a market, for purposes of examining relative dominance, may be as small as a single community—it need not be an interstate or national market. In the past, hospital officials contemplating merger have ignored these federal laws, on the legal ground that hospital activities are not matters of interstate commerce and therefore beyond their reach.[24] None of our six cases considered the antitrust implications of merger.

This indifference was justified by a series of court decisions, starting in the 1930s and 40s, that put hospitals beyond the reach of federal antitrust laws. But all that was before May 24, 1976, when the U.S. Supreme Court ruled in the case of Hospital Building Company vs. Rex Hospital (1976). The plaintiff, Hospital Building Company, operated a 49-bed proprietary hospital in North Carolina. The company brought antitrust action against Rex Hospital and the local health planning agency for violation of the Sherman Act, charging that these parties had conspired to control the total number of beds in the community, were monopolizing the market, and generally restraining the business of providing hospital services—all through blocking authorizations under certificate-of-need procedures. In brief, the company alleged that this cartel in the marketplace was doing exactly what many researchers and professionals say merged hospitals and multihospital systems should do: act as planners, allocators, and controllers of hospital resources in a community or region. The case went to the U.S. Supreme Court, which did not decide on the merits, but ruled that hospital activities are interstate in nature. This reversed the previous precedents; hospital mergers were now within the jurisdiction of federal antitrust laws.

One agency of enforcement under these laws is the U.S. Justice Department, which monitors the national economy and selects industries for aggressive attention. The department's enforcement activities are guided by a feature of the Clayton Act which defines anticompetitive effect as that which brings about substantial lessening of competition, or tendency toward monopoly. The department has separate guidelines for horizontal integrations, vertical integrations, and conglomerates.

With respect to horizontal mergers, the department's activities have the following interrelated purposes: 1) preventing elimination of any firm as an independent entity likely to be a substantial competitive influence in a market, 2) preventing any firm or small group of firms from obtaining a position of dominance in a market, 3) preventing significant increase in concentration in a market, and 4) preserving significant possibilities for eventual deconcentration in a concentrated market. The department regards a market as highly concentrated if the share of the four largest firms in that market amounts to 75 percent or more. If this is the case, the department ordinarily goes into the courts to challenge any further integrations in that market. The department will not make an exception to these guidelines based on claims of economies of scale, since there are usually severe difficulties in accurately establishing the real magnitude of claimed savings, particularly with respect to the consumer.

With respect to both horizontal and vertical mergers, the department pays particular attention to those involving new entrants into a market, since competition is seen as the greatest limitation on the exercise of market dominance by existing leading firms. The department will usually challenge any merger between a likely entrant and 1) any firm with more than 25 percent of the market, 2) either firm of a two-company combination with a combined share of over 50 percent, and 3) any of the top four firms of an eight-firm combination that shares over 75 percent of the market, provided the merging firm's share is in excess of 10 percent.

Table 10.1 shows the effect of four of our case study mergers on hospital industry concentration.

TABLE 10.1.   Degree of Industry Concentration
Produced by Four Mergers

Case	Definition of Market	Percentage of market (Non-government, General Acute Care) Held by Largest Hospital	
		Before merger (%)	After merger* (%)
Westhaven-Riviera	Eastern Los Medanos County	60	100
Seattle	First Hill area	27	47
Davenport	Scott County	40	79
Norfolk	City of Norfolk	48	58

*This assumes the Westhaven-Riviera and Davenport mergers took place.

Three other examples are instructive. In Richmond, Virginia, in 1972, one of the national investor-owned corporations constructed an acute hospital which subsequently assumed 11 percent of the inpatient days (market share) of that city. The same corporation owned another hospital in Richmond which controlled 18 percent. This produced a situation where the four largest non-governmental producers of hospital care in Richmond controlled 79 percent of the market—well within the Justice Department's guidelines for a highly concentrated market. Were another merger in Richmond to be challenged, a decision would likely hinge on the question of submarket or product differentiation. Hospital patient days are not homogeneous, but are composed of surgical, pediatric psychiatric days, etc. Further, patient days are not the only product of hospitals; there are emergency and outpatient visits, laboratory and radiology procedures, pharmacy prescriptions, etc. The extent to which each of these is considered a submarket or a separate product would be crucial.

Another example is the Kaiser Medical Program, the nation's prototype HMO. The Justice Department's view of Kaiser would be one of a vertically integrated combination of hospitals, doctors and health insurance, which controls a substantial portion of the marketplace of several communities of the western United States. This domination exceeds 40 percent in some local markets. Private antitrust action might be brought by other hospitals or by doctors not affiliated with Kaiser, against any further Kaiser acquisitions. (This would be a strange reversal of history, since in the 1930s it was Kaiser that brought action against medical societies for interfering in the right of Kaiser doctors to practice medicine by limiting hospital medical staff privileges and medical society memberships.)

In Delaware, the Wilmington Medical Center is a merger of three previously separate hospitals which represent 85 percent of the acute care hospital beds in the city of Wilmington and the County of Newcastle (Brown and Lewis, 1976). The eight general hospitals in the state of Delaware comprise slightly over 2,000 beds, and over 1,000 belong to the Wilmington Medical Center.[25]

These examples assume a local as compared to a regionally or nationally defined market. The numerous hospital combinations spanning relatively large regions, notably Catholic and other religious chains, and investor-owned hospital combinations, appear to be immune. Only if their conduct in a local market were to contribute to increased concentration to the degree outlined above would they be in antitrust jeopardy.

If situations like our cases and the above three illustrations were to be brought to court, the arguments would likely center on three legal issues. One would be the rule of reason, established in 1911 by the U.S. Supreme Court, providing that a combination cannot be held illegal just because it restrains trade, since all combinations to a greater or lesser degree do so. The test is whether the public service rendered by the proposed combination does not unreasonably restrain trade. Many integrations have been approved under this doctrine. The key question would be: "What are the public interest effects of further restricting competition among hospitals?," "Does the merger result in effects favorable to the public interest?," and "Do the public benefits from merger outweigh the effects of restricting competition?" Some of the public benefits to be argued for hospitals would be the gains derived from improved coordination, increased services, managerial efficiency, enhanced quality, and support for education. It would appear that hospital combinations in small cities and rural communities, consisting typically of small hospitals with limited services, would find defense in this rule. For others, arguments in support of the public benefit would be diminished by the lack of tangible evidence, while the mere proof of market concentration might be controlling, since only the tendency or possibility of offending the public interest need be demonstrated.

A second issue would be hospitals' inherent tendency. Since most hospitals are nonprofit, it can be argued that they do not possess the motivations leading to the consumer exploitation which antitrust laws seek to prevent. In the nonprofit sector, it is said that decisions are based solely on improved service and/or reduced cost, while in the for-profit sector, decisions are based on profit motivation alone, without concern for the public interest.

These questions are extremely difficult to settle, with conclusions usually based less on fact and more on judgment and force of argument. Phillip Areeda (1972) states:

> The key difficulty for anti-trust agencies is the claim that competition is not possible nor practical or not fully responsive to the social interest. Such claims are properly viewed with skepticism, for there never has been an anti-trust sinner who did not claim that he was serving the public good. But the claim is sometimes true, and an obvious saving in social resources can effectively immunize what would otherwise be an unlawful restraint of trade. The antitrust division, the Federal Trade Commission, and the courts face the unenviable task of distinguishing good from bad when both are indistinct. The essential fact of life is that data about the past, predictions about the future, and judgments about anything are not always extant, costless, reasonably obtainable, or very reliable. Furthermore, decisionmakers everywhere are of mixed quality and sometimes of no quality at all. [pp. 52, 53]

The third issue would be whether government has preempted any antitrust applications by establishing strict regulation. The evidence for this would be the detailed system of cost-based reimbursement by government, coupled with certificate-of-need laws at both federal and state levels. However, the mere presence of these regulations does not void the application of antitrust laws. The courts have distinguished between actions that are a government priority but cannot be said to be mandated. The standards set down in two 1976 Supreme Court cases would probably not qualify hospital mergers for a state action exemption to antitrust laws (Cantor, 1976; Ottertail Power, 1976). Health systems agencies can encourage mergers but they generally cannot command them. The difference is crucial.[26]

In short, it is now clear that federal antitrust statutes can reach local hospital mergers. Further, the application of state laws also seems likely; there is generally an open field at the state level, and there is marked variation in statutes. The possibility of legal action at both levels is enhanced by the substantial confusion concerning the extent of real competition in various segments of the hospital industry and the lack of documented evidence as to the real benefits of mergers.

There are both strong similarities and contrasts between control by regulation and by antitrust: the consumer's interest is the underlying purpose in both methods, yet assumptions about the feasibility of free competition differ in the two modes. Government regulation assumes that free and real competition does not exist. Either an industry is regulated in order to preserve competition, as is said to be the goal in the transportation industry, or it is regulated to control natural monopolies as in the telephone and power industries. Many persons immersed in government regulation of hospitals make these same assumptions, and conclude that antitrust laws have little bearing on the field. That assumption is erroneous, according to Areeda (1972).

Areeda starts instead with the assumption that antitrust laws are an expression of a broad national policy favoring competition, rooted in the nation's political and economic history. Deviations from the free market model should be undertaken only as exceptions to this general rule. Such a policy should be given appropriate weight by regulatory bodies even though they have the power to grant exemptions.

One approach to expressing this would be to stipulate that regulators value competition to the extent consistent with regulatory goals. This is reasonably straightforward where the regulatory premises are unambiguous, but they seldom are. Regulation of airlines is an example. Are airlines regulated in order to give the public the benefits of competition in the absence of a perfectly competitive market structure? Or does regulation seek the development of more elaborate equipment through cartel pricing that diverts competitive motives into a preoccupation with service and equipment variations? Or is the purpose to support rates between major markets in order to provide sufficient carrier revenues to subsidize services to unprofitable destinations? The analogy to the hospital industry is obvious.

Another policy might be that the existence of regulation supersedes antitrust law: a regulatory commission would become the exclusive judge and enforcer of the competitive rules of the game. This has the virtue of simplicity.

But improper conduct could no longer be challenged directly by injured parties; they could complain to the commission but would have no independent remedy in the courts. In place of impartial, disinterested, and skeptical judges, decisions would be made by administrators who, as Areeda notes, sometimes grow too close to their regulated clients.

A final approach could be that since regulatory and antitrust objectives are ultimately similar—as much competition as is practicable consistent with economic and technical imperatives of efficiency—judicial and regulatory guidelines about hospital mergers should be brought into closer alignment. Yet, while the basic court standard of the rule of reason is supposed to take into account an industry's particular circumstances, an agency charged with supervising that industry is presumably more knowledgeable and more expert, and thus better able than the courts to judge the reasonableness of competitive or anticompetitive behavior. The question is, then, who is best able to make an intelligent judgment about market behavior? Hospital regulators may know more, but the courts may be more appropriately objective. Areeda concludes: "The fundamental truth is this: the decision to approve or disapprove a given (merger) will often depend upon the perceptions and 'institutional' outlook of the decision-maker in the light of what he considers most important. Thus, who decides will often determine what is decided" (p. 51).

This brief discussion of antitrust is not designed to imply that there is no public gain to be realized in many communities through hospital consolidation; nor is it designed to suggest that the current dominant method of social control of hospitals—government regulation—will be totally abandoned in favor of antitrust mechanisms.

However, it does serve the purpose of pointing out that there is a limit to the appropriate degree of concentrated power among hospitals, particularly since so little is known about the real effects. Both the U.S. Justice Department and the U.S. Federal Trade Commission are examining this question; either or both can decide that there is undue concentration or the potential for such, and aggressively pursue hospital mergers. Not all mergers are in the public interest per se, given that abuses resulting from concentration of institutional power are as possible in the health care field as they are in other realms, given that provider domination of health organizations in the prevailing situation, given that consumers are relatively ignorant and unqualified to judge medical and hospital matters, given that countervailing economic forces which may exist in many realms of commerce are blunted in medical care markets by health insurance, despite the charitable institution status of most U.S. hospitals.

D.   SUMMARY AND DISCUSSION

In this chapter we have tested a number of propositions stated earlier in the

book relative to the environmental forces that dictate whether hospital mergers will take place. We have also discussed the advantages and disadvantages
of mergers relative to the larger system of U.S. medical care organization.
Finally, we have outlined some of the existing public policy options and potential initiatives to be taken vis-a-vis hospital mergers. A few generalizations
can be teased out of all of this.

We know far less than we should about the real benefits and the real
costs of various forms of hospital integration, given the magnitude of the trend
and the decibels of the rhetoric. There is no substitute for the results of large
scale and systematic research. The National Center for Health Services Research and Development should fund longitudinal studies of both specific sets
of mergers and of the impact of mergers on the more general structure of
U.S. medical care delivery. A research agenda has been proposed (Frawley
et al., 1978; Levy and Kominski, 1980).

Our reconsiderations of section C indicate that hospital mergers are
benefits, mixed benefits, or detriments depending on the community or region
of application. Whatever the gain from more research, mergers will always
require the thoughtful and careful application of findings to each specific
situation, as well as ample doses of good judgment.

In general, our six cases support the eleven propositions examined thus
far: the factors included in the propositions were present in mergers that
transpired and absent in those that did not. Even so, it is clear that the
variables described by these propositions do not entirely capture the merging
process. Our cases suggest that the residuals run to the personal leadership
that is either present or missing in a situation, and the interpersonal chemistry
of the key parties involved. Examples of these are: 1) the personal leadership
of Kauffman at Norfolk (chap. 9, D), of Dupar at Seattle (chap. 6, C), and of
Gluba at Davenport (chap. 7, D), and the absence of strong hospital or community leadership at Westhaven-Riviera; and 2) the interpersonal chemistry
of the "three families" of Palo Alto-Stanford (chap. 4, B), the "southern family" members at Norfolk (chap. 9, D), the subgovernment in Westhaven
(chap. 5, B), and the interaction of department heads Witherill, Brinkman,
and Heidebrand in Los Angeles (chap. 8, G).

Hospital mergers are enormously complex; by definition the predictive
variables will be numerous, widely different in character, and in some cases
obscure. In this chapter we have concentrated on the structural variables
necessary for merger to transpire. But while these are necessary, they are
not sufficient. Additional and more idiosyncratic process factors are also important. Structural features provide the organizational stage and the backdrop; without them, there will be no drama. Just as surely, the right players
and the right unfolding of acts are also essential.

It is these process factors that we address in the next chapter.

NOTES

1. This is something of an overstatement. In some areas RMP agencies worked closely with local and state health planning agencies to develop models and criteria for regionalization of hospital services. Also by the mid-70s some useful "Hospital Categorization Guidelines" (1975) had been developed through a grant by Regional Medical Programs to the Joint Commission on Accreditation of Hospitals. These optimal criteria for hospital resources for the care of patients with heart disease, cancer, stroke, and end-stage kidney disease were designed to advance, among other things, a cohesive, regional stratified system. The publication was intended to guide, and not to regulate standards; it thus had little direct impact. The methodology used in developing the criteria was picked up by numerous planning agencies and fashioned into certificate-of-need criteria for various specialized services and facilities. Something of the same approach was also used in 1978 by HEW Secretary Califano in issuing guidelines for certificate-of-need activity by planning agencies, as mandated by Congress in the National Health Resources and Development Act of 1975.

2. In a due process case involving certificate of need, a hospital appealed the refusal of a health systems agency to issue a certificate for rebuilding as an autonomous institution. The agency's denial was based on a finding that the hospital had failed to demonstrate cooperation with two adjacent hospitals, as mandated by the National Health Resources and Development Act. The hospital's appeal was upheld, on grounds that the agency's action was not properly founded.

3. This finding is the same as Mosher's (1967), in his cross case study of numerous government agency mergers and other reorganizations. He found that many reorganizations had been structurally effective, yet the evidence of substantive effectiveness remained elusive. He identified four factors that made substantive evaluation difficult: 1) subjective weighting of multiple and complex goals and objectives; 2) qualitative and largely subjective appraisal of results; 3) costs of reorganization which often offset gains; and 4) lags which prevented the early detection of most changes.

4. Personal conversation, John Aird, President, San Jose (California) Health Center, September 28, 1977.

5. If each of the shared services revealed by the survey reported by Astolfi and Matti were to yield a 20 percent gain in efficiency, the maximum possible gain in total hospital operations would be approximately 3 percent.

6. Even so, at Palo Alto-Stanford there were duplication costs in radiology services necessary to the equity of two medical staffs (chap. 4, C, 3). And, in Seattle the merged pavilion solution (chap. 6, C, 10) undoubtedly increased costs over what they would have been with a total physical integration of the two smaller hospitals with big Swedish.

7. Sam Tibbetts, quoted in "Looking Around . . ." *Modern Hospital*, February 1973, p. 14.

8. However, several of the nationwide investor-owned chains have recently moved to strong regionalized divisions.

9. Note for instance the final paragraphs of the numerous case descriptions in *Hospital Management Systems* by Brown and Lewis (1976).

10. An organization process model suggested by Thompson (1974) comes closest to explaining this impact of technology. He asserts that, increasingly, complex interdependencies are required by more sophisticated technologies. Homer and

Smith (1978) apply Thompson's conceptualization to the health field. Their comments are made in connection with an insightful analysis of merger dynamics in "Urban City." In 1963 Elling wrote "The Hospital Support Game in Urban City," and thirteen years later Homer and Smith updated the situation in "The Hospital Support Game Revisited." This sequence provides a longitudinal analysis of great value.

11. To be sure, the burgeoning population of the midpeninsula area in the 1960s could support if not warrant a second hospital. The point is that additional hospital services were provided through a second autonomous hospital, not as increments at Palo Alto-Stanford.

12. This type has been widely discussed as a solution to the problems facing New York City's hospital system (William, 1976).

13. The discussion that follows in this section deals with interventions that would generally require new federal legislation. These changes are thus broader and more sweeping than others that could be introduced within existing federal law, by altering the details of administrative implementation. Starting in mid-1978, staff members of the Health Care Financing Administration and of the American Hospital Association started exchanging ideas and proposals for altering the existing regulations for Medicare cost reimbursement. Several of these ideas are included in notes 14, 15, 16, 20, 21, and 22.

14. Flanagan (1978) complains that "the capital financing vehicles presently available to hospitals are not conducive to consolidations. For example, the FHA program does not contemplate the guarantee of debt incurred to acquire an existing facility" (p. 7).

15. Diamond (1978) suggests that closing costs, in the case of hospitals entering merger, might include severance pay, physician contract cancellation costs, and the purchase of pension rights. Other federal officials (Discussion Paper, 1978) have suggested cost allowances for moving equipment, demolition costs of closing an old facility, and selling and legal expenses relating to merger.   .

16. The suggestions of Boston, Edwards and Malm all call for new forms of venture capital. The ideas of federal officials are much less expansive and promotive, born undoubtedly from their concerns over both excess hospital capacity and cost escalation. Accordingly, a paper developed in late 1978 contained these ideas (Discussion Paper, 1978): "The potential regulatory changes which are discussed below provide for the reimbursement of previously uncovered consolidation costs of individual hospitals or groups of hospitals as well as selective exemptions to reimbursement ceilings for those consolidation costs. These more generous reimbursement rules would only be applied if the consolidation activity in question has planning agency approval and results in a net reduction in reimbursable costs. . . . These regulation changes will be subject to the following conditions or controls that will ensure that proper cost savings and containment will result: total discontinuance of an (acute care hospital) inpatient service; discontinuance of an identifiable unit (floor, wing) of a hospital; conversion of part or all of a facility to a lower level of care, e.g., intensive care to general patient care; acute care to nursing home care. . . . The merger or consolidation must be approved by the Health Systems Agency. This will insure that adequate health care will still be available in a given area even if a merger takes place. . . . The activity must be cost effective over a specified period of time, e.g., 5 years. The costs of the consolidated facility, including the reimbursement not previously provided, should not exceed the costs prior to consolidation. . . . Under current regulations, if a provider closes all or part (wing, floor) of its

institution the cost of any space that is deemed to be in excess of normal stand by cost is not reimbursable by Medicare. This rule often encourages providers to keep a section (or the entire institution) open and receive reimbursement for depreciation and maintenance costs on it even though it may be highly inefficient to do so. As an incentive to help providers consolidate their operations or merge with underutilized institutions, HCFA is considering allowing out-of-pocket costs (taxes, interest, maintenance) or out-of-pocket costs plus a depreciation allowance for a partially or totally closed facility even if the closed space is in excess of normal stand by requirements and the costs involved are not directly related to patient care. . . . In the case of asset demolition or abandonment (permanent retirement of an asset for any future purpose as well as relinquishing all rights, title etc., to the asset), the Medicare Bureau is in the process of tightening the rules on the payment of any remaining depreciation. Under current regulations, all undepreciated costs of the demolished or abandoned assets are reimbursed in a lump sum. More favorable treatment could be provided in instances where permanent retirement of an asset is part of a merger or consolidation effort. The lump sum payment currently recognized under Medicare principles could be retained in a merger situation as long as this payment were used in providing patient care services or facilities approved by the Health Systems Agency" (pp. 5, 6).

To some of these ideas, a staff member of the American Hospital Association offered the following comments (Flanagan, 1979): "The first provision indicates that incentive payments may occur for discontinuance of an identifiable unit. Although the potential for cost savings theoretically appears in such a situation, practical experience has shown that the discontinuance of a unit has generally not reduced overall cost. Generally, existing fixed and overhead expenses cannot be substantially reduced. Providing an incentive to close units is, therefore, of questionable merit. . . . An incentive payment for the conversion of a part or all of a facility to a lower-level care facility does offer encouragement. The concept of the swing-bed is related to this. The industry has so far met with little success in achieving an incentive or regulatory relief to achieve this and this concept needs additional attention. . . . It appears the program is trying to entice hospitals into total or partial closure by paying for such costs as taxes and maintenance. These costs are minute in comparison to total or partial closure costs. The proposal is silent on such matters as severance and other types of costs involving employees, and debt service retirement. If the HCFA is truly trying to accomplish a reduction of system capacity, it must take these and other costs into consideration in formulating a policy. . . . Tightening the rules on payment of any remaining depreciation may result in litigation. The industry would take an extremely firm stance that depreciation under generally accepted accounting principles be paid and recognized by the federal programs. The suggested treatment for permanent retirement of assets in a merger or consolidation effort is a positive one. However, it is basically the same as providers are now receiving" (Flanagan, 1979, pp. 2, 3).

17. In the extreme there is the case of charitable trusts and endowments that have been provided with stipulations concerning local use. Even if local use is not specified there may be legal problems, usually involving states' attorneys general in their roles as supervisors of such trusts (Stromberg, 1978).

18. An official of Kidder-Peabody has documented the reductions of 10–20 percent in cost of capital for loans granted to multihospital systems, over comparable nonmerged facilities (Hernandez, 1978).

19. In the long run the larger units in a merger usually get more capital funds anyway, due to their greater need for expensive technologies.
20. Flanagan (1978) suggests that the solution to this problem is for the Medicare Bureau to "publish specific guidelines for these types of hospitals to seek exceptions from routine cost limitations and thereby not inhibit their growth" (p. 6).
21. The peculiar effect of individual provider number requirements is illustrated by Flanagan's (1978) complaint: "The related organization regulation concerning interest expense also hinders the development and maintenance of multihospital systems. This occurs because of Medicare denial of reimbursement for interest expense on loans negotiated between units of the system and/or central organizations. Medicare has taken the position that if any component of a multihospital system has sufficient capital to "give" another component, interest expense on the loan negotiated between the components is not recognizable. Thus, any incentive for a system which has temporary excess cash reserves to loan money at rates equal to or less than prevailing rates is lost. Rather, the individual component will seek outside sources for its loans, because only these loans are recognized by Medicare. This again, increases patient cost and reduces cash management efficiencies for a multihospital system. . . . An interesting aside is that if a single institution borrows for non-capital expenditures from its own depreciation fund it can charge and be reimbursed for interest expense. However, if that institution borrows from the depreciation fund of a sister hospital no interest expense is allowed for Medicare cost finding." (p. 3)
22. Flanagan (1978) has put hospitals' point of view as follows: "Start up organizational expenses are not reimbursable as incurred under present regulations. This, combined with the prohibition against the build up of equity funds, is a definite impediment to the formulation of a true multihospital system. The occurrence of such cost during the initial stages of organization is a certainty and if the multihospital concept is recognized as possessing long term cost saving potentials, then the cost incurred to organize such a system, if reasonable, must be allowable. We can understand the Medicare Bureau's points in safeguarding the program from unforeseen expenses and perhaps losses from start-up costs which do not materialize effectively; but, nevertheless, this is a gamble that must be permitted." (p. 4)
23. However, there have been legal questions as to whether these plans may be so specific.
24. Likewise, they have ignored state antitrust laws, which by and large are not aggressively administered.
25. In August 1981, the Federal Trade Commission accused American Medical International of trying to monopolize the hospital market in San Luis Obisbo County, California. The Commission stated that AMI's 1979 purchase of French hospital gave the company control of 68 percent of the hospital beds and three of the five hospitals in the County. The Commission charged that the acquisition gave AMI the power to raise prices, exclude competitors, and lower quality. Further, AMI was charged with refusing to offer price and other concessions to Los Padres Group Health, a new health maintenance organization. (Wall Street Journal, 1981)
26. For a review of recent court decisions on state action defense, see Sims and Grimm, 1981. In June 1981, the U.S. Supreme Court shed some light on, but did not resolve the question (National Gerimedical . . . , 1981). In its unanimous opinion that reflected skepticism of the claim that P.L. 93-641 had implied an exemption to the normal anti-trust doctrines, the court stated (in part): (1) the

alleged monopolistic activity was, in the particular instance of the case, not required or even approved by the health systems agency; (2) Congressional intent to repeal the anti-trust laws in respect to hospital combinations, through P.L. 93-461, was not at all clear; and (3) there is no blanket exemption from anti-trust laws for all private conduct undertaken in response to the health planning process. On the other hand, Justice Powell's opinion (written for the Court) included the statement that "there are some activities that must, by implication, be immune from anti-trust attack if hsa's and state agencies are to exercise their authorized powers . . . Where, for example, an hsa has expressly advocated a form of cost saving cooperation among providers, it may be that anti-trust immunity is necessary to make the [P.L. 93-461] work (p. 4676, n. 18).

References

American Hospital Association, "Special Survey on Selected Hospital Topics." *Hospitals*, July 16, 1977.

Areeda, Phillip. "Anti-Trust Laws and Public Utility." *Bell Journal of Economics and Management Sciences*, Spring, 1972.

Astolfi, A., and Matti, L. "Survey Profiles Shared Services." *Hospitals*, September 16, 1972.

Bauer, K.G. *Cost Containment under P.L. 93–641: Strengthening the Partnership Between Health Planning and Regulation*. Final Report, Harvard University Center for Community Health and Medical Care, Cambridge, Massachusetts, 1978.

Boston, J.R., and Edwards, S.A. "Hospital Mergers, A Model for Third Party Funding." *Hospital Administration*, Summer, 1974.

Brown, M., and Lewis, H. *Hospital Management Systems*. Germantown, Maryland: Aspen, 1976.

Buchanan, J.M., and Lindsay, C.M. "Financing of Medical Care in the United States." In *Health Services Financing*. London: British Medical Association, 1970.

Cantor vs. Detroit Edison Company, 428 U.S. 579, 96 S Ct. 3110, 1976.

Clarkson, K. "Some Implications of Property Rights in Hospital Management." *Journal of Law and Economics*, October, 1972.

Connors, Edward J. "Generic Problems in the Development and Operations of Multi-Hospital Systems." Sixth Annual International Conference on Multi-Hospital Systems, San Francisco, June 17–19, 1978.

Cooney, James P., and Alexander, T.L. *Multi-Hospital Systems: An Evaluation*. Health Services Research Center of the Hospital Research and Education Trust and Northwestern University, 1975.

Diamond, Alvin D. "Keynote Address: Health Financing." American Hospital Association Invitational Conference on Multi-Hospital Systems, Washington, D.C., June 15, 16, 1978.

Discussion Paper. "Promotion of Hospital Consolidation Through Regulatory Change." Draft, Office of the Administrator, Health Care Financing Administration, Department of Health, Education and Welfare, 1978.

Flanagan, R. J. Office communication to Robert Toomey. "Regulatory and Statutory Barriers to Mergers, Consolidation, Closure, Shared Services, and Multi-Hospital Systems." American Hospital Association, August 10, 1978.

————. Office communication to Robert Toomey. "Draft Report on Reimbursement Changes . . ." American Hospital Association, January 26, 1979.

Foley, Henry A. "Multi-Hospital Systems: A Potential For Solving a Health Dilemma." American Hospital Association Conference on Multi-Hospital Systems and Shared Services Organization, Washington, D.C., June 16, 17, 1978.

Frawley, Sandra. "Research Priorities for Health Systems Management." Conference Summary Paper, National Health Care Management Center, University of Pennsylvania, Philadelphia, November 30–December 1, 1978.

Fuchs, Victor. *Who Shall Live: Health, Economics, and Social Choice.* New York: Basic Books 1975.

Havighurst, Clark C. "Health Maintenance Organizations and the Market for Health Services." *Law and Contemporary Problems*, 1970.

Hermandex, Mike, "Comments." Sixth Annual Invitational Conference on Multi-Hospital Systems, San Francisco, July 17–19, 1978.

Homer, Carl, and Smith, David. "The Hospital Support Game Revisited." *Journal of Health, Politics, Policy, and Law*, Summer 1975, pp. 257–65.

Horty, John F. "Remarks of John F. Horty, President, National Council of Community Hospitals, Regarding Multi-Hospital Systems." Washington, D.C., c. September 10, 1978.

Hospitals (Editorial Notes). "Collaborative Systems—Realistic and Opportune." June 1, 1977.

Hospital Building Company vs. Trustees of Rex Hospital. 511 f 2d 678 (4th cir.), 1976.

Illich, Ivan. *Medical Nemesis.* New York: Pantheon Books, 1976.

Jacobs, Paul. "A Survey of Economic Models of Hospitals." *Inquiry*, June 1974.

Joint Commission on Accreditation of Hospitals. "Hospital Categorization Guidelines." Chicago, 1975.

La Londe, Marc. "A New Perspective on the Health of Canadians: A Working Document." Department of National Health and Welfare, Ottawa, 1974.

Lee, L.M. "A Conspicuous Production Theory of Hospital Behavior." *Southern Economic Journal*, July 1971.

Levy, Joanne, and Kominski, Gerald. "Management of Multi-Institutional Systems." National Research Conference Summary Paper, National Health Care Management Center, University of Pennsylvania, Philadelphia, May 12–13, 1980.

"Looking Around: The Multiple Hospital is the Only Way to Go." *Modern Hospital*, November 1973.

Malm, Harvey M. "Systems Can Reduce Costs, But Need Incentives for Future Development." *Hospitals*, March 1, 1977.

McNerney, W.J. "Control of Health-Care Costs in the 1980's." *New England Journal of Medicine*, Nov. 6, 1980, pp. 1088–95.

Money, William H., et al. "A Comparative Study of Multi-Unit Health Care Organizations." *Organization Research in Hospitals.* Chicago: Blue Cross Association, 1976.

Morris, Robert. "Basic Factors in Planning for the Coordination of Health Services." *American Journal of Public Health*, February 1963 (Part I) and March 1963 (Part II).

Mosher, F.C., ed. *Governmental Reorganizations: Cases and Commentary.* Indianapolis: Bobbs-Merrill, 1967.

Mountin, Joseph, et al. "Health Services Areas: Requirements for General Hospitals and Health Centers." Public Health Bulletin #292, U.S. Government Printing Office, Washington, D.C., 1945.

National Gerimedical Hospital and Gerontology Center v. Blue Cross of Kansas City. 49 U.S.L.W. 4672. U.S. June 15, 1981, rev'd 628 F. 2d 1050, 8th Cir. 1980.

Ottertail Power Company vs. U.S. 410 U.S. 366, rehearing denied 411 U.S. 910, 1976.

Pauley, M.V., and Redisch, M. "The Not-For-Profit Hospital as a Physician's Co-operative." *American Economic Review*, March 1973.

Posner, R.A. "Taxation by Regulation." *Bell Journal of Economics and Management Sciences*, Spring, 1971.

Priest, A.J.G. "Possible Adoption of Public Utility Concepts in the Health Care Field." In *Law and Contemporary Problems (Health Care, Part II)*. Duke University School of Law, Autumn, 1970.

Roemer, M.I., and Morris, R.C. "Hospital Regionalization in Perspective." *Public Health Reports*, October, 1959.

Rosenberger, Donald. "How Mergers Begin and How They Work." *Hospitals*, July, 1966.

Schweiker, R.S. Paper (untitled). American Hospital Association Invitational Conference on Multi-Hospital Systems, Washington, D.C., June 15, 16, 1978.

Sigmond, Robert. "The Issues Facing Multi-Hospital Systems." Keynote Address, Sixth Annual Invitational Conference on Multi-Hospital Systems, San Francisco, July 17–19, 1978.

Sims, J. and Grimm, K. "Health Planning Activities Test Sherman Act." *Hospital Financial Management*, July 1981.

Somers, A.R. *The Hospital in the Evolving Health Care System*. First Mark Burk Memorial Lecture, Mt. Zion Hospital, San Francisco, 1972.

Starkweather, David. "Hospital, From Physician Dominance to Public Control." *Public Affairs Reports*, Institute of Government Studies, University of California, Berkeley, October 1975.

————, et al. "Anti-Trust Implications of Hospital Mergers: A Review and Discussion." Blue Cross and Blue Shield Assocations.

Stromberg, Ross. "Hospital Consortia Seminar: Legal Issues and the Resolution of Institutional Differences." California Hospital Association, Anaheim, August 25, 1978.

Taylor, Robert J. *Human Dynamics in Hospital Mergers*. Research Fellowship paper prepared for the American College of Hospital Administrators, 1978.

Thompson, James. "Technology, Policy, and Societal Development." *Administrative Science Quarterly*, January 1974.

Tibbetts, Sam. "Looking Around. . . ." *Modern Hospital*, February 1973, p. 14.

Vraciu, Robert A., and Zuckerman, Howard S. "Legal and Financial Constraints on Development on Multi-Hospital Systems." *Health Care Management Review*, Winter, 1979.

Wall Street Journal. "FTC says a monopoly in County is sought by American Medical." August 5, 1981.

Weisbord, M.R. "Why Organizational Development Hasn't Worked (so far) in Medical Centers." *Health Care Management Review*, Spring 1976.

Williams, Herbert. *Hospital Closures and Mergers, New York City, 1960–1975*. Health and Hospital Planning Council of Southern New York, Inc., 1976.

11.

Mergers as Bartered Solutions

The titles of the three sections of this chapter—Mergers and Motives, Mergers as Coalitions, and Mergers as Decisions—will build on the Assumptions of Discord, Exchange, and Power stated in chapter 2 (sections D, E, and F, respectively), as well as 19 of the propositions of chapter 3 relating primarily to the enabling stage of the merging process. These propositions emphasize the behavioral dynamics involved in translating whatever merger predispositions exist in communities into actual decisions to combine or not to combine.

A. Mergers and Motives

ECONOMIC MOTIVES

In chapter 2, A, we laid out the reasons underlying the assumption that hospital mergers are economically rational in the long run, but controlled by behavioral dynamics in the short run. In Propositions 6a and b (chap. 3, B) we spoke to the same peculiar interplay in another way: economic factors control the initial stages of merger, and the perception of economic advantage is a necessary though insufficient condition, while prestige factors control transitional stages and the perception of improved or at least equivalent status for participating influentials is necessary for a merger to proceed. We might be tempted to call the economic factors rational and the prestige factors irrational, but that is only from one perspective; let us instead call them type a rationality and type b rationality.

Concerning type a rationality, our cases demonstrate both the strength of economic considerations in the four successful mergers as well as the reduced importance of them in the two unsuccessful ones. At Palo Alto-Stanford, the university's initial motivations to merge included the trustees' determination to rid Stanford of the annual operating deficit of its inefficient San Francisco hospital, some 30 miles from the main campus. In addition, the city of Palo Alto wished to get out of the hospital business to avoid further capital drain (chap. 4, B). The strength of these combined type a motivations is revealed by the very heavy financial burdens placed on the newly merged operating corporation (chap. 4, C). The parties to the First Hill merger in Seattle were unequal in their economic strength. The two smaller hospitals, Doctors' and Seattle General, were convinced of their dead end economic plight; consultant Jones articulated this as a way of galvanizing the parties to action. By contrast the Big Swedish was in much sounder financial shape, and for this reason resisted merger until the last (chap. 6, C). Indeed, was it economics that motivated Swedish, or is our theory wrong? The answer appears to be a different kind of economics, a more calculating and future-oriented one relating to sufficient referrals and admissions for its costly tertiary services, rather than the present day economics of institutional survival. Because Swedish's financial situation was not so severe, its loss of institutional autonomy was less: it essentially acquired the other two hospitals (at no direct cost, only the opportunity cost of its debt limit), while continuing as the surviving corporation (chap. 6, C). In Los Angeles, economics was the initial driving force, due both to the cost squeeze of county-sponsored medical services, as an aftermath of Medicaid legislation, and to the increasing political visibility of the largest item of expenditure in the county budget (chap. 8, B). The Norfolk situation was much like that of Seattle—a whale-guppy merger—except that economics was motivating the larger Norfolk General as well as the survival-threatened Leigh Memorial: Norfolk General wanted Leigh's private paying patients to balance its costs of charity care and teaching programs (chap. 9, D).

Another way to test our propositions is to determine if our nonmerger case situations lacked strong economic imperatives. This appears to be so. In Norfolk, the King's Daughters backed off from merger because they calculated that they could survive by independent fund raising (chap. 9, D, note 7). In Davenport, both St. Luke's and Mercy hospitals were in sound financial shape. St. Luke's balance sheet was so strong that its trustees were less concerned with economic well-being than with whether their superior asset strength should obtain more influence for them in the consolidated corporation (chap. 7, C). Mercy's side of the proposed merger was complicated by the fact that the hospital was being used as collateral for investments made by the provincial house in other realms of the order's network—hardly an indication of financial weakness (chap. 7, C). In Westhaven-Riviera, the directors of the Westhaven district collaborated in merger talks only until they determined that the comprehensive health planning agency could not block their construction of a separate nonmerged facility, at which point the district directors went to the voters for capital financing approval—an economic trump card they held as a public hospital that allowed them to ignore utilization trends that would spell economic disaster for most hospitals (chap. 5, G). Thus, our cases support the proposition that economics is a driving force at the initial stages of merger, probably the sole driving force.

BEHAVIORAL MOTIVES

Our theory says that initial economic imperatives give way to behavioral ones—type b rationality—as hospital officials barter with each other using the subtle but powerful tools of identity, status, and autonomy (chap. 2, A; chap. 3, B).

The data from our cases do not clearly confirm this proposition. At Palo Alto-Stanford, the original community and university elites were willing to turn hospital affairs over to other civic leaders without apparent concern for their own standing (chap. 4, C). However, within the medical profession the drives for improved or at least equivalent status were powerful. These were the forces that led initially to the unusual two-staff medical practice organizations that allowed each town-gown group within each specialty to maintain equivalence (chap. 4, E). These were the forces that continued to disrupt the merger, starting with the impossible array of joint committees, leading to hassles over the power of the proposed medical board, and ending with Stanford's eventual purchase of Palo Alto's interests in order to satisfy the medical school faculty's continued complaints about its standing in the hospital (chap. 4, D). These factors strongly shaped the implementation period, lasting in this instance for approximately eight years.

At both Westhaven-Riviera and Davenport there were no sustained transitional periods by our definitions in chapter 3 (sec. A). Yet, in Westhaven-Riviera behavioral factors were clearly more important than economic motivators. These behaviors were rooted in the vast differences between the two communities (chap. 5, B) that were apparent in virtually all transactions: the Becker issue, the charges of racism against Dana Memorial and Riviera officials, the symbolism of sites, the parlaying of committee appointments, etc. (chap. 5, E). In a way, the roots of these behaviors were broadly cultural—not confined to questions of individuals' prestige. In another way, the concerns for individuals' roles were manifestations of the cultural clash between the two communities, best evidenced in the case by the overriding concern of the Westhaven board for equivalent status in the proposed consolidated board. This concern was so great that Westhaven interests would not go for the merger even when they had gained substantially on other points of negotiation, notably site, and when the board imbalance was perceived to be only one seat in ten (chap. 5, F).

In Seattle, as in Palo Alto-Stanford, the questions of status ran primarily to the medical staffs: fear on the part of Doctors' and Seattle General's general practitioners that led to insistence on the merged-pavilion solution rather than Swedish's merged-addition plan (chap. 6, C). The parties stood apart on this single issue for some time, with the merger hanging in the balance.

Of our six cases, Los Angeles illustrates most clearly the dynamic of prestige and status among professionals. The initial merger was forced on the professionals for reasons of perceived efficiencies as well as the county's intent to redirect health care delivery. After the merger was declared, interprofessional jockeying took over. The equivalency issues among the three groups—specialty-oriented somatic medicine, public health, and mental health—were as consuming as their fear of the giant department of hospitals (chap. 8, C, D). These resulted in the failure jointly to plan the new and experimental health centers (chap. 8, C), the problems in selecting regional directors (chap. 8, D), the role conflicts among both physicians and nurses in Dr. Finn's pilot region (chap. 8, D), the complications of decentralization, with particular reference to Dr. Brickman's efforts to preserve mental health status by resisting decentralization (chap. 8, E), the problems centering on public health's bureau system (chap. 8, C), and Witherill's multistage plan for, phasing regionalization—a plan so long in developing that few could follow its momentum and many could find opportunities for its criticism and sabotage.

The Norfolk case is in many ways a story of negotiation and exchange, with status and prestige as important chips. Within the southern family, prestige for various groups was preserved in the merger by stipulating equal numbers on the new board, even though the 102-seat result was know to be dysfunctional (chap. 9, C). Among physicians, the common status strains existed between generalists and specialists. This had blocked a merger attempt some years previous, and might have again without the last minute agreement to grandfather all of Leigh Memorial's general practitioners, and without board president Billy Dickson's efforts to bring about a medical staff unification even after the two medical groups had failed to agree on a leader and the nominating committee had struck (chap. 9, E). Perhaps more subtle were the ramifications of prestige in the medical community surrounding the various moves by the Doctors' Clinic Company, the Norfolk Diagnostic Clinic, and the Tidewater Ambulatory Surgery Partnership. At two points, Medical Center Hospitals officials were concerned that these groups might obtain, or be seen as obtaining, preferred treatment by the hospital (chap. 9, D, E).

In summary, our few case studies bear out our basic notion that behavioral determinants follow economic ones. Yet, these are not as distinct phenomena as can be read into propositions 6a and 6b. Economic factors remained compelling beyond the initial stages in Los Angeles, and to a lesser extent also in Palo Alto-Stanford, relating to capital debt burdens (chap. 4, E), and in Norfolk. Conversely, the forces of prestige-seeking and status-saving operated strongly in the early stages at Westhaven-Riviera and Norfolk. In addition, the transactions in Davenport seemed less influenced either by economics or status differences as by the expressions of community values and the politics of planning (chap. 7, F).

In our cases, status clashes among general community leaders seemed less deterministic of merger than those among physicians—contrary to much

that has been proposed in chapter 3 (sec. B). One possibility is that the prestige game among community elites is not in fact less important but appears
so from our cases because it is played better: the strains are more clearly
seen, anticipated earlier, and properly accommodated. On the other hand,
doctors are less practiced both in recognizing these games for what they are
and in making the necessary political adjustments; thus their prestige games
come through in our cases as contributing more dramatically to merger results. If this be so, it illustrates in yet another way a simple but basic theme
of this book: the element of professionalism in health care organizations
makes mergers in this field categorically different than their counterparts in
business and commerce.

Another finding relates to status barriers among administrators. It is
commonly alleged that management egos and motives of job protection block
mergers. No doubt they do in some cases. Our findings herein do not support
or reject this conclusion. In one way or another the succession of administrators made necessary by consolidation was anticipated and worked out in
every case that eventually evolved to merger. The Seattle and Palo Alto-
Stanford mergers showed evidence of planning in this regard (chap. 6, C;
chap. 4, C). Only in Los Angeles did managers conflict, and these were
former department heads who became deputy directors in the new agency.
But here the strains occurred less along strictly administrative lines than
along professional lines. In one of our two nonmergers, Westhaven-Riviera,
the issue of administrator positioning was clearly not the barrier. It is hard
to judge what it might have become in Davenport; the presence of a Catholic
order provided for the possible elimination of any final obstacle in this regard.

We can conclude from our case data that several mergers have gone
forth without major obstruction by administrators, and that two mergers have
failed for reasons other than management resistance. But we do not know
how many other mergers have floundered on this shoal.

MOTIVES OF PUBLIC BENEFIT

Proposition 6c (chap. 3, B) links economic and behavioral forces to those of
community welfare—those factors that Mosher (1967) calls substantive rather
than structural changes. Specifically, the proposition states that during all
stages of the merging process community betterment is a contingent condition
that legitimizes the merging process, and that only during the last stages does
it, in some cases, become controlling.

Our cases indicate that this is too jaded a view. In the first place,
motives of economic survival can be viewed as means to community betterment: a hospital can do no good if it ceases to exist. Understandably, those
in control of a hospital take this view; it justifies their attempts at institutional

survival whether their tactics be merger or continued separate identity. It is difficult to separate institutional survival motives as means to other ends from institutional maintenance motives as ends in themselves.

Even so, community betterment appeared to be a real rather than legitimizing force at Palo Alto-Stanford, where the three-legged stool of teaching, research and community service represented a valid synergism (chap. 4, C). Likewise, in Los Angeles the plan for using the merged agency as the basis for a new thrust towards ambulatory care and prevention seemed entirely genuine (chap. 8, C). In Westhaven-Riviera, the advantages of regionalized hospital care seemed real and obvious to most (chap. 5, B, C). In our other three cases objective community services seemed much more entwined with motives of organizational maintenance and growth.

We grant that these are very subjective conclusions, based perhaps on selective case writing or interpretation. Westhaven Hospital's behavior could easily be classified as strictly legitimizing, and the various interest groups in Davenport could just as readily be viewed as genuinely striving for the community benefits of a secondary referral system (chap. 7, C).

Whatever the forces of community betterment as original and real motivators, they seem to wane as the merging process unfolds. At Palo Alto-Stanford the dealings in organizational stress overwhelmed the discussion of objective benefit of the merger. Deehan's five principles represented a last ditch effort to recapture for the merger the benefits that had been originally conceived, but the attenuated process leading to their achievement yielded a hollow victory (chap. 4, E). By the time Stanford had bought out Palo Alto, little was heard of the original goals, and the university had essentially shifted its purposes to ones that supported its distinguished medical faculty's research, with less concern for community effect (chap. 4, E, F; app. B). At Westhaven-Riviera the merger dynamics drifted so far from original betterment goals that a carefully documented study showing obvious savings in community health care costs was completely ignored not only by the hospital decision makers but also the planners and consultant (chap. 5, H). At First Hill in Seattle, interhospital tensions diverted the merging process from the obvious community solution in the case of maternity services (chap. 6, C). This situation contained a particular irony; the biggest goal diverter, Swedish's medical director Lobb, was likewise the person who at several junctures saw and stated most clearly the issues of public benefit (chap. 6, C). At Davenport, the health care delivery objectives ended up taking a back seat to objectives stemming from religious and economic values (chap. 7, F). Goal diversion is probably most obvious in the Los Angeles case, where merger was justified in the first place on the widely accepted goals of efficiency and community service contained in the Health Services Planning Commission report (chap. 8, C). But the ensuing process within this gargantuan subgovernment was so embroiled that five years hence politicians were calling for demerger as the best means to some of the same ends (chap. 8, E).

To summarize, we cannot conclude, as stated in Proposition 8 (chap. 3, B), that community betterment is only a legitimizing force at all stages; it appears to be real at the initial stages of many mergers. We can say that it remains as a legitimator at subsequent stages, although not significantly so in complex mergers where issues of organizational means seem to overwhelm those of organizational ends. And, we can say that community betterment goals are rather easily displaced in the last stages of merger—in some cases original goals have dropped from organizational memory.

Much of this confirms the phenomena of goal displacement and goal intangibility (chap. 3, B). Our cases provide numerous examples of original goals stated only intangibly (Proposition 9a), of failure to translate these generalities into central, means-end strategies (Proposition 9b), and of resulting tension (Proposition 9c). The most obvious examples of these are in the Palo Alto-Stanford and Los Angeles cases.

We also know from our cases that the parties performed a minimum amount of evaluation to determine if goals had been achieved. Of our three successful mergers that had been operational for a time, only Los Angeles made an effort to document merger accomplishments and shortcomings (chap. 8, E). Proposition 9d (chap. 3, B) states, in part, that because of the absence of tangible goals, evaluation activities will be minimal. Our case data support this.

With vague institutional goals and minimal evaluation, it is no surprise that motives remain blurred and obscured, and results are often other than originally expected. It is also no surprise that the real behavior of merging organizations can best be seen not by looking at the way people pursue formal goals, but by examining the interactions of the major groups that form hospitals' dominant coalitions.

B.   Mergers as Coalitions

Several of our propositions assume the interaction of hospital subcoalitions as a basic merger dynamic. The Assumption of Exchange (chap. 2, E) provides the underlying theory.

Propositions 10 a-e deal with the relative congruence in goals among these different coalitions. When all hospitals have high internal congruence (Proposition 10b), each remaining organizationally intact during bargaining, freeing leaders to turn to external bargaining and the resolution of issues of redundancy and other substantive matters (Proposition 10e), mergers are more likely to occur. When differential goal congruence exists between these subcoalitions, i.e. congruence in one hospital and dissonance in the other(s), the advantage in bargaining goes to the hospital with congruence (Proposition 10a), and exchange proceeds on the assumption that the one institution is dominant and the other submissive (Proposition 10c). This leads the submissive hospital to adopt a strategy of survival of parts rather than the whole, through the formation of new subcoalitions (Proposition 10d).

Propositions 14 and 16 deal with how these coalitions reform, given that even in highly congruent hospitals mergers force new conflict, new distribution of power, and new interdependencies among subcoalitions (Proposition 14a). Those who become active in early merger proceedings seek increased power within their established coalitions (Proposition 14b), and obtain such by virtue of their control over information (Proposition 16b). This time of uncertainty gives rise to a general expansion or diffusion in the bases of power, thus increasing the number of potential influentials and causing a focus on those parties politically necessary to the proceedings (Proposition 14c). At about this time one of the several subpowers of each hospital will directly undertake or otherwise become acknowledged as the group to undertake formal merger negotiations. This party then must deal with two orientations: intraorganizational debate which preserves former identities and relationships where possible, and interorganizational debate which has the purpose of developing a merged organization (Proposition 16c). From the conflict between these two orientations both issues and parties to future bargaining and exchange will develop (Proposition 16d, e). If merger proceeds, those who control the scarce elements necessary for survival or growth of each hospital obtain influence, hold veto over the proceedings, and become the target of either cooptation or absorption, depending on whether the merger parties are balanced or imbalanced in relative power (Proposition 14e, Proposition 16e). This results in a reduction in bases of power and number of influentials, allowing the merger dynamics to focus on resolution of substantive issues (Proposition 14e). At this later stage uncertainty has been reduced and predictability increased—things most organizations crave (chap. 2, E). Out of this dynamic will emerge a dominant coalition for the new merged organization which reflects a new domain consensus and interdependencies (Proposition 16f). Also, a central figure will emerge to manage this new coalition— a person with superior political skills (Proposition 16g).

Do the dynamics in our six cases follow this rather complex pattern? For those exchanges that resulted in merger, were these dynamics important, and did they break down when merger failed?

We will contrast a successful and an unsuccessful merger in the light of these several propositions. At Palo Alto-Stanford, neither party to merger displayed high congruence, but the goal dissonance seemed greater on the Palo Alto side. The Palo Alto city council knew only vaguely that it wanted to get out of the hospital business, the Palo Alto Medical Staff was divided into a number of loose factions, notably group practice and solo practice doctors, and the hospital administration was a caretaker management (chap. 4, B). The Stanford side reached clearer initial agreement on the goals to be sought in the merger: the three-legged stool of teaching, research, and service was elucidated by Stanford leaders as a part of their intention to make Stanford's medical school nationally prominent (chap. 4, app. B). The initial merger situation, then, was one of differential goal congruence: relative dissonance within Palo Alto and relative congruence within Stanford. Thus, Stanford secured the bargaining advantages while Palo Alto remained in a more dependent state, interested in the future of its organizational parts rather than in the continuance of the hospital as a complete identity.

Diffusion of power was also apparent during this early time. Stanford changed its method of operating its hospital from the San Francisco structure, wherein the hospital board consisted of clinical department heads with the administrator functioning as a clerk-of-the-works superintendent, to the tighter structure of the Palo Alto-Stanford Hospital where a formal hospital board representing diverse interests combined with a professional management, and two hospital medical staffs. Significantly, the change greatly reduced the power of the medical school's clinical department heads over hospital affairs. This change, more than anything else, inspired new coalition dynamics and the identification of those parties politically essential to the proceedings, as witnessed by the Packard Agreements and by the Hewlett-Kaplan showdown over the formation of a new Medical Board (chap. 4, E).

Likewise Palo Alto underwent an early diffusion of power. The requirements for new capital monies brought the city manager and city council into active negotiating roles in hospital affairs, and a variety of physician groups emerged to represent interests and viewpoints other than those of the three medical families (chap. 4, C).

Our propositions state that at this stage one of the several subpowers within each party to merger becomes the merger negotiator, taking on a role of reconciling intra- vs interhospital orientations. However, it is not obvious in the Palo Alto-Stanford case that this took place. It appears that the university president's office took on this role for Stanford, and the city manager took it on for Palo Alto—probably because these parties were in the best positions to deal with the demanding fiscal and physical aspects of this merger. For each, the difficulty of melding the interests in an intraorganizational status quo with those in interorganizational change was quite apparent. The corporate arrangement separating the authorities of the two owners via the hospital corporation from the authorities of the hospital management board is one attempt (chap. 4, C). Another is the early agreement on two medical staffs (chap. 4, C). A third is the complex ownership and lease arrangement on hospital buildings: some owned outright by each owner, others owned jointly (chap. 4, C). A fourth example is the proviso about the use of private patients for teaching (chap. 4, D), and a fifth is the complex rate structure for hospital services (chap. 4, D). For most of these examples our case study identifies the issues at stake and the parties holding the scarce resource who had to be accommodated in order for the merger to proceed. This is seen very clearly in the instance of the scarce resource of teaching patients: controlled by Palo Alto physicians but needed by Stanford doctors, putting Palo Alto doctors in a position to obtain a separate medical staff with separately elected chiefs of all clinical services, and forcing a very restricted development of Stanford's outpatient clinics so as not to compete with private practitioners (chap. 4, D). However, as the merger unfolded and Stanford developed its own patient referrals, exchange between the two groups shifted to one of mutual cooptation: witness the replacement of the Joint Professional Activities Committee by the Medical Board (chap. 4, E), the abortive efforts to create a single medical staff (chap. 4, E), and the solution to the pathology crisis presented by the introduction of Dr. Eversole (chap. 4, C, D). Then, as Stanford's position in the medical marketplace grew even stronger, it purchased Palo Alto's ownership interests while preserving the same hospital corporation and medical staff structures. The new policies that flowed therefrom showed the ownership difference: reduced admitting privileges of Palo Alto medical staff physicians (chap. 4, E), and reorganization of the Stanford Clinics to replace the hospital's responsibility with medical school jurisdiction (chap. 4, E). These examples appear to fit a pattern of: 1) early veto activity by those parties in control of essential resources, 2) subsequent cooptation activity when the two parties to merger are relatively balanced, and 3) eventual absorption of some coalitions by others if balance of power becomes imbalanced.

This time period at Palo Alto-Stanford also saw dispersed power replaced by more concentrated power. The initial organization of the merger could hardly have distributed influence more broadly (fig. 4.2). Several stages of concentration then took place. One stage took place through formal changes that provided for a medical board and provided increased authority for the hospital board, via Deehan's five principles (chap. 4, E). But this was not sufficient. An informal group of influentials in both medical staffs tried to obtain a unified medical staff, to no avail (chap. 4, E). Some time after this Stanford seemed to shift its strategy with respect to the hospital. It created a new position, vice-president for Medical Affairs, and brought in a new person to fill both this position and the medical school deanship—a concentration of power (chap. 4, E). This led eventually to further concentration of influence in the hospital stemming from the University's buy out of Palo Alto. Along the way the owners took things out of the hospital board's hands, even leaving the board in the dark about the future of its own institution (chap. 4, E). Each of these changes was associated with one or more contested issues—medical staff organization, sufficient control of patient care for teaching and research, owner financial equity, etc. And, in general, each resolution led to greater predictability and control of the future, at least for the two owners who, after all, carried the risks.

Several new dominant coalitions emerged during this time, in the following sequence: 1) a coalition of owner interests taking over from the early medical families, strongly representing university and city administrators who dealt with financial and construction matters, 2) a hospital-oriented coalition headed by the board president and including medical school and hospital administrators as well as key doctors, dealing with early operational exigencies, and 3) a Stanford-oriented coalition dealing with reorganization and restructuring of the medical center. A certain functionalism can be seen in these recoalitions: they reveal changing agreements about domain and shifting dependencies. The number of changes is due to the extreme complexity and long duration of the Palo Alto-Stanford merger, a circumstance neither anticipated nor contradicted by Proposition 16f. Probably because of this long duration, we find at Palo Alto-Stanford the emergence of not one person with superior political skills as advanced in Proposition 16g, but three persons associated with each of the three major dominant coalitions that emerged over time: Stanford University president Sterling with the first, Hospital Board president William Hewlett with the second, and vice-president for Medical Affairs Robert Glazer with the third.

In summary, the fabric of the Palo Alto-Stanford situation seemed to provide for not only the identification of important coalitions but also their successful reformation. The Davenport situation differed. Where the Palo Alto-Stanford setting was coalition-fluid, Davenport was coalition-stable—except at the dramatic end.

Although Coyne's case study does not document such directly, it appears that both Mercy and St. Luke's were high congruent hospitals: each reached a high level of agreement among its subgroups. Each institution remained intact, organizationally speaking, during interhospital bargaining among institutions of roughly balanced power. Following Proposition 10e and Propositions 11a to 11d, merger dynamics moved quickly to substantive issues concerned with redundancy and organizational issues of mutual cooptation, as illustrated by the bargaining over board seats in the new corporation (chap. 7, C).

Neither hospital was desperate: Mercy could and eventually did fall back on provincial resources, and St. Luke's had a strong financial position. Relative to Proposition 5, no simultaneous crises existed. Neither party had exhausted all possibilities as autonomous institutions (Proposition 11d), and both were of relatively balanced power (Proposition 11b). Thus, no merger. These circumstances allowed each hospital to maintain high congruence relative to its internal subgroups. Little or no new coalition behavior occurred between subgroups of the two hospitals: medical staff groups remained intact, the administrations remained mutually distant, and the Joint St. Luke's-Mercy Coordinating Committee seemed not to move beyond arms length negotiations until replaced by the Consolidated Board (chap. 7, D). True, the Consolidated Board seemed to represent a new coalition, and it dealt with numerous organizational issues relating to the proposed merger. The group seemed to lack a coalition leader appropriate for the circumstances. Further, in Davenport a scarce resource was a commodity as intangible as a religious value, in that the Sisters of Mercy, backed by the entire Catholic Church, held the veto. The provincial houses' actions reflected a concentration of power on the Mercy side (chap. 7, D). Thus, there was no formation of a new dominant coalition to constitute to the merger. The only new coalition to form was an antimerger one, the Concerned Citizens—complete with a leader possessed of obvious political skills.

Our two cases seem to confirm Propositions 14 and 16 in different ways: the groupings and behaviors highlighted by these propositions were extant in Palo Alto-Stanford, a merger, and not extant in Davenport, a nonmerger. This proves nothing—we really have only two samples. But all observations support the notion that hospitals must be seen, organizationally, as coalitions, and that coalition dynamics is of the essence in the merging process. Further, domains are negotiated variously, but without domain consensus there will be either no merger or a merger destined for a stormy future.

C.   MERGERS AS DECISIONS

Proposition 13a states that merger activity will be greater in communities where private or statutory planning bodies are strong. Four of our cases are relevant to this hypothesis.

In Seattle the local planning agency undertook some minor brokering activities at one or two points at others' request (chap. 6, C). Otherwise, its involvement was peripheral (chap. 6, D). In Davenport, the planning agency initiated merger talks between three hospitals, and succeeded in obtaining funds for consultant studies that would advance the deliberations (chap. 7, C). Opponents of the merger used the planning agency as the forum for publicizing their objections, and perhaps because of this the action moved away from the agency and into the Consolidated Board comprised primarily of trustees of the remaining two hospitals (chap. 7, C). In Norfolk, the merger architects forgot to advise the planning agency of their intentions until the evening before the merger was publicly announced (chap. 9, E). Of course the agency was miffed. Its subsequent actions showed clearly that it was not on top of the possibilities for merging among hospitals in the Tidewater area, notwithstanding its feeble attempt to integrate Norfolk General and the new Chesapeake Hospital through a management contract (chap. 9, E). The Norfolk influentials had created their own private planning body, the Medical Center Planning Board, which had considerable influence on the merger. This group was really not a third party, yet it acted as such at times: a private community structure that acted something like a government. In only one of our cases, Westhaven-Riviera, was the planning agency strongly instrumental in the merger dynamics. Here the agency executive designed and implemented a special study committee, followed it with a joint negotiating committee made up of hospital officials and others, and used every power at his means to block actions on the part of either hospital that were contrary to merger (chap. 5, C, D, E). Ironically, even here the planning initiative failed, due in part to a peculiarity in the sequence of planning laws which provided one of the merger parties with a loophole (chap. 5, G), but due more fundamentally to a lack of broad community and CHP board support (chap. 5, G).

Thus, we have a mixed conclusion. Proposition 13a is perhaps true, but cannot be verified by our cases. Certainly the stronger planning bodies of our six cases appeared to be in Davenport and Westhaven-Riviera, where they stimulated merger activity. However, neither of these mergers came to pass, while consolidations did take place in our cases where planning bodies were more passive: Seattle and Norfolk. This suggests that the converse of Proposition 13a is possible: mergers are more likely where planning bodies are passive; or, mergers are less likely if discussion of them goes public. These are probably not true either; there are many other variables in each of our cases that explain the results, not just the character of the planning body.

A careful reading of the cases suggests another possibility: while Proposition 13a is probably true in the main, it is possible for a planning agency to be too strong, thus pushing merger candidates the other way. There is the hint of this in the Westhaven-Riviera situation (chap. 5, G). In addition, a planning agency may conclude that the private network of community and medical leaders will more likely bring parties to a merger than would its direct intervention. This was perhaps the calculation made in Seattle, which seems correct by hindsight, and also in Davenport, which seems incorrect. In Norfolk, any group's attempts to oppose the "southern family" would likely have failed, which planning agency officials may have realized.

Proposition 13b states that where potential merger parties are of relatively balanced power the intervention of a third power is necessary. This should have been the case in both Westhaven-Riviera and Davenport, where there was relative balance of power. We conclude from these cases that third party intervention may be necessary, but is not sufficient.

In some of our case situations, limits had been placed on local planning agency power. The agencies in Seattle and Davenport could not have denied certificates of need to the various hospital applicants for projects contrary to merger solely on grounds that the hospitals had failed to demonstrate some form of integration. Knowing this, they resorted to various promotive and brokering strategies, rather than punitive denials of franchises. Had these agencies been backed by an approved plan showing the public benefit to be gained by merger, their posture would likely have been different, and perhaps also the merger results.

The different roles and influences of both private and statutory planning bodies in our cases point to the range of vastly different constructions of community power. How the private and public systems of influence correlate is important, as well as the degree to which one depends on the other. All four of our cases indicate that the official planning agencies' actions depend on validation by private community power structures. In this sense they are not true third parties.

Propositions 12a to 12e, taken together, argue that the influentials who make up a community's power network must become involved with hospital merger decisions, because 1) hospitals are important civic enterprises, 2) they are strongly rooted in the value system of the community, and 3) the network of influentials reflects the social and economic interdependencies of a community essential to its functioning. The propositions go on to state that the network may be relatively visible when the community agrees on who makes decisions of import, or it may be relatively obscure when the community lacks consensus. The propositions indicate that this high or low consensus will influence the rate at which the merging process goes forward. This is because early in the merging process the medical and hospital subelites attempt to confine decision making to their familiar circles, but subsequently the issues must be escalated to the generic network of community influentials.

Our cases reveal something of the extent to which community power is legitimated, the degree of correlation between hospital and community elites, the extent to which the involvement of community elites is essential to the merging process, and the methods of interaction and decision making used. Some of these elements are summarized in figure 11.1, which categorizes five of our six merger situations on the two important dimensions presented in these propositions.

This figure invites us to look first at the correlation of hospital and community power. The Norfolk community influentials were also hospital trustees (chap. 9, D); their influence was clear and obvious from the start— thus, a ninety-day merger. In Los Angeles the situation was analogous: the five members of the board of supervisors were clearly in charge, sometimes aided by their county administrative officer. They pushed the merger, even over the very considerable resistance of two well established professional

FIGURE 11.1   Five Cases in Relation to Propositions
12a through 12e

CONCENTRATION OF COMMUNITY POWER

<table>
<thead>
<tr><th rowspan="2">RELATIONSHIP OF HOSPITALS TO COMMUNITY INFLUENTIALS</th><th rowspan="2"></th><th>CONCENTRATED</th><th>DISPERSED</th></tr>
</thead>
<tbody>
<tr><td>HIGH CORRELATION</td><td>NORFOLK (success)

LOS ANGELES
    (success)</td><td>PALO ALTO —
STANFORD
(success)</td></tr>
<tr><td>LOW CORRELATION</td><td>WESTHAVEN—
RIVIERA
    (failure)</td><td>DAVENPORT

(failure)</td></tr>
</tbody>
</table>

groups (chap. 8, C). In Palo Alto-Stanford the community elites clearly helped to put the merger together: the three medical families were also three important community families, and influentials like Hewlett and Packard were prominent in the merger formation (chap. 4, D). When these persons pulled back, particularly when Hewlett finished his term as president of the hospital board, conflict and confusion gained the upper hand in the postmerger period. In Westhaven-Riviera, the Westhaven representatives to the merger negotiating committee, notably Don Modrow, were not members of the subgovernment derived from the Westhaven Advancement League (chap. 5, B, E); and in Riviera the promerger activist, William Forrest, did not represent prominent industrial interests (chap. 5, E). No merger occurred in Westhaven-Riviera, despite heavy third party pressure. Likewise in Davenport, the hospital and community influentials were far from synonymous. In fact, the power at Mercy Hospital lay outside the community, and important labor and political interests were under-represented on both hospital boards, particularly St. Luke's.

The Davenport case also illustrates the second dimension of figure 11.1, relative dispersion of community power. Davenport seemed not to be jelled in this regard; the constellation of community power and its use was unclear both to Illowa and hospital influentials. In addition, the power system was dispersed. In the end the grassroots Guba coalition prevailed (chap. 7, D).

The Palo Alto-Stanford situation also contained many nodes of influence, but, unlike Davenport, enjoyed many connections between these nodes. Palo Alto-Stanford was a successful merger, Davenport was not.

The three-hospital situation in Seattle is not easily classified by our scheme. The earlier merger talks between Doctors' and Seattle General floundered (chap. 6, C), perhaps because community influentials were insufficiently involved. But when Big Swedish entered the talks, its leaders seemed to bring to bear certain sectors of Seattle's power structure, notably business interests. Yet, power in Seattle did not seem as concentrated as in Norfolk— explaining, perhaps, the difference in the interaction between hospital and planning agencies in the two cities (chap. 6, D; chap. 9, E).

In summary, review of our cases indicates that connections between persons prominent in hospital merger decisions and those in general community power, as well as the latter's endorsement, are vital to merger success (Norfolk, Los Angeles), even when the community power system is somewhat dispersed (Palo Alto-Stanford). Where these connections don't exist, a merger is unlikely. This is certainly true if there is a concentrated unsupportive network (Westhaven-Riviera), and likely in low-consensus or dispersed-power communities (Davenport). That is, the positive support of a community's power structure, whether it is concentrated and visible or dispersed, is a necessary condition of merger; the pace of merger activity is influenced by this factor.

Propositions 15 and 17 speak to forms of merger transactions and to the changing patterns of influence that take place in the process of decision making. In earlier stages, influence based on private relationships will be used (17b), an approach enhanced by a homogeneity in the influentials' personal characteristics (15a). In subsequent stages bargaining is used, and in final stages forms of public persuasion may be evoked (17b). At whatever stage, resistance to merger will come from those who believe themselves to be of lower socioeconomic or professional status (15b), and who will more readily escalate the means of resolving conflict from closed to open, visible, and public mechanisms (17c). Further, the proper method of dealing with issues will itself become an issue, and switches in approaches between substantive and process matters will be undertaken in some mergers—incongruent or imbalanced ones—that are not properly communicated between the parties (17d). When this happens, questions of mutual trust are raised (17f) which both delay the proceedings and increase conflict (17e). This can be destructive of the merger unless third party mediation is brought to bear (17f).

Figure 11.2 categorizes our six merger situations in respect to two variables included in Propositions 15 and 17, and provides a framework for examining the decision making behaviors of the merger parties. By decision

FIGURE 11.2   Decision-Making Structure and Behavior:
Six Merger Cases

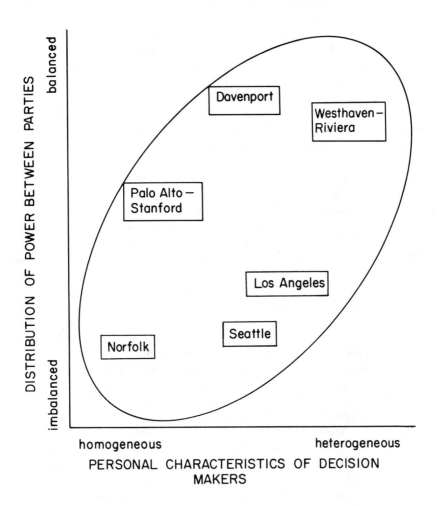

making behavior we mean the different methods identified in chapter 2 (sec. D): problem solving (computation), persuasion (judgmental), bargaining (compromise), and political (inspirational)—as well as the different kinds of influence identified in chapter 3 (sec. B): use of personal relationships, selling, and appealing to public opinion.

At Norfolk, the leaders of both hospital boards could scarcely have been more alike: old Virginia families, lawyers, grammar school chums, white males, etc. They made decisions by means of personal relationships in very private settings (chap. 9, C, D). Bargaining and rational argument were always conducted in a most civil and gentlemanly manner: certainly no third parties were welcome, and no public debate was considered necessary. Yet, our propositions suggest that if the situation was imbalanced, as clearly it was in Norfolk, the weaker party, Leigh Memorial, would escalate the decision making to more open mechanisms. That Leigh Memorial leaders did not do so suggests that where homogeneity in personal character is very high the mechanisms of decision making are confined strictly to private ones regardless of power balance. Such was also the case at Palo Alto-Stanford, where Palo Alto's power did not match Stanford's; yet even the Brown Act controversy about public meetings (chap. 4, E) found no particular support among Palo Alto city representatives.

The Seattle merger parties were also considerably imbalanced, but lacked similarities in personal characteristics among influentials that were evident in Norfolk and Palo Alto-Stanford. In Seattle, the prime decision-making mechanism was not the use of private relationships but various forms of bargaining, both directly between the parties, via the joint merger committee, and under the sponsorship of a third party—in this case a consultant. At one brief but crucial point the weaker party escalated the decision making to a public forum, the Washington State Hospital Commission (chap. 6, C). The Los Angeles case says little about the similarities in personal characteristics of the members of the board of supervisors; it is often the case that such persons are dissimilar. Certainly, the different professional groups held little in common, even though they were mostly physicians (chap. 8, C). In addition, there were vast differences in the power and size of the four departments merged into the new agency. So, given heterogeneity and imbalance, our theory predicts the use of public and open decision-making processes. This was definitely the case. But how could it have been otherwise in a government setting? For this test we should discount the Los Angeles situation.

Davenport and Westhaven-Riviera are quite alike in our two dimensions: balanced power and dissimilar personal characteristics of top decision makers. In these two cases the decision-making methods generally excluded personal and private relationships and concentrated instead on bargaining, under the sponsorship of planning agencies. These bargaining units met in closed sessions in both instances, although at Westhaven-Riviera there were frequent leaks to the public, usually via the newspaper and always by the party that saw itself as weaker: Westhaven. In both instances there was also ample use of the force of public opinion, and in the end both merger parties escalated to open and public forums (chap. 5, E; chap. 7, D).

We can conclude from this that of our two variables shown in figure 11.2, relative power and relative homogeneity of personal characteristics, the second is more important: when the decision makers are like each other the decision making will be private in spite of an imbalance of power (Norfolk, Palo Alto-Stanford). However, the converse is not true; if power is balanced, private decision making will not occur in the presence of marked differences in decision makers' personal characteristics. Put differently, our cases demonstrate a strong correlation between homogeneity among merger decision makers and private mechanisms of decision making.

Finally, we can apply to our cases a marvelous set of perceptions about organizational decision making by March and Simon (1958): "Because of the consequences of bargaining, we predict that the organizational hierarchy will perceive (and react to) all conflict as though it were in fact individual rather than intergroup conflict" (p. 131). Examples of this are: at Palo Alto-Stanford, the disputes between pathologists (chap. 4, E); in Seattle, the dislike for Dr. Lobb's style (chap. 6, C); and in Los Angeles, the strains between Affeldt, Brickman, and Heidbreder (chap. 8, G). They continue: "More specifically, we predict that almost all disputes in the organization will be defined as problems in analysis, and that the initial reaction to conflict will be problem solving and persuasion, that such reactions will persist even when they appear inappropriate, . . . and that bargaining (when it occurs) will frequently be concealed within an analytic framework" (p. 131). Examples of these include: the 26 subcommittees of the Joint Professional Administrative Council at Palo Alto-Stanford seeking to solve operational problems in the hospital instead of the real questions over the distribution of power between the two medical staffs and between the hospital and the medical school (chap.4, E); in Westhaven, the calls for objective analyses of possible hospital site locations when the question of location was in fact a chip being moved around the table of an organizational poker game (chap. 5, E); in Seattle, the last gasp use of financial consultants to analyze Swedish Hospital's balance sheet, even though the issue was obviously a political one (chap. 6, C); in Davenport, the analysis provided by Smith and Associates and the Iowa Regional Medical Programs, even though most of the data were already well known, and even though the consultants missed some obvious and crucial issues of community values and political differences (chap. 7, C); and in Norfolk, the regular use of the Medical Center Planning Board and the consultations arranged by that group, as a rational planning parallel for the political negotiations being conducted by members of the community leadership.

We can see in these several examples the relationship between rational and behavioral approaches to decision making: both must exist, and there is a subtle but necessary alternation and cross-feeding of each to the other.

D. DISCUSSION

There is a fuzziness about much that we have presented and discussed in this chapter; processes are not as easily visualized as structures, and variables like imbalanced power and homogeneity among elites need a larger empirical base for analysis than our few case studies can provide. The tests of our nineteen propositions on our six cases yield many questions.

For behavioral scientists, the discussion in the chapter points to a void in theories about decision making in complex organizations in changing environments. We have sociological theories on environmental impact on organizational structure, and on the impact of organizational structure on decision making. We have economic and management sciences approaches to rational decision making. We have the theories by psychologists of decision making and other phenomena in small groups. But all of these somehow miss the realm of organizational decision making in the context of coalitions, which in turn are both creating and responding to changing interorganizational arrangements.

For both students and managers of organizations, we have some unusual inversions of what is often taken to be preferred or predictable. One is the observation that the more open and complex the organization, the more closed and private the decision making (more on this in chapter 12). Another is the durability and influence of informal and personal status systems, despite formal and official systems based on role definitions. Another is the gap between legitimating and motivating purposes, raising the basic question of which yields which.

Negotiation is the most pervasive phenomenon in the cases discussed in this chapter. Environments are negotiated yielding domain consensus; power is negotiated yielding dominant coalitions; and decisions are made reflecting the results of barter. A view by Strauss et al. (1963) underscores this aspect of hospitals as organizations; it is even more appropriate to hospital mergers.

> The hospital can be visualized as a place where numerous agreements are continually being terminated or forgotten, but also as continually being established, renewed, reviewed, revoked, and revised. Hence, at any moment those that are in effect are considerably different from those that were or will be. . . . These agreements do not occur by chance, nor are they established between random parties. They are, in the literal sense of the word, patterned. . . . A reconstituting social order, we would hazard, can be fruitfully conceived in terms of a complex relationship between the daily negotiative process and a periodic appraisal process (yielding policies and rules). The question of how negotiation and appraisal play into each other, and into the rules and policies, remains central. [pp. 164–66]

REFERENCES

March, James, and Simon, H. *Organizations*. New York: Wiley, 1958.
Mosher, F.C. *Governmental Reorganization: Cases and Commentary*. Indianapolis: Bobbs-Merrill, 1967.
Strauss, Anselm, et al. "The Hospital and its Negotiated Order." In *The Hospital in Modern Society*, ed. by E. Friedson. New York: Free Press of Glencoe, 1963.

12.

The Management of Mergers

"Merger is not effected by vote. It is merely created,
and has a long way to go in its development."

Ernest Shortcliffe (1967)

A. INTRODUCTION

We deal here with two aspects of management: management of the merging
process, and management of merged organizations. The first assumes a broad
definition of management—perhaps better called mediation—and focuses on
activities leading up to merger. In our cases this role has been assumed
variously by a consultant, a planning agency executive, a civic leader, and a
hospital administrator. The second describes the more typical role of a chief
executive: the leadership and control of an organization created by merger.
The focus here is on those circumstances with which an administrator deals
after most merger decisions have been made and the new venture is an
operational reality. We cannot assume a predictable or smooth transition from
the first type of management to the second; a number of propositions of
chapter 3 suggest the contrary, as also have our cases.

All six cases provide the basis for discussion of management of the
merging process. For management of mergers we can draw on three cases
only—Palo Alto-Stanford, Norfolk, and Seattle—since only in these was there
actual integration of activities.

B. MANAGING THE PROCESS

For a process as complex and conflict-ridden as a merger, at least one change
agent must have a solid understanding of organizational dynamics. This strength
can reside within or without the parties to potential merger.

SOURCE OF LEADERSHIP

The initiation of change and the management of the change process are
sometimes undertaken by the same party(s) and sometimes not. At Palo Alto-
Stanford the initiators were Stanford's President Wallace Sterling and Dr.

Russell Lee, founder of the 130-doctor Palo Alto Clinic. They enjoyed a longstanding personal relationship. It was perhaps strategic on their part that once having initiated merger considerations they both withdrew from the subsequent organizational change process and remained in reserve. Others were available for this chore; if things did not move along appropriately their considerable influence could be brought to bear again. As it turned out, no widely recognized manager of organizational change was appointed or emerged, leaving the job to a series of committees. At several junctures the venture nearly failed. The organization that resulted looked like it had been created by a committee. Two examples from our case are: 1) the financial planners who succeeded in creating a corporate entity with a double burden of debt retirement and funded depreciation (chap. 4, C), and medical staff planners who succeeded in bridging two independent physician groups just enough to provide for their shared (but not joint) use of common facilities (chap. 4, C), but at the price of so much organizational discord that one medical staff eventually revolted (chap. 4, E).

In short, at Palo Alto-Stanford the initiators of change possessed community and institutional power, but the change process they introduced was almost unmanaged—to the point not only that great conflict ensued but also that the enterprise which finally evolved could hardly be controlled—the first decade of the merger saw six hospital chief executives and three medical school deans.

By contrast, the Westhaven-Riviera initiators were also the managers of change: CHP executive Hafey and his consultant colleague Starkweather. They came from outside the two communities involved (chap. 5, E). Try as these two did to identify inside change agents, they were unsuccessful; the kind of reserve influence so obvious at Palo Alto-Stanford was missing at Westhaven-Riviera—and most people knew it.

The perception of influence is as important as the reality. At Palo Alto-Stanford the perception seemed to keep the parties moving toward merger even when serious complications set in such as the surgical pathology issue and the shortages of teaching patients (chap. 4, C). At Westhaven-Riviera the parties involved in negotiations knew that the real influentials of the two communities had not been committed. So each hospital maintained two tactics, one to merge and one not to merge (chap. 5, F).

The Norfolk situation is both like Westhaven-Riviera, and like its opposite. In both cases the initiators and managers of change were identical, but in Norfolk they were all members of the "southern family" of the city's influentials (chap. 9, D). It is true that an outsider, Norfolk General's new administrator, Glenn Mitchell, did plant an important seed with one of the civic leaders, Sox Baldwin (chap. 9, C); nevertheless, the community influentials controlled the merging process from start to finish. Unlike the Palo

Alto-Stanford situation, this group was small enough and sufficiently integrated to effectively manage the process.

In between these outside/inside extremes are Los Angeles County, Seattle, and Davenport. In Los Angeles the stimulus for merger came from outside the health service agency (the county board of supervisors) (chap. 8, C). But the merging process was tightly managed by a dyad of the County Administrative Officer, L.S. Hollinger, and the head of the Department of Hospitals, Liston Witherill (chap. 8, C). How else could such a gargantuan change have been made?

At Seattle no one person could be called an initiator; rather, numerous trustees of the two smaller hospitals were involved (chap. 6, C). A consultant, Wanda Jones, undertook a good deal of effective guidance of the change (chap. 6, C). This reflected a certain inability on the insiders' parts to capture the kind of organizational leverage so apparent in both the Palo Alto-Stanford and Norfolk situations. The outsider eventually ran into some of the same problems Hafey and Starkweather encountered in Westhaven-Riviera: she could not secure the consent of the Big Swedish elites, some of whom came to resent her manipulation of the Washington State Hospital Commission to their public embarrassment (chap. 6, E). Nor could she transfer the job of change management to the professional administrators on the scene because none of them, for various reasons, were committed or qualified to taking up the task.

The Davenport situation is the opposite of Seattle's and can be compared to that of Westhaven-Riviera. Instigation for change in Davenport came from without: the planning agency. But unlike Hafey's strategy in Westhaven-Riviera, the planning agency executive then pulled back from active involvement in the merging process (chap. 7, D). Further, no recognized leadership came forth from the participating hospitals. The lack of effective guidance of organizational change might have been crucial to the end result.

We can only speculate. Did outsider activists Hafey and Starkweather merely bring on the inevitable in Westhaven-Riviera; or, had they hung back, would local change agents have emerged eventually to tip the scales in that tender merger balance? In Davenport, had the planning agency staff been more aggressive would the results have been any different? We should note that the differences in Westhaven-Riviera's and Davenport's communities were substantial. In the former there was no community power structure that embraced both hospitals; in fact, the two community structures were known to be markedly different in several important respects (chap. 5, B). By contrast, the Davenport hospitals occupied a single community—probably a better foundation for possible change. Yet this community did not have the tight decision making structure of Norfolk's network of influentials, nor the leadership density of Palo Alto-Stanford's medical and business families, nor the competent civil servants of Los Angeles County, nor the continuous consultation arranged by Seattle's leaders (the consultants in Davenport were essentially in and out). On the other hand Davenport's medical community, something like Norfolk's, was capable of sustained and determined action (chap. 7, D).

With many differences and so few similarities, what can we conclude?

1) The parties managing the merging process have greater impact on the final outcome than the parties initiating merger consideration, as shown in the Palo Alto-Stanford and Los Angeles cases. It is important that the initiating personalities be drawn from a community's power reserve, as negatively illustrated by the Westhaven-Riviera case and positively illustrated by the Norfolk case. The combination in one set of persons of both initiation and management of organizational change seems most likely to produce a successful merger.

2) Size is an important determinant of merging process management. Both Westhaven and Dana were small hospitals in small communities. Smaller institutions are less likely to have available the professional administrators or planners qualified to conduct wholesale organizational changes of this sort. In addition, the real or perceived differences between two small communities are perhaps less likely to be bridged by accepted and respected civic leaders, making difficult the instigation of merger from within the communities. At the other extreme is Los Angeles, where both agency and community were so large that a major change could take place only if guided by inside professional administrators—regardless of who originated the plan. Between these extremes range Norfolk and Palo Alto-Stanford, which were more like Los Angeles in their requirements for insiders, and Seattle and Davenport, which were more like Westhaven-Riviera in their institutional sizes and requirements for outside assistance.

3) Few individuals or groups in the typical merger situation seem to understand the need for this kind of organizational change, and how to implement it. In our cases, few administrators took the lead, Glenn Mitchell at Norfolk and Liston Witherill at Los Angeles excepted. Among boards of directors, only at Norfolk, and to a lesser extent at Seattle and Westhaven-Riviera (Dana Memorial) did the kind of community trusteeship emerge that is supposed to characterize the governance of eleemosynary hospitals. In several of our cases the medical staffs or medical societies did little more than answer surveys and pass occasional motions in favor of or in opposition to merger, despite the essentiality of hospitals to their medical practices. Only in Davenport did the medical community adopt an active

position in favor of a merger with any apparent understanding of the implications. At Palo Alto-Stanford and at Los Angeles there was strong medical involvement, but it was based more on questions of professional prerogatives than any larger sense of institutional or communitywide benefit. Only in Davenport was a community or consumer group seriously involved, and this involvement centered on one merger issue rather than on the overall array of advantages and disadvantages.

This is perhaps too broad an indictment; between the lines of our case studies there may have been more persons and groups with broad outlooks and active commitments. Yet, a reasonable conclusion remains that many parties are important to hospital and community decision making about mergers, but few appear equipped or willing to guide this kind of change. This means that persons who are so prepared and inclined are indeed precious, and occupy pivotal roles.

4) Outside managers of the merging process work against great odds, since they may likely be ignorant of some feature of community or institutional anthropology which eventually will be crucial. The Westhaven-Riviera and Davenport cases provide examples of this. Further, there is the likelihood of a rejection phenomenon, analogous to that of the human body that builds up an immune response and eventually sloughs a foreign tissue. The Seattle and Norfolk cases provide examples of this. An outside manager of the merging process may be essential at certain points; but, once involved, the outsider may easily take on too much, and the client may grant too much. Both temptations tend to lead the merging process to an organizational dead end. Conversely, a skilled outsider can manage to constantly build the insiders' capacity effectively to chart their own destinies. This is a middle ground tactic, between "let them flounder; they must learn how" and "I'll do it for them; that's what they're paying me for."

AN ESSENTIAL SKILL: MEDIATING CONFLICT

The story of most mergers can be told by tracing the conflict, bargaining, and decision making over a handful of pivotal issues. This has been the main framework for four of our case studies—Palo Alto-Stanford, Norfolk, Davenport, and Westhaven-Riviera—and, to a lesser extent, also for the remaining two.

The issues at conflict can be categorized as substantive or procedural, and the tracking of issues in our cases shows an intricate interplay between these two types. Mark Secord's postcase analysis of the Seattle merger (chap. 6, F) provides a theoretical perspective for this.

Recognizing the interrelation of these two aspects of decision making, we will deal here only with the second: how process itself can be an issue in conflict. Thompson and Tuden (1959) note that the administration's important role is managing the decision process rather than making the decision. They suggest five techniques, which we have modified and augmented. These several tactics, along with illustrations from our cases, are as follows.

1) *Providing a time frame.* Where the nature of the issue does not clearly imply a time dimension, one should be delineated, by fiction or otherwise.[1] Examples are: in the Seattle case, Jones' Decision A and Decision B timetable (chap. 6, C, B); in the Westhaven-Riviera case, Hafey's action designed to return the negotiators to the bargaining table (chap. 5, D); and in the Los Angeles case the three-phase time schedule mandated by Witherill and Avant for implementing the two pilot regions (chap. 8, D). Timing as a mediating influence acted positively on the merging process in Norfolk, and negatively in Westhaven-Riviera. There were timing problems at different stages of the process in Seattle (early on) and in Los Angeles (postmerger).

2) *Reducing alternatives.* When many alternatives are available, some machinery should be provided to eliminate all but a few. Examples are: in the Westhaven-Riviera case, the efforts of Starkweather and the lawyers to reduce the numerous legal questions and corporate options to three (chap. 5, F); in Norfolk, the role of the Medical Center Planning Board and consultant Wheeler in presenting the tangible options to federation of the three hospitals (chap. 9, C); and in Davenport, the consultants' enumeration of the three role and site options for St. Luke's, Mercy, and Osteopathic (chap. 7, C).

3) *Obtaining agreement to agree.* In a bargaining situation, this means obtaining an initial commitment to reaching subsequent agreement, and maintaining this agreement over interim periods when issues are at contest. Examples are: in the Westhaven-Riviera case, Wagner's strategy of a final locked doors meeting of the negotiating committee (chap. 5, F); in the Davenport case, the commitment obtained by CHP from the hospitals that they would merge in some way, with agreement on the nature of the consolidation to be worked out jointly in the future (chap. 7, D); and in the Palo Alto-Stanford case, Deehan's return to the administrator's post with commitment by key parties that they would promptly come to resolution on his proposed five principles of the Board (chap. 4, E).

4) *Crystallizing consensus.* Early ambiguity in a decision situation may result from lack of knowledge or from dissimilarities of values. As debate goes on, these conditions change. A mediator who can sense agreement and articulate it can play a vital part in decision making. Examples are: in the Norfolk case, Baldwin's memorandum of understanding after a year of misunderstanding and negotiation between hospital officials and physicians over the shared responsibility for development of the Kempsville site (chap. 9, E); in the Seattle case, the recitation of understandings and commitments that Jones and Dupar scheduled for the end of the first meeting of the three boards (chap. 6, C); and in the Palo Alto-Stanford case, the Packard Agreements (chap. 4, C).

5) *Redefining issues.* When an issue is too complex, it may be necessary to redefine it into a series of issues, each assigned to an appropriate decision process. Examples are: in the Westhaven-Riviera case, Starkweather's identification of five subtopics each with a task force (chap. 5, F); in the Palo Alto-Stanford case, Deehan's five principles (chap. 4, E); and in the Seattle case, Jones' Decision A and Decision B specifications (chap. 6, C).

6) *Specifying setting and format.* Setting and format can contribute or detract from decision making. Propositions 17 a-f highlight the importance of public vs. private settings. Other aspects include neutrality of setting, formal vs. informal procedures, etc. Examples are: in the Seattle case, the carefully planned educational conference (chap. 6, C); in the Westhaven-Riviera case, the agreements obtained early on about private discussions and tape recordings (chap. 5, E); and in the Norfolk case, the White Heron Inn retreat (chap. 9, C). Settings and format were positive mediating devices in Norfolk, negative in Davenport, and of mixed value in Westhaven-Riviera.

7) *Expanding or contracting the parties to decision making.* Propositions 17 a-e underscore the various pathways of influences that are available: personal relationships, bargaining, and force of public opinion. Not only do these vary with different stages of the merging process but also constitute a matter of conflict and negotiation. Proposition 17f suggests that a mediator's role in these matters is crucial. Examples are: in the Davenport case, CHP's success in having a Catholic clergyman on the joint hospital committee, in view of the abortion issue (chap. 7, D); in the Norfolk case, the more inclusive membership of the Medical Center Planning Board, and the more exclusive list of attendees to the White Heron retreat; and, in Seattle,

Jones' involvement of the chairman of the Washington State Hospital
Rate Commission (chap. 6, C).

SUMMARY

Effective mediation can make the difference in whether or not a merger takes
place. Few persons in the typical merger seem available or come forth to
provide this sort of skill. Persons with these talents and commitments often
need to be identified, encouraged, educated and supported. This can be an
important merger investment.

C.   MANAGING THE UNEXPECTED

Proposition 18a asserts that, at the approximate time a merger becomes operational, essential control passes to top management. This is the "hot potato
aspect of uncertainty absorption," to use Thompson's phrase, where management is expected to establish a new stability after a period of rapid change,
redistribution of power, and widespread ignorance and suspicion. This puts
management in a pivotal position (Proposition 18b).

Yet a main reason for merger may be the benefits of a new management
or a management shuffle. As stated by Linowes (1965), "New executives begin
looking over the shoulders of old managers, asking questions, making suggestions, and requiring answers. In effect, vitality is being purchased . . ."
(p. 7).

These transition problems are difficult enough in the business community (Weston, 1973). For hospitals, they pose several special problems: the
absence of profit as a management performance measure, the peculiar position of physicians in the organization, and the absence of stock ownership
as a determinant of board composition and enterprise authority. (See chapters 1 and 2 for full discussion.) We have posited that these features call for
management skills of the highest order, placing hospital mergers in a different
and more demanding category than their counterparts in most other realms
of enterprise.

Concerning physicians, Propositions 19a and 19b assert that merger
increases conflict between administrators and professionals, requiring new
and different forms of organizational control. Two years after the three-hospital merger that created the Wilmington Medical Center, its board chairman
reported that "the burden of decision making was almost overwhelming as
policy was standardized and the administrative structure was realigned"
(Gottshall, 1967, p. 6). At about the same time, the chief executive of the
same merger was reporting to a group of consultants, "Since the merger of
the medical staff there has been the acceleration of tremendous pressure
from the body for action leading to clinical consolidations, new programs, and

for the development of new facilities. The administration found itself inadequately organized for implementation of many of the things the medical staff had visualized as essential gains in merger itself" (Shortcliffe, 1967).

Concerning boards and board structure, our previous analyses and discussions (chap. 9, C, E) indicate that some mergers succeed only because a philosophy of institutional parity has evolved of including all prior board members. This is but one of several examples of "problem liening": commitments made early in the process in order to advance merger which become detrimental at later stages (chap. 10, B). The merger management must now face a board difficult to work with—too large, possessing enormously varied expectations and demands, and ineffective at policy setting at precisely the time when effective policy is most needed.

Given these economic, medical staff, and board features of hospital mergers (not paralleled in other realms except perhaps in university mergers, which are rare), Propositions 23a and 23b assert that the consequences of merger are other than anticipated, leading to a period of postmerger reappraisal when prior subpowers adapt a wait and see attitude, reappraise the worth of what they've done, jockey for position, test all next relationships, and reserve their full support of the new venture. At best, a period of inconclusiveness ensues when a management takes over the new operation. Worse, there is a climate of hostility. In the extreme, there is a time of anomie or spontaneous change (Proposition 22c): an organizational vacuum when change is pervasive, sudden, unpredicted, and uncontrollable.

Could any management cope under such circumstances? Is it true that the managements of hospital mergers generally fail to meet others' expectation of them (Proposition 20b), and that a concomitant of merger is management attrition (20c)? If not, what characteristics of management lead to effectiveness or survival?

In chapter 3 (sec. B) some obvious skills in problem solving, communication, and value setting were outlined, and a less obvious trait was suggested, which Thompson calls coalignment and Whistler calls the formation of order out of chaos: a creative skill involving the discernment of previously unnoticed relationships or patterns, calculating their cause effect relationships, and translating them into appropriate actions.[2]

With these propositions as a backdrop—those relating to the transition of merger control to management, the peculiar administrative problems deriving from professionalism and governance in hospital mergers, and the effect of unexpected consequences—we shall cut across our cases again to discern what we might about the characteristics, the performance, and the fates of our merger managers.

Of the three cases that proceeded to integration, Palo Alto-Stanford is the most extreme in that both a completely new organization was created and a new physical plant was built which totally replaced prior hospitals. At Norfolk, the merged corporation was derived from the larger of the two prior hospitals, and both premerger physical plants continued in operation after corporate merger while a new facility was being built to replace the smaller of the two. This merger, then, was less extreme, properly characterized not as a total fusion of two relatively equal entities but as a partial takeover of a smaller entity by a larger. Los Angeles County was yet a milder merger, since it was an amalgamation of four departments of county government which were not free-standing in their prior stages but rather units of a larger bureaucracy already in place.

Given these differences, we could expect the Palo Alto-Stanford merger to contain the greatest hot potato transition problems, the greatest management problems relating to medical staff and trustees, and the largest number of unexpected consequences. At Norfolk, we could expect the merger effects to impact most heavily on the absorbed organization—the smaller Leigh Memorial Division. At Los Angeles County, we could expect merger to be more the result of planned change than spontaneous result, since an umbrella structure with substantial power and management capacities was in place throughout the entire process. This is much the case.

At Palo Alto-Stanford the administrators of both prior hospitals were shop foremen types[3] (chap. 4, B). They had been hired to look after the books and did not concern themselves with the broader economics of hospital capital and operating financing which were impinging so obviously on both institutions' futures. Neither was equipped to guide the organizational changes on the horizon. Both rather willingly left their hospitals at the time of merger, one to be administrator of a hospital in another location very much like the one he was leaving, the other to manage a nursing home. The national search for an executive led merger instigators to Dwight Barnett, an outsider with optimal credentials, yet an insider because he was a member of one of the area's influential medical families with strong ties to both Stanford's medical school and the practicing medical community (chap. 4, C). Barnett was quite the opposite of his two predecessors: he possessed ties to the environment, and knowledge of the larger forces affecting hospitals. Yet, Barnett could not handle the very hot merger potato; nor was it clearly passed to him. Without any involvement in the design of the merger organization, Barnett came into an administrative nightmare bordering on the unmanageable. Even worse, he was not given important prerogatives necessary to making it manageable; these were held back by the hospital's two owners (chap. 4, C). But not all of what happened with Dr. Barnett can be attributed to the structure of the situation. It turned out that his management approach was derived from a prior experience which was the opposite of what he encountered at Palo Alto-Stanford: he previously had managed a hospital with a board that possessed full trustee authorities, and a hospital with a very favorable financial situation. When Barnett left his Palo Alto-Stanford post a year after the merged hospital opened, his board had concluded that he could not adjust to the kind of organization that, in the board's view, was the only kind possible under the circumstances. Dr. Barnett, in turn, had concluded that his superiors were not prepared to make the corporate adjustments essential to make the institution manageable, even granting that the original merged entity could probably not have been so designed. Between the parties to this stand-off lay nine months of operating deficit totalling a million dollars. Clearly, no one had achieved Thompson's coalignment nor Whistler's creative formation of order out of chaos.

We have, then, a transition from outside control to top management that essentially was aborted. There was, as put forth in Propositions 20 a-c, failure on the part of new trustees to appreciate the management exigencies of the merger, a management not capable of responding to these expectations, and attrition at a crucial time.

As the Palo Alto-Stanford case goes on to illustrate, the merger problems with which succeeding executives had to deal were primarily in the realms of governance and medical staff—those aspects which distinguish hospital mergers from others. Of the six issues presented in the Palo Alto-Stanford case study (chap. 4, A) four are directly in these two realms, and the remaining two are strongly influenced by them.

As for the third aspect of our most extreme situation, the impact of unexpected merger consequences, there are numerous examples of pervasive, simultaneous, and unpredictable change—clearly uncontrolled from a management point of view, and approaching anomic chaos. One example is the surgical pathology cause célèbre, which early in the proceedings should have derailed the entire merger had not the most prestigious town/gown leader— David Packard, president of Palo Alto's huge Hewlett-Packard Corporation and future president of Stanford University's Board of Trustees—stepped in (chap. 4, C). Then pathologist Stanton Eversole was brought in from the east—introduced by the chairman of the medical school's department of pathology, Alvin Cox, to an entirely suspicious group of Palo Alto surgeons, only to be subsequently rejected by Dr. Cox and a portion of the medical school faculty for being nonacademic, and warmly embraced by Palo Alto physicians for his diagnostic acumen and devotion to clinical duty (chap. 4, D). For several years Eversole operated in an organizational vacuum, without hospital contract and without firm university appointment. Then Cox resigned, partly because some of his faculty colleagues in surgery did not support his position on Eversole. Now the way was clear for the hospital to contract with Eversole, except that the medical school contract sign-off prerogatives, negotiated as part of the Packard agreements, were now assumed by Stanford's medical school dean, who for reasons entirely unrelated to the pathology problem soon announced his own resignation. Eversole finally moved away. His replacement in surgical pathology, at a medical center now judged to be among the top ten in the nation, was a panel of pathology residents—nominally supervised by a department faculty without a chairman (chap. 4, E).

Another example of unanticipated consequences at Palo Alto-Stanford is the management itself, which in the five years following opening of the hospital went through six changes in the chief executive position, three of them centering around the resignation-reinstatement-resignation-replacement of one man, Oliver Deehan (chap. 4, E), causing the organization to be managed by interim administrators three times.

The hot potato transition of control was smoother at Norfolk than at Palo Alto-Stanford, partly because Administrator Mitchell was involved earlier, partly because he was highly regarded as a professional manager, but mostly because the change from Norfolk General Hospital and Leigh Memorial Hospital to Medical Center Hospitals was not as substantial as from Palo Alto Hospital and Stanford Hospital to Palo Alto-Stanford.

In addition, those who designed the merger at Norfolk were prepared to follow through in its implementation. These persons understood the many ramifications of the consolidation, remained continuously engaged, and were steadfast in their duties. By contrast, at Palo Alto-Stanford only two persons understood in any detail the institutional ramifications of the change created by merger: early hospital board president William Hewlett and medical school associate dean Lowell Rantz (chap. 4, E). Natural turnover in board seats removed Hewlett from the scene, and death removed Rantz. Others were drawn in—new deans, new directors, new vice-presidents—but none had the same grasp or commitment.

As for Norfolk's merger management, Mitchell faced an array of classical issues: what to centralize and what to leave decentralized, management development, early losses of control over finances and personnel, and employee morale (chap. 9, E). The remaining merger management problems at Norfolk were very much involved in medical staff and professional dynamics: the unification of the medical staff (chap. 9, E), Mitchell's efforts to create a medical staff organization that would both respect the tenets of private practice and serve the purposes of the new medical school (chap. 9, E), and the numerous aspects of professional practice surrounding the Kempsville development (chap. 9, E). Yet, in all of these, Norfolk's problems were less than Palo Alto-Stanford's, due both to Norfolk's single medical staff arrangement and to its medical school's substantial dependence on the community doctors and hospitals for teaching material. At Norfolk the major postmerger events were generally predictable, usually controllable, and transpired sequentially rather than simultaneously. They did not sum to the pervasive and abortive changes which characterized Palo Alto-Stanford's stormy history.

Our third merger, Los Angeles County, was more clearly a professionally managed merger. The earliest reports and recommendations for the consolidation came from a blue ribbon commission staffed by County Administrative Office Hollinger (chap. 8, C). Later, Hollinger threatened to take over management of two of the merged departments, mental health and public health, if they did not capitulate to Hollinger's merger recommendations (chap. 8, C). A seemingly independent action, a board of supervisors' motion to establish a cooperative interdepartmental comprehensive health center, was immediately referred to the CAO for implementation. The interim planning committee organized to accomplish the merger consisted solely of the executives of the merging departments (chap. 8, C).

Thus postmerger problems were mostly those common to management directed integrations: two department chiefs in public health and mental health who knew their influence would decline (chap. 8, C), an opportunistic chief veterinarian who saw that his influence might increase (chap. 8, C), the fears of the Department of Hospitals monster (chap. 8, C), the many aspects of centralization vs. decentralization which, because of the scale of the undertaking, were crucial (chap. 8, D), the difficulties in selecting and retaining effective generalists for the new regions (chap. 8, D), and the benefits and drawbacks of the attrition of key people (chap. 8, E).

Of the three unexpected events in our description of the Los Angeles County merger—the Friends of the Friendless ambulance chasing ring, the nursing home scandal, and the intern and resident strike—none were the direct result of the merger, unless they can be attributed to oversights that come with size. Each was handled in its way; we do not sense anything of the pervasive change that characterized Palo Alto-Stanford. However, they did impact on the merger, culminating in a rather weak demand by members of the board of supervisors for the county executive to consider redividing the merged agency. This gave a new county administrative officer the opportunity to move in on the merger with a new plan for recentralization, reversing Witherill's regionalization momentum and imposing new criteria for management efficiency and standardization (chap. 8, E).

In summary, our three cases indicate that the transition of essential organizational control is not really as hypothesized in Proposition 18a: the hot potato is seldom passed as clearly to top management as proposed. Our cases also indicate that the management of hospital mergers is strongly conditioned by the peculiar features of medical staff and governance in these institutions (Propositions 20a, b); it is these features which put the greatest stress on mergers and demand most of their administrator's attention and skill.

As for executive attrition (Proposition 20c), the very high turnover in the top 20 management positions in Los Angeles, reaching 16 out of 20 in one year (chap. 8, E), and the revolving door of top executives at Palo Alto-Stanford, is revealing. Even in Mitchell's seemingly stable management at

Norfolk, of his top five trust of equals three departed and four were replaced in a relatively short time.[4] In a field characterized by career mobility, it is difficult to determine the extent to which these changes were normal. In the Palo Alto-Stanford situation most of the change resulted directly from merger,[5] as did three of the key Norfolk changes. In Los Angeles, many of the changes appeared to be the direct result of merger dynamics.

Finally, we can conclude that the effect of unanticipated postmerger problems is generally not one of organizational vacuum or anomie, as proposed in connection with Proposition 22c. Nevertheless, our cases indicate that unplanned events requiring major management response do most definitely occur, leading to general postmerger reorganization and restabilization (Propositions 23a, b).

D.   MANAGEMENT STRUCTURE

In chapter 3 we advanced the proposition that once essential transition to management occurs in a merger, a new control system must be established recognizing shifts in the distribution of organizational power and new dominant coalitions. Two essential features of this control system were discussed: patterning authority, and channeling information. We will deal with the first of these in this section, leaving the second to section E, Organizational Development.

MANAGING PROFESSIONAL AFFAIRS

Our cases indicate that it is inappropriate to speak of a single or fixed management structure for any given merger. Since major aspects of mergers cannot be anticipated and require reappraisal, and since during the postmerger time all important relations are tested and some are revised (Proposition 23b), then certainly also the pattern of management must be revised.

At Palo Alto-Stanford much of the revision was in the organization of medical staff affairs—probably the most unusual aspect of that merger. At Norfolk the medical staff structure was less the focus of attention than was the general structuring of hospital-physician relations. This was particularly evident in the efforts to strike a proper relationship between Medical Center Hospitals and the Doctors' Clinic Company. At Los Angeles the emphasis was placed on the proper reorganization and management of a large public agency. Although the physicians were largely inside rather than outside the bureaucracy, even here various professional elements intruded strongly. The strike of interns and residents is but one example (chap. 8, E).

All of this indicates that mergers do lead to increased professionalism, increased conflict between administrative and professional goals, and the requirement for new forms of organizational control (Propositions 19a, b). It also indicates that the design of medical staff and professional relations is so crucial to merged hospitals that it should become a central part of the manager's role—not something initiated and executed by physicians and accepted or rejected by administration. Our three mergers provide rich examples of this. These examples also validate another aspect of merger dynamics discussed in connection with Proposition 22e: the lag that usually occurs in the integration of medical staffs, with management consequences.

At both Palo Alto-Stanford and Norfolk the contractual relations with hospital-based physicians became extremely sensitive, both to doctors generally and to hospital functioning. At Palo Alto-Stanford the struggle was to keep these matters within the hospital jurisdiction, as witnessed by the "Packard Agreements" and the first administrations' efforts to sign a bilateral contract with pathologist Eversole (chap. 4, D). Later on, the hospital administration proposed a new affiliation agreement with the medical school in which the school would become a third party to all hospital-physician negotiations and contracts (chap. 4, E).

At Palo Alto-Stanford professional matters were not only central to management's concerns but also led eventually to a total reorganization of the merger. In response to the inadequacy of the original dual medical staff arrangement, the merger's first administrator designed a system of committee management, but eventually the 26 joint professional and administrative committees proved unworkable (chap. 4, E). The second administrator proposed a medical board with clear responsibilities for hospital professional affairs, and succeeded in this only after a showdown between the president of the hospital board and the medical school department chairmen (chap. 4, E). The next administrator, sensing the medical school faculty's dissatisfaction and using a new affiliation agreement as the instrument of change, revised his predecessor's medical board arrangement so that both medical staffs had direct access to the hospital board. He also cut the outpatient clinics and two other activities from the hospital's patient care jurisdiction and transferred them to the medical school's educational jurisdiction (chap. 4, E).

At Norfolk, top management saw the issue of professional contracts as a major concern. Here, hospital jurisdiction was never seriously threatened, but administrator Mitchell used his influence to be sure that dealings on such matters were regarded as the administrator's and not those of a committee of the board nor the medical staff (chap. 9, E). The general organization of the medical staff was also an important management concern. The first order of business after the White Heron meeting was to strike a set of bylaws for a new and unified medical staff. The 72-page document that resulted 1) provided validation for traditional medical democracy, with its elected officers; 2) provided a voice for the emerging medical school; 3) avoided potential standoffs between community and medical school clinical chiefs (as at Palo Alto-Stanford); and 4) provided for effective hospital functioning by designing an operationally-oriented executive committee and three standing committees matching important hospital activities (chap. 9, E).[6]

The Kempsville development clearly shows the management implications of a merger involving physicians. Some of the hospital's best doctors migrated to Kempsville; the hospital followed, after some urging by Mitchell. This put the hospital and Doctors' Clinic Company physicians cheek-by-jowl in an arrangement wherein neither could dominate the other yet each was indispensable to the other. The series of exchanges that then transpired resulted in 1) agreement jointly to plan the Kempsville site, 2) fixing responsibility for a surgicenter, and 3) agreement on the operation of certain activities in the medical office building (chap. 9, E). These were all measures to integrate the activities of a pivotal group of physicians with the hospital's functions, so as neither to drive the doctors away nor provide so many benefits that other medical staff physicians would rebel.

At Los Angeles County, the nature of professional-management interaction was not along medical staff or doctor-hospital lines, but related to differences in professional outlook among public health, mental health, and somatic physicians. To quote Marshall (1971), "Mistrust between the (former) Department of Health, the Department of Hospitals, and the Department of Mental Health was more than mere organizational conflict. It was also a conflict between different professional orientations and . . . philosophies" (p. 874). Administrator Witherill's entire regionalization plan—the most dramatic element of the reorganization other than the merger itself—was in part a response to public health concerns that without decentralization the community health point of view would be overwhelmed by traditional medical care interests established in the old Department of Hospitals. The experimental comprehensive health centers were seen as the new positions of power for former public health officials whose bureau system of organization was being dismantled (chap. 8, D). The initial arrangement of deputy directors for the department reflected parallel concerns among mental health professionals (chap. 8, D).

Interprofessional tensions were so bad that the merger almost ceased at the early operational stage: the three deputy directors of the merged agency, all former department heads, failed to plan for the integration, being unwilling to accept the leadership of Dr. Affeldt, former Department of Hospitals medical director. For the first experimental health center they merely designed separate operations for the same building, without collaboration or integration. Later, when Witherill assigned agencywide program responsibility for alcoholism and drug abuse to Dr. Affeldt, tension increased between him and the deputies for public health and mental health to the point that, as author

Johnson reports "the solution to this general conflict was to come up with the retirements of Sachs and Brickman, at which time their positions would be downgraded to staff positions" (chap. 8, C).

By way of summary, we can place all these examples, and the general matter of managing highly professionalized organizations, in the context of Lawrence's and Lorch's contingency theory. As discussed in chapter 2, section G (Assumption of Organization Effect), this theory emphasizes the blending of organization structures that permit differentiation in order to meet external conditions with patterns that provide for necessary internal integration. A simple listing in table 12.1 of all management strategies noted in this section illustrates this idea.

The proper mix of these two orientations—one advancing differentiation and one obtaining integration—is a "constantly changing equilibrium" (Hage, 1974). And, the proper blending of these two patterns is one of the creative arts of merger management.

ORGANIZATIONAL DESIGN

In chapter 3, section B, we noted the management complication of dealing simultaneously with the professional and institutional aspects of a massive reorganization. In many ways solutions in one realm become problems in the other, particularly if we recognize the need for more organic approaches to the first while granting the appropriateness of more mechanical methods for the second. We will focus here on only one aspect of our three cases: centralization/decentralization.

In chapter 3 we reviewed 1) the tendency of new mergers first to centralize and then to decentralize; 2) the need to choose which functions to centralize and which to disperse; 3) the problems top executives face when attempting to make certain centralized services work effectively that separate staffs previously accomplished; and 4) the job of selecting second and third level managers suited to the new merged conditions. For hospital mergers, we argued that a relative dispersion of power, both lingering from premerger times and built into the new organization, poses a basic limit on management discretion: top management has difficulty delegating powers it does not itself hold.

With the heavy requirement for management strength on the one hand, and for constraints on the full exercise of management discretion on the other hand, control will tend to remain (or become) centralized despite operating circumstances which call for decentralization (Proposition 20a). We will want to look at our three mergers in this light, and, further, to examine them for those activities in which there were at least attempts to retain decentralized status after merger, if they were so organized beforehand, or achieve decentralization anew, if not.

TABLE 12.1.   Management Patterns in Respect to Professional Affairs:
Three Hospital Mergers

	Differentiation	Integration
Palo Alto-Stanford	Recognizing the medical school as a party to hospital-doctor contracts	Bilateral contracts with hospital-based specialists
	Recognizing the independent relationship of both medical staffs to hospital board reorganization of outpatient clinics	Establishing a medical board to replace numerous joint committees
		Policy that two patient-care wings to be operated as one hospital
Norfolk Medical Center	Purchase of Kempsville land and development of satellite hospital	Negotiations with hospital-based specialists the administrator's responsibility
	Separate initial development of surgicenter	The composition of the merged medical staff executive committee
		Joint planning with Doctors Clinic Company of Kempsville development
Los Angeles County	Regionalization by geography	Making three former department heads deputy directors of merged agency
	Experimental health centers	Method of planning experimental health centers
		Appointing Affeldt agencywide program head of alcoholism and drug abuse

Some useful information exists on this second matter from studies of mergers not included in this book. Reflecting on the large merger creating the Wilmington Medical Center, its chief executive reported to a group of hospital consultants as follows (Shortcliffe, 1967):

> I believe you will agree with me that there is trauma in merger from the point of view of former relatively independent hospital administrators, assistants, department heads, and their employees. We wrestled philosophically with this problem prior to merger and debated at length whether or not we would follow the pattern of some of the major local industries in extending almost total local autonomy to the individual units, or whether we would centralize all administrative decisions.
>
> We settled on a compromise and moved to centralize personnel administration immediately after merger in order to gain control over the standardization of

policies and over wage administration. It took 18 months, however, for us to accomplish much more than that. What we have done is to move in the direction of increasing centralized authority but not "centralization for its own sake." We have attempted to be selective in our decision about centralization and, in the process, we have repeatedly traumatized the stature and the traditional role of the individual hospital administrator. [p. 10]

Dagnone's (1967) study concentrated on the management problems of multiunit hospital systems, both those created by merger and those developed through satellites (chap. 1, H). Respondents to his survey of 28 managements (40 percent merger-type, 60 percent satellite-type) indicated that their greatest management problems were deciding what to centralize and what to decentralize. Of the 28, 22 described their organizations as decentralized, but of the 22 only 5 were decentralized to the point of having no central staff other than the chief executive and his office. Seventeen management structures were based on a balance between centralized policy formation and decentralized operations. The remaining six hospitals reported a highly centralized form.

Dagnone concluded that specific allocation of functions between corporate and divisions varied according to the function, the circumstances at the time, the executive's personality and the geographic placement of the units (p. 33). Nonetheless, patterns emerged. Administrative functions such as accounting, personnel, and payroll were found to be centralized in 70 percent of the hospitals, while purchasing was a central function in 85 percent of the cases. Decentralization of functions among hospital units was most evident in admitting, housekeeping, and dietary: 85 percent of the hospitals noted that these functions were a unit responsibility. Nursing functions were decentralized in 80 percent of the hospitals. Pharmacy, medical records and maintenance were also predominantly unit responsibilities.

As for problems in striking the correct balance, Dagnone's respondents reported their most serious problems to be: 1) a chief executive attempting to centralize day-to-day decision making at the top; 2) absentee administration and control; 3) friction between central staff and unit line personnel; 4) different units with unequally able administrators; 5) the "notable determination of branches to imitate the central unit"; 6) subunits that "show their dependency needs only when they have urgent requirements, but resist control at other times as interference and undue domination"; and 7) the difficulty faced by management in attempting to develop a "Weltanschauung"[7] among all system personnel. Dagnone concluded that a certain amount of all of this is inevitable and good. "It appears that no matter what decisions are reached, problems such as these will remain. Vying or jockeying for power among hospital branches are by-products of their ambition and pride" (p. 64).

Of our three case study mergers, we will comment briefly on the Palo Alto-Stanford and Norfolk situations, and deal more extensively with Los

Angeles. The merger at Palo Alto-Stanford yielded one hospital operation in one location. After approximately two years of merger operations, a satellite unit (the former Palo Alto Hospital) reopened as a nonsurgical acute-care facility, located less than one mile from the main hospital. When the satellite was first opened it was managed and operated entirely as an extension of each of the functioning departments of the main hospital: there was no local management and all decision making was channelled through existing supervisors to the central administration. This was so arranged partly because both administrator Barnett and his successors wanted the satellite to be used by the medical school faculty as well as by the community practitioners; they were fearful that a decentralized local management would identify with or be captured by Palo Alto physicians, eventually excluding Stanford-admitted patients. This management reasoning fits our explanation of why initial merger management structures tend to be centralized.

Three years later, after complaints mounted about hospital services at the satellite, top management switched its thinking and hired an administrator for the satellite and placed all on-site supervisors under his management for operational concerns, while leaving them responsible to their central department heads for technical matters. At about this same time plans developed within the hospitalwide nursing department for a unit management system, which was installed two years later throughout the organization.

So, at Palo Alto-Stanford the management structure changed over the course of seven years from a centralized decision-making structure organized by function to a more decentralized decision-making structure, organized in part by geography.

At Norfolk, administrator Mitchell came to the merger with a strong management philosophy against establishing a large central administration (chap. 9, E). Yet, pressures ran strongly against this approach, notably in finance and personnel. In both cases he could not achieve the degree of control he felt was necessary. In the first instance it was the exigencies of working capital control that forced his centralization to a corporate director of finance (chap. 9,E). In the second, there was no single dramatic event, although some time prior to his reorganization there had been an official charge and investigation of discriminatory hiring practices. Differences between the Norfolk General and Leigh Memorial divisions in wages and personnel policies had become a problem. Perhaps also Mitchell's centralization of the personnel function expressed his own keen interest in this aspect of management (chap. 9, E).

Despite these two important centralizations, Mitchell sought otherwise to achieve a decentralized organization. Shortly after the merger when Warren Oliver resigned as administrator of the small Leigh Memorial Division, Mitchell did not hesitate to replace him with another manager with similar responsibilities and authorities. (Note the difference between this strategy and the one used at Palo Alto-Stanford.) And, in subsequent management developments, maximum authority remained vested in the two division administrators (chap. 9, E).

The questions of management structure found their greatest test in the Los Angeles case. Witherill's approach to decentralizing authority was meshed entirely with his concepts of geographically regionalized health care delivery. As Jo Ann Johnson writes in her case study:

> Witherill opted for geographic decentralization for several reasons: to develop a responsive health care delivery system meant that care be provided in the community where it was needed. To monitor need, organizational decisions needed to be delegated . . . as close to the consumer as possible. Geography was chosen as the form of decentralization because Los Angeles had a dispersed population which tended to identify with particular areas.
>
> Health service regions were designated to serve as the basic organization through which the Department of Health Services was to discharge the bulk of its health service activities. Regions were to be divided into health service districts. Each district was to contain a comprehensive ambulatory care program along with a network of neighborhood health centers which would make extensive use of para-professionals.
>
> Deputy Director Avant added details to Witherill's broad guidelines for regional development.
>
> "The general rule of thumb is that everything should be regionalized unless there is some specific reason why they should not. In other words, non-regionalized functions are exceptions to the rule." [p. 68]

Witherill's concept faced some very rough sledding. His main obstacles were 1) internal resistance, not to decentralization but to its form in regionalization; 2) proper definition of regional boundaries; and 3) external resistance from the county administrative officer.

In the first category, Witherill's form of regionalization stood in marked contrast to the long tradition of public health services organization. What Johnson describes as a bureau organization refers to a funtional-type management structure in which several deputy or associate public health directors are each given substantial line authority for the operation in various locales of their different specialties of nursing, sanitation inspection, epidemiology, laboratory services, etc. In the classical form of this structure (Hanlon, 1969), administration consists primarily of providing support services to these specialties. With both former public health directors of Los Angeles County having been long used to this method, along with all their local public health officers, it is understandable that they had troubles comprehending, working towards, and implementing a management structure so completely different— even when that structure so obviously provided the best pathway to future maintenance of the public health viewpoint (chap. 8, C).

The method of organizing mental health services also contradicted Witherill's form of decentralization, primarily because of its pattern of funding. While both public health and hospital services were funded by county government—a legal mandate in California for health services for the poor—mental health programs were funded largely by state and federal government, stemming from special legislations. Mental health officials regard these special funding authorities as the main political bulwark against two constant threats: the tendency of somaticists, in charge of most local health care activities, to underallocate to mental health, and the view of public health traditionalists that mental health is just another aspect of public health's broad jurisdiction over preventive efforts. So, Los Angeles County's mental health chief Brickman resisted a merger reorganization that would deliver mental health back to where it had been prior to its long-fought efforts to achieve independence.

The former Los Angeles County public health and mental health departments shared a mutual fear of the influence of somatic medicine, strongly entrenched in the mammoth Department of Hospitals and now transformed in the personage of Witherill and his deputies to positions of highest power in the new agency.

Witherill's second major obstacle to regionalization was boundary definition. He faced at least four conflicting forces in the drawing of regional lines in such a way that deputy director Avant's 1972 criteria would be met: relatively self-sufficient, encompass a full range of health services, number between five and ten, and contain two to be selected as pilots (chap. 8, D). The old public health department regions made the most sense from a rational management point of view, since the long-standing legal reporting requirements in public health provided the best basis for information gathering on health outcomes. Yet, these regions did not jibe with another set of boundaries that would provide at least one county hospital for each region, making it easier to meet Avant's criterion of encompassing a full range of health services. A third basis related to the population distribution of racial minorities. Racial caucuses and various community-based advocacy groups applied pressure to be on one side or another of a boundary in order to maximize access to certain health care resources. And, there was some possibility that the total flow of funds for the agency's activities would be affected by the racial mixture of designated subareas. The fourth method was the "rule of five": a well known political guideline in Los Angeles County that said boundaries and resource allocations had better closely match the five supervisorial districts from which board of supervisor members were elected, or proposals would have little chance of obtaining the necessary approvals. On the other hand, to acquiesce entirely to the rule of five invited interference from individual supervisors in the management of their health services.

Witherill's boundary-drawing had to walk a fine line among these four forces. The process delayed and complicated the entire regionalization effort. Even after initial approval, the boundaries became the object of regular questioning and restudy (chap. 8, E).

With these circumstances as a backdrop, Witherill adopted a three-phase approach to decentralization: 1) new administrative organization for each region, casting aside old relationships; 2) change in focus away from hospitals and toward ambulatory health care delivery; and 3) reassignment and relocation of headquarters personnel (chap. 8, D).

Should the sequence have been reversed? Did not this form of transition set up a situation where, for the first two phases, the regions were robbed of the personnel necessary to make regionalization work effectively, while at the same time the personnel still inclined to traditional central office control were striving to prove decentralization unworkable? The requirement to conduct two pilot regional operations complicated the matter, serving both to stretch out the reorganization and place key personnel simultaneously under different management structures.

Both the sequence of phasing and the commitment to pilot experiments are entirely sensible management approaches. Yet, the combined impact of these strategies in the context of the size and inherent obstacles of the Los Angeles County situation raises the question whether a sudden-death transition would not have been the preferred strategy.

Would such have been possible?

A long line of management doctrine, backed by the assertions of behavioral scientists, states that gradualism and pilot testing is to be preferred: people can better participate in the developments, mistakes can be corrected before applied wholesale, and new approaches become comfortable because they have been around for awhile. The counterargument states that, for mergers and perhaps other forms of severe adjustment where organizational interdependencies are so great, nothing short of sudden, systemswide change is appropriate; without this, the reorganization always falls short of the mark. Gradualism may obtain acceptance, but it seldom yields all of the original aims of reorganization.

The two pilot regions described in our Los Angeles case illustrate how different the effects of decentralization can be in two circumstances which outwardly appear the same.

The San Gabriel Valley region director was former public health officer Finn; the Coastal region director was former hospital administrator Smith. Finn was not experienced or trained in management; he did not lay out a clear management plan, as did Smith. Things got bogged down in the task force approach which Finn used and which was customary in public health administration. He rather bungled the redefinition of roles for community health nursing, sanitarians, and mental health counselors, and he did not see the eventual management problems in letting Supervisor Shabarum do some of his bidding (chap. 8, D). In action more typical of public health than of hospital administration, he established active and effective working relationships with community and consumer groups, which paid off when the continuance of his job as permanent regional director was in jeopardy. Finn had much less with which to work than did Smith: without a county hospital in his region he had fewer resources upon which to draw, and he had the difficult job of reorienting district public health officers, mostly in their senior years, toward clinical roles.

In the Coastal region, Smith had more resources and thus fewer problems of implementation. Where Finn had to compensate for the absence of a hospital and thus the shortage of personnel to deliver mandated medical care, Smith had the opposite problem of breaking up a hospital dynasty complete with its emphasis on clinical specialization and acute care therapies. Smith's management design, a combination of program, resources, and geographic emphasis, was complex, novel, and led to a degree of confusion; but it provided the basis for decisions about changing personnel roles comparable to those faced by Finn in San Gabriel Valley (chap. 8, D). Smith did not have to deal as much with supervisorial intervention.

The outcome of the two experiments, or at least the destinies of their acting directors, was bizarre. Despite his effectiveness in a new and difficult position, Finn scored poorly in the exams of permanent regional director. This could have been his performance or a bias in the test. He was temporarily continued in his post only through bureaucratic maneuvering, but subsequently moved to another post in the agency. Toward the end of the San Gabriel Valley region's pilot phase, Finn presented a paper on administrative pitfalls in regionalization which, according to Johnson, revealed his teeter-tottering between a wish for greater headquarters guidance and a wish for greater autonomy (chap. 8, C). Smith gained wide respect for his performance as acting regional director of the Coastal region, but then caught the rap for the Friends of the Friendless ambulance chasing ring, through his demotion and replacement as regional director. Subsequently, he left the county's employ.

Decentralization in Los Angeles was certainly not going as envisioned. Witherill's lack of discretion in matters of internal organization reduced his credibility. This, combined with the aftermath of the intern and resident insurrection at Martin Luther King Hospital, caused a cover-your-ass attitude to pervade the rank and file—counterproductive to decentralization efforts. But more than this, Witherill's third major obstacle to regionalization was now surfacing: the county administrative office's increasing concern for operating costs. Stimulated in part by the CAO's management study of the agency's public health function, the CAO's original liaison position to the agency was expanded to a full-blown health services division assigned to study and monitor the agency (chap. 8, E). Concern for costs grew into criticism of the agency's management control, which signaled a switch in Witherill's four-year efforts to regionalize operations. The CAO forced a redefinition of regional director positions away from policy autonomy and towards a day-to-day supervision and follow through on central office decisions (chap. 8, E). He also forced a restructuring of the agency's top management towards re-centralizing staff and imposing tighter controls over the regions, as well as introducing two new positions and persons at the deputy director level, including Jerry Chamberlain, the standardization man (chap. 8, E). All of this seemed to be Witherill's price for the CAO's continued support of the merger.

What can we derive from our three cases about management centralization and decentralization of mergers?

Two of our merger cases (Palo Alto-Stanford, and to a lesser degree, Medical Center Hospitals of Norfolk) support our hypothesis about initial centralization following merger. It is neither supported nor refuted by the Los Angeles County case, that merger not being one of previously independent corporations.

Our proposition about the limitations on management's ability to follow initial centralization with effective decentralization are generally confirmed by the Los Angeles case, to a lesser extent by the events at Palo Alto-Stanford, and not at all by Norfolk. (What will happen in Norfolk after the new satellite hospital is opened at some distance to the main operation remains to be seen.) Los Angeles certainly is a situation where there were constraints on the full exercise of management discretion, leading to a situation where control remained centralized despite circumstances which called for decentralization (Proposition 20a).

In all three of our cases decentralization was attempted by geography rather than by function.

Certainly at both Norfolk and Los Angeles top management faced serious personnel problems in making central services work where local activities were previously the pattern, and vice-versa. Whatever the original plans were in this regard, they usually had to be modified as difficulties in implementation emerged.

Sociologists and management theorists assert that there is a tendency for enterprises to overreact to one extreme of centralization/decentralization by imposing the other: the oft-quoted pendulum swing. This is undoubtedly dysfunctional. Only one of our merger cases, Los Angeles, revealed this behavior, suggesting that the phenomenon is limited to extremely large organizations, and that in hospitals (and other highly professionalized organizations) the phenomenon is blunted by the counterforces of dispersed power and coalition-based decision making.

Little evidence from our cases suggests the relative superiority of either centralization or decentralization. Our cases show wide variation in management practice. Clearly, varying circumstances call for different mix strategies.

E. ORGANIZATIONAL DEVELOPMENT

The suggestion persists from social scientists that the deliberate practice of organizational development would reduce or eliminate many of the communication and morale problems that pervade mergers (Levinson, 1970). Among employees it would reduce resistance to change and increase performance of the merged organization (Roos, 1975), for board members it would reduce interhospital identity strains and advance mutuality of goals, and for medical staffs it would deal with the institutional problems commensurate with increased professionalization (Hage, 1974).

By organizational development we mean the application of behavioral science techniques aimed at increasing communication and feedback, broadening decision making through participation, sharing individual and organizational goals and maximizing their commonalities, developing person-based rather than office-based authority, strengthening relationships based on mutual trust, and developing team as compared to individual efforts. These approaches are all based on the assumptions of organic rather than mechanistic organizations, as discussed in chapter 2, section C (Assumption of Conduct), and the assumption that attention to interpersonal and group processes will lead eventually to better organizational performance than attention solely on production.

Several of our propositions run in this vein. Propositions 19a–19d state that the increased professionalization which comes with merger demands a shift from sanction-based controls to socialization-based controls, and that failure to make this shift leads to organizational instability and attrition. Propositions 21a, 21b, and 22c assert that rank and file employees and supervisors have little knowledge or influence during early stages of hospital merger, so that at a critical stage the sudden adjustment of these nonvalid perceptions to organizational reality causes unanticipated stress and, in the extreme, spontaneous and uncontrolled change.

These hypotheses all suggest that more attention to organizational development is warranted. The same conclusion stems from the study of mergers conducted by the American Hospital Association-Northwestern University Health Services Research Center: merger managers should pay more attention to the phenomenon of alienation that seems inevitably to accompany merger, and they should do this by concentrating more on broadly based information and feedback and by employing specialists in organizational development (Cooney and Anderson, 1975).

But arrayed against these ideas is another set of propositions indicating that such is hardly possible, and may not even be appropriate. Proposition 22a points to the high degree of redundancy in hospital mergers, leading inevitably to the behavioral reactions associated with organizational disintegration. Organizational development might mitigate these effects, but the techniques would have to be more powerful or more effective than most known applications in order substantially to alter these consequences. Proposition 22b indicates that leaders will actually make or imply organizational protections for people, which can be predicted not to hold. If this is done knowingly it smacks of unethical and dishonorable behavior, and no amount of human relations management will make any difference. More likely, this behavior is not intentional deceit but rather an expression of hope, coupled with ignorance on leaders' parts as to what actually will happen. Either way, the short term easing of strain by making manifestations of protections will inevitably have its consequences (Propositions 22c, d) which seem unlikely to be cured by organizational development.

Beyond this, there is the question of whether high turnover and attrition—usually taken as the measure of a poorly developed organization—is indeed bad. Proposition 22f argues that attrition can be both functional, eliminating persons who would otherwise sabotage the merger, and dysfunctional, eliminating persons with useful organizational intelligence.

We have here quite a contrast: a line of argument that organizational development is much needed, and another that it is either futile or, in a peculiar twist, damaging. This second line says that mergers would seldom develop if all parties knew what they were getting into, and that merger decisions would never get made if the assumptions of egalitarianism, harmony-seeking, and goal congruence which are basic to organizational development were substituted for the assumptions of elitism, conflict, and bargaining that run through much of our conceptual material and our cases.

Does organizational development work in hospital mergers?[9] Has it been tried?

The evidence is sketchy. We have the experience of Golembiewski and Blumberg, reported in chapter 3 (note 55), in which the deliberate application of organizational development is said to have made a positive difference. We have Schneider's (1969) report of a merger of two Canadian hospitals in which a specific educational program was launched well in advance of a merger, but serious problems based on feelings of insecurity by staff were still encountered. And, we have Mosher's (1967) study of the reorganization and integration of numerous government agencies:

> The stage at which participation was most frequent and most consciously sought in the cases was that having to do with putting proposals into effect. In about half the cases, considerable effort was applied to bringing officers and employees into decision-making at some point in the implementation pro-

cess, and in some, fairly elaborate ad hoc organizational arrangements were made. Some participation of persons whose behaviors are to be modified is almost by definition essential in the implementing phases of reorganizations. . . . While some reorganizations involving a considerable amount of participation were fully or moderately effective, others with little or no participation were also effective. [pp. 523-26]

There are some gleanings from our several merger studies. The West-haven-Riviera merger failed. One author of the case study suggested in an epilogue to the case that game playing was the dominant underlying behavior of most of the participants (chap. 5, H). The merger transactions at West-haven-Riviera certainly contradicted the behavior recommended by Levinson (1970):

> At the bargaining table, the prospective partners would do well to indicate to each other what they wish from the merger, how they see each other's orga-nizations, how they feel about apparent differences, and how important those differences are to them. In particular, both organizations should be able to answer with psychological honesty, "What does he want me for really?" Then the prospective partners can jointly evolve their modes of compromise and integration. Such a process also creates a mechanism for the continuing so-lution of problems which arise subsequently. [p. 146]

If organizational development techniques had been applied to that small group of Westhaven-Riviera negotiators who flailed at each other for almost two years, the outcome might have been different. Yet, it might not have: more open sharing of feelings might simply have brought earlier to the fore the vast differences in the two communities, reflected by their respective leaders.

At Palo Alto-Stanford there was no deliberate organizational develop-ment, and there is some question as to whether efforts at informing or solic-iting the participation of key actors was undertaken (chap. 4, D, note 8). The case study is clear on the outcome: medical school faculty members felt betrayed by their university superiors, and felt that they had been forced into a set-up that made running a high quality medical school impossible. They succeeded eventually in getting their university to extricate them from the arrangement by buying out the city's assets and control (chap. 4, E).

At Norfolk, the problems of employee and medical staff reaction cen-tered predictably at the smaller Leigh Memorial Hospital. Statements made to Leigh employees shortly before the merger (chap. 9, E) were as hypothe-sized in Proposition 22b. And, last minute changes in the medical staff bylaws for Medical Center Hospitals were designed to accommodate Leigh's general practitioners (chap. 9, E). The problems these and other transactions had on the subsequent merger led administrator Mitchell to muse three years later: "I wish we had de-emphasized the myth of parity (between the two merged hospitals) and been more honest about de facto takeover" (chap. 9, E). There was no defined organizational development effort at Norfolk.[10]

At Los Angeles, efforts at organizational development were influenced by the civil service system of government. Both lower level and professional employees enjoyed job securities not available to their counterparts in our other mergers. While their jobs were protected, work location and organizational assignment were not. The response to merger was thus less one of fear of job loss due to redundancy and more one of resistance to reassignment to tasks and organizational setting. There are numerous examples of this, including the sanitarians, public health nurses, and mental health social workers of the San Gabriel Valley region (chap. 8, D), the hospital-oriented physicians and nurses of the Coastal region (chap. 8, D), and the long-term employees of the centralized offices of the several departments making up the new agency (chap. 8, D). The morale problems in our nongovernment mergers peaked at about the time of actual merger; in Los Angeles they were manifest much later. Indeed, an ongoing resistance seemed built into the merger at all levels of both the former public health and mental health departments, sufficient to hobble Witherill's regionalization plan (chap. 8, D). There was no defined organizational development at Los Angeles, although the top nurse of the agency performed this task at times (chap. 8, D).

In all our cases severe morale problems existed, stemming generally from the development of inaccurate fate assessments (Proposition 22c). We are struck by the long duration of these organizational problems: eight years with the Stanford faculty, six years (to date) with the key employees of Los Angeles County and five years with several groups within the Norfolk medical community. In each case the long duration is primarily among physicians. This supports Proposition 22e, that there is organizational lag in the medical staff aspects of hospital mergers.

Why was organizational development not used in our combinations, and why is it not in mergers generally? Merger managers are generally progressive and enlightened, and the benefits of this approach seem obvious.

The answer seems to be that organizational development is a strategy of planned change, while mergers involve many changes that are unplanned and unexpected. Further, organizational development assumes an ultimate harmony of goals—both between organizations and between individuals and organizations. Its techniques are those designed to bring out this harmony: open sharing, feedback, etc. Yet, in mergers, goals are often incompatible, and clash of goals is inevitable; the techniques of negotiation and exchange are often applied instead.

Even so, there are certainly aspects of this applied behavioral science that our cases indicate would be useful. One is simple communication. We distinguish this approach from broad scale participative decision making, which seems impossible in many aspects of hospital merging: the bargaining and bartering that go on in most mergers lead key decision makers to play their information cards close to the vest, but this yields information vacuums with serious consequences. The employment of behavioral scientists to increase the amount and type of communication could be a useful management strategy. Two veteran merger administrators have written as follows:

> The best public relations is face to face, and experience indicates that small and personal group meetings of employees of the merging units is essential and effective. [Rosenberg, 1966, p. 86]

> It is my opinion that we did in fact overlook the importance of direct and personal communication with those who have been so deeply involved in the operations of the pre-merger institutions. We could have avoided much difficulty had we been astute enough from the very beginning to have established a well-organized program of repetitive contact so that the ultimate decision in . . . consolidation would have come as no surprise. While we have now appointed a director of information services, this appointment should have been made prior to merger itself. I should like to add the comment that from the point of view of a professional in hospital administration I wish very much that I had at my side a medical sociologist. [Shortcliffe, 1967]

The timing of this communication is important. Premature communication of information that might turn out to be wrong will likely do more harm than good. Not only will the rank and file be misled, but merger managers run the risk of losing people's trust—the one factor that research indicates correlates strongly with acceptance of change (chap. 3, B). Communicating anything but the reality that is known at the time—harsh though it may be— can have serious aftereffects (Wyatt and Galski, 1977). There is a difference between 1) not knowing all the future realities of merger and communicating honest confusion about these, along with what is known, 2) knowing the probabilities for the future but not communicating them fully because to do so would side-track the merger, and 3) purposely misleading people, even with good intention, who are not in positions to know better and whose organizational lives are at stake.

In hospital mergers the costs and benefits of each are crucial.

In a way, the differences between each are differences in management tactics. But in another way, the differences are those of management ethics.[11]

F.   THE STYLE OF MERGER MANAGEMENT

Executive style remains as varied and elusive of measurement in merger management as it does in other realms of administration. Our discussion here will cover two approaches which summarize and contrast the many and varied ideas about style: strong persona and low profile.

As discussed in chapter 3 (sec. B), some theoreticians identify a particular requirement for personal or charismatic leadership at the early stage of a new organization's development. This strong persona view also finds many adherents among practitioners. Lowell Bellin (1970) summarizes this view:

It is imperative that in our analysis of interorganizational behavior we do not neglect this human element. You all recall the favorite chestnut of college sophomores as to whether within the context of human history heroes produce events or events produce heroes.

Which is the primary causal agent with respect to how two organizations deal with one another: the organization or the human being? Are we prepared to accept the notion that the major determinants of the mode and the extent of the interagency cooperation or competition lie in the nature of the organizations themselves? In the rewards and sanctions the organizations can theoretically impose upon one another? In the perceived self-interest of these same organizations? And in their inventory of things to be exchanged? Perhaps. But, if so, there is an implication to be derived from such an analysis: in order to achieve desirable objectives, either for the sake of our own specific organization, or, more altruistically, *pro bono publico*, we must concentrate on tinkering with bureaucratic structures and their formal tables of organizations. In such a scheme individuals are of secondary importance. Function follows administrative form . . .

If the pendulum swings the other way, one may anticipate that future holistic theories of interorganizational behavior will address themselves more to the individual human being as a determinant of how organizations react.

Consider the following examples:

1. In one city, the municipal health department and the municipal urban renewal authority worked out an arrangement whereby health department sanitarians routinely inspected and certified a dwelling unit for occupancy before a family would be relocated to this dwelling unit. By local policy, the urban renewal authority would withhold relocation funds from that family until the health department verified that the new home to which the family was about to move was not in violation of the state housing code. This arrangement prevented the normal phenomenon of governmental sponsorship of family displacement from one slum about to be razed by urban renewal to another slum. An obvious area of interagency cooperation? To my knowledge, up to the present time only one city in the country has such an interagency arrangement. And yet urban renewal authorities and city health departments, at least in structure and powers, are not too dissimilar from city to city.

Could it be that what facilitated this interagency cooperation was the fortuitous circumstance 1) that the top administrators of both agencies shared identical social commitments? 2) that coincidentally the administrators of both agencies had been close friends for some years prior to their appointment? 3) that the appointment of these two administrators to their offices occurred within two months of one another? 4) that because their respective offices represented the first public position for each of them, they were neither burdened nor prodded by knowledge of agency tradition?

2. In one city serious interagency tension developed over a period of a few months between the municipal health department and the visiting nurse association. Ultimately involved in this strife were the city public health council, the board of trustees of the municipal hospital, and the mayor of the city.

Previous relationships between the two agencies had been superb—so much so that the municipal health department a few years back had granted space at nominal cost within its own building to the visiting nurse association.

What happened? Was this merely a disagreement attributable to competition between two agencies for the scarce resource of desirable space within the health department, as some opined at the time? Or was the regrettable chemical reaction between the personalities of the agencies' top administrators the primary factor and the space issue merely incidental? [pp. 106–8]

The low profile view is more popular with organization theorists. Perrow's multiple leadership concept discussed in chapter 3 (sec. B) is in this vein, as is Lawrence and Lorch's contingency theory of management. An analyst of several cases of government reorganization (Mosher, 1967) concluded that personalities must operate within contexts of organizational structure and situation that are in some degree compatible.

Richard Wittrup is a merger manager with a low profile view. He made the following comments in response to an interview question about his management style (*Health Care Management Review*, 1975):

Well, I suppose the thing that's special about handling a hospital merger is that you have what is essentially a voluntary environment. That is to say, you're really in a situation where the parties can't be compelled to do anything. Whereas in the ordinary bureaucracy you've got some kind of sanctions that you can impose: You give somebody a raise or you don't give them a raise, or you promote somebody or you don't promote them, or if they have a request you can approve it or disapprove it. Those kinds of sanctions are not available to you in a merging situation. . . . In other words, what you have to do is to think in terms of how you create a situation so that behavior oriented toward your objective of merger is, if not more rewarding, at least less problematic than behavior in the opposite direction.

Viewing the dynamics of a merger as a set of social pressures you can guide is the most productive approach. If you're trying to quarterback this thing, the main thing to recognize is that the merger isn't happening because you willed it. The merger is happening because there a lot of planets out there with the right alignment. If you stay out of their way and just nudge them, you get your results. If the planets are not in their right alignment, you might as well forget it—it's not going to happen, at least if they're so far out of alignment that even with a little nudge from you they won't get in.

Between these two strong persona and low profile views, there is the obvious possibility of mutual causality: organization patterns are adjusted to reflect strong individual's behavior, while also the major determinants of individual's behavior lie in the nature of the interacting organizations. But this is too vague. We can examine the choices made in our merger cases to see if what followed was determined by individual's discretionary action or was declared by the situation.

Our richest test of this is in the Palo Alto-Stanford case. Barnett was initially accorded a strong persona role—the situation seemed to call for it—but his style was otherwise. His resignation from the hospital was quite precisely on this point (chap. 4, D). His successor, Oliver Deehan, was not so much a charismatic leader as professional manager who sought to emphasize the importance of the administrator's office. Deehan's principles of hospital authority (chap. 4, E), had this orientation—in theoretical terms, they emphasized Weberian rationality and hierarchy. Deehan felt strongly about this; in fact, he resigned twice over the failure of the merged hospital to follow his lead. His replacement, Leroy Bates, carefully blurred rather than sharpened organizational distinctions; he preferred negotiated solutions to ones based on principles, as shown by his handling of both the outpatient clinics situation and the affiliation agreement (chap. 4, E). Bates generally made no decisions where many seemed to be called for, and saw value in refusing to force every issue to sharp resolution.[12]

It appears that at Palo Alto-Stanford, changing circumstances were more deterministic than the personalities. In the early postmerger time a strong charisma seemed to be needed. At all times a blurring of rational management concepts seemed to be called for. In the ten-year history recorded in the case, the match of personalities to the situation's requirements was more often unsuccessful than successful.

At Norfolk, these two determinants seem more balanced. Mitchell was seen as a professional manager whose influences were apparent in the basic decision to merge, in his success in reversing an earlier decision taken against building a satellite at Kempsville, and in his strong impact on the initial medical staff organization (chap. 9, E). Yet, the constraints on Mitchell's behavior were also clear: the "southern family" was going to run things in a certain way regardless what Mitchell did; in addition, the evolving patterns of medical practice determined certain hospital responses, and the medical school had its inevitable impact.

In Los Angeles, the personal management style of top leaders seemed of little importance; role definition determined more than person—an inevitable consequence of size. At the regional level, the different circumstances Finn and Smith confronted seemed more controlling than their behavior as individual mergers. And, the movement of key people—at times summing to managerial migration—seemed to flow inevitably from the system.

In the Westhaven-Riviera case, a merger did not result, nor was there a high profile personal leader. Had there been a charisma in the situation the result might have been different.

However, all of these comparisons must be strongly qualified: the case method of analysis leaves ample room for writers to see and report with varying emphasis on cults of personality. Granting this, a tentative generalization may be advanced stating that merged organizations—and perhaps others—vary in the latitude within which personal leadership can operate. The latitude at Palo Alto-Stanford was wide, Norfolk's was middle-range, and Los Angeles' narrow. Latitude and size seem to be correlated, although perhaps there is also a correlation with complexity, after adjustment for size.

Another variable seems to be the clarity of a situation: Palo Alto-Stanford's organization was murky, making it difficult for managers to figure out the limits of their discretion and difficult to determine the impact of their actions. By contrast, the situation's constraints in Norfolk were more obvious, as were the results of individual actions. The other cases appear to fall between.

Our cases suggest that effective merger management depends less on a particular management style and more on a careful matching of management approach to situation. In many instances this matching seems to have been left to accident. Many mergers' successes and failures can be viewed as histories of good and bad matches. Matchmaking is very difficult business, often requiring more candor and evaluation of both organizational and personal characteristics than leaders are able or willing to undertake at the time. Yet, the importance of effective matching is not diminished by the difficulty of achieving it. As put by Connors (1978), "There has emerged a body of knowledge, a set of beliefs, and some hard evidence that: management style does make a difference in effectiveness, productivity, and morale, there are distinguishing characteristics of effective managers, and leaders of organizations can now make conscious choices on matters of management style, processes, and politics" (p. 8).

Finally, if there is any special management skill that seems called for by our case studies it is the one sketched by Whistler and discussed in chapter 3 (sec. B): the discernment of hitherto unnoticed relationships or patterns, the calculation of their cause and effect, and the creative translation of them into appropriate programs and actions.

NOTES

1. Richard Wittrup (*Health Care Management Review*, 1975), an experienced merger manager, provides the following discussion of timing: "Some fellow said there are three criteria for buying real estate: Location, location and location. We convert that and say there are three major things we regard in adminstration: Timing, timing and timing. It's a judgment call. If it gets out too soon, you blow your cover and you get a lot of people offended about it. But there will come a time probably when they will want to keep it quiet and you're better off to let it leak, because if the milieu is conducive to it, then the fact that it's being discussed brings pressure to bear on whoever is doing the negotiating to produce something, either do it or not do it. . . . Another thing that creates pressures to act are deadlines. Around the flimsiest kind of rationale you can often get a date

set and a deadline established, and that deadline shouldn't be too far out there, because that just improves geometrically the chances of something coming up that would bollix it up. So you have a short deadline, you can reduce the risk of unanticipated events and you keep everybody's nose right hard against those deadlines" (p. 95).

2. Thompson's (1967) discussion of this is worthwhile: "Perpetuation of the complex organization rests on appropriate co-alignment of time and space not simply of human individuals but of streams of institutional action. Survival rests on the co-alignment of technology and task environment with a viable domain, and of organization design and structure to that domain. . . . Each of the elements involved in the co-alignment has its own dynamics. . . . Now if the elements . . . are in part influenced by powerful forces in the organization's environment, then survival requires adaptive as well as directive action in those areas where the organization maintains discretion. Since each of the necessary streams of institutional action moves at its own rate, the timing of both adaptive and directive action is a crucial administrative matter. The central function of administration is to keep the organization at the nexus of several necessary streams of action; and because the several streams are variable and moving, the nexus is not only moving but sometimes quite difficult to fathom. . . . The configuration necessary for survival comes neither from yielding to any and all pressures nor from manipulating all variables, but from finding the strategic variables . . . (pp. 147, 148).

3. One had the title of "superintendent"; the other had succeeded in changing this to "administrator" only a few years previous.

4. Replacement of the Leigh Division's administrator, replacement of the corporate finance director, replacement of the Norfolk General Division administrator, and, not reported in the case study, resignation and replacement of the corporate director of personnel.

5. Author's personal knowledge.

6. This fourth result portends what Shortell (1977) predicts for the hospitals of the 1980s: "Medical staff organizations will continue to evolve toward more structured forms. They will be increasingly organized along matrix lines, with an individual physician being both a member of a traditional clinical department (for example, general surgery) and a functional hospital unit (for example, admissions surveillance, process control, or outcome control)" (p. 71).

7. German sociology: the purpose of the world as a whole.

8. This being their feeling, Witherill must at times have approached regionalization humming that old love refrain, "Health is a Many-Splintered Thing"!

9. Does it work in nonmerged hospitals? The title of Weisbord's (1976) paper is revealing of one conclusion by an experienced practitioner of organizational development: "Why Organizational Development Hasn't Worked (So Far) in Medical Centers." For a contrasting view see Margulies' (1977) "Managing Change in Health Care Organizations."

10. However, Mitchell believes that the application of behavioral sciences to hospital management will and should play a more prominent role in the future. Personal conversation, May 3, 1976.

11. For an excellent discussion, see Bok (1978).

12. Theorists of decision making call this a decision not to decide, rather than inaction. It can be a deliberate strategy.

558   THE RAMIFICATIONS

REFERENCES

Bellin, Lowell. "Discussions of William J. Reid's paper 'Interorganizational Coop-
eration: A Review and Critique of Current Theory'." In *Interorganizational Re-
search in Health*, ed. by Paul White and George Vlasak. Conference Proceedings,
Johns Hopkins University. National Center for Health Services Research and
Development, U.S. Department of Health, Education and Welfare, 1970.
Bok, Sissala. *Lying: Moral Choice in Public and Private Life*. Vintage Books: New
York, 1978.
Conners, Edward J. "Generic Problems in the Development and Operation of Multi-
Hospital Systems." Sixth Annual Invitational Conference on Multi-Hospital Sys-
tems, American Hospital Association, July 17–19, 1978.
Cooney, James P., and Alexander, Thomas L. *Multihospital Systems: An Evaluation*
(Part I). Health Services Research Center of the Hospital Research and Educa-
tion Trust and Northwestern University, Chicago, 1975.
Dagnone, Antonio. "A Study of Multiple Unit Hospital Systems," Master's thesis,
Program in Hospital Administration. University of Toronto, 1967.
Gottshall, Ralph K. "Merger Benefits Outnumber the Problems." *Trustee*, November
1967.
Hage, Jerald. *Communication and Organizational Control: Cybernetics in Health and
Welfare Settings*. Wiley: New York, 1974.
Hanlon, John J. *Principles of Public Health Administration*. St. Louis: Mosby, 1969.
Health Care Management Review. "The Way Dick Wittrup Sees It." Winter, 1975.
Levinson, Harry. "A Psychologist Discusses Merger Failures." *Harvard Business
Review*, March-April 1970.
Linowes, David F. "Is Merger Necessary?" *Academy of Management Journal*, April
1965.
March, James G., and Simon, Herbert A. *Organizations*. Wiley and Sons: New York,
1965.
Margulies, Newton. "Managing Change in Health Care Organizations." *Medical
Care*, August 1977.
Marshall, D.R. "Attempting a Merger: Reorganizing Health Services in Los Angeles
County." *Health Services and Mental Health Agency Reports*, October 1971.
Mosher, F.C., ed. *Governmental Reorganizations: Cases and Commentary*. Bobbs-
Merrill: Indianapolis, 1967.
Roos, N.P. "Two Models for Understanding the Hospital Merger." Working Paper
No. 75–51. Graduate School of Management, Northwestern University, Evanston,
1975.
Rosenberg, Donald. "How Mergers Begin and How They Work." *Hospitals*, July
1966.
Schneider, R.A. "Anatomy of a Merger." *Canadian Hospital*, November 1969, pp. 23–
25.
Shortcliffe, Ernest C. "Hospital Merger—Some Personal Observations." The As-
sociation of American Hospital Consultants, Chicago, 1967.
Shortell, Stephen. "The Researcher's View." In *Hospitals in the 1980's: Nine Views*.
Chicago: American Hospital Association, 1977.
Thompson, James D. *Organization in Action*. New York: McGraw-Hill, 1967.
————, and Tuden, Arthur. "Strategies, Structures, and Processes of Organiza-
tional Decision." In *Comparative Studies in Administration*, ed. by James D.
Thompson *et al*. University of Pittsburgh Press: Pittsburgh, 1959.

Weisbrod, M. "Why Organizational Development Hasn't Worked (So Far) in Medical Centers." *Health Care Management Review*, Spring 1976.

Weston, J. Fred. "The FTC Staff's Economic Report on Conglomerate Merger Performance." *The Bell Journal of Economics and Management Science*, Autumn, 1973.

Wyatt, Janice, and Galski, Thomas. "The Psychosocial Impact of Hospital Expansion." *Health Care Management Review*, Summer 1977.

13.

A Summary Comment

Professionals in health services planning, regulation and administration have developed a certain faith in hospital integrations. A momentum has grown around this conventional wisdom—one that inspires these professionals to promote an upward sizing of hospitals by whatever means, including mergers. This is perhaps rooted in a national culture equating size and corporate ingenuity with the American way of life. This culture prevails despite several countercultures: the attraction of "new age" people to the intimacy of human-centered small groups, the attraction of intellectuals to the idea that small is not only beautiful but perhaps economical, the attraction of ecologists to the possibilities of self-sufficiency of small living and production units, and the growing disdain of virtually everyone for large bureaucracies. It also prevails despite the failures of the late 1960s of the conglomerate era in the business community, perhaps best illustrated by the total collapse of the seventh largest U.S. corporation, Ling-Tempco-Vaught. More surprising for our field, it prevails despite the cottage industry of American medical practice, rooted in the small business interaction of a single professional and a single patient.

Just as all mergers are not all good, so they are not all bad. The growth culture seems to have masked from the merger phenomenon the arguments and the evidence that could lead to a more sensible matching of types of hospital integration to varying circumstances. As an example, a misfit currently on the health care landscape is the horizontal merger of hospitals in widely dispersed locations rather than the vertical integration of hospitals with other provider enterprises in local regions.

Despite this general imperative toward merger, all sorts of behavioral blocks exist at the institutional level—blocks with which this book has dealt extensively. The irony is that these behavioral barriers seem to impinge most strongly on those close in or tight mergers which make the most sense in terms of both operating efficiency and health care delivery effectiveness. The reading of this book will, it is hoped, help people involved in hospital mergers to understand these dynamics so that they can reduce the behavioral obstacles and achieve the gains inherent in most merger situations.

The hospital merger phenomenon is not simply a cultural imperative or a labyrinth of institutional psychosocial dynamics. It is also a proper and useful response to the economic, demographic, and technological forces characterizing the United States in the late 1900s. The question, then, is not whether we have hospital mergers but what kind they will be and what impact they will have on the entire industry structure of medical care delivery. In this, the public's concern must be paramount. Hospital mergers strongly impact such political-economic choices as: regulation by government or by the invisible hand of the marketplace, the enhancement or reduction of competition, and the power balance of divergent interest groups such as consumers, hospitals, physicians, and reimbursers.

The U.S. medical care system has many virtues; however, one of its defects is its lack of a regionalized structure. Many nations achieve this regionalization through a combination of socialized medicine and government operation of all hospitals. The U.S. has rejected this. However, regionalized health care remains possible without state domination. The twentieth century history of U.S. health care legislation is dotted with a great variety of efforts to accomplish this, most of which have failed. Corporate reorganization could achieve regionalized health care delivery; such would be a uniquely American approach. The beginning efforts have started with hospitals, but too much has centered thus far on the hospitals alone. The combination of institutional power residing in hospitals and corporate enterprise that is a part of our economic culture could achieve a very worthwhile transformation.

As this effort unfolds, the challenge for the corporate rationalizers—health planners and hospital trustees—will be properly to match enterprise inventiveness to the true medical care needs of the populations to be served. The challenge for regulators will be to obtain the advantages of a more concentrated industry while avoiding the public exploitation that is made possibly by monopolies. The managerial challenge will be to achieve the advantages of specialization that come with size without incurring the rigidity of bureaucracy. The social scientists' challenge will be not only to understand this complex phenomenon but also to turn their knowledge to the usefulness of policy makers and operators.

These are but some of the many opportunities afforded by the hospital merging process.

Index

Health planning agencies
Trade-off agreements, definition and examples, 37
Trade restraint. *See* Antitrust
Transactional analysis of mergers, 127 n. 40
Transitional phases of mergers, 57, 530, 531
Trust as a predictive variable, 518
Trust busting, 488-94
Types of mergers and multihospital systems, 35-38, 474-76

Umbrella corporations, definition, 37, 38
Unanticipated consequences, 96, 119, 531
Uncertainty
    as basis of strategy, 59
    different perceptions in merged hospitals, 71 n. 11
    effects organizational bargaining, 64
    limits decentralization, 116
    reason for coalitions, 103
    reduction through merger, 510
    relationship to environment, 60

role of merger managers in absorbing, 111, 127 n. 41, 530
    in Seattle, 287-93
Uncontrollable change, 531
Undepreciated costs of demolition, 497 n. 16
Unification of medical staff, 534
Unit costs. *See* Diseconomies of scale; Economies of scales; Efficiency
Unplanned change, 551
Urban vs. rural differences, 26-28, 87, 88

Vertical integrations
    as defined by antitrust laws, 490
    definition and examples, 35
    relationship to cooptation, 71 n. 10
    vs. horizontal integrations, 462-67 passim
Volunteerism, 487

Wilmington Medical Center, Delaware, 23, 24, 120, 491, 530

About the Author

David B. Starkweather has served as a consultant to numerous hospitals and health care organizations on topics related to mergers and multi-hospital systems. These include the National Center for Health Services Research and Development and the National Health Care Management Center. Currently Professor of Hospital Administration at the School of Public Health, University of California, Berkeley, Dr. Starkweather is the author of numerous articles and monographs on the subject of hospital mergers. He is currently on the advisory boards of both the Institute of Industrial Relations and the Institute of Business and Economic Research at the University of California as well as the Board of Trustees of Herrick Memorial Hospital in Berkeley. Dr. Starkweather received his Dr.Ph. from UCLA in 1968.